THETWO WORLDS OF THE POET

THE TWO WORLDS OF THE POET
NEW PERSPECTIVES ON VERGIL

ROBERT M. WILHELM
AND
HOWARD JONES,
EDITORS

WAYNE STATE UNIVERSITY PRESS
DETROIT

Classical Studies
Pedagogy Series

GENERAL EDITOR

Norma Goldman
Wayne State University

ADVISORY EDITORS

Herbert W. Benario
Emeritus, Emory University

Sally Davis
Wakefield High School
Arlington, Virginia

Judith Lynn Sebesta
University of South Dakota

Meyer Reinhold
Boston University

Finley Hooper
Wayne State University

Books in this series

Caesaris Augusti Res Gestae et Fragmenta, second edition, revised and enlarged by Herbert W. Benario, 1990.

Roman Letters: History from a Personal Point of View, by Finley Hooper and Matthew Schwartz, 1990.

Cicero's Verrine Oration II.4: With Notes and Vocabulary, by Sheila K. Dickison, 1992.

Copyright © 1992 by Wayne State University Press
Detroit, Michigan 48202. All rights reserved.
No part of this book may be reproduced without formal permission.
Manufactured in the United States of America.

99 98 97 96 95 94 93 92   5 4 3 2 1

Library of Congress Cataloging-in-Publication Data

The Two worlds of the poet : new perspectives on Vergil / Robert M. Wilhelm and Howard Jones, editors.

    p. cm. — (Classical studies pedagogy series)

  Essays in English, French, German, and Italian, with some of the original Latin from Vergil.

    Includes bibliographical references and index.

    ISBN 0-8143-2450-9 (alk. paper)

    1. Virgil—Criticism and interpretation. 2. Pastoral poetry, Latin—History and criticism. 3. Didactic poetry, Latin—History and criticism. 4. Aeneas (Legendary character) in literature. 5. Epic poetry, Latin—History and criticism. 6. Latin literature—History and criticism. 7. Rome in literature. I. Wilhelm, Robert M. II. Jones, Howard, Ph.D. III. Series.
PA6825. T85 1992
873'.01—dc20

92-30789

te sine nil altum mens incohat

TABULA GRATULATORIA

Antonio and Maria Alessio
Ernst Badian
Viola Bartelme
Barbara Bayne
Janeene R. Browne Blank
Dr. and Mrs. A. Bourns
Bruce Brace
Frederick E. Brenk, S.J.
John Breuker, Jr.
William M. Calder, III
Raymond J. Clark
Margaret R. Conner
Gwen Daluge
Mary M. Dowd
J.A.S. Evans
M. Elizabeth Franck
Brent and Gail Froberg
Lawrence and Ruth Froberg
Sophia Furman
Elizabeth Giedeman
Mark A. Greenwood
Michael Grant
Karen Grimsrud
Mr. and Mrs. J. Guenther
Jane H. Hall
Eric Handley
Jayne I. Hanlin
Edward L. Harrison
Susan I. Hengelsberg
Bernice K. Jefferis
Howard Jones
Ross S. Kilpatrick
Mr. and Mrs. Walter Kowalski
Karen H. Laner
Gilbert Lawall
Dr. and Mrs. Alvin Lee
Robert B. Lloyd
Philip and Elizabeth Lockhart
Flora Lutz
Elizabeth Masters
Victor Matthews

G. Joette McDonald
Anne S. Morrissett
Elizabeth R. Murphy
Joan W. Newey
John F. and Jacqueline S. Pach
G.M. Paul
Michael C.J. Putnam
Margaret E. Reesor
Meyer Reinhold
Thomas G. Rosenmeyer
Marina Salmon
Donald M. Shepherd
Jean and James Showkeir
Arlene E. Silness
R.J.A. Talbert
George Thaniel
Alan Walker
James Warren
Mr. and Mrs. K.H. Wellesley
M.M. Willcock
Alexander R.M. Wilhelm
L. Berniece Wilhelm
Celeste R.M. Wilhelm
Robert M. and Michelle P. Wilhelm
Catherine B. Williams
A. Geoffrey Woodhead

McMaster University,
   Office of the President
Miami University,
   Office for the Advancement of
   Scholarship and Teaching
Miami University,
   College of Arts and Science
Miami University,
   School of Fine Arts
Miami University,
   Department of Art
Ontario Classical Association
Queen's University,
   Department of Classics

CONTENTS

Introduction
    Robert M. Wilhelm and Howard Jones 11
Biography: Alexander Gordon McKay 15
A Bibliography of the Published Writings of
Alexander Gordon McKay 17

PART ONE

Sola . . . multis e matribus: A Comment on
Vergil's Trojan Women
    Charles L. Babcock 39
Les Amours de Didon ou les Limites de la Liberté
    Pierre Grimal 51
Dido and the Representation of Women in Vergil's *Aeneid*
    J.P. Sullivan 64
Minerva in the *Aeneid*
    Michelle P. Wilhelm 74
Seven Suffering Heroines and Seven Surrogate Sons
    M. Owen Lee 82
Aeneas at Rome and Lavinium
    Karl Galinsky 93
Aeneas at Carthage: The Opening Scenes of the *Aeneid*
    E.L. Harrison 109
Dardanus, Aeneas, Augustus and the Etruscans
    Robert M. Wilhelm 129
The *Aeneid* and the Concept of the Ideal King:
The Modification of an Archetype
    J.A.S. Evans 146

The Similes of *Aeneid* 5
  Ward W. Briggs, Jr. 157
Vergil, *Aeneid* 6: The Bough by Hades' Gate
  Raymond J. Clark 167
Aeneas in Purgatory
  Colin M. Wells 179
War and Peace in *Aeneid* 10
  Susan Ford Wiltshire 189
Sur Trois Passages de Virgile: L'Archéologie des Anciens
  Raymond Chevallier 206
Gilbert Highet's Raising of Italy: *Aeneid* 3.523-524
  William R. Nethercut 229
Ductor Rhoeteius: Vergil, *Aeneid* 12.456
  Robert J. Rowland, Jr. 237
Plautus and Terence in Vergil: A Servian Perspective
  Robert B. Lloyd 244

PART TWO

Book 2 of Horace's *Odes*: *amicitia, urbanitas, humanitas*
  Janice M. Benario 257
Ovidius in Tauris: Ovid *Tr.* 4.4 and *ex P.* 3.2
  R. Elaine Fantham 268
Philomela's Web and the Pleasures of the Text:
Ovid's Myth of Tereus in the *Metamorphoses*
  Charles Segal 281
Two Notes on Roman Elegy: Catullus 67 and
Propertius 1.9
  Ross S. Kilpatrick 296
The Death of the Paraclausithyron: Propertius 1.16
  Howard Jones 303
Le concept de prose poétique dans la *Rhétorique* d'Aristote
et *La Composition stylistique* de Denys d'Halicarnasse
  Maurice Lebel 310
δειλός and οὐτιδανός in the Language of Achilles
  Valerie M. Warrior 320
Principatus and *imperium*: Tacitus, *Historiae* 1.1
  Herbert W. Benario 328

Cybele und Attis im All: Zur Patera von Parabiago
  Erika Simon 335
Prayer and the Living Emperor
  Duncan Fishwick 343
The *Other* Spas of Ancient Campania
  George W. Houston 356
Vasa Fictilia: Ollae Perforatae
  Wilhelmina F. Jashemski 371
From Vergil to Ausonius: Poets on World-Politics
  Charles-Marie Ternes 392
Gemina pictura: Allegorisierende Aeneisillustrationen in Handschriften des 15. Jahrhunderts
  Antonie Wlosok 408
Dismal Decorations: Dryden's Machines in *Aeneid* 12
  W.R. Johnson 433
Reception of Gibbon's *Decline and Fall* in America in the Early National Period
  Meyer Reinhold 448
Tradizione e originalità negli studi canadesi su Virgilio
  Mario Geymonat 458
A Late Twentieth-Century Reading of Vergil's *Eclogues*: The Shepherd As Artist
  Harry C. Rutledge 467
Fallgruben für den klassischen Philologen
  Viktor Pöschl 478
Four "Neoclassical" Poems
  George Thaniel 489

List of Illustrations 493
Index Keyed to Line Numbers 495

INTRODUCTION

In a recent review of yet another translation of Homer's *Iliad* the Oxford scholar, Jasper Griffin, underscores the importance of every generation engaging afresh the works of the first of the Greek poets. Griffin is right, and not only for Homer but for all the creative minds of the classical past, not least the Roman poet, Vergil. Moreover, in the case of Vergil, it is particularly fitting that as a millennium draws to a close we revisit the world of an artist whose own generation witnessed a transition from one millennium to another. It was a transition, to be sure, of which the poet and his contemporaries were unaware, an accident of computation, and yet with an artist's prophetic vision Vergil seems to have sensed the coming of a different age, or at least the return of the *saturnia regna*.

Like Janus, Vergil's world presents two faces, each inseparable from the other—the world which formed the poet and the world which the poet himself created—and it is proper that a volume which commemorates a scholar whose own work has illuminated both of these worlds should address itself to each in equal measure. Accordingly, the volume divides itself into two roughly equal parts.

The first consists of a series of essays which examines the poet's *modus creandi*—his use of the simile; his assimilation of the language and motifs of Roman comic drama; his exploitation of the rich store of Greek, Etruscan and Roman mythological, legendary and historical material; and his treatment of a variety of themes which touch upon the very essence of the human condition. The organization of the essays in this first part is designed both to reflect the broad themes of the poet's world (the role of women [mothers, Dido and Minerva] in the *Aeneid*, patterns of heroism, the character of Aeneas from a variety of vantage points) and to offer a re-examination of specific books and passages from the *Aeneid* and the *Georgics*, all of which show how Vergil's poetic art manifests itself in the text.

The essays which comprise the second part of the volume touch upon various aspects of Vergil's material and cultural environment, a consideration of which enables us to place his created work in a broader perspective: the Augustan aesthetic as it manifests itself in the work of his contemporaries, Horace, Ovid and Propertius; the Greek literary legacy viewed through the eyes of Homer, Aristotle and Dionysius of Halicarnassus; the principate in historiography and the visual arts; the architecture and landscape of Campania where the two worlds of the poet are deeply embodied in the monuments and the topography. There follows a group of essays which offer new perspectives on the post-classical treatment of Vergilian themes, essays which show how the reception of Vergil varied as successive eyes engaged anew the poet and his world. The volume concludes with the reflections of the senior statesman of Vergilian criticism upon the scholars' art and mission.

Vergil knew that to understand the present it was essential to break out of the narrow circle of the moment and to reach into the past. By reaching into the past we affirm our own humanity and our place in the world and find paths into the future. It has been argued that "to live intellectually only *in one's own time* is as provincial and misleading as to live intellectually only *in one's own culture.*"[1] Vergil and his poetry create an evocative nexus of associations and connections that cut across temporal and cultural boundaries so that the many voices of his poetic vision provide entry into the multicultural and international experience of the human story. The two worlds of the poet which this volume of essays seeks to address become a mirror into the timeless and universal concerns of humanity, reflecting the shared legacy of the past and the present. On the one hand the essays of this volume explore Vergil's own struggle to find his place in the world and chronicle the pathway by which we gain entry into the world of the poet; on the other hand the essays carry us into the future and examine how the world of the poet has influenced and enriched another world.

This collection of studies in honour of Alexander Gordon McKay is intended to offer new perspectives on that larger Vergilian world which his own scholarship has so richly illuminated.

—The Editors

1. W.R. Parker, "The Case for Latin," *PMLA* 79.4 (1964) 6.

ALEXANDER GORDON MCKAY

BIOGRAPHY: ALEXANDER GORDON MCKAY

PROFESSOR EMERITUS OF CLASSICS
MCMASTER UNIVERSITY
HAMILTON, ONTARIO, CANADA

Alexander (Sandy) McKay was born in Toronto, Ontario, on Christmas Eve, 1924, the son of Alexander Lynn McKay (B.A., M.D., F.R.C.P.C.) and Marjory Maude Redfern Nicoll McKay. He attended Upper Canada College and was admitted to Trinity College, University of Toronto, as Duke of Wellington Scholar in Classics in 1942. He was graduated from the University of Toronto in Honours Classics in 1946. He received an M.A. in Classics from Yale University, where he was Kellogg Fellow in Classics, in 1947, and an A.M. from Princeton University, where he was a Woodrow Wilson Fellow, in 1948. He holds earned and honorary doctorates from several universities: Doctor of Philosophy, Princeton University (1950), Doctor of Laws (honoris causa) from The University of Manitoba (1986), Brock University (1990), and Queen's University (1991), and Doctor of Letters (honoris causa) from McMaster University (1992).

Professor McKay joined the McMaster faculty in 1957 after holding posts as lecturer and assistant professor at Wells College, the University of Pennsylvania, Mount Allison University, Waterloo College, The University of Western Ontario, and The University of Manitoba. He became Professor of Classics at McMaster University in 1963 and served as Chairman of the Department from 1962-1968, and from 1976-1979. He served McMaster University's newly established Faculty of Humanities as its founding Dean from 1968-1973.

He was visiting lecturer at the University of Colorado on several occasions and lectured widely in Canada, the United States, the United Kingdom, Europe and Australia. He was

Professor-in-Charge of the Intercollegiate Center for Classical Studies in Rome (Stanford University) in 1975, and held a Killam Senior Fellowship during 1979-1980. He has been a Visiting Member at the Institute for Advanced Study in Princeton and at the Fondation Hardt, Vandoeuvres-Geneva, and he was elected a Visiting Fellow of Trinity College, Cambridge, in 1988. In 1986 he was a member of the Core Faculty at *The Aeneid Institute* and in 1989 a member of the Core Faculty at *The Ovid Institute*; both institute programs were funded by the National Endowment for the Humanities and were held at Miami University, Oxford, Ohio. Upon retirement from McMaster University he was appointed Adjunct Professor of Humanities and Classics at York University, Toronto (1990) and Distinguished Visiting Scholar at Concordia University, Montreal (1992).

Dr. McKay has been widely honored for his scholarship in Roman literature, art and archaeology. In 1965 he was elected a Fellow of the Royal Society of Canada. He served as President of the Classical Association of Canada (1978-1980), the Vergilian Society of America (1973-1974), and the Classical Association of the Middle West and South (1972-1973), and was Vice President of the International Union of Academies (U.A.I.) from 1984-1986. He has been Honorary Editor of the Royal Society of Canada (1970-1984), and Contributing Editor to *The Classical World, Vergilius,* and *Classical Journal.* For his frequent role as Director of the Classical Summer School sessions at Cumae (Baia/Napoli) and for his constant services to the Vergilian Society of America and to Vergilian scholarship, he was elected the Society's Honorary President for Life in 1989. He was elected to a three-year term as the one-hundredth president of the Royal Society of Canada, the National Academy of Arts and Sciences, in 1984. He was awarded the Silver Jubilee Medal in 1977. Dr. McKay was appointed Knight Commander of the Order of St. John of Jerusalem in 1986, and was invested as Officer of the Order of Canada in Ottawa on 12 April 1989. In May, 1991, he received the Doctor of Laws, *honoris causa*, from Queen's University at Kingston, Ontario, and in June, 1992, he received the honorary degree Doctor of Letters at the Convocation of the Faculty of Humanities and the Arts and Science Programme at McMaster University, Hamilton, Ontario.

Alexander McKay married Helen Jean Zulauf on Christmas Eve in 1964; he has two stepdaughters, Julie Brott and Danae Fraser, and four grandchildren. The McKays live in Hamilton, Ontario.

A BIBLIOGRAPHY OF THE PUBLISHED WRITINGS OF ALEXANDER GORDON MCKAY

—1943—

Poems:
"Metaphysique," *Trinity University Review* 56 (Summer) 32.
"Dedication," *Trinity University Review* 56 (Autumn) 11.

—1944—

Poems:
"Reverie," *Trinity University Review* 56 (February) 23.
"Introversion," *Trinity University Review* 56 (Summer) 19.
"Capriccio," *Trinity University Review* 57 (Christmas) 11-13.

—1945—

Poems:
"Poem," *Trinity University Review* 57 (January) 16.
"New Directions," *Trinity University Review* 57 (January) 16.
"Fantasie-Impromptu," *Trinity University Review* 58 (Summer) 15-17.

Article:
"Modern Criticism," *Trinity University Review* 58 (Summer) 12-13.

—1946—

Review:
Latin Songs and Carols, by J.C. Robertson, *Phoenix* 1.2: 20.

—1950—

Dissertation:
Athens and Macedon: A Study of Relations from the sixth to the mid-fifth century B.C., Princeton University, *Dissertation Abstracts* 5 (1955) 564.

—1952—

Article:
"The Tale of Troy Divine," *Manitoba Educational Association 47th Annual Convention* (Easter) 35-38.

Review:
Aeschylus' Eumeniden, by P. Groeneboom, *CW* 46: 140.

—1953—

Review:
The Iliad of Homer, by Richmond Lattimore, and *The Aeneid of Virgil*, by C. Day Lewis, *Phoenix* 7.1: 154-156.
Aeschylus' Eumeniden, by P. Groeneboom, *CW* 46.9: 140.

—1954—

Bibliography:
"A Survey of Recent Work on Aeschylus (1947-1954)," *CW* 48: 145-150, 153-159.

Reviews:
Sophocles: A Study of Heroic Humanism, by C.H. Whitman, *CJ* 50: 43.
Sophocles and Greek Pessimism, by J.C. Opstelten, *CJ* 50: 43-44.
Sophocles and Pericles, by V. Ehrenberg, *CJ* 50: 44.
Sophocles the Dramatist, by A.J.A. Waldock, *CJ* 50: 44-45.
Three Scenes in Sophocles' Ajax, by I.M. Linforth, *CJ* 50: 45.
Die Persönlichkeit des Chors. Grundlage der Einheit der Handlung in Oedipus auf Kolonos, by I. Errandonea, *CJ* 50: 45-46.
Das 4 Stasimon der Antigone *von Sophokles* (944-987), by I. Errandonea, *CJ* 50: 45-46.
Aspects of Euripidean Tragedy, by L.H.G. Greenwood, *CJ* 50: 46.
A New Chapter in the History of Greek Tragedy, by D.L. Page, *CJ* 50: 46.
Aeschylus: Oresteia, translated and with an introduction by Richmond Lattimore, *CJ* 50: 46-47.
Sophocles: Three Tragedies... "Oedipus the King" (translated by D. Grene), "Oedipus at Colonus" (translated by R. Fitzgerald), "Antigone" (translated by E. Wyckoff), with an introduction by D. Grene; *CJ* 50: 47.
Sophocles: Electra and Other Plays (a new translation), by E.F. Watling, *CJ* 50: 47.
Euripides: Alcestis and Other Plays (a new translation), by P. Vellacott, *CJ* 50: 47.

—1955—
Article:
"The Man in the Ivory Mask," *Waterloo College Cord* 30: 3, 8-11, 52.

Review:
Histoire du Texte de Pindare, by J. Irigoin, *AJP* 76: 106-108.

—1957—
Article:
"The Greeks at Cumae," *Vergilian Digest* 3: 5-11.

Reviews:
Greek Civilization, by A. Bonnard, *CJ* 53: 134.
Pindar and Aeschylus, by J.H. Finley, Jr., *Phoenix* 11: 176-178.
Alcestis and Other Plays by Euripides; The Bacchae and Other Plays by Euripides, by P. Vellacott, *Yearbook of Comparative and General Literature* 6: 80-82.

—1958—
Guidebook:
Ancient Campania, Rome, Latium and Etruria: An Anthology of Classical Texts.

Reviews:
Ten Greek Plays in Contemporary Translations, edited by L.R. Lind, *Yearbook of Comparative and General Literature* 7: 71-73.
Twilight in Italy, by D.H. Lawrence, *Waterloo Review* 1: 7-8.

—1959—
Guidebook:
The Cities of Greek and Roman Sicily: History and Monuments.

Article:
"Director's Report: Summer Sessions," *Vergilius* 5: 3-4.

Reviews:
Gate to the Sea, by W. Bryher, *Waterloo Review* 2: 73-75.
Thoreau's Translation of "The Seven Against Thebes" (1843), edited by L.M. Kaiser, *CW* 53: 260-261.
The Book of Job as a Greek Tragedy, by H.M. Kallen, *CW* 53: 128.
Greek Civilization, II: from the Antigone to Socrates, by A. Bonnard, *CW* 53: 128.
Euripides V (The Complete Greek Tragedies), edited by R. Lattimore and D. Grene, *CJ* 55: 278-279.

Greek Portraits II: To What Extent Were They Faithful Likenesses?, by G.M.A. Richter, *CW* 53: 193.
Selections from Greek and Roman Historians, edited by C.A. Robinson, Jr., *CB* 35: 35.
From Homer to Mycenae, by T.B.L. Webster, *Bulletin of the Humanities Association of Canada* (April) 19-20.

Abstracts:
"In the Journals," *CW* 53: 268-270, 294-295.

—1960—

Guidebook:
Greek and Roman Antiquities in the National Museum of Naples: A Selective Guide.

Article:
"Director's Report: Summer Sessions," *Vergilius* 6: 2-3.

Reviews:
"Old Loyalties, New Directions," *Waterloo Review* 2: 53-61.
Pompeianische Wandinschriften, edited and translated by H. Geist, *CW* 54: 298.
Pompeian Wall Paintings, by A. Maiuri, *CW* 54: 297.
Greek Portraits III: How Were Likenesses Transmitted in Ancient Times? Small Portraits and Near-Portraits in Terracotta, Greek and Roman, by G.M.A. Richter, *CW* 54: 157.
The Motif of Io in Aeschylus' Suppliants, by R.D. Murray, Jr., *Phoenix* 14: 251.

Abstracts:
"In the Journals," *CW* 53: 294-296.
"In the Journals," *CW* 54: 28-30, 67-69, 100-103, 134-137, 161-163, 195-197, 231-233, 268-270, 301-302.

—1961—

Reviews:
"Western Ontario Drama," *Waterloo Review* 5: 13.
Römische Porträt-Plastik aus sieben Jahrhunderten, by H. von Heintze, *CW* 55: 125-126.
Das Schöpferische in der römischen Kunst: Zwischen Republik und Kaiserzeit. Römische Kunst I-II, by G. Kaschnitz von Weinberg, *CW* 55: 258.

Abstracts:
"In the Journals," *CW* 55: 23-26, 56-58, 91-92, 127-129, 148-150, 181-183, 220-222, 262-263.

—1962—

Books:

Naples and Campania: Texts and Illustrations.

Ancient Rome: The City and the Monuments, Ancient Latium and Etruria.

Articles:

"Latin Studies in Canada," *Humanitas: Revista de Cultura Romana* 5: 323-331.

"Director's Report: Classical Summer School," *Vergilius* 8: 16-17.

Reviews:

Pompeian Frescoes, by T. Copplestone, *CW* 56: 140-141.

The Orestes Plays of Aeschylus: The Agamemnon, The Libation Bearers, The Eumenides, translated by P. Roche, *CW* 56: 218, 220.

The Masks of Tragedy: Essays on Six Greek Dramas, by T.G. Rosenmeyer, *CW* 56: 289.

Abstracts:

"In the Journals," *CW* 55: 25-26, 55-56, 89-90, 148-149, 191-193, 228-230, 264-265.

—1963—

Bibliography:

"Vergilian Bibliography, 1962-1963," *Vergilius* 9: 33-36.

Necrology:

"Amedeo Maiuri, 1886-1963," *Vergilius* 9: 15.

"Pellegrino Claudio Sestieri," *Vergilius* 9: 27.

Reviews:

Aeschylus, Prometheus Bound, translated by W.D. Anderson, *CW* 57: 16, 24.

Ein Satyrspiel des Aischylos?, by A. Greifenhagen, *CW* 57: 354-355.

The Art of Crete and Early Greece: The Prelude to Greek Art, by F. Matz, and *The Art of Rome and Her Empire,* by H. Kaehler, *CW* 57: 375-376.

Aeschylus, Prometheus Bound, translated by P. Roche, *CW* 57: 378-379.

Die Grundlagen der republikanischen Baukunst: Die Baukunst im Kaiserreich. Römische Kunst III-IV, CW 57: 360.

The Unicorn, by I. Murdoch, *Tamarack Review* 28: 91.

Abstracts:

"In the Journals," *CW* 57: 73-74, 167-169, 283-285, 363-364.

—1964—
Book:
Roman Lyric Poetry: Catullus and Horace, with D.M. Shepherd.

Article:
"Vergil's Roman Monuments," *Proceedings of the Virgil Society* 4: 68.

Bibliography:
"Vergilian Bibliography, 1963-1964,"*Vergilius* 10: 40-44.

Reviews:
Vergessenes Pompeji: Unveröffentlichte Bilder römischer Wanddekorationen in geschichtlicher Folge, by K. Schefold, *CW* 58: 19.
Die maritime Bildersprache des Aischylos, by D. Van Nes, *CW* 58: 162.
La Casa Reg. IX.5, 18-21 a Pompei e le sue pitture, *CW* 58: 142-143.

Abstracts:
"In the Journals," *CW* 58: 146-147, 178-179, 261-262.

—1965—
Bibliography:
"Aeschylean Studies, 1955-1964," *CW* 59: 40-48, 65-75.
"Vergilian Bibliography, 1964-1965," *Vergilius* 11: 40-47.

Necrology:
"W.F. Jackson-Knight: Discipulus discipulis," *Vergilius* 11: 38-39.

Reviews:
Virgil: A Study in Civilized Poetry, by B. Otis, *Phoenix* 19: 330-332.
The Art of Greece, 1400-31 B.C.: Sources and Documents, edited and translated by J.J. Pollitt, *CW* 59: 219.
The Art of the Romans, by J.M.C. Toynbee, *CW* 59: 317-318.
Die maritime Bildersprache des Aischylos, by D. Van Nes, *Phoenix* 19: 95.

Abstracts:
"In the Journals," *CW* 59: 95-96, 170-172.

—1966—
Article:
"The Achaemenides Episode: Vergil, *Aeneid* III, 588-691," *Vergilius* 12: 31-38.

Bibliography:
"Vergilian Bibliography, 1966-1967," *Vergilius* 12: 39-45.

Reviews:
Die Aischyleische Gestalt des Orest und ihre Bedeutung für die Interpretation der Eumeniden, by H.J. Dirksen, *CW* 60: 214.
Bei Töpfern und Zieglern in Süditalien, Sizilien und Griechenland, by R. Hampe and A. Winter, *CW* 60: 67, 70.
The Furniture of the Greeks, by G.M.A. Richter, *Vergilius* 12: 52-53.
The Art of the Romans, by J.M.C. Toynbee, *Vergilius* 12: 54-55, and *CW* 60: 317-318.
Roy Thomson of Fleet Street, by R. Braddon, *Canadian Commentator* 10.1: 28.
"The Canadian Theatre in 1965," *Canadian Commentator* 10.1: 10-11, 28.

—1967—

Book:
Victorian Architecture in Hamilton (Centennial Publication).

Article:
"Aeneas' Landfalls in Hesperia," *G&R* 14: 3-11.

Bibliography:
"Vergilian Bibliography, 1966-1967," *Vergilius* 13: 35-41.

Necrology:
"William Sherwood Fox, 1878-1967," *Phoenix* 21: 235-236.

Reviews:
The Ancient World, by H.A. Grönewegen-Frankfort and B. Ashmole, *CW* 61: 10.
Minoan and Mycenaean Art, by R. Higgins, *CW* 61: 248.
Art Forms and Civic Life in the Late Roman Empire, by H.P. L'Orange, *CW* 61: 115-116.
The Poetry of the Aeneid, by M.C.J. Putnam, *CN&V* 11.1 (1967): 21-22.
Sarsina: La Città Romana, Il Museo Archeologico, by G.V. Gentili, G.A. Mansuelli, G. Susini, and A. Veggiani, *Phoenix* 21: 321.

—1968—

Articles:
"Vergilian Landscape into Art: Poussin, Claude and Turner," *Studies in Latin Literature and Its Influence: Virgil*, edited by D.R. Dudley, 139-160.

"Vergil and Vitruvius," *Canisius College Language Methods Newsletter* 5.3 (1968) 1, 11.

"Director's Report: Classical Summer School," *Vergilius* 14: 53-56.

Bibliography:
"Vergilian Bibliography, 1967-1968," *Vergilius* 14: 16-27.

Review:
Mythologisches in Vergils Georgica, by W. Frentz, *CW* 62: 194-195.

—1969—

Book:
Roman Lyric Poetry: Catullus and Horace, with D.M. Shepherd, revised and reprinted.

Article:
"Report of the Dean of Humanities," *President's Report, McMaster University* (1968-1969) 13-15.

Bibliography:
"Vergilian Bibliography, 1968-1969," *Vergilius* 15: 42-52.

Reviews:
Vibia Sabina: Funzione politica, iconografia e il problema del classicismo adrianeo, by A. Carandini, *CW* 63: 96.

Die römischen Bronzen aus Österreich, by R. Fleischer, *CW* 63: 174-175.

Aeneas, Sicily, and Rome, by G.K. Galinsky, *CW* 63: 242.

Aeneisstudien, by E. Kraggerud, *Phoenix* 23: 408-410.

Euripides: Helen, with introduction and commentary by A.M. Dale, *AJP* 90: 245-248.

—1970—

Book:
Vergil's Italy, Greenwich, CT.

Articles:
"Report of the Dean of Humanities," *President's Report, McMaster University* (1969-1970) 15-17.

"Foreword," *Masters and Scholars*, by Sir Eric Ashby, v-vii.

"Director's Report: North Italy," *Vergilius* 16: 53.

Bibliography:
"Vergilian Bibliography, 1969-1970," *Vergilius* 16: 33-39.

Editions:
Proceedings of the Royal Society of Canada: Délibérations de la Société Royale du Canada, Fourth Series, volume 8.

Transactions of the Royal Society of Canada: Mémoires de la Société Royale du Canada, Fourth Series, volume 8.

Reviews:
The Arch of Septimius Severus in the Roman Forum, by R. Brilliant, *CW* 64: 170.
The Portraits of Septimius Severus (A.D. 193-211), by A.M. McCann, *CW* 64: 170.
Time in Greek Tragedy, by J. de Romilly, *AJP* 91: 239-241.

—1971—

Book:
Vergil's Italy, Bath, England.

Articles:
"Applied Science and Humanities: A Study of Vergil's *Georgics*," *Chancellor's Lectures, Brock University* 24-33.
"Report of the Dean of Humanities," *President's Report, McMaster University* (1970-1971) 14-16.

Bibliography:
"Vergilian Bibliography, 1970-1971," *Vergilius* 17: 13-21.

Editions:
Proceedings of the Royal Society of Canada: Délibérations de la Société Royale du Canada, Fourth Series, volume 9.
Transactions of the Royal Society of Canada: Mémoires de la Société Royale du Canada, Fourth Series, volume 9.

Review:
Mythos und Zeitgeschichte bei Aischylos: Das Verhältnis von Mythos und Historie in Eumeniden und Hiketiden, by C. Gülke, *AJP* 92: 754-755.

—1972—

Books:
Ancient Campania, Volume I: Cumae and the Phlegraean Fields.
Ancient Campania, Volume II: Naples and Coastal Campania.

Articles:
"Vergil's Glorification of Italy (*Georgics* II, 136-174)," *Cicero and Virgil: Studies in Honour of Harold Hunt*, edited by J. Martyn, 149-168.
"Vergil's *dulcia limina*," *Classical Association of the Empire State Newsletter* 8: 5.
"Report of the Dean of Humanities," *President's Report, McMaster University* (1971-1972) 12-14.

"Director's Report: Classical Summer School, Greek Session," *Vergilius* 18: 61-62.

Bibliography:
"Vergilian Bibliography, 1971-1972," *Vergilius* 18: 16-30.

Necrology:
"George Eckel Duckworth, 1903-1972," *Vergilius* 18: 15.

Editions:
Proceedings of the Royal Society of Canada: Délibérations de la Société Royale du Canada, Fourth Series, volume 10.
Transactions of the Royal Society of Canada: Mémoires de la Société Royale du Canada, Fourth Series, volume 10.

—1973—

Articles:
"Apollo Cumanus," *Vergilius* 19: 51-63.
"An Unpublished Statue Base at Cumae," *Vergilius* 19: 63-64.
"Piranesi's Impressions of Rome," *City and Society in the Eighteenth Century*, edited by P. Fritz and D. Williams, 39-58.

Bibliography:
"Vergilian Bibliography, 1972-1973," *Vergilius* 19: 33-40.
"An Index of *CW* 'Surveys of Scholarship,'" *CW* 221-224.

Necrology:
"Robert Francis Paget, 1890-1973," *Vergilius* 19: 33-34.

Editions:
Proceedings of the Royal Society of Canada: Délibérations de la Société Royale du Canada, Fourth Series, volume 11.
Transactions of the Royal Society of Canada: Mémoires de la Société Royale du Canada, Fourth Series, volume 11.

Reviews:
The Speeches in Vergil's Aeneid, by G. Highet, *ACR* 3: 193
Patterns of Action in the Aeneid*: An Interpretation of Vergil's Epic Similes*, by R.A. Hornsby, *AJP* 94: 315-317.

—1974—

Book:
Roman Lyric Poetry: Catullus and Horace, with D.M. Shepherd, second edition, revised.

Articles:
"Foreword," *The Nemesis of Empire*, by E.T. Salmon, v-viii.
"Director's Report: Cyprus and Turkey," *Vergilius* 20: 54-55.

Bibliography:
"Recent Work on Vergil, 1964-1973," *CW* 68: 1-92.
"Index of Classical World Surveys of Scholarship," *CW* 67: 221-224.
"Vergilian Bibliography, 1973-1974," *Vergilius* 20: 33-44.
"Bibliography of Books and Articles Written by Edward Togo Salmon," *Polis and Imperium: Studies in Honour of Edward Togo Salmon*, edited by J.A.S. Evans, 3-9.

Editions:
Proceedings of the Royal Society of Canada: Délibérations de la Société Royale du Canada, Fourth Series, volume 12.
Transactions of the Royal Society of Canada: Mémoires de la Société Royale du Canada, Fourth Series, volume 12.

Review:
Perspectives of Roman Poetry: A Classics Symposium, edited by G.K. Galinsky, *CJ* 72: 176-178.

—1975—

Book:
Houses, Villas, and Palaces in the Roman World.

Bibliography:
"Vergilian Bibliography, 1974-1975," *Vergilius* 21: 51-59.

Editions:
Proceedings of the Royal Society of Canada: Délibérations de la Société Royale du Canada, Fourth Series, volume 13.
Transactions of the Royal Society of Canada: Mémoires de la Société Royale du Canada, Fourth Series, volume 13.

Review:
From Croesus to Constantine: The Cities of Western Asia Minor and Their Arts in Greek and Roman Times, by G.M.A. Hanfmann, *CJ* 71: 362-365.

—1976—

Books:
Roman Satire: Horace, Juvenal, Persius, Petronius, and Seneca, with D.M. Shepherd.
The Royal Society of Canada: A Summary Statement (1882-1975).

Articles:
"The Aims of a Liberal Education," *Hillfield-Strathallan Review* (Fall-Winter) 17, 19-20.
"Director's Report: Roman Spain and Provence," *Vergilius* 22: 59.

Bibliography:
"Vergilian Bibliography, 1975-1976," *Vergilius* 22: 2-13.

Editions:
Proceedings of the Royal Society of Canada: Délibérations de la Société Royale du Canada, Fourth Series, volume 14.
Transactions of the Royal Society of Canada: Mémoires de la Société Royale du Canada, Fourth Series, volume 14.

Reviews:
Vitruvius and Later Roman Building Manuals, by H. Plommer, *CJ* 72: 68-69.
The Altar and the City: A Reading of Vergil's Aeneid, by M. Di Cesare, *CJ* 72: 270-271.
Perspectives of Roman Poetry: A Classics Symposium, edited by G.K. Galinsky, *CJ* 72: 176-178.
Sicily: An Archaeological Guide, by M. Guido, *CW* 70:490.
Süditalienkunde (1. Band. Campanien und seine Nachbarlandschaften . . .), by E. Kirsten, *CW* 70: 490.
The Towns of Roman Britain, by J. Wacher, *CW* 70: 214-215.

—1977—

Article:
"Archaeology and the Creative Imagination," *New Perspectives in Canadian Archaeology*, edited by A.G. McKay, 227-234.

Bibliography:
"Vergilian Bibliography, 1976-1977," *Vergilius* 23: 55-69.

Editions:
New Perspectives in Canadian Archaeology: Proceedings of a Symposium Sponsored by the Royal Society of Canada, October, 1976.
Proceedings of the Royal Society of Canada: Délibérations de la Société Royale du Canada, Fourth Series, volume 15.
Transactions of the Royal Society of Canada: Mémoires de la Société Royale du Canada, Fourth Series, volume 15.

Reviews:
The Roman Villa: An Historical Introduction, by J. Percival, *Archaeological News* 6: 127-128.
Essays on Roman Culture: The Todd Memorial Lectures, edited by A.J. Dunston, *EMC* 21: 98-99.
A Vergil Concordance, by H.H. Warwick, *CJ* 72: 371-372.

—1978—

Book:
Vitruvius, Architect and Engineer: Buildings and Building Techniques in Augustan Rome.

Articles:
"The Trojans at Carthage," *Humanitas* (Ohio Classical Conference) 3.1 (1978) 15-16.
"McMaster University Archaeological Team in Italy," *EMC* 22: 4.
"Director's Report: North Africa and Sicily," *Vergilius* 24: 88-89.

Bibliography:
"Recent Work on Vergil: Bibliographical Survey, 1964-1973," republished in the *Classical World Bibliography of Vergil*, edited by W. Donlan.
"Vergilian Bibliography, 1977-1978," *Vergilius* 24: 62-76.

Editions:
Proceedings of the Royal Society of Canada: Délibérations de la Société Royale du Canada, Fourth Series, volume 16.
Transactions of the Royal Society of Canada: Mémoires de la Société Royale du Canada, Fourth Series, volume 16.

Reviews:
Country Life in Classical Times, by K.D. White, *Vergilius* 24: 85-86.
The Golden Age of Augustus, by M. Reinhold, *EMC* 22: 117-118.

—1979—

Article:
"Director's Report: Cities of Vesuvius A.D. 79," *Vergilius* 25: 82.

Bibliography:
"Vergilian Bibliography, 1978-1979," *Vergilius* 25: 46-60.

Editions:
Proceedings of the Royal Society of Canada: Délibérations de la Société Royale du Canada, Fourth Series, volume 17.
Transactions of the Royal Society of Canada: Mémoires de la Société Royale du Canada, Fourth Series, volume 17.

Review:
Greek and Roman Coins in the Athenian Agora, by F.S. Kleiner, *Cornucopiae* (Ancient Coin Society of Canada) 4: 66-67.

—1980—

Book:

Römische Häuser, Villen und Paläste, Deutsche Ausgabe von R. Fellmann, Atlantis Verlag: Zürich und Freiburg.

Articles:

"Quadrangles Where Wisdom Honours Herself," *The Written Word / Prestige de l'Écrit*, edited by A.G. McKay, 140-149.

"Director's Report: Greece and the Aegean Islands," *Vergilius* 26: 90-91.

Bibliography:

"Vergilian Bibliography, 1979-1980" *Vergilius* 26: 56-73.

Editions:

The Written Word: Prestige de l'Écrit, (Proceedings of a Symposium sponsored by the Royal Society of Canada).

Selected Papers from the Proceedings and Transactions of the Royal Society of Canada: Anthologie des Mémoires et Comptes Rendus de la Société Royale du Canada, volumes I-III (general editor).

Proceedings of the Royal Society of Canada: Délibérations de la Société Royale du Canada, Fourth Series, volume 18.

Transactions of the Royal Society of Canada: Mémoires de la Société Royale du Canada, Fourth Series, volume 18.

Review:

Fathers and Sons in Virgil's Aeneid, by M.O. Lee, *Vergilius* 26: 77-79.

—1981—

Bibliography:

"Vergilian Bibliography, 1980-1981," *Vergilius* 27: 57-71.

Editions:

Proceedings and Transactions of the Royal Society of Canada: Délibérations de la Société Royale du Canada, Fourth Series, volume 19.

Transactions of the Royal Society of Canada: Mémoires de la Société Royale du Canada, Fourth Series, volume 19.

—1982—

Book:

The Royal Society of Canada: Centennial Summary Statement (1882-1982).

Articles:
"Scholars and Scholarship in Retrospect," *Transactions of the Royal Society of Canada: Mémoires de la Société Royale du Canada, Fourth Series*, volume 20: 323-332.
"Vergil Translated into European Art," *Transactions of the Royal Society of Canada: Mémoires de la Société Royale du Canada, Fourth Series*, volume 20: 339-356.
"Director's Report: Classical Summer School: Magna Graecia, Sicily, and Tunisia," *Vergilius* 28: 93-95.
"Vergilian Commemorative Session at Cumae II," *Vergilius* 28: 95-96.

Bibliography:
"Vergilian Bibliography, 1981-1982," *Vergilius* 28: 65-80.

Editions:
Proceedings of the Royal Society of Canada: Délibérations de la Société Royale du Canada, Fourth Series, volume 20.
Transactions of the Royal Society of Canada: Mémoires de la Société Royale du Canada, Fourth Series, volume 20 (Centenary Volume).

—1983—

Article:
"Camilla and Aristaeus," *Listy Filologicke* 106: 20-23.

Bibliography:
"Vergilian Bibliography, 1982-1983," *Vergilius* 29: 55-76.

Editions:
Proceedings of the Royal Society of Canada: Délibérations de la Société Royale du Canada, Fourth Series, volume 21.
Transactions of the Royal Society of Canada: Mémoires de la Société Royale du Canada, Fourth Series, volume 21.

Reviews:
Cosmos and Tragedy: An Essay on the Meaning of Aeschylus, by B. Otis, edited with notes and preface by E.C. Kopff, *CJ* 79: 155-156.
Virgil: His Poetry Through the Ages, by R.D. Williams and T.S. Pattie, *Phoenix* 37: 91-92.
Capri: from the Stone Age to the Tourist Age, by A. Andrén, *EMC* 27: 262-264.

—1984—

Articles:
"The Vergil Portrait," *Vergilius* 30: 1-9.
"Vergilian Heroes and Toponymy: Palinurus and Misenus," *Mnemai: Classical Studies in Honor of Karl K. Hulley*, edited by H.D. Evjen, 121-137.
"The Villa Vergiliana and the Vergilian Colloquium," *Vergilian Bimillenary Lectures, 1982 (Vergilius, Supplementary Volume 2)*, edited by A.G. McKay, 179-206.
"Apollo," *Enciclopedia Virgiliana* 1: 220-222.
"Canada: Studi filologici," *Enciclopedia Virgiliana* 1: 645-646.

Bibliography:
"Vergilian Bibliography, 1983-1984," *Vergilius* 30: 44-60.

Edition:
Vergilian Bimillenary Lectures, 1982 (Vergilius, Supplementary Volume 2).

—1985—

Book:
Vitruvius: Architect and Engineer, revised and reprinted by Bristol Classical Press, by permission of Macmillan Education Limited (1978).

Articles:
"formido," *Enciclopedia Virgiliana* 2: 560-561.
"Classics," *The Canadian Encyclopedia* 1: 352.
"Classical Studies in Canada" (Italian version), *Il Veltro: Rivista della Civiltà Italiana* 29: 239-246.

Bibliography:
"Vergilian Bibliography, 1984-1985: In Memoriam, Charles T. Murphy, 1985," *Vergilius* 31: 62-80.

Review:
Catullus: Selections, and Teacher's Handbook, by R.O.A.M. Lyne, *New England Classical Newsletter* 12-3: 29-30.

—1986—

Book:
Roma Antiqua: Latium and Etruria, A Source Book of Classical Texts.

Article:
"Art and Architecture as Severan Coin Types," *Ancient Coins of the Graeco-Roman World* (The Nickle Numismatic Papers), edited by W. Heckel and R. Sullivan, 241-260.

Bibliography:
"Vergilian Bibliography, 1985-1986: In Memoriam, Robert Deryck Williams (1917-1986)," *Vergilius* 32: 79-87.

Necrology:
"Charles Theophilus Murphy," *Vergilius* 32: 3-4.

Review:
Vergil and His Influence: Bimillennial Studies, edited by C. Martindale, *Vergilius* 32: 100-101.

—1987—

Articles:
"metuo/metus," *Enciclopedia Virgiliana* 3: 509-510.
"pavor/pavidus," *Enciclopedia Virgiliana* 3: 1036-1038.
"The Vitality of the *Aeneid*," *Augustan Age* 6: 6-14.
"Book Illustrations of Vergil's *Aeneid*, A.D. 400-1980," *Augustan Age* 6: 227-237.
"Vergil's Northern Route to Hesperia," *Augustan Age* 7: 19-30.
"Can Poets Move Mountains? Reflections on the 'Two Cultures,'" (Presidential address), *Transactions of the Royal Society of Canada: Mémoires de la Société Royale du Canada, Fifth Series*, volume 2: 3-10.
"Director's Report: Special Session for the (N.E.H.) Fellows of the *Aeneid* Institute," *Vergilius* 33: 163-167.

Bibliography:
"Vergilian Bibliography, 1986-1987: In Memoriam, Raymond Victor Schoder, S.J. (1916-1987)," *Vergilius* 77-100.

Necrology:
"Raymond Victor Schoder, S.J.," *Vergilius* 33: 3-5.

—1988—

Books:
Selections from Vergil's Aeneid, *Books I, IV, and VI: Dido and Aeneas*, with J.H. Hall, Longman Latin Readers, edited by G. Lawall.
Teacher's Guide to the Latin Readers: Vergil, Longman Latin Readers, 147-172.

Articles:
"Vergil's Aeolus Episode," *Daidalikon: Studies in Honor of Raymond Victor Schoder, S.J.*, edited by R.F. Sutton, 68-80.
"Towards the Centenary: Sortes Vergilianae," *The Vergilian Society of America: The First Fifty Years*, edited by R.M. Wilhelm, *Vergilius, Supplementary Volume* 3: 55-57.

"Pleasure Domes at Baiae," *Studia Pompeiana et Classica in Honor of Wilhelmina F. Jashemski*, edited by R.I. Curtis, *Classica,* volume II: 155-172.

"Houses," *Civilization of the Ancient Mediterranean*, edited by M. Grant and R. Kitzinger, volume III: 1363-1383.

Bibliography:
"Repertori Bibiliografici," *Enciclopedia Virgiliana* 4: 443-444.
"Vergilian Bibliography, 1987-1988," *Vergilius* 34: 139-178.

Necrology:
"Edward Togo Salmon, 1905-1988" *Journal of the Classical Association of New South Wales and of the Classical Languages Teachers' Association* 14.2: 55-57.
"E.T. Salmon, In Memoriam," *American Philological Association Newsletter* 11.3: 9.

—1989—

Article:
"Italy-Canada Research," closing address at the Tenth Anniversary Conference of the Canadian Academic Centre in Italy, December, 1988, *Canadian Mediterranean Institute Bulletin* 9.3: 4-5.

Bibliography:
"Vergilian Bibliography, 1988-1989," *Vergilius* 35: 89-120.

Necrology:
"E.T. Salmon, In Memoriam," *American Philological Association Newsletter* 12.1: 15-16.
"Edward Togo Salmon, 1905-1988," *Transactions of the Royal Society of Canada: Mémoires de la Société Royale du Canada, Fifth Series*, volume 4: 425-428.

—1990—

Articles:
"timeo, timor, timidus," *Enciclopedia Virgiliana* 5: 180-181.
"vereor," *Enciclopedia Virgiliana* 5: 506-507.
"Director's Report: Vergil's Hesperia," *Vergilius* 36: 178-187.

Bibliography:
"Vergilian Bibliography, 1989-1990," *Vergilius* 36: 104-128.

Reviews:
The Rhetoric of Space: Literary and Artistic Representations of Landscape in Republican and Augustan Rome, by E.W. Leach, *CO* 67: 97-98.

Roman Spain, by S.J. Keay, *CO* 67: 101.

—1991—
Bibliography:
"Vergilian Bibliography, 1990-1991," *Vergilius* 37: 77-111.

—FORTHCOMING—
Books:
Vergil: Aeneid XI, Introduction, text, translation, and notes: Aris & Phillips.
Vergil: Aeneid XII, Introduction, text, translation, and notes: Aris & Phillips.
A Quarter-Century of Vergilian Scholarship, 1965-1990, with R.M. Wilhelm, Garland Publishing, Inc.
The Tradition of Vergil in the Nineteenth Century: Scholarship, Translation, Literature, Art, and Music.
The Tradition of Vergil in the Twentieth Century: Scholarship, Translation, Literature, Art, and Music.
Housing for the Spirit: A History of Christ's Church Cathedral, Hamilton, Ontario (1835-1990).

Articles:
"Classical Education in English Canada," *The Classical Tradition and the Americas: Aufstieg und Niedergang der Roemischen Welt*, volume 5.
"Classical Archaeology at Home and Abroad: Canada's Contribution," *The Classical Tradition and the Americas: Aufstieg und Niedergang der Roemischen Welt*, volume 6.
"The Liri Valley: Landscape and People in Roman Literature."
"Kyme I (Aeolis), Kyme II (Cumae, Campania), Misenos (Misenum)," *Lexicon Iconographicum Mythologiae Classicae* 6 (1992).
"Vergil's Campania and the Art of J.M.W. Turner," *The Gail A. Burnett Lectures in the Classics, 1969-1990*, ed. E.N. Genovese, San Diego, CA.
"Caverns and Grottoes in Vergil's *Aeneid*."
"Prometheus Then and Now," *The Augustan Age* 12 (1992).
"Figures in an Italian Landscape: Horace, *Satires* 1.5."
"Grand Tourists in *The Flaming Fields*."
"Canada: Studi filologici," *Enciclopedia Oraziana*.
"*Aeneid* (Virgil); *Satyricon* (Petronius); *Pro Caelio* (Cicero); *Ajax* (Sophocles); *Electra* (Sophocles); *The Persians* (Aeschylus); *Oresteia* (Aeschylus); *The Trojan Women* (Euripides); *Orestes* (Euripides)," *Reference Guide to World Literature*, volume I, *Writers*; volume II, *Works*. London: St. James Press, 1993.

Biographical Notes:

"Sinclair MacLardy Adams; James Wilfred Cohoon; John Alexander Ernest Crake; Ernest Abell Dale; William Sherwood Fox; William Meredith Hugill; Maurice Hutton; Skuli Johnson; John McCaul; Humfrey Michell; Robert Duff Murray, Jr.; Gilbert Norwood; Eric Trevor Owen; Edward Togo Salmon; Clement Hodgson Stearn; Marcus Donald Campbell Tait; Herman Lloyd Tracy; Edith Mary Wightman," *Biographical Dictionary of North American Classicists*, eds. Ward W. Briggs, Jr. and Robert L. Fowler, New York: Garland Publishing, Inc.

Reviews:

Community and Society in Roman Italy, by Stephen L. Dyson, *Vergilius*.

The Classical Epic: An Annotated Bibliography, by Thomas J. Sienkiewicz, *Classical Outlook*.

Rome's Desert Frontier from the Air, by David Kennedy and Derrick Riley, *Classical Outlook*.

PART ONE

Vergil Mosaic, Bardo National Museum, Tunis

SOLA... MULTIS E MATRIBUS:
A COMMENT ON VERGIL'S TROJAN WOMEN

Charles L. Babcock
The Ohio State University

In *Aeneid* 9.216-218 Nisus, while remonstrating with Euryalus for his insistence on joining Nisus on his proposed mission to take a message to the absent Aeneas and to obtain both loot and *gloria* on the way, raises as one of his objections a plea to Euryalus' sense of *pietas*:

> *neu matri miserae tanti sim causa doloris,*
> *quae te sola, puer, multis e matribus ausa*
> *persequitur, magni nec moenia curat Acestae.*

Nisus here informs the reader for the first time that Euryalus has a mother who has accompanied him (Euryalus himself has just mentioned his apparently dead father by name, Opheltes [201]), having chosen not to remain with Acestes in Sicily in the new town named for Acestes and founded to receive those whom Nautes terms *longaeuosque senes ac fessas aequore matres* (5.715). From Book 5 we know that Aeneas decided to leave behind those who had no heart for further travels, just as he had left a few unspecified followers behind in Crete (*paucisque relictis*, 3.190). Nisus' statement above suggests that alone of all the *matres* the unnamed mother of Euryalus has accompanied Aeneas as he left Sicily and sailed at last for Italy. John W. Zarker cites Vergil's variety of terms for groups of women, not only *matres*, but also *Iliades, Troades, Latinae* and *matronae*.[1] Although Nisus seems to be saying that of the many mothers only Euryalus' chose to follow him to Italy, Vergil's usage would make the interpretation "of the many women" a possibility as well. Zarker (p. 18) speaks of the ultimate end in the Underworld for all the Trojan women and lists three groups: "for those left in Crete and for those left in Sicily as well as for those going to Hesperia." And the mother of Euryalus is not the only Trojan woman who appears after Book 5. But the count is slim indeed. Caieta, the nurse of Aeneas, appears at 6.900 and at 7.2, the first revealing that a port is named after her, and the second that she dies upon arrival in Italy and is honored with a tomb at that site. At only one other place, 11.34-35, do Trojan women appear subsequently, as mourners for the dead Pallas:

> *circum omnis famulumque manus Troianaque turba*
> *et maestum Iliades crinem de more solutae.*

Page, in his note on 9.217, is aware of the problem in *sola*:

> "In 5.715 Aeneas leaves behind with Acestes *longaeuosque senes et fessas aequore matres* to found a city of the same name, but in 5.750 he adds *transcribunt urbi matres*, which clearly marks that only some of the women were selected to be left there. Hence *sola* here must mean 'alone' of those who, like herself, were old and widowed."[2]

So also Conington, drawing the conclusion from his predecessors:

> "Spence (Polymetis) finds a difficulty here, as in 11.35 the Trojan women are mentioned as being in Italy. But Heyne rightly remarks that Virg. cannot have meant the Trojans to have sailed without their wives, but only that the aged women were left in Sicily."[3]

In what follows we will look at that which Vergil chooses to say about the women who accompanied Aeneas as he left Sicily for the main part of his task, settling in Italy, and the significance this choice may have for the latter part of the epic.

That Aeneas, in his progress from the ruins of Troy to the site of Rome, must symbolically and actually discard elements representative of the past has long been a given in the interpretation of the poem. The most notable of these, Anchises, is dead before the narrative begins but remains a dominant figure throughout the first six books. It is in connection with his funeral games in Book 5 that the most sweeping and most literal of these gestures separating the past from the future takes place (604-778). While the Trojan males are engaging in the games themselves the women withdraw to a secluded part of the beach to mourn the dead Anchises and there are stimulated by a messenger of Juno to release their pent-up resentment against constant displacement by attempting to burn the instrument of that displacement, the beached ships. First Pyrgo, the nurse of Priam's sons and a voice of the past, then Ascanius, the obvious future, and then the present's Aeneas try to bring them to their senses. Only with the intervention of Jupiter, who must see to it that the fated voyage continues, is there a brake placed on their actions. Four ships have been lost; Aeneas has in despair called for his own destruction if that be the will of the gods.[4] Somewhat characteristically it is up to a representative of the past, Nautes, who, like Anchises, is apparently an instrument of the gods, to make the crucial statement to Aeneas: a reaffirmation of fate, and a suggested path out of the crisis:[5]

> *Nate dea, quo fata trahunt retrahuntque sequamur;*
> *quidquid erit, superanda omni fortuna ferendo est.*
> *est tibi Dardanius diuinae stirpis Acestes:*
> *hunc cape consiliis socium et coniunge uolentem,*
> *huic trade amissis superant qui nauibus et quos*
> *pertaesum magni incepti rerumque tuarum est.*
> *longaeuosque senes ac fessas aequore matres*
> *et quidquid tecum inualidum metuensque pericli est*
> *delige, et his habeant terris sine moenia fessi;*
> *urbem appellabunt permisso nomine Acestam.*
> 5.709-718

Nautes seems to enter here (and only here) for a number of purposes. First, he is *senior Nautes,* of Anchises' generation, and therefore to be listened to. Then, he is goddess-trained as orator and perhaps as seer (although as an orator he is unusually terse). And he is practical, balancing the inevitability of fate with the expediency of eliminating those elements (many of his own age group) that are likely to hinder the carrying out of that fate. Finally, he provides a prologue with a different emphasis to Anchises' speech (724-739), which advises Aeneas to accept Nautes' suggestions but stresses the choice of young and brave companions rather than the rejection of old and tired ones.[6] It is Nautes, however, with his stern but realistic *longaeuosque senes ac fessas aequore matres* who makes it clear (on behalf of the gods' understanding of fate?) that not all of those who set out with Aeneas are required by fate to stay with him all the way to Italy; what is more, it is not only the old, but also those shattered by shipwreck who have lost their stomach for the great enterprise and/or have become weak or afraid. Anchises only echoes with the reverse:

> *lectos iuuenes, fortissima corda,*
> *defer in Italiam.*
>
> 5.729-730

Otis points out (279) that the next words explain this choice, "the true reason for the elimination of the weak and the unwilling":

> *gens dura atque aspera cultu*
> *debellanda tibi Latio est.*
>
> 5.730-731

After Anchises concludes with his summons to the Underworld and complete knowledge, Aeneas properly places this manifestation in divine context and moves quickly to follow instructions. Acestes agrees to the plan, and then, in a remarkable shift from Aeneas as actor to the whole now-eager Trojan band as subject of the action:

> *transcribunt urbi matres populumque uolentem*
> *deponunt, animos nil magnae laudis egentis.*
> *ipsi transtra nouant flammisque ambesa reponunt*
> *robora nauigiis, aptant remosque rudentisque,*
> *exigui numero, sed bello uiuida uirtus.*
>
> 5.750-754

In this brief shift of subject Vergil shows clearly the importance of the change of composition of the company. It is vital to Aeneas that he have companions who are able to act and function eagerly in the wake of near disaster. Not that they do not need a leader; indeed Aeneas and Acestes have set the task, and both reappear as ritual and actual founders of the city in lines 755-761. But those who are described in 750-754 *belong* in the groups defined, the ones remaining behind and the ones preparing to go.

In the scene immediately following (5.762-778) Vergil presents an especially important moment, and one of exceptional emotion, for the survivors of Troy:

Sola . . . multis e matribus: A Comment on Vergil's Trojan Women

> *Iamque dies epulata nouem gens omnis, et aris*
> *factus honos: placidi strauerunt aequora uenti*
> *creber et aspirans rursus uocat Auster in altum.*
> *exoritur procurua ingens per litora fletus;*
> *complexi inter se noctemque diemque morantur.*
> *ipsae iam matres, ipsi, quibus aspera quondam*
> *uisa maris facies et non tolerabile numen,*
> *ire uolunt omnemque fugae perferre laborem.*
> *quos bonus Aeneas dictis solatur amicis*
> *et consanguineo lacrimans commendat Acestae.*
> 5.762-771

Vergil uses *genus* and *gens* with great frequency in the *Aeneid*, often in close proximity and often with almost indistinguishable meaning. There is a particularly interesting collocation of these words in this part of Book 5:

(a) in 624-625 the false Beroe, whose *genus* has been mentioned in 621, addresses the Trojan *matres* as *o gens / infelix*;
(b) in 730 Anchises describes the people the Trojans will find in Italy as *gens dura*;
(c) in 737 Anchises promises that Aeneas will learn of his whole race (*genus omne tuum*) in the Underworld;
(d) in 762 all the Trojans (*gens omnis*) have feasted;
(e) in 785 Venus complains of Juno's destroying the city *media de gente Phrygum*;
(f) in 801 Jupiter reminds Venus of her origins in him (*unde genus ducis*).

This focus on *gens/genus*, each strongly placed in its line, and in particular the movement from *genus omne tuum* to *gens omnis*, leads me to suggest that we should understand in *gens omnis* an emphasis on the last formal act of almost all the remaining Trojan people undertaken together.[7] We have noted that a few were left behind after the mistaken attempt to settle in Crete (3.190, the cryptic and completely undeveloped *paucisque relictis*). With the exception of these, who were the victims of the pestilence on Crete (3.140, a number undetermined) and Orontes and the bulk of his shipmates lost in the Book 1's storm (113-119), the company has been remarkably stable in the face of enormous opposition and difficulties. Now, in the rite offered to Anchises, the presumed residue of Troy, in a last unified action, salutes the departed past, and then regretfully accepts the division agreed on. Significantly the group that stays behind will be led by someone of Anchises' generation, or near it; Acestes is regularly distinguished in one of two ways: his Trojan or Dardanian origin, and his age (*aeui maturus*, 5.73, *senior*, 5.301 and 573, and perhaps *grauis*, 5.387). Those who go on, and they are few, are distinguished by their excitement for and courage in war; their significance is emphasized by their description in a line (754) with hypermetric elision preceding and itself containing a strong alliteration:

exigui numero, sed bello uiuida uirtus.

These are the *Aeneadae* who sail from Sicily to Italy.[8] The bulk of them must be of Aeneas' age or younger, although not all; a few are cited with epithets of age, such as *senior Thymbris* in 10.124 and in 12.420 *longaeuus Iapyx*, the physician.

To this group of men one must, as Page and others note, add an uncertain number of wives and sisters, and perhaps more distant female relatives or hangers-on. Two factors in Book 2 suggest that despite Aeneas' comment on his surprise at the numbers, there cannot have been too many at Mount Ida. First, Book 2 presents a series of Trojan women whose survival of the disaster must almost certainly lead to slavery, or who die in the event. Some are named: Cassandra, Andromache, Hecuba and her other daughters, Creusa; another group appears without names in the palace, the wailing women's voices and mothers wandering in fright in the corridors (486-490). Second, Vergil chooses to leave as the last impression of the defeated Trojans the glimpse Aeneas has of long lines of captive boys and mothers observed as he seeks the lost Creusa (766-767). Special point is given to this sad group by the words of Creusa's ghost that follow almost immediately. Creusa's vital prophecy/farewell (by Highet's classification) speaks specifically to Aeneas when she says that he has by will of the gods lost her, his wife, but that a new wife awaits him at the end of his fated voyage. But in the light of the context in which this occurs we must be expected to read the more general from this specific. Many women and children will have been separated from the men in their families (cf. the pitiful crowd in 766-767 and those killed, perhaps best represented dramatically by Creusa herself and Astyanax, mentioned in 457 and mourned by Andromache in 3.489). As Lavinia awaits Aeneas, so with final victory in Italy women must be found by the widowed or unmarried Trojans from among their allies or from among the defeated. Zarker concludes his article (p. 21) on Trojan and Italian *matres*, "the real victims of epic heroism," with such an assumption:

> "These Italian *matres* are fit ancestors for the fighting Romans of the Augustan age and for the strong-willed women of imperial Rome."

Zarker is commenting on the desperate courage of the Latin women defending their walls against attack in 11.891-895. But the implication is there: the two races are to become one, an outcome represented by the union of Aeneas with Lavinia. Juno's acceptance of this in Book 12 focuses on those unions:

> *cum iam conubiis pacem felicibus (esto)*
> *component ...*
> *sit Romana potens Itala uirtute propago.*
>
> 12.821, 827

Conubiis must be read to include all those marriages across racial lines that will make possible the peace now in sight. That there will be widows or unmarried women among the Trojans who may unite with Italian spouses is probable, but Vergil certainly chooses to place no emphasis on them.

We have seen that the Trojan women who appear after the great divestment of Book 5 are very few indeed, yet each appearance plays a significant part in the story, however brief it may be, and each is tied to the symbolic transfer from the Trojan past to the Roman future.

First, Caieta: To build the transition between Books 6 and 7 on the shadowy figure of Caieta has caused at least one critic to assume that Vergil had not completed his thinking about that transition.[9] With Palinurus and Misenus she satisfies the Vergilian audience's apparent fascination with aetiological, geographic and family assumptions.[10] That like Anchises she represents the closing out of the past at the moment of arrival in Italy seems now to be accepted.[11] We can perhaps add that she, like Orontes, Palinurus and Misenus, serves as a sacrifice to the demands of the gods as the Trojans pursue their inevitable course; this sacrifice of an aged nurse may seem less severe, but that she takes with her a part of Aeneas' emotional life and shuts the final door to the "Trojan" phase of his life as he emerges from the

Underworld heightens its impact. That she is mortal, aged, and parallels Anchises as the nutritive element in Aeneas' growth is clear when one considers the ever-present and somewhat exasperating involvement of his divine parent, Venus. It is appropriate that these elements of Trojan mortality be excised from his environment and his thinking now that he seems clearly and finally to have accepted the uncomfortable burden placed on him by fate that will, in time, lead him to godhead and to Olympus. On this aged Trojan woman, then, the only one honored with a name after the debacle of Book 5 and its political and psychological resolution, Vergil places a multiple burden.

And what of the mother of Euryalus, whose husband is named while she is not, and to whom the honor of a scene and a speech is given? The popularity of the Nisus/Euryalus episodes has given a certain prominence to the scene after their death when Euryalus' mother addresses her son in death and also the Rutulians who carry the heads of the dead pair about the walls of the Trojan camp.[12] Since W.R. Johnson, following on suggestions by Henry and Fecherolle, argued for Vergil's use of *pietas* to mean something akin to "compassion" in some passages, including the speech of Euryalus' mother, a number of scholars have been attracted to such an interpretation of the word in Vergil (granted that other authors so used it).[13] Two, writing from quite different points of view, have made this *pietas* focal to their theses. Barbara Pavlock, looking at the episode in Book 9 through its literary background, notably Homeric and Euripidean sources, discusses the weaknesses as well as the strengths of the two men, and stresses Vergil's understanding of the inherent tension between *gloria* and *pietas*.[14] Having noted Nisus' injunction to *pietas* in 9.217-218, which Euryalus is to ignore, she suggests that the speech of Euryalus' mother essentially continues Vergil's examination of familial *pietas,* but that it introduces "the 'unclassical' meaning of *pietas* as 'pity'" when she calls upon the Rutulians to slay her as well (p. 221). R.B. Egan, concerned with episodes of the last four books, looks at the mother's speech with the warning that, in effect, *pietas* means *pietas* and does not readily cross cultural boundaries in definition.[15] In contrasting the acts or omissions of the Rutulians with those of *pius Aeneas*, Egan concludes that Euryalus' mother is brought in for her apostrophe to her son and her lament as a major introduction to (quoting Duckworth on the Nisus and Euryalus episode itself) prepare "for Vergil's treatment of character and event in IX-XII" (p. 176).

Highet places his discussion of the speech (153-155) and the apostrophes of Aeneas and Evander to the dead Pallas together, implying (as others have noted) that the mother's speech is a preparation for the (perhaps more significant) addresses to Pallas. When M. Owen Lee turns to the role of women in Vergil it is with a consideration of Euryalus' mother, which leads to a discussion of the archetypal hero-myth.[16] She is, alas, only a grace-note to the discussion, although Lee favors the pathos of Nisus to that of the mother at the moment of extreme hysteria.

It is its location within the larger action that gives the scene of Euryalus' mother a particular importance. This is really the start of the almost continuous war that will result in Turnus' death and, presumably, the marriage of Lavinia to Aeneas, whose mission will be all but accomplished. The deaths of these two men, who were so intriguingly introduced in Book 2, are the first of a series that is to include Lausus, Pallas, Camilla, and finally Turnus, a demonstration of the awful consequences of war to all generations and all peoples and a measure of the cost set for the task of Aeneas and the Trojans. In a work skillfully designed to focus our attention through past and present into the future, the time for today's youth, this episode slams home the toll of youth required to reach and achieve that future. It is, in a curious way, the beginning of the end for the mother's generation, for we are to hear the mournful cadence of her *"tune ille senectae / sera meae requies"* three more times:

>   *sors ista senectae*
> *debita erat nostrae.*
>   11.165-166

>   *spes tu nunc una, senectae*
> *tu requies miserae . . .*
>   12.57-58

>   *Dauni miserere senectae*
>   12.934

The words are those of Evander to Pallas' corpse and the Trojans, of Amata in desperation to Turnus to keep him from going to almost certain death, and of Turnus asking Aeneas to send him (or his body) back to his father Daunus. Each represents that terrible moment when a parent confronts the loss of his or her hope for the future. And, finally, in her scene this unnamed

Trojan mother delivers the last lament of her generation for a son fallen for a Trojan cause, since she alone of all the mothers dared to follow her son to Italy. Vergil grants her the privilege of high drama, a perfect speech (seven questions, Highet notes, and Pavlock quotes Servius that the speech fulfills Cicero's requirements for arousing pity), the keening expected of a mother at the death of a son, the depth to shake the hearts of those who hear her, return to the shelter where she had dropped her spindle at the summons of Fama, and then, the last distinctive Trojan woman in the epic, disappearance from the action, but not from the effect of her brief moment before us.[17] We do not know whether she benefitted from Ascanius' extravagant promise that she would be a mother to him in all but the name of Creusa; only the silence of the absolutely bereft.

Finally, the *Iliades* of 11.34-35 at the bier of Pallas:

> *circum omnis famulumque manus Troianaque turba*
> *et maestum Iliades crinem de more solutae.*

Why do these Trojan women appear at this juncture, the first to be named as a group since the *matres* of Book 5 initiated the crisis that was to divide the followers of Aeneas permanently? First, this is a state occasion, and Aeneas makes its importance clear:

> *"ite," ait "egregias animas, quae sanguine nobis*
> *hanc patriam peperere suo, decorate supremis*
> *muneribus, maestamque Euandri primus ad urbem*
> *mittatur Pallas, quem non uirtutis egentem*
> *abstulit atra dies et funere mersit acerbo."*
>
> 11.24-28

Aeneas sees this as a decisive moment in the war, one which has in fact won for them the position they seek and a new *patria*. While one may well quarrel with this, it is the position taken by the Trojan commander. It is appropriate, therefore, that the Trojans turn out in force and honor this adopted Trojan prince with all due ceremony. Michael Putnam has recently argued persuasively for a far closer personal relationship between Aeneas and Pallas than has been usually understood.[18] Putnam demonstrates through careful analysis of the poetry that Aeneas' final act of vengeance is in good part personal, not simply *pietas* owed to Evander. Aeneas' impassioned farewells to Pallas seem confirming of this, and certainly we can expect that he would call out the Trojans to honor his companion, whose death has so moved him. Next, Pallas' death erases a hope for the future, an aid for Iulus (cf. lines 57-58), and a key element in the amalgamation of peoples that is to emerge. They are all there to do him honor:

> *tum maesta phalanx Teucrique sequuntur*
> *Tyrrhenique omnes et uersis Arcades armis.*
>
> 11.92-93

Only the Latins and Rutulians are missing from this glimpse into the future, and Turnus must go before they can join with the others. Lastly, and somewhat paradoxically, although the death of Pallas re-evokes the Trojan *furor* in Aeneas, this is the last time in which the Trojan women will really appear as Trojan. In the rapid denouement from this solemn moment their identity must inexorably fade, until we realize from Juno's conversation with Jupiter in *Aeneid* 12 that she has finally won . . . Troy is no more.

In that part of his poem in which a major focus is on the impact of this war on the women of Italy, whether queen, princess, warrior, farm girl, wife or mother, Vergil has counterpoised three references to Trojan women that mark the evanescence of their existence as "Trojans" as the inevitability of their destiny emerges.

NOTES

1. J.W. Zarker, "Vergil's Trojan and Italian *Matres*," *Vergilius* 24 (1978) 23, n. 1.
2. T.E. Page, *The* Aeneid *of Virgil, Books VII-XII* (London, 1900) *ad loc.*
3. J. Conington, rev. H. Nettleship, *The Works of Virgil* (London, 1883) *ad loc.*
4. See K. Quinn, *Virgil's* Aeneid: *A Critical Description* (Ann Arbor, 1968) 14-16, for an interesting discussion of what Quinn calls a *death-wish* as part of the "heroic impulse."
5. Nautes is trained as an orator by Minerva and seems here to play the role of interpreter of fate; for Anchises as an instrument of the gods, see B. Otis, *Virgil: A Study in Civilized Poetry* (Oxford, 1964) 278-279.
6. Despite the importance of this speech G. Highet does not treat it in *The Speeches in Vergil's* Aeneid (Princeton, 1972); on Nautes' advice see M.A. Di Cesare, *The Altar and the City* (New York, 1974) 77-78, and Quinn 158 (the negative tone).

7. The group under Antenor which settled Patavum is not known to Aeneas and must be discounted; cf. Venus' speech in Book 1, esp. 242-249.
8. And these are the remnants of those whom Aeneas met at Mount Ida:

    Atque hic ingentem comitum adfluxisse nouorum
    inuenio admirans numerum, matresque uirosque
    collectam exsilio pubem, miserabile uulgus.
    2.796-798

    Despite the numbers here implied and the many ships, one must be careful not to take too literally the large specific numbers, such as the many instances of *mille* respecting troops in the latter half of the epic.
9. Quinn, *op. cit.* 176, n. 1.
10. See, e.g., G. Williams, *Technique and Ideas in the* Aeneid (New Haven, 1983) 107; on 209-210 Williams also pursues the philosophic tone introduced by the poet's somewhat ambivalent remark on the "honor" of burial *"si qua est ea gloria"* in line 4; see also the excellent section on Caieta/Gaeta by A.G. McKay, *Vergil's Italy* (Greenwich, CT, 1970) 160-161.
11. Di Cesare comments effectively on this point, *op. cit.* 123 and 216.
12. For a convenient summary of work that looks at the Nisus/Euryalus episodes themselves, see the citations of J. Makowski, "Nisus and Euryalus: A Platonic Relationship," *CJ* 85 (1989) 1-15.
13. W.R. Johnson, "Aeneas and the Ironies of *Pietas*," *CJ* 60 (1965) 360-364.
14. B. Pavlock, "Epic and Tragedy in Vergil's Nisus and Euryalus Episode," *TAPA* 115 (1985) 207-224.
15. R.B. Egan, "Euryalus' Mother and *Aeneid* 9-12," *Studies in Latin Literature and Roman History II*, ed. C. Deroux, *Collection Latomus* 168 (Bruxelles, 1980) 157-176.
16. M.O. Lee, *Fathers and Sons in Virgil's* Aeneid: *Tum Genitor Natum* (New York, 1979) 113ff.
17. It should be noted here that the arrival of Fama with devastating news for Euryalus' mother in 9.473-475 anticipates Fama's arrival at Pallanteum with news of Pallas' death in 11.139-141.
18. M.C.J. Putnam, "Possessiveness, Sexuality, and Heroism in the *Aeneid*," *Vergilius* 31 (1985) 1-21.

LES AMOURS DE DIDON OU LES LIMITES DE LA LIBERTÉ

❦

Pierre Grimal
Academie des Inscriptions et Belles-Lettres, Institut de France

Peut-on dire du nouveau sur le célèbre épisode de l'*Enéide* où sont contées les amours de Didon et d'Enée, l'une des parties du poème le plus souvent lues et commentées? Ces pages recèlent-elles encore quelque secret? Mais, même si tout a déjà été dit, il n'est peut-être pas inutile de revenir, une fois de plus, sur cette aventure qui a fait l'objet de si nombreux commentaires.

Le récit de ces amours, occupe, on le sait, tout le livre 4 de l'*Enéide*, qui se termine par le départ d'Enée et la mort de la reine. Mais il est déjà question de ces amours au livre 2, qui les annonce et les prépare. Dès le premier livre, Vénus y fait allusion, lorsqu'elle promet à son fils que la reine l'accueillera[1] et, de son côté, Didon, aussitôt qu'elle connaît l'arrivée du célèbre Troyen, l'attend, souhaite sa venue et, déjà, l'admire—condition favorable à la naissance d'une passion plus tendre.[2] De plus, Didon est présente, bien que muette, pendant que se déroule, aux livres 2 et 3, le long récit de la prise de Troie et du voyage d'Enée, depuis la Phrygie jusqu'en Sicile et à Carthage. Puis, encore, après la catastrophe, elle réapparaît, au livre 6, parmi les ombres, aux Enfers, où elle a retrouvé son premier mari, le Tyrien Sychéc.

Pour toutes ces raisons, la reine fondatrice de Carthage ne peut manquer d'apparaître comme un personnage majeur de l'épopée, ne serait-ce que par la place qu'elle y occupe. Ce qui, à la réflexion, ne laisse pas de surprendre. Dans les poèmes homériques, ni Hélène, ni Andromaque, ni Pénélope ne jouent un tel rôle. Les commentateurs antiques s'étonnaient déjà de ce qu'ils considéraient comme un manquement aux lois de l'épopée. Servius se fait leur porte-parole lorsqu'il écrit:

> Apollonius a composé des *Argonautiques*, et, au livre 3, fait figurer Médée amoureuse; c'est de là que vient, tout entier, le présent livre (le livre 4 de l'*Enéide*).... Il consiste entièrement en manoeuvres et en finesses, et le style en est presque celui de la comédie, ce qui n'est pas étonnant puisqu'il est question d'amour.[3]

La référence à Apollonios de Rhodes a été souvent commentée, et les rapprochements que l'on fait, depuis l'Antiquité, entre les deux poèmes, sont évidents et certains. Ces rapprochements, toutefois, restent assez formels. Ils concernent essentiellement la "peinture" de l'amour naissant, puis le cheminement d'une passion qui, finalement, poussée à son paroxysme, devient cause de mort. Lorsqu'il s'inspire des *Argonautiques*, Virgile se souvient, d'avoir été un *poeta novus*. Comme Catulle dans l'épisode d'Ariane abandonnée,[4] il transpose dans un poème de caractère épique une analyse de la passion que la littérature grecque classique réservait plutôt à la tragédie. Au-delà d'Apollonios, c'est la *Phèdre* d'Euripide que l'on aperçoit. Il n'est pas douteux que Virgile se soit complu à cette peinture. Il avait des garants et à Alexandrie et à Rome. Mais faut-il en conclure que son dessein s'est borné à traiter, avec autant de vérité que d'ingéniosité, une aventure d'amour, pour elle-même, l'un de ces ἐρωτικὰ παθήματα que Parthénios de Nicée, une trentaine d'années, environ, avant l'*Enéide*, proposait à son ami Gallus? Les élégiaques, et tout particulièrement Properce, s'étaient engagés dans cette voie. Virgile voulut-il, consciemment, suivre leur exemple? Se trouva-t-il, un peu malgré lui, entraîné par la mode littéraire de son temps? Ou bien a-t-il utilisé pour ses propres fins un thème de la poésie amoureuse? Mais, s'il en est ainsi, quel fut son dessein? Pourquoi a-t-il cédé à la tentation d'insérer un roman d'amour dans la grande épopée qui méditait sur la naissance—et la re-naissance—de Rome?

Chacun sait, depuis les récentes études sur Naevius,[5] que la venue d'Enée à Carthage et sa rencontre avec Didon figuraient déjà dans le *Bellum Punicum* et que le Troyen offrait à la reine de riches présents d'hospitalité—ce qu'il fera aussi dans la version virgilienne de l'aventure.[6] Or, Naevius composait cet épisode aux environs de l'année 207 av. J.C., en un temps où la seconde guerre punique faisait encore rage, même si les jours des plus grandes angoisses étaient passés. A ce moment-là, parler de

Carthage, dans un poème à la gloire de Rome, et dont l'un des buts était de rendre aux Romains la confiance en eux-mêmes et en leur destin impérial,⁷ c'était évidemment poser le problème des relations entre les deux grands puissances de l'Occident méditerranéen. Un problème que Virgile ne pouvait manquer de rencontrer, dans la mesure où il reprenait cet épisode du poème de Naevius, ce qu'il avait fait, si nous en croyons les témoignages antiques. Certes, l'acuité du débat s'était fort émoussée, en deux siècles, et une fois Rome maîtresse du monde, mais les guerres puniques n'en restaient pas moins un moment décisif dans le destin de Rome, et un poème qui tentait de retracer celui-ci, sous la forme d'une épopée riche en symboles, ne pouvait se dispenser de l'évoquer.

Aussi peut-on facilement découvrir, dans cet épisode des amours de Didon, des allusions à deux événements dominants de ces guerres. Il n'est pas douteux que les flammes du bûcher de Didon, qui illuminent le ciel, tandis que s'éloignent les navires troyens n'évoquent celles de l'incendie qui détruisit la Carthage punique, après la victoire romaine, à la fin de la troisième guerre menée par Rome. Mais il est une autre allusion, plus insistante, à ce qui fut un thème majeur de la "propagande" romaine, la "perfidie" des Carthaginois, qui justifie que toute la responsabilité de la querelle soit rejetée sur ceux-ci. Ainsi, dès le livre 1 de l'*Enéide*, Vénus avoue les craintes qu'elle nourrit envers cette "maison ambiguë" et les "Tyriens au langage double."⁸ Tous les commentateurs reconnaissent dans ces vers la condamnation de la *fides punica* et, plus particulièrement, peut-être, l'évocation du plus célèbre manquement commis à la loyauté, celui d'Hannibal violant le traité de l'Ebre et déclanchant ainsi la seconde guerre punique. Peut-être aussi le poète songe-t-il à ce qui fut la cause de la troisième guerre, le réarmement de Carthage, contrairement aux clauses du traité conclu après Zama.

Didon, par conséquent, reine de Carthage, peut, elle aussi, commettre une trahison. Vénus le craint. Ce même thème apparaît une seconde fois, au moment où Enée, décidé à partir et une fois tout préparé, s'attarde, sans penser que la reine peut changer d'avis et attaquer les Troyens. Mercure lui apparaît alors en songe et le met en garde contre une telle possibilité. Didon ne va-t-elle pas essayer d'incendier la flotte et de massacrer les compagnons d'Enée, et, pour se venger, recourir aux ruses caractéristiques de son peuple?⁹ Mercure parle de "ruse" (*dolus*) et de crime (*nefas*). Ce crime, ce serait un manquement aux devoirs de l'hospitalité. Didon a accueilli les Troyens, elle a conclu avec eux une sorte de pacte, solennisé par des sacrifices[10] et des échanges de présents, dont les dieux ont été les témoins. Le ressentiment, personnel, qu'elle éprouve envers Enée ne concerne que ses rapports avec lui; il ne saurait justifier ni religieusement ni moralement qu'elle prenne l'initiative de les traiter en "ennemis," en *hostes*, c'est-à-dire en étrangers "hors-la-loi"—ce qu'ils ne sont plus. Si elle le faisait, elle manquerait à l'ordre divin, au *fas*. Ce n'est donc pas un abus de langage lorsque Mercure, dans l'apparition que nous avons dite, prononce le mot de *nefas*. Aucun mortel, surtout s'il se trouve chef d'un peuple, et, par conséquent, intermédiaire entre celui-ci et les dieux, n'a le croit de rompre un *foedus*, au gré d'une passion ou d'un caprice.

Mais, dira-t-on, Enée est coupable, puisqu'il "trahit" la reine. A ce moment, nous devons nous garder d'apporter, pour comprendre Virgile, des notions et des sentiments d'un autre siècle. Les relations d'Enée avec Didon ne relèvent que de sa personnalité humaine, de *privatus*; elles ne mettent pas en jeu sa qualité et ses responsabilités de conducteur d'hommes, de *dux*. De même Didon se conduit en femme trahie, non en reine. Comme reine, elle doit respecter les engagements politiques qui la lient, et la guerre qu'elle songe un instant à déclancher ne serait pas un *iustum bellum*; elle n'aurait pas l'agrément des dieux.

Ce qui montre clairement la division qui existe entre le domaine des sentiments privés et celui des engagements d'Etat. Un *dux*, dans la conception romaine, doit suivre l'ordre divin, dont il est l'interprète et l'exécutant par l'intermédiaire des auspices, dans l'exercice de son *imperium*. Et tout le drame des amours de Didon et d'Enée repose sur cette dualité. Enée n'a pas le droit, plus que Didon, de céder aux sentiments qu'il éprouve. Didon ne peut utiliser son pouvoir royal pour tirer vengeance de ce qui reste une offense privée; si elle a la tentation de le faire, c'est parce que l'âme punique, qui est en elle, lui suggère "d'user d'un langage double." Enée, en Romain, fait taire la passion qui l'anime et refuse de céder à son immense désir de demeurer près de la reine:

>   . . . *et obnixus curas sub corde premebat.*[11]

On sait la force du mot *cura*. Chez Virgile, il s'applique, par exemple, à la passion nourrie par Gallus pour Lycoris, une passion qui entraîne Gallus dans les bois où il gémit et pleure, sans souci de ses devoirs.[12] Et le terme, on le sait, appartient au vocabulaire de l'élégie amoureuse. Enée est un amant véritable, sensible, passionné, comme l'est Properce au même moment,[13] à l'égard de

Cynthie, un amant qui souffre, et non pas seulement un amant qui désire.[14] Virgile n'a pas voulu qu'Enée apparaisse comme un amoureux volage, qui ne chercherait que son plaisir. Le Troyen fugitif est véritablement, en pensée et en intention, devenu l'époux, l'associé de la reine dans les tâches du gouvernement. Il en accepte les devoirs et travaille à construire la ville.[15] Son amour et son instinct profond de conducteur de peuple s'accorderaient donc, s'il s'agissait de *son* peuple. Mais il n'en est pas ainsi, et s'il reste à Carthage, s'il en devient le souverain de fait, alors il n'est plus en accord avec l'ordre du monde ni avec le Destin. C'est ce dont Mercure vient l'avertir.

Ce destin, qui veut que naisse Rome, et qu'elle obtienne l'empire du monde, se réalisera quelles que soient les péripéties du devenir historique. Mais la manière dont il se réalisera et dont la race d'Enée s'élèvera au-dessus de tous les autres peuples n'est pas déterminée à l'avance. Elle ne peut pas l'être si la liberté humaine est une réalité, si Enée, en ce moment crucial, peut, ou non, obéir à l'avertissement des dieux.

Les longues guerres entre Rome et Carthage, qui ont duré pendant des siècles, s'étaient terminées par la victoire de Rome, et elles ne pouvaient se terminer autrement, puisque Jupiter avait déclaré solennellement, en s'adressant à Vénus, qu'il "a donné (aux Romains) un empire sans fin."[16] Il faut donc que le Troyen ne demeure pas à Carthage, qu'il aille, dans cette Hespérie qui lui est promise, fonder son propre empire. Mais il peut aussi ne pas le faire. Les moyens par lesquels s'accomplira le destin restent contingents, seul le résultat final est déterminé. Entre temps, interviennent les sentiments et les passions humaines, et ce sont eux qui fondent la poésie, épique ou tragique.

Quel est donc, dans ce grand débat, le rôle des divinités? Sont-elles toutes puissantes, régissent-elles à leur guise l'âme humaine? Une certaine tradition des interprètes de Virgile semble l'admettre, mais, croyons-nous, à tort, comme il apparaît au moment où Vénus explique à son fils, le dieu Amour, qu'elle redoute un revirement de la part de Didon, même si, pour le moment, elle l'accueille de manière amicale. Pour éviter cela, elle veut lui inspirer un amour violent, qui déterminera sa conduite:

. . . et cingere flamma
reginam meditor, ne quo se numine mutet.[17]

Vers que nous traduisons ainsi: "j'ai l'intention d'environner la reine d'une flamme, pour qu'elle ne change pas de volonté," alors que l'on comprend, en général, d'une manière différente. La majorité des commentateurs et traducteurs voient dans le mot *numine* la mention d'une divinité dont l'action va pousser la reine à changer d'attitude, et ils pensent que c'est une allusion voilée à une intervention possible de Junon. Mais est-ce bien cela que dit le texte? Servius, à propos de ce passage, s'interroge sur le sens de *quo*, mais reste muet sur l'essentiel, la signification du mot *numen*. On sait (et cela était clair depuis longtemps) que ce terme ne désigne pas, d'abord et forcément, une divinité, mais une "volonté agissante." G. Dumézil l'a rappelé, à juste titre, et l'on ne peut que lui donner raison.[18] Ce sens est bien attesté, notamment chez Cicéron, dans le *Discours au peuple après son retour*[19] et dans la troisième *Philippique*;[20] le *numen* du peuple romain, celui du sénat sont des "volontés agissantes," qui "informent" l'avenir, instaurent une politique déterminée. Virgile désigne ainsi, dans le passage qui nous occupe, le parti que prendra Didon à l'égard des Troyens, sa "politique": ou bien leur donner l'hospitalite, ou bien les combattre.

De plus, l'emploi de *mutare*, dans ce texte, avec un ablatif, est semblable à celui que nous voyons dans l'*Art poétique* d'Horace: *ut silvae foliis pronos mutantur in annos.*"[21] De même que les forêts "changent de feuilles" selon les moments de l'année, de même Didon pourrait "changer de volonté," et cela sans que Junon intervienne. La reine est libre de se montrer accueillante ou bien hostile. Cela ne dépend que d'elle, et c'est précisément pour cette raison, parce que les déesses ne peuvent pas la contraindre, et que cela dépasse leur pouvoir, qu'elles vont ruser, et faire naître en elle l'amour. Vénus se chargera de l'amour-passion (car c'est là son domaine), Junon de l'amour conjugal, auquel elle préside.

Ainsi, il est clair que la contrainte exercée par les divinités sur la liberté humaine reste limitée: d'abord, qu'elle s'exerce seulement dans la sphère d'action de chacune d'elles, ensuite qu'elle ne provoque pas un acte particulier, déterminé, mais qu'elle agit sur l'esprit en créant des conditions psychologiques favorables à la décision souhaitée. Selon le cas, elles prendront comme "relais" soit la passion soit la raison, soit d'autres arguments, d'autres sentiments capables de persuader. Vénus, Junon, Mercure lui-même, ne sont que des tentateurs. Il est possible de leur résister, lors du combat qu'ils livrent dans l'âme sur laquelle ils veulent agir. Qu'il y ait bien un combat, que tout ne soit pas acquis d'avance, c'est ce dont témoigne Virgile lui-même, dans le discours de Junon à Vénus, lorsque la reine des dieux reproche à celle-ci d'avoir remporté sur une femme une victoire trop facile.[22] Fallait-il deux divinités pour vaincre Didon?

L'action de Mercure sur l'esprit d'Enée est semblable. Il n'utilisera pas la passion, pour le déterminer à reprendre sa route vers l'Italie et accomplir les destins, mais des instincts plus profonds, qui sont ceux d'un homme et d'un Romain.

Qu'Enée quitte Carthage pour l'Hespérie dépendra d'une décision du héros, qu'il prendra "librement." Ce qui est déterminé de toute éternité, c'est la fondation de Rome, non les moyens de cette fondation. Le destin n'exclut pas le contingent. Aussi faut-il que Mercure provoque la décision d'Enée. De même que Vénus et Junon agissent sur la reine en réveillant en elle ses instincts de femme, le désir charnel qui la porte vers le beau héros, et, plus profondément encore, l'espoir de trouver en lui cet appui, ce secours qu'une épouse attend d'un époux, de même le discours de Mercure à Enée s'adresse aux instincts qui forment son être même. Les arguments qu'il emploie font appel aux catégories morales qui ont toujours animé les conducteurs d'hommes de la cité romaine. Catégories fixées une fois pour toutes, auxquelles nous donnons les nom de "devoirs" (mais dans une perspective kantienne et, finalement, chrétienne) et qui sont bien plutôt que des obligations morales, des pulsions irrésistibles, irrationnelles et affectives.

Le discours de Mercure à Enée[23] se limite à dix vers, mais il suffit à réveiller des sentiments profonds, qui sommeillent au fond de cette conscience, engourdie dans le confort de son aventure carthaginoise. Deux arguments essentiels. D'abord, un appel à la gloire qui attend le fondateur d'un grand royaume. Aucun Romain ne saurait être insensible à cet appel. La gloire, en effet, croit-on alors, fait de celui qui la mérite l'objet de l'admiration universelle et, par là, lui confère une véritable immortalité. Une page célèbre de Cicéron, au premier livre des *Tusculanes*, montre que le désir de gloire, inné chez les humains (du moins à Rome), implique qu'il existe en nous une croyance instinctive à la survie des âmes. Et la gloire, en fait, assure cette survie, dans la mesure où, selon le mot, souvent répété, d'Ennius, elle fait "voler, vivant, le nom (du défunt) sur les lèvres des hommes."

Le second argument de Mercure s'appuie sur le souci, inné lui aussi chez tout Romain, du sort de sa descendance. Pour décider Enée à accomplir son destin, il y a d'abord Ascagne, le fils déjà né, il y a aussi Iulus (qui n'est autre que ce même Ascagne, de son nom "italique," mais Enée l'ignore), qui symbolise, d'une manière mystérieuse, mais d'autant plus efficace, le royaume à venir. Mais, indépendamment de ces espoirs lointains (qui ne sont assurément pas clairs pour Enée, mais ont pour lui valeur d'oracles) aucun Romain ne peut rester insensible à l'avenir de ceux qui seront issus de lui. Tout Romain sait bien qu'il est seulement un maillon d'une longue chaîne, que sa mission, en cette vie, est d'assurer la continuité du nom, de transmettre le *"patrimonium"* dont il est dépositaire, et que symbolisent les masques des ancêtres déposés dans le *tablinum*. Mis en face de cette responsabilité, à laquelle il ne saurait se soustraire sans un déchirement intérieur, Enée ne peut pas résister. Il faut abandonner la reine et reprendre les chemins de la mer. Il est confirmé dans cette décision par les rêves qui lui montrent, précisément, Anchise, son père[24] et lui rendent sensible, matériellement, cette continuité gentilice qu'il ne saurait briser.

On voit que Virgile a mis, dans cet épisode des amours de Didon et d'Enée, tout autre chose qu'un roman de la passion et de la trahison. Il en a fait non seulement un mythe politique, préfigurant des siècles d'histoire, mais un mythe moral illustrant, de manière exemplaire, les instincts les plus profonds de l'âme romaine, ceux qui régissent le déroulement même de chaque vie. Les rapports qui s'établissent entre Didon et Enée reflètent, par exemple, la conception que l'on se fait alors de la vie conjugale. Celle-ci, pensait-on, dans la plus ancienne tradition, encore vivante au temps d'Auguste, ne devait pas être fondée sur l'amour-passion;[25] un tel amour n'était pas exclu, il ne pouvait l'être, mais il était regardé avec suspicion, comme une sorte de faiblesse, passagère, instable et dangereuse. Le véritable but du mariage était la continuité de la "race." Rappelons la formule dont usaient les censeurs pour demander aux citoyens s'ils avaient une épouse *"liberorum creandorum causa."* Rappelons aussi quelques exemples illustres, et particulièrement significatifs: celui de Marcia, que Caton consent à abandonner pour qu'elle puisse donner des enfants à Hortensius, parce qu'elle est "d'une fécondité éprouvée." En sens inverse, on connaît le dilemme posé par les devins à Sempronius Gracchus, le mari de Cornélia. Des deux serpents, l'un mâle, l'autre femelle, qui étaient apparus dans sa maison, s'il tuait le premier, c'est lui-même qui mourrait, s'il tuait le second, ce serait sa femme. Il choisit, en tuant le serpent auquel était lié son destin, de mourir lui-même. Sacrifice qui ne lui fut pas dicté par l'amour ni la passion, mais par le "bon sens": lui-même était vieux, Cornélia était encore jeune et par conséquent, plus à même que lui d'assurer l'éducaton de leurs enfants (elle en avait eu douze!). C'est donc elle qui devait demeurer auprès d'eux.

En vertu de la même morale, Énée comprend qu'il doit quitter Didon, moins pour réaliser les destins ou pour obéir à Jupiter (qui, d'ailleurs, ne charge pas Mercure d'apporter au héros un ordre formel) que pour accomplir son destin de fils et de père, vis-à-vis d'Anchise, qui l'en presse, et d'Ascagne, qui attend.

A aucun moment Énée n'est contraint. Il est libre, lui aussi, comme Didon. Celle-ci, finalement, reconnaît qu'elle a commis une faute, en s'abandonnant à la passion;[26] elle a été victime d'une illusion, à laquelle elle a consenti, et elle sent bien que là est son crime. Les dieux ne sont pour rien dans sa propre responsabilité. Ce n'est pas la première fois, dans l'histoire humaine, celle de la légende, qu'ils ont égaré les humains. Troie n'a-t-elle pas été édifiée sur la Colline d'Atè, la Colline de l'Erreur?

Et, à ce moment, c'est tout le problème de la théodicée qui se trouve posé, et auquel Virgile tente d'apporter une solution. Ce problème, toute la tradition légendaire grecque le posait. Il se retouve un peu partout, dans l'épopée, dans la tragédie, surtout. Virgile ne pouvait l'éviter. Dès les premiers vers de l'*Enéide*, il s'interroge sur ce qui forme la trame même de l'*Enéide*, la colère de Junon, qui voit son projet d'élever sa ville, Carthage, au-dessus de toutes les nations, définitivement ruiné par la prédiction que vient de faire Jupiter,[27] et il s'écrie: "Peut-il y avoir de si violentes colères dans les âmes célestes?" Question indignée, qui revient à mettre en question toute la théologie poétique, la vision des dieux que les poètes, depuis Homère, imposent aux mortels. C'est là un très ancien débat, instauré par les philosophes mais aussi des sculpteurs, comme Phidias, et quelques poètes, depuis le siècle de Périclès. Virgile, donc, pose la question, mais quelle est sa réponse?

Nous avons vu que Virgile refusait d'accorder aux divinités la toute-puissance sur l'âme humaine. Vénus et Junon, sans doute, abusent Didon, elles ne font pas, à elle seule, que la reine se laisse aller à sa passion. La liberté humaine est préservée, pour le bien comme pour le mal, le bien étant ce qui donne à l'âme la paix, la sérénité, le mal étant ce qui la déchire. Enée, en poursuivant sa route vers l'Italie, retrouvera le calme intérieur. La reine, au contraire, sera torturée jusqu'à la mort. L'un et l'autre sont les artisans de leur destin personnel, et les dieux n'y sont pour rien, pas plus que la fatalité.

Virgile, ici, nous semble suivre l'enseignement d'Epicure, qui a toujours défendu l'existence de la liberté chez les humains, comme source de leurs bonheurs. Nous lisons en effet dans la *Lettre à Ménécée*:

"Mieux vaudrait. . . . accepter docilement les mythes relatifs aux dieux que de s'asservir à la fatalité des physiciens, car le mythe nous laisse l'espoir que les dieux se laisseraient fléchir par les honneurs du culte, tandis que la seconde opinion ne comporte qu'une nécessité inflexible; il (le sage) ne considère la Fortune ni comme une divinité (car un dieu ne fait rien sans règle) ni comme une cause inconsistante, car il ne croit pas que ce soit elle qui donne aux hommes ni le bien ni le mal, et par conséquent qu'elle contribue à les rendre heureux, mais seulement qu'elle fait naître les causes qui sont à l'origine des grands biens ou des grands maux."[28]

Ni la volonté divine ni le Destin ne sont en effet contraignants dans l'*Enéide*, puisque, pas plus que les dieux, la Fortune de Rome, fixée depuis l'origine des Temps, ne dicte aux personnages leur conduite—celle-ci, librement choisie, réalise cette Fortune, mais elle reste de l'ordre du contingent. D'autre part, en refusant aux divinités le pouvoir sur les âmes, Virgile restait fidèle, une fois encore, à l'épicurisme. Sans doute, puisqu'il écrivait une épopée, il devait en conserver les conventions, remontant au modèle homérique, et les règles du genre voulaient que les divinités interviennent à tous les instants. C'est ainsi que la tempête qui disperse la flotte d'Enée est voulue par Junon et réalisée par Eole, que Vénus ménage à son fils un bon accueil de la part de Didon, avant même de faire naître chez celle-ci la passion que l'on sait. Et l'on pourrait multiplier les exemples. Mais ici encore il ne s'agit que de facteurs contingents, et l'on en vient à se demander si les dieux que Virgile met en scène sont réellement de "vrais dieux," s'il ne s'agit pas de conceptions théologiques que nous connaissons bien par ailleurs, mais sans les associer ordinairement à l'auteur de l'*Enéide*.

Lorsqu'il paraît s'indigner que l'opinion vulgaire attribue des passions aux divinités, aux "âmes célestes" (c'est-à-dire, sans doute, les âmes des êtres célestes), il suit, une fois encore, la doctrine d'Epicure. La *Lettre à Ménécée* en apporte le témoignage: "En premier lieu, écrit Epicure, persuade-toi que la divinité est un être éternel et bienheureux, ainsi que la notion commune du dieu se trouve gravée en nous, et ne lui attribue rien qui soit en contradiction avec l'immortalité ni en désaccord avec la béatitude."[29] Or, ce qui est "en désaccord avec la béatitude," pour reprendre les mots dont se sert Epicure, ce sont précisément les passions, tout ce qui provoque le trouble dans l'âme et détruit le "plaisir" serein, souverain bien et des dieux et des hommes.

Mais, dira-t-on, les divinités que nous voyons agir dans l'*Enéide* sont des êtres de passion. Nous l'avons vu à propos de Vénus et de Junon. Il est facile de le constater à propos de presque toutes les autres, par exemple Diane, qui gémit sur la mort de Camille,[30] mais aussi de Neptune lui-même, qui éprouve, en s'apercevant qu'une tempête s'est déchaînée sans son ordre, une émotion violente,[31] en vif contraste avec l'expression majestueuse et calme de son visage (*placidum caput!*). Mais on notera que Jupiter seul apparaît comme exempt de passions. Lorsque Vénus vient se plaindre à lui des manoeuvres de Junon, il l'accueille avec un sourire comme si les affaires humaines, et les émotions de ses "enfants" divins ne pouvaient l'affecter réellement. Virgile montre ainsi que Jupiter est le plus "véritable" des dieux, le plus "épicurien," simple témoin de la réalisation des Destins, dont il n'est à aucun degré l'agent.

Tout se passe donc, en dernière analyse, comme si les divinités, dans l'*Enéide*, n'étaient (à l'exception de Jupiter) que des "démons," et non des dieux au sens le plus plein—celui que donnait Epicure à ce mot. Ces "démons" sont intermédiaires entre les dieux et les hommes, ils agissent sur le monde, ou du moins le tentent, leur pouvoir est supérieur à celui des humains, mais il n'est pas sans limite, et chacun ne peut agir que dans la sphère de ses attributions—un trait qui nous paru caractéristique de la manière dont se manifestent Vénus et Junon pour intervenir auprès de Didon. Le texte le plus célèbre relatif aux démons se trouve, on le sait, dans le *De deo Socratis* d'Apulée,[32] mais cette doctrine n'est pas née au second siècle de notre ère. Apulée se réfère à Platon, et il pense sans doute à Eros, tel que le décrit le *Banquet*, ou encore au Démiurge, et non au seul démon de Socrate. Finalement, on entrevoit assez bien comment se sont formées de telles idées, dans une Grèce où l'on rencontrait partout des héros, des demi-dieux, des puissances invisibles, qui n'appartenaient pas à la "famille" des divinités majeures, mais entretenaient avec elles des rapports de subordination. Il est bien certain que les épicuriens ne croyaient pas à de tels démons, puisqu'ils n'attribuaient aucune existence séparée aux âmes, alors que, selon les stoïciens, les "démons" étaient souvent des âmes libérées de leur corps. Mais on peut imaginer que, dans l'univers d'Epicure, il y eût place malgré tout pour des êtres divins "incomplets"— malheureusement, aucun témoignage ne vient appuyer l'hypothèse! Quoi il en soit, il est probable que Virgile, comme les philosophes, et les poètes d'alors, ne répugnait pas à opérer des synthèses entre les différents courants d'idées. Platon, au moment où l'*Enéide* prenait forme, n'était pas loin de sa pensée. Très sensible aux arguments épicuriens sur la nature des divinités et à leur valeur exemplaire pour les humains, il n'en accepte pas moins l'existence d'un Destin, d'une finalité du monde, comme le veulent les stoïciens. Mais, en même temps, il sauvegarde la liberté des âmes, et les montre, vivant d'une vie propre, au fond des Enfers, ce qui est en mythe platonicien.

Et c'est précisément aux Enfers qu'Enée, une dernière fois, rencontrera Didon. La reine est guérie de sa passion. Enée, lui, ne l'est pas, et pleure lorsqu'elle refuse de répondre à ses propos, trop évocateurs du passé. C'est que la magie de Vénus et celle de Junon ont cessé de s'exercer dans cette âme. Didon est désormais libre, et sa liberté la porte, à nouveau, vers Sychée.

NOTES

1. *Enéide* 1.387 et suiv.
2. *Ibid.* 1. 375-376: *atque utinam rex ipse, Noto compulsus eodem / apparet Aeneas.*
3. Servius, l'*Eneide* 4.1.
4. Catulle, poème 64.
5. En particulier M. Barchiesi, *Nevio epico* (Padoue, 1962).
6. *Bellum Punicum,* fr. 24 Marmorale: *pulchramque . . . ex auro uestemque citrosam.* Cf. *Enéide* 1.647.
7. C'est ainsi que des livres prophétiques (Sibyllins?) y étaient remis par Vénus à Anchise. Le thème du Destin de Rome y est donc bien présent.
8. *Enéide* 1.667: *quippe domum timet ambiguam Tyriosque bilinguis.*
9. *Ibid.* 4.563: *illa dolum dirumque nefas in pectore uersat.*
10. *Ibid.* 1.632 et suiv.
11. *Ibid.* 4.332.
12. *Eglogue* 10.22 et suiv.
13. *Elégies* 1.15.31.
14. *Ibid.* 3.15.3.
15. *Enéide* 4.260 et suiv.
16. *Ibid.* 1.279: *imperium sine fine dedi.*
17. *Ibid.* 1.673-674.
18. *La religion romaine archaïque* (Paris, 1966) 43 et suiv.

19. Ciceron, *Ad Quirites* 18.
20. Ciceron, *Philippiques* 3.32.
21. *Art Poétique* vers 60.
22. *Enéide* 4.95.
23. *Ibid.* 4.265-275.
24. *Ibid.* 4.351-353.
25. V. notre ouvrage, l'*Amour à Rome* (Paris, 1963).
26. *Enéide*, 4.550; cf. 596: *nunc te facta impia tangunt.*
27. *Ibid.* 1.8-11.
28. *Lettre à Ménécée*, trad. L. Robin, par. 134.
29. *Ibid.* par. 123.
30. *Enéide* 11.835 et suiv.
31. *Ibid.* 1.123 et suiv. ("*grauiter commotus*").
32. *De deo Socratis, passim.*

DIDO AND THE REPRESENTATION OF WOMEN IN VERGIL'S *AENEID*

J.P. Sullivan
University of California, Santa Barbara

The ideological basis of Vergil's *Aeneid* (*haud iniussa cano*) should have meant that the poet's attitudes towards women in his epic would be relatively uncomplicated, perhaps simply reflecting standard Roman views. Put bluntly, Woman—the Other— whether Creusa, the disheartened Trojan women in Sicily, Dido or Cleopatra, should be construed as an obstacle to the fulfilment of Man's creative vision and goals, whether political, artistic or moral. Yet the forces, conscious and unconscious, philosophical, social, literary and political, that guide Vergil's pen in writing the *Aeneid* are unexpectedly complex. The critical challenge then is to explain why his portraits of women are often so unexpectedly subtle.

Clues to his predictable evaluation of the battle of the sexes are to be found in the *Eclogues*, particularly the tenth, on Gallus' hopeless love for the fickle Lycoris (*sollicitos Galli dicamus amores*, verse 6), the name being a pseudonym for Volumnia, mistress not only of her own patron, but also of Gallus and Mark Antony. Vergil, being a card-carrying Epicurean, would surely have shared Lucretius' attitude to romantic passion. It was a madness, and an obstacle to the good life of moderate pleasures, friendship and philosophical inquiry. The best Vergil can do for Gallus is to comfort him with the thought that, although he cannot help himself (*omnia vincit Amor* [*Ecl.* 10.69]), out of this there may come the consolations of Art: immortal poetry can be fashioned out of a passion such as his (*Ecl.* 10.72). Vergil, of course, is writing just when the glorification of the pleasures and pains of romantic love by Catullus, Gallus, Tibullus and Propertius had so captured the imagination of the Roman literary public. Horace and Vergil might be seen as the almost officially appointed opposition to this regrettable tendency to prefer the pleasures of private life and passionate love over the call to duty and patriotism. *Make Love, Not War* is the message spelled out in the other elegists, even Ovid; *Make War, Not Love* is therefore one of the messages to be encoded in the *Aeneid*.

Dido, the central figure dominating most of the first six books of the *Aeneid*, must be examined first. Why was she introduced at all into the story of Aeneas and the founding of Rome? She was not an integral part of the myth.

Explanations abound and there is no doubt that Dido is heavily freighted with symbolism. Vergil, we are told, had to emulate Apollonius Rhodius' depiction of the passion of Medea for Jason (and look how badly that ended!); romantic love, thanks to the elegists, was a hot topic in Rome, and would not be out of place in a modern epic. Vergil was also self-consciously challenging Homer, so Dido could stand for the Sirens, Circe and Calypso all at once. Most great literary works are, in the psychologist's term, "overdetermined," and there is perhaps some truth in all of the above explanations. It was once fashionable in Vergilian scholarship to stress literary influences, but poets *choose* their models as well as their materials, and the very *choice* of models, and how they are reworked, will illuminate the processes of artistic creation.

Vergil understandably refashioned the mythic history of Troy for his political purposes. He made Aeneas a valiant hero who fought his way out of the doomed city, and not the actual betrayer of Troy, as some sources claimed. Even more radical was his transformation of the mythic portrait of Dido. For Christian authors, such as Tertullian and Ausonius, Dido was always an example of perfect chastity.[1] The sad epigram translated by Ausonius (*Epig.* 118) from the Greek (*AP* 16.151), written to decorate a portrait of Dido, tells the story, narrated in full by Justin (18.6.1-18):

> *Illa ego sum Dido vultu, quam conspicis, hospes,*
>   *assimulta modis pulchraeque mirificis.*
> *talis eram; sed non, Maro quam mihi finxit, erat mens,*
>   *vita nec incestis laeta cupidinibus:*
> *namque nec Aeneas vidit me Troius unquam,*
>   *nec Libyam advenit classibus Iliacis;*
> *sed furias fugiens atque arma procacis Iarbae*
>   *servavi, fateor, morte pudicitiam,*

> *pectore transfixo, castus quod perculit ensis,*
> *non furor aut laeso crudus amore dolor.*
> *sic cecidisse iuvat: vixi sine vulnere famae;*
> *ulta virum, positis moenibus, oppetii.*
> *invida cur in me stimulasti, Musa, Maronem,*
> *fingeret ut nostrae damna pudicitiae?*
> *vos magis historicis, lectores, credite de me,*
> *quam qui furta deum concubitusque canunt*
> *falsidici vates, temerant qui carmine verum*
> *humanisque deos assimulant vitiis.*

Dido, a *univira*, according to this version of the myth, never enjoyed an illicit liaison with Aeneas as Vergil described; Aeneas didn't even get to Libya in her time. Dido killed herself to preserve her chastity and fidelity to the priestly Sychaeus (or Acerbas) against the passionate African chief Iarbas, who wanted to marry her, not because she was love-crazy about Aeneas. It was her own people, anxious for the protection of Iarbas, who had tried to trick her into agreeing to the marriage for the common good. The historians have the true story, not lying poets like Vergil.

Why does Vergil change the myth of Dido? Surely not just because Naevius (fragments 17-21) had introduced the motif to explain the historical hostility between Rome and Carthage. It is more likely that Vergil wanted Dido to stand for the eternal Female that obstructs the hero's quest, whether it be the *nostos* of Odysseus returning to his faithful Penelope and, just as important, to his overlordship of Ithaca, or Aeneas' quest to refound Troy in the more magnificent vision of Rome. The hero must spurn these alluring feminine temptations or, seen through sterner eyes, these fearsome female dangers, these overt or disguised Sirens and temptresses. Aeneas' duty is to complete his divinely ordained mission and his behaviour has to fit an established mythic pattern of the final rejection by the hero of the heroine who had helped him, whether this is Jason's discarding Medea for another Creusa and the kingdom of Corinth, once the Golden Fleece was won, or Theseus' abandonment of Ariadne (a constant presence in the Dido episode) on the island of Naxos after the Minotaur was slain, or even the executions of Scylla, princess of Corinth, by Minos and the Vestal Virgin Tarpeia by the Sabine Tatius. Aeneas similarly deserts Dido, despite all the help she had given him and his shipwrecked crew. An analogous, more moral theme manifests itself in Roman historical legend in such instances as Lucretia's suicide after rape, Virginia's slaughter by her father to save her from Appius Claudius, and Horatius' killing of his sister because of her lament for her betrothed, one of the Curiatii whom he had slain. Women, clearly, may have to be sacrificed in the interests of patriotic or moral goals.

As part of this divine mission, Aeneas had first to be rid of his Trojan wife, Creusa; this is easily enough managed in the confusion of the sack of Troy. In the escape, she was lost or sat down exhausted, but Aeneas never sees her again alive (*Aen.* 2.736ff.). Aeneas, however, takes good care of his young son and his aging father, Anchises, which helps build up his reputation for piety, just as Augustus' bloody revenge on the assassins of his adoptive father, Julius Caesar, would help his own propaganda image as a dutiful son: always an appealing message in a patriarchal society. Aeneas supposedly goes back to look for Creusa, but instead he is greeted by a dutiful phantom, who explains to him that, by the will of heaven, he can't take her with him, because there is a more advantageous bride awaiting him in Italy. The sad fact is that Creusa and Lavinia are interchangeable; indeed they *have to be* for the underlying text of the *Aeneid*, which is the Founding of Rome and the justification of the contemporary political situation. The mythic accounts even vary as to whether Creusa or Lavinia gave birth to Ascanius/Iulus; in Vergil's version Lavinia is given instead a son named Silvius Aeneas (*Aen.* 6.764). (The Roman myths about the relationship between Silvius and his half-brother, Ascanius/Iulus and how they share power became immensely complicated.) It was perhaps the preferable version that the Julian *gens* have a solid Trojan ancestry. Creusa belongs to the past. Aeneas may shed tears over her, but he has no problem with forgiveness, for Creusa gives it freely, when she predicts—and willingly accepts—the *regia coniunx* awaiting Aeneas in Italy (*Aen.* 2.772). The virgin daughter of King Latinus belongs to the future, but she is also a shadowy figure, a political convenience, like Creusa, and an aetiological pretext for the naming of places (*Aen.* 12.194). Essentially, she is a prize to be fought over by warriors such as Turnus and Aeneas, just as Dido is also made out to a prize to be fought for by Iarbas and Aeneas.

It has been asked why both Creusa and Lavinia are made such uncomplaining and colorless figures. First of all, because Vergil's epic canvas is necessarily limited, if indeed it was ever finished. Secondly, too much sympathy lavished on these pivotal, but externally shaped, female figures would distract from the heroic thrust and from Vergil's creation of more autonomous female heroines.

Both Creusa and Lavinia then are pawns in the game of masculine politics. But not content with portraying the handing over of Lavinia by father Latinus to the foreigner Aeneas—an example of filial Roman obedience often seen in the dynastic arrangements of the late Republic—Vergil has to twist the knife. Turnus is portrayed not just as a gang-leader defending his turf, but also as a jealous suitor for Lavinia's hand. What does the colorless, but decorous virgin, Lavinia, who blushes easily, now become? She is accused of being the *causa mali tanti* (*Aen.* 11.480): the "cause" of this great evil, the war. It is not Aeneas' Trojan imperialism or Turnus' fanatical nationalism that brings on the war that occupies the last six books of the *Aeneid*, but a girl, a peace-maker, easily saddened by military reverses. The scapegoating of Helen in the myths of the Trojan War is the mythic pattern Vergil follows here. Similarly it is Dido's curse on Aeneas that *causes* the imperialistic and mercantile wars between Rome and Carthage, and Cleopatra will later be blamed for the civil wars between Antony and Octavian that culminated in the battle of Actium. On the shield of Aeneas there is the depiction of Antony with his barbarian resources and motley army (*hinc ope barbarica variisque Antonius armis* [*Aen.* 8.685]). He brings with him the forces of the East, and behind him trails his Egyptian bride, Cleopatra, an unholy sight (*nefas* [*Aen.* 8.688]).

Later Vergil presents Cleopatra with her sistrum of Isis encouraging the troops and he alludes to her suicide with the help of a couple of snakes. He adds a final touch by suggesting that she began the panicky rout that led to Augustus' victory (*Aen.* 8.695-713). There is an implication here that women crack under the pressure that the tougher male would resist. Aeneas survived the test with Dido, but Dido, racked by the pangs of love for Aeneas, could not endure the separation and committed suicide, and in the underworld she bears, for Aeneas, an incomprehensible grudge. Aeneas' defence, in addressing her shade in the underworld, is fascinating:

> "*infelix Dido, uerus mihi nuntius ergo*
> *uenerat exstinctam ferroque extrema secutam?*
> *funeris heu tibi causa fui? per sidera iuro,*
> *per superos et si qua fides tellure sub ima est,*
> *inuitus, regina, tuo de litore cessi.*"
>
> *Aen.* 6.456-460

"Unlucky Dido," he says, "was the news true then that you had fatally stabbed yourself? Was I, alas, the cause of your death? I swear by the stars and by the gods and by whatever is sacred in the nether regions that I left your shores, O Queen, *against my will.*"

Generations of sentimentalists have interpreted this as the words of a noble leader, putting duty above the call of passion and affection, and then apologizing, along the lines of Sir Richard Lovelace: "I could not love thee, dear, so much / Loved I not Honour more." But where did Vergil borrow this protesting line? From Catullus' translation of the mock-epic Callimachean poem on the *Coma Berenices*, on the wifely sacrifice by Berenice of a lock of her hair, which supposedly became the constellation that the astronomer Conon had just discovered, the poem that became the inspiration for Alexander Pope's even more humorous mock-epic, *The Rape of the Lock*. The relevant line of Catullus is: *invita, o regina, tuo de vertice cessi (Carm.* 66.39), which may be translated, roughly, as "It wasn't my idea, Ma'am, that I left your topknot." Any sophisticated Roman reader would recognize the allusion to this playful context. What then would he make of the supposed "sincerity" of Aeneas' plea for forgiveness and of Vergil's deliberate subversion of his own text?

Another example of a strong woman who tries to compete on male terms but who fails in her endeavors is Camilla, again a virgin (which gives her magical potency), but one who aspires to male roles (cf. *Aen.* 7.805ff.). Camilla is on the wrong side, of course, but her portrayal by Vergil, who provides her, through Diana, with a whole life story, is not a purely literary digression particularly since she appears to be largely a Vergilian invention.[2] First of all, she represents the amazingly popular Amazonian theme in the epic cycle, the fierce uncivilized natural forces that have to be tamed by the stronger, and more civilized, forces of the male. Camilla has an important symbolic role in the *Aeneid*; indeed, she dominates much of Book 11. A Volscian female warrior of royal descent and dramatic history, she serves to remind the audience of other Amazonian fighters, such as Penthesilea, the actual Queen of the Amazons (*Aen.* 1.490 and 11.661); Harpalyce, the fleet huntress, daughter of the exiled Thracian king, Harpalycus (*Aen.* 1.317, 11.535); and Atalanta, whose story is also brought to the reader's attention (*Aen.* 11.535). Vergil seems fascinated by such strong women, and their portrayal transcends their status as defenders of the primitive order standing in the way of the male avalanche that will sweep them aside.

The dirty trick, it would at first appear, is that it is not an heroic opponent who kills this Amazon, as Achilles, with loving tears in his eyes, killed the Amazon Penthesilea, but an Etruscan nonentity, Arruns, who is later himself eliminated by one of Diana's minions, Opis. Did it seem artistically appropriate to Vergil that a great female warrior should be brought low by an unworthy opponent simply because she was challenging males? Is the lesson that even the lowliest male is a match for the doughtiest human female?

To the contrary, her killer Arruns not only meets an early death in condign revenge, but he is subtly but unmistakeably linked with Aeneas himself, and his fate foreshadows the hero's own death after the slaying of Turnus.[3]

There are other female obstacles to Aeneas' mission to found Rome. The discouraged and weary Trojan women in Sicily are fed up with this mystical quest and try to burn the ships that will carry them from that prosperous and welcoming island to the unknown perils of mainland Italy (*Aen.* 5.615ff.). Admittedly, Juno has a hand in this but again, the stronger will, that of Jupiter prevails. These treacherous and ashamed Trojan women and some other faint-hearts on the expedition are abandoned to their disgraceful ease in Sicily (*Aen.* 5.750ff.), and Aeneas' mission goes forward.

Near the end of the *Aeneid*, Amata, who strongly objected to Aeneas as a son-in-law, because of Lavinia's prior betrothal to her favourite Turnus, does away with herself, like Dido (12.493ff.). Another obstacle to the mission is eliminated, this time by the noose. Vergil, in her case as in Dido's, invokes images of madness (12.499ff.), suggesting that women are particularly prone to derangement when faced with the inevitable.

As for the workings of female forces on the divine plane, Juno and Venus are both part of the epic machinery and also of the Augustan perception of the political world. Juno is initially modelled on the Argive Hera, hostile to Troy, whatever new or old shape it takes. Her connection with Carthage, which has now become her beloved city, is almost non-existent outside the *Aeneid*. Venus, however, is *ROMA/AMOR*, and the female ancestor (through Iulus, whoever he is) of the most powerful family in Rome when Vergil was writing.

Now we must come to the dominating male in the story, Aeneas himself. *Pius* Aeneas is ruthless, for all his professed qualms, and Piety as a justification for ruthlessness is omnipresent in the *Aeneid;* as it was also in the bloody reign of Augustus. Aeneas saves his father and son, even while losing his wife; Augustus avenges his adoptive father, Caesar, but sacrifices his sister, Octavia, to gain political advantage with Antony and he had divorced his first wife, Claudia, in 41 B.C., step-daughter of Antony, since she no longer served his political ends. Are the women in Vergil's *Aeneid* similarly dispensable? It has often been suggested that Vergil's tragic or ambivalent treatment of Turnus as the betrayed suitor of Lavinia and the nationalist opponent of the invading Trojans, subverts Aeneas' patent claim to the reader's sympathy. The hero's claim on us is not enhanced by the distress of the victimized Lavinia (*causa mali tanti* [*Aen.* 11.480]) and the suicide of Amata, who goes to her death blaming herself for the tragic war (*se causam clamat crimenque caputque malorum*, 12.600). Perhaps the more central character of Dido and the marginal, yet symbolic figure of Camilla are also subverting in different ways the manifest and dictated purpose of the *Aeneid*— to justify Rome's ways to Man.

From the legal, that is, male point of view, Dido and Aeneas were not properly married. In Aeneas, at least, the *adfectio coniugalis* was absent. Vergil underlines Dido's moral blindness, caused by her romantic passion. She protests to her sister Anna her devotion to her dead husband, saying she would rather die than violate her vows (*Aen.* 4.15ff.)—according to some, she did precisely this. Vergil's account is different: with Anna's encouragement and after the portentous sexual episode in the cave, Dido apparently abandons her self-respect, calls her liaison with Aeneas a marriage, and so hides (notice Vergil's insistence) under cover of this word, her adultery: *coniugium vocat, hoc praetexit nomine culpam* (4.172). The blame for all her future misfortunes seems firmly placed on Dido's shoulders by Vergil—note again the use of the word *causa* at *Aen.* 4.170. All Aeneas has to say later is that he never entered into a solemn marriage contract (4.339); his future country, Italy, is his true love (*hic amor, haec patria est*, verse 347), to which the tearful Dido had now become a barrier to be carefully crossed. At first glance Vergil's portrayal of women, when seen as responses to the dictates of the basic hard message of the *Aeneid*, seems somewhat negative or even patronizing. But on deeper inspection, it is Vergil the artist who triumphs over the propagandist. It is the poetic ambiguity of the *Aeneid* that saves it from being a vehicle of either political ideology or phallocratic misogyny.[4]

Vergil's treatment of Camilla is the most suggestive pointer here in the latter part of the *Aeneid*, but just as illustrative of Vergil's art is the quick sketch of Juturna. In mythic tradition a water nymph of some power, Vergil chose to make her also the sister of Turnus and she plays an extended role towards the end of the poem (12.138ff.). There in disguise she causes the truce to be broken to save Turnus from death, and then, as Aeneas approaches, she takes over as charioteer for her brother (469ff.), impersonating his driver, Metiscus. Vergil compares her to a foraging swallow in a palace: she orchestrates her brother's appearances around the battlefield, but carefully keeps him from combat with Aeneas. When Turnus is finally apprised of the Trojans' burning the city of Latinus, she continues to play her part as his saviour, and urges him to fight on far away from Aeneas. Once recognised, her attempt to protect the determined, and therefore doomed, Turnus has to be abandoned. His last words to her express his determination to make her proud of him (676ff.). It is she who also comes to his rescue when he is beset by Aeneas and hands him his own sword (785), while Venus helps Aeneas recover his spear. Juturna is only deterred from her efforts when she is forced to do so by Jupiter's despatch of one of the Dirae. In heart-felt distress, she finally bursts out into a long despairing speech, rebuking Jupiter and bemoaning her immortality which will not allow her to accompany her brother into death (872ff.). A moving final speech. But Juturna is impressive, because she is depicted in action rather than through words alone, and her changes of emotion are vividly reflected in what she does and how she reacts. Again, this effective introduction of a non-pivotal female character tells us almost as much about Vergil's attitudes to women as does his delineation of the women who advance the plot of the epic. Dido's sister, Anna, is another case in point.

To stress the latent misogyny of the *Aeneid*, conditioned by the contemporary social and political environment, is therefore to underrate the power of Vergil's poetic genius and his human sympathy. The artist deliberately transcends the Augustan ideologue; the portrait of Dido remains one of the most impressive literary depictions of a woman that we have in ancient epic. The other examples of this phenomenon in the *Aeneid*, when the energized and sympathetic art of the writer takes over and transcends the originally satiric, ideological, theological, misogynistic and other goals, serve to support this reading. The Augustan propagandist, Vergil, who so cleverly attacks Cleopatra, develops, as does his friend Horace, a curious sympathy of his own for the African queen (*non humilis mulier*), and conveys it unforgettably to later generations of readers; witness St. Augustine's tears over the death of Dido!

NOTES

1. Christian references to a pro-Dido tradition are to be found in Tert., *anim.* 33.9; cf. Prisc. *paneg.* 185f. For pictures of Dido, Macrob., 5.175.
2. On Camilla as a Vergilian invention, see. G. Arrigoni, *Camilla* (Milan, 1982). The stress on virginity in warrior women (or huntresses) is a standard mythological theme: Artemis and Pallas Athene being divine prototypes.
3. On the depiction of Camilla and the reverence of Arruns, see W.P. Basson, "Vergil's Camilla: A Paradoxical Character," *AC* 29 (1986) 57ff.
4. An obvious analogy is the presentation of Lucifer in *Paradise Lost*. Theological considerations dictate the manifest direction of the epic, but the defiant Republicanism and social heterodoxy of the poet, who was, later, the Lord Protector Cromwell's Latin secretary and the eloquent apologist for divorce and *Glasnost* and freedom of the press in his *Areopagitica*, radically subvert the message of the epic, as W. Empson points out in *Milton's God* (Cambridge, 1961).

MINERVA IN THE *AENEID*

Michelle P. Wilhelm
Miami University

At the center of *Aeneid* 8, the most Roman book of his poem, Vergil describes Vulcan rising from Venus' bed to get to work in his forge in the middle of the night, the very same hour at which a Roman matron, busy at the work of Minerva, pokes the embers of the fire beside which she and her household toil:

> *Inde ubi prima quies medio iam noctis abactae*
> *curriculo expulerat somnum, cum femina primum,*
> *cui tolerare colo uitam tenuique Minerua*
> *impositum, cinerem et sopitos suscitat ignis*
> *noctem addens operi, famulasque ad lumina longo*
> *exercet penso, castum ut seruare cubile*
> *coniugis et possit paruos educere natos:*
> *haud secus ignipotens nec tempore segnior illo*
> *mollibus e stratis opera ad fabrilia surgit.*
>
> 8.407-415[1]

The exact point of comparison in this simile is the time when both Vulcan and the Roman housewife are at work;[2] but more significantly the simile points to their actual handiwork: Vulcan is about to create the shield etched with so many of the most crucial events of Roman history; the woman is spinning and weaving, as she does uneventfully every night, in order to ensure the maintenance of her home and of her children. One task points to the war ahead, the other to the constant chores of everyday life—both necessary to guarantee the foundation, continuance and growth of the Roman nation.

Minerva, the Roman goddess of arts and crafts and also the warrior goddess[3] and one-third of the Capitoline triad (as she appears on Aeneas' shield: 8.699) underscores in the *Aeneid* the Romans' struggle to combine their domestic and military pursuits. She does not have a pervasive role in the *Aeneid* as a whole, but throughout the poem weaving imagery and references to Minerva and her realms serve to juxtapose scenes of war and domesticity, contrasts which poignantly lay bare the sacrifices exacted from individuals for the sake of Rome.

In the *Aeneid* Minerva is described in both favorable and inauspicious terms, with both the olive branch (7.154)[4] and the Gorgon head (2.616 and 8.435-438) serving as her emblems; she is depicted as acting only in accordance with fate and the will of her father Jupiter. The first reference to her in the poem, although ominous in tone, reveals her as a just goddess; unlike Juno, she does not play favorites or hold unreasonable grudges. At line 39 of Book 1 Juno expresses envy of Pallas' vengeance against the Greek Ajax after the fall of Troy. At that time Pallas was on the side of the Greeks, but later, after Ajax had defiled her shrine, she did not hesitate to punish him swiftly and completely. Later in Book 1 we meet Minerva again as Aeneas views scenes of the Trojan War in Juno's temple and sees Minerva averting her gaze from the suppliant Trojan women, their hair all dishevelled and beating their breasts, as they bring Minerva her robe (1.479-482). Here Minerva is described as *non aequa* (479) and as keeping her eyes fixed on the ground: *diva solo fixos oculos aversa tenebat* (482).[5] Thus in both appearances in Book 1 Minerva is inexorable, and these scenes prepare us for her decisive role in the destruction of Troy recounted in Book 2.

Book 2 can be characterized as Minerva's book,[6] for it is Minerva with whom both the horse and the snakes, agents and symbols of Troy's downfall, are closely linked. Aeneas begins his account to the Carthaginians of Troy's final agony with a description of the horse, woven together by the Greeks with the help of Pallas' divine skill (*divina Palladis arte*, 15); he soon calls it the fatal gift of Minerva (*donum exitiale Minervae*, 31). Three times a form of the verb *texere* (to weave) describes the fabrication of the horse: *intexunt* (16), *contextus* (112) and *textis* (186), clear references to Minerva's connections with weaving and craftsmanship. Thus the skill and careful planning connected with domestic pursuits are necessary also for the construction of this destructive war machine. Minerva's merciless disposition during the war is emphasized not only by her part in the ruse of the horse, but also in Sinon's explanation of the offering of the horse, namely previous actions by the Greeks concerning the Palladium, another of Minerva's creations. Sinon recounts how the Greeks had based all their hope and confidence on Pallas' help: *Palladis auxiliis semper stetit* (163); but Diomedes and Odysseus, after taking the sacred statue from its shrine and slaughtering the guards, had polluted the goddess' image with their bloody hands, and the goddess had turned against them: *aversa deae mens* (170), a phrase reminiscent of Minerva's stance against the Trojan women as described in Book 1.482. Sinon continues his elaborate lie by relating how, once in the Greek camp, the statue's eyes burst out in flickering flames, salt-sweat ran down over her limbs, and three times she lashed out with her shield and spear (171-175). Thus according to Sinon the horse was created as an act of atonement to the insulted goddess, who, though favoring the Greeks, could quickly turn against them. Sinon's story is immediately corroborated for the Trojans by the two serpents which strangle Laocoon and his sons and then slither up the citadel to Minerva's statue and nestle under her feet and shield (225-227). Aeneas describes the Tritonian goddess as savage (*saeva*, 226) as he details the Trojans' realization that she sent the serpents to punish Laocoon for hurling his accursed spear against the sacred oak of the horse.[7]

Two others receive no support from the fierce goddess during Troy's last hours: Cassandra, who is dragged from Minerva's temple with arms uplifted to the heavens (404-405) and whose violation is alluded to twice elsewhere (1.41 and 6.840); and Coroebus, who is slain at the altar of the warrior goddess (*divae armipotentis*, 425). But it is the final appearance of Minerva in Book 2 which provides the greatest proof of her unswerving hostility. Venus reveals to her son Aeneas that it is the gods, Neptune, Juno, Jupiter and Minerva, who are overturning Troy. Venus points to Minerva sitting above the others on the highest towers observing the final moments of the slaughter (615-616). She is *nimbo effulgens et Gorgone saeva* (616), a phrase very difficult to translate and still convey her terrifying stance: "brilliant in a dark storm-cloud and grim-Gorgoned." This then is the picture Aeneas paints of Minerva and her role in the fall of Troy: she is deceptive, ruthless and implacable.[8] But Minerva will not pursue the Trojans further, and out of the annihilation she directed at Troy will come the creation of Rome.

Aeneas mentions Minerva once more in his account to Dido and the Carthaginians. This is when he and his fellow Trojans land at Castrum Minervae in Calabria, site of a temple to Minerva (Strabo, 6.281) and of their first landing in Italy. The first thing Aeneas sees are four white horses grazing on the plain. Anchises interprets this as meaning that this land portends war; then he adds that there is also hope of peace, for the horse is both armed for war and can be placed under the yoke.[9] It is significant that the Trojans' first sighting of Italy and their initial landing involve Minerva. Her part in the fall of Troy is in the past; Minerva is already in Italy,[10] and Italy will involve peace as well as war. Aeneas, Anchises and the others pray to the armor-clashing goddess, and she is the first to welcome them to Italy: *quae prima accepit ovantis* (3.530-545). Eventually she will fight on the side of Rome at the battle of Actium (8.699).

Minerva's divine skill, with which she created the deceptive horse, from now on is linked to more positive pursuits, although an association with the hostilities of warfare is frequently present. Such is the case with the gifts Andromache gives to Ascanius and the Trojans as they depart from Buthrotum. She gives them robes, a scarf and other gifts from the loom, gifts which she wove herself, memorials of her handiwork, (*manuum . . . monumenta mearum*, 486) and the last gifts of their people: *dona extrema tuorum* (488). She sends her fellow Trojans on to Italy with the final reminders of a previous kingdom and family destroyed by war, and these gifts are all the more important because they are the products of Andromache's own hand: personal, family heirlooms which will now find their way into the harsh and sometimes impersonal world of conflict in Italy.

Other woven gifts in the poem reveal a significance equal to that of Andromache's. First, in Book 4 Mercury, sent by Jupiter to force Aeneas back to reality and leave Carthage, finds Aeneas busy building towers and houses, wearing a cloak ablaze with Tyrian purple and interwoven with gold thread, which had been created by Dido as a gift. Mercury characterizes Aeneas as *uxorius* (266), a very telling word: Aeneas has become too much like Dido, as symbolized by the robe he wears, her creation. And in Book 11, Aeneas drapes a robe of purple and gold around Pallas' corpse (72-77), a robe which Dido had once woven for him in happier times. The tragic deaths of Dido and Pallas are here linked by the repetition of line 75 from Book 4.264: *fecerat et tenui telas descreverat auro* and by the description of Dido as *laeta laborum* (73) when she had toiled at the weaving. At this time of sorrow it is a cloth woven by a loved one which offers a bit of solace amid the tumults of war.

This antithesis between the everyday work of weaving and the horrors of the battlefield is nowhere more poignantly depicted than in Book 9, when Euryalus' mother learns from Fama of her son's death. At that moment, sitting at her loom, she drops the shuttle and the thread unwinds (476). She rushes among the ranks of the soldiers, shrieking that she won't be able to bury Euryalus' corpse, bathe his body or even cover him with a robe she had been working at night and day (as a gift for him while alive, not a shroud for him in death). She says that she worked at the robe to comfort the cares of old age (*tela curas solabar anilis*, 489). Her grief affects everyone, who groan and whose strength for battle is crushed (499). Iulus weeps profusely and several Trojans carry her away. The focus then abruptly shifts to the trumpet's call to battle: *At tuba terribilem sonitum procul aere canoro / increpuit* (503-504). In this scene we can discern not only the stark contrast between the domestic and military spheres, but also the fact that these spheres cannot be totally separated. What was woven for the living, and could at times be used for the dead, in this case cannot be employed for either, so great is the disruption caused by the war.[11]

There are other briefer references in the *Aeneid* to the arts of Minerva which are more removed from the battlefield. Two occur in Book 5, where first, as the reward for winning the ship race Sergestus receives from Aeneas a slave woman described as not unskilled in the works of Minerva: *operum haud ignara Minervae* (284), a simple reference to the importance of women's skill at handicrafts. And later Aeneas is counseled after the burning of the ships by the old man Nautes, who was taught by Tritonian Pallas all the knowledge concerning her lore, including the meaning of the gods' anger and the fates' demands (704-707). According to Dionysius of Halicarnassus (6.69) it was Nautes who brought the Palladium from Troy to Italy, and hence his descendants, the Nautii, were later the priests of Minerva at Rome.[12] Nautes' skill is pivotal in convincing Aeneas to continue with his goal of reaching Italy, and here it is clear that Minerva's providence includes even fate, which will be on Rome's side.

As the Trojans finally near the Tiber at the beginning of Book 7, they sail closely past Circe's shores where they hear her ceaseless song as she runs the shuttle through the loom (7.10-14); they also hear the angry growls and ragings of lions, boars, bears and the howling of monstrous wolves, all animals which Circe through her magical herbs had changed from human beings (15-20). Neptune fills their sails with favorable winds so that the

Trojans can escape such a fate themselves (21-24). The mystery and magic associated with the weaving process, which creates a final product so different from the original threads, intensifies the aura of enticement and danger created by the sounds coming from Circe as she weaves. Although the Trojans avoid this peril, these first noises from central Italy portend greater threats to come. One such threat will be from the Volscian Camilla, who is characterized in the parade of Latin warriors at the end of Book 7 as a warrior maiden, a *bellatrix* (805), who has never accustomed her hands to Minerva's distaff or to a basket of wool: *non illa colo calathisue Mineruae / femineas adsueta manus* . . . (805-806). Why does Vergil mention this? Possibly in order to indicate that she is not a true warrior maiden in the tradition of Minerva, because Camilla is interested at this point only in war and nothing else. Prowess only in the arts of war is not enough; this will not sustain a nation. Other types of toil are also necessary, and by denying this Camilla seals her fate.[13]

The final reference to Minerva in the *Aeneid* underscores her unswerving support of the fates. In Book 11.477-485 a throng of Latin mothers led by Queen Amata with Lavinia at her side rides up to Minerva's temple bearing her gifts and offering incense and prayer. They beg the goddess, whom they address as *armipotens, praeses belli* (484), to utterly destroy Aeneas, the leader of their Trojan enemies. The next line of the poem turns to Turnus and his preparations for entering the battle. There is nothing more about the Latin mothers, no reaction to their plea from Minerva—we don't even know if she heard them. It is very evident that Minerva is now on the side of the Trojans. How ironic it is that the Latin mothers should invoke this goddess, and not Juno! Minerva does not even avert her gaze away from her beseechers this time—she simply is not present at all.

In light of this review of Minerva's role in the *Aeneid*, it is clear that the simile at the center of Book 8 comparing the work of Vulcan and the Roman housewife is a significant one. Not only is there the contrast between the unchaste bed Vulcan has just left and the chaste bed, *castum cubile* (412) of the virtuous and hardworking Roman woman, who is an *univira* and the antithesis of Dido and Cleopatra;[14] but it is the importance of the work Vulcan and the woman do, causing them to be up in the middle of the night, which this simile also highlights. It is the housewife's burden to make life bearable with her spindle and the humble work of Minerva: *cui tolerare colo vitam tenuique Minerva / impositum* (409-410). This woman must also rear her sons through this toil: *possit parvos educere natos* (413). These are the children whose history will be shown on the shield Vulcan is about to carve, and for whom Aeneas and his fellow Trojans will wage war in Italy.[15]

NOTES

1. All quotations from the *Aeneid* are from R.A.B. Mynors, *P. Vergili Maronis Opera* (Oxford, 1972).
2. For discussions of this simile see the following: M. Putnam, *The Poetry of the Aeneid* (London, 1965) 139-140; K.W. Gransden, *Virgil: Aeneid VIII* (Cambridge, 1976) 39-41, 138; V. Pöschl, *The Art of Vergil: Image and Symbol in the Aeneid* tr. G. Seligson (Ann Arbor, 1962) 170; C.J. Fordyce, *P. Vergili Maronis Aeneidos Libri VII-VIII* (Oxford, 1977) 251-252; R.D. Williams, *The* Aeneid *of Vergil, Books 7-12* (Glasgow, 1973) 255; J. Conington, *P. Vergili Maronis Opera*, vol. 3, ed. H. Nettleship (London, 1883) 125-126; R. Cruttwell, *Virgil's Mind at Work* (New York, Inc., 1969) 101-102; G. Williams, *Technique and Ideas in the* Aeneid (New Haven, 1983) 83, 126-128; S.F. Wiltshire, *Public and Private in Vergil's* Aeneid (Amherst, 1989) 42-43, 112-113; M. DiCesare, *The Altar and the City: A Reading of Vergil's* Aeneid (New York, 1974) 153-154.
3. C. Bailey, *Religion in Virgil* (Oxford, 1935) 152-157, reviews all of the appearances in the *Aeneid* of Minerva, as both the Italian and Etruscan goddess of handicraft and women's work and as the Greek warrior goddess Pallas. Bailey points out that when Vergil refers to her as the genuine Italian goddess he always calls her Minerva, never Pallas, and that he never speaks of Athena (153). See also E. Henry, *The Vigour of Prophecy: A Study of Virgil's* Aeneid (Carbondale, 1989), 90-107, for an in-depth study of Minerva in the *Aeneid* focussing on three episodes which she thinks may be original to Vergil: the snakes' destruction of Laocoon and his sons (2.199-227); the omen of the four white horses at the temple at Castrum Minervae (3.530-540); Minerva's rejection of the Latin mothers' appeal (9.477-485); for a concise summary of the various theories about the etymology of the name Minerva, see p. 214.
4. See also *Georgics* 1.18-19; 2.3, 179 and 420-425.
5. Cf. *Aeneid* 6.469, where Vergil says of Dido: *illa solo fixos oculos aversa tenebat*. Like Minerva, Dido would not be appeased.
6. G.S. West, in *Women in Vergil's* Aeneid (diss., University of California, Los Angeles, 1975) 95-111, carefully analyzes Minerva's role in *Aeneid* 2 and then discusses how Minerva's actions throughout the poem serve both to parallel and contrast the conduct of Juno.

7. For a review of Pallas Athena's association with snakes, see E. Henry, *op. cit.* 98.
8. E. Henry, *ibid.* notes that "In the *Aeneid* Minerva's characteristic gesture is rejection, as individuals and peoples are found wanting." This is in contrast to Homer's Athena, who offers protection to many Greeks, to Odysseus above all ". . . in a personal way that is quite alien to the cold detachment of Virgil's Pallas-Minerva" (94).
9. See R.D Williams, *P. Vergili Maronis Aeneidos Liber Tertius* (Oxford, 1962) 167-168, for a thorough discussion of this omen.
10. Minerva's early presence in Italy, as attested by Lycophron, *Alex.* 1261-1262 and Strabo, 6.1.14, has recently been confirmed by the discovery of statues of Minerva at Pratica di Mare (ancient Lavinium). See G. Dumézil, *Enea nel Lazio: Archeologia e Mito.* Catalogue of the Bimillenario Virgiliano exhibition (Rome, 1981), esp. 187-196.
11. S.F. Wiltshire, *op. cit.* 38-55, in her chapter on "Grieving Mothers and the Costs of Attachment," explores the actions and feelings of Euryalus' mother, the only mother who chose not to remain in Sicily but to travel on to Italy, and she points out that Vergil makes many connections between death and the handwork of women: "In each of these cases the private world of family affections—of women's work and women's love—intrudes into the events of history" (54).
12. See Conington, *op. cit.* 403.
13. For discussions of the character of Camilla, see Williams, *op. cit.* 226-227; Wiltshire, *op. cit.* 62-64, 119; G.S. West, "Chloreus and Camilla," *Vergilius* 31 (1985) 22-29.
14. See Fordyce, *op. cit.* 251; Gransden, *op. cit.* 138.
15. An earlier version of this paper was given at the April 1989 meeting of the Classical Association of the Middle West and South.

SEVEN SUFFERING HEROINES AND SEVEN SURROGATE SONS

M. Owen Lee
St. Michael's College, University of Toronto

Seven, the traditional number of the planets in mythology, became in the language of myth a symbol for cosmic and psychic order. In his *Dictionary of Symbols*, J.E. Cirlot speaks of a septenary as a "spatial order of six dynamic elements, plus one which is static," a device in art and myth which "has the quality of the mandala about it, comparable with the notion of 'squaring the circle,'" and he adds, "It would be impossible to name, even in brief or in sum, all the innumerable applications of the septenary, or the ways in which this cosmic 'model' figures in myths, legends, folktales and dreams."[1]

Seven is, not surprisingly, a Virgilian number. From the *Aeneid*'s seven-line prologue onwards, mazes of sevens await the Crutwellian[2] reader tracing his way through Virgil's mind. Perhaps because Rome was built on seven hills (*Geo.* 2.535 and *Aen.* 6.783), Virgil has seven ships make their way with Aeneas out of the storm (1.170 and 383), and the hero slays seven deer to feed the crews (1.192). But other uses of seven seem to owe more to the mythological notion of a cosmic septenary, ordering events in Virgil's story. Aeneas wanders for seven years over the sea (1.755), and a year later his people still remember the voyage as lasting seven years (5.626). The serpent at his father's tomb draws a length of seven coils in seven folds (5.85). Later, his god-crafted, goddess-bestowed shield has seven orbs (8.448), and so, we discover at the poem's end, has that of his chief opponent Turnus (12.925). And there are other passages where the number seven may have special significance.[3]

Two patterns of seven, and the *loci* which bear directly on them, will be my concern here: Dido appears with seven mythic heroines in the underworld, and Aeneas loses, by my count, seven surrogate sons in the course of his adventures after leaving Dido.

The *locus* that anticipates these patterns is the description of the golden doors of the temple at Cumae at the beginning of Book 6, an elliptical and obscure *ecphrasis* that, like the description given another temple relief in Book 1, uses figures from the past to tell Aeneas' evolving story.

The figures on the temple in Book 1 are from the Trojan War of the hero's own experience, and their significances for his future are relatively easy to see.[4] But the figures on the temple doors in Book 6 are mythical emblems, and they are much more difficult to interpret.[5] They were fashioned in gold by the exiled Athenian, Daedalus, who landed at Cumae after his winged escape from Crete and the loss of his son, Icarus, to the sea. Daedalus is clearly something of a figure for Aeneas, who has landed here after his flight from Carthage and the loss of his helmsman, Palinurus, to the sea.

On the first door Daedalus has depicted happenings in his native Athens:

> *in foribus letum Androgeo; tum pendere poenas*
> *Cecropidae iussi, miserum! septena quotannis*
> *corpora natorum; stat ductis sortibus urna.*
>
> Aen. 6.20-22

There appear to be two panels here. The story briefly indicated on the first is familiar enough: Androgeos, prince of the royal house of Crete, was killed while competing in athletic competitions in Athens. Two separate traditions developed about Androgeos' death, one pro-Athenian (that he was fatally gored by the bull of Marathon, which he challenged in combat), and one pro-Cretan (that he was murdered by his Athenian rivals in the games).[6] Whatever the case, in the second panel on Daedalus' door (*tum*, line 20) we see the consequence of this death: Athens was required by the more powerful Crete to provide a yearly tribute, a human sacrifice of seven youths and seven maidens.[7]

At least, that was the established tradition. Virgil chooses to limit the number of Athenian victims from fourteen to seven,[8] makes all the victims male, and stresses their sonship: they are *septena . . . corpora natorum*, and their lots are already drawn.

Then, in two panels on the other door, we see depicted some of the tragic story of Crete. Dominating the myths once again is that planetary symbol,[9] the bull, which in the myths of Crete is also sacred to Neptune and so perhaps emblematic of Cretan sea power, perhaps even of Crete's unnatural lust for sea power and the consequences it brought:

> contra elata mari respondet Gnosia tellus:
> hic crudelis amor tauri suppostaque furto
> Pasiphae mixtumque genus prolesque biformis
> Minotaurus inest, Veneris monumenta nefandae;
> hic labor ille domus et inextricabilis error;
> magnum reginae sed enim miseratus amorem
> Daedalus ipse dolor tecti ambagesque resolvit,
> caeca regens filo vestigia.
>
> Aen. 6.23-30

Once again, the myth is treated in two panels, the first familiar in its details. The queen of Crete, Pasiphaë—whose name means "she who gives light to all"—was overwhelmed by a *crudelis amor,* a *Venus nefanda,* a passion for a beautiful bull sent out of the sea by Neptune. Instead of sacrificing it, as Neptune intended, King Minos kept it, and Queen Pasiphaë mated with it secretly, and produced that *mixtum genus,* that *proles biformis*, the Minotaur. In the second panel (*hic,* line 27) we see the consequence of this. Daedalus, the Athenian artist who had crafted the likeness of a cow for Pasiphaë's seductive purposes, crafted then a labyrinthine maze to house the monstrous offspring of her union. Every year the seven Athenian youths sent as tribute were imprisoned in those windings from which there was no return, and eventually were devoured by the Cretan Minotaur—until one year the prince of the royal house of Athens, Theseus, came as one of the seven youths, killed the Minotaur, and, with a thread clandestinely provided by the Cretan princess Ariadne, found his way out of the labyrinth.

At least, that was the established tradition. Once again, Virgil changes the myth in his second panel. There is no mention of Ariadne providing the necessary thread. Instead the artisan Daedalus, who had pitied the passion of Queen Pasiphaë[10] and provided the artificial cow for her, provides now for the Athenian prince[11] the thread that will lead him out of the labyrinth.

The symmetrical contrasts between the two doors are now complete: the bull of Athens kills the prince of Crete; the prince of Athens kills the bull of Crete. But Virgil seems less interested in such parallels than he does in changing the old myths so that they will cast the story of his *Aeneid* in relief. If, as some commentators suggest,[12] Athens subjected and rising anew under Theseus is meant to stand for Troy defeated and rising anew under Aeneas, then it seems likely that Virgil reduces the old myth's fourteen youths and maidens to seven *corpora natorum* because his Aeneas will lose seven *corpora natorum* as he moves onward to found his city. And if, correspondingly, Crete is meant to stand for the sea power, Carthage, that will someday be the enemy of that city, then perhaps Virgil omits the Cretan details which do not fit his Carthage story so as to emphasize the destructive passion of the Cretan queen, a figure for Dido.

He seems also to have wanted to put himself in the picture. While Daedalus the refugee crafting the doors is a figure for Aeneas the refugee contemplating the doors, more importantly Daedalus the artist pitying the Queen and guiding the hero through the labyrinth is a figure for Virgil pitying Queen Dido and guiding Aeneas through the underworld. Virgil is an artist who, like Daedalus, provides the clue for the solving of his own labyrinthine work of art.

Let's take then, as our thread through the maze that spreads outward from this thought-teasing *ecphrasis,* the mythic number seven, remembering that, when the Sibyl interrupts Aeneas' contemplation of the doors and speeds him on to his labyrinthine underworld, she proscribes the sacrifice of "seven bulls from a herd unbroken, and seven ewes properly chosen" (6.38-39).

Dido is accompanied in the underworld by seven women properly chosen:

> *hic, quos durus amor crudeli tabe peredit,*
> *secreti celant calles et myrtea circum*
> *silva tegit; curae non ipsa in morte relinquunt.*
> *his Phaedram Procrinque locis maestamque Eriphylen*
> *crudelis nati monstrantem vulnera cernit*
> *Evandnenque et Pasiphaen; his Laodamia*
> *it comes et iuvenis quondam, nunc femina, Caeneus*
> *rursus et in veterem fato revoluta figuram.*
> Aen. 6.442-449

Until recently, critics have thought these seven ladies not "properly chosen." One editor went so far as to say: "This crowd scene of seven heroines irrelevant to the action of the *Aeneid* serves to focus the attention very sharply on the one who is not irrelevant."[13] Actually, the ladies are, in accordance with the Sibyl's command, very relevant. Their myths tell Dido's story[14] as closely, and in as close a sequence, as do the figures which, on the temples in Books 1 and 6, tell the story of Aeneas.

That is to say, Dido was, like Phaedra, prevailed upon by her confidante to give way to her unqueenly passion. Like Procris (fatally wounded when, on a hunt, her husband mistook her for a beast), Dido was symbolically wounded by the man she loved, a man cast by Virgil as a hunter and she as a wounded deer.[15] But Dido was also, like Eriphyle *crudelis nati monstrantem vulnera*, wounded by the god of love cruelly disguised as that man's son. Like Evadne, Dido threw herself on the pyre of her "husband"— as she always thought him to be. Like Pasiphaë, Dido had given way to a god-sent passion with the power to destroy a whole civilization. Then, like Laodamia, she was restored in death to her true husband.

Finally, there is a surprising seventh figure, Caeneus, for whose appearance in this company Virgil adds the details in lines 448-449; we gather that, as Caeneus was turned by *fatum* from woman to man and then again to woman, so the loving Elissa was renamed Dido (*id est 'virago' Punica lingua*[16]) when *fatum* called her to the manly mission of founding and ruling Carthage, and then in death she was restored to her womanly position at the side of her Sychaeus. Thus the seventh figure in the cosmic septenary rounds off the device, squaring the circle.

There can be little question that this underworld setting for Dido is meant to correspond in detail to the Cretan story told on the second temple door. In the underworld we have *hic quos durus amor crudeli;* on the door, *hic crudelis amor*. In the underworld, *secreti calles;* on the door, *inextricabilis error*. In the underworld, *rursus et in veterem fato revoluta figuram;* on the door, *mixtumque genus, prolesque biformis*. Both the lives of the ladies below and the details on the temple door above tell, in the elusive ways of myth and symbol, Dido's tragic tale.

Then, as the fates of seven ladies ("ewes properly chosen") and the second temple door tell of Dido, the fates of seven youths ("bulls from a herd unbroken") and the first temple door may be thought to tell Aeneas' story,[17] especially the tragic truth in it: for anything good to come in Virgil's world, there must be sacrifice, loss, death—the breaking of the young and innocent. *Stat ductis sortibus urna.*

Aeneas' seven lost "sons" group themselves into pairs, in a series of memorable deaths. The first two link Books 5 and 6. Aeneas' helmsman Palinurus falls into the sea as a sacrifice to

Neptune to secure the hero's safe voyage to Italy, and, so soon after as to seem almost simultaneous, Aeneas' trumpeter Misenus falls into the sea as a victim of Triton, so that the hero can find the golden bough that will grant him safe passage through the underworld. The two sacrificial victims are not flesh-and-blood sons of Aeneas, yet their special filial relationships to him are nicely established in the *pater* given Aeneas as he wakes to find Palinurus lost at sea (5.867) and the *pius* twice given him as he buries Misenus (6.176, 232).

The second pair, Nisus and Euryalus, die in Book 9. They are *Aeneidae* (9.180), "sons of Aeneas" who fall together on an unsuccessful mission to find *pater Aeneas* (9.172). They are caught in a forest described in terms that call to mind the labyrinth (9.391-393), and Virgil, pitying their great love for each other, assures them that their fame shall never die, so long as Rome shall last and a *pater Romanus* (9.449) shall possess imperium.

The third pair, who die in the battle in Book 10, are symbols of the young Romans lost on both sides in the civil wars of Virgil's own day—the Arcadian Pallas and the Italian Lausus. The first of these "sons" is the boy Aeneas took from his father's arms into his own service and protection; the second is an enemy's son whom Aeneas kills, but gives his hand to in death, and lifts tenderly from the earth. A whole series of father-son relationships attends the first death—Evander/Pallas, Aeneas/Pallas, Hercules/Pallas, Jupiter/Hercules, Jupiter/Sarpedon, Aegyptus/his fifty slain sons. In the second death, Aeneas' fatherly role is established when, after killing many sons impiously on the battlefield, he is moved by this son's *pietas* for his father (10.812). Virgil then restores to him, after many acts of *furor*, the patronymic *Anchisiades* (10.822) and the epithet *pius* (10.826).

So Aeneas loses six surrogate sons. Who is the seventh that the *ecphrasis* seems to demand? According to the mythic idea of the septenary, there should be a "spatial order of six dynamic elements" and a seventh "one who is static." Should our seventh son then be the one who, like Theseus among the *septena . . . corpora natorum,* does not die, but survives to rule his people? If so, the figure that comes instantly to mind is the only young man in the poem who does not die—the prince who is the hope for the future, Aeneas' own son Iulus.

The identification is attractive but unsatisfying. The Sibyl commanded that seven untouched bulls be slain (6.38) in sacrifice. We need a boy who dies, and one who will be, like the others, not a flesh-and-blood but an adoptive son, a surrogate son. There is one such, a compelling seventh figure, a symbol for the others because he dies, not in the narrative, but in the history the narrative illuminates. He is the adoptive son of the man for whom the poem was written, Augustus' heir Marcellus, dead of undiscovered causes at age nineteen.

Virgil encourages this identification—Marcellus as the figure who embodies all the surrogate sons—by another pattern of subtle linkings. When, in Book 6, Aeneas looks into the future and hears of the death of Marcellus, his father Anchises calls the doomed boy *miserande puer* (6.882), a phrase given in the poem to both Lausus (10.825) and Pallas (11.42) as they lie in death. Anchises then asks to strew the body of Marcellus with lilies and purple flowers (6.883-884). The deaths of the six adoptive sons in the narrative are marked, successively, by a branch dipped in dew from Lethe (Palinurus, 5.854); the golden bough itself (Misenus, 6.187-189); a purple flower cut down by the plough (Euryalus, 9.435) or two poppies weighed down by a chance shower (Nisus and Euryalus, 9.436-437); a violet or hyacinth amid arbutus and oak leaves and fronds, plucked by a young girl's finger and still keeping its hue and its beauty (Pallas, 11.65-70) and, more subtly, the expression on a face grown pale in the wondrous ways of death (Lausus, 10.821-822).

Is it Iulus or Marcellus then who is the seventh son predicted in *septena . . . corpora natorum* on the temple doors? Iulus would fit the optimistic interpretation of the *Aeneid* as a glorification of empire, Marcellus the view, more in fashion today, that the poem is a pessimistic meditation on the cost in human lives required by any forward movement in history. But logically (though admittedly logic is not the prime consideration in such patterns as we are considering), Marcellus should not figure among the seven victims on the temple doors. He should be the royal son whose death (also of undiscovered causes) brought all the other deaths in its wake—Androgeos. The three lines on the first door at Cumae become a summary of everything to follow in the *Aeneid* if for Androgeos we substitute Marcellus, and think of Virgil as bidden to expiate that death in his verses, and deciding to do it seven times over:

> *in foribus letum Androgeo; tum pendere poenas*
> *Cecropidae iussi, miserum! septena quotannis*
> *corpora natorum; stat ductis sortibus urna.*
> Aen. 6.20-22

If, then, neither Iulus nor Marcellus can be the seventh victim, who is the last surrogate "son"? Remembering the seventh lady, the virago Caenis-Caeneus that accompanied Dido, I'd like to suggest for the seventh "son" the virago Camilla. Virgil suppressed the seven female victims of tradition, but to include one, Camilla, as a seventh "son" would be to give to the list of *septena . . . corpora natorum* the sexual ambivalence Virgil liked to have in his work. Certainly Camilla fits the patterns we have noted. Like Marcellus, Pallas, and Lausus, Camilla in death is called *miseranda* (11.593). Like Nisus and Euryalus in death, the purple color leaves her face (11.819) and she lets her head droop (11.829-830). Like them, too, she is a votary of Diana, and connected with the moon. (11.532f., 663).[18] And though she fights against father Aeneas, her death, like those of the other "sons," saves his life: Turnus, when he hears Camilla is dead, deserts his place of ambush just at the point where he had the chance to kill *pater Aeneas* (11.904).

And just at the point when we wonder whether all of this can have resulted from conscious planning, Virgil, with the architectural skill that makes us doubt whether there is any incident, any line, any word in the poem that does not have its Crutwellian significance, gives us a minor figure to sum up *mutatis mutandis* much of what we have traced: in Book 10, a warrior of Cretan ancestry, Cydon, is about to die in battle at the hand of Aeneas when suddenly his brothers, "seven in number, and seven the weapons they cast" (10.329-330), come in force to save him. Like Marcellus, Nisus and Euryalus, Lausus and Camilla, Cydon too is directly addressed (325); like Nisus and Euryalus, his love is homosexual (326-327); like Marcellus, Lausus, Pallas and Camilla, he is given the epithet *miserande* (327).

Virgil never put the *ultima manus,* the finishing touches, to his Roman epic, and for that reason our schemata must always remain tentative. For that reason, too, Virgil's final comment on the *ecphrasis* in Book 6 is so moving. Daedalus too never puts the *ultima manus* to his masterwork, the temple doors at Cumae. There is one more lost son that should have had a place there but never found it because his grieving father couldn't finish the work. Virgil, as he had addressed Nisus and Euryalus, Lausus and Camilla, addresses that missing son:

tu quoque magnum
partem opere in tanto, sineret dolor, Icare, haberes;

bis conatus erat casus effingere in auro,
bis patriae cecidere manus.
Aen. 6.30-33

Two lost sons thus frame Book 6, and each stands outside the narrative as a symbol for the seven lost sons within it—Icarus at the beginning of the book, Marcellus at the end.

Twice, Virgil says, the father's hands fell from their task. Perhaps twice because the surrogate sons, as we've noted, fall in pairs.[19] Perhaps twice because the fugitive Daedalus who made the figures was so like the fugitive Aeneas who is contemplating them—each has lost a son to the sea. Perhaps twice because the artist Daedalus who made the figures is so like the poet who is writing the poem—each leaves his work of art unfinished. Or perhaps twice because the poet writing the poem grieved with the man who asked for the poem and, in the midst of its writing, lost an adoptive son. Both the Icarus of myth and the Marcellus of history die seven times over in the windings of the *Aeneid*.

NOTES

1. *A Dictionary of Symbols*, tr. Jack Sage (New York, 1971) 283. Cirlot's attribution of the magical qualities of the number seven to a planetary model helps explain the importance of Pasiphaë ("she who gives light to all") to the sacrifice of seven Athenian youths and maidens, as well as her presence among the "seven suffering heroines" in the underworld where Dido is glimpsed as if by moonlight. It may also help explain one of the contentions of this paper, that Camilla (connected with the moon in 11.663 and, by cross-reference, in 1.490) should be thought to be one of the "seven surrogate sons." A mythic parallel to all of these concerns is the slaying of the seven sons and seven daughters of Niobe by the sun and moon deities, Apollo and Diana.

2. For R.W. Crutwell, who traces the labyrinthine ways of *Virgil's Mind at Work* (Oxford, 1947), "the idea of continuity, as of a single thread persisting throughout some complicated pattern" (specifically the thread Troy/Rome) is "the keynote of the *Aeneid*" (39). Crutwell discusses patterns of seven on pages 88-91. In following his footsteps I haven't, unfortunately, followed his lead in dispensing fearlessly with footnotes.

3. Orpheus' lyre has seven strings (*Aen.* 6.646) and Pan's pipe seven stalks (*Ecl.* 2.36). The Nile has seven mouths (*Aen.* 6.800 and *Geo.* 4.292) and the Ganges seven streams (*Aen.* 9.30). The Sicilian *caestus* is made from seven ox hides (*Aen.* 5.404-405). The Scythians

live under the seven stars of the Wain (*Geo.* 3.381), where the snow and ice pile up seven cubits high (*Geo.* 3.355). Bees live for seven summers (*Geo.* 4.207). Orpheus mourns the twice-lost Eurydice for seven months (*Geo.* 4.507).

4. Achilles (468) foretokens Turnus in victory; the night raid on the tents of Rhesus (469-473) is the night raid of Nisus and Euryalus; the death of Troilus, "no match for Achilles" (474-478), is the death of Pallas, no match for Turnus; the wailing Trojan women (479-482) represent the mother of the dead Euryalus; Hector defeated (483-487) is Turnus going down in defeat. Finally, the *ecphrasis* in Carthage foretells the situation that lies immediately in store there for the hero: the figures of himself, black Memnon, and the virago Penthesilea (488-493) foretoken those of himself, black Iarbas, and Dido, whose name, conferred on her by her subjects, means "virago." For Turnus prefigured first in Achilles and then in Hector, see W.S. Anderson, "Vergil's Second *Iliad*," *TAPA* 88 (1957) 17-30.

5. A good discussion of the problem, with extensive bibliography, is M. Paschalis, "The Unifying Theme of Daedalus' Sculptures on the Temple of Apollo Cumanus," *Vergilius* 32 (1986) 33-41.

6. See Apollodorus 3.15.7, especially as commented on by J.G. Frazer in *Apollodorus,* vol. 2 (London, 1921) 116-117.

7. So Catullus 64.78, and also Plutarch, *Thes.* 15, Pausanias 1.27.10, Diodorus 4.61.3, Apollodorus 3.15.8 and Hyginus *PA* 2.5. Euripides *HF* 1326 keeps the number of Cretan victims fourteen, but makes all the victims young men.

8. Only Hyginus (*Fabulae* 41) among extant writers speaks of seven victims, and they are children.

9. Cirlot (above, n. 1) 34 finds support in Near Eastern mythologies for the bull as both a lunar and solar figure.

10. Most commentators insist that *reginae* in line 28 refers to Ariadne, who provides the thread in the traditional version of the myth. But Ariadne is not a *regina*, and Virgil, adapting line 445 from Homer, *Odyssey* 11.321, explicitly deletes Ariadne's name. See also B. Otis, *Virgil: A Study in Civilized Poetry* (Oxford, 1964) 284, n. 1: "*Regina* applies much more naturally to Pasiphaë and the whole passage refers to her." Virgil, as usual, is changing the old myth to suit his purposes.

11. Otis, *ibid.*, derives from *magnum reginae . . . miserum amorem* an interpretation that is unusual and in the end unhelpful, but certainly faithful to the text: Daedalus gave the thread, not to Theseus, but to Pasiphaë, pitying her desire to visit her monstrous offspring.

12. See especially V. Pöschl, *The Art of Vergil*, tr. G. Seligson (Ann Arbor, 1962) 149-150, and R.W. Crutwell, *op. cit.* 179-182.

13. R.D. Williams, ed., *The* Aeneid *of Virgil, Books 1-6,* (London, 1975) 487.
14. Many of the details that follow were first noted by J. Perret, "Les compagnes de Didon aux enfers," *REL* 42 (1964) 249-261; E. Kraggerud, "Caeneus und der Heroinenkatalog, *Aeneis* VI 440 ff.," *Symbolae Osloenses* 40 (1965) 66-71; and G.S. West, "The Significance of Vergil's Eriphyle," *Vergilius* 26 (1980) 52-54 and "Caeneus and Dido," *TAPA* 110 (1980) 315-324.
15. The motif of Aeneas as hunter and Dido as wounded deer, so close to the myth of Cephalus and Procris, has been detailed by Otis, *op. cit.* 72-80, W.S. Anderson, *The Art of the* Aeneid (Englewood Cliffs, 1969) 26-27, and many others.
16. Servius *ad Aen.* 1.340. Dido as virago is a pattern developed in Virgil's text (cf. *dux femina facti* in 1.364, *saepta armis* in 1.506, *Dido dux* in 4.165) and even more in the figures associated with her by patterns of hunting and moon imagery—Venus as huntress, Diana, Penthesilea, Camilla.
17. Crutwell, *op. cit.* 90-91, connects the Cretan labyrinth with Aeneas' Trojan games via "a very ancient Etruscan vase found at Tragliatella" on which a drawing "represents a procession of seven beardless warriors dancing." Cirlot, *op. cit.,* notes that in Scottish sword dances St. George conquers the dragon in the company of seven saints.
18. See M.O. Lee, *"Per nubila lunam:* the Moon in Virgil's *Aeneid,"* *Vergilius* 34 (1988), especially 11-12.
19. *bis patriae cecidere manus* could also refer to such dying pairs as Laocoön's two sons (2.213-217); the Trojan brothers Pandarus and Bitias (9.672f.), the Italian twins Larides and Thymber (10.390-396) and the Italian brothers Lucagus and Liger (10.576-601). The saving death of Palinurus, the clearest instance of a surrogate son dying to save his "father," is beautifully completed by the story of Iapyx in Book 12. Palinurus and Iapyx may be brothers. See M. Owen Lee, "The Sons of Iasus and the End of the *Aeneid,"* *The Augustan Age* 1 (1981-1982) 13-16. Virgil's Crutwellian patterns expand ever outward from their source, finally beyond our abilities to schematize them.

AENEAS AT ROME AND LAVINIUM

Karl Galinsky
University of Texas

Since I wrote on this subject last,[1] several well-known scholars, especially Solmsen, Momigliano, and Horsfall,[2] have made major contributions to the subject which, because of its many ramifications, continues to attract lively and ongoing discussion. It has proved fruitful not only in its own right but because it is a methodological paradigm in its combination of several major disciplines of *Altertumswissenschaft* in the best sense: history, art, archaeology, religion, epigraphy, literature and philology. This perspective also characterizes Sandy McKay's work. It is a pleasure, therefore, to offer him this contribution on the current state of the question of the Aeneas legend not in the least because his adventures as the *pius dux* of assorted travellers on Mediterranean shores have made him the subject of legend himself; may I recall, in the mood of *Aeneid* 1.203, our joint *labores* at the Algiers airport *anno a.u.c.* 2730.

Although Lavinium and Rome interacted, the genesis of their Aeneas legends must be considered separately because the origins of the legends were different in each case. Let us turn to Rome first.

The version that Aeneas actually founded Rome occurs only in the earliest mention of Rome's origins in our extant Greek sources, i.e. that of Hellanicus (*FGH* 4.F84) quoted by Dionysius of Halicarnassus (*A.R.* 1.72.2). It is not found later anywhere in the Greek tradition and Sallust is the only Roman writer who refers to it (*Cat.* 6.1). A reliable date for Hellanicus' account is the middle of the fifth century B.C. By the time of our next Greek source on the founding of Rome, the Sicilian Alcimus (c. 350 B.C.), the indigenous Romulus legend is too strong to be ignored but, anticipating many subsequent attempts of this sort, the Trojan and the Latin lines of descent are melded: Romulus is the son of Aeneas and, significantly (as we shall see shortly), of Tyrrhenia, the personification of Etruria.[3]

The attempt to dismiss Hellanicus' testimony as the result of some confusion on the part of Dionysius has deservedly not met with any success.[4] Quite on the contrary, this is a very meaningful account and a useful springboard for the discussion of some of the major perspectives relevant to the Aeneas legend in Latium.

The current climate of the pertinent scholarship, represented most articulately by J. Poucet, is that of "hypercriticism."[5] According to this view, literary testimonia such as Hellanicus' are best understood as *matière non historique* and relevant archaeological finds, such as the heroon of Aeneas at Lavinium (on which see below), should simply be described instead of being related to the (unreliable) literary and historical traditions with new hypotheses as a result. As so often, this tendency is the almost inevitable reaction to the *jeu* and *joie des hypothèses* which greeted the arrival of archaeological finds pertaining to the Aeneas legend in Latium. Consider the well-known votive statuettes from Veii. With one of history's ironies, they arrived on the scene virtually at the same time as Perret's monumental *thèse* (still the best collection of literary sources) according to which the Trojan legend of Rome did not predate King Pyrrhus. The pendulum swung against Perret: to Bömer, Alföldi, and others the statuettes were proof positive of Aeneas as a founder hero in Etruria, of an Etruscan Aeneas cult, of the Romans' adoption of Aeneas in the fifth century as their ancestor because of his *pietas*, and so on. The basic premise was ignored that knowledge of the legend on the part of a people, such as the Etruscans, cannot simply be identified with any such functions without further evidence.[6]

Two factors contributed to these interpretations. One was the lack of the full archaeological context, which was not published until 1971.[7] In the votive deposit at Veii, Lucia Vagnetti has identified about 150 major categories for the more than 3,000 ex-voto. The Trojan statuettes do not even constitute such a category and the cult, or more properly, the concerns of the faithful, center on the usual problems of fertility and health. Secondly, after decades of hearing that Aeneas somehow was imposed on the

Romans by the Greeks and their mythographers, scholars reacted by trying to legitimatize him as an indigenous hero with full force. Hence the overinterpretation of the statuettes; they seemed to provide the tangible clarity that was so conspicuously missing in the morass of contradictory versions which already irritated Dionysius (A.R. 1.4.2).

This brings us to a central issue concerning Hellanicus' account. On what was it based? One *a priori* answer has been: on nothing more than Hellanicus' own imagination. As E. Bickerman demonstrated in a fundamental article,[8] Greek mythographers and historians habitually assigned to various newly discovered places and regions around the Mediterranean foundation stories in which Greek heroes were prominent. The procedure reflects the hellenocentrism typical of archaic and classical Greece; any place worthy of notice perforce had to have a Greek connection. Native legends were customarily ignored in the process unless they could be connected somehow with the world of Greek myth. Conversely, so far from feeling imposed upon, the natives often welcomed this immediate entrée into the world of Greek civilization since it bestowed cultural legitimacy.

An important point is that the legend of Aeneas' founding of Rome is indeed the product of Greek historians such as Hellanicus.[9] The very nature of his version, however, suggests that there is more involved than the routine schema I have just described, for, according to Hellanicus, Aeneas founded Rome with Odysseus. Aeneas, as Solmsen has well demonstrated, is the main founder;[10] the addition of Odysseus—and here I follow Momigliano[11]—indicates the opposition between the Trojan Aeneas and the Greek sphere, represented by Odysseus. In other words, Odysseus is the counterweight, coming out of the hellenocentric culture, to Aeneas. In much of Greek mythography, the Trojans were just as Greek as the Greeks, but such is not the case here.[12]

Is is very unlikely that Hellanicus simply invented such a story one late evening on Lesbos because he needed to give Rome a Greek pedigree rooted in Greek mythology. Nor is there any likelihood that his version in some way reflects the Romans' own choice of Aeneas as their founder at this early time. Hellanicus' version, which also involves Aeneas' coming from the land of the Molossians and a Trojan woman's, Rhome, burning the ships is best considered as a synthesis of accounts received over time from Greeks in Italy and his own creative adaptation.[13] Lionel

Pearson once surmised that the informants were Greeks from Campania.[14] Today, further explanations are possible in view of our knowledge of the archaeology of early Rome, i.e. especially the surprising intensity of Greek contacts with archaic Rome, and of the well-known evidence relating to Aeneas in Etruria. Hellanicus' version is not mere literary fantasy, but an allusion to these two elements. Aeneas stands for the Etruscan associations of early Rome; Odysseus, for the Greek. Both deserve a closer look.

Aeneas in Etruria

Without needing to be overinterpreted, the archaeological evidence pertaining to Aeneas in Etruria is significant. His legend was known and well received in southern Etruria from the last quarter of the sixth century on. The relevant objects are: [1] The vases with his representation as a fugitive from Troy as well as in exploits such as the warfare at Troy and the abduction of Helen.[15] The choice of these subjects reflects the predilection of the clientele or, at least, the exporters' anticipation of the preferences of the eventual consumers rather than the choice of the vase painters; the workshop of Nicosthenes, which is roughly contemporary, provides a documented example of this procedure.[16] In a similar vein, Mauro Cristofani aptly entitled his book *L'arte degli Etruschi: Produzione e consumo* (1978). We know that the majority of extant Greek vases come from the area of Etruria and that there were many more vases with images of Hercules and Achilles, for instance, but that does not detract from a perceptible increase in demand for vases with the image of Aeneas especially in the last quarter of the sixth century in the territory of Vulci. The Etruscans themselves depicted the subject on their vases; a good example is the red-figure amphora in Munich, although the object carried by Creusa is not a *doliolum* (with the household gods) but a generic carrying-case.[17] [2] On the Etruscan scarab in Paris, however, the *cista mystica* is clearly represented; this is an exquisitely crafted piece of work that can be reliably dated to the beginning of the fifth century.[18] [3] Similarly, in the case of the votive statuettes from Veii, preference must be given to the dates determined by archaeological experts who were not influenced in their judgments by various hypotheses about the Aeneas legend. For that reason, the date determined by Vagnetti—i.e., the first half of the fifth century—who published the entire votive deposit of the more than 3,000 ex-voto and had ample basis for stylistic comparison recommends itself more readily than Torelli's.[19] Torelli supports his fourth-century date with reference to the Roman resettlement of Veii in 387 B.C. and interprets the statuettes as a reflection of the Romans' consciousness to be the new Aeneases; hence they brought him along as the patron of their migration. As we have seen, so far there is no evidence whatsoever that the Romans adopted Aeneas as their founding hero in the fifth century unless we resort to circular arguments.

What we can safely deduce from the evidence, however, is that Aeneas was well known and perhaps even favored by the Etruscans. By the fifth century, Rome had reached its early heyday while being under Etruscan domination. That, in my opinion, is the basis for the association of Aeneas with Rome in Hellanicus and his sources, most likely Greeks familiar with Rome.[20]

The Greek Acquaintance with Early Rome

The archaeological discoveries in the past twenty years have fundamentally altered our knowledge of early Rome as regards its commercial and even cultural contacts with Greece from the eighth to the fifth centuries B.C. To focus again on the second half of the sixth century: the finds from the Sant' Omobono area, in the Forum Boarium in particular, demonstrate the intensity of this contact.[21] An outstanding example is the acroterial group with Herakles and Athena, which may represent his introduction to Olympus and probably was the product of a Greek workshop at Rome.[22] Already in the eighth century, even before the founding of Cumae and Pithecusae, the northern vanguards of the Greek colonization in Italy, the presence of Greek traders and craftsmen is attested in the area of Rome.[23] They came especially from Euboea, which was well known at this early time for its far-flung trade. Interestingly enough, the other area where such trade and cultural contacts are evident is that of Vulci, to which we referred earlier in connection with the Aeneas vases. The imports of Greek pottery increase even more in the seventh century in Rome; the provenience is Attic, Ionic, and Laconic. From the eighth to the fifth century, the continuity and intensity of Greco-Roman relations is remarkable. The adoption by the Romans of the Greek cult of Castor and Pollux in 484 B.C. and the similarities between the Roman Comitium and the Athenian Pnyx,[24] datable to the first half of the fifth century, also belong in the context.

The strength of such a Greek presence, especially as early as the eighth century, was greeted with a great deal of surprise.

Eugenio La Rocca, who published these finds in 1977, stated correctly that it was difficult—to the extent of our knowledge in 1977—to determine, what the Greek traders were looking for at the time. He assumed it was salt, vegetables, wood, milk products, and grain.[25]

Today we can provide an answer which is both more general and more specific. Led by Professor Carandini of the University of Siena, excavations are now taking place in the Roman forum which reach down to the eighth-century level past the strata where Boni's excavations had stopped. According to preliminary reports,[26] remains of a fortification wall have been found which was built and rebuilt in the eighth century. The wall was further demarcated by a broad ditch in which several votive gifts were found. We have, therefore, an indication of a significant settlement with its religious boundary, the *pomerium*, at a much earlier time than had been previously suspected. It is the same time—the eighth century—in which the founding of Rome took place according to the literary and historical tradition.

All this makes it clear that early Rome was anything but a nebulous entity to the Greeks. By the time of Hellanicus, there had been a long and unbroken history of Greco-Roman contacts. It is this continuing Greek presence that is reflected, I believe, by Hellanicus' reference to Odysseus as the co-founder of Rome. Etruria was the dominant power in Rome until the fifth century; hence Aeneas had precedence over Odysseus. But the Greek element had to be recognized also and that led to the inclusion of Odysseus for more than the generic reasons discerned by Bickerman, although Odysseus is associated in that vein with many other places in Italy too.[27] At any rate, the peculiar nature of Hellanicus' *testimonium* makes excellent sense in the context of what we presently know about early Rome and about Aeneas in Etruria.

As we saw earlier, however, the Romans did not adopt the story of Aeneas as the founder of their city. The local story of Romulus prevailed, but the Trojan and the Latin legends were combined so that Aeneas became not the founder, but the ancestor. Again, as we saw earlier, the next extant Greek *testimonium* after Hellanicus, that of Alcimus, makes Aeneas Romulus' father while Tyrrhenia, i.e. Etruria—for good reasons, as we now can see—is his mother. The date of this version is around the middle of the fourth century and it is exactly for that period that good case can be made for Aeneas' emerging as the founder of Lavinium.

In terms of the mixture of cultural influences—Latin/Italic, Greek and, to a lesser extent, Etruscan—Lavinium in the archaic period is similar to Rome. Castagnoli, for instance, has incisively highlighted the general parallelism between the urban and cultural development of Rome and Lavinium in the sixth century without, wisely, positing any "influence" of one city on the other.[28] Connections with Greece are again documented by ceramic imports and, among other examples, the bronze votive tablet to *Castorei Podlouqueique qurois*, which dates from the late sixth century and was found by Altar VIII.[29] Another superb example of the dissemination of even fairly recondite Greek mythological versions to Lavinium is the statue of the warlike Athena from the eastern sanctuary.[30] The iconography is special. Besides the heavy emphasis on the chthonic aspect as evidenced by the profusion of serpents, her shield rests on the head of a young boy. The best explanation is that the latter represents the river Triton. According to a local legend in Boeotia, Athena was born from that river and already Homer knows her as Tritogeneia. It is a type that is also known to us from the Athena Rospigliosi. The statue at Lavinium is a local product. Its style is late archaic and the most sensible date is the first quarter of the fifth century.

It can be reasonably assumed, therefore, that the legend of Aeneas, just like other Greek myths, was known at Lavinium by the sixth century. Its identification at that early time, however, with a foundation legend or cult once more is an *argumentum ex silentio*.[31] As usual, our literary sources are late. The earliest is Timaeus, who visited the sanctuary of the Penates at Lavinium and was shown "iron and bronze heralds' wands and Trojan pottery" there (*FGH* 566.F59). Those who tend to hypercriticism have tried to down-date his visit to the early third century; I still prefer Karl Meister's date of the late fourth century (by approximately 310 B.C. at the latest) at which the German scholar arrived irrespective of the current scholarly controversies about the Aeneas legend.[32] The conventional date for the composition of Lycophron's *Alexandra*, who alludes to Aeneas' founding of Lavinium in line 1259, is the early decades of the third century, but Stephanie West's recent arguments for a late first-century date of the "Roman" passages of the poem deserve serious consideration.[33]

Next we have Naevius, Fabius Pictor, Ennius, and Cato. They all know of Aeneas' arrival in Latium. Servius *auctus* reports that *Naevius et Ennius Aeneae ex filia nepotem Romulum conditorem urbis tradunt* (ad Aen. 1.273); here is Aeneas, the Roman ancestor. One or possibly two of the fragments of Naevius contain references to objects that Aeneas was able to salvage from Troy. They are mostly vessels:

> *pulchraque (vasa) ex auro vestem citrosam* (fr. 10 M.)
> (*vasa* is Reichardt's emendation)
>
> *ferunt pulchras creterras, aureas lepistas* (fr. 7 M.)

These objects, as well as the *anclabres* (fr. 8 M.), a special kind of triangular table, "were clearly essential for Aeneas and his clan, if they were to continue the cult of their gods in a foreign country."[34] They belong in the same context, therefore, as the *keramos Troikos* attested by Timaeus at Lavinium a few decades before Naevius. Fabius seems to have invented the list of Alban kings to bridge the chronological gap between the fall of Troy and the founding of Rome, whereas Cato in the first book of the *Origines* systematized Aeneas' landing and exploits in Latium. The problem is that this literary evidence, which of course also includes Dionysius, Vergil, and some annalists, is, for the most part, later than the archaeological finds at Lavinium. What light do these shed on the Aeneas legend?

Most of the recent debate has centered on the so-called heroon of Aeneas.[35] Without taking up every argument in the controversy, I want to focus briefly on some salient aspects.

We are dealing with a seventh-century tomb which despite depredations gives enough evidence of the high social status of its inhabitant and which was incorporated into a fourth-century heroon in a special manner: the corner of the new cella abutted directly into the tomb. We have no secure evidence of worship at the tomb before the fourth century; the sixth-century oinochoe of *bucchero pesante* may indicate a gift of expiation for disturbing the grave rather than prove the existence of a cult. In the second half of the fourth century, the tumulus was restructured and the heroon proper was built. The site apparently was part of the precinct of the Thirteen Altars since the latters' inception in the sixth century. This complex reached a new height precisely at the time the heroon was built and the old grave literally became cornerstone of the latter: the construction of four new altars and the renovation of some of the older ones date from that period also. The decades soon after the middle of the fourth century provide, as we will soon see, the relevant historical context.

The coincidence between the archaeological realities of this heroon and Dionysius' description of the heroon of Aeneas at Lavinium (*A.R.* 1.64.5) is too close to be dismissed. With all deference to hypercriticism, it simply does not happen that often that we find a heroon/tumulus. Furthermore, Dionysius is an excellent topographical and historical source. The two principal objections are:[36] (1) the references in other writers, such as Livy, have been taken to indicate that the heroon should be located right by the Numicus. In fact, however, phrases such as Livy's *super Numicum flumen* (1.2) cannot be so pressed. Besides some ancient parallels, which I have cited elsewhere, let me adduce a modern one. Napoleon said expressly *"je désire que mes cendres reposent sur les bords de la Seine."* His tomb is about 800 meters from the Seine, about the same distance as Aeneas' is from the Numicus. Perhaps we should leave to the excavators of the Invalides in the far future to consider this odd as Napoleon's contemporaries and subsequent generations obviously haven't taken notice. (2) The inscription cited by Dionysius mentions only a *Pater Indiges*, and not Aeneas, by name, but that is precisely the title he has in the *elogium* set up in his honor at Pompeii (*CIL* 10.8348 = *ILS* 63). Besides, Aeneas was worshipped under a variety of names at Lavinium, including *Iuppiter Indiges*.[37] *Lar Aineias* was not one of them; that inscription, which was found at quite a distance from Lavinium anyway, will not hold up to scrutiny, and its precipitate interpretation, in conjunction with the inscriptions on the cippi of three Fata, as the consecration of the *sacra principia populi Romani* and an anticipation of Vergil's connection between Aeneas and *fatum* has not helped the credibility of archaeological and epigraphic testimonia which have been brought to bear on the Aeneas legend.[38] Conversely, if we look upon Aeneas *Indiges* under his various names as overshadowing, if not supplanting, Sol *Indiges* at Lavinium we are back to the rivalry between Aeneas and Odysseus: since Hesiod, Odysseus was known as the father of Latinus by Circe, the daughter of Sol.[39]

The principal event to which the "Trojanization" of the objects in the Lavinian sanctuary, the new building phase of the sacred area of the Thirteen Altars,[40] and the restructuring of the old tumulus into a heroon for Aeneas are related is the *foedus* between Rome and Lavinium in 338 B.C. (Livy 8.11.15). It was preceded by the first treaty between Rome and Carthage in 348 B.C. which makes specific mention of the territory of the Laurentes.[41] The *foedus* signalled the end of the Latin League and thus, of whatever political power Lavinium may have had.[42]

At the same time, it gave emphasis to Lavinium's special role in the area of cult and religion. Connected with this, I would argue, was the establishment of the legend of Aeneas as the founder of Lavinium and the ancestor of Rome.

We saw earlier that, as for the founding of Rome, the native legend of Romulus and Remus prevailed. Hence the compromise by Alcimus, which can be dated to the period we are now discussing, i.e. 350 B.C. and after: Aeneas is Romulus' father. Aeneas, therefore, had to find, and did find, another city. That city, as Timaeus' account from the late fourth century attests, was Lavinium. Our sources reflect the Roman connection of the procedure. Lavinium was promoted to the Roman ancestral city in Latium: *oppidum, quod primum conditum in Latio stirpis Romanae, Lavinium* as Varro puts it (*L.L.* 5.144). Similarly, a Pompeian inscription from the time of Claudius refers to the *foedus* and connects it with the *sacra principia populi Romani Quiritium nominisque Latini quae apud Laurentes coluntur* (*CIL* 10.797 = *ILS* 5004).

The procedure would hardly have seemed forced to anyone at the time. The venerable character of Lavinium is confirmed by its archaeology: it was one of earliest inhabited sites in Latium (since the 14th century B.C.)[43] and it was the site of a federal sanctuary. Cults such as those of Athena Ilias and the Aphrodision contributed to effecting a Trojan ambiance;[44] the place-name *Troia*, nearby, is probably a result of the Trojanization of Lavinium after the *foedus* in 338 B.C. rather than a contributory cause. Besides, as we mentioned before, there was the affinity or parallelism, documented again by the recent archaeology, between the urban and cultural development of Rome and Lavinium especially in the sixth century. Some coincidences are striking: the height of the earliest Altar (XIII) at Lavinium is the exactly the same as that of the podium of the modified temple of the Sant' Omobono area.

The Romans, then, could retain Romulus as their founder and claim Trojan descent at the same time. But some Greeks never gave up and pointedly continued to give this version a Greek and, not surprisingly, Ulyssean equivalent. Xenagoras, who can be dated to the late fourth and early third century B.C., knows of Rhomos' founding Rome, but Rhomos' father is not Aeneas, rather Odysseus (the mother again is Circe).[45] Or, to give another example, Demetrius of Skepsis in the second century B.C. was so ornery as to deny that Aeneas had ever left the Troad at all.[46] Others tried to reconcile the two pedigrees. One Kleinias, for example, had Aeneas marry Rhome, a daughter of Odysseus' son Telemachus, and Rome was named after her.[47] Still in the fourth century, Heracleides of Pontus called Rome a *polis Hellenis* (Plut., *Cam.* 22.3). And why not? Even around 290 B.C. the Romans set up statues of Alcibiades and Pythagoras on the Comitium (Pliny, *N.H.* 34.26). Finally, Pyrrhus' contemporary Callias (of Syracuse) made Romulus the son of Latinus and the Trojan woman, Rhome (*FGH* 564.F5 = 840.F14).

It is against the background of this contentious debate that we must view Pyrrhus' famous pronouncement. So far from creating the legend of Rome's Trojan ancestry he was reacting to it. If the Romans did not want to be Greeks, despite many helpful hints from Greek historiographers, their claim to Trojan descent would have its repercussions: he was going to be Achilles about to destroy this latter-day Troy. With this, the vocabulary of the legend became political: in the third century and the second, it helped the claims of Rome over Sicily and became part of the discourse on foreign policy between Rome and various Greek states with varying degrees of initiative on both sides.[48]

Let me conclude with a few perspectives on the *Aeneid*. While critics go on debating the "political" aspect of the *Aeneid* as Augustan or anti-Augustan, Vergil's merit is precisely to have taken a figure, who had been used politically both by the Roman state and the *familiae Troianae*, and fleshed him out as a multi-dimensional human being. Vergil transformed Aeneas both into a truly popular hero in Rome and into a paradigm of the complexity of the human existence.[49] There is a connection between this and Rome's choice of Trojan ancestry in the late fourth century. That choice, as Momigliano has formulated it so well, was one of self-definition: "It was a proclamation of noble origins combined with the recognition of diversity from the Greeks."[50] The process of self-definition is carried forward immensely in the *Aeneid*. Aeneas did appear in the epics of Naevius and Ennius, but we have no indication of a full-blown character there. For all we can tell from the fragments, the emphasis seems to have been, understandably enough, on the tradition of the wanderings and the basic story of his landing in Italy including, in Ennius, his relations with the king of Alba.[51]

That raises another point. By the second century B.C., the sanctuary of the Thirteen Altars and the heroon of Aeneas at Lavinium had fallen into desuetude and there certainly is no trace of an Augustan restoration. The Julii claimed their descent from Alba and the rivalry between Alba and Lavinium for Trojan legitimation percolates through our sources.[52] In this context belong the references by the annalist Fabius Maximus Servilianus and by Dionysius to Lavinium as a barren and unpromising place that causes Aeneas considerable anguish.[53] The upshot is that Vergil, while mentioning the *Lavina litora* as the goal of the voyage, has Aeneas land in a *locus amoenus* at the mouth of the Tiber and later proceed directly to Rome.[54] There he is received by the Greek Evander, the founder of proto-Rome.

That brings us back full circle to Hellanicus. Once more, Aeneas is coming to Rome, not, however, with the *polymetis* Odysseus but with the *pius* Evander. Their union stands for the symbiosis of the two great civilizations, a symbiosis which is one of the hallmarks of the Augustan culture[55] (hence the allusions to the Augustan buildings during Aeneas' tour, guided by Evander, of the site of Rome in Book 8).[56] The beginning of the *Aeneid* still sounds the reverse note of Pyrrhus' pronouncement (1.283-285):

> *veniet lustris labentibus aetas*
> *cum domus Assaraci Phthiam clarasque Mycenas*
> *servitio premet ac victis dominabitur Argis.*

But in Book 8, the real end of the Odyssean *Aeneid*—which started with a firm rejection in *Troiae qui primus ab oris* of the Ulyssean claim to have come to Latium first—[57] Greece and Rome are reconciled. Aeneas receives not nearly the military help from Evander for which he had hoped. It is more important that they are spiritual, cultural, and human allies.[58] Evander lives at the site of Rome; Aeneas is his true heir and ally, becoming even a surrogate father to Pallas; Romulus will found Rome, and Augustus will restore it. And Odysseus is in no way connected with Rome; in the Odyssean part of the *Aeneid*, Aeneas has superseded him.

Resilience, however, had always been one of Odysseus' hallmarks. In Ovid's reaction to the *Aeneid*, the *Metamorphoses*, he regains his ascendancy over Aeneas. And Tiberius may have had the same reaction to Augustus: instead of the latter's role model Aeneas, a huge Odysseus Group becomes Tiberius' favorite at Sperlonga.[59] One final lesson we can learn from the dynamic polyphony and interplay of the historical, mythographical, literary, and artistic traditions is that there is still much more to be explored usefully before we turn into narcissistic critics and concentrate on our own polyphonal reader responses to the *Aeneid*.

WORKS CITED BY NAME ONLY

A. Alföldi, *Die trojanischen Urahnen der Römer* (Basel, 1957); *Early Rome and the Latins* (Ann Arbor, 1965); *Römische Frühgeschichte* (Heidelberg, 1976).
F. Castagnoli, *Lavinium I* (Rome, 1972); *Lavinium II: Le tredici are* (Rome, 1975); "La leggenda di Enea nel Lazio," *Studi Romani* 30 (1976) 1-15; also in *Atti del Convegno mondiale scientifico di studi su Virgilio* 2 (Milan, 1984) 283-303.
T.J. Cornell, "Aeneas' Arrival in Italy," *LCM* 2 (1977) 77-83.
G. D'Anna, "Il ruolo di Lavinio e di Alba Longa nei primi scrittori latini," in *Problemi di letteratura arcaica* (Rome, 1976) 43-143.
G. Dury-Moyaers, *Enée à Lavinium*, Coll. Latomus 174 (Brussels, 1981).
Enea nel Lazio. Archeologia e mito (Rome, 1981).
G.K. Galinsky, *Aeneas, Sicily, and Rome* (Princeton, 1969); "Troiae qui primus ab oris," *Gymn.* 81 (1974a) 182-200; "The 'Tomb' of Aeneas at Lavinium," *Vergilius* 20 (1974b) 2-11; "Aeneas in Latium: Archäologie, Mythos und Geschichte," in V. Pöschl, ed., *2000 Jahre Vergil*. Wolfenbütteler Forsch 24 (Wiesbaden, 1983).
N.M. Horsfall, "Some Problems in the Aeneas Legend," *CQ* 29 (1979) 372-390; "The Aeneas Legend from Homer to Virgil," in J.N. Bremmer and N.M. Horsfall, *Roman Myth and Mythography. BICS* London Suppl. 52 (1987) 12-24 (Italian version in *Enciclopedia Virgiliana*).
B. Liou-Gille, *Cultes héroiques romains. Les fondateurs* (Paris, 1980).
A. Momigliano, "How to Reconcile Greeks and Romans," *Settimo Contributo* (Rome, 1984) 437-462 = *Meded. Kon. Nederl. Akad. Wetenschappen, Afd. Leterkunde* n. r. 45.9 (1982) 231-254; "The Origins of Rome," *Settimo Contributo* (Rome, 1984) 380-436 (also in *CAH*[2] vol. 7 [1989] 52-112).
J. Perret, *Les origines de la légende troyenne de Rome* (Paris, 1942) 281-331.
J. Poucet, *Les origines de Rome. Tradition et histoire* (Brussels, 1985); "La diffusion de la légende d'Enée en Italie centrale et ses rapports avec celle de Romulus," *LEC* 57 (1989) 227-254 (reached me only after the completion of this article).
W.A. Schröder, *M. Porcius Cato: Das erste Buch der Origines* (Meisenheim, 1971).
F. Solmsen, "Aeneas Founded Rome with Odysseus," *HSCP* 90 (1986) 93-110.
L. Vagnetti, *Il deposito votivo di Campetti a Veio* (Florence, 1971).

NOTES

1. Galinsky (1983). Part of this paper was delivered as a lecture at the Johannes Gutenberg Universität in Mainz in May 1989; I should like to thank especially A. Wlosok for helpful suggestions.

2. Solmsen (1986), Momigliano (1982) and (1984), Horsfall (1987).
3. *FGH* 560.F4; cf. Momigliano (1984) 384.
4. Horsfall (1979) 376-383; *contra*, Solmsen (1986), Momigliano (1982) 444 and *Settimo Contributo* 107-109.
5. Poucet (1985); see my review in *Phoenix* 41 (1987) 71-74.
6. Details in Galinsky (1983) 38. On a related matter, Horsfall (1987) 12-13 makes another brave attempt at positing a strong tradition of Aeneas' piety in Greece, but his case is circumstantial at best; besides, see W. Fuchs' sober assessment of the artistic evidence in *ANRW* I.4 (1973) 615-632.
7. Vagnetti (1971).
8. "Origines gentium," *CP* 48 (1952) 65-81.
9. I have refined this point since my book (1969), p. 105, and article (1974a) for reasons that will be clear from the following argument. Cf. Castagnoli (1982) 15 and Dury-Moyaers (1981) 176.
10. Solmsen (1985) 94-95.
11. Momigliano (1982) 447. Momigliano, however, allows for the possibility of Hellanicus' version being the reflection of a Latin legend.
12. The variant reading *met' Odysea* reflects the recognition that the conjunction of two disparate founder heroes is unusual. This solution makes the version more hellenocentric yet, but is awkward and has rightly been dismissed.
13. Details in Solmsen (1986); cf. Galinsky (1983) 41-42.
14. *Early Ionian Historians* (Oxford, 1939) 192.
15. For the most recent tabulation see Horsfall (1987) 18.
16. M. Eisman, *Archaeology* 28 (1975) 76-83; R.M. Cook, *Greek Painted Pottery* (London, 1960) 273.
17. Antikensammlungen Inv. 3185. See Horsfall, *Antike Kunst* 22 (1979) 104-105 after B.B. Shefton, *Wiss. Zeitschr. Rostock* 16 (1967) 534 n. 25.
18. Bibl. Nationale, Coll. des Luynes, Inv. 276. P. Zazoff, *Etruskische Skarabäen* (Mainz, 1968) 41-43.
19. Vagnetti (1971) 88; cf. Canciani in *LIMC* 1 (1981) 395; Torelli, *DArch* 7 (1973) 399-400.
20. The version according to which Remus founds Aineia (the later Janiculum; D.H., *A.R.* 1.73.3) may belong in the same context rather than indicate the fusion of the Latin and Trojan legends.
21. Good survey in *Enea nel Lazio* 115-154.
22. A. Sommella Mura in *BMCR* 23 (1977) 3-15; further references in Galinsky (1983) 52 with nn. 29 and 30.
23. Details in E. LaRocca, *PP* 32 (1977) 375-397.
24. E. Sjöqvist, *Studies D. M. Robinson* (St. Louis, 1951) 400-411.

25. LaRocca (n. 23, above) 389.
26. See *Archeo* 48 (1989) 50-59; *Bollettino di Archeologia* 1.2 (1990) 160-163.
27. E.D. Phillips, *JHS* 73 (1953) 53-67; Galinsky (1974a) 186-190.
28. *PP* 32 (1977) 340-355.
29. Castagnoli (1975) 441-443.
30. Details in Castagnoli, *Acc. Naz. Lincei. Problemi attuali di scienza e di cultura* 246 (1979) 3-14; *Enea nel Lazio* 187-191.
31. See my review of Dury-Moyaers (1981) in *AJA* 86 (1982) 598-599.
32. Cf. L. Pearson, *The Greek Historians of the West: Timaeus and His Predecessors*. APA Monograph 35 (Atlanta, 1987) 37-38. Timaeus was in exile in Athens for 50 years starting in the years after 317 B.C. and did not return to Sicily until 263/262. Modern scholars should be careful not to arrange field trips to Lavinium for him too cavalierly during this period.
33. *JHS* 94 (1984) 127-151.
34. G. Luck, *ICS* 8.2 (1983) 272.
35. Published by P. Sommella, *Rend. Pont. Acc. Arch.*, ser. 3.44 (1971/ 1972), 47ff. and *Gymn.* 81 (1974) 173-197; cf. Galinsky (1974b) and the Catalogue of the Exhibition, *La Civiltà del Lazio Primitivo* (Rome, 1976) 305-311.
36. Detailed discussion with reference, e.g., to Cornell (1977) in Galinsky (1983) 43-45.
37. Good compilation of sources in Schröder (1971) 129; cf. R.M. Ogilvie, *A Commentary on Livy Books 1-5* (Oxford, 1965) 41; Liou-Gille (1980) 86-134.
38. Lar Aineias inscription: Degrassi *ILLRP* 10-12 and 1271; detailed discussion in Galinsky (1983) 42.
39. *Theogony* 1011-1016 with D.L. West's commentary; see *Latomus* 26 (1967) 627-628.
40. Castagnoli (1975) 89-174; *Enea nel Lazio* 169-177.
41. For further discussion see Alföldi (1965) 350-355; F.W. Walbank on Polybius 3.22.1-3.
42. Liou-Gille (1980) 130-132 makes the good point that Lavinium's role traditionally lay more in the area of cult than political power.
43. Good survey in Dury-Moyaers (1981) 98ff.
44. Castagnoli (1982) 9-10; Horsfall (1987) 19 with n. 90.
45. *FGH* 240.F29. For the date of Xenagoras, see Gisinger, *RE* 2.18, 1410.14ff.
46. Cited by Strabo 13.1.53; see Momigliano (1982) 451-452.
47. FGH 819.F1, probably third century B.C.; see Schröder (1971) 67-68.

48. E. Weber, *WS* n. s. 6 (1972) 213-275; Momigliano (1982) 453; H. Kirchner, *Die Bedeutung der Fremdkulte in der römischen Ostpolitik* (*Diss.*: Bonn, 1956) 13ff.
49. See *ANRW* II.31.2 (1981) 997 and the bibliography listed there.
50. Momigliano (1982) 447.
51. Naevius: M. Wigodsky, *Vergil and Early Latin Poetry*. Hermes Einzelschr. 24 (1972) 22-34; G. D'Anna, Rendic. Acc. Naz. Lincei 8, 30 (1975) 1ff. Ennius: O. Skutsch, *The Annals of Quintus Ennius* (Oxford, 1985) 176-191; Horsfall (1987) 22 with nn. 130-132.
52. Full discussion in D'Anna (1976); also Alföldi (1976) 131-143.
53. Fabius Maximus Servilianus (cos. 143): Serv. *auct. ad Aen.* 1.3 (= fr. 1P.); see F. della Corte, *La mappa dell'Eneide* (Florence, 1972) 131. D.H., *A.R.* 1.56.2. Cf. Liou-Gille (1980) 128-129 who suggests that Fabius may be Fabius Pictor.
54. *Aen.* 7.25-36 with the excellent discussion of V. Buchheit, *Vergil über die Sendung Roms*. Gymn. Beiheft 3 (1963) 177-182.
55. For the arts, see now P. Zanker, *The Power of Images in the Age of Augustus* (Ann Arbor, 1988); cf. the articles by R.R.R. Smith on the Sebasteion at Aphrodisias in *JRS* 77 (1987) and *JRS* 78 (1988); cf. *ICS* 14 (1989) 77-78.
56. See now Christine Renaud, *Studies in the Eighth Book of the* Aeneid (*Diss.*: Texas, 1990).
57. Galinsky (1974a). For the *Aeneid* as *Odyssey* see now F. Cairns, *Virgil's Augustan Epic* (Cambridge, 1989) 179-214.
58. In Cato's *Origines* (F6) the Aborigines, with whose king Latinus Aeneas makes an alliance, are from Greece; see Schröder (1971) 91, 108-110.
59. Cf. B. Andreae, *Laokoon und die Gründung Roms* (Mainz, 1988) 67ff. and my review in *AJA* 94 (1990) 164-165.

AENEAS AT CARTHAGE:
THE OPENING SCENES OF THE *AENEID*

E.L. Harrison
University of Leeds

Writers on the *Aeneid* disagree about the role of Aeneas in both its opening and closing scenes, and in particular the anger which drives Aeneas to kill his suppliant adversary at the end of the epic has been much discussed.[1] Here I should like to consider how the hero is presented to us at the start, concentrating on his earliest speeches, on the Homeric models used by Vergil to produce them, and on the discordant reactions among critics to what Aeneas has to say.

To begin the action the poet tells how, when Aeolus frees the winds in response to Juno's overtures, the resultant storm drives the Trojans onto the North African coast. While the winds are still doing their worst, Aeneas reflects aloud in a monologue with a carefully organized climax[2] whose own growing violence seems to compete with that of the surrounding chaos (passage 1):

> *incubuere mari totumque a sedibus imis*
> *una Eurusque Notusque ruunt creberque procellis*
> *Africus, et uastos uoluunt ad litora fluctus.* . . .
>
> 1.84-86

> *extemplo Aeneae soluuntur frigore membra;*
> *ingemit et duplicis tendens ad sidera palmas*
> *talia uoce refert: "o terque quaterque beati,*
> *quis ante ora patrum Troiae sub moenibus altis*
> *contigit oppetere! o Danaum fortissime gentis*
> *Tydide! mene Iliacis occumbere campis*

non potuisse, tuaque animam hanc effundere dextra,
saeuus ubi Aeacidae telo iacet Hector, ubi ingens
Sarpedon, ubi tot Simois correpta sub undis
scuta uirum galeasque et fortia corpora uoluit!"
talia iactanti stridens Aquilone procella
uelum aduersa ferit, fluctusque ad sidera tollit.
                                                    1.92-103

As his primary model for this speech Vergil naturally took the matching episode in the *Odyssey*, where Odysseus reacts to a similar sea-storm produced by another persecuting deity, in this case Poseidon, angry with Odysseus for the blinding of his son, Polyphemus (passage 2):

σὺν δ' Εὖρός τε Νότος τ' ἔπεσον Ζέφυρός τε δυσαὴς
καὶ Βορέης αἰθρηγενέτης, μέγα κῦμα κυλίνδων.
καὶ τότ' 'Οδυσσῆος λύτο γούνατα καὶ φίλον ἦτορ,
ὀχθήσας δ' ἄρα εἶπε πρὸς ὃν μεγαλήτορα θυμόν·
 "Ὤ μοι ἐγὼ δειλός, τί νύ μοι μήκιστα γένηται;
δείδω μὴ δὴ πάντα θεὰ νημερτέα εἶπε,
ἥ μ' ἔφατ' ἐν πόντῳ, πρὶν πατρίδα γαῖαν ἱκέσθαι,
ἄλγε' ἀναπλήσειν· τὰ δὲ δὴ νῦν πάντα τελεῖται,
οἵοισιν νεφέεσσι περιστέφει οὐρανὸν εὐρὺν
Ζεύς, ἐτάραξε δὲ πόντον, ἐπισπέρχουσι δ' ἄελλαι
παντοίων ἀνέμων. νῦν μοι σῶς αἰπὺς ὄλεθρος.
τρισμάκαρες Δαναοὶ καὶ τετράκις οἳ τότ' ὄλοντο
Τροίῃ ἐν εὐρείῃ, χάριν Ἀτρείδῃσι φέροντες.
ὡς δὴ ἐγώ γ' ὄφελον θανέειν καὶ πότμον ἐπισπεῖν
ἤματι τῷ ὅτε μοι πλεῖστοι χαλκήρεα δοῦρα
Τρῶες ἐπέρριψαν περὶ Πηλείωνι θανόντι.
τῷ κ' ἔλαχον κτερέων, καί μευ κλέος ἦγον Ἀχαιοί.
νῦν δέ με λευγαλέῳ θανάτῳ εἵμαρτο ἁλῶναι.ὢ
 "Ὣς ἄρα μιν εἰπόντ' ἔλασεν μέγαν κῦμα κατ' ἄκρης
δεινὸν ἐπεσσύμενον, περὶ δὲ σχεδίην ἐλέλιξε.
                                          Odyssey 5.295-314

Vergil's echoes of his model, already noted in antiquity,[3] seem obvious enough. The Homeric description of the gathering storm is closely matched; Aeneas, like Odysseus, reacts to it with a highly emotional monologue; and once more that unforgettable cry, "Three times and four times blessed," introduces a hero's wish that he had fallen in battle at Troy. But there are the usual deviations from the model. Some seem close to Alexandrian word-play: Βορέης, for example, is plucked from the introductory Homeric narrative (296), and its equivalent is given a role in the Vergilian sequel (Aquilone, 102), while in that same sequel *fluctusque ad sidera tollit* (103) now reverses the direction of the matching κῦμα κατ' ἄκρης / δεινὸν ἐπεσσύμενον (313f.). But other changes are more pointed. For example *extemplo Aeneae soluuntur frigore membra* (92) seems a clear word-for-word approximation to the Homeric καὶ τότ' Ὀδυσσῆος λύτο γούνατα (297), except that now *frigore* has been added to make it clear that Aeneas has lost control over his limbs not through any terror but because of the extreme conditions produced by the sudden storm. This interpretation of Vergil's addition to his model is supported by several corresponding omissions. For on the one hand the internalizing καὶ φίλον ἦτορ (297), which indicates that Odysseus is indeed terrror-stricken, finds no equivalent in the new context;[4] and on the other Vergil also avoids echoing Odysseus' matching preoccupation with his own apparently impending death, producing no equivalent of "What is to become of me in the end?" (299), or "Now my utter destruction is certain" (305), or "Now I am doomed to be seized by a dismal death" (312). Throughout his monologue Aeneas is concerned, not with any immediate mortal danger, but with the hero's death he wishes he had achieved at Troy.[5] Comparison with the Homeric model thus confirms that there are no grounds for the commonly held view that on his first appearance Aeneas is in the grip of fear. There is no basis for such comments as "In the sea-storm he appears as a terror-stricken incompetent," "An ordinary man . . . frightened of the elements," "filled with terror," and even "collapsing in a mortal chill of terror."[6] For a very short time Aeneas is physically affected by the severe conditions prevailing during the storm, but once that is over and he is ashore he is soon himself again, and as active as ever (180ff.).

Because Aeneas' experiences at Carthage are in general based on the *Odyssey*'s Phaeacian episode, the contribution of the *Iliad* is perhaps liable to be underestimated at this early stage.[7] But not only is it involved in the familiar kind of imitation in the very first episode (with Juno's approach to Aeolus based on that of Hera to Hypnos in Book 14), but from the start the *Aeneid* is presented as a sequel to the *Iliad*, with the same inexorable goddess still persecuting the same long-suffering race, even though now her name has changed and her victims have left Troy far behind: *ueterisque memor Saturnia belli* (1.23). So too, we find that in composing Aeneas' monologue Vergil has also drawn on Achilles' confrontation with the river Xanthus, the closest parallel the *Iliad* could provide, and the earliest in this trio of passages portraying a hero's reaction to the prospect of being ignominiously drowned[8] instead of dying on the battlefield (passage 3):

ποταμὸς δ' ὑπὸ γούνατ' ἐδάμνα
λάβρος ὕπαιθα ῥέων, κονίην δ' ὑπέρεπτε ποδοῖιν.
Πηλείδης δ' ᾤμωξεν ἰδὼν εἰς οὐρανὸν εὐρύν.
" Ζεῦ πάτερ, ὡς οὔ τίς με θεῶν ἐλεεινὸν ὑπέστη
ἐκ ποταμοῖο σαῶσαι. ἔπειτα δὲ καί τι πάθοιμι.
ἄλλος δ' οὔ τίς μοι τόσον αἴτιος Οὐρανιώνων,
ἀλλὰ φίλη μήτηρ, ἥ με ψεύδεσσιν ἔθελγεν.
ἥ μ' ἔφατο Τρώων ὑπὸ τείχεϊ θωρηκτάων
λαιψηροῖς ὀλέεσθαι Ἀπόλλωνος βελέεσσιν.
ὥς μ' ὄφελ' Ἕκτωρ κτεῖναι, ὃς ἐνθάδε γ' ἔτραφ' ἄριστος.
τῶ κ' ἀγαθὸς μὲν ἔπεφν', ἀγαθὸν δέ κεν ἐξενάριξε.
νῦν δέ με λευγαλέῳ θανάτῳ εἵμαρτο ἁλῶναι
ἐρχθέντ' ἐν μεγάλῳ ποταμῷ, ὡς παῖδα συφορβόν
ὅν ῥά τ' ἔναυλος ἀποέρσῃ χειμῶνι περῶντα."
Iliad 21.270-283

Achilles' bitter cry and glance heavenwards (272), as opposed to the formulaic monologue indicator preceding Odysseus' outburst (298), doubtless inspired Vergil's *ingemit et duplicis tendens ad sidera palmas* (93); and Aeneas' wish that he had died at Troy, killed by Diomede, "bravest of the Greeks" (96f.), similarly has no equivalent in passage 2, but recalls Achilles' corresponding wish centered on Hector (279). This early association of Aeneas with Achilles in itself has little impact at this stage, in view of the context and the dominance hereabouts of the association with Odysseus. But it is the first hint of a process which will gather impetus in the second half of the epic, and become decisive when the action reaches its climax. As for the other point—the *Aeneid's* functioning as a continuation of the *Iliad*—Aeneas' monologue is composed throughout in that spirit and with that perspective. His wish that he had died at Troy in his confrontation with Diomede (to which we shall return shortly), and the references to Achilles' killing of Hector, to Sarpedon's death at the hands of Patroclus, and to the clogging of Troy's river with dead warriors and their weapons, all take the reader's mind back to specific passages in the *Iliad*.[9]

If we turn now to the reaction of critics to this first appearance of Aeneas, we find that in general it is regarded as remarkably negative, and the despair which seems to have overwhelmed him is especially noted. Knauer refers to Aeneas' "Ausdruck grösster Verzweiflung,"[10] and Liebermann to his "Verzweiflungsmonolog."[11] Gossage comments: "For most of the first book Aeneas' mental condition alternates between bewilderment and despair. Here it is despair."[12] W.W. de Grummond draws attention to the bathos thus produced: "By the time this as yet unidentified hero of *arma uirumque cano* appears the reader's expectations are high, but are at once dashed by an Aeneas who is in the depths of despair and helplessness."[13] Almost a century ago, indeed, Heinze suggested that such an opening amounted to "a slap in the face for the conventional but distorted notion of Roman magnanimity and strength of character";[14] and although critics in the meantime seem not to have endorsed this view, preferring to confine the issue to the context of the epic, they have for the most part accepted the negative evaluation of Aeneas' first appearance which underlies Heinze's comment.[15]

There has, however, been significant support for a more positive assessment of Aeneas' monologue, though the argument involved varies considerably in approach. V. Pöschl,[16] for example, sees the speech as above all an illustration of the hero's *pietas*. Whereas Odysseus in his speech (passage 2) is concerned only with the loss of glory and burial honours, Aeneas in his dwells lovingly on home, family ties, and the heroes who died at Troy fighting in their defence. But while emphasis on this appealing concept of *pietas* might carry conviction if we were considering some isolated vignette, in fact the speech stands at the beginning of a national epic, where the demands on Aeneas' *pietas* are of a totally different order, and where nostalgic yearnings, however loving, are simply not enough. Indeed, to be more precise, before he can make any real progress in this epic, *pius Aeneas* must first get such retrospective tendencies out of his system and confront a new and very different future.

A. Wlosok is also concerned with the retrospective aspect of Aeneas' speech, but concentrates exclusively on what she regards as the implications of his wish that he had died at the hands of Diomede while fighting in defence of Troy.[17] Her view is that this reference to Diomede involves further implicit reference to the way in which, in *Iliad* 5, Aphrodite and Apollo rescued Aeneas from that same hero when he was in mortal danger, and that this further reference should then be extended to take into its scope consideration of the mission which those same two deities have in the meantime been helping him to pursue in the context of the

Aeneid. At this point, then, we are to infer that Aeneas, deeply conscious that this divinely ordained mission has just been placed in jeopardy by the gods (cf. 3.715: *"hinc me digressum uestris deus appulit oris"*), feels that they have betrayed him. "Not a syllable of this doubt is expressed. But the cryptic reference to Diomede guarantees that we are not imposing it on Aeneas' attitude."[18] Thus "Aeneas stands before us as a sensitive man who suffers beyond all human comprehension for his fated mission, yet bows in obedience to the divine."[19] But it is difficult to accept that so much can be deduced from the reference to Diomede in what is, after all, an instantaneous response to a sudden catastrophe. Confronted with the immediate threat of an unheroic death, Aeneas' instinctive reaction is to wish that he had died a hero's death at Troy: and Diomede naturally springs to mind, since he once came so close to providing him with just that (cf. *Iliad* 5.311ff.). It is difficult, too, to see how Aeneas' death-wish can be construed as "bowing in obedience to the divine," since it naturally implies indifference to the mission which in this context is inseparable from the concept of "the divine."

Finally H.-P. Stahl has produced the most recent rejection of the notion that this monologue shows Aeneas to be, as he puts it, "the hero in despair."[20] He insists that Aeneas' association with Sarpedon and Hector, and his wish that he had been killed at Troy by Diomede (elevated for the purpose, with Homeric precedent,[21] to "the bravest of the Greeks"), are positive indications of his heroic stature: Vergil thus emphasizes from the start "that his hero's attitude is that of a full-scale Homeric warrior."[22] Stahl argues, that "decisive" confirmation of the positive character of the monologue is provided by the echoes of Achilles' comparable speech in *Iliad* 21 (passage 3, above),[23] although, as I have already suggested, in view of the context this allusion can scarcely amount to more than a hint of things to come.

In rejecting the views of such interpreters as R.G. Austin, R.D. Williams, and W. Clausen, Stahl draws attention to Clausen's comment: "A strange speech for a hero to make, especially a hero sailing towards a new world," and suggests that such reactions might arise from "a predetermined notion of what Aeneas' role is (or rather is not) supposed to be like."[24] But if a predetermined notion of Aeneas' role influences the approach of these scholars, it is one predetermined, not by themselves, but by the poet, and set by him in the most emphatic position possible, the poem's opening lines. There we are introduced to a hero who qualifies for that role in the new epic context by virtue of his *pietas*: and he is to manifest this, not by shouting out in the middle of a storm "I am the greatest on this side" (Stahl's version of what Aeneas' reference to Diomede really conveys),[25] but by dutifully transferring from Troy to Italy the gods of his nation, and establishing there the basis for the future Roman world. Thus any searching investigation into the possible subtleties behind Vergil's employment of Homeric reminiscences in this and other relevant passages, however interesting and revealing it may be in other respects, merely circles round the central problem without ever touching it. For the way in which Aeneas formulates his death-wish when he first appears on the scene counts for nothing compared with the crucial *fact* of that wish: and the real problem facing the interpreter of the monologue is why, having so emphatically prepared us for the arrival of a hero with a mission, the poet confounds our expectations and presents us instead with one so unmindful of that mission that he is preoccupied with thoughts of death. We will of course bear that question in mind, and return to it later.

When we turn to Aeneas' second speech (1.198ff.), we again find fundamental disagreement about its significance. Once more, too, the Homeric influence is clear, with deviations from it of varying interest. *Odyssey* 10.133ff. provides the general background: there Odysseus puts in at Aeaea with the single ship and crew that survived the onslaught of the Laestrygonians, and after two days spent recovering from the ordeal climbs a rocky height in order to view the surrounding territory. He sees smoke emerging from what will prove to be Circe's house, but postpones further investigation, and on his way back, when he has almost reached his ship, brings down a large stag with his spear. The poet then describes how he weaves a rope of willow withes with which to lash the beast's feet together, carries it the short distance back to his ship slung over his shoulder, and finally flings it to the ground in front of his crew, reassuring them that they will not after all be dying of starvation just yet, or, as he puts it, will not be visiting the house of Hades—a nice ironical touch, since they will be doing precisely that, in a literal sense, at the end of their stay with Circe. In the matching *Aeneid* scene, after Neptune has ended the storm, Aeneas manages to reach a natural harbour with seven of his ships and go ashore. Like Odysseus he climbs a height to extend his view, but does so at once, anxious about the other ships and crews, and he has Achates with him carrying weapons. In the account which follows (1.184ff.), the most striking feature of Vergil's employment of his model is the way in which unavoidable modifications soon take him into what would seem to be dramatic difficulties. Since Aeneas has to provide for seven crews rather than Odysseus' one, he naturally has to encounter a herd; and the quest for seven beasts soon develops into a full scale hunt using bow and arrows, until Aeneas at last finds himself at some distance from his ships with seven *ingentia corpora* lying about the woodland awaiting collection and delivery (190ff.). Whereupon, undaunted by such prosaic considerations, the poet concludes the episode with the line (194):

hinc portum petit et socios partitur in omnis.

Aeneas also dispenses wine to his men (given to the Trojans by Acestes as they were leaving Sicily, their last port of call), and then addresses them (passage 4):

> "*o socii (neque enim ignari sumus ante malorum),*
> *o passi grauiora, dabit deus his quoque finem.*
> *uos et Scyllaeam rabiem penitusque sonantis*
> *accestis scopulos, uos et Cyclopia saxa*
> *experti: reuocate animos maestumque timorem*
> *mittite; forsan et haec olim meminisse iuuabit.*
> *per uarios casus, per tot discrimina rerum,*
> *tendimus in Latium, sedes ubi fata quietas*
> *ostendunt; illic fas regna resurgere Troiae.*
> *durate et uosmet rebus seruate secundis.*"
> *Talia uoce refert, curisque ingentibus aeger,*
> *spem uultu simulat, premit altum corde dolorem.*
> 1.195-206

The model for Aeneas' speech is provided by *Odyssey* 12, when Odysseus' ship is approaching Scylla and Charybdis.[26] The hero himself is aware of the danger, having been warned by Circe to keep close to Scylla's cliff, even though she will snatch away six of his crew as the ship passes; for the alternative is to be sucked down to total destruction by Charybdis (73ff.). When the crew hear the din from the direction of the great whirlpool, they collapse in terror and drop their oars. Odysseus tries to reassure them before issuing more specific instructions (passsage 5):

> "ὦ φίλοι, οὐ γάρ πώ τι κακῶν ἀδαήμονές εἰμεν.
> οὐ μὲν δὴ τόδε μεῖζον ἔπι κακὸν ἢ ὅτε Κύκλωψ
> εἴλει ἐνὶ σπῆϊ γλαφυρῷ κρατερῆφι βίηφιν.

Aeneas at Carthage: The Opening Scenes of the Aeneid 117

ἀλλὰ καὶ ἔνθεν ἐμῇ ἀρετῇ βουλῇ τε νόῳ τε
ἐκφύγομεν, καί που τῶνδε μνήσεσθαι ὀίω.
νῦν δ' ἄγεθ', ὡς ἂν ἐγὼ εἴπω, πειθώμεθα πάντες.
ὑμεῖς μὲν κώπῃσιν ἁλὸς ῥηγμῖνα βαθεῖαν
τύπτετε κληΐδεσσιν ἐφήμενοι, αἴ κέ ποθι Ζεὺς
δώῃ τόνδε γ' ὄλεθρον ὑπεκφυγέειν καὶ ἀλύξαι.
σοὶ δέ, κυβερνῆθ', ὧδ' ἐπιτέλλομαι. . . .

Odyssey 12.208-217

The association of Aeneas with Odysseus in passage 4 is especially strong and has two quite distinct aspects. On the one hand, as a comparison quickly shows, some of Aeneas' words clearly echo what Odysseus says in passage 5; and on the other, his words also indicate that during their voyage to Italy, Aeneas and his companions have, in the later stages, taken the same route as Odysseus and even acquired first hand knowledge of some of his more bizarre experiences. With regard to the second point, Aeneas' reference to Scylla (200) is in fact cited by G. Highet to illustrate the principle that "in every important speech of the *Aeneid* intended to persuade, there is at least one lie."[27] But it would be pointless for Aeneas to lie to an audience who were themselves aware of what really happened, and, as D. Feeney has pointed out,[28] all that Aeneas claims is that the Trojans approached (*accestis* [201]) the area concerned, which is consistent with his later version of events in Dido's court (3.554ff.). But when Aeneas continues: *"uos et Cyclopia saxa experti"* (201), the issue becomes more complex. Aeneas' listeners know that *Cyclopia saxa* is a topographical reference, and that the switch to *experti* is justified, since they did in fact go ashore in the rocky area inhabited by the Cyclopes. But for the reader who up to this point has only the *Odyssey* to guide him, *"uos et Cyclopia saxa experti"* must surely conjure up the vision of a frantic departure from the region, evading "the rocks hurled by the Cyclops." Only later does the less impressive truth of Book 3 emerge (569ff.).[29]

In addition to the already mentioned echoes of the Homeric model in passage 4 there are the usual differences. Odysseus' sole concern in passage 5 is with survival, whereas Aeneas tries to rouse his men with the prospect of renewing Troy's fortunes in Latium. Odysseus suggests that Zeus might possibly come to the rescue of his followers (another ironical touch, since in fact he will kill them all after their very next stop), while at the same time making it clear that it was his own courage and cunning that rescued them from their most recent and perilous experience in the cave of the Cyclops. Aeneas, on the other hand, says simply, "*dabit deus his quoque finem*," and makes no reference to himself or to his contribution as leader. But his speech, and the varied reaction to it, need separate treatment, to which we can now turn.

V. Pöschl's assessment of Aeneas' second speech is no less positive than his earlier view of the monologue, though now he sees a different quality in the hero's performance: whereas previously Aeneas showed his *pietas*, now it is his *magnitudo animi* that comes to the fore, and Vergil portrays Aeneas as "eine grosse Seele die auf ein grosses Ziel drängt."[30] In view of this verdict it might be useful to recall here the familiar distinctions between the various forms of *pietas* exhibited in the *Aeneid*. For convenience we can call *pietas* involving human relations "social," that concerned with the gods "religious," and that concerned with the fulfillment of *Fatum* and the Roman mission "heroic," since it constitutes the essence of Aeneas' heroic status in the *Aeneid*. With such basic distinctions in mind, it is difficult to understand Pöschl's approach in this context. For irrespective of whether his assessment is correct or not, the contrast on which it is based seems a strange one, since, if Aeneas is indeed "pressing on to a great goal," then in doing so he is surely displaying heroic *pietas* in its clearest form.

F. Klingner is similarly impressed by Aeneas' encouragement of his men. "What he keeps a firm grip on," he writes, "is not simply life, but the inner presence of determination and goal. Thus does the nobler life distinguish itself from the more ignoble."[31] A. Wlosok concludes: "In all his misfortune, and in spite of outward appearance, Aeneas remains truly committed to his mission."[32] Brooks Otis, after stressing Aeneas' total despair in the storm, thinks this second speech marks a transformation: "With the calm, *pietas* returns. Now he reverses his mood, and himself encourages the others. . . . Now he accepts and insists upon his mission and fate."[33]

In other words, then, these and other scholars with similar views[34] insist that when Aeneas is introduced into the action at Carthage, what I have called his heroic *pietas* is intact and beyond question. Since Aeneas is in fact given the epithet *pius* on two occasions in these early scenes, it should perhaps be stressed that this has no bearing on the present issue. In both cases it is clearly Aeneas' social *pietas* that is involved, first, when he shows his deep concern for the other crews who could be victims of the storm (220), and then (305), when he resolves to explore the neighbourhood and take back to his *socii* (309) any information he may acquire. Indeed, he clearly qualifies for the epithet in that sense in these earlier lines, too, when he continues his deer-hunt until he can supply all seven crews with food (192ff.), and then tries to raise their spirits with the speech which we are now considering.

In discussing this second speech of Aeneas some critics find a parallel in Horace's seventh *Ode*, where Teucer, forced into exile by his father, is about to set out under Apolline instruction in order to establish a second Salamis in Cyprus.[35] In a speech of encouragement to his followers on the day before their departure Teucer addresses them with the words "*o fortes peioraque passi*" (30), of which Vergil's "*o passi grauiora*" is taken to be an echo. But more revealing than any minor similarity is the difference in the way the ode ends, as compared with passage 4. Horace, having sung the praises of Tibur, goes on to advise its most celebrated son, Plancus, to find relief from the pressures of affairs in the enjoyment of mellow wine; and Teucer finally makes his entrance as the mythological *exemplum* who presses the point home, ending the speech in question with the words:

> "*o fortes peioraque passi*
> *mecum saepe uiri, nunc uino pellite curas:*
> *cras ingens iterabimus aequor.*"
>
> *Odes* 1.7.30-32

Whereupon, having gone off at this loosely attached tangent, Horace in familiar fashion ends where it takes him, and makes no further comment. But the case is very different in the *Aeneid* passage. There the poet adds two remarkable lines of comment to guide the reader:

> *talia uoce refert, curisque ingentibus aeger*
> *spem uultu simulat, premit altum corde dolorem.*
> *Aeneid* 1.208-209

In other words, Aeneas' external performance, in both speech and appearance, is a pretence adopted for the benefit of his audience: in reality the despair that overwhelmed him during the storm still has him in its grip. Thus "*dabit deus his quoque finem*" (199) cannot really rate as a simple affirmation of faith, but is there to trigger off an argument aimed at justifying the injunction "*reuocate animos, maestumque timorem / mittite*" (202f.), just as "*tendimus in Latium, sedes ubi fata quietas /*

ostendunt; illic fas regna resurgere Troiae" (205f.) is scarcely a genuine conviction, but serves to justify the closing "*durate et uosmet rebus seruate secundis.*" (207) Such an interpretation would no doubt explain why Vergil put such a clear frame round Aeneas' first two utterances, suggesting that they belong together as a unit, forming the introduction of a hero who has lost any real confidence in the future. For the formula *talia uoce refert* introduces the monologue (94), concludes this *cohortatio,* and makes no further appearance in the epic.

The view that the poet's editorial comment on Aeneas' second speech in effect invalidates its content has been advanced by several critics, with varying degrees of emphasis.[36] But since this interpretation has tended to lack elaboration, we can pursue the question further here. Some might perhaps feel that Vergil's comment need not be taken so far, and agree for example with C.J. Mackie's verdict: "Both men and mission are foremost in his mind, but at this stage he sees that the prospects are bleak."[37] But if we test the interpretation by considering evidence elsewhere in Book 1, and in particular the two speeches in which Aeneas introduces himself, first to the disguised Venus, and then to Dido, it will emerge, I believe, that the book places before us a hero who has not simply become pessimistic about the likely outcome of his mission, but one who feels so cruelly betrayed by the gods behind it that, for the present, as far as that mission is concerned he has lost both interest and commitment.

Aeneas' introduction of himself to Venus marks the culmination of Vergil's treatment of the motif of the hero whose *pietas* has produced an unacceptably harsh response from Juno, although in Aeneas' speech the identity of the god is naturally missing.[38] The motif makes its first appearance in the epic's opening lines, where the poet, in a manner reminiscent of Euripides, seems to challenge the very principle on which retardation of the action of his epic is chiefly based:

> *Musa, mihi causas memora quo numine laeso*
> *quidue dolens regina deum tot uoluere casus*
> *insignem pietate uirum, tot adire labores*
> *impulerit. tantaene animis caelestibus irae?*
>
> 1.8-11

The question then acquires more urgency as it is integrated into the action to form the climax of Venus' bitter complaint to Jupiter:

> "nos, tua progenies, caeli quibus adnuis arcem,
> nauibus (infandum!) amissis unius ob iram
> prodimur, atque Italis longe disiungimur oris.
> hic pietatis honos? sic nos in sceptra reponis?"
>
> 1.250-253

The most stiking feature of these lines is the way in which Venus identifies herself so completely with her son. It is, after all, not she, but Aeneas who has been promised a future place in heaven (cf. 295f.), and in the meantime a kingdom in Italy (cf. 263ff.), just as it is he whose reward for his *pietas* is to find himself so far from his intended destination.

Finally the poet puts the complaint into the mouth of the one most entitled to formulate it, the hero himself, as he addresses his mother without realizing who she is:

> "sum pius Aeneas, raptos qui ex hoste penates
> classe ueho mecum, fama super aethera notus;
> Italiam quaero patriam, et genus ab Ioue summo.
> bis denis Phrygium conscendi nauibus aequor,
> matre dea monstrante uiam data fata secutus;
> uix septem conuulsae undis Euroque supersunt.
> ipse ignotus, egens, Libyae deserta peragro,
> Europa atque Asia pulsus."
>
> 1.378-385

In these lines the indignant rhetorical questions posed earlier by the poet and by Venus are replaced by the simple juxtaposition of two series of statements whose very juxtaposition is enough to expose the intolerable injustice inflicted on *pius Aeneas*. In the Homeric model Odysseus, identifying himself in the Phaeacian court, claims to enjoy fame reaching to the heavens (*Odyssey* 9.19f.), and to have won it because of his unfailing resourcefulness. Aeneas claims fame on a similar scale, but for a very different quality, his heroic *pietas*: and the statement which follows "*sum pius Aeneas*" not only vindicates his claim, but in effect defines the special and quite specific nature of that form of *pietas*. Having rescued the Trojan *penates* during Troy's fall, with them on board he made for Italy, his ancestral fatherland, seeking to establish there a race descended, through him, from Jupiter. He set out with twenty ships, and followed the guidance given him by his divine mother[39] and by oracles. At this point (382) a semicolon is usually printed to mark the contrast involving the ships:

but it should not obscure the fact that all of what follows stands in stark contrast with the high expectations roused by the preceding lines. Seven ships out of the original twenty have just managed to survive the storm,[40] and Aeneas now finds himself an unknown wanderer in a Libyan wasteland, expelled from one continent and barred from another.

In discussing this passage A. Wlosok rejects W.B. Anderson's view that Aeneas is here protesting against his treatment by the gods, and adds the further comment: "Aeneas identifies himself with his mission. His will is firmly directed towards it. . . . As a matter of course he holds firm to the goal required of him."[41] But as Anderson noted, Venus herself clearly takes Aeneas' speech as such a protest, hence the opening words of her reply: *"quisquis es, haud, credo, inuisus caelestibus auras / uitalis carpis . . ."* (1.387f.).[42] Indeed, Aeneas' juxtaposition of the divine guidance and the situation in which he now finds himself seems enough to justify Anderson's point. As for the notion of Aeneas' enduring enthusiasm for his mission, perhaps the best answer to that is provided by the hero's own words when he once more introduces himself, this time to Dido. There is no question now of using his mission in order to encourage his audience, or as the basis for complaint: here then we might have expected at least a brief reference to it that was devoid of rhetoric. Instead, after identifying himself to the queen, and thanking her for the kind reception of his followers, Aeneas ends with the words: *"semper honos nomenque tuum laudesque manebunt / quae me cumque uocant terrae"* (1.609f.). However conventional such words may be in general, "whatever lands summon me" is hardly the expression of a hero who knows exactly where he is going, and is preoccupied with getting there.[43]

If it is true that Aeneas is so alienated from the gods at the beginning of the *Aeneid* that he loses interest in his mission, then this attitude ought to be reflected in the familiar area of his *pietas* which was already acknowledged in the *Iliad*, namely his constant attention to their cult:[44] and we find that throughout his stay in Carthage he neither prays nor sacrifices. It is true of course that he is in Dido's kingdom, and we could hardly expect him to be allowed to encroach on the queen's prerogative in such matters. But on more than one occasion the opportunity was there without his needing to do that. Once on dry land, for example, he could have acknowledged his escape from drowning with some pious gesture, or perhaps sought the favour of the unknown local deities on arrival in a strange land. Later, especially in view of Helenus' urgent insistence on the need to appease Juno (3.433ff.), he might have paid some respect to her in her new temple at Carthage, as he does to Apollo in his temple Delos (3.84), instead of confining his attention to the pictures on its walls (1.453ff.). So too, during the feasting in Dido's court, there is no question of Aeneas being associated with such procedures as the invocation of deities and the pouring of libations (1.730ff.), as he is, for example, along with his followers, when he enjoys the hospitality of Evander (8.278f.). Indeed, not once while he is on Carthaginian soil does Aeneas invoke a god. For after Mercury's second visit, when at last he cries:

> "sequimur te, sancte deorum,
> quisquis es, imperioque iterum paremus ouantes.
> adsis o placidusque iuues et sidera caelo
> dextra feras."
>
> 4.576-579

he is already on board ship, and on the very point of departing.

Apart from that, the closest Aeneas gets to his customary piety[45] is when he expresses the wish that the gods will reward Dido for the kind reception she has just given to Ilioneus and others of his followers; but it is difficult to accept Austin's assertion (*ad loc.*) that the conditions attached to the wish are merely conventional:

> "di tibi, si qua pios respectant numina, si quid
> usquam iustitiae est et mens sibi conscia recti,
> praemia digna ferant . . ."
>
> 1.603-605

For in view of earlier events, Aeneas' general bearing in this book, and the heavy preponderance of the clauses in question over the actual wish, this looks very like a final echo of the "divine injustice towards *pius Aeneas*" motif already mentioned.

One last point regarding Aeneas' religious *pietas*, and it concerns the significance of the very first gesture the hero makes in the epic. Before he begins his opening monologue (cf. passage 1), he is described as *duplicis tendens ad sidera palmas* (1.93); and because such a gesture ususally implies subsequent prayer, that is how Aeneas' monologue is in fact sometimes categorized. R. Heinze, for example, refers to it as "more of a quick prayer than self-address";[46] E. Paratore (*ad loc.*) calls it "the first prayer in the *Aeneid*"; and K. Büchner notes that Aeneas "lets a prayer escape from his lips."[47] But clearly, what Aeneas goes on to say bears no real resemblance to a prayer, since unlike the *Iliad* model (cf. passage 3), which begins with a comparable gesture heavenwards, at no point does it involve the invocation of a deity, or mention of one, in its content. In this respect,[48] at least, the Servian comment seems apposite: *quis ad caelum manum tendens non aliud precatur potius quam dicit "o terque quaterque beati?"* This clash between the gesture and what actually follows is brought out especially clearly if we compare the passage in question with others in the *Aeneid* introduced by a similar gesture. There are no less than eleven such passages, involving Sinon, Anchises, Iarbas, Cloanthus, Turnus, and Mezentius, in addition to Aeneas.[49] In only two cases does a clearly recognizable prayer fail to materialize: they are the first and last in the epic, and they bring together in a fleeting but nevertheless extraordinary pairing, on the one hand, *pius Aeneas*, and on the other *contemptor diuum Mezentius*.[50] Without noting this remarkable link, or their common lack of a following prayer, F.A. Sullivan interprets both passages in a positive spirit.[51] In Mezentius' case he accepts Lejay's view that the upraised hands involve a denial of his former ways of thinking, even though the defiant cry *"nec diuum parcimus ulli"* soon follows (10.880). Similarly with Aeneas: "Vergil wishes to represent his hero on his first appearance, in an attitude that will, so to speak, define him all through the poem and set him apart from Homer's heroes. He is *pius Aeneas,* a man who instinctively prays to heaven in every crisis. A Roman reader would have readily caught the meaning of the gesture: it is a *precatio* without words, a despairing appeal for help." But the fact remains that seven and one half lines of speech follow Aeneas' prayer signal, and like those spoken by Mezentius, they are entirely secular in their content. If Aeneas had time for these lines, and the idea behind the scene was to imprint on the reader's mind an image of *pius Aeneas*, why was the introductory prayer gesture not followed by a genuine prayer? Sullivan's point about its impact as Aeneas' very first gesture is a valid one, but his interpretation does not go far enough. For the highly unusual absence of any following prayer is a crucial part of the signal involved, and the resulting message warns us that, for the time being at least, there is something about *pius Aeneas* and his *pietas* that is out of joint.

Now that we are back at our starting point, we ought to recall here that earlier question: Why does Vergil in the opening lines of the *Aeneid* lead us to expect the appearance of a hero with a mission, and then introduce one who in his very first utterance is so unmindful of his purpose in life that he is preoccupied with thoughts of death? And to that question we can now of course add others: Why does that same hero then go on to refer to his mission only in order to raise the spirits of his followers, or in order to justify a complaint against the gods, rather than for its own sake, and out of genuine enthusiasm for it? And finally why does Aeneas go on to reveal that, for the time being, his ambition is limited to emerging safely from possible danger, and improving his immediate plight,[52] so that his cry on seeing the Carthaginians at work on their new city (*"o fortunati quorum iam moenia surgunt!"* [1.437]) proves in the event to be an early hint, however faint, that he is already inclined to join them (cf. 4.259ff.)? The answer, I take it, is to be found in the necessary preparation of Aeneas for the approaching drama at Carthage. On the personal side his isolation is already far advanced when he reaches there, with his city and many friends lost, and his wife and father dead. Shortly what he takes to be his own mother's cruelty in placing the barrier of a disguise between them will take that isolation further.[53] But above all, disillusioned by the disastrous storm which is allowed to strike just when his divinely ordained goal is in sight, and with his *pietas* towards the gods and his mission as a result reduced to a state of quiescence, he will now be all the more disposed to respond, first to Dido's sympathy, and then to her love, when the occasion arises. In short, just as Book 4 opens with the disappearance on Dido's side of the sole obstacle to a liaison with Aeneas (her *pudor* [cf. lines 24ff. and 55]), so also Book 1 opens with clear indications that any corresponding inhibitions which Aeneas' concern for his mission might have interposed on his side have likewise disappeared: and nothing could indicate more vividly his lack of such concern than the death-wish he expresses on his very first appearance.

NOTES

1. Cf. G. Thome, *Gestalt und Funktion des Mezentius, mit einem Ausblick auf die Schlussszene der Aeneis* (Frankfurt am Main, 1979) 274ff.; C. Renger, *Aeneas und Turnus: Analyse einer Feindschaft* (Frankfurt am Main, 1985) 73ff.; P. Hardie, *Virgil's Aeneid: Cosmos and Imperium* (Oxford, 1986) 147ff.; P. Burnell, "The Death of Turnus and Roman Morality," *G&R* 34 (1987) 186ff.; G.K. Galinsky, "The Anger of Aeneas," *AJP* 109 (1988) 321ff.; F. Cairns, *Virgil's Augustan Epic* (Cambridge, 1989) 82ff.

2. For the structural features see G. Highet, *The Speeches in Vergil's Aeneid* (Princeton, 1972) 189.
3. See Servius *auctus* on *Aeneid* 1.92.
4. G.K. Galinsky, *Latomus* 28 (1969) 16, suggests that Vergil produced the line *extemplo Aeneae soluuntur frigore membra* by adapting Livius' translation of the Homeric line: *igitur demum Ulixi cor frixit prae pauore* (fr. 16, Morel). If so, then he handled it in a spirit of *oppositio*, with *demum* changed to *extemplo*, *pauore* rejected in favour of *frigore*, and in keeping with that, the unheroic inner "freezing" (cf. *cor*) now transformed into an external and purely physical one (*membra*).
5. Cf. *Aen.* 2.431ff.
6. Cf. G. Howe, *CJ* 26 (1930) 187; Austin, *Ad Aen.* 2.93; C.J. Mackie, *The Characterisation of Aeneas* (Edinburgh, 1988) 19; J.W. Hunt, *Forms of Glory* (Carbondale, 1973) 4.
7. See M. Lausberg, "Iliadisches im ersten Buch der *Aeneis*," *Gymnasium* 90 (1983) 203ff.
8. On this topic see A.J. Gossage, *Phoenix* 17 (1963) 132ff.
9. Cf. *Il.* 5.242ff.; 22.337ff.; 16.477ff.; 21.218ff. and 12.22ff.
10. Cf. G.N. Knauer, *Die Aeneis und Homer* (Göttingen, 1964) 321.
11. Cf. W.-F. Liebermann in *Studien zum antiken Epos*, ed. by H. Görgemanns and E.A. Schmidt (Meisenheim-am-Glan, 1976) 188, n. 68.
12. Cf. Gossage, *op. cit.* 134.
13. Cf. W.W. de Grummond, *Hermes* 105 (1977) 226f.
14. Cf. R. Heinze, *Virgils Epische Technik* (Leipzig, Berlin, 1915) 486.
15. In addition to works mentioned already in the text and in n. 6, above, cf. also e.g. W.W. Fowler, *The Religious Experience of the Roman People* (London, 1911) 413; K. Büchner, *P. Vergilius Maro der Dichter der Romer* (Stuttgart, 1966) 318; W. Clausen, *HSCP* 68 (1964) 139; G.B. Conte, *The Rhetoric of Imitation: Genre and Poetic Memory in Virgil and other Latin Poets,* ed. by C. Segal (Ithaca, London, 1986) 65f. n. 32; B. Otis, *Virgil: A Study in Civilized Poetry* (Oxford, 1964) 232; K. Quinn, *Vergils Aeneid: A Critical Description* (London, 1968) 102f.; and R.J. Rowland, *The Augustan Age* 6 (1987) 144.
16. Cf. V. Pöschl, *Die Dichtkunst Virgils* (Vienna, 1964) 57ff. and 68.
17. Cf. A. Wlosok, *Die Göttin Venus in Vergils Aeneis* (Heidelberg, 1967) 18ff.
18. *Ibid.* 19.
19. *Ibid.* 20.
20. Cf. H.-P. Stahl, "Aeneas: An Unheroic Hero?" *Arethusa* 14 (1981) 157-177: 164.

21. Cf. *Il.* 6.98f., where Helenus considers him to be more formidable in his *aristeia* than Achilles himself.
22. Stahl, *op. cit.* 162.
23. *Ibid.* 163.
24. *Ibid.* 161; cf. Clausen, *op. cit.* 140.
25. Stahl, *op. cit.* 164.
26. Knauer, *op. cit.* 176, n. 2, suggests that *Aen.* 1.198ff. should be referred to *Od.* 10.174ff., where Odysseus tells his crew that they will not be dying just yet, and 189ff., where he describes his reconnaissance of Circe's island, with an additional contribution coming from 12.298ff. But it seems clear enough that *Od.* 10 simply suggests the dramatic setting, with *Od.* 12 supplying the only significant model for the actual speech. On this, and some possible further minor sources, see Highet, *op. cit.* 195.
27. Highet, *op. cit.* 287f.
28. Cf. D. Feeny, *CQ* 33 (1983) 217, n. 91.
29. Knauer, *op. cit.*, assumes that *saxa* here must refer to missiles, and thinks that, since there is no rock-throwing in the *Aeneid* 3 episode, and in the *Odyssey* the Cyclops throws only one rock, there may be an allusion to the Laestrygonians involved here. But Polyphemus in fact throws two rocks (*Od.* 9.480ff., 537ff.); and in any case cf. e.g. *Aen.* 3.432 and 555 for *saxa* in a topographical sense.
30. Pöschl, *op. cit.* 68f.
31. F. Klingner, *Virgil: Bucolica, Georgica, Aeneis* (Zürich, Stuttgart, 1967) 389.
32. Wlosok, *op. cit.* 24.
33. Otis, *op. cit.* 232.
34. E.g., T.R. Glover, *Virgil* (London, 1904) 320; E.K. Rand, *The Magical Art of Virgil* (Cambridge MA, 1931) 352; V. Cleary, *CB* 40 (1964) 87; Hunt, *op. cit.* 4.
35. Cf. Rand, *op. cit.* 352; Klingner, *op. cit.* 392; B. Otis in *Virgil*, ed. by D.R. Dudley (London, 1969) 56; Highet, *op. cit.* 195.
36. Cf. Heinze, *op. cit.* 274; W.B. Anderson, *CR* 44 (1930) 4; K. Büchner, *Der Schicksalsgedanke bei Vergil* (Freiburg, 1964) 6; F.A. Sullivan, *AJP* 80 (1959) 155; W. Kühn, *Götterszenen bei Vergil* (Heidelberg, 1971) 88 n. 24.
37. Mackie, *op. cit.* 23.
38. Cf. his remark at 3.715: "*uestris deus appulit oris.*" Although this conforms with the epic principle that normally knowledge of such matters is beyond mortals, one might have expected Helenus' remarkably emphatic warning about Juno (3.435ff.) to have made the identity of the hostile deity only too clear.
39. For Varro's account of Venus' stellar guidance (not used by Vergil in the *Aeneid*) cf. Servius *auctus ad Aen.* 2.801. V. Henselmanns,

Die Widersprüche in Vergils Aeneis (Würzburg, 1913) 33, points to this allusion as a typical aberrant detail of the kind Roman poets under Hellenistic influence liked to admit into their work, letting consistency on occasions give way to a fleeting display of erudition. In this case the dramatic irony no doubt appealed to Vergil, since *matre dea monstrante uiam* spoken by Aeneas involves him in unconsciously accusing the one he is addressing of helping to guide him into his present plight.

40. In fact Aeneas has lost just one ship, as he soon discovers.
41. Wlosok, *op. cit.* 79.
42. Anderson, *op. cit.* 4.
43. For the importance of this phrase in the developing Dido tragedy see E.L. Harrison in *Vergilian Bimillenary Lectures* (*Vergilius* Supplementary Vol. 2, 1984), ed. by A.G. McKay, 3ff.
44. Cf. *Il.* 20.297ff., where Poseidon, before rescuing Aeneas from Achilles, asks: "Why does this man, who is guiltless, suffer woes? . . . He is always making offerings to the gods who rule the broad heavens."
45. When Aeneas meets Venus in her disguise as a young local woman out hunting, Vergil lets him echo Odysseus' words on meeting Nausicaa (*Od.* 6.151), combined with those of Telemachus when he meets Odysseus (*Od.* 16.183ff.). The result is a mixture of lavish flattery and somewhat heavy irony, as Aeneas ventures guesses about which deity the stranger might be, and even promises her lavish cult for any information she might give him (1.326ff.). This highly contrived scene, designed as an introduction to the divine "prologue" at 338ff., can hardly be regarded as involving the kind of religious *pietas* which concerns us here.
46. Heinze, *op. cit.* 430.
47. Büchner, *op. cit.* 318.
48. For the general superficiality of Servius *auctus ad Aen.* 1.92 see Gossage, *op. cit.* 131f.
49. Viz. 1.92ff., 2.152ff., 2.687ff., 3.176ff., 3.263ff., 4.203ff., 5.232ff., 5.685ff., 9.16ff., 10.667ff., 10.844ff.
50. 1.192ff., 10.844ff. For the latter phrase cf. 7.648, and the similar 8.7.
51. Cf. F.A. Sullivan, "*Tendere manus*: Gestures in the *Aeneid*," *CJ* 63 (1968) 360.
52. Cf. 1.450ff. Note also his words to Achates (463), and Achates' reassuring response later (583). This preoccupation with safety passes on in due course to Venus, hence her intervention at 657ff.
53. Cf. 1.470: "*crudelis tu quoque . . .*"

PLATES

Plate 1 (Fantham): *Orestes and Pylades: detail of copy of the Timomachus painting (see Plate 5) from Casa del Citarista, Pompeii.*

Plate 2 (Fantham): *Iphigenia before the Temple of Artemis; detail from copy of the Timomachus painting, Casa del Citarista, Pompeii.*

Plate 3 (Fantham): *Orestes and Pylades before Iphegenia; pinax from House of Vettii, Pompeii.*

Plate 4 (Fantham): *Orestes and Pylades are led before Iphigenia; sarcophagus (307 A.D.) from Glyptotek, Munich.*

Plate 5 (Fantham): *Orestes and Pylades before Iphigenia: copy of the Timomachus painting from Casa del Citarista, Pompeii.*

Plate 6 (Kilpatrick): *"Vendita di amorini" (from Stabiae), Museo Nazionale, Naples: Inv. No. 9180; Andreae, Kat. Nr. 267, pp. 192, 217.*

Plate 7 (Kilpatrick): *"Erotenverkauf" (copy by Tischbein), Dusseldorf: Andreae, p. 223; Trevelyan, pp. 45, 125.*

Plate 8 (Kilpatrick): *"La Marchande d'Amours" (by Vien, 1763), Fontainbleau: Trevelyan, p. 62.*

Plate 9 (Simon): *Abbildungslegende: Mailand, Soprintendenza Archeologica della Lombardia Inv. ST. 5986. Patera von Parabiago. Hirmer Fotoarchiv Nr. 562.3110.*

Plate 10 (Houston): *Artist's rendering of a silver plate from Spain showing various ways in which a spring served the community.*

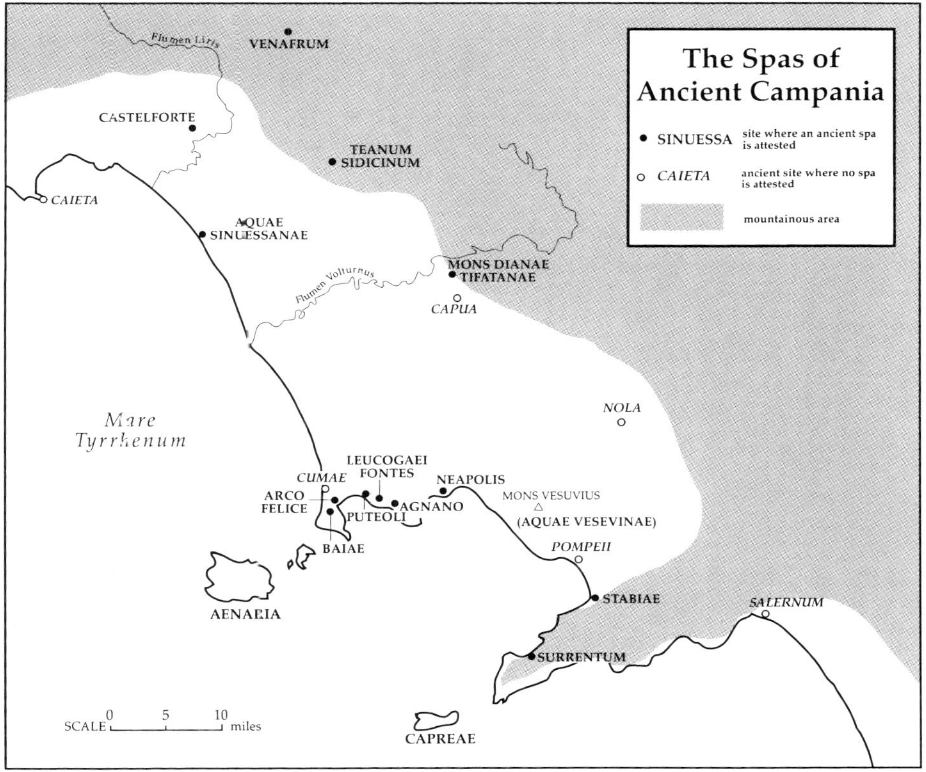

Plate 11 (Houston) left: *Map of the known spas of Roman Campania.*

Plate 12 (Jashemski) below: *Restored terra-cotta pot with four holes found in garden in House of the Ship Europa, Pompeii. (Photo: Stanley Jashemski.)*

Plate 13 (Jashemski) below: *Restored pots from Garden of Hercules, Pompeii. (Photo: S. Jashemski.)*

Plate 14 (Jashemski): *Cast of tree root in pot in Garden of Hercules. (Photo: S. Jashemski.)*

Plate 15 (Jashemski): *"Sombrero" formations in garden in House of Polybius, Pompeii. (Photo: S. Jashemski.)*

Plate 16 (Jashemski): *West part of peristyle garden in House of Polybius. (Photo: S. Jashemski.)*

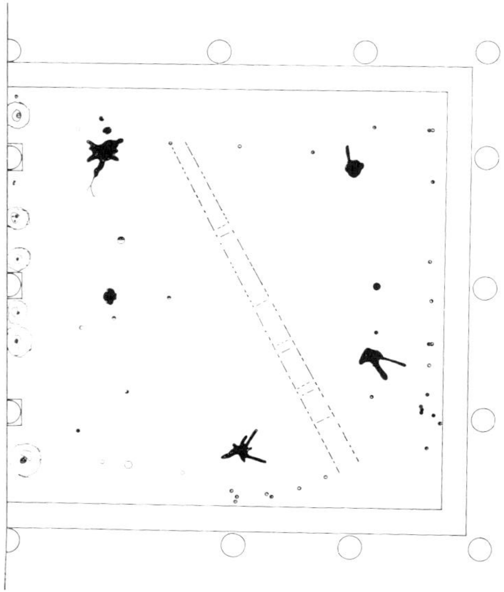

Plate 17 (Jashemski): *Plan of peristyle garden in House of Polybius; roots are indicated in black, stakes by circles. (Plan courtesy Soprintendenza alle antichità della Campania-Napoli; garden details by S. Jashemski.)*

Plate 18 (Jashemski): *Southeast portico garden in villa at Oplontis. (Photo: S. Jashemski.)*

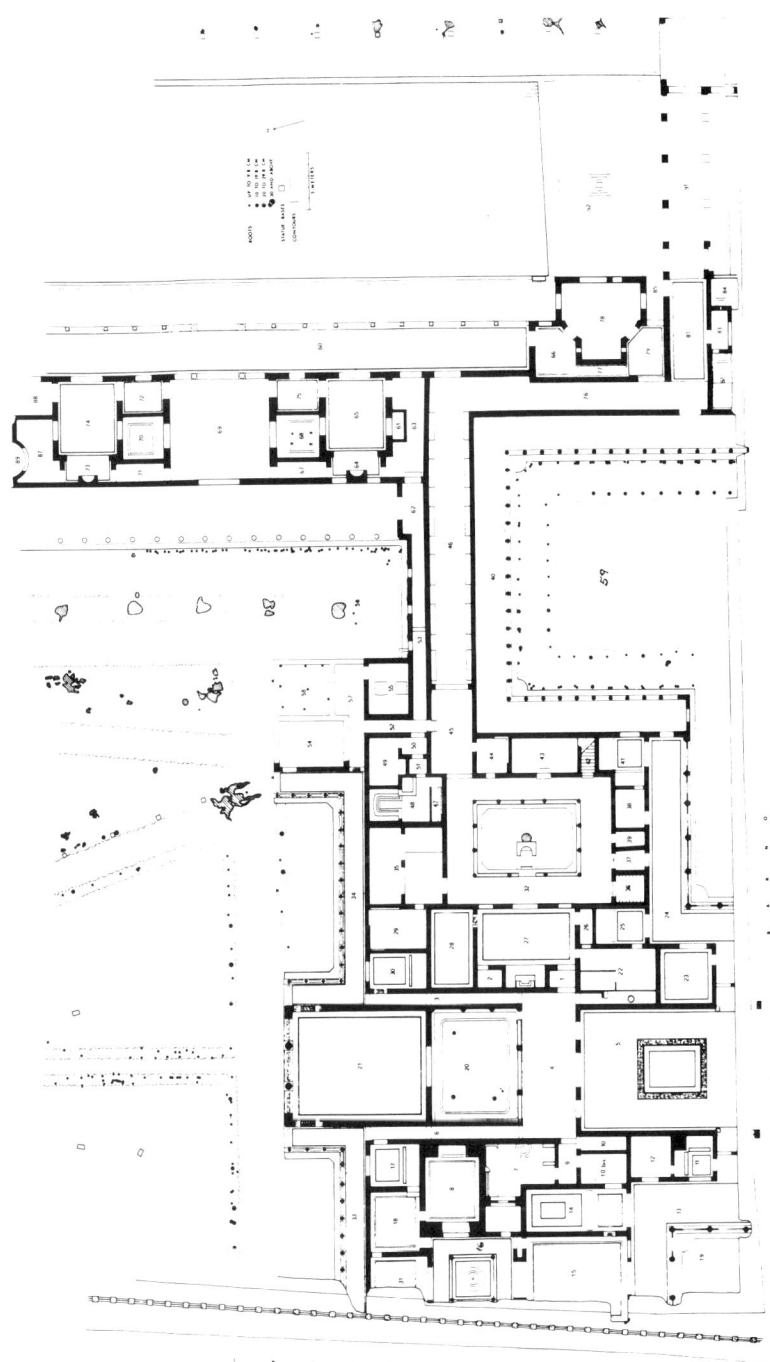

Plate 19 (Jashemski) preceding page: *Plan of villa at Oplontis. (Plan courtesy Soprintendenza alle antichità della Campania-Napoli; garden details by S. Jashemski.)*

Plate 20 (Jashemski): *Pots each with two small stake cavities, found in garden of villa at Oplontis. (Photo: S. Jashemski.)*

Plate 21 (Jashemski) above: *Pots found in planter-pool garden in villa at Oplontis. (Photo: S. Jashemski.)*

Plate 22 (Jashemski) left: *Ornamental pots in Casa dei Cervi, Herculaneum. (Photo: S. Jashemski.)*

Plate 23 (Jashemski) below: *Pots found in garden in winter palace of Herod at Jericho. (Photo: courtesy E. Netzer.)*

Plate 24 (Jashemski) right: *Pot found in garden in Hadrian's villa. (Photo: F. Luciolli.)*

Plate 25 (Jashemski): *Cast of tree root in half amphora, in sculpture garden in villa at Oplontis. (Photo: F. Hueber.)*

Plate 26 (Jashemski): *The Canopus in Hadrian's villa. (Photo: F. Luciolli.)*

Plate 27 (Jashemski): *Discarded amphoras, cut in two, and used as planting pots in Canopus garden. (Photo: F. Luciolli.)*

Plate 28 (Jashemski): *Adonis gardens. (Furtwängler-Reichhold, Griechische Vasenmaleri, pl. 78.1.)*

Plate 29 (Wlosok): *Bibliothèque municipale de Lyon. Ms. Palais des Arts 27. Virgile. L'Enéide. Fol. 137r°. Descente aux Enfers et reconcontre d'Enée et de Didon. (8.9 x 9.8 cm.). Phot. Bibliothèque municipale de Lyon.*

Plate 30 (Włosok): *Cambridge, MA, Houghton Library, Harvard University, ms. Richardson 38, fol. 135v (8.4 × 9.5 cm.). By permission of the Houghton Library, Harvard University.*

Plate 31 (Wlosok): Paris, Bibliothèque Nationale, ms. fr. 861, fol. 33v (14 x 19 cm.). Phot. Bibliothèque Nationale, Paris.

Plate 32 (Wlosok): Valencia, Biblioteca de la Universitat de València, ms. 837, fol. 161r (13.1 x 13.9 resp. 17.4 cm.). Phot. Biblioteca de la Universitat de València.

Plate 33 (Wlosok) preceding page: *London, British Library, King's ms. 24, fol. 131v. (6.8 x 10 cm.). By permission of the British Library.*

Plate 34 (Wlosok) left: *Cambridge, MA, Houghton Library, Harvard University, ms. Richardson 38, fol. 174v (9.7 x 9.5 cm.). By permission of the Houghton Library, Harvard University*

Plates 35 and 36 (Wlosok): *Biblioteca Apostolica Vaticana, Vat. lat. 3225, pict. 36 u. 37 in den Stichen von Carolo Ruspi (19. Jh), aus: T.B. Stevenson, Miniature Decoration in the Vatican Virgil (Tübingen, 1983) 72f. (verkleinert im Verhältnis 4:5).*

DARDANUS, AENEAS, AUGUSTUS AND THE ETRUSCANS

Robert M. Wilhelm
Miami University

Scholars have long recognized that the story of Aeneas as presented in the *Aeneid* is Vergil's own creation and that he had a plethora of legends upon which to draw when creating and shaping his poem.[1] Vergil's use of Dardanus in the *Aeneid* seems an excellent example of the way in which he exploited to the fullest the legends surrounding this ancestor of Aeneas while at the same time in all probability creating a new tradition.[2] By focusing on Aeneas' Homeric descent from Dardanus on the one hand (cf. *Il.* 20.208ff.), and on the other by devising for Dardanus, and so by implication for the central hero of his epic, an Etruscan origin, and then emphasizing this cultural heritage, Vergil was able to further his general purpose of giving a special prominence in the *Aeneid* to the Etruscan contribution. Vergil's motivation for thus highlighting the Etruscans was probably as much personal as it was political: Vergil's own Etruscan heritage and his friendship with the retinue of Etruscan friends and advisors in the court of Augustus would naturally have stimulated his creative imagination to the possibilities inherent in presenting Dardanus as Etruscan ancestor of an Aeneas who returns home to Italy to reclaim his legacy.[3]

The story of Dardanus, as treated by Vergil, is an integral part of the journey of Aeneas from Troy to Italy. When Aeneas lands on the island of Delos he prays to Apollo for guidance and direction. Immediately Apollo himself gives to Aeneas and his *Dardanidae duri* the most emphatic prophecy yet to be received concerning their final destination:[4]

'Dardanidae duri, quae uos a stirpe parentum
prima tulit tellus, eadem uos ubere laeto
accipiet reduces. <u>antiquam exquirite matrem.</u>
hic domus Aeneae cunctis dominabitur oris
et nati natorum et qui nascentur ab illis.'
haec Phoebus.

Aen. 3.94-99

Anchises interprets the *antiquam . . . matrem* to mean that they should go to Crete, the cradle of Trojan civilization (*gentis cunabula nostrae*, 3.105) and the homeland of Teucer, the *maximus pater* (3.107) of the Trojan race. What is significant about Anchises' interpretation of the oracle is that it is based on a genealogical tradition that traces the origins of the Trojan royal house back to Cretan Teucer through Bateia who was married to Dardanus:

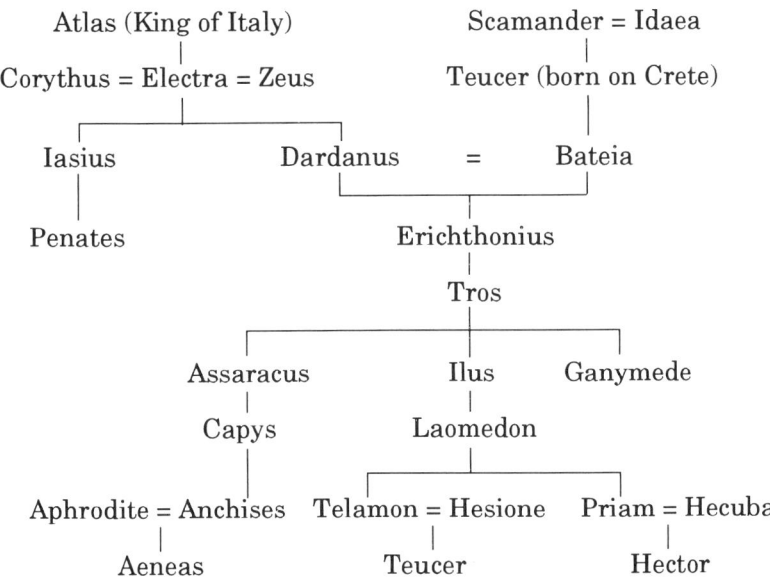

According to the traditional legend, Teucer, born in Crete, was the son of the river Scamander and Idaea, the nymph of Mt. Ida; he emigrated from Crete at the time of a famine and settled in Phrygia (Troy) where he became king.[5] And so, in pursuit of their maternal roots, Anchises gives orders to sail to Crete from where he says that Cybele, *mater cultrix* (3.111), and her Corybants emigrated to Troy; furthermore, Anchises traces Troy's devotion to Cybele and her religious rites and the practice of conveying the goddess in a chariot drawn by lions to Cretan origins (3.111-115). Thus, Anchises' belief that Crete is the *antiqua mater* is based on a genealogical and religious connection which is frequently recalled throughout the poem. At various places in the *Aeneid*, Vergil recognized the Teucrian heritage of Aeneas who is called *rex Teucrorum* (1.38), *pater optime Teucrum* (1.555), *dux inclute Teucrum* (6.562), *maxime Teucrorum ductor* (8.470) and *o Teucrum atque Italum fortissime ductor* (8.513). In *Aeneid* 6, amongst those in the Groves of the Blessed, Vergil included Ilus, Assaracus and Dardanus, whom he described as descendants of the *hic genus antiquum Teucri, pulcherrima proles* (6.648); furthermore, throughout the epic Vergil frequently called the Trojans, themselves, Teucri and by this designation drew upon the ancient tradition that Teucer was the ancestor of the Trojan race. Thus, in letting Anchises ignore the crucial clue in the opening word of the oracle (*Dardanidae duri*) Vergil is able to make use of an alternative literary and historical tradition that was well-known and established, i.e. the Trojan descent from Teucer. The immediate designation in the oracle of the Trojan wanderers as *Dardaniae duri* focuses attention on the alternative descent from Dardanus—a descent which Anchises fails to realize and whose significance encompasses at once the mythical, historical and political heritage of Aeneas and Augustus. It is this alternative descent from Dardanus which Vergil creatively underscores in epic. The alternative Dardanian genealogy is a key element in ancestral linking of Aeneas to Italy.

When Aeneas, Anchises and his men arrive on Crete, Aeneas receives another prophecy: this time, it is the Phrygian Penates, sent by Apollo, who appear to Aeneas in a dream and inform him about Hesperia and the origins of Dardanus and Iasius in Italy:

> *mutandae sedes. non haec tibi litora suasit*
> *Delius aut Cretae iussit considere Apollo.*
> *est locus, Hesperiam Grai cognomine dicunt,*
> *terra antiqua, potens armis atque ubere glaebae;*
> *Oenotri coluere uiri; nunc fama minores*
> *Italiam dixisse ducis de nomine gentem.*
> *hae nobis propriae sedes, hinc Dardanus ortus*
> *Iasiusque pater, genus a quo principe nostrum.*
> *surge age et haec laetus longaeuo dicta parenti*
> *haud dubitanda refer: Corythum terrasque requirat*
> *Ausonias; Dictaea negat tibii Iuppiter arua.*
>
> *Aen.* 3.161-171

In this prophecy Aeneas is told for the second time that he must go to *Hesperia* where the Oenotrians live and which is called *Italia*.[6] The Penates tell Aeneas to seek Italy since this is the home of his ancestors Dardanus and Iasius; in this prophecy Aeneas is specifically told to go to Corythus. Aeneas informs Anchises about his dream; Anchises immediately realizes that he had mis-interpreted the oracle which ordered them to seek the "ancient mother":

> *Anchisen facio certum remque ordine pando.*
> *agnouit prolem ambiguam geminosque parentis,*
> *seque nouo ueterem deceptum errore locorum.*
> *tum memorat: 'nate, Iliacis exercite fatis,*
> *sola mihi talis casus Cassandra canebat.*
> *nunc repeto haec generi portendere debita nostro.*
> *et saepe Hesperiam, saepe Itala regna uocare.*
> *sed quis ad Hesperiae uenturos litora Teucros*
> *crederet? aut quem tum uates Cassandra moueret?*
> *cedamus Phoebo et moniti meliora sequamur.'*
>
> Aen. 3.179-188

The ancient mother, as Anchises is now aware, is not Crete,[7] the homeland of Teucer, but the homeland of Dardanus and Iasius: Hesperia. The double ancestry and two-fold parentage of the race (*geminos parentis*, 3.180) which Anchises recognizes, refers to the maternal and paternal roots of the Trojan nation: on the one hand through Bateia to Teucer and Crete; and, on the other through Dardanus to Corythus and Etruria. In the *Aeneid*, however, Crete is associated with deceit and becomes a symbol of a false homeland—a homeland which epitomizes the futility of returning to a false past. The story of Idomeneus driven out of Crete to Italy (3.121-123; cf. Servius, *ad Aen.* 3.121), the Cretan setting of the simile in which Dido is wounded like a deer (4.68-74), the simile comparing Aeneas to Apollo amongst his Cretan followers (4.144-146), the labyrinth suggestively illustrated by the *lusus Troiae* (5.588-593) and the doors on the Temple of Apollo at Cumae (6.14-33) include verbal overtones and thematic images that reiterate throughout the *Aeneid* that Teucrian Crete is a false homeland.[8]

The probability that Vergil himself created the legend of Dardanus which appears in the *Aeneid* has already been noted.[9] According to his version of the Dardanus legend, Atlas is a king of Italy whose daughter Electra is doubly loved by Zeus and

Corythus, an Etruscan. Dardanus and Iasius are the sons of Electra, Iasius by the mortal father Corythus and Dardanus by Zeus. The brothers leave Italy to become the eponymous founders of two cities: in one version Dardanus goes to Samothrace and to Troy while in another version Dardanus goes directly to Troy and Iasius goes to Samothrace. In *Aeneid* 7 Vergil employs the first version, making Dardanus go to Samothrace and then Troy:

> *atque equidem memini (fama est obscurior annis)*
> *Auruncos ita ferre senes, his ortus ut agris*
> *Dardanus Idaeas Phrygiae penetrarit ad urbes*
> *Threiciamque Samum, quae nunc Samothracia fertur.*
> *hinc illum Corythi Tyrrhena ab sede profectum*
> *aurea nunc solio stellantis regia caeli*
> *accipit et numerum diuorum altaribus auget.*
> Aen. 7.205-211

In these lines Latinus, sitting on his ancestral throne and speaking to the *Dardanidae*, recalls an old legend in which Dardanus, the ancestor of Aeneas, was born in these fields (206) and emigrated to Troy and Samothrace; Latinus quite specifically states that Dardanus set out from "the Tyrrhenian site of Corythus" (209). The first reference, although oblique, to Aeneas' ancestral Italian kinship occurs when Aeneas is addressing his disguised mother at Carthage:

> *sum pius Aeneas, raptos qui ex hoste penatis*
> *classe ueho mecum, fama super aethera notus;*
> *Italiam quaero* patriam, *et genus ab Ioue summo.*
> Aen. 1.378-380

In these lines Aeneas is stating his genealogical credentials; the reference to his *patria*, which is based on his descent from Dardanus, is an indication that Aeneas has recognized and accepted his genealogical heritage following Anchises' revised interpretation of the Delian Apollo's prophecy.[10] The uniqueness and the importance of the oracle to seek the *antiqua mater* rests in the fact that Vergil locates the home of Dardanus and his brother Iasius, the ancestors of the Trojans, in Italy at the Etruscan site of Corythus (3.167). There has been recent scholarly debate about the exact location of Corythus which has long been identified with Cortona and more recently with Tarquinii.[11] Despite the topographical problems associated with locating the site, the important fact is that the city of Corythus is unquestionably Etruscan—an ethnic designation that Vergil deliberately keeps in the foreground of his treatment of the Dardanus story.

The birth of Dardanus and Iasius at the Etruscan city of Corythus appears for the first time in Vergil's *Aeneid*; the traditional story regarding Dardanus is given by Dionysius of Halicarnassus, who relates that Dardanus was born in Arcadia; according to this version of the legend, Atlas was King of Arcadia and it was his daughter, Electra, who united with Zeus to produce Dardanus. After a flood, Dardanus went to Samothrace and then to Phrygia where he helped Teucer in a war after which he married Bateia, the daughter of Teucer. Dardanus inherited the kingship of Phrygia through his wife and thus becomes one of the founders of the Trojan race.[12] Throughout his history Dionysius stresses the Greekness of Roman civilization and even of Rome itself; Dionysius' version of the Dardanus story makes the Trojans themselves Greek, with the result that Rome is ultimately of Greek origin through Aeneas.[13] In light of this traditional version of the Dardanus story current in Vergil's day and expounded by Dionysius who was, in fact, following Varro,[14] Vergil's variant version of the Dardanus story is all the more remarkable and suggestive: why did Vergil create this opposing "tradition" that Dardanus and Iasius came originally from Corythus? Even more important, why did Vergil equate the "ancient mother" with the Etruscan homeland of Dardanus and therefore make Aeneas a descendant of the Etruscans?

Vergil's purpose in creating this "new tradition" was, I suggest, to highlight the Etruscan legacy to Italian civilization in general and to the Augustan Age in particular. Furthermore, this "new tradition" builds on the association between the Trojans and the Etruscans—a two-fold cultural legacy of special importance to Augustus, who not only stressed his own Trojan descent through Iulus and Aeneas to Ilus, Assaracus and Dardanus, but who also developed and cultivated his Etruscan connections. The identification of Etruria (Corythus) as the *antiqua mater* was a bold innovation on Vergil's part in order to underscore the contribution of the culture, civilization and people of Etruria to Rome and the Roman nation; Vergil's fascination with this *antiqua mater* was determined as much by his personal background as by his friendships: Vergil's family probably was of Etruscan descent and he lived in the city of Mantua that claimed an Etruscan heritage;[15] Vergil's friendship with Maecenas, his Etruscan patron, undoubtedly instilled in Vergil sympathetic feelings towards a people whose devotion to the gods offered a paradigm of pre-Roman *pietas*.[16] During the Augustan Age the allure of the ancient Etruscans finds visible evidence in the many men of Etruscan background such as Maecenas and Agrippa who are amongst Augustus' most loyal supporters; even Augustus and Livia could claim to have Etruscan blood in their veins.[17] There is little question but that Augustus actively favoured this group and Vergil's partiality to the Etruscans in the *Aeneid* no doubt contributed to the august role of Dardanus and his descendants.

In the *Aeneid* Etruria is portrayed as the cradle of civilization: four times Dardanus is designated *auctor* (3.503, 4.365, 6.650, 8.336)—an epithet which highlights his role as founder, equates him with Aeneas whose mission is to found the Roman race (*Romanam condere gentem*, 1.33) and links him with Augustus who will establish the Golden Age (*aurea condet / saecula*, 6.792-793). Dardanus' role as founder is especially underscored in *Aeneid* 6 where Aeneas sees his ancestors, Ilus, Assaracus and Dardanus, in the Groves of the Blessed. Furthermore, in Anchises' discourse on the great, future Romans, the significant point is made that he is expounding Dardanian history (*Dardaniam prolem*, 6.756): the Dardanian dynasty culminates in Augustus, Aeneas' Trojan and Etruscan descendant. Iasius, the brother of Dardanus, is called *pater* by the Phrygian Penates (*Iasius pater, genus a quo principe nostrum*, 3.168). The attribution of *pater* and the relative clause *genus a quo principe nostrum* to "the comparatively unimportant Iasius" has caused surprise in most commentators.[18] In the context of Vergil's new tradition the claim of the Phrygian Penates, the *penus Vestae*, (5.744, 9.259) that the Trojans are the children of Iasius reinforces the Etruscan associations. In the *Aeneid* the Penates have an important role which commentators have traditionally regarded as providing a link between Rome and Troy: Aeneas brings the Penates with him from Troy to Italy.[19] Throughout his journey Aeneas and Anchises pay constant attention to the Penates: as they leave Troy, Aeneas commends them into his father's hands (*tu, genitor, cape sacra manu patriosque penatis*, 2.717) and as they start the journey Aeneas declares that he is an exile "with my comrades and son, the Penates and the great gods" (*cum sociis natoque, penatibus et magnis dis*, 3.12). As we have seen when he meets his mother, Venus, in Carthage he declares himself to be *pius Aeneas, raptos qui ex hoste penatis / classe ueho mecum* (1.378-379); and, it is the Penates who reveal to Aeneas the true origin of Dardanus and the location of his home (3.148-168); moreover, when he arrives in Italy he offers prayers of thanksgiving to the Penates who had promised him (3. 148ff.) that he would find his home in Italy: *o fidi Troiae, saluete, penates: hic domus, haec patria est* (7.121-122).

The Penates are generally regarded as genuine Italian spirits of the household, and it has been thought as curious that they accompany Aeneas on his journey from Troy to Italy.[20] But, since the Penates originally belonged to the home of Iasius, as Vergil indicates, the Penates are indigenous, not foreign, deities; moreover, returning to their original homeland is an event as important as Aeneas' own homecoming. When this Etruscan heritage of the Penates is noted, a new and significant dimension is added to their role in the poem: the Penates are no longer imported deities from the eastern world but rather native gods important in every Roman family's home as well as in the Roman state. The active role which the Penates exerted in guiding and directing Aeneas on his journey (i.e., the prophecy in Crete in *Aeneid* 3) is matched only by the picture of Augustus at the battle of Actium "leading the Italians to battle, with the fathers and the people, the Penates and the great gods":

> *hinc Augustus agen Italos in proelia Caesar*
> *cum patribus populoque, penatibus et magnis dis,*
> *stans celsa in puppi, geminas cui tempora flammas*
> *laeta uomunt patriumque aperitur uertice sidus.*
> *parte alia ventis et dis Agrippa secundis*
> *arduus agmen agens, cui, belli insigne superbum,*
> *tempora nauali fulgent rostrata corona.*
>   Aen. 8.678-684

By returning the *Penates et magni di* to their homeland, Aeneas has ultimately contributed to the future greatness of Rome and specifically to Augustus' defeat of Antony and Cleopatra at the Battle of Actium. Through the Penates Vergil has linked Aeneas and Augustus; a significant point in the association is that the Penates have an Etruscan legacy that must have been appealing to Augustus.

Archaeology, topography and sculpture support Vergil's depiction of the Penates in association with Aeneas and Augustus: Aeneas is credited with the establishment of a temple for the Penates at Lavinium;[21] in a relief on the Ara Pacis Aeneas is shown sacrificing a sow in front of a temple that has been identified as the Temple of the Penates on the Velia where the Penates were worshipped as the household gods of the state;[22] the Velia shrine of the Penates had special significance for Augustus who records with pride in the *Res Gestae* that he had restored the temple.[23] The significance of Vergil's linking of Augustus and Aeneas to the Penates, with their Etruscan origins, should not be underestimated, for in this homage Vergil has subtly portrayed the Etruscan legacy and contribution to Rome, appealed to Augustus' predilection for *res et viri Etrusci*[24] and betrayed his personal feelings for the glorious house of Dardanus.

The Etruscan overtones of the Dardanus story are revealed in another important way. Vergil has portrayed the return to the ancient mother as a *nostos*—a real *nostos*, in fact, that makes parallels between Homer's *Odyssey* and the Odyssean *Aeneid* even more poignant and suggestive.[25] The similarities between the *nostos* of Aeneas and the supposed route of the Etruscans are no less remarkable: both started their odyssey from Asia Minor, and travelled through the Aegean and thence to the western shores of Italy, "the Hesperia of poetry and oracles."[26] A real historical relationship between these two odysseys does not exist but it has been noted that these "unrelated movements into the western Mediterranean, centuries apart, may have fused and been suggestively identified in the poetic imagination."[27] In *Aeneid* 7 the *nostos* of the *Dardanidae* is highlighted in the speech of Ilioneus:

> *sed nos fata deum uestras exquirere terras*
> *imperiis egere suis. hinc Dardanus ortus,*
> *huc repetit, iussisque ingentibus urget Apollo*
> *Tyrrhenum ad Thybrim et fontis uada sacra Numici.*
> *dat tibi praeterea fortunae parua prioris*
> *munera, reliquias Troia ex ardente receptas.*
>   Aen. 7.239-244

Dardanus' over-the-seas journey eastward, stopping along the way to found cities, provides a worthy parallel to his descendant's reverse journey generations later. In making Aeneas' arrival in Italy a return to the homeland of his ancestor Dardanus, Vergil has emphasized the idea of "an Etruscan home-coming": it is Dardanus, says Vergil, who *returns* (*repetit*, 7.241) to the place of his birth. The emphasis on the return of Dardanus is a significant element throughout Vergil's treatment of the story: in Apollo's prophecy in *Aeneid* 3 the *Dardanidae* are informed that their homeland (*prima tellus*, 3.95) will welcome them back (*reduces*,

3.96); upon hearing the prophecy the men ask to where are they to return (*reuerti*, 3.101); in *Aeneid* 8 Tiber welcomes Aeneas back to Italy (*reuehis*, 8.37) and recalls again the Italian origin of Dardanus.[28]

Aeneas' Dardanian heritage and his return to Italy are also an underlying motif in the relationship between Dido and Aeneas. Dido's first words to Aeneas betray his destiny to return to Italy:

> *tune ille Aeneas, quem <u>Dardanio</u> Anchisae*
> *alma Venus Phrygii genuit Simoentis ad undam?*
> Aen. 1.617-618

Dido's designation of Aeneas as Dardanian in this spondaic line effectively elevates the family genealogy from Dardanus into a position of prominence. Five times in close succession in *Aeneid* 4, Dido refers to Aeneas' Dardanian heritage and his followers:

> *exoriare, aliquis nostris ex ossibus ultor,*
> *qui face <u>Dardanios</u> ferroque sequare <u>colonos</u>,*
> *nunc, olim, quocumque dabunt se tempore uires.*
> Aen. 4.625-626

> *sacra Ioui Stygio, quae rite incepta paraui,*
> *perficere est animus finemque imponere curis*
> *<u>Dardaniique</u> <u>rogum</u> capitis permittere flammae.*
> Aen. 4.638-640

> *[Dido] . . . ensemque recludit / <u>Dardanium</u>*
> Aen. 4.646-647

> *felix, heu! nimium felix, si litora tantum*
> *numquam <u>Dardaniae</u> tetigissent nostra carinae!*
> Aen. 4.657-658

> *hauriat hunc oculis ignem crudelis ab alto*
> *<u>Dardanus</u> et nostrae secum ferat omina mortis.*
> Aen. 4.661-662

The emphasis on Aeneas' Dardanian background at this point can not be ignored, for it draws our attention to the Italian traditions of the story, Aeneas' home-coming and his future in Italy. Dido's curses, which *aliquis ultor* (6.625) is to expiate, are made against the *Dardanios . . . colonos* (4.626) and surely look forward to Hannibal and the Carthaginian war[29] as well as to the war between Antony and Cleopatra and Octavian, the ultimate descendant of Dardanus. The immediacy and poignancy of Aeneas' Dardanian heritage is highlighted by Vergil in the actions and adventures of Dido and Aeneas where there are many thematic points of comparison: the journey across the seas in search of a new home, the founding of a nation and the building of a city. Dido has accomplished all of these but in a new world to which she has had no previous attachments, whereas Aeneas is linked to the elusive Etruscan land of Dardanus which has not only an historical association but also a contemporary political reality.

This Etruscan heritage is subtly, but effectively, suggested by the oracles of Apollo which urge the Trojans to seek the Tuscan Tiber and the land of Numicus. In the speech of Ilioneus, quoted above, the phrase *Tyrrhenum ad Thybrim* (7.242) is important, for the emphasis is on the Etruscan aspect of the Tiber river which has its own origins in Etruria. The Tiber is one of the many recurring motifs of the epic[30]—a motif which integrates Aeneas' *nostos* with the Dardanian, Etruscan and Augustan elements of the poem. In *Aeneid* 2 Creusa in her prophecy to Aeneas informs him that he will come to Hesperia where the Lydian Thybris flows with its gentle stream:

> *longa tibi exsilia, et uastum maris aequor arandum,*
> *et terram Hesperiam uenies, ubi Lydius arua*
> *inter opima uirum leni fluit agmine Thybris.*
> *illic res laetae regnumque et regia coniunx*
> *parta tibi. lacrimas dilectae pelle Creusae.*
>
> *Aen.* 2.780-784

In these lines Vergil alludes to the Lydian origins of the Etruscans and suggestively brings to the reader's mind the Herodotean story of the migration of the Etruscans from Lydia to Etruria. In *Aeneid* 3 Aeneas echoes Creusa's words by referring to the Tiber as a place where his city walls will rise (*si quando Thybrim uicinaque Thybridis arua / intraro gentique meae data moenia cernam*, 3.500-501). In the *laus Tiberis* in *Aeneid* 7 (25-36) Vergil highlights the pastoral and idyllic nature of the promised land, and he depicts the table-eating prophecy as actually fulfilled at the mouth of the Tiber. Aeneas' words are noteworthy, for his prayer is to the Penates:

> *continuo 'salue fatis mihi debita tellus*
> *uosque,' ait, 'o fidi Troiae, saluete, penates:*

> hic domus, haec patria est. genitor mihi talia namque
> (nunc repeto) Anchises fatorum arcana reliquit:'
> Aen. 7.120-123

These poignant lines mark Aeneas' recognition that he has arrived home; only at his destination does he comprehend the significance of the omen which his father had foretold.

Once home Aeneas wastes little time in renewing ties with Etruscans of whom Tarchon, the eponymous founder of Tarquinia, is the "repository of Etruscan *pietas*"[31] and the leader of the Etruscan army. Aeneas meets with Tarchon in a sacred grove and gains his support. It has been noted that Tarchon is an *alter Aeneas* who has "the same vision of civilization and similar views of fate, the gods and proper behaviour."[32] Together Aeneas and Tarchon exhibit a shared legacy and heritage that underscores the Etruscan contribution to the Roman state. The meeting and alliance between these two leaders is followed by Venus' presentation of Vulcan's arms to Aeneas. It is not without some significance that Aeneas receives his miraculous armour in the grove of Silvanus, an ancient Etruscan nature god, Selvans, whose sacred grove was located near Caere. Such Etruscan landscape details contribute a topographical precision to the poem that contemporary Romans would have appreciated and recognized to no less a degree than they did the Cumaean sites in Campania.[33]

Vergil's emphasis on the Etruscan origins of Dardanus and Aeneas culminates in the Etruscan catalogue (10.163-214) in which Vergil displays a distinct partiality for the Etruscans. In the catalogue eight leaders are described: four Etruscans (Massicus: 166-169, Abas: 170-174, Asilas: 175-180, Astyr: 180-184); two Ligurians (Cunarus: 185-186, Cupavo: 186-197); and two Mantuans (Ocnus: 198-206, Aulestes: 207-212). The nine cities represented by these leaders are important Etruscan sites, all of which have some connection with Augustus and his retinue of Etruscan supporters: Clusium (167), Cosae (168), Populonia (172), Ilva (173), Pisae (179), Caere (183), Pyrgi (184), Graviscae (184), Mantua (200, 201).[34] The catalogue may have been intended as a tribute to the Etruscan contribution to the political and cultural development of Rome; the historical friendship of the Etruscan cities and Rome during her many internal and external wars is a unifying theme which no doubt appealed to Vergil. It is also possible that with this catalogue Vergil is paying homage to Maecenas, his literary patron of Etruscan origin and to Agrippa, a descendant of Etruscan Pisa and architect of Augustan victories at land and on sea;[35] and it is not unlikely that the catalogue, with its antiquarian, ethnographical and geographical connections and legendary details, was meant to appeal to Augustus. And finally, Vergil's inclusion of Mantua is of special significance for not only does Vergil come from Mantua (and therefore Vergil himself can be included in the catalogue of Etruscan supporters) but so do Ocnus, founder of Mantua and son of Manto and Tiber, and Aulestes, the only Etruscan leader to appear as a king (*regisque insigne gerentem*, 12.289). It is curious that Tarchon is missing from this catalogue, but Vergil has shown (*Aeneid* 8) how Aeneas and Tarchon have pledged their joint support against Turnus; and in *Aeneid* 11 Aeneas and Tarchon are united in common cause as leaders "to add civilization to peace" (*pacique imponere morem*, 6.852).[36]

In the Etruscan catalogue Vergil highlights the Augustan symbolism of the leaders. Massicus is described as *princeps* (10.166), clearly an Augustan epithet used sparingly in the *Aeneid* and with political overtones.[37] Abas rides in his ship gleaming with a gilded Apollo—an image recalling Augustus himself at the battle of Actium standing in the lofty prow of his ship with his brow pouring forth a double flame and on his head his father's star. The parallel with Agrippa (8. 684-686) is equally deliberate and suggestive. Asilas, who is called *princeps* in *Aeneid* 11.620 is here identified as *hominum divumque interpres* (10.175); the first epithet connects Asilas with Augustus and the second recalls the Etruscan contribution to Roman religion.[38] But what is most significant about the Etruscan catalogue, however, is that Aeneas stands at the head of the catalogue and is portrayed leading the Etruscans:

> *haud fit mora, Tarchon*
> *iungit opes foedusque ferit; tum libera fati*
> *classem conscendit iussis gens Lydia diuum,*
> *externo commissa duci. Aeneia puppis*
> *prima tenet rostro Phrygios subiuncta leones,*
> *imminet Ida super, profugis gratissima Teucris.*
> *hic magnus sedet Aeneas secumque uolutat*
> *euentus belli uarios.*
>
> Aen. 10.153-160

Aeneas has returned home to lead his Etruscans to Augustan victory.

NOTES

1. See, for instance, W.A. Camps, *An Introduction to Virgil's* Aeneid (Oxford, 1969) 85-104; W.R. Nethercut, "Vergil's Use of the *Odyssey* in Shaping the *Aeneid*," *Augustan Age* 7 (1987) 108-122; W.R. Nethercut, "Vergil's Use of the *Iliad* in Shaping the *Aeneid*," *Augustan Age* 7 (1987) 123-141; N. Horsfall, "The Aeneas-Legend and the *Aeneid*, " *Vergilius* 32 (1986) 8-17; R.J. Rowland, Jr., "Aeneas Before Vergil: Part I," *Augustan Age* 6 (1987) 155-164; R.J. Rowland, "Aeneas Before Vergil: Part II," *Augustan Age* 6 (1987) 165-175.

2. V. Buchheit, in *Vergil über die Sendung Roms. Untersuchungen zum Bellum Poenicum und zur Aeneis* (Heidelberg, 1963), argues at length that the story of Dardanus and Corythus is a Vergilian innovation (151-172). R.W. Cruttwell, in *Virgil's Mind at Work* (Oxford, 1947) discusses the thematic possibilities associated with the Dardanus story (41-54). Cf. M.A. Di Cesare, *The Altar and the City* (New York, 1974) 244, n. 19. See also N. Horsfall, "Corythus: The Return of Aeneas in Virgil and His Sources," *JRS* 63 (1973) 75 (hereafter: "Corythus"). Epigraphic evidence collected by J. Heurgon suggests that Vergil may have drawn on existing traditions: "Les Dardaniens en Afrique," *REL* 47 (1969) 284-294 and "Inscriptions étrusque de Tunisie," *Académie des Inscriptions et Belles-lettres: Comptes rendus* (1969) 526-551.

3. On the Etruscan elements in the *Aeneid*, see: R. Enking, "P. Vergilius Maro: Vates Etruscus," *MDAIR* 66 (1954) 65-96; A.G. McKay, *Vergil's Italy* (Greenwich, CT) 1970) 78-112; J.F. Hall, "P. Vergilius Maro: Vates Etruscus," *Vergilius* 28 (1982) 44-50; J.F. Hall, "The *Saeculum Novum* of Augustus and Its Etruscan Antecedents," *ANRW* II.16.3 (1984) 2564-2589; A. Dalzell, "Maecenas and the Poets," *Phoenix* 14 (1960) 96-106; P.T. Eden "Mezentius and the Etruscans in the Aeneid," *PVS* 4 (1945-1946) 31-40; J. Gagé, "Les Étrusques dans l'Énéide," *Mel. d'archeol. et d'histoire de l'École Fr. de Rome* 46 (1929) 114-144.

4. All quotations from the *Aeneid* are from R.A.B. Mynors, *P. Vergili Maronis Opera* (Oxford, 1972).

5. G. Thilo and H. Hagen, eds., *Servii Grammatici Qui Feruntur in Vergilii Carmina Commentarii* (Leipzig, 1883-1923) *ad Aen.* 3.108 (hereafter: Servius).

6. In Creusa's prophecy, Aeneas is first informed about Hesperia: *et terram Hesperiam venies* (2.781).

7. Cf. W.H. Semple "A Short Study of *Aeneid* Three," *Bulletin of the John Rylands Library* 38 (1955) 225-240, in which he argues that "by this deliberate and planned error Vergil makes them sail to the extreme south of the Aegean, avoiding by this central route all the populous and hostile parts of the Greek mainland" (231).

8. L.P. Day, "Deceptum Errore: Images of Crete in the *Aeneid*," in *Classical Texts and Their Traditions: Studies in Honor of C.R. Trahman* (Chico, CA, 1984) 39; cf. also D. Shillington, "The Wanderings of Aeneas," *Akroterion* 20 (1975) 35-41; P.V. Cova, "Il tema del viaggio e l'unità del libro terzo dell'Eneide," *Aevum* 39 (1965) 441-473, has good comments on the importance of the Cretan settlement and also on Aeneas' journey.
9. Servius, *ad Aen.* 3.167; V. Buchheit, *op. cit.* 151; N. Horsfall, "Corythus," *op. cit.* 74-75.
10. Cf. E.L. Harrison, "Aeneas' Pedigree," *CR* 22 (1972) 303-304.
11. Servius, *ad Aen.* 3.167; V. Buchheit, *op. cit.* 151; N. Horsfall, "Corythus," *op. cit.* 74-75.
12. Dion. Hal., *Ant. Rom.* 1.61-62.
13. H. Hill, "Dionysius of Halicarnassus and the Origins of Rome," *JRS* 51 (1961) 88-93.
14. Servius, *auct. ad Aen.* 3.167: *Graeci et Varro humanarum rerum Dardanum non ex Italia, sed de Arcadia, urbe Pheneo, oriundum dicunt.*
15. J.F. Hall, "P. Vergilius Maro: Vates Etruscus," *op. cit.* 44-46.
16. Cf. R. Syme, *The Roman Revolution* (Oxford, 1939) 341f.; J.-M. André, *Mécène: Essai de Biographie spirituelle* (Paris, 1967) 15-61; K.P. Nielson, "Tarchon Etruscus—Alter Aeneas," *Pacific Coast Philology* 119 (1984) 28.
17. J.F. Hall, "The *Saeculum Novum* of Augustus and Its Etruscan Antecedents," *ANRW* II.16.3 (1984) 2579; See also J.F. Hall, *The Municipal Aristocracy of Etruria and Their Participation in Politics at Rome, 91 B.C.-A.D. 14.* (Diss., Pennsylvania, 1984); on Maecenas, see R.G.M. Nisbet and M. Hubbard, *A Commentary on Horace: Odes Book 1* (Oxford, 1970) 3-4; K.J. Reckford, "Horace and Maecenas," *TAPA* 90 (1959) 195-208; on Agrippa see M. Reinhold, *Marcus Agrippa: A Biography* (Geneva, New York, 1933) 1-19. On the Etruscans, see R. Bloch, *The Etruscans* (London, 1958) 126f.
18. R.D. Williams, *P. Vergili Maronis Aeneidos Liber Tertius* (Oxford, 1962) 91.
19. E. Thraemer, "Dardanos," *RE* 4.2176-2177; St. Weinstock, "Penates," *RE* 19.1 (1937) 440-451; G. Wissowa, "Die Überlieferung über die römischen Penaten," *Hermes* 22 (1887) 29-57; J. Perret, *Les origines de la legende troyenne de Rome* (Paris, 1942) 27-30; N. Horsfall, "Corythus," (*op. cit.*) 79; cf. Servius, *ad Aen.* 3.15: *SOCIIQVE PENATES vel propter supra dictam coniunctionem Ilionae et Polymestoris, vel quia cum omni hereditate maiorum diviserant etiam deos penates Dardanus et Iasius frates, quorum alter Thraciam, alter Phrygiam incoluit occupatam.*
20. C. Bailey, *Religion in Virgil* (New York, 1935) 31, 94-95.

21. G.K. Galinsky, *Aeneas, Sicily and Rome* (Princeton, 1969) 146-149, 154-156.
22. J. Sieveking, "Zur Ara Pacis Augustuae," *JOAI* 10 (1907) 186-188; I.S. Ryberg, "The Procession of the Ara Pacis," *MAAR* 19 (1949) 80-81; R.B. Lloyd, "Penatibus et Magnis Dis," *AJP* 77 (1956) 45.
23. Augustus, *Res Gestae* 4.7; S.B. Platner and T. Ashby, *A Topographical Dictionary of Ancient Rome* (Oxford, 1929) 388-389; H.F. Rebert, "The Velia: A Study in Historical Topography," *TAPA* 56 (1925) 54-69; P.B. Whitehead, "The Church of SS. Cosma e Damiano," *AJA* 31 (1927) 11-12.
24. For Augustus' interest in Etruria, see I. Bitto "Municipium Augustum Veiens," *RSA* 1 (1971) 109; E. Rawson, "Caesar, Etruria and the *Disciplina Etrusca*," *JRS* 68 (1978) 147-148; M. Torelli, "Senatori Etruschi della tarda repubblica e dell'impero," *DArch* 3 (1969) 285-363.
25. W.S. Anderson, "On Vergil's Use of the Odyssey," *Vergilius* 9 (1963) 1-8; R.D. Williams, "Virgil and the Odyssey, "*Phoenix* 17 (1963) 266-274; B. Otis, *Virgil: A Study in Civilized Poetry* (Oxford, 1964) 215-312, esp. 251-252.
26. A.G. McKay, *Vergil's Italy* (Greenwich, CT) 93.
27. *Ibid.* 93.
28. F. Cairns' *Virgil's Augustan Epic* (Cambridge, 1989) has commented upon "Virgil's italianisation of Aeneas" (116) and the fact that Italy is Aeneas' "true *patria*" (116). Aeneas is thus not a foreigner or stranger but a native to Italy—a fact which makes Turnus the *externus* (7.367-370).
29. M.A. Di Cesare, *op. cit.* 28.
30. H.W. Benario, "Vergil and the River Tiber," *Vergilius* 24 (1978) 4-14.
31. K.P. Nielson, *op. cit.* 32.
32. *Ibid.* 32
33. A.G. McKay, *op. cit.* 77-96.
34. C. Saunders, *Vergil's Primitive Italy* (New York, 1930) 64-86; W.P. Basson, *Pivotal Catalogues in the Aeneid* (Amsterdam, 1975) 157-192; W.P. Basson, "Vergil's Catalogue of Etruscan Forces: Some Observations," *AC* 25 (1982) 51-60.
35. R.E.A. Palmer, "On the Track of the Ignoble," *Athenaeum* 61 (1983) 343-361, provides considerable supportive evidence to suggest that Marcus Agrippa came from Pisa; see also J.F. Hall, *The Municipal Aristocracy of Etruria and Their Participation in Politics at Rome, B.C. 91-A.D. 14* (Diss., Pennsylvania, 1984) Appendix I.101. The origin of the *nomen* and the ancestry of the *gen Vipsania* has stirred much controversy. Etruscan, Marsian and Venetic backgrounds have been proposed: see: M. Reinhold, *Marcus Agrippa: A Biogra-*

phy (New York, 1933) 1-11, esp. p. 9 and n. 37; J.-M. Roddaz, *Marcus Agrippa* (Rome, 1984) 17-29; T.P. Wiseman, *New Men in the Roman Senate* (London, 1971) 275. W. Schulze, *Zur Geschichte lateinischer Eigennamen, Abhandlungen der Kgl. Gesellschaft der Wissenschaften zu Göttingen* (Berlin, 1904) 256, finds a connection between Vipsania and the Etruscan *visanie* and the variant *visnie*.

36. Cf. R.D. Williams, *The* Aeneid *of Virgil, Book 1-6*, (London, Basingstoke, 1972) 513; R.G. Austin, *P. Vergili Maronis Aeneidos Liber Sextus* (Oxford, 1977) 263-264.

37. *Princeps* is used with the following: Gyas, 5. 160; Palinurus, 5.833; Turnus, 9.535; Cybele, 10.254; Asilas, 11.620.

38. Asilas comes from Pisae which is the home town of Agrippa. Cf. W.P. Basson, *op. cit.* 176-177.

THE *AENEID* AND THE CONCEPT OF THE IDEAL KING: THE MODIFICATION OF AN ARCHETYPE

J.A.S. Evans
The University of British Columbia

Since I shall be dealing with the concept of the "perfect prince," it is not altogether unfitting to start with a few words of tribute to "Sandy" McKay.[1] At McMaster University, with which his family has had close ties going back to early years of this century, and he himself has taught since 1954, he has served as chairman of the department of Classics, and dean of Humanities; on the national level, he has served as president of the Classical Association of Canada, and president of the Royal Society of Canada, and he was named an officer of the Order of Canada by the Governor-General in 1989. He has served as president and stalwart upholder of the Vergilian Society of America, and he has put all Vergilian scholars in his debt by producing an annual bibliography of Vergilian studies since 1963, thereby making it unnecessary for dabblers like myself to read all the vast production of Vergilian scholarship with my own eyes. Indeed, I shall with your permission, I hope, invert the usual line of thanks that goes, "I would like to thank Professor 'X' etc., etc., though any errors I must claim for myself," and assert that if I have misunderstood any recent work on Vergil, it is no doubt because I have misread my indispensable McKay, and I am not sure whether he or I am responsible.

"Les Anciens ont beaucoup réfléchi sur la royauté et nombreux furent les ouvrages qui en traitaient dans une optique pythagoricienne ou stoïcienne."[2] The authors who contributed to the royal ideal include Xenophon, Plato and Isocrates, and in Latin literature, we should not forget Cicero, who was mining the same metaphysical lode when he envisioned a *rector et gubernator civitatis*: a *bonus et sapiens* who would act as guardian of the state,[3] even though he also acknowledged that Rome was firmly anti-monarchical. In fact, if we look forwards at the history of imperial Rome, we can detect a dual concept behind the office of emperor that continues up until the fifth century A.D. and does not disappear from Roman law until the time of Justinian: on the one hand, the emperor was a Roman magistrate subject to the laws, and on the other hand, he was himself the source of law: *nomos empsychos*, or law incarnate. It was this latter postulate that was eventually to dominate: the conceptualization surrounding the late Roman emperor owes more to Hellenistic kingship than it does to the *res publica* that Augustus is thought to have restored in an ambivalent sort of way.[4] That was long after Vergil's day; yet the influence in Roman political thought of this speculation on the proper royal persona is as early as the principate itself. The ideal kingship archetype is already discernible in Nicolaus of Damascus' biography of Augustus with its marked emphasis on Octavian's hereditary rights[5] which his rival, Antony, lacked, and since Nicolaus had read Augustus' own autobiography published in 25 B.C., I think it very probable that Augustus himself may have made judicious use of these notions in his attempt to shape the concepts surrounding his own position. When Augustus said (of Cato) that the man who did not want to change the existing political order was both a good citizen and a good man,[6] he was sharing the constitutional views of the ruling class to which he belonged, and no doubt in one part of his mind, he was sincere. But no one who looks at the way he arranged dynastic marriages within his own bloodline, can doubt that he conceived of his position in quasi-monarchical terms, and from there it was an easy intellectual jump to the ideal royal archetype. Not for nothing was the seal of Augustus a sphinx!

I have long suspected that some of this speculation about ideal kings helped shape the character of Aeneas, and Francis Cairns' new book, *Virgil's Augustan Epic*, has now placed my suspicion beyond doubt. The problem of making Aeneas into an ideal king, however, is very like the old problem of making him into an ideal Stoic: he does not quite fit either archetype. His victims are far too attractive to be Stoic "sinners," and Aeneas himself is no imperturbable "captain of his soul."[7] We are constantly reminded of the cost, both to himself and to others, of his devotion to duty, summed up by the one word *pietas*. Nor is he altogether an ideal king. Yet, the concepts of ideal kingship helped shape his character, and if we require proof of that, we need only look at the way Vergil used Hercules as a model for his hero. Aeneas, like Hercules, is a strong man persecuted by Juno, and his quest is treated as a labor. The chief purpose of the Cacus episode (8.184-305), Brooks Otis[8] has argued, is to endow Aeneas with the aura of Hercules. But Hercules had already been developed by the Cynics and Stoics as the paradigm of the ideal hero-king who labored and served for the good of his subjects. Antigonos Gonatas of Macedon, who had a properly royal penchant for philosophers, and leaned towards Stoicism, defined kingship for his son as a "noble servitude"[9] and it was this variety of kingship which took Hercules as its model, rather than cosmic kingship, that informed the characterization of Aeneas.[10] Hercules was the servant of the human race. This was a view that antedated Stoicism; it went back at least as far as Antisthenes, who was Socrates' pupil, and was the founder of the Cynic school.[11]

However, it seems to me that, when we look at Vergil's models, it is less important to ask ourselves how he adheres to them than to document the ways in which he differs. Let us take one example. It is now virtually a cliché that the *Odyssey* provides a model for the first six books of the *Aeneid* and the *Iliad* for the last six. The *Iliad* and the *Odyssey* are both ring compositions. The *Iliad* starts with Achilles' rage at having to return Briseis, and ends with him willingly returning Hector's body to Priam. The *Odyssey* starts with Athena flashing down to Ithaca to rouse Telemachus, and ends in Ithaca again, with Athena imposing a reconciliation between Odysseus and the families of the murdered suitors. But the *Aeneid* presents us first with a defeated Aeneas, terrified, helpless in a storm at sea, and ends with Aeneas in triumph, in the act of slaying Turnus. The *Aeneid* is linear; it begins with its hero at his nadir, and ends with his victory, and with Aeneas merciless and vengeful. The view of the historical past in the *Aeneid* is not cyclic. Rather it is teleological.[12] History progresses onwards and upwards towards a great destiny, and the rule of Rome, we are assured, will be without end. Rome has escaped the cycle of history.

Let us take another example. The scene in the *Aeneid* where Venus presents her son with new armour made by Vulcan is modelled on *Iliad* 18, but with two significant differences. The first is that Thetis got a new panoply for her son, Achilles, because he needed it, for Patroclus had borrowed his old armour and lost it. Aeneas, however, already possessed a perfectly good suit of armour. What we have in the *Aeneid* is a variation of the folk-tale motif where the hero is given a magic weapon of supernatural origin, which marks him as specially chosen for a quest. Usually it is a piece of equipment: for example, a sword, like King Arthur's Excalibur, or a magic lance or cuirass, whereas in the *Aeneid*, it is a complete panoply. That detail, we must concede, comes from the *Iliad*, from which Vergil has borrowed the literary architecture of this incident. But another element of the motif also seems to be missing: I find, by checking Stith Thompson's *Motif-Index of Folk Literature*,[13] that in tales of magic weapons, the weapon usually gives the hero some advantage: it protects him from attack, or gives victory, or in one case, protects the soul from hurt.[14] Aeneas' new armour seems to have no special property of this sort.

But here we have the second difference. Achilles' shield had shown scenes from life in Homeric Greece. Aeneas' shield showed a panorama of Rome's future. In particular, it showed Augustus at the the battle of Actium, crowned with the *patrium sidus*, the comet which had appeared for seven days in late July, 44 B.C.,[15] and, if we can believe Pliny the Elder, Augustus regarded it as his own star, and a beneficent one.[16] Opposing him were Antony and his Egyptian wife with the barbarian host of the East. When Aeneas shouldered his shield, he, all unknowing, shouldered Rome's destiny, and it was Rome's destiny that was the magical property which his armour possessed. Rome's destiny, and the future success of Augustus which it portended, protected Aeneas from harm, and helped him play his heroic role quite as much as Excalibur helped King Arthur.

In these two instances, it is the difference between Vergil's models and the *Aeneid* which is important, and I think the same rule holds for the character of Aeneas himself. Granted that the concept of the ideal *basileus* informs the character of Aeneas, but it is the differences which should attract our particular attention.

The theoretical basis for the Hellenistic concept of the perfect prince was laid out by a crop of treatises *On Kingship*, and kings took titles such as "Saviour," "Benefactor," "Helper," even "*Philopator*" or "lover of one's father," which is not inappropriate for Aeneas. But to quote Martin Charlesworth, the royal function "could almost be summed up in one magnificent word, *philanthropia*."[17] In Rome, the concept was further shaped by the traditional rhetoric of the *laudatio funebris*, which expressed the dynastic feelings of the ruling families, and laid particular emphasis on the honor of public office. But the concept of the perfect prince that we find in the Latin panegyrics remained remarkably stable: he was to be pious, gentle, merciful, just, wise, virtuous and a good soldier, and his whole aim should be peace and prosperity for his people.[18] Augustus recorded in his *Res Gestae* that a gold shield was dedicated to him *virtutis clementiaeque iustitiae et pietatis causa*. He noted the dedication with pride: these were clearly the virtues he advertised: *virtus, clementia, iustitia* and *pietas*. More than fifty years ago, Schubart[19] published a paper on the ideal king as he appeared in Hellenistic inscriptions and papyri, and analogous virtues appear: *arete*—virtue, but in a wider sense than the Latin *virtus, eusebeia, philostorgia, eunoia, philanthropia*. The king should also provide good government. On the Rosetta Stone from Ptolemaic Egypt, the classical concept of *eunomia* has been transformed into a royal undertaking to create righteous government. Self-control is also a prime virtue. The king is called the father or the shepherd of his people. We even occasionally find the title *ktistes*: founder; founding cities was also a proper role for ideal kings.

How well does this archetype fit Aeneas? As I have noted, his quest is presented as a labor, and the comparison with Hercules whose myth was turned by the Cynics into an allegory of the solitary, poor, suffering *basileus* must have impressed contemporary readers, all the more so since this ideal by then informed Stoic thought as well.[20] But in some remarkable ways, the archetype does not fit.

Aeneas cannot be called a merciful man. What is surprising about the death of Turnus is not that Aeneas slew him in a flash of uncontrolled anger, but that he for a moment actually considered clemency. In Book 10, he killed without mercy: Magus, Tarquitius, and Liger pleaded in vain, and Lucagus he killed with a taunt. Lausus he pitied, but only after he had killed him. Mezentius he simply finished off. One may argue that Vergil here is only imitating Homer and piling up corpses. But the picture is consistent. Clemency is not a virtue to which Aeneas can make much claim. Cairns[21] makes a good effort to defend Aeneas' *ira*, urging a philosophic justification for it. Yet we should remember that *clementia* was one of the virtues to which Augustus himself laid claim, and it had been one of the weapons in Julius Caesar's arsenal. Would Vergil have made Turnus so attractive a figure if he thought him entirely unworthy of a little Augustan clemency?

Nor was Aeneas much better with those who showed him love and affection. The last mention of Dido in the *Aeneid* occurs at 11.72-75, where Aeneas uses two robes woven for him by Dido to cover the corpse of Pallas. It is a significant mention, but it does *not* mean that Aeneas still cherished some trace of love for Dido. Rather, Dido and Pallas had something in common, for both, in different ways, were sacrificed to Rome's drive for power and empire. Befriending Aeneas had destroyed them both.

The Dido episode itself is marked by ambiguity from the beginning. In the first book, Aeneas and the seven ships that were with him reached the shore of Libya, and his haven is described: a bay with great cliffs on either side.[22] We are reminded for a chilling moment of the harbour of the cannibal Laestrygonians in the *Odyssey*.[23] But Dido was not a savage queen. She would not harm the Trojans. Instead, she was the model of *philanthropia*: a queen who exemplified the virtues of kingship, at least until her royal quality of self-control was destroyed by her encounter with Aeneas, or to be more exact, by the poison disseminated by Venus' other son, for when we judge Dido, we should not forget that Vergil portrayed her as the victim of the duplicity of Venus, who took advantage of the welcome Dido gave Aeneas to substitute Cupid for Ascanius, and thus infect her with Cupid's darts.[24] Yet Dido represented a danger to Aeneas' mission that was as deadly as the Laestrygonians were to Odysseus and his men. Aeneas' weapon against her is an ascetic devotion to his duty. He represses his sexual desires with a severity worthy of a Christian anchorite. This unflinching devotion to duty was, of course, *pietas*, which was a Roman virtue displayed by a succession of Roman heroes who parade through the pages of Livy. But their *pietas* had broken Rome's enemies, not women who had shown them kindness and gracious hospitality. Like Turnus, Dido is too attractive for the role of victim of Rome's destiny. Can Vergil have been unaware of the contrast between her and the pale Lavinia, who is solidly asexual, even though her analogue in the *Iliad* is Helen of Troy?

Moreover, Roman readers must have caught an echo of their own apopthegm *Punica fides* when they read Dido's reproaches. She complained of *fides* broken by Aeneas, expressing her bitterness with unconscious irony. Not only was she using a term familiar to Roman law, but also one familiar to Roman historical tradition.[25] Dido turned one of Rome's stock calumnies against the Romans: *Punica fides*, as the Romans called it, in her experience was Trojan *fides*, and to the Roman legal mind, *fides* breached was a violation of *fas*, and should bring divine punishment upon the offender.[26]

There is also the matter of Aeneas' superhuman physical strength which flags only momentarily in the last book, when he is wounded. Compared to Aeneas, Odysseus is a weakling. On Circe's island, he slew one stag and dragged it with much sweat and effort to the shore.[27] But when Aeneas reached Libya, he shot seven stags and took them, with no apparent effort, to his men.[28] Unless faithful Achates, who helped him, was a secret bodybuilder, Aeneas' physical power must have been enormous. Turnus was no match for him: in the final book, the Rutulians contrast their hero with Aeneas as he prepares for unequal combat, and they pity him.[29] Aeneas was a huge warrior with a great spear. *Portis sese extulit ingens / telum immane manu quatiens* are the words used to describe him as he leaves for his duel with Turnus.[30] He is presented as *ingens Aeneas* when he boards Charon's boat on the river Styx,[31] and again when he enters Evander's humble home in Book 8.[32] Epithets like *pius Aeneas* and *pater Aeneas* vastly outnumber references to his size, but there can be little doubt that this is an irresistible warrior who sweeps other men before him.

Along with exaggerated strength, Aeneas has exaggerated wealth. He has no trouble producing rich gifts when he needs them, including a couple of garments that had once belonged to Helen![33] It is remarkable that Aeneas managed to extract so much property from the ruins of Troy when he failed to save his wife, Creusa! To be sure, the possession of wealth is an attribute of a Hellenistic monarch,[34] though not of the type of ideal king who, like Hercules, labors for the good of mankind. But I think the symbolism of Aeneas' wealth has a rather different symbolic meaning.

One of the themes that informs the portrayal of Aeneas is that of the rich and powerful invader from Asia, who intrudes upon Italy. Iarbas speaks of Aeneas with a sneer worthy of Juvenal; he calls him a Paris, with greasy hair.[35] Turnus calls him a Phrygian tyrant,[36] and speaks of his hair artificially curled with tongs, and of his eunuch followers.[37] Even the title *rex* which is given Aeneas in the words with which Ilioneus speaks to Dido of his leader, Aeneas:

> *rex erat Aeneas nobis, quo iustior alter*
> *nec pietate fuit, nec bello maior et armis.*
>
> *Aen.* 1.544-545

had an un-Roman sound to it, for the Romans hated the word *rex*.[38] To quote Cicero: *sic pulso Tarquinio nomen regis audire non poterat (populus Romanus)*. These slurs are reminiscent of the calumnies which Octavian's propaganda had used against Antony and Cleopatra. But we cannot dismiss them as unimportant and baseless. At the conclusion of the epic, Juno abandons Turnus, but she wrings from Jupiter the concession that the Latins will absorb the Trojans who will give up their language and Trojan dress. Jupiter concedes with words signifying a contract: *do quod vis, et me victusque volensque remitto*.[39] Juno had won what mattered. She had failed to deflect the ultimate ascendant of Augustus from Italy, and the Julian House was not to be cut off at its roots, but she had made certain that Aeneas and his Trojans would become Italian, and their great destiny would be the destiny of Italy. The danger that this rich, powerful invader from the East represented had been averted, and Jupiter acknowledged defeat.

I suggest that here we have a key to our puzzle. Vergil has used the archetype of the ideal king, but he has made significant alterations to suit his purpose. The clemency of Aeneas is so narrowly defined that it is almost non-existent. He is merciless when the destiny of Rome is at stake. He possesses little of that quality necessary for ideal kings: *philanthropia*. He is *pius*—almost monotonously so—but his Roman devotion to duty breaks a queen who has all the qualities of an ideal monarch, bringing her curse on Rome, and the consequent hatred of Carthage. His piety is not the same as the *eusebeia* of the Hellenistic kings.

He was an Asiatic, a powerful, wealthy invader, and we are not allowed to forget his foreignness. He has explained, or tried to explain to Dido that the oracles had directed him to found a Trojan settlement in Italy: *hic amor, haec patria est*.[40] But the result of his labor is not to be a Trojan colony in Italy; it will be rather assimilation of the Asian stranger with the native Italian, and concord between East and West, with the former yielding to the latter. Aeneas is a king whose noble servitude is to have as its aim his assimilation and his disappearance as a Trojan. He is to surrender his Trojan way of life, accept the finality of Troy's destruction, and make his destiny the destiny of Italy, which would thus join Europe and Asia under its aegis.

To put this in its context, we should remember that since the fifth century B.C., the Trojan War had been interpreted in terms of the struggle between Europe and Asia exemplified by the Persian Wars, and by the fourth century, the term "barbarian" had taken on the pejorative overtones we find in Aristotle. The *philanthropia* of the Hellenistic kings had always been directed towards the Greek cities! The non-Greeks usually did not share in it. But Vergil has taken this barbarian hero, Aeneas, complete with his superhuman strength, wealth and Phrygian origin, and made him into the victorious invader of Italy. But at the same time, he has manipulated the Greek concept of the ideal *basileus* in order to make Aeneas a symbol of the new relationship between East and West. His mission, which he himself never completely understood, was to be the first of the long series of great men who were to construct the Roman Empire, and just as no Roman noble should be unworthy of his ancestors, so Aeneas could not be unworthy of his descendants. But when he finally achieved victory, his destiny was not to build a new Trojan city or import his own civilization into an alien land, as Alexander the Great and his Hellenistic successors had done, all of whom shared to some degree the persona of the ideal *basileus*. Once victorious over Italy, Aeneas melded his future and his way of life with the Italians whom he had conquered in battle. His *patria* was not to be a New Troy after all.

The agreement between Juno and Jupiter that preceded the death of Turnus was to be ratified again at the battle of Actium, which was portrayed on the shield Aeneas bore. That victory would renew the union of East and West, and Asia would willingly assimilate into a reasserted Roman Empire. The union that the marriage of Lavinia and the Trojan *rex*, Aeneas symbolized, which was achieved at the cost of great suffering and labor, would at last come into being.

This was a bold vision for its day, and history eventually betrayed it. But before we label it naïve, we should remember that Rome did eventually make all the subjects of her empire her citizens, an achievement that would have been beyond the conceptual world of either classical Athens or the Hellenistic monarchies. The dream of East and West uniting in a new Latin *oikoumene* was to be a lively vision in the first two centuries of the empire, and it left an intellectual legacy behind it, even after it faded.

NOTES

1. This paper was first delivered orally at special session held in honor of Professor A.G. McKay as part of the 1989 annual meeting of the Classical Association of the Middle West and South at Lexington, KY. Since I was unable to attend in person due to illness, the paper was read for me by Professor Frederic M. Schroeder of Queen's University, Kingston, Ont., to whom I owe a

debt of gratitude. When the paper was delivered, I had not yet been able to consult Francis Cairns' fine study of the concept of ideal kingship in *The Aeneid, Virgil's Augustan Epic* (Cambridge, 1989), and I have since made some additions to take it into account. However, the substance of this paper is essentially unchanged.
2. C. Préaux, *Le Monde Hellénistique* 1 (Paris, 1987) 183.
3. *Republic* 2.29.51; cf. M.L. Clarke, *The Roman Mind* (Cambridge, MA, 1960; repr. Norton Library, NY, 1968) 47-49.
4. Cf. E.A. Judge, "'Res Publica Restituta': A Modern Illusion," in *Polis and Imperium: Studies in Honour of Edward Togo Salmon*, ed. J.A.S. Evans (Toronto, 1974) 279-311, who argues that there is no evidence that Augustus ever claimed to have "restored the republic," though he admits that among survivors of the civil wars, the phrase "restituta re publica" may have come into use as a way of referring to the settlement of 27 B.C. On Byzantine kingship, see J.A.S. Evans, "Byzantine Kingship: The Claim of Dynastic Right," *AncW* 18 (1988) 49-55.
5. Cf. Préaux, *op. cit.* 189-192 on the hereditary rights of kings.
6. Macrobius, *Saturnalia* 2.4.18.
7. M.W. Edwards, "The Expression of Stoic Ideas in the *Aeneid*," *Phoenix* (1960) 151-165; C.M. Bowra. "Aeneas and the Stoic Ideal," *Greece and Rome* 3 (1933) 8-21. For the argument that Aeneas' character develops in terms of the four cardinal virtues of the Stoics, see R.P. Bond, "Aeneas and the Cardinal Virtues," *Prudentia* 6 (1974) 67-91, who also gives a good bibliography on the subject.
8. B. Otis, *Virgil: A Study in Civilized Poetry* (Oxford, 1963) 334-336. Otis remarks that Hermann Fränkel's conjecture that the analogy between Hercules and Augustus was the main reason for the Cacus episode could be put in stronger terms (335, n. 1).
9. W.W. Tarn, *Antigonos Gonatas* (Oxford, 1912; repr. Chicago, 1969) 253-256.
10. Cf. Cairns, *op. cit.* 1-28.
11. Cf. R. Hoïstad, *Cynic Hero and Cynic King: Studies in the Cynic Conception of Man* (Lund, 1948) *passim*.
12. Cf. B. Otis, "The Originality of the *Aeneid*," in D.R. Dudley, *Virgil* (London, 1969) 27-66, who remarks how Vergil, in Books 1-6, took passages from the *Odyssey* and reworked them with a teleological message.
13. (Bloomington, IN, 1966) 6 vols.: cf. D1080-D1102.
14. D1389.11.
15. Pliny, *NH* 2.93; cf. A.H.M. Jones, *Augustus* (London, 1970) 15.
16. *Iliad* 22.25-32, which provides a distant analogy, likens Achilles to Sirius, a maleficent star.
17. M.P. Charlesworth, "The Virtues of Roman Emperor," *Proceedings of the British Academy* 23 (1937) 105-127. The quotation is from

106. Cairns, *op. cit.* 19-21, has tabulated the qualities of the royal stereotype.
18. Cf. L.K. Born, "The Perfect Prince according to the Latin Panegyrists," *AJPh* 55 (1934) 20-35.
19. W. Schubart, "Das hellenistische Königsideal nach Inschriften und Papyri," *Archiv für Papyrusforschung 12* (1937) 1-26.
20. Cf. Hoïstad, *op. cit.* 220-222.
21. *Op. cit.* 77-84.
22. *Aen.* 1.161-163.
23. 10.87-91.
24. On her *humanitas*, see R.C. Monti, *The Dido Episode and the* Aeneid, (Leiden, 1981) 15-20; cf. R. Hornsby, *Patterns of Action in the* Aeneid: *An Interpretation of Vergil's Epic Similes* (Iowa City, 1970) 89-100. Cairns (*op. cit.* 29-57) argues that Dido deteriorates from a good queen to a bad queen, where Aeneas maintained the qualities of a king, at least of the cynic variety. A better argument could be made that an ever-watchful mother Venus destroyed an ideal monarch (Dido) in order to further the interests of her son, Aeneas.
25. Monti, *op. cit.* 39. M.O. Lee. *Fathers and Sons in Vergil's* Aeneid (Albany, NY, 1979) 13, remarks that Augustus may have noted that the characters Aeneas opposes are all attractive figures.
26. H.J. Wolff, *Roman Law: An Historical Introduction* (Norman, OK, 1951) 65.
27. *Ody.* 10.158-175.
28. *Aen.* 1.184-194.
29. *Ibid.* 12.216-221.
30. *Ibid.* 12.441-442.
31. *Ibid.* 6.413.
32. *Ibid.* 8.367.
33. *Ibid.* 1.647-652.
34. Préaux, *op. cit.* 208-209.
35. *Aen.* 4.215.
36. *Ibid.* 12.75.
37. *Ibid.* 12.99-100.
38. Cf. Cicero, *Republic* 2.30.52. It is interesting to note that *rex* came eventually to refer only to barbarian kings and chieftains, while the Greek *basileus* was considered the proper translation of *imperator*: s.v. Procopius, *Wars* 5.1.26-29, where P. remarks that Theoderic as king of the Ostrogoths was a *rex*, though he had the qualities of a genuine *basileus*.
39. *Aen.* 12.833.
40. *Ibid.* 4.345-350.

THE SIMILES OF *AENEID* 5

Ward W. Briggs, Jr.
University of South Carolina

In 1965 Michael Putnam said, "Little attention has been paid to what is particularly Virgilian about the games of *Aeneid* V."[1] Though early commentators, beginning with Servius, assumed that Virgil inserted the games only because Homer had them, we now know that Virgil's adaptations of Homer are organic to the poem and in many ways show the poet at his most original.[2] The book serves as a kind of emotional breathing space between Books 4 and 6 and shows Aeneas controlling events and outcomes (just as at the end he controls the ship after the loss of Palinurus), whereas so much of Books 4 and 6 had been out of his control. Putnam has shown the linkage of elements within Book 5 (the snake at Anchises' tomb with Iris at 609;[3] Monoetes, Sergestus, and the dove killed by the arrow with Palinurus[4]) and without (the dolphins with the depiction of Actium at 8.671-674).[5] Pavlovskis has shown the contrast between old and young in the games (Entellus and Acestes represent the old Sicilian ways, the young Euryalus and Ascanius the new Roman ways).[6]

The most prominent features of Book 5 are the Roman elements in the games[7] and the distinctive use of similes. While the similes of Book 5 are unique not only to Virgil in their frequency and subject matter, they are exceptional in Latin literature by their re-use by an author of his own material. Despite these remarkable qualities, they have received only one full-length treatment in recent times, as we shall see. The frequency and subject matter of these similes clearly links them with the similes of *Aeneid* 9-12, whose serious battles they presage, for as Brooks Otis said, Book 5 "is not fundamentally a book about games."⁸ The unique structure of the similes within Book 5 reinforces the struggles of man with the elements of nature and with other men, culminating in the prodigies that announce Rome's destiny. Finally, the key to their meaning here is that each simile reverses not its Homeric, but rather its Virgilian predecessor in the *Georgics*.

The similes in question are, with their sources:[9]
- [1] (84-93) a snake from the tomb of Anchises portends doom as does a rainbow darting through the clouds (*Geo.* 3.416-424);
- [2] (137-150) a regatta is compared to a chariot race (cf. *Il.* 23.358-538; *Geo.* 3.105f., 1.511-514);
- [3] (210-219) Mnestheus' boat, as it takes the lead, darts and glides like a dove in flight (*Il.* 21.493-495, 18.86-87; *Geo.* 1.373-429; *Aen.* 2.515-517, 11.715-724);
- [4] (268-281) Sergestus' boat staggers to the finish like a trampled snake (*Geo.* 3.416-424);
- [5] (439-442) Dares, the young fighter, is like a beleaguered soldier besieging a city;
- [6] (443-452) Entellus, the giant boxer, falls like a mountain spruce (*Il.* 13.177-181, 389-391, 16.482-484);
- [7] (453-460) the blows of Entellus are like hail (*Geo.* 4.78-81);
- [8] (519-532) the arrows of Acestes are like shooting stars (*Il.* 4.75-77, *Geo.* 1.365-366, *Aen.* 2.693-694);
- [9] (580-595) the *Lusus Troiae* makes a pattern as complex as a labyrinth (*Il.* 18.590-606 [dancing floor]);
- [10] (594-595) the boys riding in the *Lusus Troiae* are like dolphins swimming (*Geo.* 1.373-429).

What immediately strikes us is the frequency of these similes: Of the first eight books, Book 5 has the most similes[10] and the greatest number of lines devoted to similes.[11] Moreover the ten similes in question occur in only the first part of the book, vv. 84-603, which describes the funeral games for Anchises;[12] the second part of the book, describing the burning of the ships and the loss of Palinurus (604-871), contains no similes at all. The description of the games comprises 512 of the 871 lines of the book, and averages one formal simile every 50 lines. While the density of the similes is not remarkable,[13] no other span of 500 lines in Books 1-8 has ten similes, although both Books 10 and 12 are comparable.[14] This frequency is set off even further by the fact that the games of *Iliad* 23.262-897 contain only five full similes to describe the action of its games.[15] Why does Virgil feel he needs to embellish his perfectly vivid action with these Homeric similes?

On the most basic level, the heightened frequency of similes in this book adds vigor and animation to the lively, even humorous action of the games, while according the games a significance for the poem as a whole. Book 5 had begun lugubriously with *dolores* (5) and *triste* (6) and of course it ends with Palinurus' death and Aeneas guiding the ship through the dark. The games are a peaceful, in some cases playful kind of battle and many of the similes (2, 4-8) are Homeric battle-similes made mock-heroic for the games, thereby prefiguring both in subject matter and quantity the similes to be used in the serious battles of Books 9-12.[16] Later I shall suggest that they have a more immediate source than Homer, upon which their function and tone depends.

While correspondences can and indeed have been noted by Otis and Putnam, among others,[17] the only systematic study of the similes is the 1952 Hamburg dissertation of M. von Duhn, *Die Gleichnisse in den ersten sechs Büchern von Vergils Aeneis*. Since this work has not been widely noticed, I may devote a little space to it here.

As she did with all six books, von Duhn found a pattern of similes within Book 5, which I have schematized on the left side of the chart on page 160. The rainbow simile within the snake prodigy suggests the founding of the city of Sergesta, which was kindred with Rome and later allied with her. When Acestes shoots his arrow into the air and the arrow turns into a comet, the founding of Sergesta is implied. She also notes parallels with other books, particularly Book 2. Just as six similes refer to the night battle for Troy in Book 2 (298-308, 347-360, 413-419, 469-475, 491-505, 624-633), three similes are respectively coordinated in three mirror-images of one another: the chariot race (A), the doves (B), and the snake (C) represent one half of the image. There is a kind of axis between the two long contests, the chariot race (248 lines) and the boxing match (242 lines) with three similes in each. The second half of the image are the similes of the boxing match, the siege-mountain, spruce-hail similes which make up (C), the comet (B), and the labyrinth-dolphin (A). Pair A plays on contemporary Roman events, the spectacles of regattas and chariot races and Augustus' efforts to reinstate the *Lusus Troiae*. Pair B is united through the image of the doves and the figure of Mnestheus, and pair C belongs together through verbal reminiscences, although the reminiscences are admittedly weak.

She also distinguishes two series of similes: one, which generally concerns wandering (the dove, snake, and dolphin similes),[18] and the second, which generally concerns the founding of a city.

One feels a straining after correspondence here, since she intends to find such correspondences throughout all the similes in each book of the first half of the poem. But the three similes of the boxing match cannot be reduced to one only, even for schematic purposes, and the correspondence with the snake simile is weak indeed.

Perhaps we could envision another scheme:

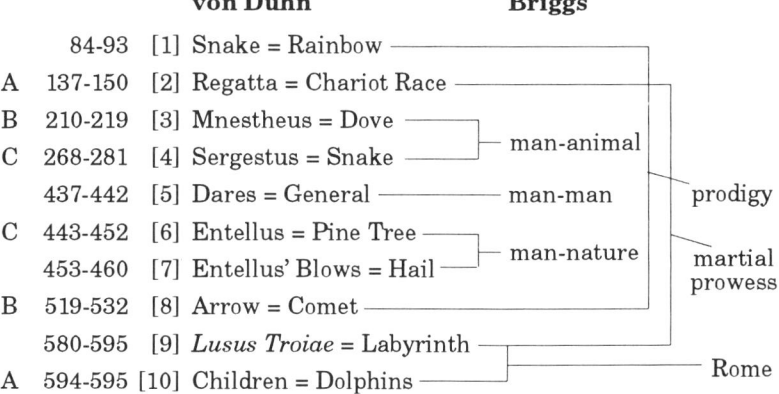

A simple arrangement pairs the two prodigies of the snake-rainbow simile [1] with the arrow-comet simile [8]. The regatta [2] and the *Lusus Troiae* [9] are both historical Roman exhibitions of martial prowess.[19] The remaining five similes (treating the dolphin simile as part of the labyrinth simile) can be seen as two similes comparing individual men to animals [3 and 4] and an individual to a natural object that happens to fall [6 and 7], flanking the relatively rare simile of a man compared to another man [5].[20]

But even if this scheme or von Duhn's scheme represents Virgil's original plan, we are no closer to an understanding of the feeling/tone of the book. For that we must look beyond Book 5 and in some cases beyond the *Aeneid* and start afresh.

Homeric battles are recalled by two of these similes: Dares compared to a besieger [5] involves, as so often happens in the *Georgics*,[21] Homeric battle-action used for a simile of peaceful activity. Entellus falling like a mountain spruce [6] is a conventional Homeric battle-simile,[22] reversed from its constructive use in the felling of the ash in *Georgics* 3.[23] (The simile comparing the *Lusus Troiae* to the labyrinth [9] is unexampled elsewhere.) The remaining seven similes all share two important and unusual characteristics: they do not recall similes of Homer nor Apollonius, but rather previous passages of the *Georgics* or the *Aeneid* (either of simile or narrative) and all seven significantly reverse both the tone and context of their previous settings to fit the mood of Book 5.

Surely the most striking example is the use of snake similes and descriptions. Bernard Knox's famous article on snake imagery in *Aeneid* 2[24] shows clearly that snakes both in the *Georgics* and in the *Aeneid* represent sudden, unforeseen lethal violence and that this image "has good precedent in the Latin tradition."[25] And yet the ominous and deadly snake image, which Virgil develops in *Georgics* 3.416-424, is part of a longer section of Book 3 (384-469) that builds up images of the cruelty and terror in nature (from thistles and briars to robbers, snakes, and diseases), and climaxes with the extended description of the plague at Noricum. Virgil speaks first of the viper that attacks the herds, then the Calabrian serpent, allied with images of the parched land and the snake's terrible thirst, Virgil's personal fear of the snake, and the horror of the famished snake on the prowl. That this is the tone of the snake (and flame) similes of *Aeneid* 2 is well known; the image there moves from concealment and deceit (Sinon) through sudden terror striking from concealment (the serpents from Tenedos) to open violence (Pyrrhus). That these descriptions develop from the *Georgics* is less well known,[26] but see what happens in *Aeneid* 5. Virgil reverses the deadly and ominous snake image from *Georgics* 3.416-424 and *Aeneid* 2. He reverses it first in the prophetic snake at the tomb of Anchises, a snake which is not threatening to man, merely one that eats already dead sacrifices.[27] The comparison of the snake to a rainbow anticipates the action of Iris in 6.701 and particularly 5.609, where she descends to encourage the Trojan women to burn the ships. But the snake at Anchises' tomb is a good omen, clearly reversed at 5.609. When the crippled barque of Sergestus hobbles across the finish line after the awards have been given, it is compared to the crippled snake in *Georgics* 3.422-424:

> *iamque fuga timidum caput abdidit alte,*
> *cum media nexus extremaeque agmina caudae*
> *solvuntur, tardosque trahit sinus ultimus orbis.*
>
> Geo. 3.422-424

> *pars volnere clauda retentat*
> *nixantem nodis seque in sua membra plicantem.*
> Aen. 5.278-279

Like the snake, the captain is embittered and frustrated in his defeat. But here the simile occurs in a light passage: the reaction of the spectators is laughter, while the reader's reaction to the crippled snake in the *Georgics* is apprehension. This is, then, one of the few light similes involving snakes in classical literature.[28] In the same way, the positive comparison of the high-spirited, at times comic, regatta to a chariot race is drawn from *Georgics* 1.511-514, the pessimistic simile of the world going out of control for want of a *moderator*, and specific lines from *Georgics* 3.103-112, a description of a chariot race, is here reversed to describe a boat race.

> *Corripuere ruuntque effusi carcere currus*
> *corda pavor pulsans? illi instant verbere torto*
> *et proni dant lora, volat vi fervidus axis;*
> Geo. 3.105-107

> *Corripuere ruuntque effusi carcere currus;*
> *nec sic immissis aurigae undantia lora*
> *concussere iugis pronique in verbera pendent.*
> Aen. 5.145-147

When Mnestheus' ship is compared to a dove, it is without the pathetic qualities that these victimized birds generally have in ancient literature[29] or elsewhere in the *Aeneid*, for instance when Camilla kills Ligus as a hawk kills a dove (11.715-724) and most notably in the simile of Hecuba and her daughters cowering about Priam's altar like frightened doves (2.515-517). In Book 5, the echo appears to be Apollonius' comparison of the Argo to a hawk (2.932-935) but, as Gordon Williams points out, Virgil uses the simile to describe the *motion* of the ship (the dove now claps its wings furiously, now glides, just as the oarsmen row madly, then cruise).[30] Again the tone is the opposite of the previous dove simile in the *Aeneid*: the tethered bird is terrified, exults to be free, then is shot. All is transformed by a miracle or confirmed by the portent of Acestes' arrow. When this arrow is compared to a shooting star, the image reverses the previously baleful quality that comets have, as in *Georgics* 1.365f., where the shooting star portends the evil that attends the death of Julius Caesar and

Aeneid 2.693f., the comet that appears as Troy falls. The simile of the Trojan boys swimming like dolphins clearly reflects the language used of the playful birds in *Georgics* 1.373-429, but with an ironic and portentous difference, as Michael Putnam has pointed out.[31] In the *Georgics* passage, Virgil is quite careful to make the various birds behave like men, gamboling, arraying like soldiers, talking like priests, down to the mention of birds that had once been human (halcyons and owls). Here in the *Aeneid*, instead of humanizing the animal, Virgil compares the joy of the boys in their darting and interweaving riding exercise to that of animals, the opposite comparison, if not a change in tone. Indeed, even when Virgil changes the tone, he does not always exchange the grave for the light. The blows of Entellus fall like hail at 5.453-460, recalling the simile of the bees descending on their enemy like hail at *Georgics* 4.78-81, but in this case, Virgil trades the generally lighter, mock-heroic description of the bees for the more serious persistent attack by the giant fighter.

These reversals of tone and context are in keeping with the character of Book 5, in which so many events will be reversed later in the poem: the ships will not be saved from burning in Book 8, and Nisus and Euryalus will have a tragic outcome in Book 9. Virgil's reversal of the feeling/tone of his previous *Georgics* and *Aeneid* material is, I think, here the controlling factor that links the similes of Book 5 together and explains the tone of the whole book, which makes something light and gay, the games, out of the funereal occasion. Between the dark beginning in the aftermath of Dido's suicide and the ending with the death of Palinurus comes the lightest of what Pöschl calls the "light" books of the *Aeneid*, and it is not surprising that the reversals of tone and context that we have seen usually alter a heavy or ominous tone to a lighter or more positive one.

Thus the similes in this book, not only by the animation that their frequency lends the action, but also by their explicit difference of mood from their previous occurrence, give the depiction of the games an added lightness that is clearly needed between the tragedy of Dido and the descent to the underworld. Just as the games make something light out of the grimness of the funeral, so Virgil has suited essentially grave and militaristic similes to the rollicking action. That this has been accomplished largely by the explicit re-fashioning of previous Virgilian material has not been recognized and may help us in some measure not only to appreciate Virgil's style but also to better understand his method.

NOTES

1. M.C.J. Putnam, *The Poetry of the* Aeneid (Cambridge, MA, 1965) 65 (= "Unity and Design in *Aeneid* V," *HSCP* 66 [1962] 206).
2. For example, the substitution of a boat race for a chariot race in the games; the competition of old and young, which is unheard of in Homer. See Z. Pavlovskis, "*Aeneid* V: The Old and the Young," *CJ* 71 (1976) 204 n. 41.
3. Putnam, *op. cit.* 75 n. 12.
4. *Ibid.* 76 and 79.
5. *Ibid.* 213 n. 12, 76, 79, 82-83, and 87.
6. Pavlovskis, *op. cit.* 193-205.
7. E.g., the use of the athletic events approved by Augustus for Roman youth and the *Lusus Troiae.* See W. Briggs, "Augustan Athletics and the Games of *Aeneid* V," *Stadion* 1.1 (1977) 267-283.
8. B. Otis, *Virgil: A Study in Civilized Poetry* (Oxford, 1964) 270 n. 1.
9. For convenience and consistency in referring to similes and in compiling my statistics, I have used the list of similes in the *Aeneid* provided by R. Rieks, "Die Gleichnisse Vergils," *ANRW* 2.31, 2 (1981) 1093-1096. I do not consider the brief similes at 242-243 (ship swifter than wind or arrow), 317 (runners like a storm cloud) and 319 (Nisus swifter than wind or thunder).
10. Book 1 has six similes, 2 has eight, 3 has one, 4 has eight, 6 has seven, 7 has seven, 8 has six, 9 has eleven, 10 has fourteen, 11 has nine, and 12 has seventeen.
11. Book 5 has 104 lines devoted to similes out of a total of 871 lines in the whole book, a frequency of one line out of every 8.37 devoted to a simile. The figures for the remaining books are Book 1: 75/756 = 10.08, Book 2: 84/804 = 9.57, Book 3 has only one simile, Book 4: 83/705 = 8.49, Book 6: 75/901 = 12.01, Book 7: 93/817 = 8.78, Book 8: 62/731 = 11.79, Book 9: 141/818 = 5.80, Book 10: 160/908 = 5.67, Book 11: 104/915 = 8.79, and Book 12: 195/952 = 4.88. The average frequency for Books 1-8 is one line out of every 11.77 is a simile; for Books 9-12 the frequency is 5.01; for the entire poem the frequency is 8.35.
12. The remaining 361 lines of Book 5, the storm which diverts the ships to Sicily (1-34), the prelude to the games, up to the snake simile (35-83), the attempted burning of the ships by the Trojan women (604-778), and the death of Palinurus (779-871), involve no similes at all.
13. For example, the ten similes of Book 5 occur within a span of 512 lines (verses 84-595), for a density of one simile every 51.1 lines *over the span,* as opposed to over the course of the whole book. For the rest of the *Aeneid,* the figures are: Book 1: six similes in a span of 454 lines = 75.6, Book 2: eight in 414 = 51.6; Book 3 has only one

simile, Book 4: eight in 607 = 75.7, Book 6: seven in 607 = 86.5, Book 7: seven in 350 = 49.8, Book 8: six in 608 = 101.3, Book 9: eleven in 777 = 70.6, Book 10: fourteen in 715 = 51, Book 11: nine in 752 = 83.5, Book 12: seventeen in 927 = 54.4. The average frequency for *Aeneid* 1-8 is 61.4; for *Aeneid* 9-12 is 64.8.

14. 10.352-610 contain 10 similes and 12.441-926 contain 11 similes. In addition, 9.329-801 and 12.1-480 contain 9 apiece.
15. 23.598-599, Menelaus' heart is gladdened as ripe corn; 692-693, Euryalus jumps like fish when struck; 712-713, wrestlers locked like rafters of a house; 760-762, Odysseus follows Ajax in foot race as closely as a weaving-rod to a young woman at the loom; 845-846, Polypoetes hurls iron as shepherd flinging crook. There are three short similes: 431-432 (discus), 455-456 (moon), and 783-784 (mother).
16. E.g., the comet and Aeneas at 10.270-278 and the hail of battle at 9.669.
17. See Otis, *op. cit.* 271-277 and Putnam, *op. cit.*, 64-104.
18. These also rely heavily on Apollonian models (*Arg.* 2.933-935, 4.1541-1546, 4.933-936).
19. See Briggs, *op. cit.* 267-283.
20. Men are compared to gods in Homer eleven times (*Il.* 2.478; 5.438ff.; 7.208; 11.295; 12.295, 298, 802; 15.605; 20.493; *Ody.* 2.5) and goddesses three times (*Od.* 6.102, 17.37, 19.54). Men are compared to to other men, principally to herdsmen (*Il.* 4.275, 12.451, 13.492, 17.65, 18.162), fathers/sons (*Il.* 23.222; *Ody.* 5.12, 394; 16.17; 17.111, 397) and hunters (*Il.* 11.292, 414, 549; 12.41, 147; 15.581; 17.282). Of the 103 formal similes in the *Aeneid*, three compare a god to a man (1.142-156, 314-320; 8.407-415), three compare men to gods (1.490-504, 6.791-807, 12.324-340) or mythical figures (10.636-644, 11.648-663), and three compare man to man (2.370-385, 5.437-442, 10.397-411) but the comparison of Dares to a besieger in the central position in the scheme, shows the essential distance between the games and the battles to come.
21. W. Briggs, *Narrative and Simile from the Georgics in the Aeneid* (Leiden, 1980) 13-14.
22. E.g., *Il.* 13.178-180, 389-391; 14.414-417; 16.482-484.
23. *Il.* 13.380-391 – 16.482-484; *Arg.* 4.1682-1688; *Aen.* 2.624-631.
24. B.M.W. Knox, "The Serpent and the Flame: The Imagery of the Second Book of the *Aeneid*," *AJP* 71 (1950) 379-400.
25. *Ibid.* 379.
26. "This is clearly a passage (*Geo.* 3.414-439) which was often present in Virgil's mind as he wrote the second book of the *Aeneid*; its presence there may be connected with the dominance which the image of the serpent assumed," Knox, *op. cit.* 399.

27. Putnam, *op. cit.* 73.
28. "A benign snake in classical literature is unusual," Putnam, *ibid.* 67.
29. As at *Il.* 21.493f., Aesch., *Suppl.* 223f.; Eur., *Androm.* 1140f.
30. G. Williams, *Tradition and Originality in Roman Poetry* (Oxford, 1968) 668.
31. Putnam, *op. cit.* 87.

VERGIL, *AENEID* 6:
THE BOUGH BY HADES' GATE

❦

Raymond J. Clark
Memorial University of Newfoundland

It is almost exactly twenty years ago that I first corresponded with Professor Alexander G. McKay. I had already read his *Naples and Campania* and visited the Villa Vergiliana at Cumae, whose continuing success in attracting Vergilians of all nationalities owes so much to his vision of providing a home in Italy for the study of Italy's greatest ancient poet. Acquaintance with this book and the Villa early in my career and a reading of Professor McKay's subsequent publications on Vergil and Campanian topography, together with discussion at times when we have met, have helped stimulate my lifelong interest in Cumaean topography. Long may he flourish and use his remarkable energy and talents to promote Classical Studies at home and abroad.

During a recent re-reading of Vergil's sixth book of the *Aeneid*, the following question occurred to me: did the Golden Bough assist Aeneas in finding and entering within the Gate of Hades? In my book on mortuary journeys, I accepted too readily (as I now believe) the consensus of Vergil's readers. "The Golden Bough," I wrote, "was to be Aeneas' passport to the Underworld. Yet curiously enough, the Bough was never so used."[1]

True, Eitrem had long ago raised the question whether the Golden Bough was a kind of key that unlocked the underworld gate. Might not Hecate, he wondered, have approached the gate as its guardian, to whom the Sibyl corresponded as κλειδοφόρος?[2] It was an attractive idea, but concerning the Sibyl, one for which there is not a shred of evidence. As for Hecate, she approaches the entrance at 6.257f., perhaps to open the gate, because in mythology and cult belief she is regularly attracted to blood.[3] There is then no need for the Sibyl even to knock with the Bough at the entrance gate;[4] for Hecate hears her name invoked (247), and flowing blood to attract her there is in plenty from the sacrifice performed by Aeneas just ten or so verses earlier.

Others have compared the Golden Bough to various beliefs attributed to mistletoe, to which plant Vergil compares the Bough at 6.205-207. On this basis, Corssen claimed that the Bough ought at least to have denoted the entrance to the cave.[5] But the chief objection properly raised to all interpretations of the Bough based on the alleged properties of mistletoe, is that supporting evidence is lacking for ancient Italy or Greece.

Corssen's claim nevertheless raises an interesting question. Did Aeneas *need* guidance to reach the cave entrance to the underworld? On the question of guidance we have Aeneas' own request to the Sibyl. Since, he says, they are in the area where the gate of the Infernal King is said to be, will the Sibyl, as Hecate's priestess in the Avernian grove, please grant him permission to visit his dead father in the realm below, and "teach the way and open the sacred gate?"—

> *unum oro: quando hic inferni ianua regis*
> *dicitur et tenebrosa palus Acheronte refuso,*
> *ire ad conspectum cari genitoris et ora*
> *contingat; doceas iter et sacra ostia pandas.*
>
> 6.106-109

Austin's view[6] on the matter is that Aeneas knows that the entrance to the underworld is at the lake where Acheron surges up, and therefore does not need a signpost thither. This supposition affects his interpretation of verse 109 above: Aeneas' request is for guidance *in* the underworld, not *to* it. Consequently, though Austin does not explicitly say so, verse 109 is an example of ὕστερον πρότερον, where the second request for the Sibyl to explain the way has been brought forward for emphasis, but actually applies to the journey after the entrance gate has been opened.

The Sibyl replies that before descending into the realm that holds his father's ghost, Aeneas must first obtain the Golden Bough (6.136ff.). And this command she prefaces with a warning; Aeneas must overcome two obstacles to his objective, in the form of a forest journey and the passage over the underworld river Cocytus. "In between," she says, "there lies a forest and pitch-black Cocytus flowing and coiling its way around":

> *Tenent media omnia silvae*
> *Cocytusque sinu labens circumvenit atro.*
>
> 6.131-132

Austin's comment on the location (*media omnia*) of this forest is cryptic—"probably the 'whole heartland' of the underworld, surrounded by Cocytus. The usual interpretation is 'all the intervening space' between the upper and lower world."[7] From what has been reported in the previous paragraph, it would appear that Austin felt that since Aeneas knew where to look for Pluto's gate (as distinct from Pluto's palace below the earth), he needed guidance past only unknown obstacles in the lower world, among which he counted the forest journey. Cocytus is, then, envisaged as surrounding a forest within the underworld itself.

The usual interpretation, which Austin rejects, is expressed more fully, and succinctly, by Conington. According to him, the Sibyl's meaning is that "between the place where they are now standing and the shades a pathless forest and the river Cocytus intervene."[8] Since the Sibyl is addressing Aeneas from her Cumaean cave, the pathless forest is or begins in the upperworld. Called Trivia's grove at 6.13, it is thus a chthonic grove, and it extends from the Cumaean acropolis, where the Sibyl prophesies in her "oracular" cave, to lake Avernus, where her "catabatic" cave is located a little under two miles away.[9] In this same forest, in some part unspecified, lies the Golden Bough which Aeneas must first obtain, before he can enter the "covered-up places of earth." Precisely where Aeneas and the Sibyl were standing Conington, writing in the last century, had no means of knowing. For the whereabouts of the oracular cave was unknown until the Italian archaeologist Amedeo Maiuri excavated it on the southern edge of the Cumaean acropolis in 1932.[10] Even so there are good reasons why Conington's interpretation should be regarded as the correct one.

Vergil appears to have had Homer in mind, and to have assigned to the Sibyl what in the *Odyssey* proceeds from the lips of Anticleia's ghost. How had her living son been able to behold her in the realm of shades? she wondered. "For in between are great rivers and dread streams, beginning with Ocean, which cannot be crossed on foot, but only by boat":

> μέσσῳ γὰρ μεγάλοι ποταμοὶ καὶ δεινὰ ῥέεθρα,
> Ὠκεανὸς μὲν πρῶτα, τὸν οὔ πως ἔστι περῆσαι
> πεζὸν ἐόντ', ἢν μή τις ἔχῃ ἐυεργέα νῆα.
>
> *Od.* 11.157-159

Vergil typically evokes these Homeric reverberations in a new context. For Aeneas has not yet crossed the great divide. He is in Trivia's chthonic grove still, standing before the doors of the Sibyl's oracular cave. It is clear that for the difficulties of Odysseus reaching his Hades across the ocean and infernal waters, the Latin poet has substituted Aeneas' journey through the chthonic forest in the upperworld and the passage of the underworld river Cocytus. Aeneas' forest journey is thus put on a par with Odysseus' ocean-crossing. And the task within it of fetching the Golden Bough is conceived as an elaborate ordeal and test, comparable perhaps to the fetching of the Golden Fleece from another oak[11] by another epic hero.

Thus Aeneas' double-request to be both shown the way and have opened for him the portal of the underworld is not taken ὕστερον πρότερον by the Sibyl. The forest journey on the approach to Avernus is part of "the way" to Anchises just as surely as is the journey beyond the gate of Dis. Butler, who anticipates Austin in confining the "intervening space" to the underworld, nevertheless confessed to being puzzled. "Of these trackless forests [in the lower world] there is no [subsequent] mention, nor are the woods on the further side of Styx [444, 638, 658] spoken of as other than the dwelling-places of shades, or mentioned with any suggestion of horror." Accordingly, he wondered "whether these *silvae* are Vergil's invention, or [are] derived from some lost Nekuia."[12] The conclusion seems inescapable that these forests of the lower world are rather the invention of commentators.

We now face a real difficulty—perhaps one which the relocation of the forest was designed to circumvent. Conington writes: "Possibly, as Peerlkamp thinks, [Vergil] may have intended to make the forest easier of entrance than of exit; but in the subsequent description the forest is not made an obstacle at all: Aeneas goes through it under the guidance of the Sibyl without a hint of difficulty, and the only real bar is the passage of the river, which the possession of the bough enables him to overcome."[13]

The substance of Conington's allegation is that Vergil has failed to carry out his original intention of making the forest journey an ordeal for Aeneas. This claim is hardly right, but to my knowledge it has not been challenged. To begin with, the affirmation that Aeneas "goes through" the forest without difficulty misses the point. True, after obtaining the Bough, Aeneas leaves the forest easily enough at verse 212 to rejoin the burial of Misenus, which was also enjoined upon Aeneas by the Sibyl. The search for the Golden Bough (in verses 185-211) in fact interrupts the Misenus episode (156-235). I have argued elsewhere that this arrangement helps divert the reader's attention from the topographical awkwardness over the finding of the body at Cumae where Aeneas landed (Vergil had transferred thither the drowning of Misenus from among the rocks of Porto di Miseno in the Bay of Baiae, the traditional site) and the place of its burial (near the traditional scene of drowning) below the mountain named after him some five miles away (*monte sub aerio, qui nunc Misenus ab illo / dicitur*, 234f.).[14] The arrangement works well, but there was a price to be paid: Aeneas leaves the grove after finding the Bough. When he re-enters the forest, as he does at verse 236, he makes directly for the catabatic cave at the lakeside, where the Sibyl awaits him. The sacrifices are performed, and they pass into the opened cave. Aeneas' *true exit* from the forest—hardly an easy one!—is by way of the awesome Gate of Death.

To say that Aeneas goes through the forest "under the guidance of the Sibyl without a hint of difficulty" is tenable only if one discounts the episode of the Golden Bough as though it were an ordeal independent of the forest journey, or in other words, if one presupposes that the discovery of the Golden Bough had nothing to do with the Gate of Hades through which Aeneas (unlike other mortals) leaves the forest. For the Sibyl makes it clear to Aeneas and to us, the readers, that for the discovery of the Bough the forest will offer the *greatest possible* difficulty. The odds against success are as great as the forest is huge, and Aeneas knows it— *aspectans silvam immensam* (6.186). Not only that, but of the Bough Conington himself remarks (on verse 138) that it is "as if the whole forest conspired to hide it." Together with the tree on which it grows (*latet arbore opaca / aureus ... ramus*, 136-137), all the others in the valley, as though acting in concert, contrive to close their shade upon it (*hunc tegit omnis / lucus et obscuris claudunt convallibus umbrae*, 138-139). To succeed, Aeneas needs far more than the Sibyl's guidance through this intimidating wood.[15] It comes, through divine intervention in answer to his prayers (186ff.), in the form of his mother's doves. Flying ahead of him, they guide him "to the jaws of pungent Avernus" (*ad fauces grave olentis Averni*, 201), where, following with his gaze their swift flight upwards through the "clear air" (*liquidum aera*, 202), he sees through the branches the gleam of the Golden Bough.

As for the presumption that the Golden Bough has nothing to do with the Gate of Hades, let us observe that the reader, though not conscious of magic, is left in no doubt that the forest conspired to conceal the underworld entrance just as surely as it did the Bough. Vergil says that it was "protected" by the darkness both of the lake and of the wood: (*spelunca* . . . / *tuta lacu nigro nemorumque tenebris*, 237-238). After his mother's doves had led Aeneas in quest of the Bough "to the jaws of pungent Avernus" (201), how thereafter did Aeneas find the cave? Could the Golden Bough have marked it? Were both in the same place within the Avernian forest?

The received view is that the Golden Bough is in a place separate from the cave entrance to Hades' kingdom. If I again quote from Austin's commentary, as representing the received view in this instance, it is because its exegesis of the issue in question has the virtue of clarifying for the reader more than any other the relevant features of this mysterious landscape that Vergil immortalizes in his poetic description. The conclusion of a long note is that the Golden Bough "grows on a tree at the entrance to the crater, before the lake is reached; the cave is within the crater, but all the countryside is wooded (188), and more densely within the crater (238)."[16] The following note on the smell of Lake Avernus adds that "the doves do not fly over it (the poisonous lake); they go only *ad fauces*."

This representation of the scene raises three interlocking questions which need to be answered before my own reconstruction of the scene is given. First, must the Bough be imagined to be at the entrance to the crater—that is to say in a place separate from the cave within the crater? There is no compelling reason why it should. Since the Bough lies concealed within a valley (see 138-139 quoted above), its most likely position is deep down beneath the crater's high wooded rim, assuredly on the inner ridge to judge from the fact that the mephitic fumes from the *fauces*, to which Aeneas is brought, affect the area within the crater.

We have already answered the second question, namely: is the forest denser around the cave (238) within the crater than wherever the Bough is elsewhere? The Bough ought not to be imagined as lying apart from the cave for this reason, since both alike are deeply hidden (138f., 238). When Aeneas enters the forest and hopes that the doves will show him where the Bough casts its shade upon the ground (195f.), it is clear that he is in a comparatively open glade. But they lead him a considerable distance from this spot into a vale where no sunlight penetrates, and they show him the Bough by other means than he had supposed they would.

Thirdly, do the doves stop short of entering the area of poisonous exhalations? The answer is problematical because no sooner have the birds brought Aeneas to the "jaws (*fauces*) of foul-smelling Avernus" (201) than they are said to fly quickly upwards through "bright, clear, pure" (*liquidum*, 202) air to where the Bough is growing. Servius offers a desperate solution: they fly up quickly (*celeres*) to escape the stench. Had Servius read on, he would have seen what he might have guessed, that the fumes rise heavenward (*ad convexa*, 241). Austin merely calls the pure air and the stench "a pretty contrast";[17] but one suspects that the contrast has had a profound effect upon his entire explanation of the scene. He remarks that the doves "go only *ad fauces*," to make the point that they do not cross the lake (where the air is imagined to be bad). But he seems to imply that they go *not even* to where the effect of the *fauces* is felt. The unwritten logic seems to be that if the *fauces* make the crater poisonous, the tree bearing the Golden Bough must be outside it, or else death ensues. It is therefore placed at the entrance to the crater (and not within it).

The relationship between the poisonous exhalations, the *fauces*, the lake, the cave, and the tree bearing the Bough, all come together in the following passage:

> *spelunca alta fuit vastoque immanis hiatu,*
> *scrupea, tuta lacu nigro nemorumque tenebris,*
> *quam super haud ullae poterant impune volantes*
> *tendere iter pennis: talis sese halitus atris*
> *faucibus effundens super ad convexa ferebat.*
> *(unde locum Grai dixerunt nomine Aornon.)*
>   6.237-242

There was a deep rugged cave, stupendous and yawning wide, protected by a lake of black water and the glooming forest. Over this lake no birds could wing a straight course without harm, so poisonous the breath which streamed up from those black jaws and rose to the vault of the sky; and that is why the Greeks named this place 'Aornos, the Birdless.'

This translation by the eminent Vergilian scholar Jackson Knight[18] yields to tradition—but departs from Vergil. Not the lake, but the cave, is what Vergil says birds cannot fly over with impunity—*quam super* refers to *spelunca*. Hence in the interpolated verse 242, the "place" (*locus*), and not the "lake" (*lacus*), is rightly glossed as Aornos, Vergil's view presumably being that the lake acquired its name from the property of the place, as though as a gateway to the Netherworld the cave has primacy. Certainly it is from the cave's own mouth that Hell's poisonous breath escapes—not from any unspecified fissure (*fauces*) somewhere in the crater, nor even from the lake itself, which is the source of the poisonous exhalations in the traditional belief repudiated by Lucretius.[19] The sole conclusion that satisfies the text is that the Avernian cave, the "black jaws" (*atris / faucibus*) of 240f., the "jaws of pungent Avernus" (*fauces grave olentis Averni*) of 201, and the "gate of the infernal king" (*inferni ianua regis*) of 106 are synonyms arranged paratactically to denote the same passageway, the jaws (or throat) of Dis (or of Orcus or Pluto or Hades) being imagined as a vertical fissure in the ground beyond and inside the opening of the cave.[20]

As though to suggest that the cave embodies a voracious throat, it is described as having a gaping mouth (*vasto ... immanis ... hiatu* [237])—imagery that is later applied to the Hydra, whose fifty mouths (*quinquaginta ... immanis ... hiatibus* [576]) seem ready to swallow any who might try to leave Tartarus. Even the reader of these two verses, remarkable as they are for their open "a" sounds, is forced in speaking them to open his jaws and throat in imitation of the imagery. Furthermore, the concept of jaws which are the Infernal King's breathing holes, from which pestilential (mephitic) vapours rise, and through which the Netherworld is reached, is typically Vergilian, as is their setting beside a lake, or spring rising from Hades in the depth of a dark wood.[21]

Far from journeying, then, through the forest under the guidance of the Sibyl, Aeneas is guided by her neither to the Bough, nor the underworld entrance. Like some hierophant, she teaches the way by warning Aeneas of the difficulties ahead, and she makes clear what he must first do. Guided by his mother's doves to where it grows within the Avernian crater beside the noisome jaws of Dis, through which he will later pass, Aeneas plucks the Bough and carries it to the Sibyl's home: *et vatis portat sub tecta Sibyllae* (211). What is more natural than that the Golden Bough, which belongs to Proserpine (142) and serves essentially as Aeneas' passport to the underworld, should grow where Vergil placed it, by Hades' Gate, and that Aeneas should take this plant to the cave to which it is adjacent? There he gives it to Hecate's priestess, the Sibyl, who has, we can presume, made her own way thither and is waiting within ready to receive it.[22]

One problem is left to be solved within this reconstruction of the scene, namely: since the Bough is in the immediate vicinity of Hell's breath, why does Vergil specify that the air, here of all places, is clear and bright and pure (*liquidum*)? Is it so *because* of the Golden Bough? Can the Golden Bough have had the power to dispel the mist and to offer divine protection to mortals called by Fate to obtain it?

In my earlier investigation into the traditions which might have affected Vergil's conception of the Bough, I made the suggestion, whose implications I did not then realize for the present context, that behind the Golden Bough the ghost of Homer's *moly* peers through.[23] It is described as a black root with a flower like milk, though Pliny says, interestingly enough, that later Greek sources represent its flower as golden.[24] It is difficult for mortals to obtain, we are told, but was uprooted easily enough by Hermes, being a god, who gave it to Odysseus on his way through the enchanted grove to Circe's palace (*Od*. 10.302-306). Aeneas obtains *his* plant himself within the chthonic grove of Hecate, though not without divine intervention to show him where to look, and not without being told by Hecate's priestess that it is impossible for mortals to pull by their own strength, unless called by the Fates. Vergil, after all, was creating a new hero of Destiny who, unlike the earlier catabatic heroes portrayed in the *Aeneid*, possesses impeccable credentials. That more of the events in the Aeaean grove should have influenced those in the Avernian than have been thought hitherto is surprising perhaps, but the influence is entirely credible. For Circe is one of Vergil's models for the Sibyl's hierophantic role. She it is who prescribes for Odysseus his ocean-crossing, to which (as we saw above) the forest journey corresponds in Aeneas' own journey to the World of Shades.

If the purity of the air in the presence of the Bough is a hint that Proserpine's plant acts as a prophylactic against the noxious emanations from the chthonic cave, the idea has a good literary precedent in Hermes' *moly*. Hermes bids Odysseus take the plant as a protection against Circe's harmful drugs, after which he is to draw his sword and rush upon her as though to kill her (*Od*. 10.287). It is a curious fact that the chthonic god never tells us, his audience, what Odysseus is to do with the magical plant. Nor is it so much as mentioned again, even when its powers are needed and presumably employed.[25] Vergil similarly does not explain to his readers how the Bough is used either. Presumably mere possession of it is sufficient to ensure Aeneas safe passage through the jaws of Hell. In the course of which the Sibyl, Hermes-like, bids him draw his sword (260), and almost as soon rebukes him for Odysseus-like behaviour in rushing against the ghosts as though to kill them (290-294). It is a brilliant stroke recalling at once the Odyssean passage and an episode in Heracles' descent.[26] The scene of the Golden Bough is brilliant too, on a grander scale. The finding of the Bough beside the cave within the crater and its divine aura of protection in warding off Hell's noxious breath, is a fitting fulfillment to Vergil's original intention to make the forest easier of entrance than of exit and as well, the first barrier for the mortal visitor on the road to Hades' kingdom.

NOTES

1. R.J. Clark, *Catabasis: Vergil and the Wisdom-Tradition* (Amsterdam 1979) 210; cf. 186.
2. S. Eitrem, "La Sibylle de Cumes et Virgile," *Symbolae Osloenses* 24 (1945) 95-97 and 103f., referring to Hecate's function as guardian of the gate to ῥηξιπύλη (*P.G.M.* 4.2751) and προθυραία (Procl., *Hymn* 6.2.14, cf. *P.G.M.* 4.2719 κλῦθι διαξεύξασα πύλας ἄλυτος ἀδάμαντος). See also T. Kraus, *Hekate* (Heidelberg, 1960), 106 on Hecate as "Schützerin von Tür und Tor."
3. Perhaps to drink it: Hecate is called αἱμόποτις in the *Orph. hymn* 294.53 Abel. Her attraction to blood is attested early, e.g., Theocr. 2.12f., describing her habit of searching for the blood of fresh corpses in their tombs.
4. The motif of knocking on the underworld door is as early as the Sumerian myth of Inanna's Descent, belonging to the second millennium B.C. (S.N. Kramer, *Journal of Cuneiform Studies* 5 [1951] 1ff.), and in Greece the motif is parodied by Dionysus' banging on the underworld door in Aristophanes, *Frogs* 460ff., 503ff.
5. P. Corssen, "Die Sibylle im sechsten Buch der Aeneis," *Sokrates* N.F. 1 (1913) 8. With Homer's *Nekyia* in mind, he describes the sacrifice at the lakeside (*Aen*. 6.243ff.) as a "blosses Ornament" (since there are no ghosts to drink the blood), which nevertheless "das Motif des Mistelzweiges unterdrückt" (13f.). As we have seen (n. 3 above), the sacrifice is not entirely an ornamental mechanism for Aeneas' descent, for its blood brings Hecate to the entrance.
6. R.G. Austin, *P. Vergili Maronis Aeneidos Liber Sextus* (Oxford, 1977) 79f. (in the course of discussing *Aen*. 6.126).
7. *Ibid*. 81.
8. J. Conington, *P. Vergili Maronis Opera*[4] revd. H. Nettleship (London, 1884) 2.442 on *Aen*. 6.131.

9. Vergil has conflated in the single figure of the Cumaean Sibyl the roles of prophet and underworld guide. As prophetess she is priestess of Apollo and her cult site is the "oracular" cave of *Aen*. 6.9-11 and 42ff.; in her chthonic role she is priestess of Hecate-Trivia, and the "catabatic" (or underworld) cave is that described at *Aen*. 6.237ff., on which Servius comments: *qua ad inferos descendebatur, non ubi fuerat Sibylla vaticinata*. On the conflation and confusion of these caves in later tradition see *Classica et Mediaevalia* 30 (1969) 300ff.; and on the Sibyl's cult ancestry see now H.W. Parke, ed. B.C. McGing, *Sibyls and Sibylline Prophecy in Classical Antiquity* (London, New York, 1988) 71-99.

10. A. Maiuri, "'*Horrendae secreta Sibyllae*': Nuova esplorazione dell' antro cumano," *B.S.M.* 3 (1932) 28.

11. With *Aen*. 6.209, cf. Ap. Rhod., *Argon*. 2.404f., 1266ff., and 4.14f., 162.

12. H.E. Butler, *The Sixth Book of the Aeneid* (Oxford, 1920) 110 on *Aen*. 6.131ff.

13. Conington, *op. cit.* 2.442 on *Aen*. 6.131.

14. R.J. Clark, "Misenus and the Cumaean Landfall: Originality in Vergil's Use of Topography and Tradition," *TAPA* 107 (1977) 63-71. On the topographical and archaeological aspects of this site (with Caieta and Palinurum) see A.G. McKay's excellent article "Aeneas' Landfalls in Hesperia," *G&R* 14 (1967) 8.

15. On the intimidating nature of "la forêt sauvage" in Vergil, see Joël Thomas, *Structures de l'imaginaire dans l'Énéide* (Paris, 1981) 83ff.

16. Austin, *op. cit.* 98f. on *Aen*. 6.201 (a note enriched by C. Hardie).

17. *Ibid.* 99 on *Aen*. 6.202.

18. W.F. Jackson Knight, *Virgil: The* Aeneid (Harmondsworth, 1956) 154.

19. Lucretius says that birds fall

> *In terram, si forte ita fert natura locorum,*
> *Aut in aquam, si forte lacus substratus Avernist.*
> *Is locus est Cumas apud, acri sulfure montes*
> *Oppleti calidis ubi fumant fontibus aucti.*
>
> De rer. nat. 6.745-748

20. That the god's jaws, or throat, extend downwards into the lower realm is shown from verse 273, *vestibulum ante ipsum primisque in faucibus Orci*, where (changing the imagery) Vergil also equates Orcus' jaws at its lower reaches with the gateway of the vestibule of his infernal palace; here the Frightful Shapes have their abode. For *fauces* in a vertical sense elsewhere in Vergil see *Geo.* 4.467, *Aen*. 7.570.

21. Perhaps developed from Ennius if the *Plutonium* described in the Ampsanctus valley at *Aen*. 7.563ff. (bearing many resemblances to

the scenery described in *Aeneid* 6) was transferred by Vergil from Ennius' *Plutonium* in the valley of the Nar, on which see now O. Skutsch, *The Annals of Quintus Ennius* (Oxford, 1985) 392ff. (frags. x-xiii).

22. The usual view is that Aeneas revisits the Sibyl in her Cumaean cave, but why should Aeneas go out of his way to take his "passport through the infernal region" to the Sibyl's "oracular" cave? Cumae is not even on the way to Misenum from the lakeside of Avernus. The fact that the Sibyl is here called *vates* is not an objection *either* to her being Hecate's priestess *or* therefore to the identification of the cave given in the text (on the distinction between the catabatic and oracular caves see n. 9 above); for it is to be observed that in blending her dual functions Vergil never allows her to lose her Apolline character. Even at the moment of descent, when she is incontestably in the catabatic cave, she is said to be "in frenzied state" (*furens*, 262) displaying behaviour more appropriate to her prophetic afflatus as a medium at Cumae (cf. *Aen.* 6.100-102).

23. R.J. Clark, *op. cit.* (above, n. 1) 211.

24. Pliny, *HN* 25.26: *Graeci auctores florem eius luteum pinxere, cum Homerus candidum scripserit.* Cf. Hom., *Od.* 10.304.

25. D.L. Page, *Folklore in Homer's Odyssey* (Cambridge, MA, 1973) 55.

26. It is worth bearing in mind that the Homeric passage may be itself an adaptation of an early version of the Heracles *catabasis*. For extant versions, see the discussion in *Phoenix* 24 (1970), esp. 245 and 252 n. 22.

AENEAS IN PURGATORY

Colin M. Wells
Trinity University

Sandy McKay is a scholar of many interests, who has written and lectured on so many subjects with such elegance and lucidity, that he deserves more than any other Canadian scholar of his generation the verdict, *nihil quod tetigit non ornavit*. To honour him with an article on Vergil is a daunting challenge, particularly for one with no pretensions to being a literary scholar. What follows derives, therefore, not from exhaustive study of recent Vergilian scholarship, but from chance concatenations of reading and teaching. To say that it is not easy to say anything original about Vergil is not even original. The best one can hope for is to say something that is new to one's own experience.

Vergil is the most complex of poets, who thus speaks to our own complexities, *cor ad cor loquitur*, so that the reader who comes back to Vergil again and again finds something new each time. When I was younger, my favourite Latin poet was Horace, and perhaps he still is, but I no longer read or teach him with the same expectation of new insights. I am comfortable with him, whereas Vergil has the power to disturb. I remember hearing the late R.D. Williams, in the last year of his life, in Ottawa as external examiner for a thesis on the *Georgics*, saying that he constantly reread Vergil and that he had found in each decade of his life, as his experience of life had deepened, a deeper understanding of Vergil. Whatever age he was, Vergil spoke to him as a contemporary, unlike Catullus, whom he said he still read with enjoyment, but without getting any more out of him than at the age of 18. And this I think is true: Catullus, like Keats, is a clever adolescent, mawkish, self-absorbed, full of adolescent self-pity. One responds to and remembers the poetry, because it is so musical, so apparently inevitable, so adhesive, but it has no depth: it is Tschaikovsky, where Vergil is Beethoven.

I happened upon Le Goff's book, *The Birth of Purgatory* (see note 4), just as I was rereading the *Aeneid*, Book 6, for a Latin literature class, whence one of these "chance concatenations." Does Vergil's account of the underworld help to shape the Christian doctrine of Purgatory? Does Aeneas, himself, in any sense pass through a purgatorial experience? Few of Vergil's works are more consistently dense, more capable of being read on many different levels, than Book 6. Let us follow Aeneas on his descent. First of all come the preparations: Apollo's temple, the sacrifice of the seven bulls and the seven sheep, the Sibyl, and the Golden Bough (lines 1-263), all of which stirred the Middle Ages to prodigies of allegorizing. Bernard Silvestris, for instance, makes much of the seven sheep. Either they are the seven members of the body, that is to say, two hands, two feet, the torso, the head, and the genitals, or alternatively "there are also said to be seven sheep which pertain to simplicity and gentleness: they are innocence, friendship, concord, piety, religion, affection, and gentleness."[1] The one thing they are not, is sheep.

Thereafter comes the poet's invocation to the gods, *di, quibus imperium est animarum* . . ., and the marvellously atmospheric descent, *ibant obscuri sola sub nocte per umbram* . . . (264-294). Thus Aeneas and the Sibyl reach Acheron, where Charon plies his trade, and see the dead, like leaves in autumn, who flock to seek passage. Aeneas is disturbed by the commotion, but the Sibyl explains that the unburied must wander the banks of the river for a hundred years before they are allowed to cross (294-332). This, of course, accounts for the presence there of those who died at sea, including Leucaspis, Orontes, and Aeneas' old helmsman, Palinurus, with whom they have a lengthy conversation (333-383). The Sibyl cheers him up by promising that Cape Palinurus shall be named after him, and then produces the Golden Bough, which persuades Charon to ferry her and Aeneas across; Cerberus is drugged to sleep, and they swiftly put the river behind them (384-425).

The place where they now find themselves is the abode of the souls of dead infants, of the unjustly condemned, and of suicides (426-439). This combination of categories has surprised some scholars but as Conington says, "There is no suffering in this part of the shades; there is merely the absence of the enjoyment of life," and those who find themselves here "are exempted alike from reward and punishment."[2] The parallel with the Christian concept of Limbo is so obvious that it is not surprising that commentators, including both Conington and Williams, do not hesitate to use the term, while recognising that in Vergil's account there are, as Williams puts it, "eschatological inconsistencies."[3] There is no suggestion in Vergil that this is a place of temporary abode, a transition between one state and another. An alternative version, followed by Tertullian and Servius, had it that people who found themselves here had to stay only for the rest of their natural lives, but that is not in Vergil's text, where the denizens appear to be there for all eternity, like the unbaptized babes in the traditional Christian Limbo.

Thereafter, Aeneas and his guide pass through the Lugentes Campi, the Mourning Fields, where they see the souls of those who died for love, *quos durus amor crudeli tabe peredit*, including Dido, reunited with her first husband, Sychaeus, and then they enter the most distant and secluded fields, *arva . . . ultima quae bello clari secreta frequentant* (477-478), where they meet the dead heroes, including Deiphobus, with whom Aeneas has a long chat, until the Sibyl suggests that it is time to be getting on, whereupon Deiphobus, picking up the cue, urges Aeneas to leave behind the past and turn to the future: *i, decus, i, nostrum: melioribus utere fatis* (440-547). They have gone as far as they can in this part of the underworld, where do they go next? In a lengthy speech, the Sibyl sets out the tripartite division of the underworld, for here is where the road divides, the left fork leading to Tartarus, which is Hell, and reserved for the great sinners like Tityos and Ixion, whom Aeneas is not allowed to visit (*nulli fas casto sceleratum insistere limen*, 548-627). The right fork, on the other hand, leads to Elysium, a place of great beauty, *devenere locos laetos et amoena virecta / fortunatorum nemorum sedesque beatas*, described at some length (628-678), where dwell the *magnanimi heroes, nati melioribus annis*.

Here it is that Aeneas finds his father, Anchises, who explains the doctrine of the purification and transmigration of souls, in language which often recalls Lucretius, although the doctrine is not his. The whole passage has much exercised commentators seeking to explain its obscurities and reconcile its ambiguities, a task which Conington hopefully suggests Vergil himself would have accomplished if he had lived to finish his poem:

> *igneus est ollis vigor et caelestis origo*
> *seminibus, quantum non noxia corpora tardant*
> *terrenique hebetant artus moribundaque membra.*
> *hinc metuunt cupiuntque, dolent gaudentque, neque auras*
> *dispiciunt clausae tenebris et carcere caeco.*
> *quin et supremo cum lumine vita reliquit,*
> *non tamen omne malum miseris nec funditus omnes*
> *corporeae excedunt pestes, penitusque necesse est*
> *multa diu concreta modis inolescere miris.*
> *ergo exercentur poenis veterumque malorum*
> *supplicia expendunt: aliae panduntur inanes*
> *suspensae ad ventos, aliis sub gurgite vasto*
> *infectum eluitur scelus aut exuritur igni.*
> *quisque suos patimur manes.*
>   Aen. 6.730-743

This is no longer a form of Limbo. Indeed, as Le Goff points out, following Norden, this passage more than any other prefigures certain aspects of the Christian doctrine of Purgatory, having in common "the mixture of pleasure and pain, the dim perception of Heaven's light, the references to imprisonment, the detailing of penalties, the combination of expiation and purification, and the idea of purification by fire."[4] Only after this purgation of their sins are the souls set free in Elysium, or Paradise, as in orthodox Catholic doctrine, although there is nothing remotely Christian in the idea that some of them are destined to be reborn on earth. It is from amongst the latter that Anchises shows Aeneas the future heroes of Rome (679-892), culminating in the famous *tu Marcellus eris* (883). This parade of Roman worthies is meant to give Aeneas something to live for, to make him feel that the sacrifice of giving up Dido was worthwhile. Does it succeed? Anchises does the honours in the manner of a conscientious tour guide, *per singula duxit*, and lays on the pep talk pretty thick, *incenditque animum famae venientis amore*. Aeneas says not a word. We are given no indication of whether he thinks the sacrifice was indeed worth it, and if he thinks his father is talking a lot of rot, he is too *pius* to say so.

And then, somewhat abruptly, and to the bewilderment of many commentators, Anchises ushers him out and up to the world above by the gate of ivory, the gate of false dreams (893-901). There is no ambiguity about it. We learn that there are two separate gates, *geminae portae*, one of them the gate of horn, the gate of true dreams, which was apparently available, but this is not the one Aeneas takes:

> *altera candenti perfecta nitens elephanto,*
> *sed falsa ad caelum mittunt insomnia manes.*
> *hic ibi tum natum Anchises unaque Sibyllam*
> *prosequitur dictis portaque emittit eburna.*
>
> Aen. 6.895-898

It happens so abruptly: once Anchises stops talking, it only takes nine lines to get Aeneas back to the ships, and he still says not one word. This suggests a certain coldness on his part. When he saw Dido a little earlier, he was not silent then. He sees her bleeding, physically and emotionally, *recens a vulnere Dido* (450), and he not only addresses her, but addresses her in strongly emotional language, as *infelix Dido*, pleading, *invitus, regina, tuo de litore cessi*, begging her to accept that he did not mean it, *nec credere quivi / hunc tantum tibi me discessu ferre dolorem*. But he cannot get through to her, the wound is still too fresh: *illa solo fixos oculos aversa tenebat*. She will not look at him, and goes back to her husband, Sychaeus, with whom she is reunited, and who comforts her, *respondet curis*. Aeneas feels the unfairness of it and grieves with her (475-476): *nec minus Aeneas casu concussus iniquo / prosequitur lacrimis longe et miseratur euntem*. If Book 4 had left us in any doubt as to the "depth and sincerity of his feelings for Dido," Book 6 removes it.[5]

The link between this farewell to Dido and his being ushered by Anchises through the ivory gate is brought out by the parallelism of both phraseology and rhythm in the the key lines, *prosequitur lacrimis longe et miseratur euntem* and *prosequitur dictis portaque emittit eburna*. Surely we are meant to understand that the vision of future glory which Anchises has shown him is indeed a false dream, and not worth having, compared with what he has lost by losing Dido. When he left her, in obedience to the concept of duty which his father had taught him, he did not yet realise what the price would be, *nec credere quivi* ... Now, when his father says in effect, "well done; here are all the kingdoms of the world and the glory thereof for your descendants," and Aeneas does not reply, are we not meant to read a meaning into his silence? *Pietas* would not let him say, even if he were thinking it, "I no longer accept your values, and now that I know what it costs, I don't think it's worth it; keep your promises of glory, I still want Dido." What are all the kingdoms of the world to him, when he might say, with Donne, "She is all kingdoms and all princes I, nothing else is"? Marcellus is not an adequate substitute.

Aeneas' concept of duty had never commended itself to Dido. She does not applaud his desertion. Neither when he left her, nor when he saw her again in the underworld, could Aeneas make her accept the logic of his decision. In the underworld (467-468) it is:

> *talibus Aeneas ardentem et torva tuentem*
> *lenibat dictis animum lacrimasque ciebat . . .*

Earlier, in Carthage, in Book 4 (393-396), and in very similar words, it had been:

> *at pius Aeneas, quamquam lenire dolentem*
> *solando cupit et dictis avertere curas,*
> *multa gemens magnoque animum labefactus amore*
> *iussa tamen divum exsequitur classemque revisit.*

It is clear that he himself is torn. Williams, commenting on this passage, translates *magno . . . amore* as "shaken to the heart by his great love," and stresses the importance of the epithet *pius*: "*Pietas* is why he must leave . . . It may be that many . . . would wish that *pietas* had not prevailed, but . . . it has done so. We might translate 'But Aeneas, because of duty . . .'" There is no doubt that the journey through the underworld has been for Aeneas himself a Purgatory, in the course of which he has had to face up to the consequences of his sins and weaknesses, for even if we excuse him for abandoning Dido, pleading the superior claim of duty, and even if we sympathise with his very human and understandable reluctance to face her openly with his decision (it would not have been an easy interview), he is guilty of monumental weakness, and knows it. But is it not possible that he has now, at the end of the journey, come to a different concept of duty? Might he not now say, with E.M. Forster, "If I have to choose between betraying my country and betraying my friend, I hope to God that I have the courage to betray my country"?

Where does Vergil stand on all this? With at least a part of himself, surely, he is among those who "would wish that *pietas* had not prevailed." He knew the human cost, *tantae molis erat Romanam condere gentem*, and it may be that he wishes us to consider the possibility that Aeneas, if he had the choice over again, would now choose differently. A concept of duty acquired secondhand from the gods via his father, and a hope of future glory, are indeed *falsa insomnia*, compared with the happiness that he had experienced with Dido, if in fact we believe that happiness has any importance in life. Wisdom is often learned too late from the suffering that a wrong choice based on false values brings, a choice in which we go contrary to our deepest self and learn too late that we can never go back again. So Lind speaks of "self-knowledge through suffering, the full realization of one's own strength and weakness through a deep and tragic emotional experience," and so too Griffin counts "the destructive cost of imperial destiny, both for the vanquished and still more for the victor."[6] It is the essence of the Christian concept of Purgatory, that we must suffer in order to accept our faults, and no suffering can be greater than the knowledge that we have hurt those that we love and cut ourselves off from God, not through conscious evil, which few of us have the strength for, but through weakness and a failure to understand, *nec credere quivi* . . .

Vergil is a poet, not a theologian, and in his account of the underworld, we should not ask for complete clarity and precision. It was to take the Christian Church many centuries of the development of its doctrine before it came up with a coherent theology of the world to come. Williams, commenting on 6.893f., suggests that the whole underworld is "in a sense . . . a dream or vision of Aeneas, personal to him," and this is an obvious modern, rational, post-Freudian way of explaining it. So too, he suggests that at another level Vergil perhaps in this account "symbolises the uncertainty of his own religious vision, a dimly seen and groping concept, based on hope not faith, of virtue rewarded and suffering to some extent explained. This is far indeed from the gloom of Homer's ghosts, but far too from the certainty of religious conviction on which Milton's *Paradise Lost* is based."[7]

Uncertain or not, Vergil's striving to express the profundity of human experience in matters of suffering and death and in the hope of eventual redemption echoes through Late Antiquity and the Middle Ages, from St. Augustine to Dante and beyond. "The tone and temper of Virgil penetrated into the very heart and soul of the boyish Augustine . . . from Virgil Augustine inherited the imagery of glory and of desolation . . . it is easy for Augustine and his disciple Newman to respond sympathetically to the sadness of the Roman poet for the world as it is and to identify themselves in part with his vision of future peace." And Newman himself speaks of Vergil's "giving utterance, as the voice of Nature herself, to that pain and weariness, yet hope of better things, which is the experience of her children in every time."⁸ Jerome cites Vergil repeatedly, using Dido as a dreadful warning to widows against remarrying.⁹ Helen Waddell notes the sensitivity to Vergil to be found at Cluny in the tenth century, which nonetheless recognises the dangers of his "luxurious eloquence," and the ultimate Vergilian was Vilgardus of Ravenna in the next century, who "taught openly that the words of the poets are in all things worthy of belief, even as Holy Writ, but expiated that heresy in the fire."¹⁰ We can scarcely overestimate Vergil's hold on the imagination of the mediaeval scholar, and it should not surprise us to find that Vergil's imagery influenced, not only such persons' individual conception of this world and the next, but also the official imagery of the mediaeval Church. It would be more surprising if it did not.

The intellectual concept and the poetic imagery of Purgatory developed over the centuries. As Protestants used to be quick to point out, it cannot be deduced from the New Testament alone. Augustine, whom Le Goff calls "the true father of Purgatory," saw it as the same place as Hell where, however, those enduring *ignis purgatorius* suffer for a limited time only. Only later did it come to be seen as a place separate from both Hell and Heaven, and not until the second half of the twelfth century, as for instance in Aquinas (died 1274), had doctrine evolved so far as "to set aside a distinctive location for Purgatory."¹¹ The imagery and topography which we find in the intervening period, in the Vision of Charles the Fat in the late ninth century, or in Alberic of Settefratri in the first half of the twelfth, or in the Irishman Tnugdal in that same century,¹² are as vaguely conceptualised as Vergil's underworld. By the second half of the twelfth century, however, and the early part of the thirteenth, Purgatory is firmly established as an actual place, with the Papal Indulgence of the Jubilee Year 1300 appearing as an unmistakeable landmark.¹³ We start to find a new emphasis on prayers for the dead and liturgical commemoration, and Dante, who began the *Divine Comedy* around 1308, already has the theology and topography of Purgatory well mapped out.¹⁴ As his guide, he chooses Vergil, but in order that Vergil may qualify, Dante feels it necessary to purify him "from more than one stain which made him obnoxious to Christian eyes," making him "far more definitely Christian than ... in the medieval tradition," so that, for instance, Vergil, who naturally knows more about life after death now than he did when he was alive, carefully explains that *desine fata deum flecti sperare precando* does not contradict the doctrine of Purgatory.¹⁵

We need to stress, not only Vergil's influence on European thought, but the extent to which different periods with different preoccupations have each gone to him to find in his multi-faceted work something which spoke to their own experience, something perhaps implicit in Vergil, but of which he himself was not necessarily conscious. So T.S. Eliot, for instance, saw Vergil as the quintessential European poet, who "led Europe towards the Christian culture which he could never know." Dryden had praised Vergil for his moral sublimity, for seeking to "form the mind to heroic virtue by example." The Romantics despised him, with Byron dismissing him as a "harmonious plagiary and miserable flatterer." The later nineteenth century, following Sainte-Beuve, stressed his pathos, his sense of the *lacrimae rerum*, "Thou majestic in thy sadness / At the doubtful doom of human kind."[16] It is a mark of his "extraordinary sensitivity and insight into man's problems" that the *Aeneid* can be praised as "a poem of honest and honourable ambivalence."[17]

The mediaeval tradition lamented that Vergil had died too soon to benefit from the Christian revelation, whence the story of St. Paul's saying, *quem te, inquit, reddidissem, / si te vivum invenissem, / poetarum maxime.*[18] He shows himself, perhaps not so much in the *Aeneid* as in the "purple passages" of the *Georgics*, in the *laudes Italiae*, for instance, or in the praises of country life, or the Aristaeus episode, fully aware of the pleasures and beauties of this world, but the world beyond is never far away. We can see him as a man "surer of eternity than of time," and the flame of prophecy still plays about his head. Of the great Latin poets, we might choose to invite Horace to a dinner party, but, like Horace himself and Dante, we might prefer Vergil as our companion in the world to come:

> . . . so Virgil died,
> Aware of change at hand, and prophesied
> Change upon all the Eternal Gods had made
> And on the Gods alike . . .
>
> Maecenas waits me on the Esquiline:
> Thither tonight go I . . .
> And shall this dawn restore us, Virgil mine,
> To dawn? Beneath what sky?[19]

NOTES

1. Bernardus Silvestris, *Commentary on the First Six Books of Virgil's Aeneid*, tr. E.G. Schreiber and T.E. Maresca (Lincoln, London, 1979) 40-41.
2. Conington's notes on lines 430 and 431 show how difficult he and other commentators find this passage.
3. *The* Aeneid *of Virgil, Books 1-6*, ed. with introduction and notes by R.D. Williams (Basingstoke, London, 1972) 485, on lines 426f.
4. J. Le Goff, *The Birth of Purgatory*, tr. A. Goldhammer (Chicago, 1983) 23-25; cf. also 53, referring to "the notion that infernal suffering serves to purify."
5. R.D. Williams, *The Aeneid* (London, 1987) 92.
6. L.R. Lind, tr., *The Aeneid: An Epic Poem of Rome* (Bloomington, 1963) xv; J. Griffin, *Latin Poets and Roman Life* (London, 1985) 159.
7. Williams, *op. cit.* (above, n. 3) 516-517, on lines 893f.
8. N. Vance in C. Martindale (ed.), *Virgil and His Influence* (Bristol, 1984) 184-185.
9. T.S. Pattie in R.D. Williams and T.S. Pattie (edd.), *Virgil: His Poetry Through the Ages* (London, 1982) 85-86.
10. H. Waddell, *The Wandering Scholars* (Harmondsworth, 1954) 103-104, 108 (first pub. 1927).
11. Le Goff, *op. cit.* 85.
12. *Ibid.* 118-121, 186-189, 190-193.
13. *Ibid.* 330-331.
14. See D.L. Sayers' introduction to her translation, *The Comedy of Dante Alighieri the Florentine, Cantico II: Purgatory (Il Purgatorio)*, (Harmondsworth, 1955) 54-71; cf. J.H. Whitfield, *Dante and Virgil* (Oxford, 1949) 29-57; and cf. Whitfield in D.R. Dudley (ed.), *Virgil: Studies in Latin Literature and its Influence* (London, 1969) 109-116.
15. D. Comparetti, *Vergil in the Middle Ages*, tr. E.F.M. Benecke (London, New York, 1895) 219-222.
16. R.D. Williams, *op. cit.* (above, n. 5) 155-161; he refers to Sainte-Beuve, 163, as "the model and foundation for literary criticism of Virgil in the past hundred years," and notes that the *lacrimae rerum* line (*Aen.* 1.462) is "the most quoted line since the time of Sainte-Beuve—but not before."
17. Williams, *op. cit.* (above, n. 5) 161.
18. Comparetti, *op. cit.* 98.
19. Rudyard Kipling, "The Last Ode (Nov. 27, 8 B.C.)," *Rudyard Kipling's Verse: The Definitive Edition* (London, 1940) 765.

WAR AND PEACE IN *AENEID* 10

Susan Ford Wiltshire
Vanderbilt University

> *I am the enemy you killed, my friend.*
> —Wilfred Owen

Vergil's *Aeneid* pivots on the injunction to the Romans, extended by Anchises through Aeneas in the Underworld at 6.852, to impose the habit of peace—*pacis imponere morem*—on the world under their sway.[1] Book 10 of the epic, however, contains as chilling an account of war as any in ancient literature. The *Aeneid* thus poses the question of whether an epic about war can promote peace—and, if so, what kind of peace could be meant in a poem commissioned to support the Roman project of Empire.

I propose to approach Vergil's treatment of war and peace by an unorthodox route. After sketching the dimensions of the problem and detailing the violence of *Aeneid* 10, I will turn to war literature of the twentieth century in order to develop a thesis against which Vergil's purposes in the *Aeneid* may be measured. My inquiry will support the conclusion that twentieth century perceptions of war—corrected by a more complex definition of peace—are not anachronistic but can offer useful insights into Vergil's political and moral dilemma of the first century B.C.E.

The issue of war and peace in the *Aeneid* is complicated by the fact that Vergil was early steeped in Epicureanism, a philosophy that in its origins is both pacifist and apolitical. The facts of

---

My choice of subject for this essay was determined in part by my affectionate respect for the truly Epicurean equipoise of the scholar in whose honor this volume is presented.

Vergil's Epicureanism are more certain than its later effects on his writing. We wish we knew more about the content and practice of that Epicurean circle gathered around Siro at Naples, a group that included not only the young Vergil but also Varius, Plotius Tucca and Quintilius Varus.[2] Probus says only that Vergil "lived for many years in leisurely freedom following the teaching of Epicurus, enjoying the remarkable harmony and companionship of Quintilius, Tucca, and Varius"—*vixit pluribus annis liberali in otio secutus Epicuri sectam, insigni concordia et familiaritate usus Quintili, Tuccae et Varii.*[3]

Apart from his admiration for Lucretius,[4] we cannot finally determine what Epicurean attitudes Vergil retained into his mature poetic life. Perhaps he simply outgrew Epicureanism as he became more closely associated with the political purposes of Maecenas and Octavian. Perhaps he remained emotionally though not intellectually an Epicurean, living quietly in Naples at a remove from the politics at Rome. Perhaps he combined an Epicurean sense of the private world with a Stoic/Roman perception of the public realm.

All of these suppositions, of course, may be moot if Epicureanism had become so adapted to Roman ways by the first century B.C.E. that both Sulla and Julius Caesar, no strangers to violence, could be said to be attracted to it. Cicero in the *Tusculan Disputations* laments the lack of philosophical successors to Socrates in Italy and says that into the vacuum came the Epicurean Amafinius and his many imitators who, with their bad writings, had swept all Italy, *Italiam totam occupaverunt* (4.6-7).[5] We can only assume that Vergil's Epicurean interests were of the more serious sort and that his commitment to peace was deeply and genuinely felt.

By the time he wrote the *Aeneid*, nonetheless, Vergil could create an Augustan hero reborn out of his own inner struggles in ways that evoke not Epicurean but Stoic psychology as well as Roman religion and the careers of Julius Caesar and Octavian/Augustus. On the cosmic scale, Vergil's understanding of Jupiter and *fatum* was also fundamentally Stoic, although in a way far more complex than simple predetermination. Even though Vergil seems fully to accept Rome's divine destiny to rule the world, he always leaves full play for human attitudes and human responses to events. In the final analysis, observes Brooks Otis, the *Aeneid* is "anything but simply Stoic."[6]

The primordial violence of *Aeneid* 10, however, silences philosophy of any stripe. Except for the two councils of the gods and

Aeneas' return with Pallas from Evander's Pallanteum, Book 10 is all battle. Of all the bloodletting in these 908 lines, the most egregious episodes are the following:

1. Aeneas lays open the ribs of Theron (*latus . . . apertum*, 314).[7]
2. Aeneas jams his spear into Pharus' mouth while he is still shouting (*intorquens iaculum clamanti sistit in ore*, 323).
3. Alcanor tries to catch his brother Maeon after the latter has been speared through the chest by Aeneas (*thoraca simul cum pectore rumpit*, 337); a spear from an unspecified thrower hits Alcanor in the right arm leaving the limb hanging by threads (*dextraque ex umero nervis moribunda pependit*, 341).
4. Clausus spears Dryopes in the throat while he is talking (*loquentis / vocem animamque rapit traiecto gutture*, 348-349); Dryopes falls face down on the earth, vomiting thick blood (*fronte ferit terram et crassum vomit ore curorem*, 349).
5. Pallas decapitates Thymber (*caput . . . abstulit*, 394).
6. Pallas severs Larides' hand, still twitching as its fingers reach for a sword (*semianimesque micant digiti ferrumque retractant*, 396).
7. Rhoetus is speared by Pallas and falls from his chariot, kicking at the ground as he dies (*curruque volutus / caedit semianimis Rutulorum calcibus arva*, 403-404).
8. Strymonius tries to choke Halaesus—who has already killed Ladon, Demodocus and Pheres—but gets his hand lopped off in the process (*Strymonio dextram fulgenti deripit ense / elatim in iugulum*, 414-415).
9. Halaesus smashes the face of Thoas with a rock, splintering bones into his bloody brain (*saxo ferit ora Thoantis / ossaque dispersit cerebro permixta cruento*, 415-416).
10. Turnus spears Pallas in the heart, then wrenches his weapon, now warmed by blood, from the wound (*ille rapit calidum frustra de vulnere telum*, 486).
11. Pallas falls dying to the ground with blood pouring out of his mouth (*et terram hostilem moriens petuit ore cruento*, 489).
12. Aeneas mows down everyone he meets (*quaeque metit gladio*, 513).

13. Aeneas takes the four sons of Sulmo to be slaughtered in human sacrifice (*viventis rapit, inferias quos immolet umbris*, 519).
14. While Magus pleads for his life, Aeneas pushes his head back by the helmet and plunges his sword into his neck up to the hilt (*cervice orantis capulo tenus applicat ensem*, 536).
15. Aeneas kills Haemonides, a priest of Apollo[8] (*lapsumque superstans / immolat*, 540-541), and has his armor stripped off as a trophy for Mars.
16. Aeneas severs the arm of Anxur; his shield falls to the ground with the arm still attached to it (*Anxuris ense sinistram / et totum clipei ferro deiecerat orbem*, 545-546).
17. Aeneas decapitates Tarquitus in mid-sentence, rolls the still-warm, headless trunk out of the way, and says to it "with a hateful heart" (*inimico pectore*):

> Lie there now, dreaded one. Your good mother
> will not bury you in the ground nor lay your
> limbs in a family tomb. You will lie there
> for the vultures, or else the sea will carry
> you beneath its wave where hungry fishes will
> lick your wounds.
>
> *istic nunc, metuende, iace. non te optima mater*
> *condet humi patrioque onerabit membra sepulcro:*
> *alitibus linquere feris, aut gurgite mersum*
> *unda feret piscesque impasti vulnera lambent.*
>   557-560

18. Aeneas kills Lucagus by slicing his groin (*tum laevum perforat inguen*, 589), taunts the corpse, then kills his brother Liger by opening his heart with his blade (*pectus mucrone recludit*, 601).
19. Mezentius smashes Latagus in the face with a rock "half as big as a mountain" (*sed Latagum saxo atque ingenti fragmine montis / occupat os faciemque adversam*, 698-699), then leaves Palmus to flop around with his knees cut off (*poplite Palmum / succiso volvi segnem sinit*, 699-700).
20. Mezentius kills Acron, who thrashes the earth with his heels as blood soaks his broken weapons (*sternitur infelix Acron et calcibus atram / tundit humum exspirans infractaque tela cruentat*, 730-731).

21. Mezentius straddles Orodes, trying to wrench his spear out of his body (*tum super abiectum posito pede nixus et hasta*, 736).
22. Mezentius, aiming for Aeneas, kills Antores with a wound just above the groin (*latus inter et ilia figit*, 778).
23. Aeneas buries his sword up to the hilt in Lausus (*validum namque exigit ensem / per medium Aeneas iuvenem totumque recondit*, 815-816).
24. Aeneas plants his spear between the temples of Mezentius' horse Rhoebus (*inter / bellatoris equi cava tempora conicit hastem*, 890-891).
25. Mezentius is still speaking when, barely conscious, he receives Aeneas' sword in the jugular and dies with blood pouring over his armor (*haec loquitur, iuguloque haud inscius accipit ensem / undantique animam diffundit in arma cruore*, 907-908).

The last word of *Aeneid* 10 is, appropriately, *cruore*.

What are we to make of all this?

Aeneid 10 begins with a council on Olympus as the gods debate the vagaries of the war below.[9] Jupiter declares that he had forbidden the Trojans and Italians to battle one another—*abnueram bello Italiam concurrere Teucris* (10.8)—even though at 1.263 he had foretold that Aeneas would fight a great war in Italy. As Venus and Juno zealously press their respective cases, Jupiter abdicates: "Since it is not permitted (*haud licitum*, 10.106) for Italians to make a pact with the Trojans," he says, "I will hold without discrimination (*nullo discrimine habebo*, 10.108) whatever outcome fortune brings today to each side." He concludes that he will be the same to all and that the fates will find a way—*fata viam invenient* (10.113).

Those who hold that cosmic *fatum* holds absolute sway over the *Aeneid* in these passages bear the burden of proof. Otis constructs an elaborate argument to keep control in Jupiter's hands:

> Do these words really mean that Jupiter has resigned all direction of events? In that case why and how will the *fates find a way*? The obvious answer is that Jupiter is here distinguishing between two meanings of fate and of his own will; one is the ultimate outcome or result such as the eventual destruction of Carthage by Rome or the eventual *foedus* of Latins and Trojans; the other is the detailed attainment of this result, the means by which it

is effected, the way in which seemingly disparate and opposite forces are made to contribute to one end. The interference of the sub-fates, especially of Juno, had deferred the establishment of a *foedus* (it cannot be made *now* as Jupiter somewhat provocatively suggests) but not deferred it permanently. For the fates always *find a way*.[10]

A more sober reading of *Aeneid* 10 suggests a different conclusion. I propose that instead of setting up a conflict between Fate and sub-fates—or greater Jupiter and lesser Juno—or permanence and provisionality—Vergil describes the human battles as unheroic, inhumane, and horrible precisely because that is in fact how people behave toward each other in wartime.

If Vergil's purposes are more descriptive than prescriptive, we cannot concur with Otis that Book 10 constitutes "the *locus classicus* of the idea, the one place where the right and wrong sides declare themselves most unambiguously as responsible for their good and bad fortunes."[11] The book is filled with ambiguity. In the representative passages detailed above, it is hard to see patterns of moral rectitude, hard sometimes even to recognize which side is committing which atrocity. Of the deaths that occur in these episodes, the Trojans and their allies are responsible for 15, the Latins and theirs, for eight—but the numbers are difficult to count and seem hardly to matter.

Much more overwhelming is the physical violence of the descriptions. Vergil names at least 19 body parts in the Latin accompanying the passages above, usually severed from the parts to which they are adjacent. One pattern does peculiarly emerge: an emphasis on confronting death face-to-face. The part of the body most commonly mentioned is the face. Forms of *os* occur five times, and on three of the occasions cited above, the casualty is still speaking to his killer when he dies. *Frons* and *facies* also appear. Vergil makes this face-to-face pattern explicit by Mezentius' refusal to kill anyone from behind. He runs in front of his victims so they will see what is coming and so that he will win not by stealth but by strength of arms: *obvius adversoque occurrit seque viro vir / contulit, haud furto melior sed fortibus armis* (734-735). With the juxtapositions of *obvius / adverso* and *viro / vir*, the word order makes the meaning concrete.

The combatants in *Aeneid* 10 may at some level be responsible for their fortunes, but the physical violence done to and by them renders moral categories meaningless. The most frightening episode is the human sacrifice of the sons of Sulmo by Aeneas.

Vergil almost certainly has in mind the precedent reported by Suetonius (*Aug.* 15) that Octavian, in retaliation for their support in 42 B.C.E. of Antony's brother Lucius, ordered all three hundred members of the town council of Perusia put to death in a ritual sacrifice on the Ides of March at an altar dedicated to the divinized Julius. R.D. Williams points out that even in the *Iliad*, where Achilles commits a similar act of human sacrifice,[12] the practice is considered barbarous, and it is even worse in Vergil. Williams suggests that "nothing could have been easier than for Vergil to omit this ghastly act of Achilles in his reworking of the story; therefore the fact that he has included it must be accorded its full significance."[13] Williams appraises the matter pointedly:

> All the lessons of the subsequent years, as Aeneas strove to find a better way, a more controlled and rational approach to crisis and danger, are now forgotten as he kills indiscriminately, taunts his defeated enemies, shows himself to have all the qualities which in Turnus caused the reader deep disquiet... It would have been easier for Virgil to pretend that even in wild grief his hero would show the self-control and humanity that we all admire; but it was truer of what Virgil knew of real human behaviour to present Aeneas otherwise.[14]

Not only Aeneas but everyone else on the battlefield is "presented otherwise."

Why?

Two responses are obvious. First, we object, of course the violence is atrocious, but this is war. What else should one expect? In wartime people do things they would not normally do otherwise. War justifies killings that in peacetime would be murder. War changes all the rules. Vergil anticipates this objection, stating it directly at *Aeneid* 10.901: *nullum in caede nefas.* Copley translates: "Killing's no crime when soldiers take the field."[15] Vergil puts the words in the mouth of the brazen Mezentius, that unrepentant warrior whose favorite torture was to bind living victims to corpses. In the mayhem of *Aeneid* 10, however, any of the other combatants could as easily have come to the same conclusion.

The second objection is that Vergil wrote this way because Homer did. It is a fair observation. Knauer catalogs seven and a half pages of Homeric parallels for Book 10, more than for any other book of the *Aeneid*.[16] The books of the *Iliad* on which *Aeneid*

10 is most closely modeled are 16, 20, and 21, where Homer's language is quite as graphic as Vergil's.

In Lattimore's translation, for example, *Iliad* 16.345-350 reads: "Idomeneus stabbed Erymas in the mouth with the pitiless / bronze, so that the brazen spearhead smashed its way clean through / below the brain in an upward stroke, and the white bones splintered / and the teeth were shaken out with the stroke and both eyes filled up / with blood, and gaping he blew a spray of blood through the nostrils / and through his mouth, and death in a dark mist closed in about him."[17] At *Iliad* 20.398-400, Achilles stabs Demoleon through the temple, and "the bronze spearhead / driven on through smashed the bone apart, and the inward / brain was all spattered forth." A few lines later, he kills Priam's son Polydorus with a slash through the belly: "The spearhead held its way straight on and came out by the navel, / and he dropped, moaning, on one knee as the dark mist gathered / about him, and sagged, and caught with his hands at his bowels in front of him" (*Iliad* 20.416-418).

While both of these arguments appear to be persuasive, they are not. The reason for this is that Vergil is a poet, not a war correspondent nor a factotum for Homer. He could have chosen to soften the ghastly language of the *Iliad*, not elaborate and extend it. Elsewhere we frequently see him recasting Homer to his own purposes. In adopting Homeric similes, for example, Vergil commonly adds a reference to bereft mothers or their young, thereby softening the tone and extending the sympathy of the similes.[18]

Vergil as poet is in control of his text. If his object is to urge peace, he has written a horrible account of war. As Otis puts it, "The tenth book, in short, is almost too Homeric to justify its anti-Homeric moral."[19] It is for clues to this contradiction that we turn to the twentieth century.

Simone Weil's response to war in this century was formed by the *Iliad*. She was the first to identify the true hero of the *Iliad* as force, that X that turns all who are subjected to it into things — the most literal things, namely, corpses. "In this work," says Weil, "at all times, the human spirit is shown as modified by its relations with force, as swept away, blinded, by the very force it imagined it could handle, as deformed by the weight of the force it submits to."[20] Weil compares force with extreme hunger in that both exercise tyranny over the human spirit.

In the midst of battle, the ends of war are forgotten and therefore one reaches the point of denying all ends.[21] The mind loses its capacity to imagine anything other than battle. It has lost all capacity to look outward. It is completely absorbed in doing itself violence.[22] The nature of force is such that it turns both those who use it and those who endure it into stones. Reason leaves, words leave, goals leave. This reification, together with the incapacity to look outward, destroys both the sense of tragic limits and the capacity for compassion. Respect for the life of others when one has had to lose all hope of life for oneself "demands a truly heartbreaking exertion of the powers of generosity."[23]

The implacable treatment of force in the epic causes Weil to consider the poem a "miracle" against which neither the *Odyssey* nor the *Aeneid* nor most other literature except Greek tragedy and the Gospels can stand. "Nothing the peoples of Europe have produced is worth the first known poem that appeared among them. Perhaps they will yet rediscover the epic genius, when they learn that there is no refuge from fate, learn not to admire force, not to hate the enemy, nor to scorn the unfortunate. How soon this will happen is another question."[24]

Weil reserves special scorn for the *Aeneid* and for the Romans in general. The Romans had no epics [!], she says, and staged gladiatorial fights instead of tragedies. She calls the *Aeneid* "an imitation which, however brilliant, is disfigured by frigidity, bombast, and bad taste."[25] She may be right about the Romans, but she is wrong about the *Aeneid*. I will argue that far from being an imitation, the *Aeneid* is the first poem in Western culture to raise the problematic nature of peace in the midst of historical circumstances that seemed, as historical circumstances always do, to forbid its very possibility.

The genius of Weil's contribution is to strip war of its attraction and to call force by its proper name. This achievement is the more remarkable since the vast majority of war literature since the *Iliad* has served to glorify rather than to deconsecrate war. Robert E. Lee is said to have remarked to a member of his staff: "It is well that war is so terrible—we would grow too fond of it."[26]

Even Vera Brittain, whose *Testament of Youth* ruthlessly reveals the emotional devastation and physical horrors of war, is acutely aware of its imaginative power:

> It is, I think, this glamour, this magic, this incomparable keying up of the spirit in a time of mortal conflict, which constitute the pacifist's real problem—a problem still incompletely imagined, and still quite unresolved. The

causes of war are always falsely represented; its honour is dishonest and its glory meretricious, but the challenge to spiritual endurance, the intense sharpening of all the senses, the vitalising consciousness of common peril for a common end, remain to allure those boys and girls who have just reached the age when love and friendship and adventure call more persistently than at any later time ... I do not believe that ... any Disarmament Conference will ever rescue our poor remnant of civilization from the threatening forces of destruction, until we can somehow impart to the rational processes of constructive thought and experiment, that element of sanctified loveliness which, like superb sunshine breaking through thunderclouds, from time to time glorifies war.[27]

In World War I it was the poets—and only a handful of those, including Wilfred Owen, Robert Graves, and Siegfried Sassoon but not Rupert Brooke—who were able to extricate themselves sufficiently from the twin hydras of resignation and romance to lay open the heart of war. One of the bravest of these was Sassoon:

Suicide in the Trenches
(1918)

I knew a simple soldier boy
Who grinned at life in empty joy
Slept soundly through the lonesome dark
And whistled early with the lark.

In winter trenches, cowed and glum,
With crumps and lice and lack of rum,
He put a bullet through his brain.
No one spoke of him again.

You smug-faced crowds with kindling eye
Who cheer when soldier lads pass by,
Sneak home and pray you'll never know
The hell where youth and laughter go.[28]

Sassoon issued "A Soldier's Declaration" in 1917, refusing further military service even though he had been awarded the distinguished Military Cross for heroism and had been so severely wounded in France that he would have been kept on home service if he had stayed in the army. His statement concluded:

"On behalf of those who are suffering now I make this protest against the deception which is being practised on them; also I believe that I may help to destroy the callous complacence with which the majority of those at home regard the continuance of agonies which they do not share, and which they have not sufficient imagination to realize."[29] In further protest, Sassoon threw his Military Cross into the Formby Links.[30]

Wilfred Owen's fragmentary vision of life in the trenches exiles forever any possible idealization of glory there:[31]

Fragment: Cramped in that Funnelled Hole

Cramped in that funnelled hole, they watched the dawn
Open a jagged rim around; a yawn
Of death's jaws, which had all but swallowed them
Stuck in the bottom of his throat of phlegm.

They were in one of the many mouths of Hell
Not seen of seers in visions; only felt
As teeth of traps; when bones and the dead are smelt
Under the mud where long ago they fell
Mixed with the sour sharp odour of the shell.

The voices of Sassoon and Owen were at the time eclipsed by the national project of support for the war, a project spearheaded by the press. Sassoon satirizes the warrior role of the press in his poem "Editorial Impressions," which tells of the exudations of the journalist just back from a visit to the trenches who has been wowed with "the splendour / Which makes us win" that he fancies he has witnessed there: "He seemed so certain 'all was going well,' / As he discussed the glorious time he'd had / While visiting the trenches." The poem concludes, "Ah yes, but it's the press that leads the way!"[32]

Paul Fussell, in *The Great War and Modern Memory*, documents the formative influence of the Great War upon British daily life even to this day. One consequence of that formation, however, was suspension of belief in the press. Fussell proposes that the devaluation of letterpress and even of language itself may date from the Great War. He quotes C.E. Montague who observed in 1922, speaking of the Battle of the Somme:

The most bloody defeat in the history of Britain ... might occur ... on July 1, 1916, and our Press come out bland and copious and graphic, with nothing to show that we had not had quite a good day—a victory really. Men who had lived through the massacre read the stuff open-mouthed.... So it comes that each of several million ex-soldiers now reads ... with that maxim on guard in his mind—'You can't believe a word you read.'[33]

In his more recent book, *Wartime: Understanding and Behavior in the Second World War*, Fussell show how sanitized the presentations of the so-called "good war"[34] have been. For example, in a widely advertised picture collection with the unwittingly ironic title, "Life Goes to War" (1977) no photographs of dismembered bodies are depicted. Although there are photographs of the three severed heads, all, significantly, are Asian. Even in the photographs of Tarawa and Iwo Jima no dismembered Americans appear. "Allied troops," says Fussell, "are never shown suffering what was termed in the Viet Nam War, traumatic amputation: everyone has all his limbs, his hands and feet and digits, not to mention expressions of courage and cheer."[35]

This denial of what really happens to bodies in war, says Fussell, began in what he calls the bourgeois age, from the paintings of the eighteenth and nineteenth centuries to the photographs of the twentieth.[36] The borders of Bayeaux Tapestry, by contrast, consist of ornamental displays of severed heads and limbs. Shakespeare, too, does not blink at the boils:

> "But if the cause be not good, the King himself hath a heavy reckoning to make when all those legs and arms and heads, chopp'd off in a battle, shall join together at the latter day and cry all 'We died at such a place'—some swearing, some crying for a surgeon, some upon their wives left poor behind them, some upon the debts they owe, some upon their children rawly left."
>
> *Henry V*, 4.1

Never in the official portraiture of World War II, but only in the journals and recollections of individuals who were there, does the truth emerge. Neil McCallum, for example, recalls a morning after a battle in North Africa. He and a friend come upon a body eviscerated by a shell blast:

> "Good God," said S., shocked, "here's one of his fingers." S. stubbed with his toe on the ground some feet from the corpse. There is more horror in a severed digit than in a man dying: it savors of mutilation. "Christ," went on S. in a very low voice, "look, it's not his finger."[37]

This suppression of smashed brains, disemboweled trunks, and severed members is of a piece with the suppression of many other unreported realities of modern war, including the numbers of civilians killed, the numbers of American deserters (20,000 in World War II), and the number of casualties caused by the oxymoron of "friendly forces," together with all the categories of information "classified" in the interest of "national security."

The real war, says Fussell, was tragic and ironic, but its meaning seemed inaccessible in unbombed America, and so the suffering—and the public maturity that could have come about from facing it directly—was wasted.[38] We were shielded from the suffering and the waste, and therefore the possibility of maturity, largely because of the public relations projects launched by all branches of the military. If disbelief in newspapers was a result of World War I, Fussell posits the origins of a public relations culture in World War II. "The postwar power of the 'media' to determine what shall be embraced as reality," he says "is in large part due to the success of the morale culture in wartime. It represents, indeed, its continuation . . . supervised by the later avatars of the PR colonels and captains so indispensable to the maintenance of high morale and thus to the conduct of the Second World War."[39]

The denial of death is qualitatively escalated as civilian populations become targeted for nuclear attack and the very notion of war becomes an abstraction. Glenn Gray speaks of the remoteness from reality, which he calls godlessness, that results when the lines between combatants and civilians are blurred and war becomes more and more abstract. "The culmination was the destruction of Nagasaki and Hiroshima with the most abstract of all death-dealing instruments.[40]

The problem with the suppression of mutilated corpses, whether through media manipulation or nuclear abstraction, is that removal from the consequences of our violence robs us of any possibility, always frail and ephemeral, of pity for the victims. If we cannot see the corpses, we are robbed of any opportunity, however remote, to acknowledge both our complicity in the violence and our kinship with its victims. And once again, all the suffering is wasted and we remain incapable of transforming sorrow into maturity and loss into new purpose.

This brings us back to the *Aeneid* and to the point where we began. The epigraph from Wilfred Owen at the head of this essay is from "Strange Meeting,"[41] a poem in which Owen, like Vergil, conceives an exchange in the Underworld in which pity, and therefore peace, is imagined as possible:

Strange Meeting

> It seemed that out of battle I escaped
> Down some profound dull tunnel, long since scooped
> Through granites which titanic wars had groined.
> Yet also there encumbered sleepers groaned,
> Too fast in thought or death to be bestirred.
> Then, as I probed them, one sprang up, and stared
> With piteous recognition in fixed eyes,
> Lifting distressful hands as if to bless.
> And by his smile, I knew that sullen hall,
> By his dead smile I knew we stood in Hell.
> With a thousand pains that vision's face was grained;
> Yet no blood reached there from the upper ground,
> And no guns thumped, or down the flues made moan.
> "Strange friend," I said, "here is no cause to mourn."
> "None," said the other, "save the undone years,
> The hopelessness. Whatever hope is yours,
> Was my life also; I went hunting wild
> After the wildest beauty in the world,
> Which lies not calm in eyes, or braided hair,
> But mocks the steady running of the hour,
> And if it grieves, grieves richlier than here.
> For of my glee might many men have laughed,
> And of my weeping something had been left,
> Which must die now. I mean the truth untold,
> The pity of war, the pity war distilled.

The poet has foreseen continuing down "some profound dull tunnel" after his own death and meeting "in the sullen hall" the enemy soldier he had recently killed in battle. The ghost speaks further of what he has lost, what they both have lost through their death:

> Courage was mine, and I had mystery.
> Wisdom was mine, and I had mastery:
> To miss the march of this retreating world
> Into vain citadels that are not walled.
> Then, when much blood had clogged their chariot-wheels,
> I would go up and wash them from sweet wells,
> Even with truths that lie too deep for taint.

> I would have poured my spirit without stint
> But not through wounds; not on the cess of war.
> Foreheads of men have bled where no wounds were.
> I am the enemy you killed, my friend.[42]
> I knew you in this dark: for so you frowned
> Yesterday through me as you jabbed and killed.
> I parried; but my hands were loath and cold.
> Let us sleep now...."

Any realistic hope for peace requires a complex and freighted definition of peace within the human situation. To define peace as the absence of conflict is faulty anthropology as well as dangerous politics. Vergil knows, and the immensely complex ending of the *Aeneid* demonstrates that he knows, that conflict and the danger of war will always inhere in the human situation. It is necessary, therefore, to look war straight in the eye, stay close to the victims, never believe that any war is a "good war" even if it has to be fought, and keep faith with the possibilities of peace—always negotiated, always precarious—in spite of the perdurance of conflict.

One way Vergil keeps faith with the possibility of peace is by keeping the corpses in view. Williams is right: Vergil could easily have avoided his repetition of the Homeric horrors. That he chose not to explains why the *Aeneid* is a great poem instead of what Weil calls a "tasteless imitation." In the *Iliad* no condition other than war is imaginable. There may be—and are—redemptive moments of grace in that incredibly beautiful and sorrowful epic. But Homer's epic could not hold the hope that Vergil maintains for his, namely, the transformation of rage into civility, killing into compromise, and ceaseless strife into negotiated settlement.[43]

Even with a more problematic understanding of peace, we can never be sanguine about its possibility. Peace may never happen in this world. Somehow it seems not accidental that both Vergil and Owen locate their expressions of hope for peace in the Underworld. Those who argue that peace is otherworldly are, in this case, geographically correct. But if the words are not uttered somewhere, they cannot be realized anywhere.

In the *Aeneid* Vergil utters the words of peace—*pacis imponere morem*. That is why the *Aeneid* finally *is* an Epicurean poem, not in the martial practice of first-century Italy but in the pacific spirit of Epicurus' Athenian garden, now imposed precariously upon Roman political realities. That is why the *Aeneid* is also a very great document in the human struggle for survival. It shows us that pity and therefore peace are possible only when we recognize the friend in the enemy because we recognize also the enemy in ourselves.

NOTES

1. Conington, Hertzel, Page and Otis, among others, adopt *pacis*. The better Mss. read *paci*. The meaning, in any event, is clear.
2. R.E.H. Westendorp Boerma collects the evidence on this in *P. Vergilii Maronis Catalepton* (Assen: Torenlaan, 1949) 10.
3. Probus, *Vita Verg.,* p. 73, Br. 10.
4. Most explicit at *Georgics* 2.490: *felix qui potuit rerum cognoscere causas.*
5. Cicero speculates about whether Epicureanism was attractive to Italians because it was easy to understand, or because of the allure of pleasures, or simply because there were no alternatives.
6. B. Otis, *Virgil: A Study In Civilized Poetry* (Oxford, 1964) 225-226 and n. 226.
7. All references to the *Aeneid* are to Book 10 unless otherwise noted.
8. This slaughter is all the more grave, given Apollo's special relationship to Augustus, and graver still because of the awful inversion of the proper meaning of the verb *immolat,* vitiated also at 519-520.
9. Otis, *op. cit.* observes that only here in the *Aeneid* does such a *concilium* take place, "an indication of the central significance of the book," 353.
10. *Ibid.* 353-354.
11. *Ibid.* 354.
12. *Iliad* 21.27ff. and 23.175ff.
13. R.D. Williams, *The Aeneid of Virgil,* Books 7-12 (Basingstoke, London, 1973) 356.
14. *Ibid.* 320-321.
15. F.O. Copley, *The Aeneid* (Indianapolis, 1965) 236.
16. G.N. Knauer, *Die Aeneis und Homer* (Göttingen, 1964) 413-420.
17. R. Lattimore, tr., *The Iliad of Homer* (Chicago, Phoenix Books, 1961) 339.
18. See S.F. Wiltshire, *Public and Private in Vergil's* Aeneid (Amherst, 1989) 38-43.
19. Otis, *op. cit.* 361.
20. S. Weil, "The *Iliad* or the Poem of Force," in S. Miles, ed., *Simone Weil: An Anthology* (New York, 1986) 163.
21. Weil, *Cahiers* I (Paris: Plon, 1970) 19.
22. Weil, *op. cit.* (n. 20) 182.
23. *Ibid.* 184.

24. *Ibid.* 194-195.
25. *Ibid.* 193, 191.
26. Quoted in G. Gray, *The Warriors: Reflections on Men in Battle* (New York, 1970; [orig. ed. 1959]) 31.
27. V. Brittain, *Testament of Youth* (New York, London, 1978 [orig. pub. 1933]) 291.
28. S. Sassoon, *The War Poems* (London, Boston, 1983) 119.
29. Included in R. Graves, *Good-Bye to All That* (New York, 1957 [orig. pub. 1929]) 260. Eventually Sassoon chose to return out of loyalty to his fellow soldiers. In his poem "Banishment," he writes: "Love drove me to rebel. / Love drove me back to grope with them through hell."
30. Graves, *op. cit.* 262. This incident was brought to my attention by Judge Walter C. Kurtz, who, in a similar protest fifty-two years after Sassoon's, threw his decorations for bravery in Viet Nam over the White House fence.
31. C.D. Lewis, ed., *The Collected Poems of Wilfred Owen* (New York, 1963) 109.
32. Sassoon, *op. cit.* 89.
33. P. Fussell, *The Great War in Modern Memory* (New York, London, 1975) 316.
34. Cf. S. Terkel, *"The Good War": An Oral History of World War Two* (New York, 1984).
35. P. Fussell, *Wartime: Understanding and Behavior in the Second World War* (New York, London, 1989) 269-270.
36. *Ibid.* 268-269. Vera Brittain (*op. cit.* 442) describes her suspicion upon hearing from a colonel that her brother was killed in battle from a shot through the head. "I looked at him in silent reproach, for I frankly did not believe him. At that late stage of the War . . . the colonels and company commanders on various fronts were so weary of writing gruesome details to sorrowing relatives, that the number of officers who were instantaneously and painlessly shot through the head or the heart passed far beyond the bounds of probability."
37. N. McCallum, *Journey with a Pistol* (London, 1959) 104.
38. Fussell, *op. cit.* 268.
39. *Ibid.* 164.
40. Gray, *op. cit.* xvi, xvii.
41. *The Collected Poems of Wilfred Owen* (*op. cit.*) 35-36.
42. An earlier manuscript version of the poem reads for this line: "I was a German conscript, and your friend"; *ibid.* 36.
43. See J.B. Elshtain, *Women and War* (New York, 1987), especially "Breaking the Deadlock," 256-258.

Sur Trois Passages de Virgile: L'Archéologie des Anciens

Raymond Chevallier
ancien membre de l'École française de Rome

Scilicet et tempus ueniet, cum finibus illis
Agricola, incuruo terram molitus aratro
Exesa inueniet scabra robigine pila,
Aut grauibus rastris galeas pulsabit inanis,
Grandiaque effossis mirabitur ossa sepulcris.
Géorgiques 1.493-497

Si quando sedem augustam seruataque mella
Thesauris relines
Géorgiques 4.228-229

ueteres tellure recludit
Thesauros, ignotum argenti pondus et auri.
Enéide 1.358-359

Ces trois passages de Virgile: Le premier faisant allusion à des découvertes fortuites sur le champ de bataille de Philippes: "Sans doute, il viendra un temps, où, sur ce terrain le laboureur, travaillant la terre avec l'araire cintré trouvera des javelots rongés par une rouille lépreuse, ou de sa herse pesante heurtera des casques vides et contemplera avec étonnement dans les tombes ouvertes des ossements gigantesques." Le second, purement métaphorique: "Veux-tu ouvrir un jour la ruche auguste, pour pénétrer jusqu'au miel la réserve de ses trésors?" Le troisième, qui montre l'ombre de son époux "ouvrant à Didon dans la Terre l'accès d'anciens trésors, monceaux ignorés d'argent et d'or." Nous ont engagé, en l'honneur d'un éminent spécialiste du poète, à tenter cette esquisse d'une archéologie des Anciens. Ces derniers ont-ils eu l'idée d'une recherche archéologique, telle que nous la pratiquons? Dans quelles conditions, avec quelles intentions?

Une réponse d'ordre archéologie existe, lorsque le fouilleur contemporain découvre des tombes violées dans l'antiquité par des chercheurs de trésors. Mon vieil ami, le regretté ingénieur C.M. Lerici m'avait signalé en Etrurie des tombes qui s'étaient refermées comme des pièges sur des "tombaroli" clandestins de toutes époques. Mais, pour rester dans les limites d'un article, nous limiterons ici notre recherche à l'examen des sources littéraires, dans le contexte gréco-romain, car le problème existe pour d'autres archéologies, par exemple en Egypte, où l'on assiste au XIIè s. av. J.C. au procès et à la condamnation de fouilleurs clandestins (*Archeo*, n°47, janv. 1989, p. 124).

GÉNÉRALITÉS—DÉFINITIONS

Opinions courantes des modernes

Elles ont été peu exploitées par les auteurs de manuels archéologiques, dans les chapitres consacrés à l'histoire de la discipline. Citons notamment:

P.E. Arias, *L'archeologia* dans l'*Enciclopedia Classica* (Turin, 1957) 99: storia della disciplina, qui renvoie à Boucher de Pertes et Darwin.

A. Laming-Emperaire, *Origines de l'archéologie préhistorique en France* (Paris, 1964): "L'histoire des recherches systématiques relatives au passé de l'homme et au passé de la terre commence vers le XVIè siècle," mais l'auteur note qu'elle remonte au Moyen Age (traditions bibliques) et ajoute: "les auteurs grecs et latins, par intuition peut-être, ou par la survivance de lointaines traditions, ou plus probablement, par comparaison avec 'leurs' barbares, ont eu des notions parfois assez justes bien que rudimentaires sur l'état de l'homme primitif." Cet ouvrage comporte cependant des renvois explicites concernant les céraunies (p. 37); nous y reviendrons.

G. Daux, *Histoire de l'archéologie*, (Paris, 1966), après avoir rappelé qu'en grec "archéologie" désigne les périodes lointaines de l'histoire, l'histoire en général et mentionné l'*Archéologie romaine* de Denys d'Halicarnasse, renvoie à Homère, le père de l'archéologie, qui nous transporte dans un lointain passé, à l' "archéologie" de Thucydide I: données sur la marine, l'architecture, le costume, le mobilier funéraire, à Aristote, aux périégètes (Pausanias), à Plutarque "qui touche plus d'une fois à des problèmes d'archéologie et d'art," à Strabon, Lucien, Athénée,

Vitruve (nombreuses références à des oeuvres classiques), Pline l'Ancien utilisant Varron, à l'Anthologie, à Cicéron, qui "témoigne d'une solide culture d'amateur," à Hadrien, dont la villa est "le premier musée d'architecture et de sculpture." L'auteur saute par dessus le Moyen Age: "Nous arrivons avec la Renaissance proprement dite au seuil de la période où l'archéologie classique va se développer peu à peu."

W. Schiering, dans le *Handbuch der Archäologie* (Münich, 1969, Ière partie, 2: *Zur Geschichte der Archäologie*), commence son historique avec Pirro Ligorio, Spon, Montfaucon, Winckelmann, Paciaudi, Caylus.

G. Ch. Picard, *L'archéologie, Découverte des Civilisations Disparues*, (Paris, Larousse, 1969), rappelle qu'en grec le mot désigne l'histoire ancienne, que les "archéologues" sont une catégorie d'acteurs spécialisés dans les pièces tirées d'anciennes légendes et que le mot resurgit, francisé, au XVIIIè s, avec J. Spon. Il observe cependant (p. 8) que "les amateurs de vieux objets, les antiquaires apparaissent dès l'époque hellénistique sans doute," qu'ils étaient nombreux dans l'aristocratie romaine, faisaient exécuter des copies, recherchaient des collections, que les temples et certains monuments publics jouaient le rôle de Musées. Pausanias était l'ancêtre des guides Joanne ou Baedeker. Des voyageurs romantiques composaient des vers sur les Pyramides. Mais cette activité demeurait d'ordre purement esthétique.

D. Whitehouse, "The Origins and Growth of Archaeology," en *The Cambridge Encyclopedia of Archaeology:* (Cambridge University Press, 1980) p. 16, note: "Speculation about the human past (including some striking anticipations of modern views) can be traced back into Classical Antiquity, but serious investigation of monuments and artifacts only began with the Renaissance..."

Glyn Daniel, *A Short History of Archeology* (Londres, 1981), signale bien (d'après J. Oates, *Babylon*, 1979, 162) une activité archéologique à Babylone, mais estime qu'il n'y eut "pas d'archéologie antique à proprement parler, c. à d. d'étude de l'histoire ancienne d'après les vestiges matériels. Hérodote et d'autres ont fait des observations ethnographiques concernant des survivances de barbares préhistoriques. Grecs et Romains avaient une idée de l'évolution de l'homme (Hésiode, Lucrèce). Les Grecs connaissaient le passé mycénien qui ignorait l'emploi du fer." On a proposé une succession des âges, spéculé sur l'antiquité de la civilisation égyptienne. Mais après Hésiode et Lucrèce, l'auteur passe à la Genèse.

H.P. Eydoux, *L'Archéologie, Histoire des découvertes* (Paris, 1985), cite lui aussi Denys d'Halicarnasse, Hérodote, Pausanias, Pline l'Ancien, Varron, dont "aucun ne procéda à une quelconque recherche comparable aux entreprises des archéologues futurs," les collectionneurs anciens (les commanditaires du navire naufragé de Mahdia, Néron, Hadrien, Constantin, Théodose).

Quant au grand atlas de l'archéologie (*Encyclopaedia Universalis*), il ne remonte pas plus haut que la fin du Moyen Age.

Définitions en grec et en latin

En grec le mot *archaiologia* est utilisé: Par Platon (*Hippias Minor* 285d.) pour définir l'histoire des anciens héros, des races, des fondations antiques: *Socrate*: "Dis-moi quels sont les sujets sur lesquels on t'écoute avec plaisir; *Hippias*: Les généalogies, Socrate, celles des héros et des hommes, les récits relatifs à l'antique fondation des cités; et d'une manière générale, tout ce qui se rapporte à l'antiquité."

Par Thucydide (1) pour désigner l'histoire ancienne avant la guerre du Péloponnèse; et par Diodore de Sicile (1.4: temps mythologiques et faits antérieurs à la guerre de Troie, antiquités barbares et grecques; 2.46: à propos des Amazones). Par Strabon, avec le sens d'histoire primitive: 10.2.9 (452): "Les auteurs les plus férus d'antiquités (hoi archaiologikôteroi) font remonter l'origine du saut de Leucade à Céphalos"; Denys d'Halicarnasse entend par "Romaikè Archaiologia" les antiquités romaines; et même emploi chez Flavius Josèphe: "Ioudaikè Archaiologia," pour les Antiquités Juives (*Proem.*): "archaiologeia ta Ioudaiôn."

Un traité des antiquités cariennes de Philippe (Strabon 14.2.28) abordait les questions linguistiques.

En latin *antiquitas* est utilisé: Par Cicéron dans le *Brutus* (60): "Notre ami Varron si exact dans ses recherches sur l'antiquité (*inuestigator antiquitatis*)," et 81: "Fabius Pictor, qui fut également versé dans le droit, la littérature et l'histoire"; dans *Diu.* 1.40 (87): "Comment rester indifférent à une opinion si ancienne et appuyée d'aussi illustres témoignages" (*clarissimis monumentis testata antiquitas*).

Cornelius Nepos, à propos d'Atticus (18.1), associe la notion au *mos maiorum*: "Il voua à la tradition des ancêtres un culte d'imitation, à tout ce qui était ancien un culte d'amour; il possédait de l'antiquité une connaissance assez complète pour en avoir exposé l'ensemble dans l'ouvrage qu'il consacra à la succession des magistrats." Juvénal (S. 4.451) lui, "abhorre une femme qui, férue d'érudition, me cite des vers que je ne connais pas" (*odi hanc quae ignoto mihi tenet antiquaria uersus*).

Tacite emploie trois fois cette notion dans le *Dialogue des Orateurs:* 21.4: des mots qui sentent leur vieux temps (*inconditi sensus redolent antiquitatem)*; "personne, je crois, n'est assez amateur de vieilles choses pour louer en Célius ce qui a vieilli: *nec quemquam adeo antiquarium puto, ut Caelium ex ea parte laudet qua antiquus est*"; 37.2: "Je ne sais s'il vous est tombé sous la main ces anciens écrits qui, jusqu'à présent, sont restés dans les bibliothèques des amateurs de l'antiquité: (*in antiquariorum bibliothecis adhuc manent)*"; 42: "Nous te dénoncerons . . . Messalla, aux partisans de l'antiquité *(antiquarii)*."

Suétone dit d'Auguste (*Vita Aug.* 86) qu'il réprouva avec un égal dédain les précieux et les archaïsants, *(cacozelos et antiquarios spreuit*).

Le mot *antiquitas* aurait donc, d'après les sources littéraires, un sens surtout philologique, ce que confirmeraient deux passages de Pline l'Ancien attestant l'intérêt pour les écrits anciens: *NH* 12.83: "J'ai vu, au bout de 200 ans environ, des écrits de la main de Ti. et C. Gracchus" et 88 (cf. AG, *NA* 1.1.9 et Denys d'Halicarnasse 4.62) à propos de la reconstitution des livres sibyllins (consultés jusqu'en 363 ap. J.C. et détruits définitivement à l'époque de Stilichon).

Emplois figurés du mot "trésor"

Nous signalerons brièvement *quelques emplois figurés du mot "trésor"*:

Cicéron, *Att.* 15.27: "Je m'occupe d'un autre travail . . ., mais il faudra le mettre dans vos trésors les plus secrets" (*quod lateat in thesauris tuis)*; *Her.* 3.28.1: *thesaurus inuentorum* (auteur incertain); *Partitions orat.* 109.5: "les lieux sont comme des trésors où l'on puise des arguments déterminés"; *De Fin.* 2.67: "les trésors d'érudition de notre cher Atticus"; 4.10: "les lieux, comme les trésors (magasins) d'où l'on peut extraire des arguments"; *De Orat.* 1.18.1: "la mémoire, trésor de toutes les connaissances."

Pétrone, *Sat.* 46: "La science, c'est un trésor et le talent ne meurt jamais de faim"; 47: "J'aime mieux mon crédit que des trésors."

Sénèque, *V.B.* 24.2.22: "Plaçons le bienfait comme un trésor profondément enfoui, que tu ne déterreras qu'en cas de nécessité?"; *BNF* I, 15.6.8: "Un bienfait n'en est pas un lorsqu'il y manque ce qui en fait surtout le prix: l'estime éclairée. Autrement une somme d'argent énorme, si la raison et la droiture d'intention n'inspirent pas le don qui en est fait, est moins un bienfait qu'un trésor trouvé"; 6.43.3.33: "Être préoccupé de rendre un bienfait, c'est supposer chez l'autre la préoccupation d'en être payé. Prêtons-nous à l'une comme à l'autre alternative: s'il veut être payé de son bienfait, apportons-en, remettons-en le prix avec joie: préfère-t-il le laisser sous notre garde: pourquoi exhumer son trésor? pourquoi refuser d'en être les gardiens?"; *Ep*. 115.5 (culte de la vertu): "Ce qu'elle veut comme honneur, ce n'est pas l'immolation en masse de taureaux bien gras, ce n'est pas les ex-voto d'or et d'argent, ni le menu tribut versé au trésor des sanctuaires, c'est l'état religieux, la droiture d'intention."

Quintilien, 2.7.4: "On aura à sa disposition une grande abondance de termes excellents . . . qui s'offrent spontanément, comme si l'on puisait, pour ainsi dire, dans les réserves d'un trésor;" 10.1.2 (modèles fournis par la lecture): "On couvera pour ainsi dire, des trésors mis sous clef;" 11.2.1: "Ce n'est pas sans raison qu'on appelle la mémoire le trésor de l'éloquence."

SHA, *Septime Sévère* 21.8: *Papianum, iuris asylum et doctrinae legalis thesaurum*; et Ammien, 17.13.32 (discours de l'empereur): "Quant à nous, grandes sont nos ressources, riches sont nos trésors, si l'on admet que nos princes et notre courage ont préservé intacts les patrimoines de tous"; 25.4.15 (qualités de Julien): "Il déclarait parfois bien haut qu'Alexandre le Grand, un jour qu'on lui demandait où il gardait ses trésors, répondit tout bonnement: chez mes amis."

Ces emplois figurés du mot ont en général une connotation morale ou philosophique, qui fait mépriser les trésors les plus matériels; cf. Sénèque, *De Ira* 3.33.4: "Si tu étalais devant moi tout l'argent de toutes les mines que nous foulons actuellement, si tu jetais à mes pieds tous les trésors cachés (car l'avarice rend à la terre ce qu'elle en avait extrait pour son malheur), je ne jugerais pas tout cet amas digne de faire sourciller un homme vertueux."

ASPECTS DE L'ARCHÉOLOGIE ANTIQUE

L'archéologie dans la Grèce antique

De très nombreux passages d'Hérodote concernent les antiquités des villes ou des sanctuaires et les trésors des souverains: 1.50: offrandes de Crésus à Delphes: une statue de lion, du poids de 10 talents (ce détail devait être connu par un ancien inventaire), placé sur un piédestal en briques d'or, deux grands cratères, l'un d'or, l'autre d'argent, quatre jarres d'argent, deux vases pour l'eau lustrale, l'un d'or avec fausse inscription et l'autre d'argent, des lingots d'argent, une statue de sa femme en or, des colliers et ceintures ayant appartenu à sa femme.

À Delphes un bouclier et une lance d'or; 1.66-68: raconte le transfert à Sparte des os du protecteur de Tégée, qui devait transmettre aux Lacédémoniens le droit qu'il avait sur la ville. Un forgeron raconte: "Je voulais creuser un puits dans cette cour; je suis tombé en fouillant sur un cercueil de sept coudées; ne croyant pas qu'il ait jamais existé des hommes plus grands que les hommes d'aujourd'hui, je l'ouvris, et je vis que le mort était de même longueur que le cercueil; je le mesurais et l'enfouis de nouveau." Mais Lichas emporte les ossements à Sparte; 2.44: les offrandes du sanctuaire d' Héraclès à Tyr; 2.106: "dans la Syrie Palestine, j'ai vu des stèles du roi d'Egypte Sésostris. Il y a aussi en Ionie deux images de cet homme taillées en bas-reliefs dans des rochers, sur la route qui va du pays d'Ephèse à Phocée et sur celle qui va de Sardes à Smyrne. De part et d'autre est sculpté un homme haut de quatre coudées; il tient de la main droite une lance, de la gauche un arc; le reste de son équipement est à l'avenant, en partie égyptien, en partie éthiopien. D'une épaule à l'autre court en travers de sa poitrine une inscription gravée en caractères sacrés égyptiens qui dit ceci: 'Moi, par la force de mes épaules, j'ai conquis ce pays.'" On a pu établir un rapprochement avec les deux bas-reliefs rupestres de Karabel, monuments hittites représentant un dieu guerrier (Ière moitié du XIIIè s. av. J.C.); 2.121: trésor royal, chambre forte et pièces; 2.129-130: le vase de bois doré de Saïs (image d'Isis). Statues colossales en bois de femmes nues . . . "Nous avons constaté nous-même que ces statues ont perdu leurs mains par l'effet de la vétusté, de mon temps encore on les voyait gisantes à leurs pieds"; 2.135: barres de métal consacrées à Delphes par Rhodopis; 2.189: offrandes d'Amasis à Cyrène, Lindos et Samos, etc.

On trouvera également maintes données de ce type chez Diodore de Sicile (1.46-49, 52, 63, 64, 66: tombeaux égyptiens; 11.62: dîme du butin des Athéniens à Delphes; 19.87: pillage des trésors du temple d'Olympie par un lieutenant d'Antigone).

Chez Strabon, 9.3.8: fouilles d'Onomarchus dans le temple de Delphes pour rechercher des dépôts de métal précieux sur la foi d'un texte d'Homère: "De violentes secousses de tremblement de terre survenues tout à coup auraient mis les travailleurs en fuite et auraient interrompu les fouilles que personne dans la suite n'eut le courage de reprendre."

Autre épisode très caractéristique: les Athéniens. sous prétexte de chercher les os de Thésée, colonisent Skyros au Vè s. (cf. *R.E., Sup.* 13.1198).

Trésors cachés et découverts: réalité et thème littéraire
L' "invention" fortuite d'un dépôt caché devait être fréquente dans la réalité pour devenir un véritable topos: Cicéron, *C.M.* 21: "Je n'ai jamais entendu dire qu'un vieillard eût oublié le lieu où il avait enfoui son trésor; ils se rappellent ce qui les intéresse"; et Horace, *S.* 2.6.2: "Oh! si quelque hasard me faisait découvrir une urne pleine d'argent, comme à cet homme qui, travaillant un champ pour un salaire, y trouva un trésor, acheta la terre et la laboura désormais pour lui, devenu riche par l'amitié d'Hercule, si ma fortune présente me plaît et me suffit, voilà la prière que je te fais."

Les allusions sont fréquentes dans la comédie: Chez Plaute, *Aulularia*, argument: "Le vieil avare Euclion, qui s'en fie à peine à lui-même, a trouvée enfouie dans sa maison une marmite avec un trésor"; 7 (c'est le dieu Lare qui parle): "Le grand-père m'a confié jadis un grand secret, un trésor: il l'a enfermé au milieu du foyer, me priant, m'adjurant de le lui garder"; 12: "il n'en a pas indiqué l'emplacement à son fils"; 26: "J'ai fait découvrir le trésor par Euclion pour qu'il puisse marier sa fille," cf. 240, 266. En *Miles* 1064: trésors plus ou moins imaginaires. En *Trin.* argument: "Partant pour l'étranger, Charmidès a enfoui un trésor qu'il recommande, ainsi que tous ses intérêts, à son ami Calliclès"; 149: "Au moment de partir pour l'étranger, Charmidès m'a fait connaître un trésor caché dans cette maison, ici, dans une chambre"; 783: "Tu déterreras le trésor sans éveiller le soupçon." Et nombreux sont chez Plaute, les emplois figurés du mot "trésor" (*As.* 277, 655; *Curc.* 676; *Merc.* 163, 641; *Most.* 865; *Poen.* 625; *Pseud.* 84, 628).

Térence utilise le thème une fois, cf. *Eunuque* 12, prologue: allusion à une pièce de Luscius, *le Trésor*, qui fait prononcer un plaidoyer au défendeur, disant pourquoi l'or est à lui, avant celui du demandeur, disant comment lui appartient le trésor en question et d'où il est venu dans son tombeau de famille.

Proche de la comédie est la fable, représentée par Esope: 62: *L'homme qui a trouvé un lion d'or:* "un avare, qui était peureux, ayant trouvé un lion d'or, disait: Je ne sais que devenir en cette aventure . . . O trésor qui ne me donne pas de plaisir . . . Cette fable s'applique à un riche qui n'ose ni toucher à ses trésors ni les mettre en usage"; 83: *Le laboureur et ses enfants* (repris par La Fontaine): "Mes enfants, je vais quitter ce monde; mais vous, cherchez ce que j'ai caché dans ma vigne, et vous trouverez tout: les enfants, s'imaginant qu'il y avait enfoui un trésor en quelque coin, bêchèrent profondément tout le sol de la vigne après la mort du père. De trésor, ils n'en trouvèrent point; mais la vigne bien remuée donna son fruit au centuple"; 84: *Le laboureur et la Fortune:* "Un laboureur, en bêchant, tomba sur magot d'or. Aussi chaque jour il couronnait la Terre, persuadé que c'était à elle qu'il devait cette faveur. Mais la Fortune lui apparut et lui dit: 'Pourquoi, mon ami, imputes-tu à la Terre les dons que je t'ai faits dans le dessein de t'enrichir? Si en effet les temps viennent à changer et que cet or passe en d'autres mains, je suis sûre qu'alors c'est à moi, la Fortune, que tu t'en prendras.' Cette fable montre qu'il faut reconnaître qui vous fait du bien et le payer de retour"; 344: *L'avare:* "Un avare convertit en or toute sa fortune, en fit un lingot et l'enfouit en un certain endroit, où il enfouit du même coup son coeur et son esprit. Tous le jours il venait voir son trésor. Or un ouvrier l'observa, devina ce qu'il en était et, déterrant le lingot, l'emporta. Quelque temps après, l'avare vint aussi, et, trouvant la place vide, il se mit à gémir et à s'arracher les cheveux. Un quidam l'ayant vu se lamenter ainsi, et s'étant informé du motif, lui dit: 'Ne te désespère pas ainsi, l'ami, car, tout en ayant de l'or, tu n'en avais pas. Prends donc une pierre, mets-la à la place de l'or, et figure-toi que c'est de l'or; il remplira pour toi le même office; car à ce que je vois, même au moment où l'or était là, tu ne faisais pas usage de ton bien.' Cette fable montre que la possession n'est rien, si la jouissance ne s'y joint pas."

Phèdre, 28: *Le chien et le trésor:* "Cette fable peut s'appliquer aux hommes avides et à ceux qui, nés dans la pauvreté, brûlent de s'entendre appeler riches. En déterrant des ossements humains, un chien trouva un trésor, et comme il avait outragé les dieux Mânes, il fut possédé de la passion des richesses, pour satisfaire par un châtiment à la Piété vénérable. C'est ainsi qu'occupé à veiller sur son or, il oublia de manger, et mourut" de faim. Un vautour juché sur son corps prononça, dit-on, ces paroles: "O chien, c'est justement que tu es mort, toi qui as désiré tout à coup des richesses royales, après avoir été conçu dans un carrefour et nourri d'ordures"; 56: *Le poulet et la perle.*

Ausone, XIX, *Epigrammata de diuersis rebus* 14: *"De eo qui thesaurum repperit cum se laqueo uellet suspendere (ex graeco). Qui laqueum collo nectebat, repperit aurum thesauriqu̇e loco deposuit laqueum, at qui condiderat, postquam non repperit aurum, aptauit collo quem reperit laqueum."*

Il ne s'agit pas là uniquement d'un thème littéraire, comme le prouve tel papyrus égyptien du Ier s. (à Berlin, Oliver, 1979): on y trouve l'inventaire de caisses d'argenterie qu'un propriétaire laisse en dépôt avant un voyage (il est question de caisses et de couvertures).

Une partie des dépôts cachés, notamment les trésors monétaires (Guelma, Tipasa, Announa . . .) et les trésors d'argenterie (Notre-Dame d'Allençon, Kaiseraugst, Beaurains, Berthouville . . .) ont fait l'objet de découvertes retentissantes. Comme exemple de trésor à valeur religieuse on citera Livius 5.40: "lors de l'invasion gauloise, des objets sacrés furent enterrés dans une chapelle voisine de la maison du flamine de Quirinus" (cf. Plut., *Cam.* 20).

Les découvertes fortuites

Comme exemples de telles "inventions" dues à des travaux divers, outre le texte de Virgile cité en épigraphe, relevons un autre cas de travaux agricoles: Liv., 40.219, à propos des livres de Numa, cf. Pline l'Ancien, NH 13.84: "Un très ancien historien, Cassius Hemina . . . rapporte que le greffier Cn. Terentius, en défonçant son champ du Janicule, exhuma un sarcophage ayant contenu le corps du roi Numa," mais Plutarque, *Numa* 22.2, parle de grandes pluies.

Autre source: les fondations de constructions: c'est le cas du Capitole (Liv. 1.55, Dion. 1.25), qui découvre une tête fatidique, ou la recherche de matériaux à remployer dans des constructions, comme la pratiquèrent les colons césariens en Campanie: cf. Suétone, *César* 81: "Comme les colons conduits à Capoue en vertu de la loi Julia démolissaient des tombeaux très anciens pour construire des maisons de campagne et le faisaient avec d'autant plus d'ardeur qu'ils découvraient en les explorant une quantité de vases anciens . . ."

L'archéologie des antiquaires et la chasse au trésor

Malgré les tabous religieux, la cupidité humaine a animé les chercheurs de trésors, à titre individuel ou collectif, notamment dans les sanctuaires et le tombeaux.

Les sanctuaires étaient munis de *fauissae*[1] dont Aulu-Gelle (*NA* 2.10), à propos du Capitole, donne la définition suivante: "C'étaient des sortes de caves et de puits qui se trouvaient en terre sous la place; on y rangeait les vieilles statues qui étaient tombées du temple, et d'autres objets vénérables provenant des offrandes consacrées. Q. Valerius Soranus disait souvent que ce que nous appelions *thesaurus* d'un nom grec, les anciens Latins l'avaient appelé *flauissae*, parce qu'on y enfermait, non pas du bronze ou de l'argent en lingots, mais de la monnaie coulée *(flata)* et frappée. Il conjecturait donc qu'on avait enlevé la deuxième lettre de ce mot, et qu'on avait appelé fauissae certaines caves ou grottes dont les intendants du temple se servaient pour garder les objets sacrés."

Les exemples de temples pillés et parfois dédommagés sont nombreux dans le monde grec comme dans le monde romain:

Tite-Live, 29.8: les Romains osèrent piller les trésors de Proserpine, restés intacts depuis tant de siècles. Pyrrhus seul les avait enlevés; mais après avoir expié son sacrilège d'une manière terrible, il avait rapporté les dépouilles sacrées; 18: le légat romain et les tribuns des soldats, qui connaissaient ce fait, ont osé néanmoins porter leurs mains sacrilèges sur ces trésors inviolables; 19: Rome promet de faire rechercher tout l'argent soustrait aux trésors de Proserpine, d'y remettre une somme double, d'offrir un sacrifice expiatoire, cf. 31.12.1, 13.1.

Strabon, 5.2.3: trésors de Delphes; 5.2.8: pillage du temple d'Ilythie à Caere par Denys; 5.2.2: temple de Junon Lacinia, naguère fort riche; 9.2.5: pillage de Delphes: les trésors des Tectosages viendraient en partie de ses dépouilles; 9.3.8: "le temple de Delphes se trouve être aujourd'hui très pauvre, sinon en offrandes pieuses . . . du moins en métaux précieux." Pillage sacrilège des Phocidiens. Nulle trace de richesse quand Onomarque et Phayllus envahirent et pillèrent le temple; 10.2.17: pillage du temple de Leucothée par Pharnace, puis par Mithridate; 13.1.30: "Antoine avait partout sur son passage et à l'intention de son Egyptienne, dépouillé les principaux sanctuaires des chefs-d'oeuvre d'art offerts et consacrés par la piété des populations, partout Auguste rendit aux dieux ce qui leur appartenait"; 15.3.7: tombeau de Cyrus pillé dans un sanctuaire; 16.18: tentative de pillage du temple de Bélus par Antiochus; 17.1.B: cercueil d'or d'Alexandre volé par Ptolémée Coccès.

Plutarque, *Sylla* 12.9: pillage de la Grèce.

Les militaires, du fait de leurs déplacements à travers tout l'empire et de leur rapacité, ont pu être des découvreurs de trésors. Citons un exemple tiré de la *Vie de Pompée* de Plutarque (2.4-5): en 81 av. J.C., Pompée est en Afrique (Tunisie) avec six légions: "On raconte qu'il lui arriva alors une aventure plaisante: quelques soldats étant, à ce qu'il paraît, tombés sur un trésor, y trouvèrent beaucoup d'argent. La nouvelle s'en étant répandue, tous les autres s'imaginèrent que l'endroit était plein de richesses, déposées là lors des malheurs de Carthage (sur les 'trésors de Didon,' cf. les vers de Virgile cités en épigraphe et Tacite, *A*. 16.1. Pendant plusieurs jours, Pompée ne put rien faire de ses soldats, occupés à chercher des trésors; il se promenait parmi eux en riant de voir tant de myriades d'hommes fouiller et retourner la plaine. A la fin, désespérant de rien trouver et se jugeant assez punis de leur sottise, ils prièrent Pompée de les emmener où il voudrait."

Les colons césariens de Capoue pouvaient avoir l'excuse de chercher des matériaux de remploi. Ils furent imités par ceux de Corinthe, mus pour la plupart par la seule avidité; cf. Strabon, 8.7.23: "Les nouveaux colons césariens de Corinthe, s'étant mis à remuer les décombres de la ville et à fouiller les tombeaux, y trouvèrent une grande quantité de sculptures en terre cuite, et aussi beaucoup de bronzes précieux. La vue de ces chefs-d'oeuvre les ayant remplis d'admiration, ils ne laissèrent pas une seule tombe inexplorée, et quand ils furent richement pourvus, ils mirent en vente à des prix très élevés tout ce qu'ils avaient trouvé, inondant en quelque sorte la ville de Rome de leurs 'nécrocorinthies.' C'est le nom qu'ils avaient donné à tous les objets retirés des tombeaux, et principalement aux sculptures en terre cuite. Dans le commencement, ces terres cuites furent extrêmement recherchées et prisées, même à l'égal des plus beaux bronzes corinthiens, mais cette vogue se ralentit dans la suite, et parce que les fouilles n'en donnèrent presque plus, et parce que le peu qu'on en trouvait encore était en général de qualité inférieure."

L'Afrique encore fut à l'ordre du jour sous Néron. Tacite raconte (*A*. 16.1-3):

1. Bientôt la fortune se joua de Néron, abusé par sa propre légèreté et par les promesses de Caesellius Bassus, un homme d'origine punique, à l'esprit déréglé, qui prit l'illusion d'un songe pour l'espoir d'une réalité certaine; il se transporte à Rome, achète une audience du prince et lui expose qu'il a découvert dans son champ une caverne d'une profondeur immense, contenant un grande quantité d'or, non sous forme de monnaie, mais en masse brute et antique: il s'agissait de lingots très lourds posés à terre, et d'autre part, de colonnes dressées, trésors cachés pendant tant de siècles pour accroître la prospérité des temps présents. D'ailleurs, selon ses explications conjecturales, c'était Didon la Phénicienne, échappée de Tyr, qui, après la fondation

de Carthage, avait enfoui ces richesses, pour éviter que le nouveau peuple ne se laissât entraîner à des excès par trop d'opulence, ou que les rois des Numides, déjà hostiles pour d'autres raisons, ne fussent, par la soif de l'or, excités à la guerre.

2. Donc Néron, sans examiner assez quelle confiance méritait l'auteur ou l'affaire elle-même, ni envoyer personne vérifier l'exactitude des faits rapportés, grossit encore la nouvelle et envoie chercher ce qu'il prenait pour une proie toute prête. On fournit des trirèmes et des rameurs de choix pour accélérer la course. Il n'y eut pas ces jours-là d'autre sujet d'entretien chez le peuple par crédulité, chez les gens avisés dans un esprit tout différent. Et comme on célébrait alors les jeux quinquennaux du deuxième lustre, les poètes et les orateurs en tirèrent leur principal thème à la gloire du prince: ce n'était pas seulement les moissons ordinaires ni l'or mêlé aux minerais que produisait la terre, mais, douée d'une fécondité nouvelle, elle prodiguait ses dons, et des richesses à portée de la main étaient offertes par les dieux-ainsi que d'autres inventions serviles, qu'ils développaient avec beaucoup de faconde et non moins d'adulation, sûrs de trouver chez Néron une complaisante crédulité.

3. Pendant ce temps, sur ce vain espoir, la dissipation ne faisait que croître, et l'on épuisait les anciennes ressources, comme s'il s'en offrait d'autres qui suffiraient aux prodigalités du prince pendant un grand nombre d'années. Il allait même jusqu'à prendre déjà sur ce fonds ses largesses, et l'attente des richesses devenait une des causes de la pauvreté publique. En fait, Bassus fouilla son terrain et tous les champs d'alentour, assurant qu'à tel endroit ou tel autre se trouvait la caverne promise, suivi non seulement par les soldats, mais encore par un peuple de campagnards, enrôlé pour effectuer le travail, enfin, revenu de son délire et manifestant sa surprise de n'avoir jamais été trompé par ses rêves antérieurs et de subir alors sa première déception, il échappa à la honte et à la crainte par une mort volontaire. Certains ont rapporté qu'il fut mis en prison, puis relâché, après confiscation de ses biens à la place du trésor royal.

ARCHÉOLOGIE ET MENTALITÉS

Archéologie et légendes

C'est un phénomène fréquent dans tous les contextes culturels: des monuments (souvent des tombeaux[2] ou objets anciens sont à l'origine de légendes explicatives). Nous avons parlé ailleurs de la "végétation folklorique" qui pousse sur les ruines.[3]

Voici quelques exemples concernant Rome et l'Italie: Liv. 1.25: tombeaux des Horaces et des Curiaces en rapport avec la légende d'Albe: "Les sépulcres existent toujours, à la place où chacun est tombé. Les deux Romains sont au même endroit, et plus près d'Albe, les trois Albains, dans la direction de Rome, avec les mêmes intervalles que dans le combat." Chez le même historien, la légende d'Arruns de Clusium (5.33.3 cf. Cato fr. 36; Diod. 14.113; app., *Celt.* 2.1) tranfère sur le plan du mythe une réalité historique certaine: les Etrusques ont attiré les Celtes en Italie en leur faisant entrevoir les avantages d'un climat plus doux, de butins fructueux et l'espoir d'un établissement sur une terre plus fertile. Cet Arruns qui introduit le vin en Gaule incarne pour nous tous les marchands méditerranéens qui ont passé les Alpes avec des convois chargés d'outres de vin, d'amphores d'huile, de sacs de figues.

Un monument ancien peut susciter une légende, par exemple la statue de Clélie, cf. Plutarque, *Publicola* 19.8: "On lui éleva sur la Voie Sacrée, en vue du Palatin, une statue équestre qui, selon certains auteurs, représentait non pas Clélie, mais Valérie." Peut-être est-ce la statue d'une déesse équestre (comme Epona) qui est à l'origine de cette légende.

Suétone rapporte, dans la *Vie d'Auguste* (72.6), que "l'empereur orna ses villas de curiosités antiques et rares, comme ces restes énormes de bêtes monstrueuses découvertes à Caprée, que l'on appelle les os des géants et les armes des héros." Il doit s'agit de fossiles. Ce texte évoque pour nous la découverte, au XVIIè s., d'ossements d'éléphants fossiles en Dauphiné qui furent attribués au géant Teutobocus (cf. E. Laming-Emperaire, o.c., citant J. Tissot), avant d'être interprétés comme le souvenir du passage d'Hannibal.

Voici maintenant des exemples empruntés à Strabon: 5.2.60 (à Aethalia): "On veut que les râclures laissées par les Argonautes quand ils firent usage de leurs strigiles subsistent encore aujourd'hui, durcies, sous la forme des graviers multicolores qui couvrent le rivage"; 4.4 et 6: légende des géants aux Champs Phlégréens (cf. 5.4.9: Typhon); 5.4.7: à Naples, tombeau d'une sirène, Parthénope; 6.1.1: à Locres, une statue du cithariste Eunomos représenté avec une cigale sur sa cithare . . . parce que, l'une des cordes de son instrument étant venue à se rompre pendant un concours, une cigale s'était posée à sa place et l'avait suppléée de son chant"; 6.3.5: source putride et légende des géants Leuterniens; 6.3.9: en Daunie, sanctuaire de Calchas et de Podalire.

L'on peut dire que l'ensemble du monde ancien est hanté de telles légendes, liées à des singularités locales: Pline l'Ancien, *NH* 5.14 (13): un rocher où l'on montre les restes des chaînes d'Andromède; 15.2: le plantane de Gortyne sous lequel Jupiter se serait uni à Europe; 34.105: "On dit qu'il existe près de l'Euphrate, dans la ville qu'on appelle Zeugma, une chaîne de fer dont Alexandre le Grand se servit pour jeter un pont"; 36.99: à Cyzique une pierre appelée "fugitive": "Les Argonautes s'en étaient servi comme d'ancre et l'avaient laissée là. Comme à maintes reprises elle avait disparu, on l'enchaîna avec du plomb."

Mentionnons aussi, chez Silius Italicus (1.273), la légende de Sagonte. La légende rapportée par Tacite (*G.* 3.3) d'un voyage d'Ulysse sur le Rhin peut s'expliquer par la découverte de runes assimilées à des caractères grecs ou par celle de tessons de céramique grecque sur des *oppida*.

Le thème du dragon gardien de trésors enfouis, auquel Cicéron (*Phil.* 18.[5]12) fait allusion (*qui domini patrimonium circumplexus quasi thesaurum draco*), se retrouve dans toutes les littératures.

Le monde chrétien a créé ses propres légendes, en interprétant à sa façon des particularités topographiques ou des monuments anciens: greniers de Joseph (les pyramides d'Egypte), gué des Hébreux au bord de la Mer Rouge.

Rappelons ici que, d'une façon générale, l'archéologie confirme les données littéraires: la légende de Tarpeia (Liv. 1.2) a pu être influencée par le voisinage du lieu où l'on châtiait parjures, incestes et crimes d'état. Au lacus Curtius (Liv. 1.13) devait exister un puits sacré à valeur infernale, car on y a retrouvé un squelette humain.

Archéologie et religion—"Les reliques"

La découverte d'objets archéologiques peut passer pour un signe des dieux. Les exemples ne manquent pas. En voici quelques-uns, par ordre chronologique:

D'abord une supercherie politico-religieuse, qui serait due à Romulus (Plutarque, *Rom.* 14.3-5: épisode de l'enlèvement des Sabines): "Romulus commença par faire répandre le buit qu'il avait découvert, caché sous la terre, l'autel d'un dieu. Le nom de ce dieu était Consus, c. à d. conseiller ... Selon d'autres, ce dieu était Neptune équestre, parce que l'autel, placé dans le Circus Maximus, reste toujours souvert, sauf pendant les concours hippiques, où on le découvre ... Romulus fit annoncer qu'il offrirait sur cet autel un brillant sacrifice, accompagné d'un concours et d'un spectacle public."

La découverte d'une tête au Capitole, "prodige annonçant la grandeur de l'empire: en creusant les fondations du temple, on mit au jour, dit-on, une tête humaine dont les traits étaient intacts. Cette découverte annonçait, à n'en pas douter, que ce lieu serait au sommet de l'empire et à la tête du monde" (Liv. 1.55). Dion (1.25) précise qu'il s'agissait de la tête d'un homme tué récemment, toute souillée de sang et de poussière. Un devin de Toscane, consulté à ce sujet, dit que cette ville deviendrait la capitale d'un grand nombre de nations; mais que ce serait par le sang et les massacres. Le nom de Capitole fut donné, à cette occasion, au Mont Tarpéien."

La découverte des livres de Numa, en 181 av. J.C. (Liv. 40.29), à confronter avec Denys d'Halicarnasse (2.58); Pline l'Ancien, *NH* 13.27.84-87: 535 ans après le règne de Numa; Varron ap. Aug., *Civ. Dei* 7.34; Festus 178L; *De uiris* 3.2; Plut., *Numa* 22; Val. Max. 1.1.11; Lactance, *Inst.* 1.22); on note quelques variantes: à l'origine de l' "invention," des travaux agricoles ou une inondation, un ou deux sarcophages. Tite-Live donne des précisions sur les dimensions des cuves, leur fermeture, leurs inscriptions, le nombre des livres, leur mode de préservation. Ce qu'il nous importe de souligner ici, c'est que les documents découverts furent brûlés comme "susceptibles de détruire les sentiments religieux" (Tite-Live, mais selon Valère Maxime, on aurait gardé les livres écrits en latin[4]).

Texte déjà cité de Suétone, *César* 81: à Capoue, on trouva dans le sépulcre où, disait-on, était enseveli Capys, le fondateur de Capoue, une tablette de bronze portant une inscription en langue et caractères grecs, dont voici le sens: "Quand on aura découvert les ossements de Capys, un descendant d'Iule tombera sous les coups de ses proches et bientôt l'Italie expiera sa mort par de terribles désastres. Cette histoire est garantie par Cornelius Balbus, un ami très intime de César."

Plusieurs "présages archéologiques" concernent *Galba*, cf. Suétone, *Galba* 8: "La foudre tomba dans un lac chez les Cantabres et l'on découvrit douze haches, symboles du pouvoir souverain"[5]; 9: "Dans la ville de Clunia, le prêtre de Jupiter, averti par un songe, avait retiré du sanctuaire le même oracle rendu de façon identique 200 ans auparavant par une jeune fille ayant le don de prophétie"; 10: "On découvrit, en fortifiant la ville (Dertosa) qu'il avait choisie pour base d'opérations, un anneau d'un travail antique, sur la pierre duquel était gravée une Victoire avec un trophée."

Un présage du même ordre intéresse Vespasien (Suétone, 7): "À Tégée, en Arcadie, sur l'indication des devins, on retira du sol, dans in lieu consacré (*fauissa*, tombeau?), des vases d'un travail antique, sur lesquels il y avait une figure tout à fait semblable à celle de Vespasien."

La découverte archéologique considérée comme un signe des dieux, peut être favorisée par telle ou telle divinité, notamment par Hercule, gardien des trésors, qui passe pour présider à leur découverte: cf. Pétrone, *Sat.* 88; "Même avant de toucher le seuil du Capitole, l'un promet une offrande s'il déterre un trésor."

La magie, les songes peuvent intervenir: *Ib.* 38: "Tu vois celui-là, qui est couché le dernier du banc (un affranchi à table). Aujourd'hui il possède ses 800000 sesterces. Il est parti de rien . . . Mais, à ce qu'on raconte, il a réussi à attraper le bonnet d'un incube, et il a ainsi trouvé un trésor"; *Ib.* 128: "Ainsi, dans la nuit qui verse le sommeil, les vains songes se jouent de nos yeux égarés: la terre, creusée, met au jour un trésor; notre main criminelle manie le fruit de son vol; elle emporte l'or, la sueur baigne notre visage, au fond du coeur palpite la crainte que quelqu'un, connaissant la cachette, ne secoue notre giron alourdi par son larcin. Puis, lorsque ce bonheur illusoire s'enfuit de notre esprit rendu à la réalité, l'âme se prend à désirer ce qu'elle a perdu, obsédée qu'elle est tout entière par le souvenir de sa vision."

Rêves et prédictions de trésors ont fourni matière à des réflexions philosophiques de Cicéron dans le *De Diuinatione* 2.7.18: "Ceux qui vous annoncent que vous découvrirez un trésor, ou qu'il vous viendra un héritage, quels indices peuvent-ils en avoir? Quelles sont les causes naturelles qui les leur font pressentir? Et s'il y a dans ces prédictions et dans d'autres du même genre quelque nécessité d'accomplissement, que restera-t-il donc à gouverner par les hasards ou par le sort?"; *Ib.* 2.14.33: "Que peut-il y avoir de commun entre le monde et la découverte d'un trésor." Cicéron pose ici le problème du rapport entre les parties de la Nature: "Quel rapport entre la fissure d'un foie et mon petit bénéfice?"

Sur ce problème complexe des rapports des vestiges ou objets archéologiques et de la religion, nous relevons un texte curieux de Pline l'Ancien, *NH* 34.137: "La famille Servilia possède un triens sacré, auquel elle offre un sacrifice annuel avec un soin et une magnificence extrêmes. On prétend qu'on le voit tantôt croître, tantôt décroître et qu'il présage ainsi la grandeur ou la décadence de cette famille." S'agirait-il d'un culte familial en relation avec une statue de divinité ou un symbole religieux représenté sur cette monnaie?

Notons enfin que les objets sortis de terre ont pu paraître maléfiques aux premiers chrétiens: l'Eglise avait imaginé des prières particulières pour leur ôter précisément ce pouvoir satanique.

Les reliques: G. Ch. Picard, dans l'ouvrage cité plus haut, écrit: "Le triomphe du christianisme tue le dilettantisme; désormais et jusqu'à la fin du Moyen Age, les objets anciens ne sont appréciés que s'ils ont une valeur religieuse. La chasse aux reliques, commencée dès le IVè s., a donné lieu assez souvent à des fouilles: l'une des plus anciennes et la plus célèbre permet à l'impératrice Hélène, mère de Constantin, de retrouver, pense-t-on, la Croix du Christ."

Ajoutons qu'il y avait déjà eu des "reliques païennes," cf. par exemple Pline l'Ancien, *NH* 7.20: le gros orteil droit du roi Pyrrhus guérissait par attouchement les maladies de la rate. Il était conservé dans un reliquaire à l'intérieur d'un temple.

Archéologie et politique—Le butin de guerre

Les vestiges archéologiques peuvent revêtir une importance politique en raison de leur signification symbolique, ce qui explique:

Restaurations, cf. Suétone, *Vespasien* 8: "Il entreprit de faire reconstituer 3000 tables d'airain détruites dans l'incendie du Capitole, et ordonna d'en rechercher partout les copies; c'était la collection d'archives la plus belle et la plus ancienne de l'Empire, qui contenait, presque depuis les origines de Rome, les sénatus-consultes et les plébiscites relatifs aux alliances, aux traités, aux privilèges accordés à quiconque." Copies, cf. Plutarque, *Pompée* 42.9: "Ravi de la beauté du théâtre de Mytilène, il en fit dessiner la forme et le plan, dans l'intention d'en élever à Rome un pareil, mais plus grand et plus imposant. Et maintes appropriations: transfert à Rome de statues, de tableaux, d'objets divers (des bijoux aux obélisques) pris comme butin à des villes ou à des princes étrangers.

Le pillage des oeuvres d'art ou de dépouilles significatives à titre de prise de guerre est attesté à toutes époques et placé sous le patronage des dieux nationaux: cf. Liv. 10.2.14: "des éperons de navires et dépouilles lacédémoniennes restèrent longtemps accrochés dans le vieux temple de Junon à Padoue"; 24.21.9: dépouilles des Gaulois et des Illyriens offertes à Hiéron par le peuple romain et déposées à Syracuse dans le temple de Zeus

Olympien; 25.40: "Marcellus, qui avait pris Syracuse, fit transporter à Rome, pour en orner la ville, les statues et tableaux dont abondait Syracuse. C'étaient, à la vérité, des dépouilles enlevées aux ennemis par le droit de la guerre."

Voici une série de références chez Strabon: 1.4.5: "beaucoup de trophées et de dépouilles encore exposées à Marseille rappellent maintes victoires navales"; 6.3.1: "au nombre des dépouilles, le colosse d'Hercule en airain, oeuvre de Lysippe, qui figure aujourd'hui dans le Capitole, et que Fabius Maximus y a déposé naguère en commémoration de l'entrée des Romains dans Tarente"; 7.6.I: statue colossale d'Apollon par Calamis transportée par Lucullus d'Apollonie au Capitole; 8.8.23: "Polybe nous a laissé un récit lamentable de la prise de Corinthe... Il dit avoir vu en passant dans les rues de la ville le sol jonché des tableaux les plus précieux, sur lequels des soldats jouaient aux dés. Il signale entre autres le *Bacchus* d'Aristide, ce beau tableau qui donna lieu, dit-on, au proverbe: "Rien comme le Bacchus" et, avec celui-ci, *l'Hercule consumé par la tunique de Déjanire*... En visitant le temple de Cérès à Rome, nous avons reconnu au milieu des riches offrandes qu'il contenait, le *Bacchus*, chef d'oeuvre d'Aristide. Par malheur, ce temple a été récemment détruit par le feu. La plus grande partie des oeuvres d'art que possèdent les temples de Rome a titre d'offrandes, et j'ajoute les plus belles, proviennent de Corinthe: On en retrouve aussi quelques-unes dans les différentes villes qui entourent Rome. Cela tient à ce que Mummius qui avait, dit-on, plus de générosité dans le coeur que de lumières dans l'esprit, fit libéralement part de ses trésors à quiconque lui en adressait la demande." (Lucullus en emprunte pour une dédicace, mais ne les rend pas.)

13.3.2: Sinope prise par Lucullus, qui enlève la sphère de Billarus et d'Autolycus, chef d'oeuvre de Sthénis; 13.3.31: joyaux de Mithridate déposés par Pompée au Capitole; 12.5.3: la statue de la Mère des dieux de Pessinus transportée à Rome comme l'avait été auparavant l'Esculape d'Epidaure (pour une fois, ce n'est pas un rapt!); 13.1.19: le lion abattu de Lysippe transféré de Lampsaque à Rome par Agrippa; 13.1.30: Antoine transporte en Egypte la statue d'Ajax de Rhoeteum, mais elle est restituée parmi d'autres morceaux précieux aux Rhoetéens par César Auguste; 14.11.19: "Dans l'Asclépieum de Cos on voyait naguère la Vénus Anadyomène, qui est actuellement à Rome exposée comme un hommage à la mémoire du dieu César. L'idée est d'Auguste, qui voulut dédier à son père l'image de l'archégète ou auteur de leur race. On raconte même à ce propos que, pour indemniser Cos de la belle peinture qu'il lui enlevait, Auguste fit remise à ses habitants de cent talents sur le tribut qu'il leur avait imposé"; 17.1.27: transport à Rome d'obélisques d'Héliopolis.

On trouvera d'autres mentions: Chez Appien, *Mithridate* 115: "lors de son 3è triomphe, Pompée revêt la chlamyde d'Alexandre le Grand, que les gens de Cos avaient donnée à Mithridate et qu'on avait retrouvée dans la garde-robe du roi pour réincarner en quelque sorte le personnage d'Alexandre dont il portait le surnom." Pline l'Ancien, *NH* 34.84: "les rapines que Néron avait disposées dans les salons de sa Maison Dorée furent dédiées par Vespasien dans le Temple de la Paix."

Suétone, *Caligula* 52: il lui arrive de porter la cuirasse d'Alexandre le Grand, qu'il a fait retirer de son tombeau; et Plutarque, *Flaminius* 1.1: un grand Apollon apporté de Carthage, en face du cirque; *Paul-Emile* 32.5: "La première journée (de son triomphe) suffit à peine à voir défiler les statues, les tableaux, les colosses pris à l'ennemi, que transportaient 250 chars"; 33.4: la vaisselle d'or de Pompée.

Archéologie et tourisme culturel

Plusieurs motifs expliquent que la visite des monuments archéologiques ou d'oeuvres anciennes fasse partie de "circuits" touristiques: leur valeur esthétique, mais aussi le "mystère" qui entoure certains aspects des civilisations disparues attirent les voyageurs.

Dans le cas de grands personnages, ces visites revêtent aussi une signification politique, cf. Strabon: excursion d'Alexandre à Ilion (13.1.26-27), à l'ancien palais de Pasargade et au tombeau de Cyrus (15.3.7), à Ammon (17.1.43).

Lucain nous représente César aux ruines de Troie, *Pharsale* 9.961: "Il gagne la côte de Sigée, plein d'admiration pour les grands souvenirs, et les rives du Simoïs, et le promontoire de Rhétée, ennobli par la tombe grecque (Ajax) et ces ombres qui doivent tant aux poètes. Il va voir les ruines mémorables de Troie brûlée, il cherche les nobles vestiges de Phébus. Maintenant des buissons stériles et des troncs pourris de chênes écrasent le palais d'Assaracus et ne tiennent plus les temples des dieux que d'une racine fatiguée. Pergame tout entière est ensevelie sous des ruines, ses ruines mêmes ont péri . . . Il n'y a pas une pierre qui n'ait un nom. Il avait passé, sans y prendre garde, un ruisseau qui serpentait dans la poussière desséchée: c'était le Xanthe; sans faire attention, il posait le pied sur un tertre de gazon: un Phrygien l'empêche de fouler les Mânes d'Hector; il y avait, dispersées sur le sol, des pierres qui ne conservaient plus trace du culte des dieux: "Tu ne regardes pas, lui dit son guide, l'autel de Jupiter Hercéen?" On retrouve le dictateur à Alexandrie (*Ib.* 15): "Intrépide il va voir les sanctuaires des dieux et les temple d'une antique majesté, qui attestent la puissance passée des Macédoniens ... Il est impatient de descendre dans le caveau funèbre. Là repose l'insensé rejeton de Philippe de Pella ... On a déposé les restes du héros dans l'asile du sanctuaire."

Le voyage de Germanicus en Orient associe inspection politique et tourisme culturel, cf. Tacite (*A.* 2.53): "À Actium il visite les trophées consacrés par Auguste et le camp d'Antoine" (cf. sa double ascendance). Il pénètre dans la Propontide et dans la bouche du Pont, désireux de connaître ces lieux antiques et partout vantés ... À Ilion il contemple tout ce que les vicissitudes du sort et le berceau de notre race lui inspiraient de respect." 59: "Il part pour l'Egypte afin de se faire une idée des antiquités (*cognoscendae antiquitatis*)" remonte le Nil; ici un excursus résume l'histoire de Canope "fondée par les Spartiates en mémoire du pilote Canopus, enseveli à cet endroit" (on devait montrer son tombeau). "Il visite les grandes ruines de l'ancienne Thèbes. Sur les constructions colossales subsistaient encore des caractères égyptiens retraçant dans son ensemble son ancienne splendeur." Germanicus se les fait traduire: "On lisait ... les tributs imposés aux nations, le poids d'argent et d'or, le nombre des armes et des chevaux, les offrandes pour les temples, l'ivoire et les parfums, les quantités de froment." 61: Germanicus visite non seulement les monuments historiques, mais aussi les curiosités géographiques: "la statue de Memnon qui, frappée par les rayons du soleil, rend le son de la voix, ... les pyramides, les lacs creusés dans le sol pour recevoir les eaux surabondantes du Nil."

Les chefs ennemis font de même: Silius Italicus, 12.13 sq. représente Hannibal découvrant le littoral de Baïes, v.2: "Il visite les merveilles voisines, où les lacs et la terre s'assemblent, s'intéresse aux noms successifs des villes, aux tombeaux des héros" aux illustrations mythologiques, aux cultes, aux *mirabilia* ... "On lui montre la chaîne du Vésuve, et sur l'extrême sommet des rocs que rongent les flammes, la montagne jonchée alentour d'éboulements; et ces blocs qui, pour tuer, rivalisent avec l'Etna. Et même il voit Misène qui garde en son tombeau les renoms de l'Ida et, sur le rivage même, Baules l'Herculéenne. Il admire les menaces de la mer et les convulsions de la terre."

Un large public semble avoir connu l'engouement du "tourisme culturel," cf. Tite-Live 25.40 (après le pillage de Syracuse): "Ce fut l'époque où l'on admira, pour la première fois, les productions des arts de la Grèce . . . On venait visiter jadis les temples dédiés par Marcellus, près de la porte Capène, à cause des chefs d'oeuvre de ce genre, dont il ne reste que des vestiges;" et Strabon, 9.2.25: "Ce qui fit longtemps la réputation de Thespies, c'est la présence dans ses murs de la belle statue de l'Amour de Praxitèle, sculptée par le grand artiste pour la coutisance Glycère, à qui il en fit hommage, et offerte par celle-ci aux Thespiens ses compatriotes. On ne montait guère autrefois jusqu'à Thespies que pour voir le fameux Amour, la ville n'ayant rien par elle-même d'autrement curieux" (à rapprocher de Pline l'Ancien, *NH* 36.12: un Cupidon de Praxitèle attirait les visiteurs à Thespies).[6]

Nous aurons l'occasion d'étudier ailleurs les rapports de l'archéologie et de l'histoire à Rome et quelques anticipations scientifiques auxquelles on a jusqu'ici peu porté attention: archéologie sous-marine, et sous-lacustre, topographie historique et typologie des sites, stratigraphie, archéologie industrielle, archéologie du paysage, ethnohistoire, notion de partrimoine et législation des fouilles en Grèce et à Rome.[7]

NOTES

1. Il s'agit, au fond, d'une extension des dépôts de fondation dont la pratique est attestée pour le Capitole, cf. Tacite, *H*. 4.53 (lors de la reconstruction du Capitole): "par monceaux on jeta dans les fondations des pièces de monnaies d'argent et d'or et des matériaux vierges, que nulle fournaise n'avait domptés encore, mais qui étaient à l'état de nature."

   Les trésors et dépôts des temples pouvaient être considérables, cf. Liv. 7.15: "C. Sulpicius en fait d'or tira des dépouilles gauloises une quantité considérable qu'il consacra, enfermée dans des pierres de taille, au Capitole." Une partie de ce dépôt a été moblisée en diverses circonstances, ce qui explique que certains sanctuaires aient pu jouer le rôle de banques.

2. C'est le cas du tumulus de l'âge du Fer de Lavinium, interprété comme la tombe d'Enée, cf. Don. Hal. 1.64.5 et F. Castagnoli, *Lavinium* I, Rome, 1972 sq. On rapprochera de Suétone, *Vesp*. 12: "Comme des flatteurs faisaient remonter l'origine de la famille Flavia aux fondateurs de Reate et à un certain compagnon d'Hercule dont le tombeau subsiste sur la via Salaria, il fut le premier à se moquer d'eux" (scepticisme notable, à l'encontre de l'attitude de maintes grandes familles de Rome).

3. Cf. *Ethnohistoire et archéologie*, *Caesarodunum*, Sup. 45, Tours, 1982.

4. Cf. R. Flacelière, *REG* 61, 1948, 426; J. Gagé, *Apollon romain*, 328-338.
5. Cf. A. Laming-Emperaire, *op. cit.*, à propos des haches préhistoriques dites "pierres de foudre."
6. Nous reviendrons plus longuement sur ce sujet dans un ouvrage sous presse: *L'artiste, le collectionnneur et le faussaire. Musées et collections dans la Rome antique.*
7. Communication sous presse dans le *Bulletin de la Société Nationale des Antiquaires de France.*

GILBERT HIGHET'S RAISING OF ITALY: *AENEID* 3.523-524

William R. Nethercut
University of Texas

No one who sat in Gilbert Highet's Vergil seminar will be likely to forget the night sailing of *Aeneid* 3 and that first glimpse, under the new day's early rose, of the dark coast of Italy:

> *Iamque rubescebat stellis Aurora fugatis*
> *cum procul obscuros collis humilemque videmus*
> *Italiam. ITALIAM! primus conclamat Achates,*
> *ITALIAM! laeto socii clamore salutant."*
>
> Aen. 3.521-524

Momentary recognition (*Itali-*), exclamation (*Italiam*!!), confirmation (*ITALIAM*!!), broke upon us in successive waves. When Highet read this passage, we reached *Italiam* at the start of line 523 and were just about to catch a breath at the period. The breath was knocked from us, we never heard the period, as Highet—who had been on board with Achates all along—knew, himself, the darkened hills toward which we were sailing. The cry "ITALY!" rang from a different level: we were there.

The grand moment of this first sighting can be placed within a developing scheme of reference to Aeneas' search for Italy. Three other passages exist in the *Aeneid* which present *Italiam* in two successive lines. The first is in Book 1 and is drawn from the speech of Ilioneus. The Trojan captain voices his hope that it may somehow be granted his people to reach Italy:

> *Si datur <u>Italiam</u> sociis et rege recepto*
> *tendere, ut <u>Italiam</u> laeti Latiumque petamus ...*
>
> Aen. 1.553-554

In both verses *Italiam* makes up the second foot: read aloud, the reinforcement of *Italiam* by the second *Italiam* is perceptible, though not as vigorous as it is in the raising of the Italian coast at dawn. The second verse has elision in the first foot (*tendere ut*), just as 3.523 does; however, *Italiam* itself is not involved in the elision, as it is in Book 3. In spite of these distinguishing features, the lines from Book 1 offer effectively the essential impulse and rhythm which reach more intense expression in 3.523. In both places *Italiam* recurs in a second verse: in both there is reinforcement of the name, as the long "i" follows its partner at the same point in its own line which we found long "i" to occupy in the first verse (*Italiam . . . Italiam* in the second foot of two lines in Book 1, and in the first foot of two lines in Book 3). We can also mention that in the first line of the citation from Book 1 we have the initial syllable in long "i," so that in 1.553 we have the same sound pattern as in 3.523: *si̱ datur I̱taliam: I̱taliam I̱taliam*. Furthermore, in the second line (1.554) we read *Italiam laeti*; in 3.524 we have *Italiam laeto*. Nor should we miss the fact that 1.553 sets *Italiam* by *sociis*, while 3.524 has *Italiam . . . socii*. What is worked out separately in a parallel arrangement in 1.553-554 (*Italiam sociis, Italiam laeti*) is combined into one sequence in 3.524 (*Italiam laeto socii*). These two lines in Book 1, then, contain the germ of what we shall see in the excitement of Book 3.

In Book 3, the prophet Helenus instructs Aeneas about his course:

> *I̱taliam cursu petitis, ventisque vocatis;*
> *ibitis I̱taliam portusque intrare licebit.*
>   Aen. 3.253-254

Where Ilioneus had little certainty, Helenus sees the future. The movement of *Italiam* in the first line to the lead position befits this change. Ilioneus' concern was with the granting of good fortune by the gods (*Si datur*), with the course to be followed (*tendere*): his dactyls were taken up by verbs. In Book 3, a seer speaks only a magic name, "Italy." Secondly, Helenus like Ilioneus delivers a hexameter in which the first two feet lead off with long "i": *Si̱ datur I̱taliam* (Ilioneus): *i̱bitis I̱taliam* (Helenus). However, in Helenus' words we find that the initial syllable does not only contain "i," but more, *is* only this sound (there is no consonant like the "s" in Ilioneus' *si datur*). In this way, Vergil lays the groundwork for a pun between the thematic vowel of *ire* and the long "i" in *Italia*. Aeneas' journeying and his new home can be joined dramatically. For the present, however (3.253-254), the pun is latent. We shall see it fully developed later.

If 3.253-254 represents a more vivid adaptation of 1.553-554, we can now see how, when Achates and the Trojans sight land, Vergil outdoes the preceding two occasions. For one thing, he triples *Italiam*, which each of the foregoing passages had stated twice. He keeps the initial *Italiam* in the first verse (3.523), which we saw in Helenus' prophecy (3.253), but which was lacking in Ilioneus' uncertainty in Book 1: but he adds the excitement of the elision which Highet exploded with such impact. Thirdly, he keeps to the practice of the two earlier passages by restating *Italiam* in the second of two lines (I refer to his third use of *Italiam* in 3.523-534), but he shifts this iteration to the first position, to reinforce the name as it comes first in 3.523. That is: where Ilioneus spoke *Italiam* twice in 1.553-554, both of which were in the second foot of their respective verses—where Helenus, with greater certainty, shifted *Italiam* to the first position of his first verse, keeping *Italiam* second to strengthen *ibitis* in the subsequent line (3.253-254)—the actual sighting of Italy moves the repeated *Italiam . . . Italiam* to occupy the first feet of both verses. We can see an apparent progression from Ilioneus (*Italiam* in both lines is second), through Helenus foreseeing the future (one *Italiam* first, one second), to the reality of raising land (both lines have *Italiam* first). Finally, Vergil has taken the collocations *Italiam sociis* and *Italiam laeti,* as we noticed before in 1.553-554, and has tied them both together in the second verse of the Trojans' first view of Hesperia: *Italiam laeto socii clamore salutant* (3.524).

We can turn now to Book 4 of the *Aeneid* and to the passionate confrontation of Aeneas by Dido. Aeneas speaks first:

> Sed nunc <u>Italiam</u> magnam Gryneus Apollo,
> <u>Italiam</u> Lyciae iussere capessere sortes."
>
> Aen. 4.345-346

The repetition *Italiam . . . Italiam* is organized still differently from what we have seen in any of the other three citations. Aeneas has put at a distance that original vision of Italy. He is now at Carthage, with Ilioneus, and his initial naming of Italy comes in the second foot of the line, just where Ilioneus had placed *Italiam* when he wondered, by no means certain it would happen, whether the gods would allow him to arrive in Italy. In this set of lines in Book 4, *Italiam* does move into the first foot in verse 346. The gods are urging Aeneas to sail to Italy: the situation in the second of the above lines resembles the prophecy of Helenus with its assurance that Aeneas has been destined to live in Italy—there is thus an urgency, an emphasis in the restatement of *Italiam*. So it is that the name in 4.346 comes first. However this emphasis derives from the god, from Apollo, and is not originally Aeneas' own.

These two verses show us at first an Aeneas who finds himself far from Italy and closer to Dido, but then echo the gods' insistence at the beginning of line 346. Aeneas in these words is not making up an excuse. On the basis of the comparisons we have been able to analyze, this second position of *Italiam* in 4.345, shows Aeneas realistically. For the present, he is indeed with her (*nunc* in the first foot, *Italiam* second). Mercury, we can believe, truly shocked Aeneas; Vergil's description of his reaction in 4.279-280 can be taken seriously: Aeneas feels as if he is choking, he shivers and finds himself unable to make a sound. Yet *nunc*, as Aeneas addresses Dido, marks also the moment in which a crescendo begins to build, from *Italiam* in less obtrusive position, to *magnam*, to Apollo, then Italy at the first of line 346, and finally a sweep eastward with allusion to Apollo's Asian associations *(Lyciae sortes)*. The resonance of names in these two lines is attached in two separate movements to the two namings of Italy. These two movements carry us back into Aeneas' past: *Gryneus* evokes Aeolia and Aeneas' sailing along the Greek coast and islands; *Lyciae sortes*, in a wider sweep, take us to Apollo's, and Aeneas', Asian provenience. The second verse we are discussing, 4.346, thus emerges to predominate in every way over the line which introduces it; not only does *Italiam* come forward into the first foot of the line, but between Italy and Asia, powerfully juxtaposed, the verse encompasses the limits of Aeneas' world. His words at this moment indicate the transformation of his thinking.

In his careful study of the speeches in Vergil's *Aeneid*, Gilbert Highet detailed the pointed rebuttal with which Dido challenges the words Aeneas has just spoken to her.[1] Verses 345 (*Italiam*) and 350 (*et nos fas extera quaerere regna*) are taken up by verse 381:

I, sequere Italiam ventis, pete regna per undas."

Though he did not elaborate his examination of Dido's fury along the path I have been following in this note, an important contribution of Highet's teaching for Columbia University Vergilians was to heighten their sensitivity to the poet's patterning of vowels. Let me score 4.381 differently:

I, sequere Italiam ventis, pete regna per undas."

Dido's words complete the development traced here. We shall not see the repetition *Italiam . . . Italiam* further in the epic, yet the force of the imperative "i," the elision at the end of the first foot into the second "i" of *Italiam*, deserve to be set beside the excited cries we hear at the sighting of Italy in 3.523. I have made, to the best of my eyesight, a scan of the whole epic, looking for the possible parallels among those lines which have at least the long "i" at the start of the first and second feet.[2] The single parallel I have discovered—and it is a good one—is Deiphobus' *adieu* and exhortation to Aeneas in 6. 546: *I, decus, I nostrum*. The imperative and iteration of this "i" reinforce Dido's expostulation above, and of course the double "i" . . . "i" recapitulates the musical note of our interest. There is, however, no elision, nor is any country named.

It is also worth the while to check the lines in which *Italia* occurs. A frequent position for the name is at the first of a verse: *Italiam fato profugus,* 1.2. However, of the times in which we do encounter *Italia* in this placement, it is elided only twice. Leaving aside the raising of Italy in Book 3, the one exception is in 12.41: *Italia, ad mortem.*[3] The sound here in no way resembles the effect of the Trojans' joy in Book 3.523. A general principle for reacting to the presence of elision should be that the emergence of *Italia* in the second foot, before the syllables of the first foot have been completed, represents augmentation or enhancement of the emerging second foot. This is nicely evident in 1.13, where *Karthago* is intruded upon by *Italiam*, and is strengthened by 1.38, where Juno speaks of her inability to keep the Trojans from Italy (*nec posse Italia*). It is ironic that the very expression of her power is cut short, pre-empted by the name which signals the fulfillment of the Trojans' journey. The pattern is evident again in 1.68, when Juno complains to Jupiter that a race hostile to her is carrying Ilium into Italy: *Ilium in Italiam portans.* Here, Juno's own words convey the accomplishment of the destiny she seeks to avert, as *Ilium*, the starting point, disappears into the passage into Italy. The landfall itself is adumbrated: *I(lium in) I(taliam)*, once appreciated within Vergil's design of sound, can add momentum and impact to the sighting of Italy under the dawn.

An interesting parallel to the Trojans' raising of land is found in 6.357, where Palinurus tells Aeneas in the underworld that he did live on after falling into the sea: on the fourth day, just at dawn, he sighted Italy (*prospexi Italiam*). The elision at the end of the first foot and the intrusion of *Italiam* parallels the first vision of Achates in 3.523. We can compare, also, 6.61, where Aeneas prays to Apollo: *iam tandem Italiae fugientis prendimus oras.* In this verse the pull and tug between Vergil's pattern for excited recognition (*Italiam, -ae,* etc. in the second foot, breaking in upon the first foot) and the description of Italy's coast as *fugientis* is wonderfully accurate: first, we are close to Italy in Book 3; then we are driven back away from her by the storm in Book 1; and now, finally (*iam tandem*), Italy herself. It is fitting, to conclude these examples, to notice that when, in Book 5, Palinurus considers his course from Carthage to Italy, *Italiam* is brought in to emerge over a preceding word in just this way:

> *Maganime Aenea non si mihi Iuppiter auctor*
> *spondeat, hoc sperem Italiam contingere caelo.*
> Aen. 5.17-18

Let us return, with our broadened sense of Vergil's practice, to the pattern "i" ... *Italiam* in 3.523 and 4.381. It remains true that in Book 3 there is a triple *Italiam,* while in Book 4 the name appears only once. But the events of Book 3 are unparalleled; a first sighting is never able to be repeated. For Dido, to name the name is enough. Especially is this effective if we suspect that Vergil now consciously parodies the raising of Italy in Book 3, causing Dido to throw this moment back in the face of Aeneas, whose psychology we have sensed through the changing position he gives to Italy in speaking to Dido (4.345-346). Vergil continues to play with the relationship of the Trojans and Aeneas to Italy, as he has Dido mock Aeneas in just such a way that she will succeed in recalling to him and to us the reality that Italy is there, and has already been seen from the first to be at hand. Aeneas once described that sighting to Dido with vivid first-foot placements of "Italy!"; Dido's anger, in fact, is a kind of sanction for destiny. Aeneas finds himself "on the hook."

In addition, there is a similar tonality in 3.523 and 4.381. In Book 3, the three "i"s in *Italiam, ITALIAM! ... ITALIAM!!* strengthen what is incipient, hesitant, and bring this to full joy (*Italiam laeto ... clamore,* 3.524). In Book 4, there is a similar, though opposed, development. Nothing is hesitant in Dido's "i." The feeling this imperative carries bursts, in the elision of *sequere,* into the name *Italiam,* in just the same way as *Italiam* is surmounted by *ITALIAM* in 3.523; the energy in both cases is explosive. Just as the added *ITALIAM* with its third long "i" in 3.524 tops everything that has come before, so can we point to a third long "i" in Dido's *"I̱, sequere I̱taliam ventis̱."* For the resonance of "i" at the ictus of the fourth foot, in a verse which begins with this same sound in a dactyl and whose second foot is *Italiam*, we can compare the words of Ilioneus in 1.553 with which we began our examination: *"Si̱ datur I̱taliam sociis̱."* Once more we have the opportunity to see how Vergil has worked into Ilioneus' lines the elements which will appear distinctive in the culminating verses when Italy is raised and Dido sends Aeneas to that land. Not only do we have *Italiam* reinforced by *Italiam* in the second foot of two successive lines, as we have noticed, but in the second verse from Ilioneus' evocation of destiny, 1.554, there is also a reinforcement of the fourth-foot ictus in "i," just as we heard this in *Si datur Italiam sociis*:

> *Si̱ datur I̱taliam sociis̱ et rege recepto*
> *tendere, ut I̱taliam laeti̱ Latiumque petamus . . .*

The music of these lines is additionally textured by the kind of "metaformation" of LAT (*Latium*)—LAET—and TAL (*Italiam*) which F. Ahl has argued can be found everywhere in Ovid's *Metamorphoses* and which Varro prescribes as a proper feature of Latin poetry.[4]

Where the sighting of Italy in Book 3 is capped positively by the triple "i," the sibilance of Dido's *sequere . . . ventis* adds animosity in a speech which otherwise is forcefully marked by angry hissing.[5] The final "s" in *ventis*, read aloud, would have interacted, even if slightly, with the initial "p" in *pete regna per undas* (4.381). If "s" is favored by Vergil for the speeches of Juno (e.g., in Book 1) and Dido to express bitterness and anger, "s" (*ventis*) plus "p" (*pete*) do not diminish the effect.[6]

Again, Dido:

> *I̱, sequere I̱taliam ventis, pete regna per undas!*

Italy is Aeneas' destination: toward Italy, through the elision of *sequere*, Dido hastens her anger. The hated *"Italiam"* breaks in to strike the beginning of the second dactyl, restating the long "i" of Dido's initial imperative. The pun latent in Helenus' prophecy (*Ibitis Italiam,* 3.254) becomes, through the elision, secure. Aeneas' journey ("i" from *ire*) echoes in the very name of Italy. The pilgrimage, Dido's dismissal, the land, become one.

NOTES

1. G. Highet, *The Speeches in Vergil's* Aeneid (Princeton, 1972), 151-152.
2. These verses can be grouped as: (1) those lines in which the first foot is a spondee (e.g., *qui primi,* 8.602; *his actis,* 12.843; *hi nostri,* 11.54); (2) those which have a dactyl in the first foot, but lack elision (e.g., *hi iaculis,* 10.130; *si qua piis,* 7.401; *dis geniti,* 6.131); (3) those which have a first-foot dactyl with elision in the first foot (e.g., *sive animis,* 12.892); (4) those which begin with a long "i"— the vowel without a preceeding consonant, as in our models—and have a first-foot dactyl (e.g., *ilice sic,* 6.209).
3. *Italia* and its inflections appear as the first foot 17 times in the *Aeneid.* Cf. H. Warwick, *A Vergil Concordance* (Minneapolis, 1975) 457. Of these 17 examples, only two exhibit elision with the second foot. By contrast, the elision of *Italia* is much more frequent in the second foot, occurring nine of 21 times. Of five instances of *Italia* in the third foot, four are elided.
4. F. Ahl, *Metaformations* (Cornell, 1985).
5. Highet, *op. cit.* 152 and elsewhere.
6. For spitting "s" with "p" in Dido's contempt, remember 4.305-306: *Di_ss_imulare etiam _sp_era_s_ti, _p_erfide, tantum / _p_o_ss_e nefa_s_?*

DUCTOR RHOETEIUS:
VERGIL, *AENEID* 12.456

Robert J. Rowland, Jr.
Loyola University, New Orleans

At *Aeneid* 12.456, Aeneas leads his troops into battle against Turnus "as when a stormcloud at sea moves toward the land and cuts the sunlight off . . . just so the Rhoeteian captain led his troops in close formation"[1] (*talis in adversos ductor Rhoeteius hostis / agmen agit*). *Rhoeteius* is a curious epithet, and commentators have been content to explain it as a synecdoche for *Troianus*,[2] from the name of the city and promontory near Troy. There may be more to it than that.

In Book 3 (106-110) it is associated with the pre-foundation of Troy by newcomers in a manner similar to the way Lavinium functions as the pre-foundation of Rome: Anchises recalls that "our first forefather, Teucrus, sailed to the coast around Point Rhoeteum and chose it for his kingdom. As yet no Ilium stood, no citadel" (*Teucrus Rhoeteas primum est advectus in oras / optavitque locum regno*). In Book 5 (645-652), when Iris assumes the appearance of Beroe and urges the Trojan women to set fire to the ships so they cannot wander any more, i.e., so they can remain in Sicily and found their city in that place, *Pyrgo, tot Priami natorum regia nutrix,* tells them that Iris is not Beroe:

An earlier version of this paper, with a different title, was read at the annual meeting of the Classical Association of Middle West and South in March 1989; this is offered as a token of esteem and friendship to Sandy McKay, *pius ductor par excellence*. I am grateful to friends and colleagues for advice and suggestions, particularly Professors James O'Hara, Gregory Staley and Eva Stehle.

Non Beroe vobis, non haec Rhoeteia, matres, est Dorycli coniunx ("Do not take her for Beroe: this is not she, the Rhoetean, wife of Doryclus"). Here, a false founding, a founding without issue, is urged by false Beroe to deter the Trojans from their true goal and destiny.

Rhoeteum's only other occurrence in the poem is at 6.505, where Aeneas informs Deiphobus, who, for a brief time, was husband of Helen, cause of so great a war, that "it was I who built on Rhoeteum Point an empty tomb and sent a high call to your soul three times" (*tunc egomet tumulum Rhoeteo litore inanem / constitui*). So, we can add to the foundation resonances of Rhoeteum, an empty tomb, widowhood and a useless war—points to which I shall return.

Servius commented on this last passage that Rhoeteum was also Ajax's *asylum*, and Norden adds the observation of a certain Wünsch about the existence of *tumuli* in the region, although it seems that at least some of these *tumuli* were nineteenth-century rockpiles.[3] Strabo (13.1.30) describes Rhoeteum as

> "a city situated on a hill, and, adjacent to Rhoeteum a low-lying shore on which are a tomb and temple of Ajax, and also a statue of him, which was taken by Antonius and carried off to Egypt; but Augustus Caesar gave it back again to the Rhoeteians, just as he gave back other statues to their owners. For Antonius took away the finest dedications from the most famous temples, to gratify the Egyptian woman, but Augustus gave them back to the gods."
>
> (*Loeb Classical Library* translation)

The detail about Antonius should guarantee that details about the topography of the site of Rhoeteum would not have been merely antiquarian lore to Vergil's audience. Save for the name of the hero and the removal of the statue, the same description applies both to the *tumulus*-shrine of Aeneas at Lavinium[4] and to the shrine of Ajax at Rhoeteum. Further, if the Tomb of Ajax is really the place called In Tepe, then there is also a stream nearby, the In Tepe Azmagi, analogous to the Numicus.[5]

So far as I can find, Lyne, in 1987, was the first to make anything of the connection with Ajax, but it is the burden of this paper to suggest that, in emphasizing the links between Aeneas and *tragic*, mad Ajax,[6] he misses the more significant one, namely, the suggestive, proleptic link between Aeneas, leading his troops as *ductor Rhoeteius*, and that Ajax whose tomb, shrine and sanctuary were at Rhoeteum. I must emphasize that much of what Lyne has to say in this regard, including his analysis of the simile with which I began, is a brilliant and perceptive piece of criticism. However, according to Lyne, *ductor Rhoeteius* is evocative of the dead and therefore the tragic Ajax; the epithet, I suggest, is at least equally evocative of the dead, enshrined and venerated Ajax and therefore might, possibly even *ought* to have implications for the conclusion of the poem, after which Aeneas will be dead, enshrined and venerated.

In fewer than five hundred lines after *ductor Rhoeteius* leads his men into battle, the poem inexorably moves to the final confrontation and the death of Turnus. Both in recent years and in the Middle Ages, for different reasons, the conclusion of the poem has been problematical: the authors of the *Irish Aeneid* and of the *Roman d'Enée*, for example, felt it necessary to alter the poem's conclusion;[7] some modern scholars, chiefly North Americans following the lead of Putnam, have considered it urgent to lament, or at least feel uncomfortable with, Aeneas' behavior at the end. The controversy is well known and need not be rehearsed here.[8]

Galinsky, in defense of a realistic reading of the poem against the pessimists, Putnam in particular, remarks[9] that "from the 'historical' point of view of Roman custom and tradition and perhaps even the literary tradition before Vergil, Turnus' death was inevitable and Vergil had no choice." The best statement of the optimistic view, twice quoted by Cornelia Renger[10] in her *Analyse einer Feindschaft*, is Warde Fowler's: "To spare Turnus would have been the betrayal of the mission of Aeneas in Italy."

But why? How would sparing Turnus have betrayed Aeneas' mission? Both Servius (*ad Aen.* 12.940) and Donatus (*ad Aen.* 12.945) ascribe the killing of Turnus to Aeneas' *pietas:* "out of respect for Evander Aeneas avenges the death of Pallas" (Servius) and "it is better to deny the benefit of life to Pallas' killer than to leave unavenged the death of a friend; so *pietas* is preserved in the person of Aeneas because he wanted to forgive, and *religio* is preserved for Pallas because his killer did not escape" (Donatus). Thus, already in late antiquity, arguably even earlier, the main prop of Aeneas' supporters was in place, and all justificatory discussions ever since have more or less followed them.

But can we really say with Warde Fowler that Aeneas' *whole mission* really depends on avenging Pallas? Moreover, that vengeance looks to the past, while the whole movement, the whole outlook, one might even say the whole point of the poem is to the future; and we should have expected that the end of Book 12 would look to the future as the endings of other even numbered books do (especially Books 8 and 6 with which schematic interpretations usually link Book 12, or Book 2, to which it is sometimes considered a mirror image) and it precisely reverses the tale of filial and paternal *pietas* with which Book 10 concludes.[11] Nor does the poem end on an "echoing silence," as Lyne said in an earlier essay;[12] it ends, as Gransden clearly saw, at the beginning of the reader's, of our *Aeneid sine fine*,[13] the endless re-interpretations of the poem—and it ends at a point that was more or less clearly delineated in the Romans' own historic and mythic consciousness.

Before Vergil, there were various traditions regarding Aeneas, the battle or battles with Turnus and the aftermath. As John Hall has suggested,[14] Cato's version represents the agreed-on historiographical and cult tradition—and in that version, Aeneas disappeared, becoming a deity, immediately after the death of Turnus. Prof. Hall went on to opine that Vergil's Aeneas *had* to survive; that may be, and Vergil certainly introduced other apparent novelties into the tradition, but "the average reader in the Roman street" (if we may imagine such a creature) would have had an expectation of Aeneas' imminent divinization.[15] It is this expectation which the poet himself may have reinforced for us by reminding us of the place of Ajax's shrine and tomb at Rhoeteum. The hint of Aeneas' enshrinement entitles us to speculate about the possible consequences if Vergil's Aeneas, like Cato's, Livy's and Ovid's, i.e., the tradition's Aeneas, became a deity after killing Turnus, fulfilling Jupiter's promises to Venus at *Aeneid* 1.259-260 and to Juno at 12.794-795: *feres ad sidera caeli / magnanimum Aenean* and *indigetem Aenean scis ipsa et scire fateris / deberi caelo fatisque ad sidera tolli*. Note the epithet *indiges*, which Williams[16] tersely explains as "a national hero who is deified," i.e., the Pater Theos Chthonios of Lavinium (Dion. Hal. 1.64.5). One consequence, to which I already alluded in connection with Deiphobus' marriage to Helen, is that Vergil's Aeneas and Lavinia don't get married—certainly a *lacrima rerum,* but, because they were betrothed and because it is Ascanius/Iulus who is of real importance for the future Roman race and the Julian house, that is of little real consequence. Still, it is striking that, on this interpretation, Lavinia becomes a widow before marriage and the war fought for her hand is, from that point of view, absolutely useless.[17] Another consequence is that neither Jupiter's prediction that Aeneas would reign for three years nor Anchises' prediction that he would have another son and be long-lived are true; in a paper entitled "Death and the Optimistic Prophecy in the *Aeneid*," James O'Hara has shown that prophecies in the *Aeneid* do not always contain the truth, and in fact regularly deceive.[18] More to the point is the (hypothetical) fact that Aeneas will not survive to provide protection for his son, for his future, against a still-extant Turnus—Turnus who must in that case be eliminated for the son's and the future's protection.

So far as I know, none of those who castigate Aeneas for killing Turnus have worried about Ascanius' potential fate were Turnus to be spared. As Aeneas prepares for his final battle, he kisses his son and, only 20 lines before he is the Rhoeteian leader, says *nunc te mea dextera bello defensum dabit* (12.436f.). Perhaps this final speech is stark, as Lyne[19] would have it, but if so it is only because it is a farewell address, delivered as Aeneas returns to the battle from which he will emerge divine, to defend his son by killing Turnus because Turnus himself had removed Pallas, who would have been Ascanius' sole source of protection in the absence of his father. It is too facile to quote *parcere subjectis et debellare superbos* (*Aen.* 6.853) and find Aeneas lacking. Much more to the point are Augustus' words (*Res Gestae* 3): *exter[nas] gentes, quibus tuto [ignosci p]otuit, conservare quam excidere ma[lui]*, the key word being *tuto*.

Lyne emphasizes that Aeneas' final speech to his son has a strong echo of Ajax's final address to his son (in Sophocles' *Ajax*, 550ff.), but he omits to observe the crucial point that it is precisely in that speech that Ajax tells his son he is leaving Teucer as *phylax* (562). Aeneas might have been able to tell *his* son he was leaving Pallas a *phylax* = *praesidium*, but Turnus himself had removed that possibility. So, Aeneas goes into his final battle as *pater Aeneas* (12.697) and as *pater Appenninus* (12.703)—both the father of Iulus and Pater Indiges.[20] Thus, in his funereal dirge over the body of Pallas, Aeneas laments "*quantum praesidium, Ausonia, et quantum tu perdis, Iule*" (*Aen.* 11.57f.); thus, the killing of Turnus is Aeneas' final act of *pietas*, acting as a surrogate for Pallas who would have been Ascanius' *praesidium*. It is a *pietas*, therefore, which looks to the future, bringing the poem to a satisfactory conclusion, terminating the incipient deity's duties by blending his private obligations to Pallas, Evander and his own son with his public obligations to the future *gens togata*.[21]

NOTES

1. All translations from the *Aeneid* are those of R. Fitzgerald, *The Aeneid* (New York, 1983).
2. R.O.A.M. Lyne, *Further Voices in Vergil's* Aeneid (Oxford, 1987) 11, with reference to R.D. Williams' note. I had just been reading Lyne's book when I heard J. O'Hara's paper (below, n. 18); this paper is the result of musings on their suggestions against the background of my interest in the legend of Aeneas.
3. E. Norden, *Aeneis VI* (repr., Stuttgart, 1957) *ad loc.* See the entire discussion of J.M. Cook, *The Troad: An Archaeological and Topographical Study* (Oxford, 1973) 79-90.
4. Dion. Hal., 1.64.5. See G. Dury-Moyaers, *Enée et Lavinium*, Collection Latomus 174 (Bruxelles, 1981) 123-127.
5. See Cook, *op. cit.* 88.
6. Lyne, *op. cit.* 9-12. For a somewhat different response to Lyne's book, see K. Galinsky's review in *AJP* 110 (1989) 174-176, suggesting that Rhoeteum might remind us of Augustus' beneficence.
7. Cf., *inter alia*, R.J. Rowland, Jr., "Some Medieval Aeneases," *The Augustan Age* 6 (1987) 176-191.
8. See W.R. Nethercut, "American Scholarship on Vergil," *Vergil at 2000*, ed. J.D. Bernard (New York, 1986) 309-314; further bibliography, G.K. Galinsky, "Vergil's *Romanitas* and his Adaptation of Greek Heroes," *ANRW* II.31.2, 992, n. 26 (selection); W. Suerbaum, "Hundert Jahre Vergil-Forschung: Eine systematische Arbeitsbibliographie mit besonderer Berücksichtigung der Aeneis," *ANRW* II.31.1 (Berlin, 1980) 151-153, 256-258; C. Renger, *Aeneas und Turnus: Analyse einer Feindschaft* (Frankfurt am Main, 1985) 107-109. For a recent statement, see A.J. Boyle, *The Chaonian Dove* (Leiden, 1986) 124.
9. Galinsky, *ibid.* 992-995.
10. Renger, *op. cit.* 73, 102, quoting W.W. Fowler, *The Death of Turnus: Observations of the Twelfth Book of the Aeneid* (Oxford, 1919) 156.
11. Cf. B. Otis, *Virgil: A Study in Civilized Poetry* (Oxford, 1963) 217, 418-419.
12. R.O.A.M. Lyne, "Vergil and the Politics of War," *CQ* 33 (1983) 202.
13. K.W. Gransden, *Virgil's Iliad: An Essay on Epic Narrative* (Cambridge, 1984) 210.
14. J.F. Hall, "The First Ending of the Aeneas Tale: Cato and the Historiographical Tradition of Aeneas," Annual Meeting of the Classical Association of the Middle West and South, April 1988.
15. For the Aeneas legend, see now J.N. Bremmer and N.M. Horsfall, *Roman Myth and Mythography*, University of London Institute of Classical Studies, Bulletin Supplement 52 (London, 1987) 12-24;

and N. Horsfall, "The Aeneas-Legend and the *Aeneid*," *Vergilius* 32 (1986) 8-17, both with full references to earlier scholarship.
16. R.D. Williams, *The Aeneid of Virgil Books 7-12* (London, 1973) 494, *ad* 12.794.
17. The theme of futility, in various guises, is important in the poem, but this is not the place for a thorough discussion.
18. Fall meeting of the Classical Association of the Atlantic States, September 1987; I am grateful to Prof. O'Hara for sending me a copy of his paper and for helping me, *per litteras*, to clarify my thoughts; cf. now his book with the same title (Princeton, 1990).
19. Lyne, *op. cit.* (above, n. 2) 192.
20. Cf. the acute observation of R.F. Moorton, "The Innocence of Italy in Vergil's *Aeneid*," *AJP* 110 (1989) 112: "By contrast (with Turnus) only once is Aeneas compared to a beast of prey (2.355), a wolf with other wolves . . ., foraging because of hunger and the needs of their young. The emphasis is on obligation, not predation . . ."
21. Cf. S.F. Wiltshire, *Public and Private in Vergil's* Aeneid (Amherst, 1988); for a different reading of the end of the poem, see 137-138.

PLAUTUS AND TERENCE IN VERGIL: A SERVIAN PERSPECTIVE

Robert B. Lloyd
Randolph-Macon Woman's College

Modern scholars have not been quick to see much relationship between Vergil and the comic poets. Few have been concerned with comic elements in the works of Vergil in general,[1] and still fewer, with any echoes of Plautus and Terence specifically.[2] No one would want to assert that Vergil's works are essentially comic,[3] but it must be conceded that there are humorous moments in the *Bucolics* (e.g., number 3 with its comic dialogue of insults between the shepherds Damoetas and Menalcas)[4] and the *Georgics* (especially in connection with the treatment of animals in fable-like and mock-epic fashion, e.g., the Battle of the Bees in Book 4).[5] Even the *Aeneid* has its lighter moments, although W.S. Anderson does well to point out that what is discussed as humor here often falls more likely under the category of irony rather than comedy.[6]

In late antiquity, however, at least in the time of Donatus and Servius, there seems to have been little reluctance to find comic elements in Vergil and to cite with great frequency parallels between his works and the earlier comic poets. Anderson[7] has carefully examined Servius' sweeping and challenging statement (*ad Aen.* 4.1) that Book 4 of the Aeneid "possesses an almost comic style" (*paene comicum stilum habet*).[8] He points out Servius' restricted view in the implication that the love-plot is a topic proper for comedy alone (*nec mirum, ubi de amore tractatur*) and he traces Servius' concept of the *comicus stilus* to his teacher Donatus' definition of it as embraced in the Terentine expression "modest diction and light touch" (*tenui esse oratione et scriptura levi: Phorm.* 5; cf. Donatus *ad loc.*). Although rejecting the view of the comic as the major stylistic effect of *Aeneid* 4,[9] Anderson does not discard Servius' remark out of hand, believing that he did "put his finger on an important aspect of *Aeneid* 4 . . . unusual in the *Aeneid* for its dramatic amatory plot and for the simple style assigned to its many lines of direct passionate speech."[10]

Be that as it may, modern scholars who would seek to establish any relationship between the extant Roman comedians and Vergil could do worse than start with parallels cited in the Servian corpus. It is the object of the present study to make such a beginning. The references to Plautus are not few: 120 in all (47 in S; 73 in D).[11] In the large majority of cases Plautus is cited to illustrate points of grammar, vocabulary and usage. Not all references on these matters signal points of similarity; they note differences as well. On the matter of varying gender, for example, Plautus can be quoted for confirmation of what is found in Vergil (*ad Aen.* 12.547), for elucidation of what is ambiguous in Vergil (*ad Geo.* 2.288; 4.296; *Aen.* 1.703, 6.383) or for deliberate contrast (*ad Ecl.* 1.58; *Aen.* 2.51, 12.519). Other grammatical items include case constructions, again to note parallels (*ad Aen.* 1.460, 4.229, 8.127, 9.399; cf. *ad Geo.* 4.170, 11.343) or less often, contrast (*ad Aen.* 4.373, 10.532). This all points, of course, to the use of grammatical handbooks by the commentator rather than indicating any deliberate borrowing of Plautine essence or style on the part of Vergil.[12]

In the matter of vocabulary, however, we can perhaps begin to speak of Vergilian verbal echoes from Plautus. Servius cites a good many word-parallels between the two authors, and if these do not indicate a conscious effort on Vergil's part to recall Plautine vocabulary in particular, they arguably point to an interest in an archaic flavor. To confirm this fact are the many instances where Plautus is cited to illustrate the manner of speaking of the *veteres*,[13] *antiqui*[14] or *maiores*.[15] The question arises, in what sense ancient? From the point of view of Vergil or Servius? On two occasions Servius is clearly speaking of his own day: *sermo Plautinus, quo hodie non utimur*.[16]

The context in which the Plautine references appear can be instructive. Plautus is most regularly cited alone, but on occasion other authors are quoted on the same point as well, especially in the D Scholia which are in general much more likely to contain fuller references.[17] Not surprisingly the coupling is with other early dramatists: Naevius,[18] Ennius,[19] Caecilius[20] and Terence.[21]

But the satirist Lucilius[22] and the historian Sallust,[23] whose works seem to have been a mine of archaisms,[24] also appear in this way. All of these, save the deliberately archaizing Sallust, can be regarded as *veteres* from Vergil's point of view. The fact, however, that, on one occasion at least, the decidedly unarchaic Cicero,[25] and the Augustan poets, Horace[26] and Ovid,[27] are similarly linked with Plautine expressions would indicate that something other than pure archaism can be involved. The *sermo Plautinus* may evince a colloquial as well as archaic flavor.

Of special interest in this connection is a locus (*ad Aen.* 8.310) where a Plautine phrase is reinforced by a reference to a *Symposium* by Maecenas. The expression is *faciles oculos*, "easy eyes," on which Servius comments:

> *physici dicunt ex vino mobiliores oculos fieri:*
> *Plautus "faciles oculos habet," id est mobiles vino.*

To which the Daniel Scholia add:

> *hoc etiam Maecenas in symposio ubi Vergilius et*
> *Horatius interfuerunt, cum ex persona Messalae de vi*
> *vini loqueretur, ita: "ut idem umor ministrat faciles*
> *oculos, pulchriora reddit omnia et dulcis iuventae*
> *reducit bona."*

The point of reference is Aeneas at the site of Evander's Rome. Fresh from the Saliar feasting at the rites of the Ara Maxima,[28] Evander and Aeneas, engaged in various conversation, return to the city where our hero marvels and is captivated by all he sees, turning his "easy eyes" all around: *facilesque oculos fert omnia circum*. The context in Plautus is not clear, since the quotation is apparently from a non-existant text (Lindsay: fr. 172), but modern commentators and translators have certainly not followed Servius' lead in rendering the expression,[29] or seeing that Aeneas is dazed or entranced as if from the effects of alcohol, perhaps even literally so from the Saliar celebration. An image has been missed, along with a highly probable Plautine recollection.[30]

It must be admitted that the parallels between Plautus and Vergil noted in the Servian corpus are seldom, if ever, on matters of substance. Rarely is it a question of similarity of thought or idea. At *Ecl.* 10.69: *omnia vincit amor*, we have the somewhat banal observation that "anything can be resisted more easily than love" and a reference to the opening lines of Plautus' *Persa*: "When a needy lover starts out on the path of Love, he outdoes in his toils the labors of Hercules." At *Aen.* 2.13: *fracti bello fatisque repulsi*, Servius lists the *fata* as three according to Plautus (*Bacch.* 953ff.): 1) the loss of the Palladium, 2) the life of Troilus and 3) the destruction of the lintel of the Scaean Gate (Laomedon's tomb). But there is little to suggest any deep connection between these Vergilian and Plautine passages.[31] It is, moreover, never a question of similarity of character or situation.

Turning to Terence, we find an even greater number of references to him in the Servian corpus than to Plautus. He is cited some 222 times and, somewhat surprisingly, the ratio is reversed with more references in S (137) than in D (85).[32] We may well suppose that Servius here is strongly under the influence of his teacher Donatus whose great interest in both poets manifested itself in monumental commentaries on Vergil (now lost)[33] and Terence. A confirmation of this interest can furthermore be found in the great number of quotations from Vergil in the "extant" commentary on Terence.[34]

In some respects the quotations from Terence in the Servian corpus are similar to those from Plautus. They most frequently call attention to similarities (occasionally differences) in vocabulary and grammatical usage between the two authors. H.D. Jocelyn[35] has asserted that Terence is here "treated . . . as an author of the classical canon rather than as a source of archaic usage," but in this he is not completely correct. As with Plautus we find Terence cited with reference to linguistic peculiarities of the *veteres*,[36] *antiqui*[37] or *maiores*.[38] Jocelyn is right, on the other hand, to note a considerable difference in the citations from Terence, primarily in their very number (more than any other early author), and to contrast Macrobius who does not mention Terence at all. In the Servian corpus, however, Terence is treated with the greatest familiarity, even in S, and is quoted frequently without the name of author or play,[39] which is never the case with Plautus. That the cause of such treatment is familiarity rather than carelessness is confirmed by the fact that the quotations from Terence are not only more frequent but of greater than usual length and accuracy.[40]

The great bulk of the references to Terence in Servius is, to be sure, like those to Plautus, involved with vocabulary and supposed verbal echoes in Vergil.[41] And, as we noted in the case of Plautus, these may be drawn from common language rather than signalling specific or intentional borrowings from the earlier poet. *Perii . . . nunc scio quid sit amor* (*Ecl.* 8.41-43; cf. *Eun.* 1053); *arrectis auribus* (*Aen.* 1.152, 12.618; cf. *And.* 933); *remordet* for *sollicitat* (*Aen.* 1.261; cf. *Eun.* 445) *ne saevi* for *ne irascere* (*Aen.*

6.544; cf. *And.* 868)⁴² all evoke a flavor, if not comic, at least of the colloquial. Dido's *Pro Iuppiter* (*Aen.* 4.590; cf. *Adel.* 196) is certainly the language of every day, as is Turnus' aphorism *audentes Fortuna iuvat* (*Aen.* 10. 284;⁴³ cf. *Phor.* 203). And the *hoc habet* (*Aen.* 12.296; cf. *And.* 83) of Messapus over the vanquished Aulestes is drawn, of course, from the language of the arena.

Fundamentally different, however, is the frequency of comparisons between Terence and Vergil on matters of style and substance. Attention is often called to parallel figures of speech in the two authors: aposiopesis (*ad Aen.* 1.135; cf. *And.* 164); pleonasm (*ad Aen.* 1.208, 4.83; cf. *Adel.* 329, 668); synecdoche (*ad Aen.* 1.399; cf. *Adel.* 966); prosphonesis (*ad Aen.* 4.408; cf. *Adel.* 665); prolixity (*ad Aen.* 6.890; cf. *And.* 980); euphemism (*ad Aen.* 3.217; cf. *Adel.* 985); ellipsis (*ad Aen.* 1.181; cf. *And.* 55); poetic plural (*ad Ecl.* 3. 106, *Aen.* 2.155, 10.848; cf. *Eun.* 48); editorial "we" (*ad Ecl.* 6.58; cf. *Heaut.* 476); reiteration (*ad Aen.* 8.84; cf. *And.* 282) and rhetorical question (*ad Aen.* 9.778; cf. *Eun.* 46).⁴⁴

More substantive still are the parallels drawn between characters and situations in Terence and Vergil. The forced tears of Sinon (*lacrimis coactis, Aen.* 2.196) are compared with the *falsa lacrimula* of Thais in the *Eunuchus* (67) which by Parmeno's account she can hardly squeeze out by rubbing her eyes. Vulcan, rising from Venus's bed like a dutiful housewife keeping her bed chaste with hard work (*Aen.* 8.412ff.) is linked with the futile struggle of Glycerium (the woman of Andros) to do the same (*And.* 74ff.: on which Servius comments, "*hinc ergo traxit Vergilius*"). The fact that Vergil can put noble sentiments in the mouths of ignoble characters (specifically Maxentius addressing his horse Rhaebus: *Aen.* 10.861ff.) is compared with Terence's habit of putting such words in the mouths of slaves.⁴⁵

That Servius is taking these parallels from earlier commentaries seems clear. Somewhere in ancient commentary on Terence and Vergil (Donatus?) a parallel seems to have been drawn between the appearance of an impoverished spendthrift in the *Eunuchus* (236ff.) and Achaemenides in *Aeneid* 3 (594ff.) which Servius (*ad loc.*) appears somehow to have garbled (cf. Eugraphius, *ad loc.*).⁴⁶ He misses entirely, however, a parallel drawn by Donatus between Venus' interruption of Aeneas' complaints in *Aeneid* 1 (385ff.) and Micio's similar treatment of Aeschinus in the *Adelphi* (679).⁴⁷

But it is particularly in *Aeneid* 4 that the Servian commentary draws substantive connections between Terence and Vergil. This follows logically from the fact, noted above, that Servius judged this book with its love-plot to have been written in a style that is *paene comicus*. We have already discussed the views of W.S. Anderson[48] on this point and his feeling that Servius is wrong not to recognize the essentially tragic tone of the book.

Anderson examines two other references to comic force in Servius on *Aeneid* 4, both of them involving quotations from Terence.[49] He is probably right in seeing that the enclitic *-met* (*Aen.* 4.606; cf. *Heaut.* 374) is not necessarily a comic expression, and that the deliberative question (*Aen.* 4.534: *En quid ago?*; cf. *Eun.* 46: *Quid igitur faciam?*) can be equally a comic or tragic device. But not all of the comic parallels that Servius draws between Vergil and Terence in his commentary on *Aeneid* 4 are wide of the mark. He is certainly on target in seeing something comic about Dido's delaying before the hunt (*ad Aen.* 4.133) and comparing *Heauton* 239-240: (*et nosti mores mulierum*:) *dum moliuntur, dum conantur, annus est*.[50]

It is not a point which Servius would make but the whole question of comic/tragic elements in Book 4 of the *Aeneid* ought to take into account the fact that comic pessimism can be very close to tragedy in the mode of its expression, and it is precisely such parallels between Terence and Vergil that Servius notes. The *Adelphi* is particularly fruitful in providing examples: Sostrata's words of despair at the supposed deception by Aeschinus: *quid credas at cui credas?* (330) are cited in relation to Dido's *nusquam tuta fides* (373); Demea's outrage at the rampant rumors about Aeschinus: *in ore esse omni populo* (93) is aligned with the dirty work of rumor in Vergil: *diffundit in ora* (195); and his apparent washing his hands of the whole matter: *profundat, perdat, pereat* (134) finds parallel in Dido's *i, sequere Italiam*, etc. (381) on which Servius comments: *satis artificiosa prohibitio, quae fit per concessionem*.[51] And in the *Andria* the desperation of Charinus and his determination to leave nothing untried before he dies: *omnia experiri certum est, priusquam pereo* (311) finds analogy in Dido's resolve to do the same: *ne quid inexpertum frustra moritura relinquat* (415).[52] Whether or not we want to regard any of these Terentine passages as having specifically inspired Vergil in his writing, it is important to note that in these instances Servius is drawing parallels of mood, situation and character rather than making points of vocabulary or usage such as might be derived from grammatical handbooks. In Servius' mind at least there were connections of thought and substance to be made between the works of Terence and Vergil and he makes them with considerable frequency.

Not all modern critics have ignored the possibility of indebtedness on the part of Vergil to the Roman comic poets. As early as 1949, W.F. Jackson Knight observed with reference to Plautus and Terence that "Vergil undeniably admits comic precedent even into the centre of tragedy." He cites, for example, the interplay between Juno and Venus.[53] Others who have more recently been concerned with comic elements in Vergil[54] have not attributed the humor that they have found there to influence by the comic poets. M.D. Macleod[55] did, on the other hand, note that Vergil's humor in the *Aeneid* is of a subtle type "akin to that of Terence" and largely concerned with character. Neither Jackson Knight nor Macleod, however, related the humor to anything specific in Plautus or Terence and none of those who have explored humor in Vergil (save Anderson)[56] acknowledged Servius as a predecessor.

A recent study by Charles Saylor[57] has demonstrated still another way in which *Aeneid* 4 is indebted to Plautus and Terence: the portrayal of Dido and Aeneas as traditional lovers derived from the comic stage. He finds the following stock elements: 1) madness and loss of reason (*furor, amentia: Aen.* 4.69, 78; cf. *Merc.* 82, *And.* 218), 2) idleness (*nequitia in otio: Aen.* 4.271; cf. *Miles* 1285, *Heaut.* 481), 3) loss of reputation (*fama: Aen.* 4.91, 221, etc.: cf. *Most.* 144, *Trin.* 642, *And.* 99) and 4) the wasting of patrimony (*Aen.* 4.267; cf. *Most.* 979, etc.,[58] *Heaut.* 465). Saylor is certainly on the right track, and his work clearly demonstrates that the whole subject of the influences of the comic poets on Vergil, not only in language and style but in thought and substance, is a fertile one and wide open to further investigation. It is an area clearly pointed to in the Servian corpus and well worth the pondering of modern scholars.

NOTES

1. See R.B. Lloyd, s.v. "Comico, stile" in *EncVirg* 1 (1984) 853-855 and bibliography there cited.
2. See R.B. Lloyd, s.v. "Plauto" in *EncVirg* 4 (1988) 138 and "Terenzo" in *EV* 5 (1990) 128f. and bibliography there cited.
3. Except P. Richard, *Virgile, auteur gai* (Paris, 1951) whose extreme views are untenable: The *Bucolics* amount to a *revue campagnarde*; the *Georgics*, a comedy in the manner of Walt Disney; *Aeneid* 6 presents an inferno not so much like Dante's but Offenbach's!

4. Cf. H.M. Currie, "The Third *Eclogue* and the Roman Comic Spirit," *Mnemosyne* 29 (1976) 411-420.
5. Cf. M.D. Macleod, "Humour in Virgil," *PVS* 4 (1964-1965) 56ff.
6. W.S. Anderson, "Servius and the 'Comic Style' of *Aeneid* 4," *Arethusa* 14 (1981) 115-125, n. 1; cf. R.B. Lloyd, s.v. "Ironia" in *EncVirg* 3 (1987) 24-25.
7. *Ibid.*
8. SD; S has *paene comicus stilus est*.
9. Cf. Anderson, "Vergil, the Best in the World for the Tragical-Comical-Historical-Pastoral," *Vergilius* 26 (1980) 16.
10. Anderson, *op. cit.* (n. 6) 124.
11. The references can be found in R.B. Lloyd, "Republican Authors in Servius and the Scholia Danielis," *HSPh* 65 (1961) 314-317; cf. H.D. Jocelyn, "Ancient Scholarship and Virgil's Use of Republican Latin Poetry I," *CQ* n.s. 14 (1964) 280-295.
12. A few references note figures of speech common to both authors: metonymy (*ad Ecl*. 3.16); synecdoche (*ad Aen*. 1.724); metaphor (*ad Aen*. 2.206, 3.46).
13. *Ad Ecl*. 8.71; *Aen*. 1.16, 233, 543, 636; 4.194, 424, 608; 8.632; 9.641, 693. *Vetuste*: *ad Geo*. 4.170; *Aen*. 1.378.
14. *Ad Ecl*. 5.58; *Geo*. 1.189; *Aen*. 1.233; 3.686; 4.301; 6.90, 229; 10.532; 11.361.
15. *Ad Aen*. 9.645.
16. *Ibid*. 3.42, cf. 2.51.
17. See Lloyd, *op. cit.* (above, n. 11) 317.
18. *Ad Geo*. 1.266 (cited as "Novius" on *fiscina*); *Aen*. 4.267 (*struix*).
19. *Ad Geo*. 4.170; *Aen*. 9.327. (Neither of these offers a real parallel.)
20. *Ad Geo*. 1.74 (*quassante*).
21. *Ibid*. 4.561 (*viam affectat*); *Aen*. 11.361 (*caput*).
22. *Ad Geo*. 1.266 (*fiscina*); *Aen*. 6.90 (*addita = inamica*).
23. *Ad Aen*. 1.378 (*pietate = religione*).
24. R. Syme, *Sallust* (Berkeley, 1964) 261-265.
25. *Ad Aen*. 1.191 (*turba = multitudo*).
26. *Ibid*. 1.435 (*pecus*), 738 (*crepo*), 10.727 (*lavit*); all three with reference to the *Carmina*.
27. *Ad Aen*. 7.715.
28. W.W. Fowler, *Aeneas at the Site of Rome* (Oxford, 1931) 66ff.
29. Thus *faciles* is translated "curious" (Dryden), "ready" (Fairclough) "ready, willing" (Page), "quick glancing" (Papillon and Haigh), "alert" (Jackson Knight); "obedient" (Williams); or, following the lead of Conington, adverbially "lightly" (MacKail), "eagerly" (Mandelbaum), "quickly" (Mantinband), "with unforced admira-

tion" (Day Lewis), "gladly" (Fitzgerald). The phrase *circumfer faciles oculos* (without the Vergilian tmesis) appears again in Manilius 1.649.

30. The Scholia Danielis call attention to other Plautine phrases in Vergil: *folles taurini* for "bellows" (*ad Geo.* 4.171; cf. *Bacch.* 10); *viam affectat* for "intendit" (*ad Geo.* 4.561; cf. *Aul.* 575, cited along with Terence, *Heaut.* 301); *alites/aves ferae* for "birds of prey" (*ad Aen.* 10.559; cf. *Capt.* 123); *vivendo vincere* for "supervivere" (*ad Aen.* 11.160; cf. *Ep.* 177).

31. Additionally on *Geo.* 1.344, Plautus, *Aul.* 354ff. is cited on the inappropriateness of a wine offering to Ceres. In Vergil's defense, see Servius *ad loc.* and Macrobius, *Sat.* 3.11.

32. For the specific references see Lloyd, *op. cit.* (above, n. 11) 318 and nn. 162, 163; cf. Jocelyn, *op. cit.* (above, n. 11) 280-281.

33. Many believe that the Daniel augmentations of the Servian text are derived from the lost commentary of Donatus. On the question see Lloyd, *ibid.* 291-293, 324-327.

34. Cf. J.F. Mountford and J.T. Schultz, *Index Rerum et Nominum in Scholiis Servii et Aelii Donati Tractatorum* (Ithaca, 1930) [*Cornell Studies in Classical Philology* 23] s.v. "Vergilius citatur." The commentary on Terence is not in its original form, but is a compilation of derived scholia.

35. *Op. cit.* (above, n. 11) 281.

36. *Ad Ecl.* 7.31; *Geo.* 1.248; 3.305; *Aen.* 1.6, 233 (with Plautus), 657; 2.424; 3.477; 9.693 (with Plautus); Cf. *ad Geo.* 1.125; *Aen.* 1.6 (*vetuste*); *Aen.* 1.233 (*antiquo more*); 12.694 (*veteri more*).

37. *Ad Ecl.* 3.1; *Aen.* 1.573; 4.31; 7.268; 12.296; Cf. *ad Aen.* 8.127; 11.361 (*antiquum*); *Aen.* 4.435 (*iuxta morem antiquum*); *Aen.* 12.342 (*antiquo more*); *Aen.* 6.544 (*antique*).

38. *Ad Aen.* 11.687.

39. *Ad Geo.* 4.459; *Aen.* 1.8, 58, 601, 647, 686; 2.3, 12, 60, 324, 463, 531, 610; 5.80, 122; 7.49, 427; 9.44; 10.529.

40. Lloyd, *op. cit.* (above, n. 11) 318-322.

41. Matters of case and gender are relatively infrequent. Case: *Ad Ecl.* 6.50; *Aen.* 1.460 (with Plautus); 3.278 (in contrast); 8.127. Gender: *Ad Geo.* 1.94; 3.305; *Aen.* 5.122.

42. Cf. also *affectat viam* for "*intendit*" (*ad Geo.* 4.561; cf. *Heaut.* 301 and note 30, above); *animas ... linquebant* (*ad Aen.* 3.140; cf. *Adel.* 498); *ecce tibi* (*ad Aen.* 3.477; cf. Servius *ad Aen.* 4.534; *Adel.* 537); *etiam* for "*heia*" (*ad Aen.* 11.373; cf. *And.* 849).

43. SD, *ad loc.* note: *et potest haec sententia et superioribus adplicari et per se separatim intellegi.*

44. For the relatively few instances of the use of Plautus in this way see above, n. 12.

45. The complaint of Euryalus' mother that she has not been able to address final words (*adfari extremum*) to her son is compared (*ad Aen.* 9.482) with Phaedria's addressing final words (*dum licet*) to his cousin Antipho in the *Phormio* (549); cf. also Servius, *ad Aen.* 8.577 (*Phor.* 575); 11.537 (*And.* 538); 12.538 (*Phor.* 74).
46. For a fuller discussion of this see Lloyd, *op. cit.* (above, n. 11) 320f.
47. Donatus, *ad loc.*; cf. G. Norwood, *The Art of Terence* (Oxford, 1923) 125, n. 1.
48. Above, p. 244 and see Anderson, *op. cit.* (above, n. 6).
49. *Op. cit.* (above, n. 6) 120ff.
50. Cf. R.B. Lloyd, "Humor in the *Aeneid*," *CJ* 72 (1976-1977) 254.
51. Additionally Sannio's mad cries: *minime miror qui insanire occipiunt ex iniuria* (197) are cited in connection with Dido's *furiis incensa feror* (376); Aeschinus' prosphonesis to his father: *quid illi tandem credis fore animi misero*, etc. (665) is related to Vergil's addressing of Dido: *Quis tibi tunc, Dido, cernenti* (408).
52. There are other substantive parallels with Terence which Servius draws in *Aeneid* 4. On the suppression of lurid detail in the cave scene (*ad* 166: *subpremit rem pudendam*) he compares Phaedria's report of the seduction in the *Eunuchus* (604); and Dido's *fuit aut tibi quicquam dulce meum* (*ad* 318: *tegit rem inhonestam*) finds parallel in *Andria* 294 with Chrysis' reported plea to Pamphilus not to forsake Glycerium: *seu tibi morigera fuit in rebus omnibus*.
53. *Roman Vergil* (London, 1944²) 144. Knight's other examples from the *Aeneid* are found chiefly on the divine level.
54. See nn. 1-4, above.
55. *Op. cit.* (above, n. 5) 59 and 61ff.
56. *Op. cit.* (above, n. 6).
57. C. Saylor, "Some Stock Characteristics of the Roman Lover in Vergil, *Aeneid* IV," *Vergilius* 32 (1986) 73-77.
58. Cf. E. Segal, *Roman Laughter: The Comedy of Plautus* (Cambridge, MA, 1968) 64-69.

Part Two

The Villa Vergiliana, Cumae, Italy

BOOK 2 OF HORACE'S *ODES*:
AMICITIA, URBANITAS, HUMANITAS

❦

Janice M. Benario
Georgia State University

For a long time I had considered working on a study of Book 2 of Horace's *Odes* as an entity apart from Books 1 and 3, all of which were published together in 23 B.C. There are many possible approaches to such a study, as is clear from the enormity of the bibliography on the *Odes*. (For the fullest recent survey, see W. Kissel, "Horaz 1936-1975," *ANRW* II.32.3 [1981] 1405-1558; Book 2 is covered on 1498-1502.) Most of the ideas pertaining to Book 2, however, are found in general commentaries, in separate studies of individual odes, or in critical works on Horace or his poetry. But few titles exist which pertain simply to Book 2 by itself.

The major recent work on this book is R.G.M. Nisbet and M. Hubbard's (N/H) detailed commentary, *A Commentary on Horace: Odes, Book II* (Oxford, 1978), which must provide reference for any such study. I had been familiar with some of the early preparatory notes on this volume, for, in the spring of 1974, I attended Miss Hubbard's Oxford seminar on Book 2. That seminar provided the genesis of my own interest. In addition, the chapter on Book 2 in M.S. Santirocco's *Unity and Design in Horace's Odes* (Chapel Hill, 1986), augmented by discussion with its author, suggested new possibilities.

Finally, it was the letter from Robert M. Wilhelm, requesting an essay to honor Alexander (Sandy) G. McKay, which prompted my renewed thinking about Book 2. For it seemed to me that those twenty odes, considered together and separate from the rest of the collection, suggest strongly some of the same characteristics mentioned by Wilhelm and which I associate with my own long acquaintance with Sandy: *amicitia,* enhanced by *urbanitas* and *humanitas.* Sandy and I met in the summer of 1959 at Cumae when he was Director of the Vergilian Society Summer Program, my husband was Assistant Director, and I did a little of everything in the position later termed Villa Hostess. In those days a pair of Directors served the whole summer for all sessions. Working together for eleven weeks allowed ample opportunity to lay the foundations for a long and strong friendship. In addition, there is my gratitude for the invitation from Sandy to become the Editor of *Vergilius* for the second time; thus we worked together again for six years. And so I am pleased to offer this brief essay in tribute to three decades of friendship.

Existing studies propose various unifying methods and themes for Book 2. On one level is the obvious preponderance of Alcaic and Sapphic meters and the resulting effects. Other writers already have noted as recurrent themes the mean, death, politics, patronage, the poet's art, along with innumerable schemes attempting to account for the arrangement of the poems. Without any attempt to deny or affirm such schemes and themes, I wish to suggest that a perceptive reading of Book 2 reveals pervasive qualities of *humanitas* and *urbanitas,* especially in regard to the *officia* and *virtutes* of *amicitia.* This aura of feeling rises over other analyses. I express here my debt to three additional studies basic to my premise: R.S. Kilpatrick, *The Poetry of Friendship* (Alberta, 1986); E.S. Ramage, *Urbanitas: Ancient Sophistication and Refinement* (Norman, 1973); W.R. Johnson, *The Idea of Lyric* (Berkeley, 1982). As to texts, one must now add to the long list the two new Teubners by S. Borzsák (Leipzig, 1984) and D.R. Shackleton-Bailey (Stuttgart, 1985). My quotations are from the former. References in Book 2 are by ode number alone, followed by line number if appropriate.

The general meaning of *amicitia* as the bond existing between friends or simply friendship is clear enough. And a friend is a person whom one knows, likes, trusts. The persons involved may be of equal rank or of different ranks. In either case they are *amici.* This is different from *amicitia* in the political sense, either between Rome and another state or between individuals for political ends rather than mutual affection. Kilpatrick, although primarily concerned with *Epistles* 1, sums up Horace's developing attitude towards his friends (xix):

Horace assumed a different mask or stance with each change of poetic form. In the *Satires* and *Epodes* the poet praises, complains, preaches, and narrates. In the *Odes*, the *vates* (a bard of inspired utterance) persuades, praises, and reflects. The poet of the *Epistles* no longer plays the *vates*, but the mature mellow gentleman. . . . The sequence of letters presumes a writer who loves his friends with a deep concern for their well-being and happiness.

Book 2 of the *Odes* illustrates particularly well this *vates* who persuades, praises, and reflects. As Kilpatrick finds in the *Epistles*, so in Book 2, there is the same "affection, tact, sincerity, and a kindly sense of humor," (x) as Horace offers advice and invitation, *recusatio* and affirmation, thoughts and reflections, all in lyric form.

Thirteen of the twenty odes are addressed to eleven different living individuals, whom Horace must have considered *amici*, and certainly he knew much about them, their personalities, their careers. Among his contemporaries, two are *potentes amici*. I refer to Pollio (1) and Maecenas (12, 17, 20, with possible allusions to him also in 18). Other friends are Sallustius Crispus (2), Quintus Dellius (3), Pompeius (7), C. Valgius Rufus (9), Licinius Murena (10), Quinctius Hirpinus (11), Postumus (14), and Pompeius Grosphus (16). Septimius (6) is a much younger man. About some we know a great deal, about others much is missing. Some have been consul, others are equestrians. Several are also writers of note. By addressing odes to them, Horace bestows honor, always with tact, moderation, and constraint, not for the purpose of *cultura potentis amici*.

In Book 2 the word *amicitia* appears only once (1.4) and then only with its political meaning. *Amicus*, however, is found along with other words expressing close association between the author and the addressee. The examples which commentators most frequently point out are in 6 and 7. The first and final strophes of 6 emphasize the friendship:

> *Septimi, Gadis aditure mecum et*
> *Cantabrum indoctum iuga ferre nostra et*
> *barbaras Syrtis, ubi Maura semper*
>   *aestuat unda:*
>
> *ille te mecum locus et beatae*
> *postulant arces, ibi tu calentem*
> *debita sparges lacrima favillam*
>   *vatis amici.*

In 7 the feeling of friendship in the first and final strophes is reinforced by the phrases throughout the ode: *O saepe mecum tempus in ultimum / deducte* (1-2), *Pompei, meorum prime sodalium / cum quo* (5-6), *tecum Philippos et celerem fugam / sensi* (9-10), *sed me. . . . te* (13-15), *recepto / dulce mihi furere est amico* (27-28). In both poems Horace has emphasized the importance of the relation by the final word, and the closeness of the association by his use of the pronouns, *ego* and *tu*, especially in the ablative with *cum*. There are other instances. The addressee in 9 is *amice Valgi* (5). In 11 Horace joins himself to Quinctius when he suggests that they relax and drink together: *potamus uncti* (17). Postumus is called *amice* (14.6). And although there are vast differences in their wealth and goals in life, Horace places himself in the same kind of situation as Grosphus in the final two strophes of 16.

The odes addressed to Maecenas display many such expressions of friendship. The first of these examples (12) reflects differing conceived abilities in the art of writing, expressed as a *recusatio:*

> *tuque pedestribus*
> *dices historiis proelia Caesaris,*
> *Maecenas, melius ductaque per vias*
> *regum colla minacium.*
>
> *me dulcis dominae Musa Licymniae*
> *cantus, me voluit dicere lucidum*
> *fulgentis oculos et bene mutuis*
> *fidum pectus amoribus.*
>
> 9-16

Horace is not willing to write of weighty matters, but will turn to the lighter themes of love. In so doing he honors Maecenas by speaking of the mutual love between him and Terentia (Licymnia). Ode 17 emphasizes the important status of Maecenas in Horace's life (*Maecenas, mearum / grande decus columenque rerum* [3-4]) and the poet's extreme gratitude that both were spared from potentially fatal experiences. *Non ego, quem vocas / dilecte Maecenas* (20.6-7) adds to the warm feeling, strengthened by its position in the last ode of the book. In addition, although there is no addressee, 18 expresses Horace's feelings for Maecenas and his gratitude for the Sabine farm.

Amicus appears three other times in Book 2, not, however, referring to the real addressee, but to a divinity (1.25, 6.18, 17.2).

Of the remaining seven poems in Book 2, two have unknown addressees: Xanthias (4), to whom, real or unreal, Horace offers advice as to a friend, and Barine (8), for whom, real or unreal, there are reflections on her questionable charms. Commentators consider that in two odes Horace is speaking to himself: 5, about Lalage, and 13, actually addressed to *arbos*, reflecting on Sappho and Alcaeus albeit in the Lower World. One ode, 19, is addressed to a god and the remaining two, 15 and 18, offer general thoughts on the same topic, luxury. Much of 18, however, speaks to *tu*, the anonymous general reader.

Throughout Book 2, this "I-You" relationship is prominent, both in poems to specific friends and in the others. In the former, "the person addressed (whether actual or fictional) is a metaphor for readers of the poem." (Johnson, 3) When Horace is offering general advice or indulging in universal reflections and maxims, the *tu* expands to include every reader or listener. Thus he is not only *vates*, but also a true *amicus*, as he includes us all in his circle of friends.

The odes in Book 2, both those addressed to *amici* and the others, are of different styles and moods, on different themes. Commentators agree that in the odes to real persons Horace adjusts his words and thoughts to suit the character or interests of the addressee. These poems also show the author as aware of the world about him, of contemporary events and trends. He is sometimes serious, sometimes humorous, as suits the occasion. These are all general attributes of *urbanitas* and *humanitas*.

To define specifically the two qualities, however, is not easy; and in Book 2 Horace does not use either word or the related adjective. The *Oxford Latin Dictionary* presents a variety of meanings for both. *Urbanitas* includes 1) the qualities typical of a city dweller such as sophistication, polish, suavity, urbanity; the condition of living in a city (esp. Rome); 2) refinement or polish or style marked by elegance, good taste, brevity; 3) elegance or smartness of humor, wit. *Humanitas* includes 1) human nature or character; 2) the quality distinguishing civilized man from savages or beasts, culture; 3) humane character, kindness, human feeling. Clearly the two qualities are closely interwoven, at least in some regards, and cannot be entirely separated.

Ramage focused on *urbanitas*. He relates in detail Horace's way of dealing with people, shows similarities to the views of Aristotle as expressed in the *Nicomachean Ethics*, and concludes thus: "it becomes clear that *urbanitas* in Horace's mind is part of the golden mean—a sensitive, sophisticated approach to relations with other men" (79); and "Horace, then, is one of a group of refined Romans who, while not advocating a return to rusticity, have a full appreciation of what the country can mean to a man from the city in terms of relief, respite, and leisure" (85). Johnson discusses the poet's relation not only to his friends but to his general public through the "I-You" poem and adds the importance of attention to the contemporary world. "Any lyric poet, and particularly a writer of literary lyric, dispenses with this place and this moment to his peril. It is a mistake Horace never made. . . . Horace is, at times, almost messianic, and the salvation he brings when this mood is upon him is that of art, of good breeding, of tact and judgment" (127, 130). I wish here to bring together some of the many examples of *urbanitas* and *humanitas* from Book 2.

The first ode, addressed to Pollio, has been the subject of much study. N/H detail the ways in which the poem echoes Pollio's thoughts and manner. Variation in tone suggests the versatility of the recipient who was known as statesman, orator, tragedian, and historian. The poem as whole praises Pollio as historian, but rejects his subject and is programmatic when Horace requests the Muse (as if a friend) *mecum Dionaeo sub antro / quaere modos leviore plectro* (39-40). Horace's use of *tractas* (7) and *ne . . . retractes* (37-38) emphasizes the contrast. Serious themes are right for Pollio, but not for Horace. Horace remains mindful of the Civil Wars and the troubles of the past, but his gentle conclusion welcomes the present peace.

The second poem is a panegyric to C. Sallustius Crispus, who is described by N/H as "munificent without being profligate" (39) and known for his generosity to poets. The first illustration in the ode, Proculeius, *notus in fratres animi paterni* (6), stresses Proculeius' generosity and humanity to his brothers. Horace then tactfully takes the opportunity to denounce materialism. Sallustius is not accused, for by changing from direct address to the second person subjunctive *latius regnes* (9) and then to *uni . . . quisquis* (22-23), Horace enjoins his whole audience to a life of moderation, generosity, humanity. Again Horace has used similar constructions *temperato usu* (3-4) and *oculo inretorto* (23) to enclose the poem and at the same time to emphasize his main thought.

Q. Dellius, the addressee of the third poem, is well-known, especially for his switching of sides in the Civil Wars. N. Collinge (*The Structure of Horace's* Odes, Oxford, 1961) and N/H present somewhat contrasting opinions. The former states, "That ode is frankly admonitory, even minatory," and, "If anyone profited from the 'wars of succession' it was he" (138). N/H, on the other hand, believe that "Dellius must have prided himself on his inner balance and resilience" and that Horace "is recommending hedonism to a hedonist" (52). "Dellius is not being taught a lesson he doesn't know or urged to a virtue he doesn't possess" (55). In his first words to the addressee, Horace joins Dellius with all of us, *moriture Delli* (4), and again in the final strophe *omnes eodem cogimur* (25). Horace's advice, all the way from *memento* (1), is most tactful.

As already stated, 6 and 7 exude friendship. So also they provide examples of *urbanitas* and *humanitas*. We may compare Horace's attitudes in the two odes, the first to a much younger Septimius, the second to Pompeius, not just any contemporary, but a contemporary who suffered with Horace on the losing side in the battle at Philippi, a most important event in the poet's life. In general, Horace contrasts youthful energy and aging in an urbane manner. "Septimius gets as much twitting as he can take" (Collinge 133); but the ode is full of warm feelings for Septimius and for Tibur and the area of Tarentum. In either place Horace and Septimius could seek refuge from the cares and follies of the world. N/H (108) describe 7 as "a masterpiece of tact" (108) and explain in detail. It is a poem in which Horace urges his friend to accept the changes which the years have brought. As there have been shared crises and pleasures in the past, so in the future there should be shared relaxation and delights together.

Valgius, the addressee of 9, was a very close friend of Horace, as mentioned in the *Satires* (1.10, 81). The poem is, in a sense, a *consolatio* for *Mysten ademptum* (10), a phrase which invites various explanations. Early in the poem Horace draws upon the common analogy between natural elements and the vicissitudes of human fortune. Unpleasant circumstances do not last forever. As an alternative to always weeping, he proposes something joyful, *cantemus Augusti tropaea / Caesaris* (19-20). "With its delicate irony and subtle allusiveness the ode is one of Horace's most harmonious and amusing poems; it marks a high point of Augustan urbanity, and makes us think with affection of the author and of the recipient" (N/H, 138).

Ode 10 is addressed to *Licini* (1), whose identity is much debated. A full discussion appears in N/H (151-57), concluding that the addressee must be Maecenas' brother-in-law, Licinius Murena. This is the ode of *auream mediocritatem* (5), and it is that phrase which puts the stamp on N/H's identification. The poem expresses a very real human circumstance, and Horace, by appealing to a common experience of humanity, does not cast aspersions on the addressee, but offers what is good advice for everyone: *auream quisquis medocritatem / diligit* (5-6) and *sperat infestis, metuit secundis / alteram sortem bene praeparatum / pectus* (13-15).

There is no sure identification of Quinctius Hirpinus, the addressee of 11. If *Epistle* 1.16 is to the same Quinctius, it can be assumed that he was prosperous and well-known. At any rate, in the ode he is advised to stop worrying about tomorrow, to enjoy a sober, sweet Epicurean life, pleasure in moderation. Wine, perfume, flowers, and music are all there in the *locus amoenus* of the poem for both Horace and his friend.

As stated earlier, in the four poems, 12, 17, 18, and 20, Horace appears affectionate and warm to Maecenas. In 17, the poet even delves into astrology, a subject of which he did not approve, in order to cheer Maecenas while reflecting on their death. In 18, the contrast between the two friends, *at fides et ingeni / benigna vena est, pauperemque dives / me petit* (9-11) is strengthened in the final general thoughts on death, *aequa tellus / pauperi recluditur / regumque pueris. . . . functum / pauperem laboribus* (32-34, 38-39) through the repetition of *pauper*. In 20, the final poem of the book, Horace is telling Maecenas that the friendship which they share will bring its reward. For the poetry will be immortal and so bring immortality to Maecenas also.

The well-known 14 is to a Postumus, not yet definitely identified, though evidence suggests that he is the same Postumus as in Propertius 3.12. If so, he is a successful equestrian. The atmosphere of the ode is deeply melancholy; this gravity of tone may reflect the character of Postumus. The poem is not addressed just to Postumus as in *places* (6), but is at the same time universal, for all mankind, as shown by the shift to *quicumque*, the first person plural, and the periphrastic:

> *compescit unda, scilicet omnibus,*
> *quicumque terrae munere vescimur,*
> *enaviganda, sive reges,*
> *sive inopes erimus coloni.*

9-12

Those forms dominate the next three strophes: *frustra carebimus* (13), *frustra metuemus* (15-16), *visendus ater flumine languido /*

Cocytos (17-18), *linquenda tellus et domus et placens / uxor* (21-22). Two general statements in the third person conclude the poem.

About 16, N/H say, "it is distinguished not only by organization and wit but by the rarer qualities of humanity and serenity" (256). Pompeius Grosphus, a prosperous Sicilian landowner, is described by Porphyrio as *eques Romanus*. The theme of the ode is *otium*, which can have both good and bad implications; Horace, however, uses only the good, such as peace, properly used leisure, a calm mind, acceptance of the present. Urbane wit is found throughout. N/H mention specifically the play on the Greek of Grosphus' name in *iaculamur* (17), the "whimsical comparison" of Horace and Grosphus with Achilles and Tithonus (29-30), the humor in the word *porriget* (32), and the barnyard noises (34-35). In the concluding strophes, after placing both *mihi* and *tibi* in the same line (31), Horace draws attention to Grosphus with *te, tibi*, and *te* in the penultimate strophe, while for himself there is but one *mihi* in the concluding strophe. As in some other odes, Horace avoids a critical attitude by the use of the first person in *iaculamur* (17) and *mutamus* (19). These words, occurring almost in the center of the ode, cast their influence over the whole.

Following are a few comments concerning *urbanitas* and *humanitas* in the odes not addressed to a friend. N/H describe 4 as "upper-class Roman banter" (68), that is, typical Horatian *urbanitas*, as Horace first consoles Xanthias regarding his love for a slave girl and then congratulates him; for, surely, the girl must be the daughter of a king. And, with his typical affability, Horace says that, at his age, he can no longer be interested. The ode to Barine, 8, is filled with humor and exaggeration, in an urbane manner. Even *ridet hoc, inquam, Venus ipsa, rident / simplices Nymphae ferus et Cupido* (13-14). Ode 13 starts with humorous (urbane) exaggeration in speaking of the person, *quicumque primum, et sacrilega manu / produxit, arbos, in nepotum / perniciem obprobriumque pagi* (2-4), before continuing to more serious reflections. Between these parts are two strophes of maxims which touch humanity in general. The construction of 15, with no addressee and written entirely in the third person, without even one *tu*, marks the ode as different from the others. But in the central strophe, Horace does display his own warm feelings for earlier times in Rome and his respect for tradition when he mentions Romulus and unshorn Cato.

An urbane man in Horace's world could not ignore the *princeps*, and there is ample ancient evidence for the close *amicitia* between Horace and Augustus. Commentators point to many possible allusions to Augustus in Book 2, but there are, however, only two lines which specifically mention him, *cantemus Augusti tropaea / Caesaris* (9.19-20) and *tuque pedestribus / dices historiis proelia Caesaris* (12.9-10). These two references are near the midpoint of the book, one before and one after. Although in neither case is the regime the main subject of the poem, these lines not only draw attention to Augustus at two rather central points, but extend this attention to him from the center out in both directions, to the beginning and to the end of the book.

Another facet of *urbanitas* in Book 2 is the poet's expression of his understanding of Rome in relation to Italy and the rest of the world. Worthy of note here is the multiplicity of proper names which cover a wide expanse of space and time; in fact, there are only five poems in Book 2 without some reference beyond Italy. For instance, Ode 1 carries the reader from Africa, *amicior / Afris* (25-26), through Dalmatia, *Delmatico peperit triumpho* (16), to the Medes, *auditumque Medis* (31), and back in time to Cato and Jugurtha, recalling both victory and defeat. Ode 2 also stretches from *Libyam remotis / Gadibus* (10-11) in the South and West to *redditum Cyri solio Prahaten* (17) in the East. Although a primary theme of 6 is to praise the Italian towns of Tibur and Tarentum, in so doing, Horace has the reader travel to the West, *Gadis* (1), *Cantabrum* (2), and South, *Syrtis, Maura* (3). References to the East in the first and last strophes delineate the ninth ode and emphasize the contrast between a condition which is desirable and one that is not. In the first strophe *mare Caspium* (2) and *Armeniis in oris* (4) are examples of bad weather; in the last five lines *Niphaten* (20), *Medumque flumen* (21), and *Gelonos* (23) provide examples for the pleasant songs about Augustus. In 11 Quinctius is to forget problems in the West, *Cantaber* (1), and the East, *Scythes* (1). In 16 Horace associates a lack of *otium* with the East, *in patenti / prensus Aegaeo* (1-2), *bello furiosa Thrace* (5), *Medi pharetra decori* (6); in 18 his illustrations of undesired luxury include the words *Africa* and *Attali* (5).

Providing multiple examples, two of the odes to Maecenas complete this part of the discussion. In 12 Horace ranges from historical examples in the West, *ferae bella Numantiae, durum Hannibalem, Siculum mare* (1-2), to the legendary wealth of the East, *dives Achaemenes, pinguis Phrygiae Mygdonias opes* (21-22) and *plenas aut Arabum domos* (24). Finally, in 20, he ranges from legendary times and travels in the North and South to the outer barbarians in the East and the learned provinces in the West:

> *iam Daedaleo notior Icaro*
> *visam gementis litora Bosphori*
> *Syrtisque Gaetulas canorus*
> *ales Hyperboreosque campos.*
>
> *me Colchus et qui dissimulat metum*
> *Marsae cohortis Dacus et ultimi*
> *noscent Geloni, me peritus*
> *discet Hiber Rhodanique potor.*
>
> 13-20

Through Horace's poetry, Maecenas will gain immortality over the known world and for infinite time in the future.

In sum, Book 2 is characterized by a display of *amicitia*. These odes portray Horace in a circle of his friends; they also include the reader of every era in that circle, for, as Johnson says, "He gathers himself and all of us into his richly meditated, richly harmonized group portrait" (142). Horace frequently advised his *amici* to do what they already were doing or think as they already were thinking. N.W. DeWitt includes many of the odes of Book 2 in his collection of "Parresiastic Poems of Horace" (*CP* 30 [1935] 312-319), but he admits that the possible reproofs and admonition were always characterized by gentleness, kindness, and courtesy. These attributes introduce a definition of *urbanitas*, including a sense of courtesy and refinement, an educated mind, a presence in the city, a clever wit and humor. In addition, Horace, an urbane Roman, is part of a larger world beyond Rome and Italy, part of the universal *humanitas* of all mankind. The other books of Horace's *Odes* may parade a greater variety of lyric meters, may deal with politics to a larger degree, may have more religious or amorous appeal, but Book 2 remains the high point of *amicitia, urbanitas, humanitas*.

OVIDIUS IN TAURIS: OVID *TR.* 4.4 AND *EX P.* 3.2

☙

R. Elaine Fantham
Princeton University

In proper tribute to our honorand I should be offering him something wise and witty either on Virgil himself or on the topography of Virgil's Italy, of which Sandy's knowledge is incomparable. I hope he will forgive me if I offer him instead an Ovidian theme from a very different part of the Roman world: I was privileged to have Sandy in the audience when I presented this in its oral form and have pleasant memories of enjoying his company on that as on many other occasions.

Among the poems composed by Ovid in exile, only a very few depart from his personal situation and the world of Augustan Rome. But one adventure narrative from Greek mythology had a special appeal for him: the story of Iphigenia's service as priestess of Artemis among the Taurians and her reunion with Orestes. This is treated twice, first at *Tristia* 4.4.63-82, then in an expanded version, at *ex Ponto* 3.2.43-96. Ovid had more than one reason to linger over this episode: it was in a sense "local" to his place of exile; it was the subject of a work of art celebrated in the Rome of Ovid's youth: it offered a model of friendship in the mutual loyalty and self-sacrifice of Orestes and Pylades that made it a favorite theme of Roman drama, popular philosophy and elegy; and finally this theme of friendship became urgently important to the poet at Tomi, forced by his circumstances to depend on the help of his friends for any hope of return to Italy or even escape from his place of relegation.

This paper has two purposes: to illustrate Ovid's narratological technique by comparing the successive treatments of the mytho-

Note: See Plates 1-5 for accompanying illustrations.

logical narrative, and to ground these narratives in the literary and artistic tradition. But since Ovid was cut off from both traditions from the moment that he reached Tomi, the difference between the first and second narrative is not one of new sources for the myth or even exposure to new literary stimuli of any kind: both versions draw on the same intellectual stock. Thus we can proceed from Ovid's first, bare narrative, seen in the light of his earlier use of the friendship-pair Orestes and Pylades, and open up the traditions behind his work before considering the artistic development of his final, more elaborate, presentation of the tale.

In *Tristia* 4.4 Ovid addresses an unnamed patron, identified by the allusion to *patriae facundia linguae* (4.4.5) as M. Valerius Messalla Messalinus,[1] to ask his help in petitioning for the poet's transfer from the cruel climate and savage neighbourhood of Tomis. Ovid's tale of Iphigenia serves to demonstrate the barbaric cruelty of the region, and is introduced by a monument which Ovid implies still stands: the Tauric altar of the archer-goddess, spattered with human blood.[2] The next couplet moves back in time: before Roman rule this was the kingdom of bad King Thoas. At first Ovid's description of the land as *non invidiosa nefandis / nec cupienda bonis* (65-66) seem mere padding,[3] but the first phrase at least is fitted to Ovid's own situation. Just as the region is now thought fit for *nefandi*, criminals, amongst whom Ovid is counted, so in the past it was neither begrudged to criminals nor attractive to honest colonists. Similarly the plain statement "it was here that Iphigenia tended the rites of her goddess" is modified by two implied judgments: *pro supposita cerva,* suggesting exchange or atonement for the doe substituted by the goddess, and *qualiacunque* stressing the negative aspect of the rites. Thus Iphigenia becomes a sort of predecessor of Ovid, in that her presence among the Taurians is paying a debt for her life, and her daily tasks are unworthy of her own moral or cultural level. Orestes too is introduced in moral terms, *dubium pius an sceleratus* (69) conventional in debating his role as father's avenger and matricide, but pointed by the implicit parallel with the poet: implicit too is the contrast between Ovid and Orestes, not exiled by authority but *exactus furiis ipse suis*. Once the moral parallels are set out Ovid moves forward, through his account of Pylades, as *exemplum veri amoris,* to the moment of the sacrifice (73).

Here Ovid interrupts the forward movement to evoke a picture whose details foreshadow the climax of the episode (73-78). The two heroes are led, their hands bound behind them (*evincti*) to the bloody altar set before the double doors (*geminas ante cruenta fores* [74]): as each fears not for himself but for his companion (75-76) the priestess stands poised with drawn sword, and the barbaric fillet of the sacrificial victim circles the young men's Greek locks.[4] It is the moment before the sacrifice, not the recognition and Iphigenia's embrace of her brother, that Ovid has chosen to present so vividly. From 79-82 Iphigenia dominates as she follows recognition with embrace, and rejoicing evacuates the image of the goddess to a happier place and circumstance. But with the last couplet Ovid is already working the transition back to his own case, by stressing the *crudelia sacra* loathed by the goddess (81 recalls 68 and *dira caede* 63-64) and the theme of transfer from that place *in meliora* [loca] (82). Iphigenia was able to do for the divine image what Ovid is asking for himself from Messalinus. The *envoi* of the poem (87-88) makes explicit the equation between Ovid and Orestes and hints at appeal to Augustus himself, as the poet wishes that the deity may be appeased[5] and the winds may carry back his ship like that of Orestes.

Thus while many elements at the beginning and end of the narrative are shaped to match Ovid's circumstances, the central tableau has no contemporary reference and must draw on another inspiration. How close is Ovid's tale to Euripides, and what other ingredients have contributed to the episode?

As a preliminary we should note that it is probably Ovid himself who introduced Orestes and Pylades into the Roman elegiac traditions: when Propertius lists pairs of heroic friends as precedents for the loyalty of Maecenas to Octavian at 2.1.37-38, it is not likely that the lacuna after 38 has lost a reference to Pylades and Orestes:[6] for the dependency of the polluted Orestes upon his friend would make him a poor parallel for Octavian. Pylades has no role to play in Hermione's letter to Orestes (*Heroides* 8) and only the proverbial role of faithful friend in *Amores* 2.6.15-16 *quod fuit Argolico iuvenis Phoceus Orestae / hoc tibi, dum licuit, psittace, turtur erat,* and *Remedia* 589 *semper habe Pyladen aliquem qui curet Oresten.* Both passages stress the service of Pylades to Orestes, but neither implies a specific episode in Orestes' post-matricidal career.

It is only in exile that Ovid begins to combine Orestes and Pylades as an equal pairing with Theseus and Pirithous, Achilles and Patroclus, adding to them the new Virgilian pair of Nisus and Euryalus. But in exile Ovid himself takes on the role of Orestes: and the praise of Pylades becomes a persuasive device to engage his friend's support. Already the first allusion introduces king Thoas and thus implies Orestes' Pontic adventures: the Princeps will not be angry at the loyalty of Ovid's unidentified friend any more than Thoas, who is said to have approved of Pylades when he heard of his faithful companionship to Orestes: *de comite Argolici postquam cognovit Orestae / narratur Pyladen ipse probasse Thoas* (1.7.27-28). This is followed by the alleged admiration of Hector for Patroclus, of Dis/Pluto for Theseus and of Turnus for both Euryalus and Nisus (1.7.29-34), none of which was attested in Ovid's literary models. The closest extant model for Thoas' approval of Pylades must be Euripides *Iphigenia in Tauris* 1477-1478, where Athena's speech *ex machina* leads the king to declare that he forgives Iphigenia and Orestes.

Nonetheless in the couplet *Tr.* 1.7.27-28 the seed is sown for Ovid's first treatment of the Taurian myth at *Tristia* 4.4. Even after the narrative that we are considering Ovid will use the pairs of heroic friends again in *Tristia* 5.4 to praise his anonymous friend as a Patroclus, a Pylades (*qui comitatus Oresten* [5.4.25]), a Theseus or a Euryalus: each of them is supporting his companion away from home, or on a dangerous enterprise. This is merely a variation on *Tr.* 1.7, but now the local connection between Pontus and the Taurians has been established; compare the incidental allusion at *ex P.* 1.2.77-78: *quid Sauromatae faciunt, quid Iazuges acres / cultaque Oresteae Taurica terra deae*. In due course, at *ex P.* 3.2.45-93, Ovid will write his final and fullest treatment of the theme.

There are good grounds for attributing an allusion such as *Tristia* 1.7.27-28 to recall of Euripides. Certainly Ovid knew and used Euripidean tragedy, drawing on *Medea*, *Hippolytus*, *Andromache* and other plays now lost, like *Hypsipyle*, for the *Heroides*, and returning to *Hippolytus* and *Hecuba* for episodes in *Metamorphoses* 15 and 13. So there is every likelihood that he would know and use the *Taurica* as material. How much does his narrative match that of Euripides?

In the play, Iphigenia, after a disturbing dream of her brother, is told by the herdsman who brings on the captured pair, how one was seized by madness and in his delirium called the other Pylades. Knowing only the name of Pylades and finding by interrogation that the young men know Argos, she plans to send "Pylades" back to her own country with a message to her (still unnamed) brother, but to sacrifice his friend. She leaves at 636 to fetch the letter which a prisoner wrote (584) for her to send to her family. In the interval, marked by a brief dialogue with the chorus, Orestes and Pylades debate who shall return to Argos, Orestes insisting that Pylades must return to marry his sister Electra and institute a funeral cult for Orestes at Argos.

Returning at 725 Iphigenia binds Pylades by an oath to give the letter to her brother, and only when he has sworn does she read it out, naming Orestes (769) and thus triggering the recognition scene that reverses the whole course of the action. Earlier Pylades has a noble speech as he refuses to live and let Orestes die (674-686), but is persuaded by Orestes: otherwise there is no real contest or exchange of identity in which each hero competes to save the other and no final approach to the sacrifice. Instead the recognition leads Iphigenia to deceive Thoas and ensure the escape of the young men with the image through a feigned ritual ablution of the image at the sea-shore.

One might single out details of the Ovidian narrative that echo Euripides: the bloodstained altar (*Tr.* 4.4.63-64) recalls Iphigenia's description in the Euripidean prologue of its stains and tufts of human scalp (*I.T.* 72-73), the bound heroes recall *I.T.* 455-457 "but this pair approaches, tied together by the hands in bonds, a new offering for the goddess"; we could compare Ovid's *vitta*, if it is that of the victims as I argued above, with the sacred apparatus in Euripides, such as the *chernibes* of *I.T.* 244 and 644. Even *transtulit* in *deae signum crudelia sacra perosae / transtulit* (80-81) could be an adaptation of *I.T.* 774-775 μετάστησον θεᾶς / σφαγίων—"remove me from the slaughter of the goddess." Finally the winds of *Tr.* 4.4.87 could recall the *pnoai* invoked in Athena's farewell at *I.T.* 1487 and the placated deity may recall Poseidon's cooperation at *I.T.* 1444-1445. However these are not details that would depend on close memory or reading of the Euripidean text. In contrast with, for example, Ovid's careful reworking of Polyxena's speech from *Hecuba* 547-552 and 563-565 into his single speech of *Met.* 13.457-472, most of these isolated features are well within Ovid's power of free invention, or could have come to Ovid from post-Euripidean versions of the Iphigenia myth.

For Euripides' play was immensely influential, starting a series of dramatic and artistic treatments of the refashioned myth. Thus Aristotle cites or praises the *I.T.* four times in the *Poetics*[7] for the drama of its recognition and reversal, but he also cites what seems to be another version of the same theme by Polyidos. This brought Orestes to the point of death before he cried out "that he must now perish sacrificed like his own sister"[8] and thus provoked recognition by an Iphigenia either on the point of killing him, or of witnessing his death. It is also possible that another Greek tragedy combined the two friends and Iphigenia and even King Thoas in a far more hazardous situation; this tragedy, known from the adaptation of the Roman republican playwright Pacuvius, has been identified with the lost *Chryses* of Sophocles.[9]

In Pacuvius' dramatization of Orestes' adventures, cited by Nonius and others as *Doulorestes*, "Orestes enslaved," the friends fled with Iphigenia from the Taurian land and sought the hospitality of Chryses, son of Chryseis, now ruler of Sminthe. There, however, they were overtaken by Thoas in pursuit of the stolen image of Artemis. Since Chryses hated Agamemnon as the ravisher of his mother, he wanted vengeance on Orestes. Hence the loyalty of Pylades and Orestes takes the form of a contest as each claims to be Orestes, in order that he, and not his friend, should be killed: finally they ask to die together, rather than be parted. The fame of this particular episode was extended at Rome by Cicero's citation of it twice in *de Finibus*[10] and again in *de Amicitia* 24, where the narrator Laelius reports the immense public enthusiasm for the scene with its contest of friendship. Although the play itself need not have been known to Ovid, the episode had passed into popular thought and contributed to the vitality of the mythical friendship, and it is likely that Pacuvius' pathetic contest of self-sacrifice became blended with the less spectacular Euripidean version in Roman popular consciousness. I would suggest that there are traces in Ovid's narrative of influence from this more dramatic and confrontational account of the friendship, with its nick-of-time escape from death.

Thus we should perhaps credit the influence of the Pacuvian scene when Ovid focusses on the motif of two hearts that beat as one: *qui duo corporibus mentibus unus erant* (72) or in his comment that each grieves not for himself but for his friend (75-76). But this is a matter of emphasis: in themselves these details are compatible with the context of *Iphigenia*.

Besides the dramatic tradition, Euripides' play gave rise almost immediately to a tradition of visual art, which entailed its own code and system of representation. We should consider whether the emphasis on position and gesture in the otherwise compressed narrative of *Tr.* 4.4.65-82 suggests that Ovid has in mind not Euripides, nor even the possible tragedy of Polyidos, but a work of visual art. Why else would he stress the otherwise irrelevant palace doors behind the altar?[11] We saw that his narrative lingers over a single tableau; this might well derive from memory of a painting or relief of the sacrifice. Because of their confinement to one moment and to what can be displayed without words, paintings often have to simplify or modify the dramatic episodes which may have been their inspiration. The sword in Iphigenia's hand conflicts with Euripides' account, but would be a necessary symbol in any painting to indicate the scene of sacrifice.

Such divergences from the literary texts are common in vase paintings or frescoes.[12] Art historians have often observed how an artist has contaminated narrative elements from successive scenes of a drama or inserted symbols (like a sword) of action to come: again the artist can conflate elements from rival versions of a myth or even different but parallel myths.

In the four centuries between the death of Euripides and Ovid's poetry of exile the visual tradition reproduced in vases, gems, reliefs, wall-paintings and sarcophagi both generic tableaux of the young men's sacrifice and other scenes corresponding to six recognizable moments or phases in the action of Euripides' play. These have been collected and analyzed by H. Philippart, "*Iconographie d'Iphigénie en Tauride*,"[13] and additional Greek vases are illustrated by Séchan.[14]

But one painting must have been uniquely influential in Augustan Rome. Pliny, *NH* 35.136 reports that the great Timomachus, whose Medea and Ajax were acquired by Julius Caesar for the temple of Venus Genetrix, also painted an Orestes and Iphigenia among the Taurians.[15] Art historians have looked for copies or derivatives of this work in the murals of Pompeii and Herculaneum, but the variety of representations of the myth leaves room for disagreement. Among the eleven Pompeian instances of the legend two of the best preserved are iconographically related. The most often reproduced is the triangular composition from an exedra of the *Casa del Citharista*, showing Iphigenia high on the temple podium at the center, looking down at Orestes and Pylades to our left, while Thoas sits, with a standing attendant behind him stage right. Orestes and Pylades are a magnificent pair, half naked, garlanded for sacrifice, with their hands bound. Orestes, turned away from the onlooker, is downcast, while Pylades, facing him and the spectators looks boldly around.[16] But a damaged painting from the *tablinum* of the house of Caecilius Iucundus is closely related. This represents only Iphigenia and the two heroes, in an arrangement that leaves no room for Thoas. Although the upper torsoes and heads of the heroes have been obliterated by damage, it is clear from their lower bodies that

this painting derives from the same original. The figure of
Iphigenia is clear: beside her a female attendant holds the sword
that will be used in the sacrifice.[17]

While scholars have agreed that the model for these paintings
is most probably Timomachus' great work, they have differed
over the inclusion of Thoas. But Robert is surely right to argue
that ancient evidence favors the version without the king;[18] not
only does Pliny speak only of Orestes and Iphigenia, but the
epigram from Planudes' supplement to the Palatine anthology
celebrates a painting of the first encounter between sister and
brother, and it is this encounter which offers the real dramatic
opportunities for the painter. As Phillipart comments "le moment
le plus simplement pathétique [c'est] la rencontre du frère et de
la soeur."

Of the remaining Pompeian treatments, that from the house
of Arrius Polites and another from the house of the Vettii resemble
the triangular composition of the *Casa del Citarista*.[19] While the
young men are shown with Iphigenia in three more instances,
another four paintings seem to feature them alone.[20] The only real
contender in popularity is again a representation of their first
entry and confrontation with Iphigenia. A frieze-like scene from
Herculaneum shows the heroes bound and approaching Iphigenia
in single file. She stands at an altar with drawn sword and an
attendant behind her. The resemblance of this composition to the
horizontal arrangement of the later Munich sarcophagus and
other related sarcophagi, suggests that this other representation
of the encounter of brother and sister was equally well known in
Ovid's day.[21]

While the pathos and physical beauty of the doomed heroes
in the vertical composition is an aesthetic argument for seeing
this as the masterpiece of Timomachus whose effect might remain
with Ovid even in his later years of exile, Ovid's actual description
provides minor discrepancies (the double doors of the palace, the
central altar) with any of the visual monuments available to us.
What is important, however, is less the role of the single great
picture in shaping the poet's imagination than the predominance
of the scene itself in the art of Ovid's time; not simply the
Taurian myth, but the special pathos of this first encounter and
the narrow avoidance of fratricide persisted in the paintings of
Hellenistic Italy to reinforce and maintain poetic interest in the
legend. If Iphigenia's rescue had entailed a metamorphosis and
had not conflicted with the geographical movement of Ovid's
Metamorphoses after Greek victory at Troy, he would no doubt

have found a place for this Euripidean theme as he did for Hecuba, Polyxena and others. But Ovid was following history westwards, escorting Odysseus and Aeneas to the future glory of Italy, and it was not until he was forced to travel to the Black Sea region that the myth related to his own life or his art.

Although investigation of the visual tradition has left only indeterminate conclusions, it is this same highly visual moment of brother and sister's first encounter that reappears, set in place as the highpoint of Ovid's final version of the encounter at *ex Ponto* 3.2, apparently conflating from drama and painting the tableau of bound and garlanded victims, altar and priestess with drawn sword. There is no substantial change of setting from that of *Tristia* 4.4, but instead the encounter and recognition scene are enriched by vivid dialogue, and the framing narrative is coloured by Ovid's bold imaginative device of telling the Greek legend from a Taurian, or shall we say Getic, point of view.

In this last version Ovid even provides a double motivation for Ovid's narrative. First, at 3.2.33-34, comes the enumeration of Theseus and Pylades (*qui comitavit Oresten*) as friends who earned immortal glory for loyalty. They will bear witness to Ovid's friend Cotta[22] that he will win glory from his aid to the poet. But as a second illustration of the honour paid to friendship Ovid introduces a local sage who answers the poet's Getic encomium[23] of his friends with the story of Orestes and Pylades, as proof that Pontic Tomis also cherished myths of heroic devotion.

The old fellow, a superb professional storyteller, begins with an ecphrasis—*est locus in Scythia*—in the best epic style, then describes the temple of Artemis, its forty steps and colonnade and empty pedestal[24] where once the statue stood. The pedestal is a sign, whether a rhetorical *tekmerion* or source of a Callimachean *aition*, that the goddess's image once stood there, just as the white stone altar discolored with human blood (53-54) commemorates the highborn virgin who slew foreigners with the sword. From the honest Gete's point of view the human sacrifice is simply *mos maiorum* and Thoas is "most renowned," whereas Iphigenia is *nescioquam* (62), a mere successor to the traditional Scythian aristocratic virgin priestess.[25] This local angle, expanded from 45-60, is the single most innovative element in Ovid's retelling of the narrative; the other vivid new component will be Iphigenia's speeches, representing the dialogue of recognition. A tabular form will indicate the relative correspondences of the first and second versions.

Tristia 4.4.63-82			*ex Ponto* 3.2.45-93
nec procul a nobis locus est	63	= 45	est locus
dira / caede ... ara	63-64	= 53-54	ara ... adfuso ... cruore
regna Thoantis	66	= 59	regna Thoans habuit
virgo ... sacra coluit	67-68	= 55-56	nescioquam Iphigenian 62
Orestes and Pylades	69-72	= 67-70	protinus ... ducuntur ad aram
protinus evincti ... ducuntur ad aram	73	= 71-72	evincti ...
		77-84	(Iphigenia's dialogue)
mutual self-sacrifice	75-76	= 85-86, 89	certamen amoris
fratrem cognovit	79	= 90, 91, 92	frater erat
deae signum	81-82	= 93-94	simulacra Dianae.

It can be seen from this parallel outline that the turning point at the center of both narratives is the almost duplicated line, *protinus evincti ... ducuntur ad aram* (4.4.73) expanded into the couplet 3.2.71-72. But in this later version Ovid builds up suspense, first with the triple anaphora of *dumque parat sacrum, dum velat ... / dum tardae causas invenit ipsa morae*, then with Iphigenia's apologies, *non ego crudelis ... ritus is est gentis* (77-79). She asks their origin and hears the name of her own country (81-82), a detail drawn from Euripides *I.T.* 508-509. At this point Ovid returns to narrative form, reporting Iphigenia's decision to spare the letter-carrier (83-90), the result in Euripides of a long exchange in stichomythia (*I.T.* 510-569) and of Orestes' outburst on his guilt. The rest of the Ovidian narrative (85-90) follows almost exactly the sequence in Euripides; the one difference is that Ovid's Iphigenia is literate[26] and writes her own letter offstage as the heroes compete to die.

The poet cuts instantly from the recognition to the theft of the image and escape by sea. But this time the moral of the story is the *mirus amor iuvenum* (95) and the old Getic sage ends as he began with the exaltation of their *magnum nomen*, a verbal echo of *nomen amicitiae* (43). Ovid improves on the occasion with an *a fortiori*: if even on this savage shore the name of friendship stirs barbarian breasts, how much the more should an Italian like Cotta, born to the obligations of nobility, feel compassion.

The story is a gem of *ethopoeia* and neat transitions. The myth that Euripides presented as an *aition* for the cult of Artemis Tauropolis has become in Ovid an *aition* for the empty pedestal in the land of the Taurians. But for Ovid, even more than for

Euripides, it is the noble self-sacrifice of the friends that animates the tale. Ovid's editorial comments, his parentheses (77 and 92), his variation of tempo between the swift opening and closing (71-72 and 94-95) and the suspenseful temporizing before the recognition—itself assumed, but not stated in 92—all are features of Ovid's most refined narrative style as displayed in *Ars Amatoria* or *Fasti*. There is no limit to the variety that a skilled artist can obtain from a familiar theme, and the telling of the myth in *ex Ponto* does honor to the highest standards of post-Callimachean invention.

NOTES

1. On Ovid's relationship with Messallinus, see Syme, *History in Ovid* (Oxford, 1978) 117-122: on this poem, 122.

2. While *dira / caede . . . spargitur* (63-64) may be historic present, the tense permits the assumption that the altar itself still stands.

3. The meaning of *invidiosa nefandis* is not clear, but by comparison with the similar antithesis at Lucilius 598, *neque inimicis invidiosam neque amico exoptabilem*, I interpret it as "not to be begrudged to criminals." This is also the interpretation of Nemethy, *Commentarius Exegeticus* (Budapest, 1913) 95: *quae non invidemus nefandis hominibus sed libenter illis concedimus*.

4. It would be syntactically easier to construe the *vitta* and the locks without change of human focus as Iphigenia's, but dramatically the fillets of the victims offer a more shocking contrast than those of the priestess, and stress what has not yet been expressed—that Greek men (abomination!) are being sacrificed to a barbarian cult. There is a similar ambiguity in *ex P.* 3.2.75: *dumque parat sacrum, dum velat tempora vittis*. Euripides *I.T.* 38-39 (even if interpolated) and 621-622 seem to support this interpretation, but should not be pressed too far.

5. The generic male *deo* nicely alludes both to Apollo, who sent Orestes to fetch the image, and the Roman *princeps,* who associated himself with Apollo.

6. On the need for a supplement after 2.1.38 see *Propertius,* ed. Butler/Barber (Oxford, 1933) 190, *Propertius Elegies Book II,* ed. W.E. Camps (Cambridge, 1967) 70-71.

7. See *Poetics* 11 (1452b 6-8, on the recognition), 14 (1454a 7), 16 (1454b 30-35, again the recognition) and 17 (1455a 18).

8. *Poetics* 16 (1455a 6-8) and 17 (1455b 10-12) tell us only of the recognition scene and Orestes' outcry. Lucas, *Aristotle's Poetics* (Oxford, 1968) 170-171, thinks both references can be explained as

comments of Polyidos, the sophist, in a non-dramatic work, without assuming that he composed a play of his own.

9. This hypothesis is disallowed by A. Lesky, *Greek Tragic Poetry*, tr. Dillon, (New Haven, 1972) 300, who believes the synopsis offered by Hyginus, *Fabulae* 120 need have no bearing on any play of Sophocles, or prior to Euripides' *I.T.*

10. *Fin.* 2.79 and 5.63: *qui clamores vulgi aut imperitorum excitantur in theatris cum illa dicuntur: "Ego sum Orestes," contraque ab altero "immo enimvero ego sum, inquam, Orestes." Cum autem exitus ab utroque datur conturbato errantique regi: "ambo ergo una necarier precamur."*

11. Cf. *ad aram / quae stabat geminas ante cruenta fores* (73-74).

12. Cf. L. Séchan, *Etudes sur la Tragédie Grecque en Rapport avec la Ceramique* (Paris, 1925) 387 on the iconography of this play: "Ces peintures de vases . . . nous renseignent . . . sur la methodes des décorateurs, en nous montrant qu'ils conservent toujours une certaine liberté à l'égard des sources lettéraires."

13. *Rev. Belge d'Hist. et de Phil.* 4 (1925) 5-33, the fullest documentation known to me.

14. Séchan, *op. cit.* 379-88. Although concerned only with vase-paintings, and dealing with this myth briefly, Séchan offers ancient references and some bibliography on the lost chef d'oeuvre of Timomachus and the Pompeian wallpaintings (380 n. 3).

15. Pliny, *NH* 35.136: *Timomachus Byzantius Caesaris dictatoris aetate Aiacem et Medeam pinxit, ab eo in Veneris genetricis aede positas. . . . Timomachi aeque laudantur Orestes, Iphigenia in Tauris et Lecythion, agilitatis exercitator.* Clearly the last sentence may refer to three paintings, not two; we would then have to hypothesize a picture of Iphigenia without Orestes, and another picture of Orestes without Iphigenia, neither of which survives in iconography.

16. I take the records of the legend at Pompeii from K. Schefold, *Die Wande Pompejis: Topographische Verzeichnis der Bildmotive* (Berlin, 1957). For the *Casa del Citharista* painting (16); see also L. Curtius, *Die Wandmalerei Pompejis* (repr. Hildesheim, 1960) 242-243, figs. 142 and 143. The best colour reproduction is in J. Charbonneaux, *Hellenistic Art 330-50 B.C.* (New York, 1973) 194, fig. 203.

17. Schefold, *ibid.* 66. Curtius, 244-245, figs. 144 and 145. Charbonneaux, 195, fig. 204.

18. C. Robert, *Archaeologische Hermeneutik* (Berlin, 1919) 193-195 (so also his earlier detailed analysis in *Archaeologische Zeitung* 33.147-148) citing *A.P.* 16.128: "Iphigenia rageth furiously, but the face of Orestes recalls her to the sweet memory of kinship. Being stirred by wrath and gazing, too, at her brother, her glance is as of one carried by mixed fury and pity." (Tr. Paton, LCL, *A.P.* 5.233).

19. See Schefold, *op. cit.* 59 (House of Arrius Polites) and 147 (House of the Vettii); this too is reproduced by Curtius, 247, fig. 146.
20. Orestes, Pylades and Iphigenia, Schefold, *ibid.* 117, 260, 278; the heroes alone, Schefold, *ibid.* 184 (at an altar) 200, 224 and perhaps 242.
21. The painting from Herculaneum is 19, fig. 3 (n. 26) in Philippart, also illustrated in a line drawing in Roscher, *Ausführliches Lexicon der Griechischen und Römischen Mythologie* s.v. Orestes 6.1001. On the Munich sarcophagus (München Glyptotek c363) see Philippart 24.G1.
22. Cotta Maximus, the addressee of *ex Ponto* 3.2, is the younger brother of the Messallinus for whom Ovid composed *Tristia* 4.4. According to Syme, *History in Ovid* (Oxford, 1978) 125f., Ovid's nine letters to Cotta begin with *Tristia* 4.5 (as it were a pair with 4.4 to Messalinus) but continue after Ovid's last letter to Messalinus with three letters in *ex P.* 3; nn. 2, 5 and 8. But just as Ovid writes no letter to Messallinus after *ex P.* 2.2, so he leaves Cotta alone after Book 3.
23. *Cumque ego de vestra nuper probitate referrem (nam didici Getice Sarmaticeque loqui / forte senex quidam . . . / reddidit ad nostros talia verba sonos* (3.2.39-42). The poetic ring of *ad nostros sonos* suggests but does not compel the reader to imagine a verse encomium like Ovid's ultimate achievement in Getic, the supposed *Laudes Augusti* featured in *ex P.* 4.9.
24. To authenticate the traveller's tale. The architectural term *basis* occurs here for the only time in Ovid.
25. For the Roman (mock-Roman?) elements in this narrative compare *femina . . . taedae non nota iugali / quae superat Scythicas nobilitate nurus* (55-56) *sic instituere parentes (mos maiorum!* [57]) and Thoas as *clarus . . . / nec fuit Euxinis notior alter aquis* (59-60).
26. In Euripides, Iphigenia can read (760-787) or at least remember what she dictated, but she cannot write; she had to have the letter written for her by a prisoner who was later sacrificed (584-847). We cannot determine whether Ovid forgot this detail, rejected it as an anachronism, or deliberately omitted it for narrative economy.

PHILOMELA'S WEB AND THE PLEASURES OF THE TEXT: OVID'S MYTH OF TEREUS IN THE *METAMORPHOSES*

Charles Segal
Harvard University

Despite the humane protests of writers like Vergil and Horace (one need think only of the *Fons Bandusiae* ode), the Romans seem to have enjoyed violence.[1] In places, Ovid seems to trade on this taste for blood; it is hard otherwise to account for the detail in which he describes the battles in the house of Phineus in *Metamorphoses* 5 and in the house of Pirithous in *Metamorphoses* 12.[2] Ovid does not deal so deeply as Vergil does with the moral problems of violence and suffering in the world-order; and the *Metamorphoses*, in fact, often makes us wonder how sensitive Ovid is to such questions. Is he aware of the problematical nature of the pleasure which his violent narratives arouse?

One of the most difficult passages in the poem for these issues is the episode of Tereus' rape of Philomela in Book 6. The details of Philomela's severed tongue and Tereus' Thyestean feasting on his son are worthy of Seneca, who in fact seems to have drawn heavily on Ovid here.[3] The story comes, appropriately, amid other tales of cruelty, torture and murder, especially within the family: the gods' killing of Niobe's children (6.218ff.), the flaying of Marsyas (6.385ff.), Tantalus' alleged cannibalistic

---

This study was prepared during a Fellowship at the Center for Advanced Study in the Behavioral Sciences, Stanford, California. I am grateful for financial support at the Center, which was provided by the National Endowment for the Humanities (No. RA-20037-88) and the Andrew W. Mellon Foundation.

slaughter of his son (6.407ff.) just before; Pelias' death at the hands of his daughters and Medea's killing of her children shortly after (7.297ff., 394ff.). Unlike these episodes, however, the tale of Philomela is also a story of sexual violence, probably the most lurid sexual violence in the poem. Ovid even intrudes his narrative presence, in the first person, to distance himself from the ugliest detail by a statement of disbelief (6.561, *vix ausim credere*).[4]

What follows on this incredulity is a re-focusing of the story on belief and evidence. Repressed into silence by the savage act of cutting out the victim's tongue, the story needs to find its proper mode of utterance. *Quid faciat Philomela*: how to narrate this horror? To conceal his crime, Tereus utters fictitious groans, and with tears wins "faith" or "credibility" for his story of Philomela's death (565-567):

> *dat gemitus fictos commentaque funera narrat;*
> *et lacrimae fecere fidem. velamina Progne*
> *deripit . . .*[5]

The juxtaposition of the undeserved *fides* of his false story with the *velamina* of Procne prepares us for the next phase of the tale, namely a mode of narration that will tell the events by non-verbal means. Philomela's "silent mouth lacks a witness to the deed" (*os mutum facti caret indice*, 574), but she "weaves purple marks upon the white threads in witness to the crime" (*purpureasque notas filis intexuit albis / indicium sceleris*, 577-578). This silent weaving answers the non-verbal device of "tears" by which Tereus won "credence" for his lie (566).

Here, as elsewhere in this highly self-conscious poem, Ovid calls our attention to the textuality of his work: his web of words recreates and includes communicative events which are spectacular for their suppression of speech. Io's proto-writing in the poem's first book or the weaving of Arachne and Minerva or the overwhelming of Orpheus' voice will be familiar examples. The *notae* of Philomela's weaving are virtually the "letters" of a written message—in fact, a "song," or a "poem," *carmen*, like the present one—which Procne "reads" (*legit*, 582), as if "unrolling" a scroll (581f.): *evolvit vestes saevi matrona tyranni / fortunaeque suae carmen miserabile legit.*[6] But she immediately represses this communication into silence—a silence which another authorial intrusion marks as extraordinary (*mirum potuisse*, 583). Unlike Tereus, she does not weep, for she has neither words nor tears, but is totally absorbed in the "image" that those "purple marks" have made her see (583-586):

> et (mirum potuisse!) silet: dolor ora repressit,
> verbaque quaerenti satis indignantia linguae
> defuerunt, nec flere vacat, sed fasque nefasque
> confusura ruit poenaeque in imagine tota est.

The self-reflexive nature of these gestures needs little comment. But Ovid does not forget the message in the medium. These *notae* are not just the "letters" of his text; they are also the "marks" of a brutal crime, to which their color bears "evidence."[7] Thus the signifying marks of the art-work (a "text" in the etymological sense) return at the end of the poem as the marks of blood that remain stamped upon the face of nature in perpetual witness of the savage deed (669-670):

> neque adhuc de pectore caedis
> excessere notae, signataque sanguine pluma est.

By shifting between these two meanings of the *notae* as both textual and extra-textual marks, Ovid also looks beyond the frame of his tale to the moral codes which surround, qualify, and certainly problematize the pleasure of his text. Philomela's weaving is both the art-work of the tale and the agency of revenge within the tale. This double function of the weaving, as a tableau of unspeakable horror and as a message that involves us in the demand and the necessity of its being read and understood, holds the contradiction between the violence and the pleasure of the text: the pleasure of and in the violence, and the pleasure in the poetry which recreates the violence. This text exemplifies the mimetic skill that, in the depiction of sadistic sexual pleasure, may invite the male reader or hearer to voyeuristic complicity in the crime,[8] as it perhaps may invite the female reader to complicity in the vengeance. But, as the web of words that calls attention to its textual origins, it also distances us from the crime and allows us, like the unbelieving narrator himself, to take the full measure of its horror. The plumage of metamorphosis that entitles Ovid to weave this tale into the "text" of his poem is forever marked with blood (669f.).

By calling attention to the perversion or suppression of speech throughout the episode, as we shall see, Ovid refuses to dignify the libidinous violence or to endow it with a prurient attraction. We are not invited to repeat the crime, as Tereus does (562).[9] Instead, the crime is doubly repressed into silence. It becomes a symbolic representation, an *imago,* which excites horror and revenge. Procne, the tale's first "reader," unrolls the woven narrative as a contemporary of Ovid would unroll the poem; and she is the model for the later reader's immediate reaction. What she finds is a tale whose horror outstrips the power of words: *silet: dolor ora repressit* (583).

The combination of physical outrage and the suppression of speech forms an indirect commentary on the events. Lust makes the Thracian warrior eloquent (*facundum faciebat amor*, 469), so that he becomes craftily persuasive through both his words and his tears (470-474). The inversion of cultural values would be appreciated by an audience for whom Athens was the home of rhetorical training. Having won Philomela by speech and by tears, Tereus is moved by neither (535). *Omnia turbasti:* his crime confuses the basic linguistic categories, as well as the sanctities, of kinship (537f.; cf. 605f.).[10]

Philomela's role henceforth is to "struggle to speak" (*luctantemque loqui*, 555f.; cf. *tua facta loquar*, 545). Tereus has used all the means of persuasion at his command (cf. 460-466); Philomela, made dumb, proves the more effective communicator. The revenge self-consciously echoes these inversions of speech and silence. Procne, as she prepares her response, "seethes with silent wrath" (*triste parat facinus tacitaque exaestuat ira*, 623). Her silence recalls Philomela's, but her "seething" links her with the violent intensity of Tereus (cf. *aestuat*, 491). Like Tereus too, she disregards the pleas of her victim, her child, Itys (640-642).

Philomela, at the climax of the vengeance, has her most intense longing for the speech of which Tereus had robbed her: *nec tempore maluit ullo / posse loqui et meritis testari gaudia dictis* (659f.). Her frustration, however, is compensated for by Procne's excessive eagerness to announce her "cruel joy" in the revenge (cf. *gaudia*, 653 and 660), so that she cannot keep silent any longer (653-655):

> *dissimulare nequit crudelia gaudia Progne*
> *iamque suae cupiens existere nuntia cladis*
> *"intus habes, quem poscis," ait.*

The failure to suppress her speech in these "joys" is not only the mirror-image of Philomela's situation; it also harks back to the eager joy of Tereus' victorious persuasion: *exsultatque et vix animo sua gaudia differt* (514). The echoes suggest the moral structure of the tale: the crime begets its own vengeance. But they also link the three main figures together in a pattern of reciprocal violence, into which they are frozen forever by the metamorphosis (cf. 666-674).

These crimes within the house not only destroy the security of domestic space; they also fit the savagery of the deed to the savagery of the land. Ovid plays the center of the civilized world— Athens—off against its dubiously civilized periphery, Thrace.[11] He introduces Tereus in a splendid verse-paragraph, listing the glorious cities of Greece, with Athens conspicuous by its absence (6.412-423). Athens is harassed by "barbarian troops," against whom "Thracian Tereus" offers his aid (6.424). Tereus thus enters the poem as *Threicius,* and as an ally against *barbara agmina* (423f.). The collocation proves ironical, for Tereus himself is the true *barbarus* and is so called as he carries out his crime (515, 533).[12] *O diris barbare factis,* Philomela calls him in the last speech that she will ever have (533).

Having entered the poem with the "victory of a glorious name" in a battle for Athens and against barbarians (*clarum vincendo nomen habebat,* 425), Tereus wins an evil "victory" over his Athenian victim, proving himself truly a barbarian (513-515):

> *"vicimus! exclamat, "mecum mea vota feruntur!"*
> *exsultatque et vix animo sua gaudia differt*
> *barbarus ...*

This cry of conquest marks a turning point. Tereus now reveals the hidden savagery of his character. He lifts the veil of assumed *pietas* (cf. 474 and 482); and the first of the episode's four animal images follows at once, comparing him to an eagle carrying off a hare in its hooked talons (516-518). The animal imagery will recur for the horrors of his crime (527-529, 559) and for Procne's revenge (636f.), until it becomes reality in the metamorphosis at the end. In the tale's pattern of mimetic violence, the birds of prey initiate and close the cycle of crimes against kin (cf. 516f. and 673f.).

These interlocking motifs of suppression of speech, corrupted *pietas,* barbarian status and animality form the thematic armature of Ovid's tale. Together they shape the structure of reversals in which violence meets its condign punishment in an almost exact imitation of itself.

Ovid also uses a more formal articulation of the action, punctuating the human events by a larger divine framework of seasonal or sacral time:

> *iam tempora Titan*
> *quinque per autumnos repetiti duxerat anni*
> *cum blandita viro Progne ...*
>
> 438-440

> *iam labor exiguus Phoebo restabat equique*
> *pulsabant pedibus spatium declivis Olympi*
>
> 486-487

> *signa deus bis sex acto lustraverat anno:*
> *quid faciat Philomela?*
>
> 571-572

> *tempus erat quo sacra solent trieterica Bacchi*
> *Sithoniae celebrare nurus: nox conscia sacris*
>
> 587-588

Of these temporal markers, the first sets the disaster into motion; the second introduces the success of Tereus' scheme; the third indicates the duration of Philomela's imprisonment; and the fourth leads her to freedom and vengeance. This temporal movement is measured by something grander than the impatience of human desire (cf. 514 and 653) or the necessary intervals of a long sea-voyage, although that too marks major stages of the narrative (cf. 422, 444-446, 511-520).[13] This sacred time could suggest a larger world-order framing the events. Yet the very remoteness of these celestial phenomena (especially in the first three passages above) also sets off the moral isolation of the human world and the absence of gods. This story takes us about as far from a clear divine justice as any tale in the poem. We are immersed in the dark night of human passions, as Ovid carefully points out at the beginning and end:

> *pro superi, quantum mortalia pectora caecae*
> *noctis habent*
>
> 472-473

> *tantaque nox animi est*
>
> 652

There is, to be sure, a kind of poetic justice in the fact that the nocturnal banquet of Tereus' deception is answered ultimately by Procne's night of Bacchic rites on the mountain (487-494 and 588-590, where *nox* is repeated three times). Yet the only god explicitly mentioned is Bacchus, in brief apostrophe (596).[14] Even the metamorphosis at the end comes without benefit of divinity.

It follows as the external manifestation, almost ratification, of the bestiality which the main actors have already been enacting among one another. Compared to an eagle seeking its prey with its talons (516f.), Tereus has already undergone an inner metamorphosis before he becomes, literally, the hoopoe with its "armed face" (*armata facies,* 673f.). The bestiality in Tereus' character has already been marked by adjectives like *ferus* and *saevus* (549, 557, 464, 581).

Procne undergoes an analogous change as she emerges from the Bacchic ritual with a new identity: not *blandita viro Progne* (440), but *Progne terribilis* (595), goaded by the furies of her grief. Tereus, for a moment, could imagine himself as a potential Paris, carrying off a Greek woman to a barbarian land for a second Trojan war: *aut rapere et saevo raptam defendere bello* (464). Procne, however, has a deeper and even more sinister register of mythical echoes to play upon. She becomes an Agave who rends her child, a Medea who kills her offspring, and a Clytaemnestra who would inflict multitudinous wounds on her faithless husband: *aut per vulnera mille / sontem animam expellam* (617f.; cf. Aeschyl., *Ag.* 866-868).[15]

To this demarcation of the story by temporal divisions corresponds an equally sharp set of spatial contrasts. The chief mechanism of Tereus' plot is to lure Philomela from the civilized city of Athens and from the safety of her father's house to the desolate forest in the wild land (520f.). This movement from a civilized house to the wild and from a great city to lonely Thracian forest also gains force from the comparison of Philomela, at her first appearance, to naiads and dryads of the forest (*quales audire solemus / naidas et dryadas mediis incedere silvis . . .,* 451-454). We may be reminded of the lament of these forest dwellers over their kinsman Marsyas at his bloody end shortly before (390-395). That lament created a contrast between painful physical violation and a tranquil sylvan or pastoral landscape: *nec quicquam nisi vulnus erat; cruor undique manat, / detectique patent nervi* (388ff.); *et nymphae flerunt, et quisquis montibus illis / lanigerosque greges armentaque bucera pavit* (394f.). For Philomela, likened to a naiad, the remoteness of nature is threatening. There are no compassionate Nymphs or Fauns in this deserted forest, and the mutilated woman is thrown entirely on her own resources.

The violence implicit in the shift from Athens to Thrace is also symmetrical with an abrupt spatial shift within Thrace. The two Athenian sisters move from enclosure to dangerous wildness, and then back to a domestic interior. When they are reunited inside Tereus' the house, their mood is very different from their previous domesticity. Procne's maenadic freedom on the mountainside puts an end to her previous identity as Tereus' complaisant wife (cf. 428ff., especially 440: *blandita viro Progne*). Philomela too had begun in the shelter of her own house, though under the authority and protection of a father, not a husband. But as the father proved unable to see through the evil designs of Tereus, the nocturnal festival of welcome blends into the dark night of lust in Tereus' heart (486ff.; cf. 472f.); and the "Bacchic" drink served in cups of gold returns as Procne's vengeful Bacchic riot in Thrace (587, 596).[16]

Philomela's slender weaving enables her to find a way through her heavily walled prison: *fugam custodia claudit, / structa rigent solido stabulorum moenia saxo*, 572f.). She had initially threatened Tereus with just such an exposure, filling the forest with her cries of accusation (544-547, especially 546f.: *si silvis clausa tenebor / implebo silvas et conscia saxa movebo*).[17] Now she breaches these walls not by sound but by a silent witness (cf. 574, *os mutum facti caret indice*), which is the product of artfulness in more senses than one (cf. *ingenium, sollertia, callida tela*, 575f.).

Procne's second response to the message is no longer stupefied silence (582-586, *supra*) but a violent exit from the house at night (*nocte sua est egressa domo regina*, 590), to join the Thracian women on Mt. Rhodope. The toponyms *Sithoniae* and *Rhodope* underline the Thracian character of the ritual. Procne takes up *furialia arma* and makes her way *per silvas* (594). "Stirred up by the wild madness of grief" (594f.), she leads the women in bacchantic rage. Later, in the infectious spread of violence, she will dress Philomela in bacchantic garb (598f.). Amid the Dionysiac howls (*exululat euhoeque sonat*, 597), she penetrates the remote forest, "breaks down the doors" of her sister's prison, and carries her off, amazed, "within her own walls" (*adtonitamque trahens intra sua moenia ducit*, 600). She, thus, exactly undoes the act of Tereus, who had "dragged" Philomela "into" the forest: *in stabula alta trahit silvis obscura vetustis* (521). Enclosure in the remote forest was previously in the service of lust. Now it becomes a fearful enclosure within the criminal's own body, which he would be only too willing to throw open: *et modo, si posset, reserato pectore diras / egerere inde dapes immersaque viscera gestit* (663f.). A crime committed across vast distances is answered by a crime committed in his own most intimate household and, finally, within his own interior flesh.[18]

The parallels and inversions between the beginning and end multiply as the tale goes on and clearly form part of the terrible mimetic violence of the revenge plot.[19] Tereus' helpful "conquest" of a barbarian army in Athens' behalf degenerates into a libidinous "conquest" of his sister-in-law (reversing the direction of his voyage) and then into his own being "conquered" by the collusion of two women (425, 483, 513, 525, 612).[20] The first appearance of Procne and her child Itys combines the motifs of the Eumenides, the marriage torch and the figurative bird of prophecy (430-434), all of which return as part of the crime and its punishment.

The Eumenides at the beginning (430f.) become the Furies (literal or figurative) who avenge the violation of marriage later (591-595, 657, 662).[21] The torches (*faces*) of marriage, coming straight from a funeral, overdetermine the ominous atmosphere (*Eumenides tenuere faces de funere raptas*, 430). They then become the metaphorical "torches" of Tereus' desire (480) and then of Procne's lust for revenge (614). And the birds, of course, recur at the cardinal point of Tereus' victorious lust (the eagle-simile of 516-518) and its defeat and punishment in metamorphosis (666-674). The *blanditiae* with which Procne appeals to Tereus for her sister's visit (*cum blandita viro Progne*, 440) returns in her horrible vengeance for the crime that she has thus innocently set into motion (*blanditiae*, 626, 632). The joyful "leaping about" of Tereus at the apparent success of his plot (*exsultat*, 514) becomes the "leaping" of his son's boiling flesh in the caldron (*pars inde cavis exsultat aenis*, 645). The displacement of speech into weaving becomes a female "unveiling" that transforms apparent feminine helplessness into decisive and bloody action (cf. 566f., 576ff., 604). The male weapon of the sword or iron (*ensis, ferrum*) undergoes a parallel shift from agent to victim (551ff., 611f., 617, 643), until it fixes Tereus forever in his role of aggressive pursuer (666). As we have already noted, the repeated motifs of *pietas*, tears, night, fire, conquest, joy, weaving, speech and silence mark the major stages of crime and punishment.[22]

How seriously are we to take this working out of an immanent moral law in the *Metamorphoses*? Is Ovid just exploiting the *grand guignol* possibilities that a Thracian barbarian's goriness would permit? Does he expect us to appreciate the violence and horror as an example of what he can achieve in his blending of tragedy and epyllion? It is, of course, hard to be certain in the case of so protean a poem. One has to acknowledge that here, as elsewhere, Ovid does not resolve the deep moral issues that his narrative raises, particularly, as in this case, the problems of innocent suffering and gratuitous violence.[23]

In one respect, at least, Ovid seems to show himself aware of the grimness of his tale, for the next episode casts a similar narrative into a very different mood. This tale, the story of Boreas and Orithyia, is virtually the comic mirror-image of the story of Tereus and Philomela. It allows us to see the murderousness of the preceding tale in comic relief and thus offers perspective on its outrageous crimes.[24]

The Tereus story contains a harsh asymmetry in its moral structure, for the parallelism between the male violence of lust and the female desire for revenge is not exact. Not only is the former individual and the latter collective, but the women's crime develops only as a response to Tereus'. He was the initiator and aggressor, the women are avengers. Horrible as their vengeance is, it has some justice on its side. The dehumanization of all three characters in the final metamorphosis, however, does not discriminate between degrees of guilt, and in fact, rather, encourages us not to judge. The closest Ovid comes to recognizing the tragedy of Procne's maternal love turned into child-murder is the brief hesitation and monologue at 624-635. Once decided, she is almost as monstrous as Tereus. Such is the effect of the tigress simile of 636f. and the pathos of Itys' death as he stretches out his arms to his mother, who does not even turn her face away as she strikes (639-642).[25]

The justice that is never mentioned in the case of the women has a prominent place at the beginning of its sequel, the story of Pandion's successor in Athens (677f.):

sceptra loci rerumque capit moderamen Erectheus,
iustitia dubium validisne potentior armis.

At the beginning of the Tereus episode these attributes of power (but not of justice) belong not to the Athenian king, but to his future son-in-law, *quem sibi Pandion opibusque virisque potentem / . . . iunxit* (426-428). The weakness of that Athenian king and father is now replaced by a strong father-figure. Erechtheus will not surrender his daughter to a Thracian husband, divine though he is (682ff.).[26] Boreas, then, like Tereus, resorts to violence. Indeed, his highly rhetorical soliloquy, in which he reminds himself that he is a big bad storm-god, full of potential *saevitia* and *vis* (687ff.), may recall Tereus' readiness to play the role of Paris and launch a massive war (cf. 461-466). Like Tereus too, he yields to the blazing fires of passion (708) and carries his Athenian beloved off to the snowy wilds of Thrace (707ff.).

Unlike Tereus, however, Boreas makes his Athenian captive his wife and the mother of twin sons (line 711 may be an intentional echo of 581). The bird-metamorphosis that follows is now gradual and happy rather than sudden and destructive (cf. 666-674 and 714-718). The two sons, Zetes and Calais, have their wings as part of the joint attributes of both parents (*gemellos / cetera qui matris, pennas genitoris haberent,* 712f.). For the young Itys, "likeness to father" meant death (*a ! quam / es similis patri,* 621f.): here it is the source of special powers that ensure heroic success. These bird-like qualities emerge only in the due course of the Boreads' maturation (714-718), just when they are useful for their spectacular and literally radiant breaking away on the Argonautic expedition (720f.):

> *vellera cum Minyis nitido radiantia villo*
> *per mare non notum prima petiere carina.*

These are the closing lines of the book; and they offer an image of bright, happy, and expansive travel, in contrast to the movement toward enclosure and darkness in the tale of Tereus (cf. especially *iubet ille carinas / in freta deduci . . .,* 443f., of Tereus' ill-fated voyage from Thrace to Greece). They also show us the children of a Thraco-Athenian union reaching a glorious adolescence rather than being cut off horribly in childhood.

In his account of Procne's *furor*, Ovid recollects, and asks us to recollect, the maenadic *furor* of Vergil's Amata and, to a somewhat lesser degree, of Dido (*Aen.* 7.385-405, 4.300-303).[27] In this way he assimilates Procne's terrible, if just, vengeance to the most familiar literary models of female violence. Because these echoes (along with others noted earlier) mark the self-conscious literariness of Ovid's narrative, they also take us back to the problem of literary pleasure, the problematical pleasure of the text in this most unpleasant tale. The sudden shift from forest to mountain to interior of the *domus* (cf. 601, *ut sensit tetigisse domum Philomela nefandam*) destabilizes the image of woman as a helpless victim, held prisoner for the sexual pleasure of a man. Rape is answered by maenadic *furor*; violation of the ties between husband and wife and between sister and sister is answered by the violation of the bonds between mother and son and between father and son. Incest is answered by filicide and cannibalism.

The maenadic imagery, however, keeps us from a fully sympathetic identification with the avengers and prefigures their total loss of humanity in the metamorphosis at the end. As Bacchants, the women become embodiments of irrationality rather than representatives of a retributive moral order. This recourse to the Dionysiac pattern, like the three-way metamorphosis that follows it, both marginalizes the women's response and minimizes its justice and its tragedy.[28] None of these transformations of identity provides a satisfactory moral resolution.[29]

Yet these armed women on the mountainside, with the irresistible strength of maenads that we know from Euripides' *Bacchae*, also show us a different image of the female body. It is not the passive object of uncontrollable, lawless male pleasure, but it is full of strange power and quite capable of murder. The Greek tragedies with similar endings—Euripides' *Medea*, *Hecuba*, *Bacchae*, and perhaps Sophocles' lost *Tereus*—do not opt for the facile solution of metamorphosis, but leave us in shocked contemplation of this enormity of female hatred and vengeful force. In the case of Ovid our aesthetic pleasure might be less, but our moral pleasure might be greater and deeper if that shock-effect were less tamed by the pseudo-resolution of metamorphosis to which the poem is committed.

NOTES

1. See the recent study by C.A. Barton, "The Scandal of the Arena," *Representations* 27 (1989) 1-36. There is a balanced discussion of the problem of violence in the *Metamorphoses* in G.K. Galinsky, *Ovid's Metamorphoses: An Introduction to the Basic Aspects* (Berkeley, Los Angeles, 1975) chapter 3, "Ovid's Humanity: Death and Suffering in the *Metamorphoses*," pp. 110-157, especially 138-140.

2. On 552-560, for example, F. Bömer remarks: "Hier beginnt ein Katalog von Scheusslichkeiten..., den Ovid, ebenso wie anderswo, in genüsslicher Ausführlichkeit schildert..."; F. Bömer, *P. Ovidius Naso, Metamorphosen, Buch VI-VII* (Heidelberg, 1976) 151. See also Galinsky, *op. cit.* 126-132; H. Diller, "Die dichterische Eigenart von Ovids Metamorphosen" (1934) in Michael von Albrecht and Ernst Zinn, eds., *Ovid*, Wege der Forschung, vol. 92 (Darmstadt, 1968) 333f.

3. See Bömer, *op. cit.* 117; also his commentary *ad* 560 (153) and 647-674 (172ff.). The similarities between Ovid and Seneca's *Thyestes* may, of course, be due to a common source, whether Accius or Sophocles.

4. On this authorial intervention and its function of distancing Ovid from the monstrous protagonist of the story, see Bömer, *ibid.* 154.
5. For the motif of *fides* and *pietas* in the episode and their corruption, see A. Ortega, "Die Tragödie der Pandionstöchter in Ovids Metamorphosen," in W. Wimmel, ed., *Forschungen zur Römischen Literatur* (Festschrift Karl Büchner) (Wiesbaden, 1970) 217 and 220-222. The motifs run throughout the tale, signalled by the repetition of *pius* and *fides* and the derivatives: cf. 474, 482, 496, 498, 503, 535, 539, 566, 629, 635, etc.
6. The identification of Philomela's web with a mode of writing seems to have been part of the tradition: see Bömer, *op. cit. ad* 582 (158).
7. I fully agree with P.K. Joplin, "The Voice of the Shuttle Is Ours," *Stanford Literature Review*, 1.1 (1984) 25-53, esp. 26ff., in her criticism of G. Hartman, *Beyond Formalism* (New Haven, 1970) 337, for eliding the violence against the female body and "celebrat[ing] Language and not the violated woman's emergence from silence" (26). My emphasis is on violence more than on gender, though of course the two cannot be entirely separated in this case.
8. See the comment on Shakespeare's version of the rape scene in *Lucrèce* by Joplin, *ibid.* 33, n. 16: "The poet's eyes are hardly less lewd than the rapist Tarquin's ..."
9. This added horror of the repeated violence may be original with Ovid; see Ortega, *op. cit.* 218 with n. 8.
10. There is also a cruel irony in the fact that Philomela's "last farewell" as she leaves Athens proves to be the last words that she will ever speak there: *supremumque vale pleno singultibus ore / vix dixit* (509f.). On the special pathos of *supremum* here, cf. 10.62 and 134, 12.526.
11. On the Thracians as uncivilized, see Bömer, *op. cit. ad* 458 (131f.). As in the incestuous births of Byblis and Myrrha, Ovid chooses a setting at the edges of civilization for the violation of basic human laws (cf. 9.640ff., 10.476ff.).
12. For Tereus as "barbarian," see Ortega, *op. cit.* 218.
13. There is also a progression here from the more or less neutral statements of the first two voyages to the third, which takes place under the sign of Tereus' lust, as his predatory eyes never leave Philomela (515). The significance of his last voyage is also marked by the *cum-inversum* clause of the arrival: *iamque iter effectum iamque in sua litora fessis / puppibus exierant, cum rex Pandione natam / in stabula alta trahit . . .* (519-521). For other aspects of narrative structure, see Ortega, *op. cit.* 215f.; B. Otis, *Ovid As an Epic Poet* (Cambridge, 1970^2) 408-410.
14. Cf. also the *insignia Bacchi* just afterwards (598) and the metonymic use of Bacchus for wine in 488f. (*Bacchus in auro / ponitur*), to be discussed later.

15. The episode also has a number of other intertextual allusions. Often noted is the echo of Apollo's pursuit of Daphne in Tereus' lust for Philomela: 6.455-457 and 1.492-495, on which see G.A. Jacobsen, "Apollo and Tereus: Parallel Motifs in Ovid's *Metamorphoses*," *CJ* 80 (1984-1985) 45-52. The ill-omened wedding at the beginning (6.429ff.) is perhaps recalled in the story of Orpheus, 10.3-8. In both cases the resemblances set off the bestiality of Tereus and the violence of this tale. Cf. also the motif of the final farewell (509), which also recurs in Orpheus' story (10.62), as well as elsewhere: see Bömer, *op. cit. ad loc.* (141). Cf. the seduction motif of 463f. with the story of Procris in the next book (7.739f.), and see Bömer, 133.

16. This passage is perhaps a possible reminiscence of the disastrous banquet of Dido at the end of *Aeneid* 1, esp. 1.685f.; cf. Bömer, *op. cit.* at *Met.* 6.488f.

17. One wonders if these lines are a reminiscence of Eur., *Hipp.* 1253f., especially as accusation by non-spoken means is involved.

18. Note too that Tereus' tears here (*flet modo*, 665) are no longer feigned, as before.

19. This structure of infectious violence could be described in the terms of R. Girard, *Violence and the Sacred* (1972), tr. P. Gregory (Baltimore, 1977), especially 41ff., 158ff., but such an analysis would perhaps only show how little the moral issues of the myth are here resolved. For a criticism of such an approach see Joplin, *op. cit.* 45-47.

20. This reversal may go back beyond Accius' *Tereus* to Sophocles' play on that subject: see Bömer, *op. cit.* 117f. and Otis, *op. cit.* 406f. If so, the plotting and vengeance of Hecuba against Polymestor in Euripides' *Hecuba* may give us an idea of how it might have been handled in tragedy.

21. On the motif of the ill-omened wedding see Bömer, *op. cit. ad loc.*, 124.

22. For example, night: 472f., 486ff., 588-590, 652; fire: 455ff., 460, 466, 492, 609, 614f., 645f.; silence: 574, 583-585, 622f., 632, 660; joy: 514, 653, 660; tears: 471f., 504, 523, 535, 566, 585, 610f., 628, 665. See also W.S. Anderson, *Ovid's Metamorphoses: Books 6-10* (Norman, OK, 1972) *ad* 671-674; Note too, how the motif of "not containing" one's passions moves form Tereus to Procne: *nec capiunt inclusas pectora flammas*, of Tereus' lust in 466; *ardet et iram / non capit ipsa suam Progne*, of Procne's vengeful wrath in 609f.; see Bömer, *op. cit. ad loc.*

23. On these questions see my "Ovid's *Metamorphoses*: Greek Myth in Augustan Rome," *Studies in Philology* 68 (1971) 371-394, especially 377ff., 384ff.

24. M. von Albrecht, "Ovids Humor und die Einheit der Metamorphosen" (1963) in Von Albrecht and Zinn, *op. cit.* 432, observes: "Vorwiegend düstere Bücher, wie das sechste und achte ... haben ein brausend-heiteres Finale."

25. Cf. 7.340-342, where Pelias' daughter, even with her good intentions, cannot look. See Galinsky, *op. cit.* 131f. on the "untragic presentation of tragic material."

26. Note too, the motif of *blanditiae* here (685). Unlike those of the Tereus story (440, 626, 632), these do not succeed. For other parallels between the two tales, see Anderson, *op. cit.* 237 and *ad* 6.717-718.

27. *Met.* 6.587, *quo sacra solent trieterica Bacchi*, seems to be a conscious echo of *Aen.* 4.302, *ubi audito stimulant trieterica Baccho* ... On Ovid's assimilation of Vergil's language of *furor* elsewhere see F. Bömer, "Ovid und die Sprache Vergils" (1959), in Von Albrecht and Zinn, *op. cit.* 192f.; see also K. Büchner, "Ovids Metamorphosen" (1957), *ibid.* 388f. On the Bacchantic imagery of Dido and Amata, see now M. Suzuki, *Metamorphoses of Helen* (Ithaca, 1989) 111ff., 130ff.

28. See the interesting feminist critique of just this literary pattern in Joplin, *op. cit.* 45-47: "The Greek imagination uses the mythic end to expel its own violence and to avoid any knowledge of its process. Patriarchal culture feels, as Tereus does, that it is asked to incorporate something monstrous when the woman returns from exile to tell her own story" (47).

29. Otis, *op. cit.* 211-215, for example, gives a good description of the dehumanization of the two women, but, in my opinion, too easily regards the metamorphosis as the "solution of their catastrophe" (215) rather than as the problematization of justice in this world of sub-human behavior.

TWO NOTES ON ROMAN ELEGY: CATULLUS 67 AND PROPERTIUS 1.9

Ross S. Kilpatrick
Queen's University at Kingston

Alexandro G. McKay O.C. Praeceptori Amicitiae Optimo Linguae Peritissimo Utriusque Gratias

---

CATULLUS AND THE "WEDDING DOOR" (Catull. 67)

The late Colin Macleod proposed in his 1982 article, "The Artistry of Catullus 67,"[1] that the tall man with reddish brows whom the talking door fears so much (45-48) should be Caecilius himself, the present owner of the infamous house of Balbus.

> This gives the poem a sting in its tail: the door, accused *in dominum veterem deseruisse fidem* (8), at last informs on its own present *dominus*; and the scandal has now come back to Verona, from where the door was trying to attract attention. Thus the coup de grace is given to the case it has so studiously made for itself. What gives the poem its point is the door's total self-defeat and the poet's air of polite detachment, rather than the scandal for its own sake.[2]

In Macleod's reading of the poem, Caecilius (9), the new and apparently unsullied owner of the house, had once been the lover of the very woman Balbus' son had brought home to Verona from Brixia as his wife; Caecilius was the very man she had embroiled at Brixia in an abortive paternity suit.

Macleod's article has attracted its share of dissent. Levine objected (1985) that Macleod "seemingly contradicts himself" in

---

Note: See Plates 6-8 for accompanying illustrations.

Two Notes on Roman Elegy: Catullus 67 and Propertius 1.9   297

this identification, since he had first concluded that Caecilius was "'apparently not involved in the poet's story.' . . . He curiously (and quite unnecessarily) confuses the medium, which is the door, with the message, which is marital infidelity. The door's self-defence is, in fact, unassailable."[3] Medium and message are not quite so clearly distinguishable, however, and Macleod's identification of the *longus homo rubris superciliis* as Caecilius does deserve serious reconsideration.

An element of *fescennina iocatio* in the poem's personal insults of Catullus 67 has been generally recognized.[4] The speaker first addresses the house door formally as if she were a bride (1-2).[5] The significance of such a salutation seems best explained if the door is "dressed" for a wedding, i.e. festooned with wool and fronds, her doorposts still gleaming with fat from the hand of the current owner's new bride.[6] The seamy marital history of the house makes the prayer to Jupiter (2) both ironic and to the point,[7] for apparently our door had not distinguished herself as guardian of the morals of her former owner when she last appeared as a bridal door on the death of old Balbus (6):

postquam es porrecto facta marita sene.[8]

Mistress Door prudently begins her *apologia* with a prayer that her present *dominus* (the new *maritus* himself) will accept her defence (9-14):

"*Non (ita Caecilio placeam, cui tradita*[9] *nunc sum)*
culpa mea est, quamquam dicitur esse mea,
nec peccatum a me quisquam pote dicere quicquam:
verum est ius populi (ianua quid faciat?)[10]
qui, quacumque aliquid reperitur non bene factum,
ad me omnes clamant: ianua, culpa tua est."

The speaker then urges the door to make a full, detailed, and persuasive case for her innocence (15-16); thus coaxed she begins her sordid tale of a former mistress' marital and premarital sins, a tale which takes us back to Brixia prior to her arrival in Verona as the wife of the late Balbus' son (31-34). The slandered door had actually overheard that woman gossiping with servants about her liaisons in Brixia with one Postumius and one Cornelius. The juiciest scandal is kept to the end, however: a notorious paternity suit launched against a certain unnamed tall, irascible, reddish-browed ex-lover.

It would be a fine piece of fescennine (or stag-party) irony if, as Macleod suggested, that red-head had been none other than

Caecilius himself, the newly-married owner of the house and door, especially if he were a Caecilius *Rufus*. Catullus did know at least one "Rufus,"[11] and we knew of at least one Caecilius Rufus at that time, mentioned both in his own extant *elogium* and by Cicero. L. Caecilius Rufus (*ornatissimus vir: Sull*. 62) had been quaestor (66? B.C.), Tribunus Plebis (63), Praetor Urbanus (57), and Proconsul (56).[12] While there is no evidence to connect that Caecilius Rufus with Verona, we do find Catullus (c. 35) addressing a Caecilius at Novum Comum in or after 59 B.C. (the year Caesar established the colonia) as a *tener poeta* busy composing a Cybele poem much praised by his local mistress (35.11-18). Catullus is urging him to come back to Verona for a heart-to-heart talk (35.3-6). A fescennine joke in 67 would be all the more delicious if the two were the same Caecilius Rufus.

If Macleod is right in his identification, as I think he is, then the *ianua marita,* the "nuptial door" provides both occasion and stick for Catullus to tease the recently-married new proprietor. The point of the poem is that very insult, a ribald sting in the poem's tail. The joke would be triggered dramatically by the astonishing sight of the nuptial door of Caecilius (once the property of Balbus' cuckold of a son), now decked out afresh in full "bridal" array. The irony of a sordid relationship, (real or concocted) between the groom and the notorious ex-*domina* of the same house and door would make Catullus' surprise attack all the more outrageous.[13]

THE WINGS OF AMOR (Prop. 1.9.23-24)

In his book *Propertius: "Love" and "War": Individual and State Under Augustus* (Berkeley, 1985) 67-68, Professor Hans-Peter Stahl offers a new interpretation of "what Amor and what the lover do to each other." The two lines in question run (1.9.23-24):

nullus amor cuiquam facilis ita praebuit alas,
ut non alterna presserit ille manu.

Stahl deals with the logic of this situation by making the lover *face* the struggling Amor, while holding the latter's spread-out wing-tips tightly with his own hands. The lithe captive strains with shorter arms to strike his adult captor, squirming to left and right to do so. Ponticus as lover "believes himself to be in control, but is being controlled." Stahl concludes: "Although I do not know of any example, I can imagine that he was inspired by a work of sculpture (or even by two scenes from real life: a human holding a bird, a human holding up a child)."

A number of imaginative interpretations of this picture have been put forward over the years. Vulpius, cited by Fedeli (1984: see also Postgate and Camps for the notion), imagines Cupid as a pet bird tethered on a thread, like Juliet's Romeo (*R&J* 2.1.220-225):

> 'Tis almost morning; I would have thee gone,
> And yet no further than a wanton's bird,
> Who lets it hop a little from her hand,
> Like a poor prisoner in his twisted gyves,
> And with a silk thread plucks it back again.
> So loving-jealous of his liberty.

Aristophanes' beetle on a string is also compared as well (*Nub.* 762). Postgate (1881), (somewhat misquoted by Butler and Barber) favoured a Platonic image of Amor as charioteer; Butler and Barber (1933), that of Amor striking his captor-captive with his wings (on the analogy of 3.10.28). Of those two solutions, the first suggests a degree of helplessness that rings false for Cupid; the second is not obviously suited to the context. The third would imply that the lover never does get a real grip on Amor, even an imaginary one. Ovid (*A.A.* 2.20.98) boasts he will pin his wings as *praeceptor amoris* and poet.

Let us reconsider Propertius' description. Is Amor facing or backing toward the lover? On the analogy of such expressions as *barbam praebere vellere* (Pers. 2.28), *manus praebere verberibus* (Ov., *A.A.* 1.16), *ubera praebere* (Sil. 14.529), *terga fugae praebere* (Ov., *M.* 10.706), *terga Phoebo praebere* (Ov., *M.* 4.715), where the positions of the *praebens* are always clear, Amor should be facing *away* from the lover in order to offer his wings to be caught, and pretending to be an easy catch he increases his captor's pain. The analogies in the passage, then, are as follows:

> *si qua tua est* (26) – *[si] facilis praebuit alas* (23b)
> *acrius illa subit* (26a) = *alterna presserit ille manu* (24b).

Propertius' text does not really support Stahl. The lover appears rather to have grasped Amor from behind by the wings, only to find himself being harassed, left and right, by the fiendishly wriggling boy who strikes out behind him at his captor. Love allows himself to be caught only for his own cruel ends, and Ponticus should not delude himself otherwise.

If this is what Propertius means, can we parallel the picture of an Amor grasped from behind by his wings in ancient art as Stahl requires? Yes. A fresco from Stabiae, "The Cupid Seller," portrays a vendeuse showing her line of Cupids for sale to the lady of a wealthy house. One putto sits quietly in his carrying cage, while a bigger one stands coaxing at the client's knee; a third is held securely out of the cage by his wings (like a rabbit by the ears), for her to inspect. A second fresco, from the *Casa dei capitelli colorati* in Pompeii, shows a Cupid held by the wings by a stout, bearded male figure. (The Stabian fresco was copied by Tischbein and later inspired a version by Vien).[14] These parallels do not support Stahl's interpretation.

Like Amor, Ponticus' mistress only pretends to be possessed in order to entrap him, when it will be too late to escape. The best start for his cure, however, is to name that woman (33-34):

> *quare, si pudor est, quam primum errata fatere:*
> *dicere quo pereas saepe in amore levat.*

The theme of the elegy, then, would be like that of Catullus 55:

> *Oramus, si forte non molestum est,* (1)
> *demonstres ubi sint tuae tenebrae*
>
> *si linguam clauso tenes in ore* (18)
> *fructus proicies amoris omnes.*
> *verbosa gaudet Venus loquella*
> *vel, si vis, licet obseres palatum,*
> *dum vestri sim particeps amoris.* (22)

Catullus had promised greater satisfactions in love through disclosure to a friend. Propertius sets out to extract Ponticus' secret with an allusive sketch of Amor's treachery. Bondage to love can be easier to bear through frank confession.

NOTES

1. C.W. Macleod, "The Artistry of Catullus 67," Δεσμὸς Κοινωνίας, ed. G. Fabiano, E. Salvaneschi (Genoa, 1982) 71-88 (repr. in *Collected Essays*. [Oxford, 1983] 187-195: citations will be made from the Oxford version).

2. *Ibid.* 191.
3. P. Levine, "Catullus 67: The Dark Side of Love and Marriage," *CA* 4 (1985) 191, 24n.
4. E.g., L. Richardson, "Catullus 67: Interpretation and Form," *AJP* 88 (1967) 423-433.
5. With *dulci iucunda viro iucunda parenti* (1) cf. *cara viro magis et minus est invisa parenti* (62.57). See E. Badian's objections to Richardson's interpretation: "The Case of the Door's Marriage (Catullus 67.6)," *HSCP* 84 (1980) 81-89.
6. See M.B. Ogle. "The House-door in Greek and Roman Religion and Folk-lore." *AJP* 32 (1911) 251-271.
7. A cake of spelt was traditionally offered to Jupiter Farreus at old-fashioned patrician weddings (Ov., *Fast.* 2.143). See D.P. Harmon. "The Family Festivals of Rome," *ANRW* 2.16.2, 1599. The *pontifex maximus* and *flamen dialis* would be present. Plutarch (*Q.R.* 2) records that prayers would be said to Jupiter, Janus, Venus, Diana, and sometimes Peitho.
8. E. Badian's emendation of v. 6 (*"postquam est porrecto pacta marita sene"*) and his article (*op. cit.*) is most challenging. I should still prefer to retain Mynor's reading here, taking (*ianua*) *marita* as "wedding door" or "bridal door" or "nuptial door." Cf. *maritae faces* (Prop. 4.11.33, Ov., *H.* 11.101); *mariti tori* (Ov., *H.* 2.41).
9. *tradita sum* (19) continues the ambiguous conceit of the "bridal" door.
10. Reading with Munro, *"verum est ius populi"*; and Voss, *"ianua quid faciat"*; "but it is the people's judgement (What is a door to do?), . . ." P.Y. Forsyth ("A Note on Catullus 67.12," *CJ* 77[1982] 253-254) reads: *"verum isto populo ianua quid faciat."*
11. See poems 59, 69, 73 and 77 for "Rufus."
12. For L. Caecilius Rufus see *CIL* 1²2.761 (= *ILS* 880) and Cic., *Sull.* 62-66; also E.S. Gruen, *The Last Generation of the Roman Republic* (Berkeley, Los Angeles, London, 1974) 172-173, 185, 219, 249n, 323, 394, 511, 515. Gruen comments (172) on "illustrious *gentilicia* combined with obscure *cognomina.*" . . . "Caecilii appear with equal frequency on the magisterial lists. No Caecilius Rufus, apart from the praetor of 57, is attested. But that worthy, half-brother or cousin of P. Sulla, was evidently of distinguished lineage."
13. The contrary views of Macleod and Levine on the persuasiveness of the door's case (Macleod, 191; Levine, 191, n. 24) do not reflect a major issue of the poem. The door is an innocent bystander *qua* door, but at the same time there is an ironic assumption on the speaker's part that she bore the same responsibilities as a flesh-and-blood *ianitrix* for the moral failures of her mistress, and has no good excuse. Thus Catullus maintains and develops what E. Badian calls the "delightful *aprosdokêton*" (Badian, 81).

14. A full description of these two paintings in the Naples Museum can be found in W. Helbig, *Wandgemälde der vom Vesuv verschütteten Städte Campaniens* (Leipzig, 1868) 164-165, *"Erotenverkauf* nos. 824 (from Stabiae) and 825 (from Pompeii, *Casa dei capitelli colorati*). A coloured reproduction of the former (824) can be found in B. Andreae, "Modelle pompejanischer Bauten," in B. Andreae, ed., *Pompeji Leben und Kunst in den Vesuvstädten* (Essen, 1973) 192, 217 (Andreae: n. 267). The Tischbein copy of this fresco is illustrated in R. Trevelyan, *The Shadow of Vesuvius: Pompeii, A.D. 79* (London, 1976) 45; for Vien's interpretation, see *op. cit.* 62. Richard Whitaker sees a "possible source for the tears of Briseis" (Prop. 2.20.1) in a wallpainting in the House of the Tragic Poet in Pompeii. See his monograph, *Myth and Personal Experience in Roman Love-Elegy: Hypomnemata*, 76 (1983) 89 n. 6; 91 nn. 12, 14; 92 nn. 15-18; 93 nn. 19, 23.

THE DEATH OF THE PARACLAUSITHYRON: PROPERTIUS 1.16

Howard Jones
McMaster University

J.C. Yardley begins a learned article printed in *Papers of the Liverpool Latin Seminar* (1979) with the words "1.16 is perhaps Propertius' most unusual poem."[1] Let me offer a perhaps unusual interpretation.

That Propertius should have included in the *Monobiblos*, a repository of amatory themes, a poem built around the motif of the paraclausithyron is not surprising. Prior treatments in Catullus, Horace and Tibullus had established for it a place in the Roman tradition and, as Copley says, Propertius "felt that he should demonstrate his mastery of it."[2]

For the most part commentators have focused upon the personality of the door, the character of the mistress, and the mood of the poet, and pronouncements on all these points have varied widely. The door has been characterised as "a shocking gossip as well as a prude," as the "personification of an ignorant and confused old woman," as "hostile to the lover" and as "a secret and helpless sympathiser with the suppliant." The mistress has been viewed at one extreme as a former lady of repute whose moral standards have declined to such a degree that she is now more debauched than the debauched age in which she lives, and at the other extreme as a woman who has tired of her youthful excesses and "exchanged the hurly-burly of the chaise lounge for

---

I am pleased to offer this paper in homage to Sandy McKay, my friend and colleague for more than twenty years. I delivered a version of it at the "McMaster Symposium on Latin Erotic Poetry" in October 1989 in a session which he chaired.

the deep peace of the double bed." As for the mood of the poet, Propertius in 1.16 has been variously described as "deeply engaged," "cheerfully irreverent," and "gently and sweetly melancholic."

As for the text of 1.16, we have the usual excess of punctuation changes, words obelised or distorted from their normal meanings, lines excised or transposed and, of course, emendations sufficient to satisfy the most voracious appetite. A single example of the critic's art may serve to give the flavour: the expression *Tarpeiae pudicitiae* in 1.2. In desperation at the seeming incongruity of any association of *pudicitia* with the well-known Vestal who opened the gates of Rome to her lover (Propertius uses the story in 4.4) commentators have dredged up from Roman legend, literature and topography no fewer than six more suitable Tarpeias, including (most desperate shift of all) "some blameless Tarpeia well-known to Propertius and his reader but not known to us." In short, the commentators have flexed their muscles with customary vigour with the result that 1.16 has suffered more than its share of the grievous bodily harm which classical scholars are wont to inflict upon innocent texts.

I have no intention of adding to the bruising. Rather than wrestle with particular *cruces*, I would like to focus upon Propertius' intention in the poem as a whole. First of all, however, let me satisfy a demand which classicists inevitably make and produce a parallel. It may seem unusual to produce the parallel before considering the poem (I shall come back to it later), but it may give an early hint as to where we are headed:

> My mistress' eyes are nothing like the sun;
> Coral is far more red than her lips' red;
> If snow be white, why then her breasts are dun;
> If hairs be wires, black wires grow on her head.
> I have seen roses damask'd, red and white,
> But no such roses see I in her cheeks;
> And in some perfumes is there more delight
> Than in the breath that from my mistress reeks.
> I love to hear her speak, yet well I know
> That music hath a far more pleasing sound;
> I grant I never saw a goddess go;
> My mistress, when she walks, treads on the ground.
> And yet, by heaven, I think my love as rare
> As any she belied with false compare.
>
> Shakespeare, *Sonnet 130*

But, to 1.16 and Copley in *Exclusus Amator*. In assigning 1.16 its place in the history of the Roman literary paraclausithyron Copley is categorical. His analysis of Catullus 32 and 67, Horace *Odes* 3.10, and Tibullus 1.2 leads him to suggest that with each successive treatment the regular Graeco-Roman paraclausithyron was required to carry more and more weight: in the Catullus poems it was an element of *diffamatio* or low gossip, with Horace an infusion of intrigue and adultery, with Tibullus the poet's wide-ranging musings on the code of love, conventional morality, and so forth. The result was that the paraclausithyron had become "top-heavy. To the simple situation of the shut-out lover bemoaning his sorrow and disappointment had been added a list of complications; first there had been the multiplication of barriers between lover and lady: the personified door, the *custos*, the *leno*, and the rival, together with all the problems, physical, moral, and psychological, which they entailed ... [t]he paraclausithyron had virtually lost its original character." Propertius' response, Copley argues, was to place his paraclausithyron in a dramatic setting that allowed for the introduction of certain of the elements which had indeed become part of the Roman tradition, while keeping it simple and uncomplicated, making it "a door song once more." "In sum," Copley argues, "Propertius has written the definitive paraclausithyron, has made it say all that it could be reasonably expected to say, and has gathered together in one poem the essential facets and features of a literary and erotic tradition some seven hundred years long."[3]

I agree entirely that Copley is right in suggesting that in composing 1.16 Propertius was responding in conscious fashion to the tradition of the literary paraclausithyron, and I agree that the key to Propertius' intention lies in the nature of that response. However, I do not believe that Copley has correctly characterised the nature of Propertius' door-song or that he has succeeded in properly relating the door-song to the rest of the poem. And the relationship between the two parts of the poem, the song *at* the door (11.17-44) and the song *of* the door, i.e. the entire poem, is in my judgment of first importance. But if we consider them for the moment as two distinct songs certain parallels are worth noting. First, they are both complaint songs. In the case of the song *at* the door this is expected. The paraclausithyron is by its very nature a *querela*. That the song *of* the door, that is, the entire poem, is a *querela* is more significant, and that significance has, I believe, been missed. More on this directly. For the moment let us note that the two complaint songs are in certain respects parallel; indeed, they are reciprocal: the lover directs his complaint at the door, the door at the lover, each pointing to the other as the cause of distress. Second, each song is an *apologia*: the lover protesting that his behaviour towards the door has been exemplary, the door protesting that it has done its duty to the best of its ability. Third, the objectives of both the lover and the door are thwarted by two parties: in the case of the lover it is the door and the mistress, the one cruel, the other crueller still; in the case of the door it is the lover and the mistress, the one outside, the other within. We have, in short, a *ménage à trois*, lover and door working against each other, mistress working against both.

Now, pertinent as these observations may be, they do not, I think, bring us essentially closer to an understanding of Propertius' intention. To that extent they are incidental. However, these parallel features do say something of Propertius' concern for structural unity. This is not to say that for Propertius structure is always of first importance. I would suggest, none the less, that in the case of 1.16 it is of particular concern to Propertius to preserve the structural unity of the poem as a whole, that it is essential that the reader not be allowed to lose sight of the fact that the song *at* the door, the paraclausithyron proper, is an integral element in the whole song of the door.

However, Propertius does not rely solely upon the presence of parallel features. He takes pains to knit the door-song proper into the fabric of the poem as a whole by employing a joining couplet not only at the beginning of the door-song (11.15-16) but also at the end (11.45-46). It is not a subtle device; indeed the obvious and mechanical nature of it may be an indication that 1.16 is an early composition. And for those who attach importance to these things the polysyllabic pentameter count of 78%, the highest for any poem in Book I, may point in the same direction. However, transparent though the device may be, it is effective, reminding the reader that throughout the door-song proper the speaker is still the door. This said, the use of parallel introductory and concluding couplets also has the complementary effect of isolating the door-song by setting it apart within its own frame. And of the two effects this is undoubtedly the stronger. For it highlights the fact that whatever other complaints the door may have—its loss of respectability, the physical abuse it suffers at the hands of drunken komasts, the garlands hung from its posts, the torches left to smoulder on its step—all these are insignificant compared with the torture of being subjected night after night throughout the night to the irksome, grating sound of the paraclausithyron, a torture so excruciating that it feels compelled to share it with the reader by giving an example.

And this brings us to the door-song itself. For Copley, Propertius' door-song is remarkable because it marks a reversion to a simple and uncomplicated version. I would suggest that what is remarkable about the door-song in 1.16 is that it is so completely *un*remarkable. There is nothing novel, nothing arresting about it. Every feature of this paraclausithyron can be readily paralleled in both the Greek and Roman traditions: the lover's charge of cruelty against both door and mistress; the reference to secret pleas (*furtivas preces*); the lover's self-pity for his physical hardships—shivering on the doorstep in the cold of early dawn; the characterisation of the mistress as more obdurate than iron or steel; the reference to the lover's gifts (*munera*); the verses left as a token; the lover's jealousy of an imaginary rival within; the lover's abrupt shift from truculence to wheedling in a last desperate effort to persuade—all of these elements, singly or in various combinations, are to be found associated with the Graeco-Roman paraclausithyron tradition in Callimachus, Theocritus, Meleager, Menander, Asclepiades, Lucretius, Horace, Tibullus, and Ovid. In short, in both its parts and its entirety the door-song in 1.16 is entirely derivative and predictable. So familiar are the features that the door finds no difficulty in giving a ready recital; though I am tempted to suggest that what we have is not, in fact, a recital of a remembered song but a paraclausithyron which the door makes up as it goes along, piecing it together from all the well-worn themes, that what we have, in fact, is not the door-song of a particular lover but a composite of all door songs; indeed in 1.45 the door suggests as much:

haec ille et si quae miseri novistis amantes.

Copley asserts that in 1.16 Propertius has composed the definitive paraclausithyron. I would suggest that what Propertius has composed is the definitively boring paraclausithyron. But this, surely, is the point. What angers the door, what causes it to lash out in frustration, is the fact that the paraclausithyron has become so utterly predictable, a tiresome parade of worn-out clichés, to the point where the very thought of being subjected to another one is beyond bearing. The irony is that it is the door which inflicts the torture on itself.

However, this is an irony set within a much larger one and it is in this larger irony that the essence of 1.16 lies. And this brings me back to J.C. Yardley, if only to prove that I went beyond his first sentence. In his second sentence he observes that "the speaker introduces himself in the first two lines not as the poet, but as a door . . . " This is a novelty. A speaking door has appeared, of course, already in the tradition, in both Plautus and Catullus. But this is the first time that the door has been made the sole speaker. Moreover, in assigning the entire poem to the door, Propertius reflects the importance of the door in the Roman as opposed to the Greek door-song tradition. However, the prominence of the door in 1.16 must not be allowed to obscure the fact that throughout it serves as the *persona* of the poet. For I would suggest that what we have in 1.16 is Propertius himself expressing his own profound *ennui* with the paraclausithyron which as an amatory motif has become worn and tedious. At least, this is what we would have if Propertius intended us to take him seriously. I am convinced that he does not. The whole is an ironic pretence. And this brings me back to my parallel. In *Sonnet CXXX* Shakespeare parades a range of conventional comparisons and turns them on their heads by negating each in turn. The result is a fresh and witty poem which gains its charm by utilising in a novel and engaging way the very stock images which it parodies. So here in 1.16 we are presented with the supreme irony that the vehicle which Propertius chooses to declare the paraclausithyron dead is a paraclausithyron which he constructs from all the self-same themes which constitute the target of his pretended criticism. Thus, through a half-serious, half-playful indulgence in parody and wit Propertius has succeeded in revitalising an erotic motif whose possibilities had been pretty well exhausted.

But we are not through. I suggested earlier that there are signs that 1.16 is an early composition, written perhaps at a stage in Propertius' development when he was experimenting with various amatory motifs. However, if at this stage Propertius' attitude towards the paraclausithyron was detached enough to allow him to indulge in a self-conscious and irreverent parody of it, his later elegies reveal that the figure of the *ianua clausa* and the images associated with it assume a position of symbolic importance in his poetry. Copley has noted that the figure of *clausae fores* occurs no fewer than 25 times in the elegies, and it is with a summarising statement of Copley that I will close: "All of these instances go to show to what degree the *vigilatio ad clausas foras* dominated Propertius' concept of love; in a very real sense it has become to him the keystone of the fabric; his thoughts return to it again and again as the most telling and most nearly all-inclusive of the lover's experiences."[4]

I suppose that this is the final irony.

NOTES

1. J.C. Yardley, "The Door and the Lover: Propertius 1.16," *Proceedings of the Liverpool Latin Seminar: ARCA Classical and Mediaeval Texts, Papers and Monographs* 3 (1979) 155.
2. F.O. Copley, "Exclusus Amator: A Study in Latin Love Poetry," *American Philological Monographs* 3 (1956) 113.
3. *Ibid.* 123.
4. *Ibid.* 79-80; see 162, n. 16, for 25 instances of the *clausae fores* figure.

Le concept de prose poétique dans la *Rhétorique* d'Aristote et *La Composition stylistique* de Denys d'Halicarnasse

Maurice Lebel, O.C., F.R.S.C.
Université Laval, Québec

Le maréchal Foch avait coutume de commencer chaque séance du Conseil de guerre par cette question vraiment socratique: "De quoi s'agit-il?" Bien avant lui, sans doute Aristote et Denys d'Halicarnasse ont-ils fait de même en abordant la prose poétique. A l'instar du philosophe de Stagire et d'Athènes, du critique littéraire d'Halicarnasse et de Rome, commençons par définir les termes. Nous entendons aujourd'hui par prose poétique cette variété de prose qui participe à certaines propriétés de la poésie; c'est la prose d'art cadencée, mesurée, rythmée, apparemment spontanée, mais savante en fait, comme celle, *en grec*, de Thucydide et de Platon, de Démosthène et d'Isocrate, d'Eschine et d'Hypéride, d'Isée et de Lycurgue, de Lysias et de Xénophon, *en français*, comme celle de Pascal, de Bossuet, de Jean-Jacques Rousseau et de Mirabeau, de Chateaubriand et de Michelet, de Renan et de Flaubert, de Charles Péguy et de Paul Claudel, de Marcel Proust et de Paul Valéry. Elle se trouve donc en plusieurs genres littéraires. C'est la prose digne d'être opposée à la poésie.

Mais qu'en pensaient Aristote et Denys d'Halicarnasse? C'est le thème que je me propose de traiter en essayant de répondre aux questions suivantes: Où ces deux auteurs ont-ils exprimé leur concept de la prose poétique? Quel est-il au juste? D'où vient-il? Dans quelle mesure ils se ressemblent et se différencient à cet égard. Je terminerai en tâchant de mesurer l'originalité de leur apport.

Disons, au départ, qu'Aristote et Denys sont deux Grecs de la diaspora, le premier, originaire de la Macédoine, le second d'Asie Mineure; le premier, fils de médecin et biologiste de métier, philosophe de génie, savant universel et précepteur d'Alexandre le Grand, le second, historien d'Halicarnasse, comme Hérodote, son compatriote, mais plutôt rhéteur, historien, professeur de grammaire, critique littéraire et esthéticien, précepteur et directeur d'un cercle littéraire à Rome, où il expliquait les grands écrivains grecs; le premier, familier avec le macédonien et l'attique, a vécu une trentaine d'annés à Athènes, tandis que le second, familier avec le grec et le latin, a vécu une quarantaine d'années à Rome. Deux auteurs bilingues qui ont laissé chacun un ouvrage de fin de carrière, le premier vers 330 av. J.C., la *Rhétorique*, ῥητορική le second, vers l'an 10 av. J.C., *La Composition stylistique*, περὶ συνθέσεως ὀνομάτων. Ni l'un ni l'autre ne furent des orateurs ou des rhéteurs, mais des professeurs, qui ont tenu École, tous les deux intéressés au style, à la prose et à la poésie, notamment à la prose d'art, bien différente de la poésie.

C'est probablement durant la seconde partie de son séjour à Athènes qu'Aristote écrivit la *Rhétorique*. Cet ouvrage, au titre incomplet et trompeur, est divisé en trois livres; le premier porte sur la dialectique puisqu'il traite de l'argumentation et de l'objet propre des trois formes de discours: académique, judiciaire et politique; le deuxième est un traité assez poussé de psychologie morale sur les caractères et les passions; le troisième est un livre fort original et pénétrant sur la prose et le style. Comme quoi, pour Aristote, faute d'argumentation solide et de connaissances précises, de psychologie et d'art, il n'existe point de véritable prose de qualité. C'est dans le troisième livre qu'il est question de prose poétique. Mais, comme dans cette partie Aristote renvoie quatre fois à sa *Poétique* περὶ ποιητικῆς, autre titre aussi incomplet et trompeur, qui signifie Poésie dramatique et épique, il faut en tenir compte, car il complète son concept de la prose poétique. Ajoutons qu'Aristote consacre, dans sa *Poétique*, quatre courts chapitres au style poétique.

Denys d'Halicarnasse, lui, écrivit son livre, *La Composition Stylistique*, vers l'an 10 av. J.C. à Rome. Il le dédia à l'un de ses élèves, Metilius Rufus, qui devint plus tard proconsul d'Achaïe. On peut le tenir pour un instrument de travail, pour une méthode de travail. Il comprend quatre sections; la première (du ch. 1 à 9) est de caractère général, puisqu'elle traite de la nature, des effets et de la méthode de la composition; la deuxième (du ch. 10 à 20) et la troisième (du ch. 21 à 24) constituent la partie centrale, car elles insistent respectivement sur les buts et les procédés, puis sur les trois variétés de la composition stylistique; la quatrième section (ch. 25 et 26) étudie les rapports et les différences entre la prose et la poésie. C'est dans le chapitre 25 que Denys aborde la prose poétique, et il le fait en une quinzaine de pages. Ce développement, annoncé à trois reprises dans les chapitres 1, 13 et 20, renvoie à plusieurs de ses essais antérieurs de critique littéraire, dont l'ensemble comprend 650 pages dans l'édition Teubner de Leipzig. C'est aussi dans la second partie de son volumineux essai sur *Démosthène* (II) qu'il développe ses vues sur la composition stylistique. Le *Démosthène* est donc un complément du *De Compositione Verborum*.

Aristote étudie la prose poétique, comme la poésie d'ailleurs dans sa *Poétique*, un peu en biologiste, sous l'angle de la fonction— l'un de ses mots favoris—comme s'il s'agissait d'un animal. Aussi n'est-il pas surprenant de relever, dans la *Rhétorique*, des mots applicables à un être animé, tels que: fonction et organe, corps et membres, signes et symptômes, mesures et excès, traits et caractères. Il écrit ce qui suit au ch. 2 du livre 3:

> "Il faut donc s'en tenir aux considérations de la *Poétique* (c'est-à-dire aux diverses parties de l'élocution et aux genres littéraires) et admettre cette définition qu'une vertu du style est la clarté. En voici un indice: si le discours ne montre pas son objet, il ne remplira pas sa fonction. Il faut en outre qu'il ne soit ni plat ni enflé, mais approprié; sans doute le langage poétique n'est pas plat, mais il ne convient pas à un discours."

De toute évidence, Aristote prend ici le mot discours dans l'acception de prose, notamment de prose d'art; il l'oppose nettement à la poésie. Il veut dire aussi que la langue poétique n'a pas sa place dans la prose oratoire. Autre est la langue de la poésie, autre est la langue de la prose: ἑτέρα λόγου καὶ ποιήσεως ἐστίν.

Et Aristote de développer sa pensée sur le sujet. Il termine ainsi cette partie de son exposé:

> "Le travail du style doit rester caché; le langage ne doit pas avoir l'air recherché, mais naturel. . . . L'art se dérobe

bien, si l'on compose son style de mots choisis dans le vocabulaire usuel; ainsi fait Euripide qui a donné le premier spécimen du genre."

Aristote est le premier, non seulement à avoir établi une nette distinction entre le choix et l'arrangement des mots, mais aussi à avoir montré que le choix des mots est la base de l'arrangement ou de la position des mots. Pour lui, les prosateurs de qualité ne doivent pas écrire comme les poètes qui parent leurs vers d'épithètes, d'images et de périphrases abondantes et éclatantes. Les premiers écrivent pour charmer, instruire et persuader, tandis que les seconds ne poursuivent pas les mêmes objectifs; le charme de la poésie n'est pas du tout celui de la prose. Aussi aucun prosateur n'a-t-il pris la liberté en Grèce d'être poète en prose, sauf Platon, dans quelques passages restés célèbres du *Banquet* et du *Phédon*.

Pour Aristote, le maître de la prose d'art grecque n'est ni Platon ni Démosthène, mais Isocrate. Il le cite 26 fois dans le livre 3 de sa *Rhétorique* et renvoie à neuf ouvrages d'Isocrate, tandis qu'il y réfère seulement trois fois à Démosthène. Pas une seule fois à Eschine, qui était pourtant vendu à Philippe et qui est un grand artiste. Pourquoi? me direz-vous? Sans doute est-ce, en partie du moins, parce qu'Isocrate était pro-macédonien et brûlait de voir Philippe et Alexandre y répandre partout l'hellénisme ou la culture grecque au-delà de la Méditerranée. Sans doute est-ce aussi parce que sa prose est cadencée, mesurée, métrique, poétique, rythmée, voire musicale. Il aurait même réglé l'arrangement de ses mots d'après la sonorité. Ce qui est sûr, c'est qu'il a voulu, comme il l'écrit lui-même, rivaliser avec la musique en prose. En effet, pendant près de 65 ans—il est mort centenaire, comme Fontenelle—il a tenu école et formé tous les orateurs attiques du IVè siècle. Faute d'être orateur lui-même— c'est à tort qu'on le classe parmi les orateurs, car la tradition ne lui attribue qu'un seul discours prononcé en public—il n'avait point de voix et était fort timide; il faisait plutôt étudier, corriger et réciter à haute voix ses propres compositions par ses élèves; on peut même tenir son école pour un gueuloir, ancêtre de celui de Gustave Flaubert, auteur de *Salammbô*. Naturellement conscient de son talent et de sa valeur, il éprouvait le sentiment aigu de n'être point reconnu comme orateur public à Athènes, qui était alors la république de la parole. Mais, loin de s'avouer vaincu pour autant, comme il était fort riche, il faisait copier ses propres textes à de nombreux exemplaires par les copistes de l'agora et d'Athènes; bien plus, il les faisait distribuer partout dans le monde grec, dans les îles de la Mer Égée, en Asie mineure et en Égypte, voire jusqu'en Assyrie, en Mésopotamie et jusqu'à l'Indus. De sorte que ses compositions ont précédé l'arrivée d'Alexandre en ces pays; Alexandre vivait encore en 330, au moment de la composition de la *Rhétorique* et du *Discours* de Démosthène *pour la couronne*. En bref, Aristote a fort bien saisi, avec Isocrate, toutes les possibilités de l'hellénisme et d'une nouvelle littérature, c'est-à-dire de la littérature écrite, car la littérature grecque avait été jusque-là une littérature orale.

Denys d'Halicarnasse qui écrivait, lui, à Rome, trois siècles après Aristote, n'a pas manqué de bénéficier de cette évolution, voire de cette profonde révolution intellectuelle. Au chapitre cinq de son opuscule, *La Composition Stylistique*, il tient pour modèle de la prose grecque non pas Isocrate, ni Thucydide ni Platon, mais Démosthène. Il le cite douze fois, tandis qu'il renvoie sept fois à Platon, six fois à Isocrate, cinq fois à Aristote et une fois à Eschine. En outre, il a consacré à Démosthène un volumineux essai, divisé en deux parties; et c'est surtout dans la seconde qu'il est question de la prose d'art. Pour lui, Isocrate représente l'harmonie polie, tandis que les représentants de l'harmonie austère sont Eschyle et Thucydide, de l'harmonie intermédiaire, Platon et Aristote. Le mot ἁρμονία implique dans son esprit la métaphore de la construction en pierres. Denys sacrifie donc Hérodote et Thucydide, Isocrate et Platon à Démosthène. Il brûle d'apprendre à son élève:

> "comment un langage non métrique peut ressembler à un beau poème épique ou lyrique, et comment de la poésie, épique ou lyrique, peut être proche de la prose. Je commencerai d'abord par la prose, en faisant appel à l'écrivain chez qui l'on trouve au plus haut point, me semble-t-il, la marque du tour poétique. Je voudrais bien citer plusieurs auteurs mais je n'ai pas assez de temps pour tous. Eh bien donc! qui refuserait de reconnaître que les discours de Démosthène ressemblent à ce que l'on fait de mieux en la matière, en particulier les discours contre Philippe et les plaidoyers composés pour les procès publics?"

Dans l'esprit de Denys d'Halicarnasse, le plus poète des orateurs grecs serait Démosthène. Bien plus, pour lui, il n'existe point de prose d'art en dehors de la prose oratoire, en dehors de la rhétorique proprement dite. Son point de vue nous paraît aujourd'hui un peu étroit. Si Démosthène a passé sa vie à parler en public, à prononcer des harangues, des plaidoyers politiques, des plaidoyers civils, Isocrate, au contraire, a passé sa vie à enseigner la belle prose d'art et à former le style des orateurs attiques du IVè siècle, à composer des essais polis comme des rails d'acier et à les faire distribuer dans le monde grec et à l'étranger. Denys a beau renvoyer souvent à la *Poétique* et à la *Rhétorique* d'Aristote, il ne conçoit pas du tout la prose d'art de la même façon que le philosophe grec. Loin d'être lui-même un penseur original, un théoricien, un philosophe, il est plutôt un grammairien, un précepteur, un directeur de cercle littéraire, un praticien, qui se pique d'enseigner des procédés ou des techniques de style, qui tient la composition stylistique ou l'ajustement musical, sonore des mots pour le *summum* de la prose d'art.

Pour lui, la prose poétique est une sorte de prose qui contient "des mètres et des rythmes discrètement introduits dans sa trame" (7-15). En guise de démonstration ou d'illustration, il analyse le préambule du discours de Démosthène *Contre Aristocratès* et le début du *Contre Ctésiphon* d'Eschine. Il insiste beaucoup non seulement sur les rapports entre la prose et la poésie, mais aussi sur la musique ou sur la succession des sons qui frappent l'oreille, comme le fait la musique vocale ou instrumentale (11.13). La qualité et la valeur des sons, leur répartition dans la durée, l'aspect phonétique des mots et les caractéristiques des rythmes propres au langage: tels sont les points qui l'intéressent le plus. De même qu'il existe une prose poétique, de même la poésie peut ressembler à de la prose (26.1-5), sans être pour autant prosaïque (26.6-10). Ce qui l'intéresse aussi, c'est le mouvement de la phrase, c'est le rôle de la syntaxe, ce dont il parle pour la première fois. Soucieux d'illustrer son point de vue, il cite un extrait d'Homère (26.11-12) pour la poésie épique, un passage d'Euripide (26.13) pour la poésie ïambique et un poème de Simonide (26.14-16) pour la poésie lyrique. Il tient la prose d'art pour une imitation de la poésie; la poésie est certainement l'origine ou la source de la prose poétique.

Les sophistes furent les premiers à s'intéresser à la prose poétique. Plusieurs d'entre eux, comme Gorgias et Protagoras, Hippias et Prodicos, jaloux de la popularité d'Homère, brûlaient de rivaliser avec la poésie et d'écrire en prose comme des poètes. Ils donnaient des leçons qui coûtaient fort cher à leurs élèves. Ion, lui, se plaisait à déclamer des chants homériques devant

20,000 Athéniens. Ils s'occupaient des problèmes de forme et de style, notamment de morphologie et de syntaxe—on leur doit l'optatif—d'étymologie, de sémantique et de synonymie; ils se plaisaient aussi à employer, par exemple, l'anaphore, l'assonance, le chiasme, l'interrogation feinte, et à développer des périodes à l'aide de propositions conditionnelles, consécutives et relatives. Incroyants et amoraux, ils aimaient la mythologie et Homère. Mais, faute de principes de philosophie morale et politique, c'étaient plutôt de vaniteux ciseleurs de phrases, la plupart du temps vides de sens. Aussi furent-ils la cible de Platon qui se moqua d'eux en plusieurs de ses dialogues.

Il fit même davantage. Soucieux de former des citoyens utiles à la vie publique, car il était convaincu de la souveraine importance de la parole dans la vie civile, il composa le *Phèdre*; qui est un grand traité de rhétorique, où il donne (*Phèdre* 265 sqq.) cette définition géniale et pittoresque de l'unité de la composition: ἐστὶ ζῷον; elle est comparable à un animal, avec une tête, un corps et des pieds, c'est-à-dire comprend un début, un développement et une fin; le mot, pris ici dans le sens de proportion des éléments entrant dans une production de l'esprit, comprend aussi, bien sûr, un ensemble de phrases composées qui forment un tout comme un cercle ou un oeuf. Isocrate partageait un point de vue identique. Platon et lui s'entendaient, non seulement pour se moquer dans leurs écrits de la prose poétique fallacieuse des sophistes qui ne rimait à rien, mais aussi pour préparer sérieusement les jeunes à mener un jour une vie utile dans la cité.

Isocrate, Platon et Aristote sont aussi conscients de la révolution intellectuelle qui débute à Athènes au début de la Guerre du Péloponnèse et se poursuit au IVè siècle; c'est l'apparition de la prose au Vè et le début de son enseignement dans les gymnases. Jusque-là on y avait enseigné exclusivement Homère, la poésie épique, didactique, lyrique et dramatique. Mais on commence alors, vers 430, à y ajouter des fragments d'Hérodote, l'archéologie de Thucydide, puis, avec le temps, paraissent des morceaux choisis de Xénophon, de Platon, d'Isocrate, de Démosthène, voire d'Aristote; comme quoi l'étude d'auteurs contemporains dans les collèges ne date pas d'aujourd'hui.

La prose d'art grecque, tard venue, soit plus de quatre siècles après Homère et la poésie, a atteint son plus haut sommet en un siècle, de 430 à 330. Prose sans école, sans prédécesseurs et sans successeurs. Elle fait alors contrepoids à la poésie épique, lyrique et dramatique. Prose variée, puisqu'elle est l'oeuvre d'historiens, de biographes, d'orateurs, de rhéteurs, d'essayistes, de philosophes, d'hommes de science, d'auteurs de dialogues, de lettres, de mémoires. En bref, la prose l'emporte d'emblée sur la poésie au IVè siècle et lui dispute aussi le rôle d'éducatrice. Les auteurs s'appellent désormais, non des ποιηταί, mais des συγγραφεῖς.

A l'instar d'Isocrate et de Platon, Aristote veut aussi réformer la rhétorique et rendre la prose plus effective, plus raisonnable et plus utile. Pour lui, la prose d'art par excellence est celle d'Isocrate, qui circule sous le manteau à un nombre limité mais important d'exemplaires. Elle se veut éducatrice, formatrice; qu'elle s'adresse à un prince ou à des citoyens, elle vise à l'instruction et à la formation du destinataire. Elle est honnête, idéaliste, juste, utile, composée pour être lue et retenue comme des préceptes moraux. Elle s'inspire d'une haute philosophie politique. L'esprit de philanthropie, de pan-hellénisme, de culture générale, une sorte d'apostolat laïque l'animent profondément. On ne peut lui appliquer la théorie de l'art pour l'art, encore moins établir de distinction entre l'esthétique et l'éthique.

Désireux de faire revivre à Rome l'âge d'or de la prose grecque qui avait fleuri à Athènes au IVè siècle, Denys d'Halicarnasse tient pour modèle de prose poétique celle de Démosthène, notamment celle de ses harangues politiques et de ses plaidoyers judiciaires. Par suite de la domination universelle de Rome et de l'arrivée d'Auguste au pouvoir, l'éloquence politique était morte. A la place on lui substitue la déclamation et la lecture publique. Denys, grâce à l'appui de puissants protecteurs romains, peut se livrer en toute quiétude dans son école ou cercle littéraire à l'étude méthodique et fouillée du style des anciens écrivains attiques. Il y développe à loisir sa théorie esthétique du style, hédoniste et impressionniste, qui est tout à fait différente de celle d'Aristote et des rationalistes qui l'avaient précédé. Sa doctrine esthétique s'accordait avec les tendances de la littérature latine contemporaine. Vivant dans un milieu conservateur, à l'époque des Caecilius et des Tubéron, il s'intéresse avant tout à la forme, aux valeurs sonores du langage, à l'étude technique des éléments constitutifs de la prose d'art, à l'effet qualitatif des phonèmes et à l'harmonie imitative. Pour lui, le problème essentiel de l'art d'écrire réside, non pas dans le choix des mots, mais plutôt dans l'arrangement, la position des mots, c'est-à-dire dans la composition stylistique. Par contraste, Aristote ne fait qu'une fois allusion à ce sujet, dans sa *Rhétorique*; cet aspect du style ne semble pas l'avoir intéressé, comme il fut aussi indifférent à son disciple et successeur, Théophraste.

Animateur d'un cercle de lettrés, membres de la haute aristocratie romaine, Denys reflète les idées et les tendances de ces élèves distingués. Son point de vue, étroitement technique, est celui d'un grammairien, d'un rhéteur, doublé d'un esthète qui étudie de façon méthodique l'arrangement ou la place des mots dans la phrase, l'alternance des brèves et des longues, le rythme, l'harmonie, la musique. Polémiste lui-même de tempérament, il considère comme idéale la prose oratoire polémique de Démosthène, de même qu'il tient l'histoire pour une dépendance de la rhétorique. Champion de l'atticisme à Rome, il y a fort bien servi l'hellénisme, au point qu'il est l'un des principaux artisans littéraires de la renaissance du IIè siècle de notre ère. C'est aussi grâce à son influence si le classicisme latin s'est exercé sur les lettres grecques. La perception par les sens, l'impression est à la base de sa théorie du style et de son appréciation de la prose d'un écrivain; celle-ci repose sur une étude approfondie et technique des procédés de composition. De là l'intérêt permanent de ses écrits. Il lit et étudie des textes pour son plaisir. Autant dire qu'il a fait école et qu'il marque une date importante dans la littérature occidentale.

L'apport de Denys d'Halicarnasse, pour avoir consacré un essai fort substantiel à la prose d'art de Démosthéne, diffère donc sensiblement de celui d'Aristote, qui n'a pas jugé bon de faire de même à propos d'Isocrate. Penseur original, philosophe, savant, théoricien, il s'en tient à de profondes observations sur la prose et le style dans le livre 3 de sa *Rhétorique*. Celle-ci, universellement connue, est même devenue un classique, c'est-à-dire un livre de base, de classe, de masse qui a été pillé à l'envi depuis des siècles par les auteurs d'ouvrages de techniques littéraires, de composition et de style. *La Composition Stylistique* de Denys d'Halicarnasse et son essai fort pénétrant sur *Démosthène* 1.2 sont sans doute beaucoup moins connus que le grand traité d'Aristote. Mais on ne continue pas moins de s'y intéresser, bien que la rhétorique, au sens péjoratif et sophistique du terme, possède aujourd'hui mauvaise presse, et non sans raison, car elle est creuse et malhonnête; c'est cette dernière que vise Victor Hugo quand il nous invite à lui tordre le cou; la bonne, la vraie, elle, a toujours sa place, fondée qu'elle est sur la connaissance, le savoir et la vérité, l'honnête, le juste et l'utile; le grand écrivain français du XIXè siécle l'a cultivée toute sa vie dans son oeuvre, aussi bien en prose qu'en poésie.

De nos jours, et en plusieurs pays d'Amérique et d'Europe, on voit chercheurs et érudits, écrivains et philosophes étudier de plus la Rhétorique de l'Antiquité païenne et chrétienne, voire la Rhétorique de la Renaissance. Ils travaillent donc, pour ainsi dire, à l'ombre ou dans le sillage d'Aristote et de Denys d'Halicarnasse qui furent les premiers, à trois siècles de distance l'un de l'autre, à traiter de la prose et tout particulièrement de la prose cadencée, mesurée, rythmée, poétique. Ces deux auteurs grecs, originaires de la Macédoine et de l'Asie Mineure, sont aussi les premiers en Occident à l'avoir étudiée, avec textes à l'appui, en profondeur et en détail, montrant ainsi la voie à leurs successeurs. Unique est leur contribution à l'étude de la prose et de la composition.

En bref, Démosthène ou Isocrate, comme tout grand écrivain, prouve que l'écriture est tout. On est soi-même, on s'appartient par les mots, par le choix et l'arrangement des mots.

δειλός AND οὐτιδανός IN THE LANGUAGE OF ACHILLES[1]

❦

Valerie M. Warrior
Boston University

Achilles' psychology and distinctive use of language have been the focus of much scholarly discussion.[2] Little attention, however, has been given to his declaration at the conclusion of his confrontation with Agamemnon at *Iliad* 1.293-294:

ἦ γάρ κεν δειλός τε καὶ οὐτιδανός καλεοίμην
εἰ δὴ σοι πᾶν ἔργον ὑπείξομαι ὅττι κεν εἴπῃς

Two of the three occurrences of οὐτιδανός in the *Iliad* are in speeches of Achilles.[3] The word δειλός occurs 24 times, the first and last two of which are in speeches of Achilles. In his address to the suppliant Priam who has come to ransom Hector's body, Achilles' first words ἆ δειλέ (24.518) are followed seven lines later by mention of "poor mortals" (δειλοῖσι βροτοῖσι) for whom the gods have spun lives that are subject to suffering (24.525). Study of the contexts of all 24 occurrences of δειλός indicates that the basic meaning is "helpless" or "hapless" and, consequently, "pitiful" or "wretched" because of what has happened or is felt to be imminent. The collocation of Achilles' usage of δειλός and οὐτιδανός suggests that these epithets may have a particular significance within the evolution and resolution of Achilles' wrath.

Achilles' speeches in Book 1 show him to be one who, through sparing and unusual vocabulary, is in full control of his rhetoric even in the heat of confrontation. The quarrel with Agamemnon is punctuated by two interventions: that of Athena who prevents

320

Achilles from drawing his sword and advises him to use verbal taunts, and that of Nestor who attempts to reason with the two contestants. Agamemnon's response to Nestor's mediation is interrupted by Achilles without any formal address:[4] "Indeed, I would be called a pitiful nonentity (δειλός τε καὶ οὐτιδανός) if I am going to give in to you in everything you happen to say."[5]

The verb καλεοίμην reveals Achilles' concern about his reputation: how society will view him if he gives in to Agamemnon. The issue for both Agamemnon and Achilles is τιμή—honour, public esteem or image. Agamemnon has earlier expressed concern about his image, telling Achilles that it would not be fitting for him to be the only one of the Greeks to be without a prize (1.118-119). His τιμή is already in jeopardy because he refused to accept ransom for Chryseis, although the people cried out in support of her father's pleas (1.22-23). Achilles poses a threat to Agamemnon's position as leader of the Greeks, since he has taken the initiative by summoning the assembly after the onset of the plague.[6]

In an attempt to mediate, Nestor sums up the relative positions of the two contestants. The honour (τιμή) of a sceptered king to whom Zeus gives glory is unequalled. Even though Achilles is stronger (καρτερός) and has a goddess as mother, Agamemnon is superior (φερτερός) because he rules over more people (1.278-281). Agamemnon's reply reflects his fear that Achilles is attempting to usurp his position: "But this man wants to be above all others, wants to control all, to rule and give orders to all; yet I think there is one who will not obey him" (1.287-289).[7] This prompts Achilles' retort that giving in would make him seem δειλός and οὐτιδανός. Echoing Agamemnon, he says: "don't give orders to me; I think I'm not going to obey you any longer" (1.295-296).

Achilles has earlier used οὐτιδανός to describe Agamemnon's subjects: "Folk-devouring king, you rule over nonentities, otherwise this would be your last outrage.[8] By declaring that he would be called οὐτιδανός if he acquiesces in everything Agamemnon says, Achilles reveals a fear that he might become a nonentity like the rest of Agamemnon's subjects.

The meaning of δειλός is more complex. Its antithesis is ἄλκιμος, as is apparent from the instance at 13.278 where Idomeneus is pointing out that ἀρετή is best discerned in an ambush: "here the man who is δειλός and the one who is ἄλκιμος are revealed."[9] In the *Iliad*, ἄλκιμος generally means powerful, mighty or valorous, and is frequently used to describe a hero in action. In the context of battle, the heart (ἦτορ) is described as ἄλκιμον.¹⁰ Patroclus is 12 times denoted as ἄλκιμος.¹¹ Thus, as a first approximation, one may say that δειλός denotes one who is ineffective or ineffectual. Significantly ἄναλκις, the negative of ἄλκιμος, occurs in conjunction with the only other occurrence of οὐτιδανός in the *Iliad*. Here Diomedes compares an arrow shot by Paris, the epitome of the non-hero in the *Iliad*, to the blunt weapon of a weakling and nonentity.¹² The implication of the phrase δειλός τε καὶ οὐτιδανός is that Achilles fears the reputation of being a nonentity: ineffectual, unheroic and, thus, pitiful.

By the time of the embassy sent by Agamemnon, fear has become reality. In highly unusual language, Achilles expresses a sense of alienation when he tells Ajax (9.647-648): "Agamemnon has treated me abominably among the Argives (μ' ἀσύφηλον ἐν Ἀργείοισιν ἔρεξεν, 9.647) as if I were a dishonoured outcast (ὡς εἴ τιν' ἀτίμητον μετανάστην)." He repeats the latter phrase to Patroclus at 16.59 where he specifically mentions Agamemnon taking Briseis from his arms. The word μετανάστης denotes one who has moved to a different community, an alien.¹³ The meaning of ἀσύφηλος can only be approximated since there is but one other occurrence in Homer, where Helen lamenting over Hector declares that she never heard a word from him that is evil or ἀσύφηλον (24.767). These two contexts suggest that the word describes behaviour or language that is an affront to the family or community, "uncivilized" or "uncivil."¹⁴ Achilles now feels not simply lacking in public esteem (τιμή) but also alienated from society, a non-person.

To Odysseus, the first speaker of the embassy, Achilles characterized Agamemnon's behaviour as an outrage, λώβη (9.387), thus recalling the verb he used in his insult to Agamemnon at 1.232: "you rule over nonentities (οὐτιδανοῖσι), otherwise this would be your last outrage (λωβήσαιο)."¹⁵ The theme of social outrage recurs at the end of the *Iliad* in the sole occurrence of the epithet λωβητός. Achilles uses this word in his speech to the suppliant Priam, whom he has greeted with the cry ἆ δειλέ. In his subsequent reflection on the suffering of "poor mortals" (δειλοῖσι βροτοῖσι), Achilles recounts the myth of the two jars and describes the plight of the man to whom Zeus has given a portion from the jar of sorrows: Zeus makes him reviled (λωβητός); terrible madness drives him over the face of the sacred earth, and he wanders honoured (τετιμένος) by neither gods nor mortal men.¹⁶

The various nuances of δειλός emerge gradually as the *Iliad* progresses. In five instances of recent or impending bereavement through death in battle, δειλός has the sense of "hapless." Thetis refers to herself as the hapless mother of a son who is soon to die (18.54). Briseis and Hecuba speak of themselves as δειλή—the former as she cries out in lamentation and throws herself on the mangled body of Patroclus (19.287), the latter as she bewails Hector's death (22.431). Achilles' lamentation over Patroclus is compared to a father lamenting a newly-wed son whose death has brought sorrow to his hapless parents (23.223). There is a similar context at 17.38, where the son of Panthous, faced with death at the hands of Menelaus, recalls the grief caused to his hapless parents by Menelaus' slaughter of his brother. δειλός does not only describe the bereaved; it is used four times of the dead Patroclus and once of the slain sons of Diocles.[17]

In the last four books of the *Iliad* mortals are δειλός in the context of their suffering or death. Apollo reflects on the lot of hapless mortals (βροτῶν . . . δειλῶν) who, like leaves, flourish only to wither away (21.463-466). The line-ending δειλοῖσι βροτοῖσι occurs three times in contexts which indicate that the repetition is more than formulaic.[18] Achilles' rush across the plain is compared to the star which brings much fever to hapless mortals (22.26-31). Priam, as he begs Hector not to engage in combat with Achilles, envisages his own corpse being mangled by his own dogs, "the most piteous thing that can befall hapless mortals" (22.76).[19] Finally, in his speech to the suppliant Priam in Book 24, Achilles reflects on the life of suffering that the gods have spun for hapless mortals (24.525-526). As the *Iliad* approaches its conclusion, δειλός becomes increasingly associated with the human predicament.

The vocative of δειλός at the beginning of the line is especially striking. The first two such uses are instances of vaunting. These occur within 11 lines of each other, and both are uttered by Odysseus over Socus (11.441 and 452). When the first spear-thrust has failed to kill his victim, Odysseus cries: "ἆ δειλέ, your father and mother will not be able to close your eyes in death, but carrion birds will tear your flesh apart, beating their wings thick and fast about you." Redfield has noted that this is the first time in the *Iliad* that a warrior has made such a threat by asserting his right to deprive his victim of a proper burial. Previously the concept of a hero becoming the prey of dogs and birds had been a remotely expressed fear, but henceforth it becomes increasingly a real and imminent threat uttered by heroes over their victims.[20] These first two occurrences of the initial vocative of δειλός mark a shift in the heroes' code of behaviour, which reaches its climax in Achilles' treatment of Hector's body.

Patroclus' cry, ἆ δειλοί, while it continues the theme of the mutilation of the corpse, is one of compassion. As he is setting out to get Achilles' permission to join in the fighting, he sees the wounded Eurypylus and exclaims: "Poor wretches, leaders and captains of the Greeks, was it your intention, far from your native land, to glut the dogs of Troy with your white fat?" (11.816-818). This cry marks the beginning of Patroclus' own tragedy.[21] Hector vaunts over the fallen Patroclus, saying that vultures will devour him: "ἆ δειλέ, Achilles for all his heroism did not help you" (16.837). This contemptuous exclamation evokes for the audience a note of pathos when, subsequently, the dead Patroclus is four times referred to as δειλός.[22]

As Hector puts on the armour of Achilles stripped from Patroclus' body, Zeus cries: "ἆ δειλέ, although death is near to you, it is far from your thoughts" (17.201). From the immediate context it might appear that Zeus is vaunting over Hector's approaching death, as Odysseus has vaunted over Socus at 11.441 and 452. However, Zeus later cries ἆ δειλώ when he sees Peleus' horses weeping for Patroclus: "You poor creatures, why did we ever give you to lord Peleus, a mortal, while you yourselves are immortal and ageless? Was it so that among unhappy men you might also feel pain? For among all creatures that breathe and crawl on earth, there is not anything more lamentable than man" (17.443-447). Zeus' "you poor wretch" for Hector should be understood as a cry of compassion; for later, when Hector is about to be slain, Zeus says that his heart weeps (22.169-170). This instance at 17.201 is the first in which δειλός is used of the Trojans in a compassionate sense.

Of the first six occurrences of the initial vocative usage of δειλός, in all cases save one it is used of individuals who have fallen into the power of others, who have become or are about to become victims, and who have been reduced to the the status of objects, sometimes in the literal sense of being food for dogs or birds. The exception is Zeus' cry for the horses of Peleus.

The seventh and last instance of the initial vocative of δειλός is Achilles' opening words to Priam.[23] The cry, ἆ δειλέ, signifies a shift in Achilles' classification of Priam from enemy, one to be vaunted over as victim, to that of a man to be pitied as a fellow mourner. After Priam's speech of supplication he and Achilles mourn together, he for Hector and Achilles for Peleus and

Patroclus. Homer twice notes Achilles' compassion for Priam: ἦκα, gently (24.508) and οἰκτείρων, pitying (24.516).

In Achilles' exclamation all the various nuances come together: pity, helplessness, haplessness, bereavement and mourning. By bringing δειλός back into Achilles' language at this point, Homer signals to the audience that Achilles recognizes in Priam the condition of a "pitiful non-person" that he had feared for himself in the original confrontation with Agamemnon. As he raises Priam by the hand, Achilles identifies with the sufferings of another and so, for the first time in the *Iliad*, shows compassion.

A mere seven lines after crying ἆ δειλέ, Achilles says that the gods have have devised lives for hapless mortals (δειλοῖσι βροτοῖσι) that are subject to suffering, whereas the gods themselves are sorrowless (ἀκηδέες).[24] He then recounts the moralizing myth of the jars of Zeus with its vivid picture of the reviled outcast.

The phrase δειλοῖσι βροτοῖσι with which Achilles prefaces his homily is an unwitting repetition by Achilles of Priam's last two words to Hector that mutilation of an aged man is the most piteous thing that can befall hapless mortals (22.76). By having Achilles unknowingly repeat Priam's own words to Priam himself, the poet signals to the audience a bond of empathy between Priam and Achilles. These words also recall Apollo's reflection on the lot of hapless mortals who, like the leaves, flourish only to wither away (21.465-466). Finally, Achilles' juxtaposition of mortal suffering with the god's freedom from care recalls Zeus' compassion for the immortal horses of Peleus which must live among men and feel pain (17.443-447).

Achilles, son of the immortal Thetis, has come to accept the pain and compassion of humanity. The poet has begun the final resolution of Achilles' wrath.

NOTES

1. This paper has its origins in my teaching of epic under A.G. McKay at McMaster University and in the NEH Summer Seminar, "Homer, Text and Context," given by J.M. Redfield in 1983.
2. D.B. Claus, *TAPA* 105 (1975) 13-28, contra A. Parry, *TAPA* 87 (1956) 1-7, esp. 25, where he describes Achilles as "a speaker fully alive to the tacit seeming of his own language and that of others"; J.M.

Redfield, *Nature and Culture in the Iliad* (1975) 11-23; P. Friedrich and J.M. Redfield, *Language* 54 (1978) 263-288, esp. 276, where they characterize Achilles' speech as "passionate and highly personal, unequivocal, aiming at self-declaration rather than at persuading others" (see also 278 on his conciseness and forcefulness); J.A. Arieti, *CJ* 82 (1986) 1-27, R. Scodel, *CP* 84 (1989) 91-99; R.P. Martin, *The Language of Heroes* (1989) 146-205.

3. Achilles: 1.231 and 292; 11.390 occurs in a speech of Diomedes.
4. On the abruptness of the interruption and lack of formal address, see M.M. Willcock, *The Iliad of Homer, Books I-XII* (1978) 193, and G.S. Kirk, *The Iliad: A Commentary*, vol. I: Books 1-4, (1985) 82.
5. The translation of δειλός at 1.293 as "coward" by A.T. Murray, *The Iliad* (Loeb Classical Library 1924), vol. 1, 25, and R. Lattimore, *The Iliad of Homer* (1951) 67, is somewhat misleading, especially for Greekless readers to whom it might initially suggest fear of battle. Neither fear of battle nor a possible allusion to Achilles' earlier threat to return to Phthia (169-171) and his subsequent withdrawal from the fighting make any sense at 1.293, where the reputation for being δειλός and οὐτιδανός is contingent upon his acquiescence to Agamemnon.
6. For a more detailed analysis of the escalation of the confrontation, see Redfield, *Nature and Culture . . . (op. cit.)* 93-97.
7. As Kirk points out, *Commentary* 82, Agamemnon "studiously ignores" all of Nestor's points, preferring to "harp obsessively on Achilles' domineering behaviour."
8. *Il*. 1.231-232: δημοβόρος βασιλεύς, ἐπεὶ οὐτιδανοῖσι ἀνάσσεις
    ἦ γὰρ ἂν Ἀτρεΐδη, νῦν ὕστατα λωβήσαιο
9. *Il*. 13.278: ἔνθα ὅ τε δειλός ἀνήρ ὅς τ' ἄλκιμος ἦτορ ἐξεφαάνθη. Murray, *Iliad* vol. 2, 23, and Lattimore, *Iliad* 278, render δειλός as coward, but with more justification than at 1.293 (see above, n. 5).
10. *Il*. 5.529; 16.209, 264; 17.111; 20.169. Cf. also ἄλκιμον ἔγκος at 3.338; 10.135; 14.12; 15.482.
11. *Il*. 11.605, 814, 837; 12.1; 16.278, 307, 626, 665, 827; 18.12, 455; 19.24. Other heroes referred to as ἄλκιμος are Diomedes (6.437), Meges, the son of Phyleus (10.110) and Telamonian Ajax (12.349, 362).
12. *Il*. 11.390: κωφὸν γὰρ βέλος ἀνδρὸς ἀνάλκιδος οὐτιδανοῖο.
13. On the concept of social alienation and Achilles' marked use of μετανάστης, see Arieti, *CJ* 82 (1986) 23-24. Cf. Lattimore's translation (215) "dishonoured vagabond" and Willcock's note *op. cit.* (283) "a refugee without any rights."
14. Cf. Arieti, *CJ* 82 (1986) 21-22, who emphasizes the element of social alienation which he considers is common to Helen and Achilles.

15. *Il.* 9.387: πρίν γ' ἀπὸ πᾶσαν ἐμοί δόμεναι θυμαλγέα λώβην. Arieti, *CJ* 82 (1986) 6, notes the unique collocation of θυμαλγής heartrending, with λώβη. In the two other occurrences of λώβη that involve Achilles, Iris tells him that failure to fight over Patroclus' body will be a λώβη (18.180) and, after their reconciliation, Achilles tells Agamemnon that it will be a λώβη to Patroclus if they do not return to the fighting immediately (19.208).
16. *Il.* 24.531-533: ᾧ δέ κε τῶν λυγρῶν δώῃ, λωβητὸν ἔθηκε.
    καί ἑ κακὴ βούβρωστις ἐπὶ χθόνα δῖαν ἐλαύνει.
    φοιτᾷ δ' οὔτε θεοῖσι τετιμένος οὔτε βροτοῖσι.
17. *Il.* 5.574; 17.670; 23.65, 105, 221.
18. Cf. Claus, *op. cit.* 105 (1975) 17, who considers that Parry's theory of oral formulaic language (see above, n. 2) "ignores the need to read the contextual components of speech that transform mere words, formulae or not, into functioning language."
19. C. Segal, *The Theme of the Mutilation of the Corpse in the Iliad* (1971) 33.
20. Redfield, *Nature and Culture . . . (op. cit.)* 168-169.
21. Segal, *op. cit.* 9, notes the significance of the appearance of the theme at this turning point in Patroclus' destiny.
22. See above, n. 17.
23. Homer, *Iliad,* Book 24, ed. C.W. Macleod (1982) 132 notes: "this form of address is a sign of strong feeling . . . Later, in comforting or admonishing Priam, Achilles uses the drier γέρον . . . or γεραιέ."
24. *Il.* 24.525-526: ὡς γὰρ ἐπεκλώσαντο θεοὶ δειλοῖσι βροτοῖσι,
    ζώειν ἀχνυμένους αὐτοὶ δέ τ' ἀκηδέες εἰσι.

PRINCIPATUS AND *IMPERIUM*: TACITUS, *HISTORIAE* 1.1

Herbert W. Benario
Emory University

—*AGM amico amicus HWB*

A little reminiscing is in order. I first met Sandy McKay in the summer of 1956, in Rome, when he was guiding the first of the Vergilian Society's grand tours, from Sicily to Hadrian's Wall. The following summer, Sandy was scheduled to assist Father Schoder in the direction of the summer school at Cumae. In early June, he underwent emergency surgery. Appy Thayer, the President of the Society, called me in desperation to see if I could go to Italy in Sandy's place. Although scheduled to teach summer school at Columbia, I was able to make other arrangements for my courses and I sailed in late June. One of the Fulbright participants in the American Academy summer session was a lady whom I had known since graduate school. When she came down to the Villa after the Academy program, we decided, on the Isle of Capri, to marry. Two years later, in 1959, Sandy McKay was Director of the summer school, and Janice and I were his assistants. It is now, as I write in the spring of 1989, a third of a century since Sandy and I were introduced to each other by a mutual friend, a third of a century of friendship and, on my part, admiration.

Among the many professional obligations which he has fulfilled over the years has been the responsibility for the *Classical World* surveys, a task which he assumed for the 1968-1969 volume and has continued ever since. As Surveys Editor he has perused and approved three Tacitus installments which I have had the honor to prepare. I offer him, therefore, a brief essay on Tacitus on the occasion of his retirement.

Tacitus concludes the first chapter of his *Historiae* with the promise that, if the years should be granted him, he will write the history of the happy period of Nerva and Trajan. That will be a pleasant change from the events of the Flavian dynasty and from the imposed limitations on one of the most cherished aspects of Roman *libertas*, freedom of speech and thought.[1] His words ring with enthusiasm: *quod si vita suppeditet, principatum divi Nervae et imperium Traiani, uberiorem securioremque materiam, senectuti seposui, rara temporum felicitate, ubi sentire quae velis et quae sentias dicere licet.*[2]

The variation which Tacitus employs to designate the rule of the two emperors has for long engaged scholarly attention. Does the choice of two different words imply a judgment on the character of each man's position in the state or the nature of his power, or is it no more than another of the many examples of Tacitean *variatio*? My attention was drawn once again to this problem some dozen years ago by the publication of a lecture delivered by a scholar of Roman law, with the intriguing title of *Politik und Gerechtigkeit bei Traian*.[3] The author denies that Trajan involved the senate in government to any significant degree. "Traian dachte über die Rolle des Senats im Verfassungsleben kaum anders als Domitian. Für Tacitus, der in Traian zunächst einen Gleichgesinnten vermutet hatte, war daher seine Regierung 'Imperium', Herrschaft, und nicht, wie die Nervas, 'Prinzipat'."[4] Wolf is applying Tacitus' vocabulary (which, he assumes, mirrors his thought) to a juridical distinction. I think it is quite wrong to do so.

A review of Tacitus' use of the words elsewhere, as well as their appearance in the works of some other contemporary writers, may prove instructive. It needs to be emphasized that the word *princeps* and the other words connected with it, such as *principatus*, have no basis in law and never appear as part of imperial titulature.[5] Augustus used it in the *Res Gestae* to describe his position,[6] and it had a familiar ring which evoked the days of the republic, with the *princeps senatus* and perhaps even the claim made long ago by Augustus that he had restored the republic.[7] In the official Greek terminology of the eastern half of the empire, ἡγεμών is the normal equivalent for *princeps*, but it essentially disappears after the Julio-Claudian period. In the second century, αὐτοκράτωρ had taken over, which is the natural match for *imperator*.⁸ The only rival was Σεβαστός, which introduces quite a different element, that of religious character.

Imperator is the official title of the man whom we call the Roman emperor. The word bespeaks his command of the army, entire or almost so, stands first in the regular accumulation of titles, and directly leads one's thoughts back to Augustus, who, while still little more than Caesar's heir, transposed the word which had indicated salutation by a victorious army in the field to a *praenomen*.⁹ It is this word which has a juridical basis.

What then does use of the words *princeps* or *principatus* imply? It refers, I suggest, to the senatorial concept of constitutional rule, the concept which is put forth in extreme form, perhaps, by Pliny in his *Panegyricus*. The emperor is *primus inter pares*; he is not a *dominus*.¹⁰ When *principatus* exists, the state is spared a *dominatio*.¹¹ This is what Tacitus meant when, early in the biography of his father-in-law, he speaks of Nerva's great achievement, *Nerva Caesar res olim dissociabiles miscuerit, principatum ac libertatem*.¹² This approach on Nerva's part toward his power and duties was responsible for the beginning of a *beatissimum saeculum*.¹³

Several other Tacitean passages help to illuminate the statement in the *Historiae*. Toward the end of the *Agricola*, Tacitus repeats the expression *beatissimum saeculum* but this time links it only with Trajan, whom he describes as *princeps*.¹⁴ In *Historiae* 1.15-16, where Tacitus presents Galba's speech with which he adopts Piso, a speech which *may* have been composed on the basis of Tacitus' knowledge of events surrounding Nerva's adoption of Trajan, the historian links *imperium* and *principatus* very closely, with no distinction of meaning.¹⁵ Both represent the supreme power of the state. Further along in the speech Galba claims that his advanced years can offer the state no greater boon than a *bonum successorem*, while Piso's age, in its prime, can offer a *bonum principem*. Selection as emperor is a better means of succession than claim by birth, for *optimum quemque adoptio inveniet*.¹⁶ This last, regardless of what weight one may wish to give it in consideration of Tacitus' political thought,¹⁷ may well have been meant to allude to Trajan, the *optimus princeps*.¹⁸

Sex. Iulius Frontinus, the distinguished senior consular who was resurrected from retirement by Nerva and Trajan to serve first as *curator aquarum* and then hold a second and a third consulate, speaks of Nerva as both *imperator* and *princeps*.¹⁹

Unfortunately, there is no instance where he speaks of Trajan with a title.

And what can Pliny tell us? Crucial in this context are chapters 44 and 45 of the *Panegyricus*. The significant word here is *princeps*, since Pliny wishes above all to focus upon that quality of the emperor which can be styled *civilis*. He was one of us, he is still one of us: *nam privato iudicio principem geris, meliorem immo te praestas, quam tibi alium precabare. itaque sic imbuti sumus, ut, quibus erat summa votorum melior pessimo princeps, iam non possumus nisi optimum ferre.*[20] It is a nice touch, to note how smoothly Pliny progresses from a good *princeps*, the word standing alone, to one better, *melior*, and finally the best, *optimus*. Later, in his *Historiae*, Tacitus echoed that idea: *optimus est post malum principem dies primus.*[21]

Further, when expatiating on Trajan's favor shown to good men, Pliny says: *aequum est esse eos carissimos bono principi, qui invisissimi malo fuerint. scis, ut sunt diversa natura dominatio et principatus, ita non aliis esse principem gratiorem, quam qui maxime dominum graventur.*[22] Trajan is *princeps* because he leads by example: *nec tam imperio nobis opus est quam exemplo.*[23] Use of the word *imperator* in this context would have defeated Pliny's purpose, namely to emphasize the character of the new emperor.

To return now to the distinction of meaning between the two words which Wolf claimed existed. He is not, by any means, alone among modern scholars to conclude this. Indeed, he follows a formidable line. Syme writes, of the succession to Domitian: "Nerva and 'Libertas' is but an episode. The strong and enduring tendencies resume their course. Although the proprieties are saved and respected, there is a breach in continuity between the 'principatus' of Nerva and the 'imperium' of Trajan."[24] Straub claimed that *principatus* and *imperium* are by no means synonymous, and therefore we must conclude that *princeps* and *imperator* are similarly distinct.[25] Shotter argued that, since Tacitus distinguished Nerva's *principatus* from Trajan's *imperium*, he contrasted Nerva not only with Domitian but also with Trajan.[26]

On the other hand, Wickert, in his magisterial Pauly-Wissowa article on "Princeps," stated that "Wenn z.B. Tacitus den *principatus divi Nervae* unmittelbar neben das *imperium Traiani* stellt (hist. I 1, 4), oder wenn er hist. I 56, 3 die Wörter *imperator* und *princeps* nebeneinander gebraucht, so ist das nur eine Variante des Ausdrucks, nicht des Inhalts."[27] But the views of

Béranger, however, weakened Wickert's resolve a bit: "Les termes qui devraient être des mots clés: *princeps, principatus, imperator, imperium* ont des emplois multiples. Parfois ils sont synonymes, parfois ils forment antithèse, parfois ils se confondent à la surface, tandis qu'ils diffèrent en profondeur. Ils offrent au virtuose une gamme riche et souple où l'enharmonie tempère les modulations et rend imperceptible le passage d'un ton à l'autre."[28] But he grants that *principatus* and *imperium* can be synonymous, and Wickert continues to believe that as well.[29] If we accept that, as I do, the question remains whether that is the case in our passage.

Any student of Tacitean style is aware that the historian repeats words, particularly words that are intellectually or emotionally suggestive, only very rarely in close proximity. Tacitean *variatio* is one of the truisms of his style. He does not, I submit, wish to distinguish two quite different kinds of principate, nor is it at all likely that Tacitus wished to stigmatize Trajan's rule as a "persönliches Regiment."[30] That would have been foolhardy, if not dangerous. Granted that when Tacitus called Trajan *princeps* in the *Agricola* the latter had only recently come to the purple and, although all would have hoped, none could have known what kind of ruler he would prove to be. Nerva's principate being so brief, Trajan's predecessor was effectively Domitian, and, as at the accession of Vespasian not three decades before, the very beginning of a new era was the best: *optimus est post malum principem dies primus.*[31] We do not know when Tacitus undertook his *Historiae* nor whether he penned the chapter at the beginning or at some later point.[32] But in all likelihood he was at work about 107; in the course of a decade or so, the argument goes, he could have become disenchanted with the emperor, and realized that his policies were no different from Domitian's, only the manner had changed.[33] Consequently, use of the word *imperator* to designate Trajan is intended pejoratively.

That argument will not do. After the Dacian Wars, when Trajan had brought Rome her greatest victories and booty and accession of territories since the days of Augustus, it was right, if not politic, to emphasize Trajan's military prowess. The opportunity which Tacitus embraced to compliment the emperor and show that he was very different from Tiberius, a *princeps proferendi imperi incuriosus,*[34] will hardly have also been employed to rebuke the emperor for despotic rule. Tacitus focuses upon the first element in the emperor's titulature, that of *Imperator.* It would have been ludicrous to have so designated

Nerva. But to seek significant differences between the principates of Nerva and Trajan because of differing emphasis and desire for stylistic variety demands more than we should require the text to give us.

NOTES

1. Tacitus, *Agr.* 2.3.
2. Tacitus, *Hist.* 1.1.4.
3. J.G. Wolf, *Politik und Gerechtigkeit bei Traian*, Schriftenreihe der juristischen Gesellschaft e. V. Berlin, Heft 54 (Berlin/New York, 1978), 24.
4. *Ibid.* 10. For similarity to Domitian, see K.H. Waters, "Traianus Domitiani Continuator," *AJP* 90 (1969) 385-405.
5. M. Hammond, *The Antonine Monarchy* (Rome, 1959) 58-63 and *The Augustan Principate* (New York, 1968²) 111-112; L. Wickert, "Princeps," *Mélanges offerts à Jérôme Carcopino* (Paris, 1966) 979-986.
6. *RG* 13, 30.1, 32.3.
7. *RG* 34.1. On the *res publica restituta*, see, *inter alios*, F. Millar, "Two Augustan Notes. 2. The 'Restoration of the Republic' in 27 B.C.," *CR* 18 (1968) 265-266 and E.A. Judge, "'Res Publica Restituta': A Modern Illusion?," *Polis and Imperium: Studies in Honour of Edward Togo Salmon* (Toronto, 1974) 279-311.
8. H.J. Mason, *Greek Terms for Roman Institutions: A Lexicon and Analysis* (Toronto, 1974) 119, 144.
9. R. Syme, "Imperator Caesar: A Study in Nomenclature," *Historia* 7 (1958) 172-188 = *Roman Papers* I 361-377; D. Timpe, *Untersuchungen zur Kontinuität des frühen Prinzipats*, Historia Einzelschriften 5 (Wiesbaden, 1962) 10-12.
10. M. Hammond, "Pliny the Younger's Views on Government," *HSCP* 49 (1938) 115-140; particularly 123, n. 5: "Pliny uses the terms *imperator* and *princeps* interchangeably for the most part."
11. H.W. Benario, "Tacitus and the Principate," *CJ* 60 (1964-65) 97-106.
12. Tacitus, *Agr.* 3.1.
13. M. Hammond, "*Res olim dissociabiles: Principatus ac Libertas—* Liberty Under the Early Roman Empire," *HSCP* 67 (1963) 93-113.
14. Tacitus, *Agr.* 44.5.
15. Tacitus, *Hist.* 1.15.1: *nunc me deorum hominumque consensu ad imperium vocatum praeclara indoles tua et amor patriae impulit, ut principatum . . . bello adeptus quiescenti offeram. . . .*

16. *Ibid.* 1.16.1.
17. R. Syme, "The Political Opinions of Tacitus," *Ten Studies in Tacitus* (Oxford, 1970) 119-140.
18. R. Syme, *Tacitus* (Oxford, 1958) chapters I-V.
19. Frontinus, *De aquaeductu urbis Romae* 88.1.
20. Pliny, *Pan.* 44.2.
21. Tacitus, *Hist.* 4.42.6.
22. Pliny, *Pan.* 45.3.
23. *Ibid.* 45.6.
24. R. Syme, *Tacitus* 12.
25. J. Straub, "IMPERIUM ET LIBERTAS: Eine Tacitus—Reminiszenz im politischen Programm Disraelis," *Regeneratio Imperii* (Darmstadt, 1972) 19 (originally published in *Spiegel der Geschichte*; Festschrift M. Braubach, edd. K. Repgen and S. Skalweit [Münster, 1964] 52-68).
26. D.C.A. Shotter, "The Principate of Nerva: Some Observations on the Coin Evidence," *Historia* 32 (1983) 215.
27. L. Wickert, "Princeps," *RE* 22 (1954) 2060,60-2061,5.
28. J. Béranger, "La Notion du Principat sous Trajan et Hadrien," *Principatus* (Geneva, 1973) 292 (originally published in *Les Empereurs Romains d'Espagne* [Paris, 1965] 27-44); L. Wickert, "Neue Forschungen zum römischen Principat," *ANRW* II 1 (1974) 23-24: "nachdem aber J. Béranger . . ., bin ich meiner Sache nicht mehr ganz sicher."
29. Béranger, *op. cit.* 293: "Aussi peut-il (*imperium*) être synonyme de *principatus*, mais cette équivalence reste occasionnelle." Wickert, *op. cit.* 24 (see n. 28): "Der Kaiser ist ebensowohl *princeps* wie *imperator*, und so darf der römische Autor, wo es ihm nicht auf scharfe Begriffbestimmung ankommt, die beiden Wörter ohne unterschiedliche Bedeutungsnuance nebeneinander gebrauchen." For Béranger's latest views, see the posthumously published chapter, "L'expression du pouvoir suprême chez Tacite," in C. Nicolet, *Du Pouvoir dans l'Antiquité: Mots et Réalités* (Geneva, 1990) 181-205, particularly 181-183.
30. E. Kornemann, *Tacitus* (Wiesbaden, 1947) 26.
31. Tacitus, *Hist.* 4.42.6.
32. R. Syme, *Tacitus* 117.
33. *Ibid.* 219. For another possible reason for Tacitus' resentment of Trajan, see R.G. Tanner, "Tacitus and the Principate," *G&R* 16 (1969) 95-99.
34. Tacitus, *Ann.* 4.32.2.

CYBELE UND ATTIS IM ALL:
ZUR PATERA VON PARABIAGO

Erika Simon
Archäologisches Institut der Universität Würzburg

Der grosse Silberteller, der als Patera von Parabiago in die Literatur eingegangen ist, wurde 1907 unweit von Mailand gefunden (Abb. 9).[1] Er hatte in der bei dem Ort Parabiago gelegenen Nekropole als Deckel einer Aschenurne gedient. Da er relativ spät und ohne Beifunde publiziert wurde, hielt man ihn zunächst für ein Werk antoninischer Zeit. Andreas Alföldi hat ihm seinen Platz im spätantiken 4. Jahrhundert n. Chr. zugewiesen,[2] der heute von niemand mehr bestritten wird. Auf Ausstellungen spätantiker Kunst, etwa in New York oder in Frankfurt, ist das in der Soprintendenza alle Antichità della Lombardia aufbewahrte Werk jeweils ein Glanzstück gewesen.[3] Seine Erforschung wurde vor allem durch Luisa Musso gefördert (Anm. 1). Jedoch die Beschreibung des besten Kenners des Cybelekultes, des holländischen Kollegen Marten J. Vermaseren,[4] befriedigt nicht, ganz abgesehen davon, dass er die verfehlte Frühdatierung übernommen hat. Im Herbst 1988, als wir uns persönlich kennenlernten, lieber Alexander McKay, sprachen wir des längeren über die Göttin Cybele. So machen Ihnen vielleicht die folgenden Ausführungen zum Geburtstag Freude, zumal Ihr Lieblingsdichter Vergil die Göttermutter mit grossem Respekt geschildert hat.[5]

Vermaseren bezeichnet die Fahrt der Göttin auf der Löwenquadriga zu Recht als *a cosmic journey*.[6] Er schreibt: *She is going from East to West (ab Oriente ad Occidentem)*. Das ist in der Tat durch die Himmelserscheinungen im oberen Teil der Patera—Sol mit dem Morgenstern und Luna mit dem Abendstern—

angedeutet. Den äussersten Westen der antiken Welt symbolisiert zudem der den Tierkreis emporstemmende "Atlant." Er verkörpert auf sehr originelle Art das Atlasmassiv, auf dem das Himmelsgewölbe ruht, ist also wirklich Atlas. Wenn Vermaseren in seiner Beschreibung jedoch fortfährt: *At the same time she starts from the side of light and life on her way to darkness and death*, so möchte ich dem widersprechen. Die Fahrt der Cybele vollzieht sich nämlich nicht einfach linear, sondern Attis und die Göttin kreisen im Kosmos, im All. Diese Tatsache wird dem Betrachter durch die gesamte Rundkomposition wie durch manches Detail klargemacht. Hier nur sieben Beobachtungen dazu, die sich wohl leicht vermehren liessen:

1. Die brüllenden Löwen des Viergespanns sind im Wenden begriffen. Die Köpfe des ersten und des dritten Löwen von links sind uns nämlich zugewandt, was gegen ein lineares Dahinsprengen spricht.
2. Weiter rechts im Bild steht eine Wendesäule (*meta*), wie sie aus dem römischen Circus bekannt ist. Sie signalisierte dem antiken Betrachter die Rennbahn, und das um so mehr, als auf der Spina im Circus Maximus in Rom Cybele präsent war.[7]
3. Die drei Trabanten der Cybele, die Korybanten, führen ihren Waffentanz im Kreis um deren Wagen auf. Der linke stürzt aus der Tiefe nach vorn, der rechte bewegt sich in das Bild hinein, hinter der Quadriga tanzt der dritte.
4. Die Spiralwindung der Schlange an der Meta allegorisiert die zyklische Bewegung der Zeit.[8]
5. Entsprechendes gilt für den von Atlas gestützten Zodiacus, in dem Aion erscheint, der Gott des ewigen Kreislaufs der Jahreszeiten und Gestirne, in dem sich Zeit manifestiert.[9]
6. Die Abfolge der vier die Jahreszeiten verkörpernden Putten unterhalb des Gespanns ist merkwürdig. Es sind von links nach rechts: Sommer, Herbst, Frühling und Winter, alle in tänzerischer Bewegung. Denkt man sie sich im Kreistanz, mit Sommer und Frühling in der einen, Herbst und Winter in der anderen Ebene, so "stimmt" die Abfolge.
7. Die Konnotation "Kreis" ist schliesslich gegeben, wenn wir den aus dem "fischreichen Meer" auftauchenden Wassergott[10] Oceanus nennen. Er war nämlich der Ringstrom, der die Erde umgab.

Die bisherigen Interpreten des Silbertellers betonen immer wieder, dass auf ihm alles in Bewegung sei. Das ist richtig, doch man sollte nach obigen Feststellungen hinzufügen: in kreisender Bewegung. Selbst die rechts unten lagernde Tellus, eine Erscheinungsform der Cybele, ist davon nicht unberührt. Um ihr Füllhorn windet sich eine Schlange, die mit der Schlange an der Meta darüber zusammenzusehen ist. Zwei weitere Tiersymbole sind zwischen Atlas und Tellus angebracht: Zikade (Tettix) und Eidechse (Sauros). Beide stehen wohl für die heisseste Stunde der Sonne am Mittag,[11] die Stunde des Pan. Gemeint ist zudem ein Mittag im Sommerhalbjahr, denn dessen Sternbilder sind auf dem Tierkreis zu sehen, von oben nach unten: Aries, Taurus, Gemini, Cancer, Leo, Virgo.

Neben dem Prinzip der kreisenden Zeit, das in der geschilderten Weise in der Rundkomposition zum Ausdruck kommt, steht das Prinzip der Genealogie. Es wurde bisher so wenig wie die zyklische Zeitbewegung auf der Patera beachtet. Neben Oceanus ragt in der Tiefe dessen Gemahlin Tethys bis unterhalb der Brust aus dem Wasser hervor. Links davon lagert ein Flussgott mit Schilf und Urne,[12] an seiner Seite, als tauche sie wie Tethys auf, eine Nymphe mit Blüte. Diese Gruppe verkörpert nicht einfach das Süsswasser gegenüber dem Meer, wie angenommen wurde. Wie im Falle des Berggottes Atlas ist ein konkreter Name zu suchen. Atlas erscheint im Westen, der Flussgott im Osten, im Heimatland der Cybele. Er ist Sangarius, der Hauptstrom Phrygiens, Sohn des Oceanus und der Tethys (Hesiod, *Theogonie* 344). Die Nymphe ist seine Tochter Nana, die einen anatolischen Lallnamen trägt; er bedeutet "Mutter," und Nana, eine Erscheinungsform der Cybele wie Tellus gegenüber, gebar den Attis.[13] Dessen Abstammung von Oceanus und Sangarius her ist also auf der Patera eindrucksvoll Bild geworden.

Attis lenkt an der Seite der Cybele die vier Löwen. Ihre Zügel führen zu seiner Linken hin, die das grosse Pedum hält.[14] Die Rechte umfasst die ihm heilige Syrinx, ein Instrument auch des Pan, den bereits Pindar Diener und "Hund" der Göttermutter nannte.[15] Wie man noch nicht gesehen hat, ist Pan, der spätantike Allgott, in der Darstellung der Patera impliziert: Unterhalb des Sitzes der Cybele ist am Wagen ein Relief angebracht, das eine lang gewandete Laufende zeigt. Man hielt sie für Victoria oder für eine Mänade.[16] Sie gleicht jedoch einer entsetzt Fliehenden. Man könnte an Daphne denken, doch ist dieser apollinische Mythos am Gefährt der Göttermutter wenig am Platze. Die Zweige, die an der Seite und aus ihren Armen entspringen, weisen mehr auf einen Nadelbaum. Daher möchte ich für Pitys, die Nymphe der Pinie, plädieren.[17] Sie wurde von dem verliebten Pan verfolgt, dem sie sich durch die Metamorphose in jenen Baum entzog. Auf der zweiten Wange des Wagens, an der Seite des Attis, dürfen wir also in Gedanken Pan ergänzen.

Die Pinie war nichts Geringeres als der Baum des Attis. In vielen Darstellungen lehnt er an ihr. Ihm diente die Priesterschaft der Dendrophoren, der Träger des Baumes, den man als Pinie verstehen muss.[18] Pinienkerne dienten wohl als heilige Speise im Kult der Cybele und des Attis. Nun liegen auf dem Schoss der Göttermutter auf der Patera von Parabiago mehrere amorphe Gegenstände, die nicht einfach Früchte sein können.[19] Es handelt sich wahrscheinlich um Teile eines Pinienzapfens, der auseinandergenommen wurde, um die Kerne herauszulösen. Damit ist ausgesagt, dass Cybele und ihr Parhedros das Kultmahl bereits eingenommen haben, dass sie dadurch um so enger verbunden sind.[20]

Die grosse Göttin hat ihrem Sohn und Geliebten die Zügel anvertraut, ein altes Symbol für Herrschaft wie der Hirtenstab. Da er diesen gleichzeitig mit den Zügeln hält, verstärkt sich die Symbolik. Der Einwand, in der Realität sei das nicht möglich, verfängt hier nicht. Das Ideelle ist in diesem spätantiken Werk sehr viel stärker als das Reale. Es sind aber, wie wir sahen, keine beliebigen Ideen, sondern solche, die zu Kult und Mythos der Cybele in Beziehung stehen. Von ihr ist Attis in jener Spätzeit untrennbar, während man ihn in den keinesfalls seltenen Erwähnungen der Göttermutter bei Vergil nicht findet.[21] Dagegen kann Macrobius, ein spätantiker Bewunderer Vergils und wohl Zeitgenosse des Künstlers, der die Patera von Parabiago schuf, die eine Gestalt nicht ohne die andere denken. "Wer bezweifelt," so schreibt er (*Saturnalia* 1.21.7ff.), "dass die Göttermutter mit der Erde gleichzusetzen ist?" Die Löwen, mit denen sie fährt, seien die Luft *qui vehit terram*. Attis aber sei die Sonne. Es folgt eine allegorische Auslegung der beiden Attribute, die er auch auf der Patera trägt, Hirtenflöte und—stab (*fistula et virga*). An einer späteren Stelle (1.22.4) kann Pan, weil er dieselben Attribute trägt, ebenfalls zu Sonne werden.

Von solchen spätantiken Auslegungen her versteht man besser die Luftfahrt des Paares auf der Löwenquadriga sowie die Anwesenheit von Sol und Tellus, Erscheinungsformen des Attis und der Cybele. Man versteht auch, dass die Beziehung zwischen Pan und Sol über Attis und dessen Attribute läuft. Anderseits verleiht die Darstellung auf der Patera den trockenen

Ausführungen des Macrobius Leben: Himmel, Erde und Meer sind zum Ruhm der Cybele aufgeboten, das heisst das All, das der Gott Pan allegorisiert. In dessen Stunde, zur heissen Mittagszeit, wenn die Zikade lärmt, ziehen sie vier feurige Löwen, Allegorien der Lüfte, auf der gewaltigen Kreisbahn. An der Wendemarke im Westen, der Meta mit der Schlange, kehrt sie bei Nacht zum Osten zurück, um wie Sol aufs neue von dort zu starten. Der Vergleich mit dem Sonnengott ist deshalb angebracht, weil ihr Wagenlenker Attis in der Spätantike mit ihm identisch war.

Als Erdmutter ist Cybele die Spenderin der Früchte, die ihre kleinen Söhne, die vier Jahreszeiten, tragen. Turmkrone und Zepter der Göttin auf dem Löwenwagen kennzeichnen sie zudem als Gründerin und Königin der Städte. Vergil hat an einer berühmten Stelle die Stadtgöttin Roma mit Cybele verglichen (*Aeneis* 6.784f.):

qualis Berecyntia mater
invehitur curru Phrygias turrita per urbes.

Servius, dessen Vergilkommentar in die gleiche Epoche gehört wie die Patera von Parabiago, bemerkt dazu, das Gleichnis sage nichts anderes aus, als dass die *duces Romani* unter die Götter zu rechnen seien. Zu jenen *duces* gehörte auch Kaiser Julianus Apostata, ein glühender Verehrer der Göttermutter zu einer Zeit, als das Christentum schon Staatsreligion war.[22] Das Bild des Silbertellers kann vielleicht zum Verständnis jener merkwürdigen Vorliebe des Kaisers beitragen. Attis, Wagenlenker der Cybele, identisch mit dem Sonnengott, bot ihm eine Möglichkeit zur Identifikation. Es ist gewiss kein Zufall, dass die beiden Lobreden des Julian auf Gottheiten der Göttermutter und dem Sonnengott gelten.

ANMERKUNGEN

1. A. Levi, *La Patera d'argento di Parabiago. Opere d'Arte* V (Rom, 1935); W.F. Volbach/M. Hirmer, *Frühchristliche Kunst* (München, 1958) 64 Taf. 107; L. Musso, *Manifattura suntuaria e commitenza pagana nella Roma del IV secolo. Indagine sulla lanx di Parabiago* (1983); *LIMC* 3 (1986) s.v. Attis Nr. 422—Durchmesser 39 cm; Gewicht 3, 5 kg.
2. A. Alföldi, *Atlantis* 21 (1949) 69ff. Etwas früher Musso (Anm.1): 350 n. Chr.

3. K. Weitzmann (Herausgeber), *Age of Spirituality*. Ausstellung New York, Metropolitan Museum of Art (Princeton, 1979) 185f. Nr. 164 (K.J. Shelton); Ausstellungskatalog "Spätantike und frühes Christentum," Frankfurt am Main, Liebieghaus 1983, 530ff. Nr. 138 (D. Stutzinger).

4. M.J. Vermaseren, *The Legend of Attis in Greek and Roman Art* (Leiden, 1966) 27ff. Taf. 17.

5. Cf. R.M. Wilhelm, "Cybele: The Great Mother of Augustan Order," *Vergilius* 34 (1989) 77-101.

6. Vermaseren (oben Anm. 4) 29 f. Anm. 4.

7. Cf. E. Nash, *Bildlexikon zur Topographie des antiken Rom II* (Tübingen, 1962) 32 f. s.v. *Magna Mater in Circo Maximo*.

8. Das Bildschema erinnert an Darstellungen des Aion, der in gleicher Weise von den Windungen einer Schlange umgeben ist: *LIMC* I (1981) 403ff. Nr. 17.21 und öfter s.v. *Aion* (M. Le Glay); vgl. ebendort Nr. 20 Taf. 315 (Detail aus der Patera von Parabiago) Dadurch, dass die Schlange unmittelbar neben dem im Tierkreis stehenden Aion auftritt, ist die Beziehung zueinander gar nicht zu übersehen. Unverständlich ist mir die Deutung der Meta mit der Schlange als *tree of Life* bei Vermaseren (oben Anm. 4) 29, ebenso unverständlich, dass Le Glay (ebendort 404 zu Nr. 20) von einer *date discutée: IIè ou IVè s. ap. J.-C.* schreibt. Die Frühdatierung der Patera von Parabiago ist aufzugeben.

9. Dazu Le Glay (Vorige Anm.) 399ff.

10. Vermaseren nennt ihn (oben Anm. 4) unzutreffend Triton. Ein solcher müsste Pferdevorderbeine haben. Stutzinger (oben. Anm. 3) nennt ihn Neptun, Shelton (oben Anm. 3) zutreffend Oceanus. Dafür sprechen die Krebsscheren in seinem Haar, die bei Neptunus nicht vorkommen. Schliesslich ist Oceanus aus genealogischen Gründen nötig, wie unten weiter ausgeführt wird.

11. Zur Eidechse als spätantikes Sonnensymbol: *RE* II A 1 (1921) 262f. 265 s.v. *Sauroktonos* und *Sauros*, mit den antiken Quellen (J. Zwicker). Zur Zikade: *RE* V A 1 (1934) 1113ff. s.v. *Tettix*.

12. Er wurde leider von A. Levi (oben Anm. 1) 11 *ninfa fluviale* genannt, was sich bis auf Vermaseren ausgewirkt hat. Die anderen Autoren sprechen zutreffend von einem Flussgott. Zur Ikonographie der Flussgötter: *LIMC* IV (1988) 139ff. s.v. *Fluvii* (C. Weiss).

13. Cf. *RE* XVI 2 (1935) 1672 s.v. *Nana* 1 (F. Schwenn).

14. Das wurde bereits von A. Levi (oben Anm. 1) 8 beobachtet: *regendo le redini della sua quadriga leonina.* aber später kaum mehr beschrieben. Am Original wie in guten Detailaufnahmen (Levi Taf. 3,1) sind die fein ziselierten, ursprünglich vergoldeten Zügel alle vier zu sehen. Eine Rekonstruktion der Vergoldung auch an den anderen Stellen bringt Levi auf Taf. 2.

15. Pindar frg. 95.96 (Snell). Bildliche Überlieferung: E. Simon, *Opfernde Götter* (Berlin, 1953) 81.
16. Victoria: Levi (oben Anm. 1) 6.—Mänade: Vermaseren (oben Anm. 4) 28.—Mänadenähnlich: Stutzinger (oben Anm. 3) 530.
17. Cf. *RE* XX 2 (1950) 1881f. s.v. *Pitys* 2 (R. Hanslik). Diese Baumverwandlung steht nicht in Ovids Metamorphosen, weshalb sie weniger bekannt ist, begegnet aber häufig in den ebendort gesammelten späteren Quellen, bis hin zu Nonnos. Sie ist m.E. auch in dem bisher unzutreffend gedeuteten Mosaik in Neapel, Mus. Naz. Inv. 27708 aus Slg. Farnese gemeint: R. Herbig, *Pan* (Frankfurt, 1949) 29 Taf. 29, 3; L. Marini, *Il Gabinetto Segreto del Museo Nazionale di Napoli* (Turin, 1971) Abb. S. 101; *Le collezioni del Museo Nazionale di Napoli* (1986) 122f. Das spätantike, wohl stark ergänzte Mosaik wird als "Pan und die Rebe" (Herbig) oder Pan mit Nymphe oder Hamadryade gedeutet. Der Baum, in den die Frau sich verwandelt, hat jedoch die Form einer Pinie, mit den angeblichen Trauben dürften Pinienzapfen gemeint sein; sie sind wohl auch zum Teil modern ergänzt. Zu Pan als Allgott: Herbig ebendort 63ff.
18. Attis und Pinie: *LIMC* III (1986) 27f. s.v. *Attis* (M.J. Vermaseren/ M.B. De Boer). Bei Ovid, *Metamorphosen* 10, 104 f. verwandelt er sich selbst in diesen Baum—die Sage von Pan und Pitys fehlt dort, wie erwähnt (Anm. 17). Pinie als Weihgeschenk für Attis: Helbig[4] IV nr. 3007 g (E. Simon). Quellen zur Dendrophorie am Fest der Mater Magna: A. Degrassi, *Inscriptiones Italiae XIII: Fasti* (1963) 428f. Es handelt sich um den 22. März, den Tag, der *arbor intrat* genannt wurde. Mit diesem Baum ist nach den ebendort im Wortlaut zitierten Stellen immer die Pinie (*pitys, pinus*) gemeint.
19. A. Levi (oben Anm. 1) 16 mit Abb. 10 auf S. 18 (beste Detailaufnahme) glaubt, es handelt sich einfach um Falten des Mantels der Cybele, die vergoldet waren: *assumono oggi la strana apparenza di un oggetto*. Die Vergoldung hätte aber dieses Objekt mit den merkwürdigen Kerben keinesfalls verdecken können. Eben diese Kerben nun besitzt der Pinienzapfen.
20. Man denke an die Sage von Hades und Persephone. Sie war mit ihm von dem Zeitpunkt an vermählt, an dem sie den Granatapfelkern gegessen hatte: *Hom. hym.* in Dem. (III) 371ff., 393ff.
21. Cf. die Behandlung der Stellen durch R.M. Wilhelm (oben. Anm. 5). Man nimmt an, dass Kaiser Claudius im Cybelekult auf dem Palatin den vorher dort kaum beachteten Attis stärker herausstellen liess; cf. Quellen bei Degrassi (oben. Anm. 18). Auch wenn einige Attisterrakotten aus dem palatinischen Heiligtum früher sein sollten, so spricht das nicht gegen diese Annahme— Vergil ist als Zeuge hier wichtiger. Im übrigen bleiben die neuen archäologischen Untersuchungen an jenem Heiligtum abzuwarten.

Vorbericht: P. Pensabene, *Quaderni del Centro di studio per l'archeologia etrusco-italica* 16 *Archeologia Laziale* 9 (1988) 54ff.

22. Cf. Iulianus Apostata, *Orationes* 4 (auf König Helios) und 5 (an die Göttermutter). Die letztere ist auf 361, die Heliosrede auf 362 n. Chr. zu datieren; cf. *KlPauly* 2 (München 1975) 1517 s.v. *Iulianus* (R. Hanslik).

PRAYER AND THE LIVING EMPEROR

Duncan Fishwick
University of Alberta

In a recent paper S.R.F. Price has argued that, contrary to the standard view, prayers had a prominent place in the ideology of the Imperial cult.[1] By prayers he means petitions asked of the emperor as of a god: "I want to argue that personal prayers were indeed made to the emperor living and dead." The topic raises a complex of problems that require analysis, Price stresses, from the point of view of theory and practice as attested by both the literary and the epigraphical sources. Suffice it to say here that there seems a distinct possibility that in popular belief, of which the poets frequently offer the most authentic reflection,[2] the deified emperor was thought capable of effective deity: in other words, men believed he could hear and answer prayers.[3] But such is hardly the case with the living emperor—not, that is, if we except one or two possible cases in Egyptian practice.

The following discussion concerns a number of literary passages that bear particularly on the question of prayers addressed to the emperor in his lifetime. The analysis to be developed will try to show that, first impressions to the contrary, none of these texts provides firm testimony to any clear belief in the living emperor as a god that could be approached in prayer. The essay is offered as a token of esteem and respect for a colleague who has himself made a distinguished contribution to our knowledge of Roman life and letters.

In a poem written ca. 14/13 B.C., when Augustus was about to return from Spain, Horace describes the blessings of peace brought by the emperor, how the countryman returns home glad of heart from his vineyard:[4]

> hinc ad vina redit laetus et alteris
> te mensis adhibet deum;
> te multa prece, te prosequitur mero
> defuso pateris et Laribus tuum
> miscet numen, uti Graecia Castoris
> et magni memor Herculis
>
> Odes 4.5.31-36

For the actual practice that lies behind the rites Horace describes the clearest evidence is provided by Petronius, *Cena Trimalchionis* 60.7: *rati ergo sacrum esse fer[i]culum tam religioso apparatu perfusum consurreximus altius et "Augusto, patri patriae," feliciter diximus*. Here the libation and the accompanying form of words come before the dessert, as also does the veneration of the Lares (60.8), whereas in Horace everything takes place at the second course *(alteris mensis)*; that this was the more normal sequence is confirmed by Servius: *apud Romanos etiam cena edita sublatisque mensis primis silentium fieri solebat, quoad ea quae de cena libata fuerant ad focum ferrentur et in ignem darentur . . . (ad Aen.* 1.730).[5] One may compare the formula given in Ovid, *Fasti* 2.637f., where Augustus is hailed in concert with the Lares:

> et bene vos, bene te, patriae pater, optime Caesar
> dicite suffuso per sacra verba mero.

What is clear from the above is that the formula behind Horace's *multa prece* was in the nature of a toast or an acclamation,[6] not a prayer addressed to the emperor, who as *pater patriae* was certainly not a god. As for *tuum numen*, the reference here is surely to the *genius* of the emperor. Dio reports that by a decree of the senate passed in 30 B.C. libations were henceforth to be poured to the *princeps* at all banquets public and private (51.19.7). What Dio actually says is that the libation was to Augustus himself;[7] but an honour that would have been in the same category as altars and shrines[8] is surely out of the question in 30 B.C., particularly on the part of the senate, and comparison with the Hellenistic custom of pouring a libation to the ruler's *daimon* at mealtimes[9] strongly suggests that, while the accompanying words were addressed to the emperor, the offering itself was strictly speaking to the *Genius Augusti*.[10] The Horace passage is therefore good evidence for the intrusion of the *Genius Augusti* into the private cult of the Roman household,[11] where its association with the Lares anticipates and points the way for the cult of the *Lares Augusti* at the crossroads of the Roman *vici*. In graphic confirmation of this, a wall painting from a private house at Pompeii shows a *genius* clad in a toga and holding a cornucopia as he pours a libation upon a lighted, cylindrical altar; below is a graffito *EX S C* (*CIL* 4.5285).[12] That the emperor's *genius* should be termed *numen*—that is, a divinity in the developed sense the word had acquired by metonymy—is by no means uncommon. The usage is particularly well illustrated by Ovid's reference to the *Lares Augusti* at the crossroads of Rome—the *Genius Augusti* with the two Lares Compitales—as *numina trina* (*Fasti* 5.145f.). The alternative view, that the reference could be to the emperor's immanent *numen*,[13] is surely unlikely when the altar of the *Numen Augusti*, the point of departure of this particular concept, was not dedicated until ca. A.D. 6 at the earliest.[14] The fact that Horace employs the term *numen* may nevertheless be an indication that the word was already associated with the emperor by the date the poem was composed.

The ritual at table, as described by Horace, emerges therefore with reasonable clarity. Along with offerings of food to the Lares—figures of these were set upon the table, usually at the second course—one now poured a libation to the emperor's *genius* with an accompanying expression of good will for his welfare, a formula that was akin to a toast. The entire procedure is well within the bounds of Republican practice and nothing goes to show that the countryman thought of the emperor as a "real" god, who could be called on in petitionary prayer. The interesting thing for the modern commentator is that in portraying this domestic scene the poet makes unrestrained use of charismatic imagery. Skillfully indulging his licence, he calls him *deus* and portrays him as the object of 'prayer' and libations of pure wine and associates his *numen* with the household gods. All of which is very much in contrast to the cautious outlook of official pronouncements on the cult of the emperor. That Horace had no inhibitions in writing as he did, suggests that, like other Augustan literary figures, he acted as the mouthpiece of an unofficial policy that was ready to turn a blind eye to open profession of the emperor's divinity when decently clothed in poetic garb.

As might be expected, several allusions to prayer in Ovid bear directly on the problem. In *Tristia* 3.8.13f., composed in A.D. 9-10, the poet says:

> *si semel optandum est, Augusti numen adora,*
> *et, quem sensisti, rite precare deum.*

The advice the poet gives himself is to adore the divine power of the emperor which had been officially recognised as a minor deity immanent within him by Tiberius' dedication of the *Ara Numinis Augusti* ca. A.D. 6.[15] Clearly Ovid is not saying that Augustus himself should be adored as a god. To address prayers to the emperor's *numen* would be theologically sound, an idea that seems to be taken up by *rite* (line 14), but the poet then slides from the *numen* of the emperor to the emperor himself, whom he calls *deus*.[16] The distinction between the emperor and the *numen* within him must have been even more precarious than that between the emperor and his accompanying *genius*, but clearly Ovid's imagination is given full reign here since he goes on to claim that Augustus can grant feathers and winged cars (lines 15f). In this context, then, it is difficult to think that the remainder of the exile's "prayer"[17] is evidence for a petitionary prayer to Augustus *ut deo*. What the passage presents is a combination of sound theology with metaphor.

In a similar passage composed A.D. 11-12 the poet turns to the emperor as an absent suppliant addressing an absent deity:

> *Adloquor en absens absentia numina supplex*
> *si fas est homini cum Iove posse loqui.*
> Tristia 5.2.45-46

The verb used is *adloqui / loqui* and Augustus is called Jupiter, but Ovid stresses that he wants him to dwell on earth and to be late in passing to the promised stars (lines 51f.). Despite the Jovian imagery, the so-called "suppliant's prayer" (lines 45-78), is clearly an entreaty to a human being for pardon, not a prayer to a god. Ovid abjectly supplicates the emperor on the grounds that he has been and might continue to be merciful. One might compare perhaps the use of the word *propitius* in the formula *habeas propitium Caesarem*:[18] though scarcely implying effective divinity the word hints in that direction inasmuch as the word is used of gods (*di propitii*). In the same way here Ovid asks mercy of the emperor in language appropriate to a deity.[19]

Thirdly, we have two poems in which Ovid makes ostentatious show of his *pietas* to the imperial house. The first, written ca. A.D. 12-13, is addressed to Cotta Maximus, from whom the poet had received what were evidently silver statuettes of Augustus,

Tiberius and Livia (*Ex Ponto* 2.8.1-4).[20] Ovid refers to these as rough metal now divine, heaven-sent, gods, public divinities (lines 2, 5-9, 52, 67). Gazing on them, he can imagine that the imperial three are present and can speak in person *quasi cum vero numine* (lines 9f.). In the same vein he asks that the divinity of Tiberius should not be hostile to his prayer (line 38) and calls upon the kind deities (Augustus and his family) to give it assent (line 51, cf. 10, 58). What that prayer amounted to was a plea to be returned from exile (lines 25-36), an abject supplication to the emperor by the name of Rome, by his wife Livia, by Tiberius his son, by his grandsons Germanicus and Drusus[21]—and by gods who are never deaf to the emperor's prayers (*per numquam surdos in tua vota deos*: line 28). Despite the elaborate metaphor of divinity which Ovid applies to Augustus and the Imperial family throughout, it is clear that the poet still distinguishes them from "real" gods. His entreaty is to a human emperor and his kin (cf. lines 43ff.), not to gods who might hear and respond in a divine way. More particularly, there is nothing here to show that Ovid addresses prayers to the statuettes *ut deis*. On the contrary, he refers to these as the faces and figures which art has given (line 60), images (*figura*) that should not be kept in a hateful place (line 64), his eagles, his standards (line 70).

This interpretation is surely confirmed by a later poem, probably dated to early A.D. 16, in which Ovid says that in his house is a shrine where stand Augustus, Tiberius and Livia—deities no less important than Augustus now that he has been made a god (*numina iam facto non leviora deo*: line 108)—along with both the grandsons, Germanicus and Drusus (*Ex Ponto* 4.9.105-110). Every day at dawn he performs rites before these: which presumably implies this had been his practice since he received the statuettes three years or so earlier.

> *His ego do totiens cum ture precantia verba,*
> *Eoo quotiens surgit ab orbe dies.*
> 4.9.111-112

If Ovid has followed standard Roman practice, which is surely to be expected, the place where he keeps the statuettes must be the household Lararium, where they will have stood beside figures of the Lares or before paintings of the Lares on the backwall of the *aedicula*.[22] Parallels can be adduced without difficulty. Suetonius reports that L. Vitellius paid cult (*coluit*) to gold images of Narcissus and Pallas among his Lares (*Vitell.* 2.5), Hadrian to a bronze likeness of the boy Augustus—a gift from Suetonius—which the emperor placed in his Lararium (*Aug.* 7.1). Marcus Aurelius set likenesses of his teachers among the Lares (SHA, *Marc. Anton.* 3.5), and images of Marcus himself were preserved among the household gods in the lifetime of the author of the Vita (SHA, *Marc.* 18.5f.). Again, Alexander Severus is said to have performed rites every day at his *lararium maius*, where were kept the images of the best of the deified emperors along with those of Apollonius of Tyana, Christ, Abraham, Orpheus, Alexander the Great and other great men (SHA, *Sev. Alex.* 29.2, 31.5). Even if false,[23] the tale is surely significant fiction to the extent that it reflects contemporary practice. For Ovid to have placed imperial figurines within his Lararium would also be in direct line with the policy of Augustus, who had stressed the importance of the Lares by joining the figure of his *genius* (in practice an image of Augustus himself) with the Lares Compitales (above, p. 344f.). Ovid's household shrine would thus have become a repository where the statuettes were housed as objects of veneration.

As for the rites Ovid describes, these fit the picture exactly, for it was at the Lararium that the master of the house addressed a prayer each morning to the household gods[24] and offered sacrifice at least once a month—notably incense but also fruits, grain or libations of wine, occasionally animal sacrifice.[25] In his attempt to impress—and he boasts that the whole land of Pontus will bear witness to his devotion—Ovid claims that he offers incense every day on the altar (before the *aedicula* of the Lares) and celebrates the *natalis* of the god, that is Augustus (lines 113-116). There is no mention of the Lares, but it would be reasonable to take *precantia verba* as the usual daily prayer to the Lares, to which no doubt Ovid joined a prayer for the welfare of the imperial family along the lines of his sentiments in *Ex Ponto* 2.8.45-50. *Mutatis mutandis* that would imply a certain similarity to the invocation which accompanied rites to the *genius* and the Lares at meals, Ovid's *sacra verba* (cf. above, p. 344). Whatever Ovid's precise words may have been, nothing goes to show that he addressed prayers to the statues as gods who might hear and answer. The figures in the Lararium are simply reminders, symbols of the imperial family, and one does not pray to symbols. The one qualification to be noted is that by the date of the poem Augustus was dead and had been made a state god by decree of the senate. As was observed at the outset, there is a real possibility that deceased emperors were believed open to prayer and that Ovid thought Divus Augustus, now admitted to the gods (line

127), could hear his prayer for forgiveness and would respond, a prophesy with which he ends the poem (lines 129-134). But the likeness in Ovid's Lararium is of the emperor as a man, not a god. It is not a cult idol,[26] nor were the figures reported to have stood in Lararia elsewhere.

For the Greek term εὐχή applied in a different sense to emperors than to gods, we can turn to a passage in the Roman oration of Aelius Aristides delivered at Rome in A.D. 143 (*Or.* 26, 32: Keil). At the mere mention of the emperor's name, he says, everyone stands up, praises (ὑμνεῖ) and reverences (σέβει) the emperor and utters a two-fold prayer, one to the gods on the ruler's behalf, the other to the ruler for his own affairs. As Oliver originally pointed out,[27] the change of preposition from ὑπέρ to περί implies a shift from the offering of a prayer appropriate to the gods to the negotiation of a request asked of a ruler.[28] That the word is employed both in its original and in an extended sense is to be explained by the fact that this is a rhetorical passage in which the orator deliberately uses language which exploits the ambiguous position of the emperor as a *Gottmensch*.

Just how far language of this sort could go is illustrated by a panegyric that Pacatus delivered to Theodosius before the senate in A.D. 389.[29]

Tibi istud soli pateat, imperator, cum deo consorte secretum; illud dicam quod intellexisse hominem et dixisse fas est: talem esse debere qui gentibus adoratur, cui toto orbe terrarum privata vel publica vota redduntur, a quo petit navigaturus serenum, peregrinaturus reditum, pugnaturus auspicium

Paneg. Lat. 12.6.4: Budé

In eulogizing him as adored by the people, the recipient of private and public vows made by the whole world, and even able to control the weather and grant favourable omens, Pacatus gives a definition of the qualities of the emperor that ascribes outright divine nature according to the criteria accepted in antiquity.[30] That it should be taken at face value, however, is surely unlikely. Pacatus had said of the emperor at the close of chapter 4: *deum dedit Hispania quem videmus*. The idea of the epiphany of the divine emperor is now elaborated in a passage that clearly belongs in a tradition of artificial, rhetorical exaggeration going back to Pliny,[31] whose panegyric on Trajan is in fact the first in this collection of Latin panegyrics, discovered by Aurispa at Mainz in A.D. 1433. There is obvious indebtedness to Pliny 4.4 in particular, where control of the elements and events is ascribed to the ideal emperor: *saepe ego mecum, patres conscripti, tacitus agitavi qualem quantumque esse oporteret, cuius dicione nutuque maria terraeque, pax bella regerentur.* Pacatus even produces a verbal echo of Pliny 5.1: *Talem esse oportuit quem non bella civilia, nec armis oppressa res publica, sed pax et adoptio et tandem exorata terris numina dedissent.*[32] To take Pacatus' eulogy as serious evidence for public belief in the divinity of the emperor in general or for prayers to him *ut deo* in particular is no more justified, then, than to infer from Pliny's exaggerations a contemporary belief in the power of the emperor to control the elements. Statements such as these are commonplace in imitative, mannered rhetoric,[33] not hard evidence for popular attitudes.[34] Significantly, the passage comes from a period when, as Nock emphasized, the imposition of Christian monotheism was accompanied by an intensification of the mystique surrounding the monarch.[35]

If none of the above passages provides indisputable evidence for prayers to the living emperor, such is hardly the case with a special category of testimonia that bear upon practice in Egypt. Here the situation is different from elsewhere in the Roman World in that the ruler of the time, as the descendant of the Pharaohs, was by definition the son of Amun-Re and could even be held a re-incarnation of Dionysus.[36] That the Roman emperor might consequently be deemed possessed of effective divinity is confirmed by Pliny, who states that at a time of drought the Egyptians invoked the aid of Caesar as they were wont to call upon the river—as a god, that is; no sooner had Caesar heard their appeals than their troubles were at an end: *Igitur inundatione, id est ubertate, regio fraudata sic opem Caesaris invocavit, ut solet amnem suum; nec longius illi adversorum fuit spatium quam dum nuntiat (Paneg.* 30.5). As a piece of panegyric, the statement might be suspect were it not that, from Pharaonic times down to the Ptolemies and Augustus, the king had been held responsible for the flooding of the Nile.[37] Much the same outlook, it may be suggested, could lie behind a puzzling passage in the *Metamorphoses* of Apuleius, who was himself a devotee of Isis (*Met.* 11.3-6; cf. *Apol.* 55f.).[38] Overcome by the burdens he has to carry in the shape of an ass, Lucius invokes the name of

Caesar. The effort was only partly successful (all he could manage was "O") but Lucius was nevertheless helped by the emperor, whom he calls *Iuppiter ille* (3.29).[39] In the end Isis restores him to human form. The episode seems to show Lucius addressing the emperor as a deity who can answer prayer, very much as the Egyptians called on him for help in the Pliny passage.[40]

Less problematical is a third piece of evidence, an assertion of Philo that the temple of Caesar Epibaterios at Alexandria—evidently the centre of the city cult of Augustus in its final form[41]—gave hope of safety to sailors when they set out to sea and returned (*Leg. ad Gai.* 22.151). The term *epibaterios*, as applied for instance to Zeus on his epiphany or to Demetrius Poliorcetes on his coming to Athens, had the connotation of felicitious arrival and the good fortune it brings; when used as a cult term, it implies that the deity is the protector of sea-farers and travellers.[42] Philo, a Jew, will hardly have invented the claim that the emperor could control the elements, and to his explicit statement on the belief associated with the temple[43] can be added the acclamation of Augustus in the bay of Puteoli by sea-farers from Alexandria, a formula that may echo ritual chants in the Augusteum there: *per illum se vivere, per illum navigare, libertate atque fortunis per illum frui* (Suet., *Aug.* 98.2).[44] What we have in sum, then, is clear evidence for prayer to Augustus as an effective deity both in his lifetime and *post mortem*. As with the above testimony, however, all this is very much in an Egyptian context. It has a parallel in an epigram of Posidippus saying that Arsinoe-Philadelphos-Aphrodite will grant safe sailing and a smooth sea for those who pray amid the storm (*Athen.* 318D), also in evidence that Arsinoe II was considered a god of saving after her death: in particular the hair-lock which Berenice II dedicated in the temple of Arsinoe-Zephyritis on behalf of her husband's safety in the Syrian Wars.[45] These are Egyptian ideas that go beyond the Roman notion that deceased rulers could hear prayers and render divine aid.

The Egyptian evidence apart, nothing of the above can reasonably be judged clear testimony to a firm belief in the divine efficacy of the living emperor. Certainly there are passages in the literary sources referring to prayers to the emperor but these reveal themselves as mere verbiage, inflated language that can be put down to poetic licence or rhetorical exaggeration.[46] Prayers to the deceased, more particularly to deified emperors such as Divus Augustus or Divus Marcus, are one thing but no living ruler was the object of prayers because no man could properly be called a god and addressed in prayer during his lifetime.[47] That surely was the essence of the complaint against Apollonius of Tyana, who is said to have been put on trial before the emperor Domitian: a charge that Apollonius answered by denying he had ever induced men by discourses or miracles to pray to him. If he was called a god, it was because he was thought to be good.[48]

NOTES

1. S.R.F. Price, "Gods and Emperors: The Greek Language of the Imperial Cult," *JHS* 104 (1984) 79-95 at 91-93.
2. F. Bömer, "Vergil und Augustus," *Gymnasium* 58 (1951) 33.
3. For discussion see D. Fishwick, "Ovid and Divus Augustus," *CPh* 86 (1991) 36-41; *id.*, "Prudentius and the Cult of Divus Augustus," *Historia* 39 (1990) 475-486.
4. The main lines of what looks the correct interpretation of these verses were laid down long ago by L.R. Taylor, *The Divinity of the Roman Emperor*, (Middletown, CT, 1931 [1981]) 182, 260.
5. L. Friedländer, *Petronii Cena Trimalchionis*, (Leipzig, 1906 [1960]) 312 *ad loc.*; G.C. Giardina, "*Augusto patri patriae feliciter*: Petronius 60.7," *Maia* 24 (1972) 67f.; M.S. Smith, *Petronii Arbitri Cena Trimalchionis* (Oxford, 1975) 168 *ad loc.*
6. Cf. *Gaio feliciter:* Petronius, *Cena Trimalch.* 50.1. A toast to Caesar (Domitian) seems implied in Martial, *Epig.* 9.93. On acclamations see in general E. Peterson, ΕΙΣ ΘΕΟΣ (Göttingen, 1926) 142ff. with later examples; Giardina, *op. cit.* 68.
7. Some scholars have taken him at his word, notably Weinstock in *RE* 23, 1 (1957) 823f. s.v. *propitius*; Smith, *op. cit.* (n. 5); E. Fraenkel, *Horace* (Oxford, 1957) 446f., makes no comment on the point but cites as a parallel Plut., *Marius* 27.9 (see further Val. Max. 8.15.7).
8. So Demochares on the honours paid by the Athenians to Demetrius Polyorcetes and his favourites. See K. Scott, "The Deification of Demetrius Poliorcetes," *AJP* 49 (1928) 137-166 at 150ff., citing Demochares *ap.* Athen. 6.252f.-253a.
9. For the use of σπένδειν with the dative of the deity to whom a libation is made see Liddell and Scott s.v. On the cups associated with the libation see V. von Gonzenbach, "Genius Augusti—Theos Sebastos," *Opuscula* (Stockholm Stud. in Cl. Phil.: Festschrift K. Kerényi) 5 (1968) 81-117.
10. D. Fishwick, "Genius and Numen" in *The Imperial Cult in the Latin West* (Leiden, 1991; *EPRO* 108) 2.1, 375f., nn. 1-2. The distinction between a man and his *genius* was inevitably a vanishing one and Dio is of course writing two and a half centuries or so after the event he reports.

11. *Ibid.* nn. 3-4, noting that in domestic cult twin Lares flank the *genius* of the *paterfamilias*, which now wears the *toga praetexta* appropriate to the *Genius Augusti*.
12. G.K. Boyce, *Corpus of the Lararia of Pompeii* (Rome, 1937; *MAAR* 14) 93 (n. 466) with refs.; A. Alföldi, *Die zwei Lorbeerbäume des Augustus* (Bonn, 1973; *Antiquitas* 14) 26, n. 108 with bibl.
13. S. Weinstock, *Divus Julius* (Oxford, 1971) 304, n. 3., cf. 213, n. 7.
14. Alföldi, *op. cit.* 43f.
15. *Ibid.* On the older view the altar was dedicated *ca.* A.D. 5 or 9.
16. For similar poetic license see *Ex Ponto* 3.1.162-164, where he encourages his wife to offer incense and unmixed wine to the great gods and of these to venerate above all Augustus (whom he calls *numen*), his offspring and his consort. See in general K. Scott, "Emperor Worship in Ovid," *TAPA* 61 (1930) 43-69, especially 58-63.
17. Cf. 11.17f.:
    si precer hoc—neque enim possum maiora rogare—
    ne mea sint, timeo, vota modesta parum.
    For similar uses of *preces* or *precare* see, for example, *Ex Ponto* 2.8.38, cf. 44; 4.8.21.
18. Weinstock, *op. cit.* 824-826.
19. See *Ex Ponto* 3.1.163-166, where Ovid associates Augustus, Tiberius and Livia with the gods and hopes that they may be kind (*mites*) to his wife in their accustomed fashion; cf. *Ex Ponto* 2.8.51, asking the *mitissima numina* (the Imperial family) to answer his timorous prayers.
20. On Cotta Maximus see R. Syme, *History in Ovid* (Oxford, 1978) 125-128.
21. Likenesses of Germanicus and Drusus are not said to have been sent by Cotta Maximus but they appear in Ovid's shrine in *Ex Ponto* 4.9.109f.
22. Daremberg-Saglio, *Dictionnaire* 3.2 (1904 [1963]) 937-949 at 947 (Hild); *RE* 12 (1924) 806-833 s.v. at 817 (Boehm). Cf. Boyce, *op. cit.*, 77 with pl. 31 (1 and 2). If the rites Ovid enjoins upon his wife (*Ex Ponto* 3.1.159-164) were to be performed at the altar before her *lararium*, it is possible that this likewise included figures of Augustus, Livia and their offspring.
23. So R. Syme, *Historia Augusta Papers* (Oxford, 1983) 72, 90, 214.
24. Cf. the prayer of Tibullus to the Lares: 1.10.15ff. For prayer formulae see in general Cato, *Agr.* CXLIII (134), CXLVIII (139), CL (141); cf. K. Latte, *Römische Religionsgeschichte* (Munich, 1967 [1976]; *Handb. d. Altertumswiss.* 5, 4) 47, 62, 206-208.
25. Plautus, *Rudens* 1206ff.; Ovid, *Fasti* 2.633f.; Horace, *Odes* 3.23.3f.; *Sat.* 2.3.164f., 5.12f.; Tib. 1.1.21f., 3.34, 10.26; Juvenal, *Sat.* 9.137f., 12.89f.; D.G. Orr, "Roman Domestic Religion: The Evidence of the Household Shrines," *ANRW* 2.16.2 (1978) 1557-1591 at 1567.

26. For the likelihood that a cult idol would have shown Augustus enthroned in the pose of Jupiter see D. Fishwick, "On the Temple of Divus Augustus," *Phoenix* 46 (1992) forthcoming.

27. J.H. Oliver, *The Ruling Power: A Study of the Roman Empire in the Second Century after Christ through the Roman Oration of Aelius Aristides* (Philadelphia, 1953; *Trans. Amer. Philosoph. Soc.*, 43) 918: G.W. Bowersock, "Greek Intellectuals and the Imperial Cult in the Second Century A.D.," in W. den Boer (ed.), *Le Culte des Souverains dans l'Empire romain* (Vandoevres-Geneva, 1972; Fondation Hardt Entretiens 19) 200f., citing a comparable passage in *Or.* 19.5 (Keil) in which Aristides distinguishes between prayers to the gods and requests of the godlike rulers. Cf. the implied distinction in the remark of Artemidorus that rulers, like gods, have the power to treat people well or badly (3.13). The view is rejected by Price, *op. cit.*, 93, n. 114.

28. For petitions laid at the foot of the emperor's statue see H.S. Versnel, "Religious Mentality in Ancient Prayer" in *id.* (ed.), *Faith, Hope and Worship* (Leiden, 1981; *Studies in Greek and Roman Religion* 2) 36.

29. *RE* 18 (1942) 2058-60 (Hanslik).

30. H.S. Versnel, "Heersercultus in Griekenland," *Lampas* 7 (1974) 153, n. 176 with bibl.

31. See in general J. Béranger, "L'expression de la divinité dans les Panegyriques Latins" in *id.*, *Principatus* (Geneva, 1973; Univ. de Lausanne, Publ. de la Fac. des Lettres) 429-444, especially 442ff.

32. For traces of other Classical authors in the speech, see Hanslik (above, n. 29) 2059 with refs., noting Pacatus' poverty of original ideas.

33. Cf. *Paneg.* 10 (2) 2.5: *Finguntur haec de Iove sed de te vera sunt, imperator*—a phrase that recalls the language of the Ithyphallikos sung by the Athenians to Demetrius Poliorcetes in 291 or 290 B.C. (Athenaeus 6.253 D-F).

34. See in general P. Herz, "Der römische Kaiser und der Kaiserkult. Gott oder primus inter pares?" in D. Zeller (ed.), *Menschwerdung Gottes—Vergöttlichung von Menschen* (Gottingen, 1988; *Novum Testamentum et Orbis Antiquus* 7) 137 with n. 68. Cf. the very practical outlook of the legate Bassus, who commanded Dasius to "venerate the feet of [the images of] our lords the emperors, who give us peace, give us our rations, and each day show concern for our every advantage": H. Musurillo, *The Acts of the Christian Martyrs*, (Oxford, 1972) 21.6 (276f.).

35. A.D. Nock, "Deification and Julian," *JRS* 47 (1957) 121 (= *id.*, *Essays on Religion and the Ancient World* [ed., Z. Stewart], Oxford, 1972, 844).

36. U. Wilcken, "Zur Entstehung des hellenistischen Königskultes," *Sonderausgabe Sitz. der Preuss. Akad. der Wiss.* 28 (1938) 13 (308); A. Henrichs, "Vespasian's Visit to Alexandria," *ZPE* 3 (1968) 58.
37. Henrichs, *op. cit.* 72-74 with refs.
38. See recently J.J. Winkler, *Auctor and Actor*, (Berkeley, 1985) 204ff. with bibl.
39. R.T. Van der Paardt, *L. Apuleius Madaurensis: The Metamorphoses III* (Amsterdam, 1971) 203-205.
40. Cf. S.R.F. Price, *Rituals and Power: The Roman Imperial Cult in Asia Minor* (Cambridge, 1984) 119. Contra M.P. Charlesworth, "Some Observations on Ruler-Cult especially in Rome," *HThR* 28 (1935) 36f., taking Lucius to invoke the *auxilium* of the emperor as an earthly governor.
41. The temple looks to have been originally dedicated by Cleopatra to Julius Caesar (see in particular CD 51.15.5 with Suet., *Aug.* 17), though Suidas (s.v. ἡμίεργον) refers it to Mark Antony. For discussion see P.M. Fraser, *Ptolemaic Alexandria* (Oxford, 1972) vol. 1.24 with n. 156; D. Fishwick, "The Temple of Caesar at Alexandria," *AJAH* 9 (1984, 1990) 131-134. *Contra,* H. Hänlein-Schäfer, *Veneratio Augusti* (Rome, 1985; *Archaeologica* 39) 203-219, following Suidas. See now D. Fishwick, "The Caesareum at Alexandria Again," *AJAH* 10 (1991) forthcoming.
42. E.M. Smallwood, *Philonis Alexandrini Legatio ad Gaium* (Leiden, 1961) 231f.; S. Weinstock, *Divus Julius* (Oxford, 1971) 297, nn. 6f., cf. 289, n. 8. The term could have been applied equally well to Julius or Octavian.
43. On Augustus as protector of shipping see J. Gagé, "Actiaca," *MEFR* 53 (1936) 90f. For a poetic allusion to Augustus as god of the sea *post mortem* see Vergil, *Georg.* 1.29-31. As a commonplace of panegyric, the idea occurs above, p. 349.
44. G. Rocca-Serra, "Une formule cultuelle chez Suétone (Divus Augustus, 98.2)," *Mélanges P. Boyancé* (Rome, 1974; *Coll. de l'École franç. de Rome* 22) 674-676.
45. See recently G. Nachtergael, "Berenice II, Arsinoe III et l'offrande de la boucle," *CE* 55 (1980) 240-253.
46. For pre-Roman examples of "prayers" to living rulers see Price, *op. cit.* (above, n. 1) 92, n. 110. For the view that such passages are to be explained as euphuistic language see Fishwick, *op. cit.* (above, n. 10), 1.1 (1987) 37f.
47. See now Hertz, *op. cit.* (above, n. 34) 138f.
48. Philostr., *VA* 8.7, 157 (310 Kayer), cf. 5, 152 (299); cited by Price, *op. cit.* (above, n. 1) 92, n. 113.

THE *OTHER* SPAS OF ANCIENT CAMPANIA[1]

George W. Houston
University of North Carolina at Chapel Hill

Readers of this volume will be familiar with ancient Baiae, the spectacular and fashionable resort of the late Republic and early Empire. Many will have toured the site under the expert guidance of Professor McKay or read about it in his *Ancient Campania*. Despite its fame (or notoriety) in antiquity, though, Baiae was not the only spa in Campania. There were many others, not as famous but probably more typical, and it is these *other* spas that I will consider in this article. Which of the mineral and thermal springs of Campania were known to the ancient Romans? How fully, if at all, were the springs developed, and who went to them? What did Romans *do* at their spas? In considering these questions, I hope both to extend our knowledge of this aspect of ancient social history and to provide something new for Sandy McKay to appreciate and enjoy, as thanks for all he has taught me about Campania and the Romans.

SOME GENERAL COMMENTS ON SPAS IN ROMAN TIMES

When we use the word "spa," we tend to think of an elaborate establishment: not just a spring of mineral or thermal water, but also buildings with baths, pools, and showers, places of entertainment (perhaps even a racetrack), and, in most cases, a hotel or inn of some sort. Much of this corresponds to what we know of Baiae, but we must not simply assume that it was true of all Roman spas. I therefore begin with a very general definition: a "spa" is any site where we find evidence indicating the use by the Romans of naturally occurring mineral or thermal water(s) for therapeutic purposes. I will also limit this study to those spas that were open to the public.

The Romans themselves were none too precise when talking about such sites. There was in Latin no specific word the exact equivalent of our "spa" in its developed sense. In general, mineral springs were referred to simply as *aquae*, and we know of dozens of towns called Aquae this or Aquae that, their names deriving from their springs.[2] If you said someone was at a spa, you used not a word for spa, but a phrase almost exactly equivalent to the English "taking the waters": *ad* or *apud aquas esse* or *venire* (Cic., *Planc.* 65; *ad Fam.* 16.24.2; *ad Att.* 14.12.2).

Roman medical writers were well aware that certain waters had distinctive qualities. Galen, for example, distinguishes between waters containing sulphur, bitumen, soda, copper sulphate, and traces of other minerals (11.392K). So also Pliny the Elder: sulphur waters are good for nerves and tendons *(nervi)*, water with alum for paralysis, and waters with bitumen or alum as a laxative (*HN* 31.59). Certain waters were recognized as beneficial in curing infertility (*Ibid.* 31.8, 31.10), in treating gallstones (*Ibid.* 31.9), in treating psoriasis (*Ibid.* 31.11), and in a great variety of other ailments.

Doctors, or those in the know, recommended various ways of using the waters. Most often, you were to drink or immerse yourself in the water, or both (so, for example, in Caelius Aurelianus, *Chron. Dis.* 2.48, 5.77; Strabo, 5.3.1; Plin., *HN* 31.9), and it is possible that the immersion might occasionally involve a kind of shower (Hor., *Epist.* 1.15.8). Sometimes, to induce sweating, you would go into an enclosed area which was filled with hot vapors that emerged from the earth (Celsus, *De med.* 2.17.1; Sen., *Epist.* 51.6).

Several aspects of life at a spa are represented on a silver plate from Spain, perhaps the only surviving ancient picture of a spa (Plate 10).[3] The name of the spring is written around the edge: *Salus Umeritana*. At the top, the nymph, *Salus*, is stretched out beneath the shade of two trees. Water flows from her urn into a sort of tank. Next to the tank, one man is decanting spring water into a jug, and at the bottom another is filling a wooden barrel with water. Clearly, the water was a commodity which could be sold, and it was valued highly enough to warrant its being carted off for some distance. At the top right is a man holding a walking stick and wearing a short tunic: his costume indicates that he is a traveller, and we can infer that one might come some distance to this spa.[4] At the left is a man in a toga, just possibly a priest. Each of these two men is making an offering at an altar, presumably making a vow in hopes of a cure, or thanking the nymph for a cure obtained. Finally, we see at the right a young man offering a cup of water to an elderly man who is seated in a chair and so, apparently, ill. Nowhere is there even a hint of a building, or of anyone immersed in water, and that may indicate that this spa was not developed in any major way.[5]

In addition to the evidence from antiquity, it will be useful to consider very briefly some comparative material from other pre-industrial contexts, for it can suggest some of the many different ways in which spas may be developed and used. When Celia Fiennes travelled around England in the late 1600s, she visited many spas. About 1694, she toured the area around Oxford: ". . . thence I went to Astrop where is a Steele water much frequented by the Gentry . . . there is a fine Gravell Walke that is between 2 high cutt hedges where is a Roome for the Musick and a Roome for the Company besides the Private walkes; the well runnes not very quick, they are not curious in keeping it, neither is there any bason for the spring to run out off, only a dirty well full of moss's which is all changed yellow by the water; there are lodgings about for the Company. . . ."[6] Here, at a popular spa, with various buildings for both lodging and entertainment, there is almost no development of the spring itself, not even, as Celia pointed out, any attempt to direct the course of the water.

Despite that, the spa at Astrop was still clearly "upscale." For an idea of what a poor man's spa might be like, we can turn to nineteenth-century Ethiopia. The bathing establishments there were very simple, usually consisting of one or two natural (or rarely man-made) pools and low sheds of straw or branches over the water. Spa-goers drank the water and soaked in it for as much as seven hours at a time. In general, access to the water was free, and the spas were quite popular: at a given spring there might be forty persons in the water, another hundred waiting for their turn. Occasionally a number of huts or tents were set up near the spring, but we do not hear of inns or of the other amenities so familiar from European contexts.[7] A similar picture of casual development emerges from the descriptions of some modern Campanian spas. At Acerra, for example, by about 1870, there were some inns nearby, but no major, systematic development of the spot, and the bathers ". . . jump into the water without a thought . . . The waters are also taken away in kegs.

Each year they build a structure of wood with tubs and pools inside it, and it is very crowded."[8]

It would be a mistake, of course, to assume that spas in Roman Campania were exactly like those of England or Ethiopia or even modern Campania, but evidence from those sites may alert us to the possible types of spas in antiquity. It is to those ancient spas that I will turn now.

A CATALOGUE OF THE KNOWN SPAS OF ROMAN CAMPANIA (See Plate 11)[9]

Aenaria (modern Ischia)

In Roman times, the numerous hot springs on the island were believed to be good for gallstones (Plin., *HN* 31.9; Strabo, 5.4.9); Caelius Aurelianus (*Chron. Dis.* 5.77) recommends that you drink or bathe in waters containing salt or nitrum, such as those on Ischia. When drunk, the water of Ischia was also good for internal bleeding or ulcers (Cael. Aurel., *Ibid*. 5.126).

We have a series of votive offerings, some certainly and others probably from Ischia, which spa-goers, happy in their cures, offered to the divinities who had helped them. They consist of low reliefs, usually depicting Apollo and one or more nymphs, together with short inscriptions (*CIL* 10.6786-6799). Typical of the inscriptions is *CIL* 10.6786: *APOLLINI ET NYMPHIS NITRODIBVS / C(aius) METILIVS ALCIMVS V(otum) S(olvit) L(ibens) A(nimo)*: "Gaius Metilius Alcimus gratefully fulfilled his vow [by making this offering] to Apollo and the Nymphs of the Nitrate Water."

Of the persons who made these dedications, at least two men were certainly freeborn Roman citizens (*CIL* 10.6795, 6797), one woman was a freedwoman of Nero's wife Poppaea (*CIL* 10.6787), and one woman was probably a slave (*CIL* 10.6793). Seven men were probably, but by no means certainly, freed slaves, since they have Greek *cognomina* such as Diomedes, Alexander, and Dionusius [sic] (*CIL* 10.6790, 6796, 6798). We have, then, a cross-section of Roman society, although no one of the upper classes—no senator, equestrian, municipal magistrate, or anyone else with a title—is represented in this limited sample. Two of the stones seem to belong to the first century A.D. (*CIL* 10.6787, 6797).

Agnano (ancient name uncertain, but perhaps *Aquae Ang[u]lanae*)

Just south of the crater of Agnano, and across the road from the modern Terme Nuove, are extensive remains of an ancient set of baths. In 1898 Giuseppe Schneer cleared the site, but he never published the results of his work. V. Macchioro examined the area carefully in 1911, and he was able to show that the ancient baths were supplied principally by water from the Aqua Serino, but that the Romans did also use the thermal springs on the site.[10] In particular, Macchioro found a series of rooms in the northwest section of the baths which seem to have been designed to take advantage of the natural hot vapors: in one room, you could apparently sit in and breathe the hot fumes (p. 239), and other rooms were heated by the passage of the natural hot air under the floor.

This establishment was clearly what we would call a spa, for it was not within a town: you had to travel to it, and you could hope to take advantage of natural thermal springs at it. Its use for therapeutic purposes is almost certainly referred to in connection with a certain Bishop Germanus of Capua, whose doctors told him, about A.D. 500, to go *pro corporis salute* to a certain "Thermae Angulanae," by which, Macchioro argued (pp. 252-254), the baths at Agnano were meant. Several pieces of sculpture were found on the site, enough to indicate that the establishment was once elegantly decorated: two Venuses, a Ganymede, a Hermes, an altar with low relief decorations, and two heads, one of them from a satyr (pp. 266-284). The baths seem to have been in use at least from the time of Augustus on (p. 262).

Aquae Vesevinae (Mount Vesuvius)

As part of a course of physical therapy in cases of paralysis, Caelius Aurelianus recommended that patients drink, or swim in, the warm water of the *Aquae Vesevinae* (*Chron. Dis.* 2.48). Thus somewhere on or near Mount Vesuvius, probably in the period after the eruption of A.D. 79,[11] there was a natural hot spring, large enough to swim in. We have no other evidence concerning this spring.

Arco Felice (ancient name uncertain, but perhaps *Aquae Ciceronianae*)

Pliny the Elder (*HN* 31.6-8) tells how, shortly after the death of Cicero, a spring burst forth on what had once been Cicero's villa, somewhere east of Avernus but west of Puteoli. When applied as drops to the eyes, this water helped restore vision that had become weak or blurred.

Castelforte (ancient name unknown)

In the 1880s, as workers began construction of a modern spa about ten kilometers west of Castelforte, they uncovered a large

Roman bath. The site was cleared and described briefly by L. Fulvio.[12] The bath building included the traditional hot, warm, and cold bathing rooms; there were furnaces, and some rooms had raised floors and hollow walls. At least part of the complex, then, functioned as an ordinary bath building. There is no indication in Fulvio's account that he discovered a direct link between any of the thermal springs on the site and any part of the bath. That this was a spa, however, is virtually certain: quite apart from the presence of mineral waters, and the fact that the establishment was out in the country, the workers turned up fragmentary statues of Asclepius and a nymph, suggesting healing and water respectively. Also included in the building complex were an *ambulacrum* where patients could walk and a set of rooms which Fulvio took as bedrooms, of either a *hospitium* or a *valetudinarium*. Coins found on the site indicate that the building was probably built in the first century A.D., and that it continued in use at least until the late Empire.

Leucogaei Fontes

Known to us only from a reference in Pliny (*HN* 31.12): "The Leucogaean [= White-earth] Springs, between Puteoli and Naples, are good for eyes and wounds." Presumably, then, this water was applied externally, either as drops (for eyes) or by immersion (for wounds).

Mons Dianae Tifatanae (modern S. Angelo in Formis; the name of the springs is not known)

Velleius (2.25.4) tells us that Sulla dedicated to Diana (who had a temple on the hill) the springs that are "famous for their wholesome quality and ability to heal." Thus the tutelary divinity of these springs was Diana, but we also have brick stamps (*CIL* 10.3811, *addit.* p. 976) from this vicinity inscribed with MEFITV SACRA, which seems to mean "the holy [spring] of the Mefites," taking *Mefitu(m)* as genitive plural and *sacra* as nominative singular. Whether these were different springs, or Diana and the Mefites shared one spring, we cannot say.[13]

Neapolis (modern Naples)

According to Strabo (5.4.7), Naples had thermal springs and bathing establishments that were the equal of those at Baiae in quality, though not in quantity,[14] and many people retired to Naples from Rome because of old age or poor health. We may perhaps infer that, while Naples had first-rate spa facilities, its clientele was markedly different from that at Baiae—not the young and lively but the elderly and retired.

Puteoli (modern Pozzuoli)

Pausanias mentions two hot springs here. One first appeared during his lifetime, and was so acidic that it corroded the lead pipes through which it ran within a few years (4.35.12). The very existence of these lead pipes shows that an attempt was made to control and exploit this spring. The second spring came up from the bottom of the Bay; the Romans, says Pausanias, built an artificial island and thus were able to control it (8.7.3). Solfatara, the volcanic crater in northeastern Puteoli, is described by Strabo, who calls it the Forum of Vulcan (5.4.6), but neither he nor any other ancient writer mentions the Romans using its natural emissions of sulphurous fumes.

There were numerous bathing establishments at Puteoli, and some of them may have incorporated natural springs. We know of three from souvenir vases: *Thermae (Traiani?)*, *Aquae Pensiles* (where *aquae* definitely suggests a spa), and *Balneum Faustinae*.[15] A number of *thermae* at (or probably at) Puteoli appear on inscriptions (e.g., *CIL* 10.1707), and archaeological remains of various bathing establishments and reservoirs have been found. None of these, however, can be securely connected with any natural spring.[16]

Sinuessanae Aquae (modern Sinuessa)

Clearly an important spa, Sinuessa is mentioned by Pliny (*HN* 31.8; cf. Strabo, 5.3.6), who claims that its waters are good against sterility in women and madness in men. The baths were established by the time of Livy and perhaps much earlier, for Livy cites them in narrating events of 217 B.C.

In the first century A.D. Sinuessa seems to have been at least as fashionable as Baiae. When Seneca had to leave Rome for a time in A.D. 54, he chose to go to Sinuessa (Tac., *Ann.* 12.66). Similarly, Tigellinus, having abandoned Nero and Rome in A.D. 69, made his way to Sinuessa, where he was taking the waters *(apud Sinuessanas aquas)*, surrounded by his concubines, when word reached him that he should commit suicide (Tac., *Hist.* 1.72). There is no reason to assume that either of these men would choose less than the ultimate in luxury when selecting a spa (despite Seneca's praises, *Epist.* 86.8-11, for simple baths such as old Scipio had used).

The *aquae Sinuessanae* may have been sacred to the Nymphs, for an inscription probably of Sinuessa (*CIL* 10.4734), dated to A.D. 71, is a dedication to the *Nymphae sanctissimae*.

Stabiae (modern Castellamare di Stabia)

The *Aqua Dimidia*, a cold spring, was, Pliny tells us (*HN* 31.9), useful in treating gallstones. Columella (10.133) refers to Stabiae as "famous for its springs," so we can assume both that there were several springs and that they were well known by Columella's day, and therefore probably from at least the late Republic. Nearby was Mons Lactarius, famous (as its name implies) for its milk. People came from far away to drink the milk, and it formed an important part of the cure at Stabiae (Symmach., *Epist.* 6.17; Galen, 10.363-366K).

Surrentum (?) (modern Sorrento)

In describing the Surrentine villa of his friend Pollius Felix, Statius (*Silv.* 2.2.18-19) mentions a bathing establishment and fresh-water spring by the sea. This was presumably a private spa, but it shows that Surrentum was a place to which Romans might go to take the waters; and if one man had a private spa here, there may have been other spas, perhaps public, as well.

Teanum Sidicinum (modern Teano)

Pliny (*HN* 31.9) tells us that about four miles from Teanum there is a cold spring called *Aqua Acidula*, the water of which is useful in treating gallstones. Caelius Aurelianus recommends that patients drink the mineral water from the territory of Teanum in cases of persistent ulceration resulting from an internal abscess *(Chron. Dis.* 5.126).

In 1907, excavations southeast of Teano uncovered a Roman bathing establishment in the immediate vicinity of mineral springs.[17] The complex included at least twenty-seven rooms, and the excavator, Gabrici, found substantial evidence of elegant decorations: walls of some rooms were covered with varicolored marble veneer; floors were of mosaic or marble; apses and vaults were decorated with paintings or stucco; and several pieces of sculpture were recovered. These included a Cupid with a goose, a river god, a young satyr, two statue bases or altars (each decorated with a *patera* and a *praeferculum*), a Venus, and numerous smaller fragments. The building in its present state seems to date from the late second or early third century A.D., but Gabrici thought that an earlier stage was likely.

As at Castelforte, the excavators did not discover any direct connection between a thermal or mineral spring and any rooms of the bath, and several of the rooms clearly were standard for baths: a frigidarium, tepidarium, caldarium, and so on. But there can be no doubt that this was a spa: it is too far from any ancient town to have served solely as a regular bath; mineral springs still run through the area; and a few hundred yards away were buildings which, since they certainly included at least one eating area (a *taberna*), may have served as an inn. A hoard of coins, many depicting the head of Hercules, was found elsewhere in Teano, and, since many of them were corroded through contact with mineral water,[18] they may indicate that the springs of Teanum, and perhaps the spa excavated by Gabrici, were sacred to Hercules.

Venafrum (modern Venafro; assigned to Campania in Strabo, 5.4.3 and Ptolemy, 3.1.68)

Pliny (*HN* 31.9) mentions a cold spring called *Fons Acidulus* which, he says, is useful in treating gallstones. We have no other certain reference to healthful waters here, although inscriptions mention both a *balneum* and *thermae* (*CIL* 10.4865, 4884), and remains of a bathing establishment (the Terme di S. Aniello) are known.

THE NATURE OF SPAS IN ANCIENT CAMPANIA

We have no evidence to indicate who built, financed, and administered our spas, but ordinary baths in Italy were often built and run for profit by individuals. In other cases, towns provided the funding, then leased the bath to a *conductor* to run it; or a wealthy benefactor might build a bath and give it to a town, again to be rented out.[19] By analogy, we can assume that the development of mineral springs might be financed in any of these ways; but some springs may simply have been left open, with free public access. We hear nothing of fees at our spas, but at Rome and elsewhere there was a small charge even for state-subsidized *thermae*,[20] so it seems reasonable to assume that some fee was charged at any spa that was privately owned or leased.

Both men and women went to spas. There were, though, many more men, to judge from the Umeri plate, which depicts three men and no women, and from the inscriptions of Aenaria, where we find twelve men and only two women spa-goers. Almost all socio-economic classes are represented somewhere: influential senators at Sinuessa; retirees (presumably wealthy) at Naples; freeborn citizens, freed slaves, and slaves on Aenaria. The exact social mix at any one spa surely must have varied according to the nature of the facilities and changing fashions.

At least some of the patrons of spas came from some distance away and stayed for extended periods. Obvious for upper-class spa-goers such as Seneca and Tigellinus, this is confirmed for other classes by the presence of lodging or dining facilities at Castelforte and Teanum and by the traveller on the Umeri plate. Once *at* a spa, one might undertake any of a number of activities. Drinking the water and soaking in it are mentioned often and were presumably the basic activities, found at every spa. It seems likely that there were some very simple spas, like those in Ethiopia or nineteenth-century Acerra, and that at such places large crowds of mostly local folk might gather and just jump in. But there were also more elaborate facilities: at Castelforte there seems to have been an *ambulacrum*, so walking for your health (and, one might guess, to display yourself) may have been a regular activity.[21] At Agnano, there is evidence for the use of natural fumes to create a hot room or *sudatorium*. It also seems safe to assume that the spring water could usually be bought and taken away. Such trade in mineral water is certainly indicated on the Umeri plate, and it may be implicit when doctors recommend specific Campanian waters, such as those from Aenaria, Stabiae, or Teanum Sidicinum: perhaps you could buy these (in Rome, say) without actually going to the spring itself. On the other hand, it seems unlikely that mineral water was ordinarily transported very far: the costs of land transport were just too high. This assumption receives some support from the fact that we do not have amphorae with stamps indicating that they contained mineral water, although surviving amphorae do attest to a lively long-distance commerce in wine, oil, and fish sauce.

Religion was central in the activities at a Roman spa. Springs in general were regarded as being divine and thus as having tutelary divinities, and there is ample evidence that many Romans made vows to such divinities when they went to a spa. The Umeri plate shows two men sacrificing, one of them perhaps a priest. At Campanian sites, we have specific evidence for (tutelary) divinities at several sites: Apollo and Nymphs on Aenaria, Asclepius and Nymphs at Castelforte, Diana and perhaps the Mefites at Tifata, Nymphs at Naples and at Sinuessa, and perhaps Hercules at Teanum. There was an altar in the baths at Agnano, and offerings in the form of ex-votos have been found on Aenaria and perhaps at Teanum. From Teanum we also have two statue bases with relief sculptures of vessels (*paterae* and *praefercula*) used in making offerings, pointing to religious activity. All of this is significantly different from what we imagine when we think "spa." A Roman spa, with altars and statues of various divinities, with people (and perhaps priests) making and fulfilling vows, and with smoke from offerings drifting about, must ordinarily have had quite a different tone from, for example, Celia Fiennes' Astrop.[22]

At all three of the Campanian sites where we have extensive archaeological remains (Agnano, Castelforte, and Teanum Sidicinum), the mineral and thermal waters play a subordinate role: the main part of these sites consists of standard bath complexes, with the familiar sequence of rooms and water heated by a furnace. At least at these sites, then, ordinary bathing in hot or cold water was even more important than using the mineral waters. This makes sense in the Roman context: hot water in and of itself was considered therapeutic, and doctors far more often prescribed ordinary baths than they did a course of baths in mineral or thermal water.[23] It is thus likely, though a bit surprising, that at some developed spas Romans spent most of their time in ordinary baths, with the mineral waters of secondary importance.

Given that at least some of our spas were developed also as regular baths, we might justifiably assume the presence at these spots of the regular range of activities that are attested for baths in general. Thus, at the larger and fancier spas, there may have been masseurs, slaves to pluck the hair from your armpits, exercise grounds, vendors of food (Sen., *Epist.* 56.1-2), prostitutes, and at least informal entertainments. A cultural side is suggested by the fragmentary statues found at Agnano and Teanum Sidicinum, but there is no hint of a theater or odeon at any Campanian spa other than Baiae, and no trace of a library at any of our Campanian sites. All the evidence seems to point to a variety of spas, rather than to a single, easily recognizable, type: variety in the degree of development (from open springs to elaborate and elegant baths), in the clientele (from the fashionable and powerful to the genuinely ill), and in the activities of that clientele (from Tigellinus' partying to devout praying). But if we consider our spas together as a single medical and social institution, can we assess their importance in the Roman world?

It would be easy, because of the fame of such sites as Baiae and Bath, as well as the role of spas in early modern times, to overestimate the importance of spas in the Roman world and in Campania. Ordinary baths were not only more numerous than spas, they were far more often recommended by doctors. Similarly, doctors may suggest mineral waters as part of a course of treatment, but they are just as likely to recommend that their patients drink milk.[24]

We should note too that, although some sites were developed extensively, it is probable that others were left relatively open: at Tifata, no trace of spa buildings has yet been found, though the area is not built over; and the parallels from Ethiopia suggest how a spring might be used with no elaborate permanent structures.[25] This same relatively infrequent development of springs is suggested by the inscriptions of Campania. We have ample record of the building by towns or individuals of a great variety of structures, among them numerous *thermae* and *balnea*;[26] but there is no clear record of the building of a spa. Spas *were* built and repaired, of course, but the relative frequency with which the various types of building appear on inscriptions is some indication of their relative importance in the eyes of the Romans. Finally, I have yet to find clear evidence for any staff member of a spa in Campania, although there are numerous references on inscriptions to other professions;[27] again, there must have *been* staff (they are shown on the Umeri plate and were essential at sites like Castelforte and Teanum), but they were apparently, as a group, few enough in number or importance that they have left no trace in the epigraphical record.

In sum: as we would expect, the Romans did appreciate the perceived benefits of various spring waters. Perhaps many would travel to a given spring if their need, and the reputed health-giving powers of the water, were great; such is implied by the votive deposits at Aenaria and by the depiction of a traveller on the Umeri plate, and such has been the case even in poor countries like Ethiopia. Spas as holiday resorts are another matter, more difficult to assess. We find clear evidence for several such resorts—all three of our archaeological sites are extensive enough to qualify, and Sinuessa should certainly be added—and for the well-to-do a visit to a health spa may well have formed an important part of the social year. For most Romans, however, there was neither the time nor the money for such an indulgence, and we should probably imagine lower-class Romans travelling to distant or famous springs only when necessary, and more often going to some *local* spa, sacrificing to the divinity of the place, drinking and soaking in the mineral water in a shallow pool, and perhaps buying some of the water to take home with them. And when they were cured, we can assume that they offered thanks to the god, and made an end of their stay.

NOTES

1. An earlier version of this paper was given at the annual meeting of the Classical Association of the Middle West and South in Lexington, Kentucky, in April of 1989, at a special session to honor Professor McKay. My thanks to Robert M. Wilhelm for organizing that session and for inviting me to be a part of it.
2. Thus, for example, *Aquae Albulae* = Acque Albule near modern Tivoli, and *Aquae Calidae* = Vichy in France. Baiae itself seems originally to have been known as *Aquae Cumanae*. For a list of nearly a hundred such towns in the Roman Empire, see Huelsen *et al.* in *RE* 2 (1896) 294-307, s.v. *Aquae*.
3. The plate (a *patera*) was found in the late 1700s in the province of Santander, on the north coast of Spain. I am most grateful to Professor Lidio Gasperini for permission to use the drawing of the plate by Mario Chighine (fig. 1). A photograph of a copy of the plate, and useful comments, are in M. Rostovtzeff, *The Social and Economic History of the Roman Empire* (Oxford, 1957^2) 212, no. 2. (My thanks to T. Robert S. Broughton for calling this to my attention.)
4. Alternatively, one might interpret the stick as a sign of, for example, rheumatism, the reason for his visit to the spa; but the short tunic and walking stick are standard iconographical elements to indicate a traveller.
5. The plate, however, presents several problems of interpretation, so that conclusions based on it must remain tentative. I am grateful to my colleague, Nancy de Grummond, for discussing it with me, and I owe to her the suggestion that the figure at the left might be a priest.
6. C. Morris, ed., *The Illustrated Journeys of Celia Fiennes 1685-c. 1712* (London, Sydney, 1982) 55.
7. The evidence on Ethiopian baths is assembled by R. Pankhurst, "The Thermal Baths of Traditional Ethiopia," *Journal of the History of Medicine* 41 (1986) 312-317.
8. I translate from Plinio Schivardi, *Guida descrittiva e medica alle acque minerali ed ai bagni d'Italia* (Milan, 1875^2) 53-54.
9. This catalogue includes those sites that can with some confidence be identified and classed as spas. It could be expanded considerably by conjecture: places where *balnea* or *thermae* are attested on inscriptions (see n. 26 below), sites where some remains of bath buildings have been found (such as those at Atella, Capua, or Pompeii), and places where thermal or mineral springs are to be found now (as, e.g., at Solfatara) could all be added, but they would be conjectural and so endanger the validity of our conclusions. Also, place names ending in *-ernus/-ernum*, such as Avernus,

Liternum, and Tifernum, may indicate springs: F. Castagnoli, "Topografia dei campi flegrei," in *I Campi Flegrei nell'archeologia e nella storia* (Rome, 1977) 47-49 with n. 27.

10. V. Macchioro, "Le Terme romane di Agnano," *Monumenti Antichi* 21 (1912) 225-284.

11. Caelius is generally assigned to the fifth century A.D., but much of his material comes from the work of Soranus of Ephesus, who was active in the time of Trajan and Hadrian, and it was probably Soranus who prescribed the use of Vesuvian waters. (Cf. I.E. Drabkin, *Caelius Aurelianus On Acute Diseases and On Chronic Diseases* [Chicago, 1950] xi and xiv with n. 5.)

12. "Di un edificio termale riconosciuto nel comune di Castelforte," *Notizie degli Scavi di antichità* (1887) 406-410. No plan or formal excavation report seems ever to have been published.

13. In origin, Mefitis seems to have been Oscan, a benevolent goddess of both sweet and sulphuric springs. She evolved, in Roman times, into a goddess associated especially with volcanic springs: M. Lejeune, "Méfitis, déesse osque," *Comptes Rendus de l'Académie des Inscriptions et Belles-Lettres* (1986) 202-213. I take the plural on the brickstamps from Tifata as an indication that Mephitis was similar to a nymph: there might be one or several at any given spring.

14. For this interpretation of Strabo's comment, see J.H. D'Arms, *Romans on the Bay of Naples* (Cambridge, MA, 1970) 141 with n. 114.

15. S.E. Ostrow, "The Topography of Puteoli and Baiae on the Eight Glass Flasks," *Puteoli* 3 (1979) 124-125 and 132-133.

16. A medieval account attributes as many as 27 springs to Puteoli (Ostrow, *op. cit.* 124-125 with n. 166). Some of these, however, may have been near, rather than in, Puteoli; and we have no way of knowing how many of them were mineral springs that had been developed by the Romans.

17. E. Gabrici, "Teano. Avanzi di un grande edifizio termale dell'antico 'Teanum Sidicinum,' scoperti in contrada Santa Croce," *Notizie degli Scavi di antichità* 5 (1908) 399-415.

18. A. Sambon, *Les monnaies antiques de l'Italie* (Paris, 1903) 369-370.

19. On the ownership of baths, see J.P.V.D. Balsdon, *Life and Leisure in Ancient Rome* (London, Sydney, 1969) 27. A privately owned bath is attested on *CIL* 11.3003; a public slave was assigned to the baths at Brundisium (*AE* 1978.217), so those baths were probably owned by the town.

20. L. Friedlaender, *Darstellungen aus der Sittengeschichte Roms*, Vol. 2 (Leipzig, 1920) 375.

21. Ancient doctors sometimes recommended walking for one's health. Thus Sen., *Epist.* 78.5: *medicus tibi quantum ambules, quantum*

exerceas monstrabit; other passages are cited in *Thesaurus Linguae Latinae* 1, col. 1874, s.v. *ambulo* I.B.1.

22. M.P. Duminil, "Les médecins de la Grèce antique et les sources," *Revue Archéologique du Centre de la France* 21 (1982) 73-80, argued that the earliest use of thermal springs, in Greek times, was religious in nature, and not for medical reasons at all. That is certainly consistent with the strong religious element present in our spas.

23. For the value placed on hot water, see T. Kleberg, *Hôtels, Restaurants et cabarets dans l'antiquité romaine* (Uppsala, 1957) 104-105. On ordinary bathing as therapeutic: Vladimír Křížek, "History of Balneotherapy," pp. 131-159 in *Medical Hydrology,* ed. Sidney Licht (New Haven, 1963), esp. 139: "In ancient times . . . hydrotherapeutic interest . . . centered on the curative use of ordinary water . . ."; cf. M.T. Fontanille, "Les bains dans la médecine gréco-romaine," *Revue Archéologique du Centre de la France* 21 (1982) 121-130. Ordinary bathing was, of course, much more likely to be available than was a mineral spring.

24. The index to Galen's works is indicative: Galen is aware of many mineral waters, but most of the entries under *aqua et aquae* (20.50-54K) refer to sweet water, not mineral. The references to the use of milk (20.343-46K) are substantially more numerous than those to mineral and thermal waters.

25. The same situation is found at some springs in northern Italy. A. Marchiori, "Le acque salutifere nella *Venetia:* l'utilizzazione razionale di una risorsa," pp. 77-84 in *Misurare la terra: centuriazione e coloni nel mondo romano. Il caso Veneto,* ed. R. Bussi and V. Vandelli (Modena [n.d.]), noted that the Baths of Comano were developed only partially (78, 82), and that mineral springs near the village of Caldiero, despite the name of that town and the proximity of the Via Postumia, were never developed at all (78-79).

26. Thus, for example, *balnea* on *CIL* 10.4792, 4884; *thermae* on *CIL* 10.1707, 3714, 4559, 4718, 4865 (all in Campania). Hundreds of other buildings or structures are listed in the index s.v. *"aedificia et donaria," CIL* 10.1177-1180. (Not all, however, are in Campania.)

27. Index 13, *"Artes et Officia Privata,"* in *CIL* 10.1163-1164, lists the professions attested on the inscriptions of Campania and other regions of south Italy. It is possible that some of these people—doctors or barbers, for example—worked in spas; but there is no clear sign of any doctor, attendant, or staff member in such inscriptions as survive.

VASA FICTILIA:
OLLAE PERFORATAE

Wilhelmina F. Jashemski
University of Maryland

Humble objects, until recently almost completely ignored by archaeologists and scholars of antiquity—but objects that were very important in the landscaping of the gardens of the houses, villas, and palaces of the ancient Romans, about which Professor Alexander McKay has written so eloquently[1]—are the subject of my small tribute to him.

I shall never forget finding my first ancient flower pot (in 1966). It was embedded in the soil in a corner (110 cm. from the south and west walls) of the large garden connected with a house at Pompeii (I.xi.14) that had a Hebrew graffito in the *fauces*. A *testa*, my workmen exclaimed as it came out of the soil. It was a strange looking object, somewhat like a flower pot, the preserved height 12 cm., with a hole 4 cm. in diameter in the bottom. But it also had four holes, each about 1.5 cm. in diameter in the sides, and the sides were curved in at the top, not straight as those of the modern flower pots that I knew. When I excitedly reported our find to the Italian archaeologists at the *ufficio*, they did not know what I was talking about. The word *testa* was unfamiliar to them. But when I described the object, they said that I had found a *vaso*,[2] the first one, to their knowledge, to be found in the excavations. We searched, but none could be found either in the museum or in a *deposito*. In 1971 I found a smaller, almost complete, reddish black pot embedded in the soil near the north wall of the large garden with an impressive masonry triclinium and two spectacular mosaic fountains (II.ix.6), located to the west of the palaestra. This pot, 13 cm. in height, had a base 5 cm. in diameter, a hole about 3 cm. in diameter in the bottom, and three small holes each about 1.5 cm. in diameter in the sides.

It was not until the next year (1972) when we excavated the garden of the House of the Ship *Europa* that we found a large number of pots.[3] This once beautiful and noble house takes its name from the large graffito of a ship (1.50 x 1.05 m.) labeled *Europa* found on the north wall of the peristyle when it was excavated in 1957. The French naval architect Jacques Thurneyssen remarked to me that the graffito was so carefully drawn that it could have been made only by a person who was intimately acquainted with the large merchant ships in use at the time. The name *Europa* probably belonged to a specific ship. It was commonly believed that the graffito reflected the commercial activity of the occupant of the house, but the exact nature of the activity to which the house had been converted by the time of the eruption was not known.

There are two houses in the *insula* (I.xv.1-3), the House of the Ship *Europa* at entrance 3, with its shop at 2, and a second house at 1. Both houses appear to be a single property, and they have a common split-level area at their rear, which occupies most of the *insula*. This was commonly believed to be an integral part of the commercial establishment, but our excavations in 1971 showed that it had been planted.

This site had been hurriedly excavated in 1957, but parts of the area still had a shallow covering of original lapilli. I have found that if a previously excavated site has not been overgrown with large weeds and trees with destructive roots it is possible to make subsoil excavations and recover evidence of the ancient roots. When the trees and plants growing at the time of eruption died, their roots decayed, and the volcanic debris which covered the site gradually filled the cavities. The first step in excavation is the removal of the lapilli until the level of the garden at the time of the eruption in A.D. 79 is reached. At this point the lapilli-filled cavities are clearly visible. We carefully empty the root cavities with special tools, reinforce the cavities with heavy wire, then fill them with cement. This is allowed to harden for three or four days. Then the soil around the cast is removed and the shape of the ancient root is revealed.

The unusual split-level topography of the *insula* is due to the marked difference in the level between the street in front and the one at the rear of the property. In the lower garden we found two vegetable gardens, with distinct plots separated by furrows. But most of the lower garden was planted in a young vineyard. The cavities in the upper garden, as well as those in the ramps along the side walls leading to the lower garden, and at the rear of the lower garden were either the cavities of tree roots or of old vines, perhaps some of both.

The considerable amount of carbonized material that we found helps us to identify what was grown in the garden. This material was identified by Dr. Frederick G. Meyer, research botanist in charge of the herbarium at the U.S. National Arboretum in Washington D.C. There were pieces of filbert shells (*Corylus avellana* L.), a piece of carbonized fig (*Ficus carica* L.), a carbonized almond (*Prunus dulcis* (Mill.) D.A. Webb), perfectly preserved grapes and grape seeds (*Vitis vitifera* L.). The large number of broad beans, or horse beans (*Vicia faba* L. var. *minor* (Peterm. & Harz) Beck), found in the garden strongly suggests intercultivation among the vines and trees, which is practiced extensively in the Pompeian area today. From the hole of one of the ancient beans entomologists at the Smithsonian Institution in Washington D.C., with tiny tweezers, extracted the hind leg of a bruchid, or strawberry weevil, and from another bean they extracted a large part of a bruchid. Our discovery of a date seed (*Phoenix dactylifera* L.), with a portion of the edible fruit which was caramelized still adhering, was surprising for dates do not mature at Pompeii. It must have come from the gardener's lunch. Carbonized dates have been found in the shops, so we know that the Pompeians imported them. Perhaps our proprietor, in addition to the nuts and fruits raised in the garden, also sold imported dates in his shop by the front entrance. The ship *Europa* may have been closely associated with this business.

But the most exciting discovery in this garden were the twenty-eight terra-cotta pots that we found embedded in the soil at varying depths, at intervals along the four walls. Eight of the pots were only slightly below the surface of the ground. Fourteen were found at the bottom of root cavities raging in depth from 17 to 42 cm.. A cluster of six appeared to be half pots. With one exception, the pots have one hole in the bottom and three on the sides (Plate 12). Thirteen of the pots were sufficiently complete to be restored. All were of a coarse clay and vary from red to black. The largest is 15.5 cm. high with a base diameter of 6 cm., a mouth diameter of 10.5 cm., and a maximum diameter of 14.5 cm. The smallest is 13 cm. high with a base diameter of 6 cm., a mouth diameter of 9.5 cm., and a maximum diameter of 10 cm. But there was one pot with five holes, and it was of an entirely different shape, fabric and color. It was apparently the lower part of a small yellow clay amphora, with a flat base. The base is 7 cm. in diameter, the maximum preserved height 18 cm. and the maximum preserved diameter 13.4 cm.

This is the first time to my knowledge that a large number of pots had been found in a garden at Pompeii, or at any Vesuvian site. The only previous mention of pots that I was able to find, in a careful search through the excavation reports, was to those found by a gardener in the peristyle garden of the House of the Centenary (IX.viii.6).[4] Paribeni says that this is the first time that such pots had been found. But neither the number or size of the pots is reported, nor have I been able to locate them. They are described as having the form of an *urceus*, with a swelled paunch, drawn in at the bottom. There was a hole in the bottom, and about one-third of the way up on the sides they had three holes, equidistant from each other, made in the clay either with a stick or a finger before firing. The holes, according to Paribeni, were for drainage. There is also the brief mention by Maiuri, many years later, of some pots found in the House of the Lovers (I.x.10) in the soil in the top of a low wall that enclosed the peristyle garden.[5] But he does not give the number, the dimensions, nor does he say if the pots had holes. I have been unable to locate them.

The use to which the pots found in the garden of the House of the Ship *Europa* were put must still be explored. The eight pots that were embedded only slightly below the surface of the soil and the six half pots, which had been somewhat disturbed by the original excavators, were filled with soil. The other pots or fragments of pots were found in tree-root cavities filled with lapilli. The pots filled with soil had apparently been planted with seed, or a very small plant, for we found no root cavity filled with lapilli.

I have searched carefully for all the references to pots in the ancient writers but such references are extremely rare. Pliny (*HN* 17.64) recommends planting pine nuts in pots with holes (*in ollas perforatas*). In the same passage he adds that the citron is grown from seeds or from layers and says that it needs a warm situation. Cato, in two very similar passages (*De agri cultura* 51, 52 and 133) gives instructions for layering the fig, olive, pomegranates, quinces, plums, and other fruit trees; laurels, myrtles, hazel and Palestrina nuts; and the plane tree. There are two kinds of layers. Scions which spring up from the ground around a tree can be bent down and pressed in the soil, with the tip elevated, so that it will take root; but if you wish to layer more carefully, the scions should be planted at once in pots or baskets with holes in them, and put in a trench. The second type of layer is that made on the tree by making a hole in a pot or basket, pushing the branch to be rooted through it, and filling the basket or pot with soil. When it is two years old, Cato says to cut off the branch below the basket or pot; cut the basket down the side and through the bottom, or if it is a pot, break it, and plant the branch with the basket or pot. It is interesting that Cato uses *aulla* (the old form of *olla)* and *calix* interchangeably for pot. Pliny (*HN* 17.97, 98) quotes Cato (but refers to the pots as *vasa fictilia*) and adds that when the first method of layering is used, if the layers are to be carried a considerable distance, they should be planted at once in baskets or pots. He says that the savin (*Juniperus sabina* L.), the rosemary, and the oleander too can be grown by layering. Pliny delights in the idea of branch-ends forming roots in pots at the top of the tree, a "daring device of creating another tree a long way off the ground."

The ancient Romans knew various methods of propagating trees. In addition to layering and seeds, they also used grafted stock. They realized that seedlings were often of inferior quality. The grafting of choice varieties on mature under-stocks grown from seed produces trees that bear fruit of superior quality. A tree grafted on a mature understock requires less water than seedlings or layers rooted in pots. Columella (*RR* 5.10.6) stresses the superiority of grafted trees. Grafting made it easy to establish new varieties of well-known fruits as well as fruits previously unknown in Italy. Many new fruit and nuts trees had been recently introduced in Italy by A.D. 79.

Pliny (*HN* 12.16) tells us that "various nations have tried to acclimatize the citron in their own countries, importing it in earthenware pots (*fictilibus in vasis*) in which a breathing space had been provided for the roots by means of holes." This sounds like a description of our Pompeian pots with their several holes. Is it possible that in the garden of the House of the Ship *Europa* that we have some exotic trees, such as the citron (*Citrus medica* L.), which was imported in pots? Citrus fruit often requires protection from frost in the Pompeii area today. This may explain the presence of the protecting roofs or frames built out from the walls of this garden. According to Pliny (*HN* 12.14-16, 23.105), among the exotic fruits, the citron was the one most valuable for health. In addition to its various medicinal uses, when taken in wine it counteracted poisons, it was used as mouth wash, also to protect stored garments from being injured by insects. It was not, however, eaten. The citron was also in great demand among the Jews in antiquity, as it still is today, for ceremonial purposes. At the Feast of the Tabernacles (Sukkoth) the Jews carried a bouquet of myrtle, willow, palm and citron (Josephus, *Jewish Antiq.* 3.245, 13.372). The "fruit of the goodly tree" in Leviticus 23.29-40 was interpreted by the rabbis as referring to the citron (*ethrog* in Hebrew). Could it be significant that a pot with five holes was found in the house in which the Hebrew graffito was found?

Pliny (*HN* 12.15) says that the citron refused to grow except in Media and Persia, but, as we have seen, in another passage (*HN* 17.64) he says that the citron is grown from seeds and by layering. S. Tolkowsky, in his *History of the Culture and Use of Citrus Fruits*, points out that the citron did grow in Italy at this time:

> Of all the citrus species, the citron was the first to reach the Mediterranean world, during the century following Alexander the Great's conquest of western Asia; its culture rapidly spread through the Levant, northern Africa, Greece, and Italy chiefly owing to its inclusion into Jewish ritual toward the middle of the second century B.C.[6]

The modern Pompeian frequently does his own grafting, removing buds from a choice tree, which he grafts on an understock, using methods recommended by the ancient agricultural writers. Or he may buy a grafted tree in a pot. He also propagates trees by layering. It was with great excitement that we discovered pots with three holes on the sides in a modern nursery supply store at Pompeii in 1973. The pots, which have straight sides, are used by nursery men for growing shrubs and trees, including grafted trees. We were told that the holes permitted the roots to grow outside the pot, and give the plant more air. When we visited a nearby nursery, which specialized in ornamental shrubs, we saw huge shrubs planted in such a pot almost completely embedded in the soil. The pot, however, had been broken by the pressure of the growing roots in the same way that some of our pots appear to have been broken. We saw shrubs in other pots that were embedded a little less than half in the soil. According to the nursery man, a plant in an embedded pot requires less water. These pots were much larger than those that we had found in the ancient gardens. We also saw smaller pots shaped like ours, but with only a hole in the bottom. There were also some small bowl-shaped pots, with a hole in the bottom similar to the half pots found in a cluster near the west wall of the upper garden at the rear of the House of the Ship *Europa*.

The ancient pots, which were narrower at the top, could not be removed as can the modern straight-sided pots. In some cases the ancient pots appear to have been broken before the plant was put in the soil (as Cato recommended), for in some root-cavities we found only fragments of a pot. This would indicate that when the pot was broken some of the pieces fell away from the pot and were not put in the planting hole. The depth at which some of the pots were found is difficult to explain, but these pots were always found in root cavities. Specialists have suggested to me that perhaps the pots held varieties that were stem-rooting. But we were to find many more pots, and before we speculate further as to what may have been planted in the pots, it would be well to note the context in which the other pots were found.

We next found pots in the Garden of Hercules (II.viii.6), so named from the statue of Hercules found near the large garden shrine.[7] This garden, too, had been previously excavated, but buried in the soil near the walls we began to find pots (Plate 13) similar to those that we had found in the garden of the House of the Ship *Europa*. The largest pot was 17 cm. high, with a base diameter of 6 cm., a mouth diameter of 11 cm. and a maximum diameter of 13 cm. The pots were at the bottom of cavities ranging in depth from 16 to 24 cm. A total of ten pots was found. There was one makeshift pot, similar to the one we had previously found, made by cutting holes in the bottom part of a small broken amphora. We left one pot in the soil, for we did not want to destroy the root cavity in removing the pot. The next year when we excavated the cast of the root it was most impressive to see a large tree-root growing out of a small pot (Plate 14). We were surprised to find a second pot nearby. The young tree that had been started in this pot had not grown, so the ancient gardener had planted another pot nearby. Dr. Carlo Fideghelli of the Istituto Sperimentale per la Frutticoltura, Ministero dell'Agricoltura at Rome, who has made a study of the shape of modern roots, examined our root cavities, and then later the casts. He immediately remarked on the similarity of the cast of this root to the shape of the citron or lemon tree root. Lemon trees with golden fruit are pictured in Pompeian garden paintings. Perhaps this is another example of the ancient Pompeian depicting on their walls the same plants that grew in their gardens. A mosaic, now in the Terme Museum in Rome, depicting a basket of fruit which included a lemon and a citron,[8] shows that Romans knew both of these fruits.[9]

In the garden of a modest house (I.xiv.2), portions of which were still covered with original lapilli, which I excavated in 1972, we found a variety of orchard trees and vines.[10] Near the north wall there were fragments of planting pots that had been badly damaged at the time of the original excavation. They may indicate that a few special or exotic trees that had been propagated by grafting or air-layering in pots had been planted here.

We next found evidence of earthenware pots with multiple holes in a very different type of garden, the peristyle garden in the House of Polybius (IX.xiii.1-3), which I excavated in 1973.[11] This was the first undisturbed peristyle garden to be scientifically excavated, and it is also of considerable importance because our knowledge about what was grown in peristyle gardens is far from complete. We first uncovered the soil next to the west wall; the garden is enclosed by porticoes on the other three sides. What we found as we removed the final covering of lapilli looked like a large sombrero; the soil had been carefully shaped in a high mound, surrounded by a channel for water, and in the high mound we found a small tree root cavity (Plate 15). The "sombrero" formations continued along the west wall (Plates 16, 17). It was obvious that something important had been planted here. The trees were still young, and provision had been made for them to get considerable water. When the lapilli was removed from the root cavities we found in two of them terra-cotta fragments, which I recognized as parts of pots with "breathing holes" such as we had previously found. During the summer of 1978 we pulled the soil away from the casts and then took the casts out of the ground in order to study them better. Near the first cast to the south we found most of the pieces of a complete pot in the soil, where it had fallen into the planting hole at the time the young tree was put in the soil. But part of the pot had clung to the roots and this we found embedded in the cast. It was obvious that a young tree had been started in a pot, the pot broken before the plant was put in the soil, and that the fragments of the pot had fallen into the planting hole. There were also fragments of planting pots in the soil near two other casts. On the wall above the root cavities there were many nail holes, which indicated that the trees had been espaliered. The Romans were acquainted with this practice. Professor Frank Brown, Director of the American Academy in Rome, when he visited our excavations, suggested to me that the trees could well have been lemons, a relative of the citron. Lemons are espaliered in the same manner on garden walls in the Mediterranean today. In the Pompeii area today they are started in pots, and they are planted along the walls for protection, if at all possible.

Much to our surprise, since we have become accustomed to low, formal planting in the restored peristyle gardens, we found a total of five large tree-root cavities, in addition to those in the sombrero formations, as well as various small cavities, several of which were clearly those of stakes to prop up the branches of trees heavy with fruit or nuts (Plate 17). Dr. Fideghelli identified two of the large tree-root cavities as those of figs. It was only much later that Dr. Meyer reported that he had finally identified the misshapen chunks of charcoal that we had found around one of these cavities. When he examined a cross section under high magnification, the many tiny seeds of a fig were clearly visible. Two other tree-root cavities definitely had the appearance of fruit trees—cherry, pear, or apple, but not apricot or peach, according to Dr. Fideghelli. A cherry or pear tree would explain the presence of the tall slender ladder, the imprint of which we found in the garden soil (Plate 17). The fifth cavity had the appearance of an olive tree. When Professor G.W. Dimbleby, of the Institute of Archaeology of the University of London, analyzed soil samples from this garden, he found olive pollen present.

In 1976 I found still another pot at Pompeii.[12] When we excavated a vineyard in Region III, *insula* vii, near the triclinium in this vineyard we found a small planting bed and in one corner a pot with one hole in the bottom and three on the sides. It was 13 cm. high, and 12 cm. in its widest dimension.

At the luxurious villa at Torre Annunziata (ancient Oplontis), believed to have belonged to Poppaea, wife of the Emperor Nero, we again had the opportunity to excavate largely undisturbed gardens, and here we found still more pots.[13] In 1975 and 1976 we excavated the large garden (59 on plan) to the east of the main entrance of the villa. The garden is enclosed on three sides by a portico supported by white columns, their upper portion fluted. At the edge of the garden near the columns, we found two parallel rows (2.6 m. apart) of root cavities (Plate 18) outlining the three sides of the portico (Plate 19). Except for necessary adjustments at the corners, the cavities were directly in front of the columns. In most locations we found evidence of terra-cotta pots with multiple holes. The pots missing or badly damaged had been destroyed before we excavated the garden by holes that had been dug for posts placed to hold the scaffolding used in erecting the fallen columns. The pots appear to have been broken before the plant was put in the ground, and parts of some pots had apparently dropped off, for all the fragments of a complete pot were not found in each location.

The big surprise came in 1978 when we began to pull the soil away from the root casts. In the inner row nearest the columns, at most locations, we found a second pot. The pots were not placed with their bases standing firmly in the ground, as were the first pots, but they were placed somewhat aslant, each one pointing toward a column, and always to the left of the first pot. They had obviously been placed in the ground intact, and many were still in perfect condition. Our first explanation was that these pots had contained plants which were no longer growing at the time of the eruption, for we found no root cavities filled with lapilli. But when we removed the intact pots, still full of soil, we discovered in each of them, at opposite edges of the rim, two tiny cavities (about 1.5 cm. in diameter) that reached to the bottom of the pot (Plate 20). Close examination showed that the cavities were not those of roots, as we first thought, but more probably of tiny stakes, used to support and guide the little plant, which was too small to leave a root cavity. The problem of identifying the plants grown in these pots is difficult to solve, but the fact that these pots were pointed toward the columns suggests a climbing plant that was trained on the columns. A total of 85 pots (complete or in fragments) were found in this garden. They were 11 to 16.5 cm. in height, the base diameters 5 to 7 cm.; most of the pots had a hole in the bottom and three on the sides. One pot had four holes in the sides, and one had six.

The size of the root-casts in the pots in the two rows directly in front of each column indicates that these pots contained either very large shrubs or small fruit trees of the size usually found in the area today. Some of the pots were as deep as 60 cm. in the soil, which seemed very deep to me. This, however, was vehemently denied by the workmen, even the youngest, who told me that that was the depth that they planted trees today. Dr. Fideghelli verified that this was indeed the current practice in Campania. Local farmers insist that deep planting is good, because of the long dry season, in spite of the warning that it cuts off oxygen from the roots. The Italian Department of Agriculture is trying in vain to change a practice that is many centuries old and apparently works. It is interesting to note that the ancient writers advised deep planting (Cato, *De agri cultura* 43; Pliny, *HN* 17.80).

In the west side of this villa where the family quarters were located there was a small portico supported by four columns which enclosed a deep pool (16 on plan); this contained a most unusual little garden—a round masonry structure with a depression which served as a shallow planter.[14] The planter enclosed another pool in the center of which was a pier with a jet fountain. In the planter there were five small terra-cotta pots (13 to 14 cm. high), with a hole in the bottom and either three or four in the sides. But in only one pot, the tallest one, had the holes been made before the pot was fired (Plate 21). These pots appear to have had a somewhat different use. Because of the shallow bed of soil, this area was used for temporary plantings. Plants with tired foliage or faded blossoms could easily be replaced when they were planted in pots. The plants would have been low, so as not to obstruct the view of the little pool and the fountain in the center. This small planter-pool garden reminds us of the pots that Maiuri found at Pompeii in the House of Lovers in the shallow soil in the depression in the top of a low wall that enclosed the peristyle garden.

A few pots have also been found at Herculaneum. These were found by Professor Tran Tam Tinh in two previously excavated houses that he was studying.[15] There were two pots, but not *in situ*, in the garden of the Casa dei Cervi. In the garden of the Casa del Salone Nero he found ten, two of which were complete; four were upright in the soil at a depth of 25 to 30 cm. and they may have been in their original position. They were not located, however, opposite the columns of the peristyle. The Herculaneum pots all have a hole in the bottom and three in the sides. They vary in height from 12 to 16 cm.

About eight terra-cotta pots were found in the large, partially excavated peristyle in the Villa of San Marco at Stabiae. They were found in the soil at the edge of the garden, near the gutter at the foot of the columns. They too had a hole in the bottom and three on the sides of each pot.[16]

As we review the pots with multiple holes that have been found thus far in Campanian gardens, we find that with very few exceptions the holes had been made in the pots before they were fired. The hole in the bottoms of the pots were larger than needed for drainage. They had obviously been made large enough for a branch to be pulled through them for layering. Since most of the pots were found fairly deep in the soil, and in many cases with varying amounts of the pot missing, it appears that the plant had been grown in a pot, but the pot had been broken before the plant was put in the ground. At other times, however, the pot was left partially or completely intact, because it would tend to conserve water for the young plant.

The location of the pots that were found *in situ,* and the type of garden in which they were found is of importance in trying to determine what may have been planted in them. The largest number of pots were found in the peristyle garden of the villa at Oplontis, where they were placed at the edge of the garden directly opposite the columns. The location of the pots found in the garden of the House of the Centenary is not reported, but it is tempting to speculate that they too were found at the edge of the garden in front of the columns. At most sites the pots were near a garden wall, as in the informal peristyle garden in the House of Polybius, in the two large commercial gardens (the garden of the House of the Ship *Europa* and the Garden of Hercules), in the backyard home garden I.xiv.2, in the garden at the rear of the house with the Hebrew graffito, and the one in II.ix.7. A pot was also found near the edge of the rear garden (56) of the villa Oplontis. The only pot found in the interior of a planted area was the one that we found in the vineyard III.vii. but it was near the low masonry wall that on two sides contained a small planting bed near the triclinium.

We can now, perhaps, draw some conclusions as to what had been planted in these pots. Dr. Fideghelli pointed out that both the size and shape of the cavities of roots growing out of the pots found near walls definitely indicated that they were those of trees. It is true that both Pliny and Cato suggest that various fruit and nut trees that were propagated by layering should be started in a pot if it were to be done carefully and the tree was to be transported a long distance. But of the many, many fruit and nut tree-root cavities that I have excavated through the years in the vineyards, orchards and vegetable gardens in the Vesuvian area, I have not found a single one that was started in a pot, except those found along walls. This would seem to indicate that a tree that required special protection was planted there. This, as we have seen, is true of the lemon and citron, which makes it tempting to think that the cavities of roots growing out of the pots along the walls were those of lemon or citron trees. Dr. Fideghelli points out that today most fruit trees are started from seed and then grafted, but they are transplanted bare-root during their dormant period from November to March. Citrus trees, however, which are evergreen, are transplanted in pots today. This may be another of the many examples, that we have found so striking, of the continuity of agricultural practices in the Vesuvian area from antiquity to the present, some of which were contrary to the recommendations of the ancient agricultural writers,[17] perhaps due to the unique growing conditions in Campania.

What was planted in front of the columns in the formal, ornamental peristyle garden at Oplontis? Pliny mentions that the laurel, myrtle, rosemary and oleander can all be propagated by layering. The root cavities do not have the appearance of oleanders, which we found growing in clumps in the large rear garden (56) in this villa. We were fortunately able to identify various oleanders in the large sculpture garden (93) of this villa. Plentiful partially carbonized, woody twigs and branches made it possible for Dr. Francis Hueber, Curator of Paleobotany at the Smithsonian Institution, Washington D.C., to identify the oleanders (see below), not a one of which was started in a pot. Dr. Fidegehelli thought it very unlikely that the plants growing in front of the columns in the peristyle garden were laurels; they root so easily in the Vesuvian area. It is of course possible that such a large number would have been ordered in pots. The root cavities do not have the appearance of those of myrtles or rosemary. Dr. Fideghelli suggests that the root cavities may possibly be those of lemon trees, or perhaps of the citron tree, which Pliny said was transported in pots with breathing holes for the roots. It is pleasant to speculate that the two rows of roots that outlined the portico might have been those of lemon trees. The glossy green foliage dotted with fragrant white flowers and bright yellow fruit would have presented a striking picture placed in front of each white column. It is hoped that future excavations, perhaps elsewhere, will help to answer what was planted in these pots.

To complete our enumeration of the pots found in Campanian sites, we should mention the four ornamental terra-cotta pots, or vases, in the Casa dei Cervi at Herculaneum that are displayed on bases connected with the pilasters that support the pergola in the middle of the loggia overlooking the sea. These vases which have holes on the sides would have held decorative plants (Plate 22).

When I first found a large number of pots in the garden of the House of the Ship *Europa,* I thought immediately of the pots that Dorothy Thompson had found in the rock cuttings on the south side of the Temple of Hephaistos, above the Agora in Athens.[18] The pots were directly opposite the columns of the temple. Ten pots were nearly complete. Fragments were found in another cutting. The pots varied in height from 17 to 21 cm., the diameter of the rim from 23 to 35 cm.; the top of the pot was 30 to 50 cm. below the ancient ground level. But these pots were different from the Campanian pots for they had all been roughly cut off the wheel with a string. Mrs. Thompson believed that the pots had been used to make air-layers in the way described by Cato and Pliny. She dates the replanting of this garden in the Roman period, during the first century after Christ, which would be the same period as that of the Campanian pots. A similar pot was found in the Agora to the south of the Stoa of Attalos.

When I reported on the Garden of the House of the Ship *Europa* at the annual meeting of the Archaeological Institute of America in Philadelphia in 1972, I expressed an interest in hearing from any archaeologist who might have found pots in their excavation. John W. Hayes told me of similar pots that he had found in 1963 at a kiln-site at Prima Porta, which was hurriedly excavated by the British School at Rome, when it was exposed briefly during road-works.[19] Fragments of six pots were found. One had remains of three holes on one side and one at the bottom, and he said that another could have been similar. Another type apparently had no holes in the sides. Associated finds showed that this kiln was active around or just after the mid first century after Christ. The pots are now in the British School in Rome.

I am also indebted to John Hayes for information about the pots found in Eccles, Kent, in 1973. About ten have been completely restored and there are fragments of eight others. These pots had a rounded hole in the bottom, and three triangular ones on the sides.[20] All the holes were cut before firing. The excavator was puzzled as to their use, and suggested that the most likely function that could be suggested was that they were to be used inverted over a source of light, perhaps a candle, as the diameter at the lip is only sufficient to encompass a very small lamp. He pointed out that no particular care had been taken to finish their bases, which was neither smooth, nor quite flat, as if the pots had not been intended to stand on them. But he adds that the function of the pots was open to discussion. The pots were found in the backfill, but identical wasters from the kiln-site show that the pots were of local manufacture. The pots are so similar to those found in Campania that it seemed to me that they were planting pots, an identification with which the excavator agreed after the publication of the pots in the garden of the House of the Ship *Europa*.[21] The Eccles pots are slightly smaller, about 12 cm. in height. Only rarely had one that small been found in Italy. They are usually 13 to 16 cm. in height. The Eccles pots date from approximately the same time as those at Pompeii. They can be definitely dated as not later than A.D. 65. During the early post-conquest we might easily expect direct influence from Italy in Britain. G.W. Dunning had earlier published two similar pots (12.5 and 13.5 cm. high) found in Watling Street, London.[22] He identified them as chimney pots, possibly medieval, but according to Detsicas they can now be regarded as Roman,[23] and they are certainly planting pots.

When my article on the garden in the House of the Ship *Europa* appeared in the *American Journal of Archaeology*, Professor Edmund Netzer wrote to me telling of the pots that had been found during the excavation of the Hasmonean and Herodian winter palaces at Jericho (Tulul Abu el-Alayik).[24] Some had been found by Professors Kelso and Baramki in 1950 and by Professor Prichard in 1951. In 1973 Dr. Netzer began a new series of excavations and exposed a section of garden in which 15 pots were found. These were in a pre-Herodian complex which included "a swimming pool surrounded on three sides by a large paved, platform-like courtyard." This courtyard was originally paved, but "in the Herodian period it was covered with earth; the many flower-pots, some still *in situ*, found here give evidence that it was a garden." The pots near the pool were arranged in two parallel rows, with 2.5 m. distance between them, and with a distance of 1.2 m. between the pots in each row. In a few instances there were pairs of pots close together. The second pot may have held a replacement for a plant that had died, such as we found in the garden of Hercules. The pots were 13 to 15 cm. in height. Some pots had a hole in the bottom only, some had in addition holes (usually three) bored in the sides, made before the pots were fired. The arrangement of these pots is similar to the two parallel rows of pots that we found at the edge of the garden near the columns in the villa at Oplontis where the rows were 2.6 m. apart, the pots in each row 1.5 m. apart.

More recently (1985 and 1987) Kathryn Gleason found still more pots at Jericho.[25] In a peristyle (B64) in the early Herodian palace where Netzer had found pots, her soundings revealed the basic layout of the garden: seven rows of as many as eleven pots each. The rows were roughly 1.5 m. apart and the pots in each row about 1 m. apart. The analysis of the soil for pollen and the study of the carbonized fragments of plant material found in the soil have thus far given no clues as to the plantings, but she suggests that the famous Judean balsam believed to be *Opobalsamum gileadensis* is the most intriguing possibility.[26]

Trial trenches showed that the monumental garden (B6) contained perforated pots of the same size and description as those found in the peristyle garden B64 and elsewhere in the palace. The Jericho pots, which were made locally,[27] are similar to the Campanian pots with one notable exception. The Jericho pots tapered to a small foot (3.5 cm. in diameter) that was "more like a neck, in that it is open and has a rim of its own, like an inverted bottle" (Plate 23).[28]

In an effort to locate any other pots that might have been found in the provinces I wrote letters to various archaeologists who had excavated at sites where peristyle gardens had been found, but in every instance the reply was that no pots had been found. This may be due in part to the fact that subsoil excavations were not made in most of these gardens, which were identified only because of their architectural context, and pots still *in situ* would not have been found.

The number of holed flower pots, however, known in Italy was increased in the course of excavations (1982-1984) in the Villa of Livia at Prima Porta. Among the evidence left by the nineteenth-century excavators in their disorderly search for antiquities were the considerable fragments of 35 pots, which the excavator Gaetano Messineo describes in detail.[29] Some were still *in situ* in the soil, others had been shifted as a result of ploughing. Messineo wonders if there might be some connection between the pots at Livia's villa, and the laurel grove at this villa said to have been propagated from the laurel twig which the white hen, that an eagle dropped into the lap of Livia from the sky, held in its beak. (Pliny, *HN* 15.136-137; Suetonius, *Galba* 1; Dio 48.52, 63.29). The emperors held a branch of the original tree and wore a wreath of its foliage in triumphs; after the triumph the twigs that they held were planted.

The discovery of the pots at Prima Porta led Massineo to search for other pots that might have been found in Rome or nearby. The search in the Museo Nazionale at Rome for the holed pot, 14 cm. high, from the Esquiline, cited and reproduced by Lafaye[30] led to unexpected results. Not only the pot cited, but 15 examples were listed in the Inventory of the Museo Nazionale as coming from the Esquiline, and 13 of these were found in the magazine of the museum. The provenance of six other pots was not given. A third group of eight was listed as coming from S.

Suranna. It was an even greater surprise to discover that three little pots reproduced in the catalogue of the Antiquarium Communale were part of a large group (at least 74), 68 of which were whole. The provenance of only one of these pots is given and that is vague: 30-VII-1875; Esquiline. Two old photographs (1933) show a large number of pots found above the the octagonal hall in the Domus Aurea. The first photo shows the pots *in situ,* arranged in rows, a few upside down, which would suggest that the pots had been stored, awaiting use. The second photo shows them after they had been collected and assembled in a heap. These pots may be among some of those mentioned above, with provenance not given. Messineo also learned of three pots that had been found *in situ* at Ostia in 1972, each in front of the column of the peristyle in a building near the Tempio Rotundo. Another pot, provenance unknown, was found in the *deposito* at Ostia, and another was found in 1983. He concludes with a brief enumeration of several other pots found recently in sites near Rome.[31]

In the recent excavations in the gardens of Hadrian's villa made by Dr. Salza Prina Ricotti and myself (see below), we found fragments of similar pots in several gardens. Dr. Ricotti found a small, almost complete pot, 9 cm. high (Plate 24), in the garden of the so-called Throne Room.

The number of ancient planting pots, the majority with one hole in the bottom and three on the sides, continues to grow. A careful examination of unpublished objects in museum storerooms throughout the Roman Empire may result in the discovery of still more pots. With increasing interest in Roman gardens, excavators are now beginning to excavate carefully the gardens in their sites, and all garden evidence, including any pots found, will be carefully recorded. It is hoped that future excavations will help solve the problem of what was grown in these pots.

But the Romans used another type of planting pot, which I first discovered in the luxurious villa at Oplontis. The rooms in the east wing, built during the Empire (A.D. 50-70), looked out on an Olympic-size swimming pool (60 m. long and 17 m. wide) and two handsome gardens, one at the south end of the swimming pool, and, to the east of the pool, a great sculpture garden (93 on plan, Plate 19). Here we found the cavities of an avenue of 13 trees. In front of each tree was a statue base. Six of the life-size statues that stood on these bases have been found.

The ornamental plantings behind statue bases VI to IX, which were opposite the luxurious salon (69) in the middle of the east wing, were carefully planned to provide a colorful and dramatic picture when viewed across the water. A scanning electron microscope (SEM) photo of a tiny scrap of the branch of tree VI, which I extracted from a small cavity in the cut of the unexcavated lapilli, was identified by Dr. Hueber as oleander (*Nerium oleander* L.).[32] Root IX, which was similar in size and shape, also appears to have been an oleander. At a distance of approximately 3.4 m. behind statue bases VI and IX, in a subsequent season, we found a low base, and behind each of these bases were the plentiful branches, partially carbonized, of a small tree, which SEM photos showed were also oleanders.[33] None of the oleanders had been started in a pot.

SEM photos of the woody material from the tree behind the statue base VIII indicated to Dr. Hueber that this could be either a laurel (*Laurus nobilis* L.) or a lemon (*Citrus limon* L. (Burm. f.)), but when we excavated the root cast we found that this tree had been air-layered in a pot. Laurels root very easily and are never started this way in this area. Lemon trees, however, are air-layered. We were surprised to find, however, not the type of small pot that we had become accustomed to finding, but a makeshift pot; the top half of a broken amphora had been turned upside down and used as a pot (Plate 25) and the root grew out of the mouth of the amphora. It was exciting to discover that adjacent to our excavations, lemons were today being air-layered in large makeshift containers. Old tin cans and discarded plastic containers are the broken amphoras of modern Campania. The root cavity behind statue base VII was similar in size and shape and appeared to be of the same tree as VI.

The complexity of this garden, which extends farther to the north, south, and east, will become clearer only with further excavation. But we are charmed by the portion already uncovered. Dramatically placed, as a focal point, behind each of the two central statue bases was an important tree, which appears to be the lemon, esteemed both for the fragrance of its blossoms and the beauty of its golden fruit. Completing the picture, behind the statue base on each side of these trees, was a lovely oleander, with still more oleanders behind the small bases at the rear. The oleanders would have been the pink one, ever present in the garden paintings, and so often depicted amid sculptures. This colorful central picture was framed on each side by three stately plane trees, which furnished shade to those strolling along the pool, and cast shadows on the shining marble statues.

The only reference that I have been able to find in the excavation reports to amphoras being used as planting pots is in

Fiorelli's description of an area in Pompeii from which construction had been cleared after the earthquake of A.D. 62.[34] This area (VII.xi.1) was identified by Fiorelli as a plant nursery. Soil contours, still preserved at the time of excavation (1862-1863), showed rectangular beds separated by furrows. The bed at the right of the entrance was outlined by twelve amphoras, whose tops had been broken off, filled with soil, and sunk in the ground; in these, seedlings were started. Unfortunately the "pots" were neither described nor saved.

The excavations made by Dr. Salza Prina Ricotti and myself in 1987 and 1988[35] in the Canopus area of the Emperor Hadrian's villa near Tivoli, about 27 kilometers to the east of Rome, revealed terraced gardens along the banks of the Canopus where special shrubs or trees had been planted in discarded amphora (Plates 26, 27). They had been cut in two, both the upper and lower parts serving as planting pots. Half amphoras used as planting pots, as well as several smaller pots, had previously been found by Danish archaeologists in the west bank of the Canopus in their unsuccessful search for the tomb of Antinous, the beloved of Hadrian.[36] The use of discarded amphoras as planting pots had long been practiced in the ancient world, as a vase painting on a *lechythos* in Karlsruhe showing a scene from the festival of Adonis gives witness (Plate 28). Eros holds an "Adonis garden," which is the bottom part of a broken amphora, filled with soil and planted with lettuce and fennel. At his feet is another "Adonis garden," the top of the amphora similarly planted. In the Canopus garden three holes had been cut in the sides of most of the discarded amphoras, and an additional one at the end of the bottom half of the amphora. In the top half of the amphora the mouth provided an additional opening. Again we are reminded of Pliny's description of planting pots "provided with breathing holes for the roots."

NOTES

1. A.G. McKay, *Houses, Villas and Palaces in the Roman World* (Ithaca, NY, 1975). Professor McKay's appreciation of plants is displayed in the audio-visual presentation of "Ovid's Transformations: Trees and Flowers," which he and Professor Robert Wilhelm produced for the NEH Mythology Institute on "Myth and Its Transformations: Ovid's *Metamorphoses*" held at Miami University, Oxford, Ohio, in summer 1989.

2. The Italian word *vaso* is used for both the elegant vase and humble terra-cotta flowerpot. *Testa* is the picturesque Neapolitan word for a humble terra-cotta pot, as attested by Biagio and Maria Sgariglia of the Villa Vergiliana.
3. W. Jashemski, *The Gardens of Pompeii, Herculaneum, and the Villas Destroyed by Vesuvius*, vol. 1 (New Rochelle, NY, 1979) 233-242.
4. *Notizie degli Scavi* (1902) 567.
5. A. Maiuri, *A Primo Convegno Nazionale del Giardino: Varese; Septembre 15, 1937* 6.
6. S. Tolkowsky, *Hesperides. A History of the Culture and Uses of Citrus Fruits*. (London, 1938) 323.
7. Jashemski, *op. cit.* 279-288.
8. *Ibid.*, fig. 419 on 281.
9. For Roman knowledge of the lemon see Tolkowsky, *Hesperides* 98-103.
10. Jashemski, *op. cit.* 94-97.
11. *Ibid.* 25-30.
12. *Ibid.* 228-232.
13. *Ibid.* 293-296.
14. *Ibid.* 292-293.
15. Letter from Professor Tran Tam Tinh dated February 20, 1979.
16. I am indebted to Dr. Paola Miniero for information about these pots.
17. For example, Columella (*RR* 3.21.11) insists that fruit trees may be planted only "at the very end of the rows, on that side of the vineyard, which lies to the north, so they may not shade it." But in the numerous vineyards I have excavated in Campania, there were numerous trees not only around the edge of the vineyard, but also within the vineyard.
18. D. Thompson, "The Garden of Hephaistos," *Hesperia* 6 (1937) 396-425. She was told that holed pots had been found in Ponza, Italy.
19. Letter from Dr. J.W. Hayes dated January 4, 1973.
20. A.P. Detsicas, *Antiquaries Journal* 54 (1974) 305-306.
21. A.P. Detsicas, "A Group of Pottery from Eccles, Kent," *Roman Pottery Research in Britain and Northwest Europe: Papers Presented to Graham Webster*, eds. A.C. Anderson and A.S. Anderson, BAR International Series 123 (II), (Oxford, 1981) 441-445.
22. G.W. Dunning, "Medieval Chimney-pots," *Studies in Building History*, ed. E.M. Jope (London, 1961) fig. 5.4 on 82 and 83-85.
23. A.P. Detsicas, *Antiquaries Journal* 54 (1974) 305, n. 1 (communication from Dunning).

24. Letter from Professor Ehud Netzer dated August 4, 1976 (quoted in Jashemski, *op. cit.* 360, n. 16). Also see Netzer, "The Hasmonean and Herodian Winter Palaces at Jericho," *Israel Exploration Society* 25 (1975) 92; J.L. Kelso and D.C. Baramki, "The excavation of New Testament Jericho," *Annual of the American Schools of Oriental Research* 29-30 (1955) 17.
25. K.L. Gleason, "Garden Excavation at the Herodian Winter Palace in Jericho, 1985-1987," *Bulletin of the Anglo-Israel Archaeological Society* 7 (1987-1988) 21-39.
26. For a discussion of the identification of the Judaean balsam, see Gleason, *op. cit.* 31 and n. 40.
27. J. Yellin and J. Gunneweg, "The Flowerpots from Herod's Winter Garden at Jericho," *Israel Exploration Journal* 39 (1989) 85-90.
28. Gleason, *op. cit.* 28 and n. 23.
29. G. Messineo, "Ollae perforatae," *Xenia* 9 (1983-1984) 65-82.
30. Daremberg-Saglio, *Dictionnarie*, vol. 5. 359, fig. 7011.
31. Messineo, *op. cit.* 68-72.
32. Jashemski, *op. cit.* 314 and figs. 486-488 on 312.
33. Jashemski, *op. cit.* vol. 2 (New Rochelle, NY, 1992) 299-300.
34. G. Fiorelli, *Gli Scavi di Pompei dal 1861 al 1872* (Naples, 1873) 24; Id., *Descrizione di Pompei* (Naples, 1875) 276-277.
35. W. Jashemski and E. Salza Prina Ricotti, "Excavations in the Gardens of Hadrian's Villa: The Canopus Area and the Piazza d'Oro," *American Journal of Archaeology* (in press).
36. N. Hannestead, "Über das Grabmal des Antinoos: Topographische und thematische Studien im Canopus-Gebiet der Villa Adriana," *AnalRom* 2 (1982) 80. For a strong negative reaction to Hannestad's thesis that the Canopus area was a memorial to Antinous and that the tomb or cenotaph and the obelisk of Antinous were on the left bank of the Canopus, see M.T. Boatwright, *Hadrian and the City of Rome* (Princeton, 1987) 148-149 and Appendix, "The Obeliscus Antinoi," 239-260.

FROM VERGIL TO AUSONIUS: POETS ON WORLD-POLITICS

Charles-Marie Ternes
Centre Alexandre Wiltheim, Luxembourg

THE IDEAL VISION OF THE WORLD

Man's ideas gain a political dimension when they come to devising a more or less systematic *imago mundi*, an ideal vision of the world.

Rome had reached that stage in the last century B.C., when its expanding power forced citizens and their representatives to think over its political structures for the most evident purpose of adapting them to an apparently entirely new situation. I say "apparently" because, for themselves, none of the Romans, who had to decide or to support decisions in this vital matter, wanted a true revolution[1] to take place; but somehow the *polis-character* of traditional Rome had to be kept alive[2] and, at the same time, ways and means to be found by which this unique city could be made the capital of the *orbis*.[3] They did not take long to understand that this could be done with the help (or under the constraint, or both, alternately or simultaneously) of ambitious men (Marius, Sulla, Caesar, in some ways Cicero, then Mark Antony and Octavianus) who were—somehow—borne along by a wave of feeling, thought, theory, hope, reflection as well as longing for economic profit and social upheaval.

This paper was given at a faculty-seminar at Miami University in Oxford, Ohio, on April 7th, 1987. I am proud to offer it in this revised version to Professor Alexander Gordon McKay.

We cannot go into the details of the work done by each of these men who were (or regarded themselves as, or pretended to be) *"outstanding individuals"* chosen and shaped by Destiny to be the leaders of their peoples, in the hellenistic sense of post-alexandrine politology,[4] charismatic *"soteroi"* playing the part of saviors, "kings" between gods and humans, benefactors in the euhemeristic sense of the word;[5] but all, apart and aside from this self-interpretation or self-identification[6] often imposed upon them by devout disciples, were sons of their time, i.e. of troubled, unquiet, turbulent times, with crisis permanent in Rome since the reforms of the Gracchi had been, let us say "postponed." Viewed through more or less contemporary literature, they remind us of kings and rulers of the post-alexandrine centuries in Asia Minor and the Near East; in fact they cannot be understood outside of Rome.[7]

For a hundred years there was civil dissent;[8] then, finally, civil war broke out, in its full and horrible, bloody and irrational destructiveness, so that, when Brutus (an "honorable man") died, there was nothing left to do but to proceed to a final contest between Mark Antony and Octavianus—the latter being by far the weaker, particularly lacking in the aura of oriental providentialism, Egyptian sun-godliness which raised Mark Antony to the full prestige which later descendants and/or imitators (Nero) tried to restore to their own benefit.[9]

Octavianus had but one chance: to outdo this glittering mirage by stubbornly sticking to different, *Western value*s which had been Roman long ago and could not be just re-animated, freshened up and dusted off. They had—most urgently—to be brought (back) to actual life, which means made to fit a situation wholly different from the one they had grown up in centuries ago.

This succeeded, by virtue of Augustus' clever, sometimes ruthless, decisive though altogether prudent tactical process; by virtue of the men who surrounded him and among whom M. Vipsanius Agrippa and Maecenas may have played a decisive part;[10] and, most of all thanks not to "the" people, but to a group of citizens who felt ready to enter into Roman history at the moment when the old aristocracies had lost power and new lobbies, from a new bourgeois social group, *novi homines*, acceeded to political power.

They were interested in big business, but they themselves or their fathers had been farm-tenants or craftsmen, and, though reaching for the Future, they remained true to the Past. With them, Augustus, "he who augmented" Rome, built up a new regime[11] and made Rome enter a new era.[12] Most of the Romans didn't notice; one hundred years after Actium, the un-Roman excesses of the Julio-Claudian "emperors" woke them up . . . to become—at last—conscious of what had happened. Tacitus was the very sharp (and tendentious) "anti-imperial" observer of this evolution which I have had many an occasion to point out in lectures or papers.[13] Writing when Trajan was nominated to be emperor, he reproached the late Republic and the Empire for not having clearly chosen either peace or war, for having been endlessly talking about the one and the other, but not to have acted. In his final report, the so-called *Res Gestae,* Augustus had pretended to have given peace to mankind.[14] He had intended to, and even if he did not succeed, his attempt is worth going into in some detail.

NON INIUSSA CANO. POETS HELPED HIM . . .

Poets helped Augustus. Horace and Vergil did,[15] but not as members of some kind of propaganda or publicity staff, even if Vergil wrote: *non iniussa cano*—I do not sing a song nobody wants, but, on the contrary *a song everybody was longing for.*[16] It should not surprise us that poets supported a political plan; poetry was not then the delicate privilege of beauty-seeking aesthetes, the "happy few" communicating with the poets' soul via cryptic, coded signs. It was a means to divert, to sing, to express emotions, to criticize and also to teach. This corresponds to one of the most typically Roman literary features: the need to tell, to convince, to guide.[17]

I choose a number of texts from Vergil and Ausonius to support my point; they cover the period of Augustus and of Valentinian I, who lived 350 or 400 years later. Though a few scholars remain convinced that Vergil was "just a poet," i.e. in the (more or less) "modern" sense of the word, a gentle writer of lyrical verse, describing nature, gods and "the deeds of the man who became the ancestor of all Romans," most of us are now certain that he decided once and for all to contribute to the work of the *princeps.*

As he did when he dealt with Scipio,[18] Horace,[19] Seneca[20] and Cicero,[21] Professor Pierre Grimal, my revered master at the École Normale Supérieure and at the Sorbonne thirty years ago, in his 1985 *Virgile ou la seconde naissance de Rome,*[22] left no doubt about this fundamental thesis clothed in Tityrus' statement in the first *Eclogue*:

> *Urbem, quam dicunt Romam, Meliboee, putavi*
> *stultus ego huic nostrae similem, quo saepe solemus*
> *pastores ovium teneros depellere fetus.*
> *sic canibus catulos similis, sic matribus haedos*
> *noram, sic parvis componere magna solebam.*
> *verum haec tantum alias inter caput extulit urbes,*
> *quantum lenta solent inter viburna cupressi.*
>
> 19-25

The city they call Rome, Meliboeus, stupid as I was, I considered similar to ours, where we shepherds used to take the small ones of our flock . . . I was comparing *parvis . . . magna*, small things to big ones. In fact, that city raises its head as high among other cities as flexible willow next to cypress trees.[23]

The motif to go to Rome is *libertas*, the freedom to be a citizen among citizens, to take part in the progress brought to them, to be part of this fundamental life animating Earth and Heaven, springing from matter, budding, blossoming, copulating, dying;[24] or to be totally dependent on themselves, freed from the fear of death or the longing for wealth and power, a *zoon politicon*, made for society, totally ready for it (this is the experience after 49 B.C. in the Epicurean circle of Siro in Baiae). Epicureanism was less keen on political commitment than the Portico. It did not forbid it, but advised its followers to cultivate *ataraxía* over competition, perhaps envy and the quest for influence and wealth. Whoever felt strong enough to resist these tremendous temptations, could be both Epicurean and political on theoretical grounds.

> "There was no other means [—says Tityrus in the same first *Eclogue*—] (except going to Rome) to leave my slavery and to meet equally generous gods."[25]

ACCESS TO ELYSIUM

The *Culex*, the story of the fly (or the gnat, or the mosquito) was, according to Pierre Grimal, written in 49 B.C. It concludes the *Appendix Vergiliana*,[26] and was perhaps to conclude Vergil's literary "career."[27] The Siro circle made him say good-bye to the Muses; he resumed writing in 43 or 42 B.C.

The little epic called *Mosquito* is dedicated to Octavius, whom Vergil met before 50 B.C. and who, in spite of a nine years' difference in age, was called a schoolmate of Vergil's at Epidius' rhetorical school in Rome.

Phoebus Apollo and the Muses, the Naiads, Pales and Octavius, *sancte puer* (blessed boy [26]), are to promote *per ludum* (4), for fun, the story of the mosquito. Imitating Homer's descriptions of sunrise, the poet introduces a shepherd climbing a mountain. His sheep are busy eating the grass of the slopes, while he himself, conscious of his luck, is aware of simplicity without *cura luxuriae* (60) being the secret of it. "It is not by art but by the work of his fists that he honors God," a god living in groves, among garlands of fruit and flowers, where *dulcis requies* (sweet calm [89]) and *pura voluptas* (untroubled pleasure [89]) reign.

The flock goes down to drink at a source: praise of blue water over green moss which once upon a time saw more or less innocent fighting between satyrs and nymphs, Pans and Dryads. The shepherd falls asleep without noticing; in his dream a giant dragon—directly "imported" from the shores of Troy—is about to devour him, when the *parvulus alumnus (h)umoris* (183), the small creature born from humidity, bites him so that he wakes up . . . and instinctively kills his savior before becoming aware of the much greater danger threatening him. He fights the dragon and falls asleep again. In his second dream appears the *effigies Culicis* (208), the phantom of the mosquito. He complains about having lost his life, even if this gave him access to the Elysium where he met the long series of famous heroes, from Achilles to Rhesus and Dolon, Agamemnon, Minos and Mucius Scaevola. The *complaint* is the first of our texts:

> *"quis," inquit, "meritis ad quae delatus acerbas*
> *cogor adire vices? tua dum mihi carior ipsa*
> *vita fuit vita, rapior per inania ventis.*
> *tu lentus refoves iucunda membra quiete,*
> *ereptus taetris e cladibus; at mea Manes*
> *viscera Lethaeas cogunt transnare per undas;*
> *praeda Charonis agor, vidi et flagrantia taedis*
> *limina: conlucent infernis omnia templis.*
> *obvia Tisiphone, serpentibus undique compta,*
> *et flammas et saeva quatit mihi verbera. pone*
> *Cerberus, et diris flagrant latratibus ora,*
> *anguibus hinc atque hinc horrent cui colla reflexis,*
> *sanguineique micant ardorem luminis orbes.*
> *heu, quid ab officio digressa est gratia, cum te*

> *restitui superis leti iam limine ab ipso?*
> *praemia sunt pietatis ubi, pietatis honores?*
> *in vanas abiere vices, et rure recessit*
> *Iustitiae prior illa fides. instantia vidi*
> *alterius, sine respectu mea fata relinquens*
> *ad parilis agor eventus: fit poena merenti.*
> *poena sit exitium; modo sit tum grata voluntas,*
> *exsistat par officium.*
>   Culex 210-231

No doubt this is parody: this is a jest of a cultivated youth who knows his classics and means to make equally cultivated friends laugh at what all of them naturally revere. This being said and granted, it is not our intention to work out a hundred comparative annotations on *loci similes*, to count the number of borrowings from X or Y; rather we wonder why the game was played, and how.

The *vocabulary* may be most helpful: the topic is merit; once it was honored, rewarded, respected: *gratia, honor, pietas, fides.* *Fides* was "justice" in the countryside, the deep, ancestral link between people who had to trust each other without written covenants. *Pietas* was the link with gods as well as with parents, who gave life as the gods gave life and secured life from the *vices,* the negative turn imposed upon things as soon as they are left to themselves. Life is considered a supreme good; it has to be preserved by all means, even if it is a mosquito's, apparently minor to a man's. The will to save life should prevent the savior from the terrifying monsters of Hell.[28]

Back from his dream-journey, the awakening shepherd "could not bear the pain caused to his soul by the brave mosquito's death" and so built a circular tumulus on which acanthus, roses, violets, myrtle, hyacinth, saffrons, laurel, lilies and rosemary, ivy and other odorant and sacred flowers surround the epitaph (413-414):

> *"parve Culex, pecudum custos tibi tale merenti*
> *funeris officium vitae pro munere reddit."*

This very Roman idea—that funeral honors are a means to establish just and sacred relations between the dead and the living—is the subject of several of Ausonius' familiar poems, e.g., the *Parentalia,* named after a very old religious celebration attributed to Numa, the second king of Rome.

Apart from all this, the thematic structure (shepherd-flock; water-life-security-wealth; dream-revelation of superior truth in the contest with the evil dragon) clearly sets out the frame of a possible interpretation, both political (in a general though clear way) and moral—the shepherd's task being to make sure that life, wealth and good do coincide.

THE ANTIQUE LINE OF TEUCER

Professor Grimal assigns the fourth *Eclogue* to the year 40 B.C.,[29] the year of the Brindisi agreement between Octavianus and Antony, a "strange poem"—so he writes—". . . whoever may be the Child (if it is a child) whose birth announces a progressive return to the golden age."

I do not intend to add one more interpretation to the scores already issued, most of them brilliant, astute, worth thinking over but, finally unconvincing.[30] Let us sidestep the fundamentally difficult question of who exactly was the *puer* (4.18), who was the *virgo*, and who inspired Vergil to write these lines of his poem.[31] I am not certain that anybody can supply answers because I suspect that Vergil's intention was in no way to proclaim his candidate for the world's renewal, but only to give words to a probably *general feeling* that now the way to peace seemed open— any *puer* favored by *casta Lucina* (4.10) would see the Ages run down and the *gens aurea* rise *toto mundo*. Maybe this almost uncommented detail was more (or equally) important to the poet than a—somewhat perilous, in no way clever—choice of a pretendant, and pretendant to what? Nobody (in 40 or 39 B.C.) could predict who would provide leadership.

My concern is again rather with the vocabulary: the invocation of the Muses, this time, meant to announce *paulo maiora,* a more solemn matter, not *arbusta* (4.1), bushes, but *silvae* (4.3), a woodland; *nascitur ordo* (4.5): a new state of things is being born, superseding the preceding *ferrea gens*.

Ovid gave immortality to the Roman *ordo aetatum* in his *Metamorphoseon Liber* 40 years later;[32] Lucina and Apollo are to preside over the birth of the *nova progenies*, a new and ultimate generation. Lucina is *casta virgo*, much more Artemis than Hera, dangerous to women about to give birth and sister to Apollo with whom she killed the Niobides. Moon and Sun have to be placated in order to allow the birth of a new world. The child to be born, any child, will live in the golden age, among gods *et regnet orbem patriis virtutibus*, and he will govern the Earth thanks to the (good) qualities of his fathers.

The gifts of the Earth shall be a profusion of ivy and acanthus; as if Orpheus were playing his magic flute, lions and sheep shall live in peace together, the serpent shall die, poisons perish. And the child's—any child's—very first and most urgent duty shall be to read about the heroes' exploits and his father's virtues. To assume that the Achilles sent *iterum* against Troy is Mark Antony means that Vergil was conscious *very early* of his oriental plans, perhaps earlier than Octavianus himself.

The continuity from the *Culex* to *Eclogue* 4 is obvious but the innovation and the level of meaning has been considerably uplifted. Vergil was admittedly a political philosopher. He had renounced a political career, but he would never cease to incorporate his strong convictions in a poetical language which was sure to be "heard" more readily than any Ciceronian treatise, e.g., *De Re Publica*.

The fourth book of the *Georgica* concentrates on bee-keeping. A naïve reader might consider all this as simply a chapter on the Roman technique of getting honey. But commentators have long emphasized that what really interested Vergil was the depiction of a commonwealth, a community, a *res publica* which possessed a number of decisive characteristics of a future Roman state.

In *Georgic* 4.210, the fatal word *rex* is pronounced, even though *odium regni*[33] was one of the Roman mind's oldest components:

> *praeterea regem non sic Aegyptus et ingens*
> *Lydia nec populi Parthorum aut Medus Hydaspes*
> *observant. rege incolumi mens omnibus una est;*
> *amisso rupere fidem, constructaque mella*
> *diripuere ipsae et cratis solvere favorum.*
> *ille operum cistos, illum admirantur et mones*
> *circumstant fremitu denso stipantque frequentes,*
> *et saepe attolunt umeris et copora bello*
> *obiectant pulchramque petunt per volnera mortem.*
> Geo. 4.210-218

This was not the case in everybody's mind; it was certainly no longer the case in the year of Actium (especially in association with Egypt) quoted by Vergil as a term of comparison to the *rex*, the king of bees (nobody knew that the king was a queen, and—who knows—this might have changed the fate of Rome); for *rege incolumi* (4.212), as long as he, the king, is well, *omnibus mens una est* (4.212), there is but one spirit in all the others.[34] *Amisso* (213), if he is "lost," *fidem rumpere soluerunt* (213-214), they would break their faith and undo their own work. There is motivation for a kingdom: *illum admirantur omnes* (215), admiration, prestige; personal commitment to success. The effect: care, protection, self-sacrifice. And there is *Fides:* a convention between king and people: he shall be *operum custos* (215), he shall control and thus protect the common work.

> *His demum exactis, perfecto munere divae,*
> *devenere locos laetos et amoena virecta*
> *Fortunatorum Nemorum sedesque beatas.*
> *largior hic campos aether et lumine vestit*
> *purpureo, solemque suum, sua sidera norunt.*
> *pars in gramineis exercent membra palaestris,*
> *contendunt ludo et fulva luctantur harena;*
> *pars pedibus plaudunt choreas et carmina dicunt.*
> *nec non Threicius longa cum veste sacerdos*
> *obloquitur numeris septem discrimina vocum,*
> *iamque eadem digitis, iam pectine pulsat eburno.*
> *hic genus antiquum Teucri, pulcherrima proles,*
> *magnanimi heroes, nati melioribus annis,*
> *Ilusque Assaracusque et Troiae Dardanus auctor.*
>
> Aen. 6.636-650

A good part of the sixth book is devoted to religion. Aeneas, in Cumae, confronts the Sibyl and asks her to give him entry to the world of the dead, so that he may meet Anchises again. [35] The Roman theme of *pietas erga parentes* converges with an iconographical *topos* possibly inherited from the Etruscan period, showing the young warrior (Aeneas) carrying the old man (Anchises) on his shoulders. The topic was not new: Homer,[36] Plato,[37] in the Tale of Er the Pamphylian, had imagined this—basically orphic—highly ritualised passage through both types of life *post mortem*, long before Vergil did. It seems essential to me to emphasize precisely that: Vergil, while creating *the* national epic, had primarily to "tighten up" the cultured world's spiritual tradition, to make sure that his audience (or readers), feeling themselves at ease within a familiar frame of mental structures, would be *ipso facto* ready to accept the new ideas, the new proposals and rules for a peaceful and powerful Rome to come.

The dead had to be soothed after the Civil War and the reward of the Blessed to be put into clear light. It was obvious that the sole feature would be all the more efficient, the clearer it alluded to that past and to those people that Rome now intended to live up to.

The *Aeneid* is more than a mere appeal to tradition. It is oriented from the reign of shadows towards those *campi* where air and light and sun set up the scenery of happiness: such was to be Italy (for Aeneas: Rome), even beyond Italy for Augustus, to whom—among others—verses 851 to 853 of the same sixth book must have sounded like the best political slogan ever written: *imperio regere populos*—by military power govern peoples; *pacique imponere morem*—and if this be refused, *debellare superbos*—defeat the arrogant, but *parcere subiectis*—be indulgent to those who submit to Roman rule.

Attention should be drawn to the importance of *landscape* in all of this:[38] there is an appropriate scenery for each feeling, for each action, for ideas and plans. The light of Apollo opposed to the dark, dusty inconsistency of Hell/Tartarus, is the symbol of what appears to be—according to Roman lyricists—Nature's true part in poetry. I tried to make this point when lecturing before the Société des Etudes Latines de Paris, by choosing Propertius and tracing his songs on nature's beauty down to the time of Ausonius' *Mosella*.[39] Here there was no interest in fierce, savage rocks, oceans and woods, but rather more of Pompeian painting styles, of sacred landscapes where men meet with gods.[40]

SACRED AND SECRET

In the *Mosella*, Ausonius provides our texts:

> *Iam liquidas spectasse vias et lubrica pisces*
> *agmina multiplicesque satis numerasse catervas.*
> *inducant aliam spectacula vitea pompam*
> *sollicitentque vagos Baccheia munera visus,*
> *qua sublimis apex longo super ardua tractu*
> *et rupes et aprica iugi flexusque sinusque*
> *vitibus adsurgunt naturalique theatro.*
> *Gauranum sic alma iugum vindemia vestit*
> *et Rhodopen proprioque nitent Pangaea Lyaeo;*
> *sic viret Ismarius super aequora Thracia collis;*
> *sic mea flaventem pingunt vineta Garumnam.*
> 152-160

> *laeta operum plebes festinantesque coloni*
> *vertice nunc summo properant, nunc deiuge dorso,*
> *certantes stolidis clamoribus. inde viator*

riparum subiecta terens, hinc navita labens,
probra canunt seris cultoribus: adstrepit olliis
et rupes et silva tremens et concavus amnis.
                                           163-169

Gods are present, and when *igneus Sol* (178), the fiery Sun, pauses in the middle of its *cursus*, Nature belongs to Pans, Satyrs, Nymphs and Naiads, while men rest after *negotium*.

Here too Nature is present everywhere, so persistently present that I could show you the exact place where Ausonius saw all this, reliefs and mosaics which gave him the inspiration for more than one passage, ruins of superb *villae* excavated by archaeologists and corresponding to the three types the poet described (320-329); anyone who boards a ship gliding slowly down the Moselle river, will see the landscapes that excited and inspired the poet's verses. We do not speak about utopic countries, cities of the spirit, in which all times have indulged; we are not in Plato's *Politeia*, fascinating, ideal, but never existent. Both our poets are men grappling daily with actual, decisive problems connected with the best way to govern a (real) state, relying less on abstract rules or concepts than on the virtues of the men supposed to guide and lead their fellow-citizens.

Nor is it mere lyricism: the comparison of the Moselle sites to the most famous vine-growing sites in the then known world (near Naples, in Greece and Macedonia), by itself lifts the debate to the level of the above quoted *paulo maiora* (*Ecl.* 4.1); the poems are not meant to be a visitor's guide; Vergil's *labor improbus*,[41] the daily round of plain and unheroic work,[42] is integrated into Ausonius' natural scenery and the epithet is *laetus*; gods and men share this landscape, not "children of a lesser god" nor "minor" gods, but the oldest, familiar with and dear to common people, familiar gods acting more or less as humans do. Nature helps Man to unfold, in a "natural" way, consistent with his true destiny. No doubt, this was the political message which Ausonius took over from Vergil, and Cicero: if the people are not to be *omnis hominum coetus quoquomodo congregatus* but a live part of a community directed by a *princeps* who ought to be *tutor et procurator rei publicae* (the protector and the warrant of the state), *rector et gubernator* (the master and the helmsman),[43] then the success of the formula depends not on the Prince alone, but on the qualities of the people under his care. *Concordia* (harmony) is less between opposing and conflicting political parties than between the *ordines*, decisive social groups. So, the *limes* could be defended, not by (more or less) Roman troops, but by the common will to make the Rhine again a *verus limes*, a true frontier.[44]

The first 22 verses of the *Mosella*, provide a summation to the foregoing argument:

> *Transieram celerem nebuloso flumine Navam,*
> *addita miratus veteri nova moenia Vinco,*
> *aequavit Latias ubi quondam Gallia Cannas*
> *infletaeque iacent inopes super arva catervae.*
> *unde iter ingrediens nemorosa per avia solum*
> *et nulla humani spectans vestigia cultus*
> *praetereo arentem sitientibus undique terris*
> *Dumnissm riguasque perenni fonte Tabernas*
> *arvaque Sauromatum nuper metata colonis:*
> *et tandem primis Belgarum conspicor oris*
> *Noiomagum, divi castra inclita Constantini.*
> *purior hic campis aer Phoebusque sereno*
> *lumine purpureum reserat iam sudus Olympum.*
> *nec iam, consertis per mutua vincula ramis,*
> *quaeritur exclusum viridi caligine caelum:*
> *sed liquidum iubar et rutilam visentibus aethram*
> *libera perspicui non invidet aura diei.*
> *in speciem quin me patriae cultumque nitentis*
> *Burdigalae blando pepulerunt omnia visu,*
> *culmina villarum pendentibus edita ripis*
> *et virides Baccho colles et amoena fluenta*
> *subterlabentis tacito rumore Mosellae.*
>
> 1-22

Ausonius quotes the sixth book of the *Aeneid*,[45] to give us the impression of extraordinary relief which he felt when he had left the foggy Rhine valley to plunge into the Apollonian ecstasy of verses 11 to 22, preparing and leading to the *salutatio* in verse 23. Here again, there are more than brilliant descriptions of natural phenomena; Germany should be left to castles and barbarians, culture is here, in the hinterland, where emperors dwell and vine-growers work. The Future may lie in accepting this already happy state of things, but wouldn't it be a good policy to try and secure all this by resuming activity along (and perhaps on the right bank of) the Rhine? The case of the Trier country was the *exemplum imitandum* of a provincial success. It ought to be and (Ausonius leaves no doubt about this) it could be repeated farther east.

Vergil and Ausonius were poets close to emperors, to decisive emperors both—Augustus as well as Valentinian—who were ready to listen to advisers capable of giving their policy a human credibility born from a clever mixture of Past and Future. Both poets were concerned not to sketch out a regime, but rather a *status rerum*, a way of life, a balance of things to which history gave its assent.

NOTES

1. In the view of Sir R. Syme, *The Roman Revolution* (Oxford, 1939), the last century B.C. was characterized by trouble, anarchy, breakdown of social, economic and moral patterns (Cf. D.C. Earl, *The Moral and Political Tradition of Rome* [London, 1967]), but through "outstanding men" and by the conjunction of moral forces, it was oriented towards a providential savior, Augustus. The fact is that not only after Augustus' death (Tacitus, *Ann.* 1.11.2 sq. is to be taken literally and to be considered the expression of a deep and sincere conviction on behalf of Tiberius), but again and again for over two centuries, every time somebody became an emperor the question *de statu rei publicae* was raised anew (Cf. W. Suerbaum, *Vom antiken zum frühmittelalterlichen Staatsbegriff. Uber Verwendung & Bedeutung von 'res publica,' 'imperium' und 'status' von Cicero bis Jordanes* [Münster, 1961] = *Orbis Antiquus* 16/17 esp. 279-305) by a strong senatorial lobby, anxious to regain power and influence at the expense of the "emperors" and "all their men."

2. Both by the soteric "principes" or *"primores"* (Marius, Sulla, Pompeius, Caesar, Augustus), ideologically close to hellenistic monarchy (cf. F. Taeger, *Charisma. Studien zur Geschichte des antiken Herrscherkultes* [Stuttgart, 1960] vol. 2) as well as by such political groups (*equites*, partly *populares*) who intended to strengthen Rome against rival cities (mainly Oriental), and by social *factiones* interested in municipal structures, moral pressure-groups wanting a clear distinction to be drawn between Roman gods and those imported from the shores of the Nile, the Tigris and the Orontes.

3. Politically speaking, this was (again, very gradually) achieved *via* the evolution of relations between Rome and her first ten provinces. Thus a new system was put forth, non-repressive, not (entirely) submissive, (in some way) associative, based on the capacity and the readiness of part of the local or native nobility to perceive and to accept a net of contractual boundaries, with space left for social and economic development as well as for the interests of the *res publica*. Tacitus' *Germania* renders obvious Rome's generic claim

to possession from the very moment of the first major Roman military operations towards the Eastern parts of central Europe. The frame was set, whatever the contents might happen to be or however quickly it might happen to be filled up. A similar process led to the Roman claim to be *caput orbis*.

4. Cf. Taeger, *op. cit.* vol. 1, 234 sqq.
5. This includes, as in the case of late Attic tyranny, a consensus on behalf of the *cives*, a mechanism based on the elimination or outwitting of the ochlocracies traditionally "inserted" between king and people.
6. The combination of all these elements has been perfectly described by J. Carcopino in his *César: Histoire romaine. II. La république romaine de 133 à 44 avant J.-C.* (Paris, 1950⁴) e.g., on 780 sqq. and in chapter 10, 958 sqq.: "La révolution de César." For earlier periods, see P. Grimal, *Le siècle des Scipions. Rome & l'hellénisme au temps des guerres puniques* (Paris, 1975²); for religious connections, see J. Ries, *Théologies royales en Egypte et au Proche-Orient & hellénisation des cultes orientaux* (Louvain, 1986), esp. 35-43, 135-144 and 173-182. For general discussion consult: "Le roi" in *Le monde hellénistique. La Grèce & l'Orient 323-146 av. J.-C.* (Paris, 1978) 181-293.
7. A closer analysis of measurable influences on Roman politology *via* Sicily and Magna Graecia is requisite. For a very long while, the Greeks did nothing to "seduce" the Romans, nor did they easily surrender to their superiority. (Cf. J. Deininger, *Der politische Widerstand gegen Rom in Griechenland* 217-286 v. Chr. [Berlin/ New York, 1971]). In fact nobody did.
8. I consider the period reaching from 132 B.C. to January 49 B.C. as a period of "civil dissent"; from 49 B.C. to the day of Actium as "civil war."
9. Cf. P. Grimal, *Sénèque ou la conscience de l'Empire* (Paris, 1979), esp. 119-132 and 160 sqq. Professor Grimal has traced this particular (though essential) aspect of this type of Roman ideology back to Mark Antony. See, among others, his: "Le *de clementia* et la royauté solaire de Néron," *Revue des Etudes Latines* 49 (1971) 205 sqq.
10. Thanks to Cassius Dio (54.29.3) we know that Agrippa did not really approve of all Augustus' government. Maecenas *atavis edite regibus* (Horace, *Odes* 1.1.1) was rather in charge of diplomacy and, in the absence of the *princeps,* master of Rome; known for his "oriental" display of luxury, he was the center of a circle of poets (Vergil, Propertius and Horace) who may, on more than one occasion, have embarrassed the *princeps* by their insistence on topics (a national epic, *prisca virtus Romana*, Ciceronian *concordia* etc.) which were rather hard to transform or integrate into a sensible pragmatic policy.

11. The best study on all aspects (tradition, innovation) remains P. Grenade's *Essai sur les origines du principat. Investiture et renouvellement des pouvoirs impériaux* (Paris, 1961).
12. In his *Virgile & le mystère de la 4è* Eclogue, J. Carcopino (Paris, 1953) 21-107, has marshalled all the components of the widespread expectation of the *redeunt Saturnia regna*, the *novus ordo* etc. Cf. *infra*.
13. Cf. e.g., "*Tamdiu Germania vincitur*. La critique tacitéenne de la politique romaine en Germanie," *Colloque Histoire & Historiographie* (Paris, 1980), 165-176; more recently in *Römisches Deutschland. Aspekte seiner Geschichte & Kultur* (Stuttgart, 1986) 37-162.
14. Cf. Chapter 13 (p. 94 in the 1935 edition by J. Gagé): *cum per totum imperium populi Romani terra marique esset . . . parta . . . pax*.
15. As well as: Plotinus Tucca, Quintilius Varius, Aristius Fuscus, Valgius Rufus, Domitius Marsus and Aemilius Macer. The idea (the Prince taught and guided by the Poet) has persisted through literature in subsequent periods. Cf. H. Broch's "Der Tod des Vergil," and *Présence de Virgile*, ed. by R. Chevallier (Paris, 1976) 457-468.
16. Maecenas may have insisted on and be in some way (cf. infra) responsible for Vergil's resuming his poetic work.
17. From this point of view B. Effe's most instructive book *Dichtung & Lehre. Untersuchungen zur Typologie des antiken Lehrgedichtes* (= Zetemata, vol. 69, Munich, 1977) devotes only 17 pages to Vergil (80-97); fortunately he emphasizes (86 sqq.) the various levels of meaning (cf. infra) and clearly points out that the ultimate goal was to cooperate with the Augustan project of (re-) creating a "heile Welt."
18. Cf. above, n. 6, about the Scipiones.
19. *Essai sur l'Art Poétique d'Horace* (Paris, 1968) esp. chapter 5, 133-212; *Le lyrisme à Rome* (Paris, 1978) 169-196.
20. Cf. above, n. 9.
21. *Cicéron* (Paris, 1986) 259-278; 377-414.
22. Paris, 1985.
23. We might prefer to translate (v. 23): "I used to compare" so as to render the idea of a (bad) habit.
24. *Ecl.* 1.27 sqq. insists on the strong contrast between a short (though pleasant) love-affair and even some money (*gravis aere,* v. 35) and *libertas* which is beyond *pinus, fontes, arbusta* (*ibid.* v. 38 sq.).
25. *Ecl.* 1.40.
26. Professor Grimal (*Virgile,* 67 sq.), considers the *Appendix* (as well as the *Catalepton*) not only as authentic but vital for the comprehension of young Vergil's enthusiasms . . . and weaknesses. We

meet with the same type of work in the case of Ausonius who left us numerous obscene verses supposedly written under similar conditions; there is more than one point of possible comparison between the *Culex* and the *Cento nuptialis*, which H. Evelyn-White refused to translate for his Loeb edition in 1919.

27. Cf. Grimal, 69 sqq.
28. Made at the very moment when civil war started (cf. supra), this statement takes its full programmatic meaning.
29. Together with 6.9 and 1.
30. Cf. Carcopino's book quoted in n. 12.
31. *Ecl.* 4.6-17.
32. Cf. C.-M. Ternes, "La théorie des âges et l'autopsie de l'histoire romaine par Ovide," *Présence d'Ovide* (Paris, 1982) 65-78.
33. See now: P.M. Martin, *L'idée de la royauté à Rome. De la Rome royale au consensus républicain* (Clermont, 1982) 289-388.
34. This reminds us of Plato's criticism of democracy as resembling an *himation poikilon* but essentialy leading to tyranny. The poet's delicate task is to avoid the confusion of these various types of monarchy.
35. 5.10 sqq.
36. *Il.* 20.215-240; 307 sq.; *Od.* 16.1 sqq., esp. 210 sqq.
37. Cf. "La République," éd. Robin/Moreau, *La Pléiade*, vol. 1, 1231 sqq.
38. Cf. B. Otis, *Virgil: A Study in Civilized Poetry* (Oxford, 1963); P. Grimal, "Les Métamorphoses d'Ovide et la peinture paysagiste à l'époque d'Auguste," *Revue des Etudes Latines* 16 (1938) 145-161; C.P. Segal, "Orpheus and the Fourth Georgic: Vergil on Nature and Civilization," *AJP* 87 (1966) 307-325; id., *Landscape in Ovid's Metamorphoses. A Study in the transformations of a literary Symbol* (Wiesbaden, 1969 = *Hermes Einzelschriften,* vol. 23), important for its commentary of Ausonius' *Mosella*.
39. C.-M. Ternes, "Le lyrisme dans l'oeuvre d'Ausone," *Revue des Etudes Latines* 64 (1986) 196-210.
40. See B. Teolato Maiuri, *Museo Nazionale. Napoli* (1971) 96 sqq.
41. Verg., *Geo.* 1.146: *labor omnia vincit inprobus.*
42. Cf. Ausonius' *Ephemeris id est totius diei negotium,* and my contribution "Aiôn: Le temps chez les Romains" (Paris, 1976) 239-252.
43. Quotations from Cicero, *De republica* 1.25 and 29 in the Teubner text.
44. Aus., *Mos.* 435 and my commentary "La notion de 'verus limes' dans la *Mosella* d'Ausone: la civitas des Trévires comme exemple d'une réussite provinciale." *La patrie gauloise, d'Agrippa au 6è siècle* (Lyon, 1985) 355-374.
45. *Aen.* 6.640.

GEMINA PICTURA: ALLEGORISIERENDE AENEISILLUSTRATIONEN IN HANDSCHRIFTEN DES 15. JAHRHUNDERTS

Antonie Wlosok
Johannes Gutenberg Universität, Mainz

In Kommentaren zu Vergils Aeneis aus Spätantike, Mittelalter und Frührenaissance begegnet immer wieder die These der *gemina doctrina*. Gemeint ist damit, dass der Dichter mit seiner poetischen Fiktion, in erfundenen Geschichten, Fabeln und Bildern, philosophische Wahrheit verkünden wolle, dass er somit als Dichter zwar den Regeln der Poetik und der poetischen Tradition folge, dabei aber der Wahrheit der Philosophie diene. Mit den in der Folgezeit oft wiederholten Worten des *Macrobius: ut geminae doctrinae obseruatione praestiterit et poeticae figmentum et philosophiae ueritatem (Somn. Scip.* 1.9.8).[1] Das heisst nun aber, dass der Text oder gewisse Textpartien allegorisch aufzufassen sind und einen zweifachen Sinn aufweisen, einen vordergründigen, auf der Ebene der epischen Erzählung, welcher der gewöhnlichen Wortbedeutung entspricht, und einen hintergründigen, tieferen Sinn, welcher vom aufmerksamen Leser erschlossen werden muss. Die Textpartie der Aeneis, welche sich philosophischer Interpretation in besonderer Weise anbot und darauf auch vom Autor selbst angelegt war,[2] ist das 6. Buch, Vergils Unterweltsbuch, in dem Aeneas unter der Führung der Sibylle von Cumae in die Unterwelt hinabsteigt und durch die einzelnen Regionen des Totenreiches wandert, um seinen Vater Anchises im Elysium aufzusuchen, der ihm Auskunft über sein letztes Ziel geben soll.

Die Welt der Schatten, durch die Aeneas und die Sibylle im Verlauf der epischen Handlung gehen, erscheint in der populären

Gestalt des mythologischen Hades, das ist der unter der Erde gedachten Dominiums des göttlichen Herrscherpaares Dis und Proserpina. Seine traditionellen Elemente sind: die Unterweltsströme, monströse Schreckgestalten wie der dreiköpfige Wachhund Cerberus, diensttuendes Personal wie der Fährmann Charon und die strafende Furie Tisiphone, die am Eingang des Tartarus wacht, der furchtbaren Strafstätte, in der die Frevler ewige Qualen erdulden; schliesslich das Elysium, der freundliche Aufenthaltsort der Seligen, mit grünen Wiesen, lieblichen Hainen und hellem Licht, in dem edle Heroen, mythische Sänger der Vorzeit und andere Fromme ihren Lieblingsbeschäftigungen nachgehen.

Die Gebildeten zur Zeit Ciceros und Vergils hielten diese Geschichten für Ammenmärchen, konnten sie im Wortsinn also nicht ernst nehmen. Aber für diejenigen, die an ein Fortleben der Seele nach dem Tode glaubten, gab es längst geläuterte philosophische Eschatologien. Besonders verbreitet war damals in Rom ein kosmologisches Konzept stoisch-platonistischer Prägung, in dem der alte, mythologische Hades umgedeutet und als postmortaler Aufenthaltsort der Seelen in kosmische Regionen transponiert war.[3] Dabei ergab sich folgendes Bild: Grundlegend ist die Unterscheidung zwischen einer dunklen Luftregion unter dem Mond und einer oberhalb des Mondes (oder mit dem *circulus lunaris*) beginnenden hellen Ätherregion. Die sublunare Zone, der Bereich zwischen Erde und Mond, ist Hades. Die Grenze wird durch den *circulus lunaris* gebildet. An dieser Grenze liegt der Palast des Dis, der auch die Residenz der Proserpina ist. Proserpina "ist auf dem Mond und Herrin der Monddinge," zugleich ist sie die "Grenze des Hades."[4] Als Elysium wird auch die von der Sonne beschienene Himmelsseite des Mondes bezeichnet oder die Mondregion überhaupt.

Die spätantiken Kommentatoren Macrobius und Servius haben die vergilische Unterwelt in diesem kosmischen Sinne ausgelegt und sich dafür auf die vom Dichter in den Text eingestreuten Hinweise berufen.[5] Der Kommentar des Servius geleitete Vergils Aeneis sozusagen in und durch das Mittelalter. In ihm wird der Leser zu Beginn des 6. Buches ausdrücklich auf die besondere, philosophisch-theologische Bedeutung dieses Buches hingewiesen: "Der ganze Vergil ist voll gelehrten Wissens, worin dieses Buch den ersten Platz einnimmt . . . , in welchem einiges einfach gesagt ist (d.h. ohne tieferen Hintersinn), vieles aus der Geschichte kommt (d.h. der historischen Instruktion dient) und vieles dem tiefen Wissen der Philosophen, Theologen und Ägypter entspricht."⁶ Im 12. Jahrhundert gibt John of Salisbury dieser Überzeugung eine pointierte Formulierung, indem er das 6. Buch als das Buch umschreibt, in dem Vergil "die Geheimnisse der ganzen Philosophie ergründet" (*totius philosophiae rimatur archana, Policr.* 2.15 p. 90, 22f. Webb). Sein Zeitgenosse Bernardus Silvestris⁷ nimmt sie zum Anlass, dieses Buch eingehender zu kommentieren als die ersten fünf Aeneisbücher.⁸ Ebenso verfährt im späten 15. Jahrhundert der florentinische Platoniker Cristoforo Landino in seinen *Disputationes Camaldulenses*.⁹

Zu der bei Servius und Macrobius befürworteten kosmologischen Auslegung der vergilischen Unterweltsbeschreibung kam noch ein zweiter Strang exegetischer Tradition, die ihre Textgrundlage in der *Expositio Virgilianae continentiae secundum philosophos moralis* des Fulgentius (um 500) hatte und vermutlich an neuplatonischen Odyssee-Allegoresen mit einer mehr ethischen oder anthropologischen Ausrichtung orientiert war.¹⁰

Dieser Tradition zufolge ist in dem an Gefahren, Leiden und Irrungen reichen Weg des Aeneas von Troia nach Italien der Weg des Menschen durch die Bedrohungen und Versuchungen dieser Welt dargestellt und als stufenweise Annäherung an das ihm gemässe Ziel begriffen, mag dieses nun als sittliche Vervollkommnung, als Weisheit, als Glückseligkeit oder als Erkenntnis des Göttlichen bezeichnet sein. Zur Unterstützung einer solchen Interpretation wurde der Name Aeneas etymologisch zerlegt in die vermeintlichen griechischen Bestandteile *ennos* (offenbar von ἐνναίω) = *habitator* und *demas* = *corpus* und erklärt als "der Bewohner des Leibes," was die Gleichung Aeneas = *spiritus humanus* oder *animus* ermöglichte. Im 12. Jahrhundert wird diese Erklärung, die sich nicht bei Fulgentius findet, im *Policraticus* des John of Salisbury und im Aeneiskommentar des Bernardus Silvestris vogetragen.¹¹

In dieser anthropologischen Konzeption kommt dem Abstieg in die Unterwelt eine Schlüsselfunktion zu. Er steht für die Erreichung der letzten Erkenntnis- und Läuterungsstufe¹² und beschreibt *per integumenti figuram* (Bern. Silv. p. 30.20f.) den Aufstieg des Geistes zur Erkenntnis Gottes, zunächst—so bei Bernardus Silvestris—als des Schöpfers und Lenkers der Welt.¹³ In der platonisierenden Aeneis-Interpretation des Cristoforo Landino wird daraus ein spiritueller Aufstieg, der nach kathartischer Konfrontation mit den Lastern und Sünden und den Stufen eigener Verirrung zur *divinarum rerum cognitio* im Elysium führt (*Disputationes Camaldulenses*, p. 253.12, Lohe; vgl.

p. 255, 1f.). Schon Fulgentius offeriert die Erklärung des Namens Anchises als "*ano scenon*," "der in der Höhe Wohnende," und bezieht das auf Gottvater, der im höchsten Himmel thronend vorgestellt ist (*habitans in excelsis*, p. 120.12). Bernardus Silvestris greift die Erklärung auf: *Anchises enim celsa inhabitans interpretatur, quem intelligimus esse patrem omnium omnibus presidentem* (Commentum, p. 9.8f.; vgl. p. 118.11f.). Sein anonymer Fortsetzer[14] lokalisiert das Elysium in der kosmischen Ätherregion oberhalb des Mondes (p. 116.23-117.1f.: *illa tamen que super lunam sunt non solum hominis eloquentiam verum etiam hominis scientiam excedunt. Ibi Elisii sunt, id est campi solares et lucidi vel perpetua tranquillitas*).

Damit sind kosmologische und anthropologische Aeneisinterpretation zusammengeführt und ist der zum Aufstieg umgedeutete Descensus des Aeneas in den Vorstellungshorizont des christlichen Mittelalters eingepasst. Dante konnte in seiner Divina Commedia daran anknüpfen, und er hat nach der Ansicht seines Kommentators Cristoforo Landino sich nicht nur Vergil zum Führer auf seiner Jenseitswanderung gewählt, sondern auch die Struktur seines kosmischen Weges zum *summum bonum* aus der Aeneis übernommen: *ab imis Tartaris ad supremum usque caelum* (Disput. Camald. IV p. 190.9f. Lohe; vgl. 254.1f.: *Danthes, qui primum ad inferos descendat atque inde emergens nullam aliam viam nisi per purgatoria loca ad caelum inveniat*). In der Auslegung Landinos wird Vergils Aeneas nach Betreten des Elysiums "zur Erkenntnis der Dinge geführt, die in den Himmeln sind" (*ad earum rerum cognitionem . . ., quae in caelis sunt*, p. 255.1f.). Das hermeneutische Problem, dass im Text nicht vom Himmel, sondern den Elysischen Gefilden die Rede ist, löst auch Landino im Anschluss an Macrobius mit Hilfe der *gemina doctrina*, der Vergil als Dichter verpflichtet sei (*qui eodem tempore et figmento suo et veritati inserviat*, p. 255.3f.). Dabei verfahre er mit solcher Kunst, "dass er, obwohl er nirgends von der (poetischen) Fiktion abweiche, trotzdem der philosophischen Wahrheit folge" (p. 255.7f.). Landino stand mit der allegorischen Auffassung des Weges des Aeneas in Humanistenkreisen nicht etwa allein. Boccaccio, Petrarca, Coluccio Salutati vertraten sie vor ihm, wenn auch mit anderer Akzentuierung und primär mit moralisierender Abzweckung.[15] Es wäre merkwürdig, wenn diese Auffassung überhaupt nicht in den Illustrationen der Aeneis-Handschriften zum Ausdruck käme.

Die Mehrzahl der illuminierten Aeneis-Handschriften,[16] die detaillierte Illustrationen des Textes enthalten, stammen aus der zweiten Hälfte oder gar vom Ende des 15. Jahrhunderts und wurden im Umkreis humanistischer Zentren zumeist für fürstliche Auftraggeber hergestellt. Einige dieser Handschriften— es sind diejenigen, welche nicht nur zu Beginn eines jeden Buches eine historisierte Initiale oder eine tafelbildartige Eingangsminiatur mit charakteristischer Einzelszene haben, sondern ein Buchfrontispiz mit dichtgedrängter Inhaltsübersicht bieten oder fortlaufende Textillustrationen in unregelmässiger Folge— verraten durch herausragende Illustrationsdichte ein besonderes Interesse an der Thematik des 6. Aeneisbuches.[17] In diesen Handschriften vor allem finden sich bildliche Hinweise auf ein allegorisches Verständnis des illustrierten Textes. Die Illustrationen fungieren somit als Bildkommentare, die dem zeitgenössischen Leser eine bestimmte Auslegung suggerieren und für den späteren Rezeptionsforscher das Textverständnis ihrer Urheber bezeugen.

Wie das vor sich geht, soll hier an einigen Beispielen vorgeführt werden. Sie lassen sich auf drei Rubriken verteilen: (1) moralisierende Kommentierung (sie findet sich auch zu *Aen.* 4, dem Didobuch); (2) kosmische Konzeption der Jenseitswanderung; (3) Übersetzung in christliche Vorstellungen.

MORALISIERENDE KOMMENTIERUNG

Die grösste moralische Krise des Aeneas fand man in seinem Aufenthalt in Karthago am Hofe der Königin Dido dargestellt. Hier erlag er vorübergehend den Verlockungen der sinnlichen Lust, die ihn vom Tugendweg abzubringen drohten. Erst durch den Anruf Merkurs, ausgelegt als Stimme des Gewissens, der Vernunft oder eines Freundes, vermag er sich loszureissen und die Begierden zu überwinden.

Dido verkörpert in dieser Interpretation die Lebensweise der *luxuriosi* oder einfach die Laster *libido* und *luxuria,* die im mittelalterlichen Tugend- und Lastersystem einen wichtigen Platz einnahmen. Ihr Lebensweg bietet ein Gegenexemplum zu Aeneas: sie erliegt dem Laster und findet ein klägliches Ende, dem ein ewiges Nachspiel in der Hölle folgt, während Aeneas, der Prototyp des *vir virtutis amator,*[18] als Sieger über das Laster, mit Petrarcas Worten als *carnis victor,*[19] aus dem Konflikt hervorgeht.

Die moralistischen Interpretationen der Dido-Episode in den allegorisierenden Kommentaren und darauf fussenden Äusserungen sind ziemlich einheitlich. Ich führe die einflussreichsten Stimmen hier an: **Fulgentius**, *Virg. cont.* p.

94.17ff. Helm: ... *in quarto libro et uenatu progreditur* (sc. Aeneas) *et amore torretur, et tempestate ac nubilo, uelut in mentis conturbatione, coactus adulterium perficit. In quo diu commoratus Mercurio instigante libidinis suae male praesumptum amorem relinquit; Mercurius enim deus ponitur ingenii;* ... p. 99.18ff. zur Begegnung des Aeneas mit Dido in der Unterwelt: *Illic etiam et Dido uidetur quasi amoris atque antiquae libidinis umbra iam uacua. Contemplando enim sapientiam libido iam contemptu emortua lacrimabiliter penitendo ad memoriam reuocatur.*

Bernardus Silvestris *Commentum* p. 95.12ff. Jones, zu *Aen.* 6. 450: *Dum (Aeneas) hec varia libidinis genera* (vgl. p. 93.22: *Diversa genera luxuriosorum diversis exemplis notavit*) sc. Virgilius; dazu die Ausführung p. 94.12ff.) *contemplatur, imaginatio preterite libidinis sue cernitur et hoc est quod inter hec umbra Didonis esse videtur.*—p. 24.7-10, zu *Aen.* 4: *Tempestatibus et pluviis ad cavernam compellitur, id est commotionibus carnis et affluentia humoris ex ciborum et potuum superfluitate provenientis ad immundiciam carnis ducitur et libidinis. Que immundicia carnis cavea dicitur quia serenitatem mentis et discretionis obnubilat.*—p. 25.1.18-20: *Tandem post longam monetur hiemem a Mercurio ut discedat ... Discedit a Didone et desuescit a libidine. Dido deserta emoritur et in cineres excocta demigrat.*

John of Salisbury behandelt im *Policraticus* 8.6 das üppige Gastmahl, das Dido dem Aeneas gibt, unter der Rubrik *de luxuria et libidine* als *luxuriosum muliebris intemperantiae conuiuium* (p. 261.13f.) und stellt ihm das frugale Mahl des Euander *Aen.* 8 gegenüber. Zu *Aen.* 4 bemerkt er ib. 8.24: *Quarta (sc. etas) illicitos amores conciliat et ignem imprudenter conceptum in pectore ad amantis infelicem producit rogum. Neque enim inconcessis fatalem beatitudinem esse sub typo Mercurii ratio persuadet* (p. 416.16-19); und zur Antwort des Aeneas: *Ergo et uirilis etas puerilia et iuuenilia erubescit et, si a peruersa uoluptate et immundo amore nauigii sui soluere non potest anchoram, praecidit et funem* (p. 416.27-29).

Dante setzt diese Einstufung Didos voraus, wenn er sie *Inferno* 5.61f. in den zweiten Höllenkreis unter die Sünder der Fleischeslüste und des Wohllebens (vizio di lussuria) verdammt, vereint mit den Königinnen Semiramis, Cleopatra, Helena und anderen Liebessündern.

Auch **Boccaccio**, der sich immer wieder mit der Gestalt Didos beschäftigt hat und in seinen späteren lateinischen Schriften die vergilische Darstellung zugunsten der von Iustin überlieferten vermeintlich historischen Version, der zufolge die phönizische Witwe ein Musterbeispiel für *pudicitia* und Gattentreue geliefert hat, als poetische Fiktion verwirft,[20] hält an dem traditionellen Verständnis der Rolle Didos bei Vergil fest und räumt ein, dass sie für die allegorisch verhüllte Absicht des Dichters notwendig war: *... quod sub velamento latet poetico, intendit Virgilius per totum opus ostendere quibus passionibus humana fragilitas infestetur, et quibus viribus a constanti viro superentur. Et ... volens demonstrare, quibus ex causis ab appetitu concupiscibili in lasciviam rapiamur, introducit Dydonem ... etate iuvenem ... et viduam, quasi ab experientia Veneris concupiscentie aptiorem. ... Et sic intendit pro Dydone concupiscibilem et attractivam potentiam, oportunitatibus omnibus armatam. Eneam autem pro quocunque ad lubricum apto et demum capto. Tandem ostenso, quo trahamur in scelus ludibrio, qua via in virtutem revehamur, ostendit, inducens Mercurium ... Per quem Virgilius sentit seu conscientie proprie morsum, seu amici et eloquentis hominis redargutionem, a quibus, dormientes in luto turpitudinum, excitamur, et in rectum pulchrumque revocamur iter* (*Genealogie deorum gentilium* 14.13 p. 722.27-723.12 Romano).

Für **Landino** (*Disput. Camald.* p. 183f. Lohe) hat Vergil mit Didos Preisgabe der Selbstbeherrschung und Sittsamkeit (*postremo victa amore incontinens ita redditur, ut demum in summam intemperantiam incidat; ... ut victa in incontinentiam prolaberetur; ... impudentissima effecta turpem libidinem honesto nomine appellet*) ein warnendes Beispiel setzen wollen, "welch grosser Schaden den Untertanen erwächst, wenn ihre Fürsten statt Tatkraft und Anstrengung der Üppigkeit (*luxuria*) und trägen Säumigkeit (*ignavia*) verfallen."

Durch Dantes Einstufung Didos unter die Sünder der *luxuria* im zweiten Höllenkreis dürfte die Verdammung der Königin für viele geradezu kanonische Geltung erhalten haben. Illustrierende Darstellungen des Danteschen Inferno selbst in öffentlichen Gebäuden (z.B. Santa Maria Novella, Florenz, Cappella Strozzi) verliehen ihr jedenfalls eine traurige Popularität. Hier erscheint sie, sogar durch Namensbeischrift gekennzeichnet, in der Gruppe der Liebessünder, die in spezifischer Weise zu büssen haben: sie werden in einer Sturmwolke herumgewirbelt.[21]

Sichtbare Spuren dieser Auffassung finden sich auch in Aeneisillustrationen. In mehreren illuminierten Handschriften ist die Verurteilung der Dido amorosa (Dante, *Inf.* 5.60) unmissverständlich zum Ausdruck gebracht, und zwar auf unterschiedliche, zum Teil recht originelle Weise.

So wird die Königin in der Frontispizminiatur zum 6. Aeneisbuch aus einer Handschrift der Bibliothèque municipale zu Lyon (ms. 27, fol. 137r)[22] im leibhaftigen Rachen der Hölle vorgeführt (Abb. 29). Der Illustrator hat zwei Stationen der Unterweltswanderung ausgewählt: die Ankunft am Fluss (Acheron oder Styx) beim Fährmann Charon und die Begegnung mit Dido. Aeneas und die Sibylle erscheinen zweimal im Bild. Aeneas, mit Krone, trägt als Zeichen seiner Berechtigung zur Katabasis den goldenen Zweig, der jedoch als szepterförmiger Stab mit Kreuzaufsatz gebildet ist.[23]

Die Begegnung mit Charon, der schon bei Vergil als furchterregender Dämon auftritt, sich in dem mittelhochdeutschen Aeneas-Epos Heinrich von Veldekes[24] in einen grässlichen Teufel verwandelt hat und sich in Dantes *Inferno* und zahlreichen Illustrationen der betreffenden Textpartie (*Inferno* 3.82-177), ja selbst in einigen Aeneis-Illustrationen in Teufelsgestalt präsentiert[25]—Charon erscheint in unserem Bild ganz harmlos und geradezu verniedlicht. Der kleine Fährmann in seinem winzigen Boot wirkt wie ein ergebener Diener vornehmer Herrschaft, die ihn zum Landesteg beordert hat.

Die Begegnung mit Dido dagegen überrascht durch unerwartete infernalische Züge. Die Königin, nackt mit Krone dargestellt, balanciert an der Spitze von zwei weiteren weiblichen Figuren auf der Riesenzunge eines imposanten, weit aufgesperrten Tierrachens (im Profil), hinter dem aus einer Felsöffnung Qualm und Feuerwolken aufsteigen. Die Botschaft des Bildes ist eindeutig: Dido befindet sich im Rachen der Hölle,[26] sie ist verdammt als Liebessünderin. Die Sibylle doziert, Aeneas greift sich ans Herz. Seine niedergeschlagenen Augen bekunden Scham und Nachdenklichkeit: *contemplando quam turpi amore dudum teneretur* (Bern. Silv. p. 95.16; vgl. 20: *penitens quia in tam turpi erravit*). Die Abberufung des pflichtvergessenen Liebenden durch Merkur und sein Gehorsam gegen den Befehl stehen in derselben Handschrift im Mittelpunkt der narrativen Frontispizminiatur zu *Aen.* 4 (fol. 108r).

In einer anderen Eingangsminiatur zu *Aen.* 4 aus einer im Loiretal entstandenen Handschrift, jetzt ms. Richardson 38 (fol. 135v; Abb. 30)[27] der Houghton Library, Harvard University, hat der Illustrator vor die Höhle, in der Dido und Aeneas sich der Liebe hingeben, ein drachenartiges Ungeheuer gesetzt. Dadurch wird der Vorgang moralisch und zugleich theologisch kommentiert. Der höllische Drache, dessen über den ganzen Leib verstreute Augen noch an Vergils allegorisches Monster Fama erinnern (*Aen.* 4.173-188), ist ein klares Signal, dass die Höhle als Stätte des Bösen, hier der sündigen Lust zu verstehen ist.

Die Miniatur, die geradezu ein gemaltes Buchargumentum darbietet, das den Inhalt des ganzen Buches in fortlaufenden, dichtgedrängten, nicht immer scharf voneinander getrennten Szenenfolgen bildlich nacherzählt, sei hier in ihrer Gesamtheit beschrieben. Die Bilderzählung ist auf zwei übereinander angeordnete Felder verteilt, die ihrerseits durch Architekturelemente jeweils in der ungefähren Mitte unterteilt sind. Sie beginnt links oben im Hintergrund mit einem Rückgriff auf die Ausgangssituation zu Beginn des 2. Buches: den Bericht des Aeneas; das Paar sitzt eng beieinander auf einem Sofa. Dann folgt links oben im Vordergrund die Eröffnungsszene des 4. Buches: das Gespräch zwischen Dido und Anna (beide tragen weisse spitze Hauben); rechts daneben die Konspiration der Göttinnen Iuno und Venus (zwei nackte weibliche Gestalten); weiter: Dido mit Aeneas, ihn durch die Stadt führend. Rechts hinter der Mauer folgt dann der Auszug zur schicksalhaften Jagd—ganz rechts das Paar in der Höhle, vor der der Drache liegt. Im unteren Feld sieht man (von links nach rechts) ganz oben Iuppiter (in ätherischem Rund), der Merkur (ein Vielflügelwesen) zur Abberufung des Aeneas entsendet; dieser ist aufmerkend den Göttern zugewandt und weist gehorsam auf das abfahrbereite Schiff; links daneben, im Vordergrund, ist sein Abschied von Dido dargestellt, ganz links diese allein in Trauer. In der Mitte ist ein das Bildfeld teilender Turm, auf dem ein hohes Feuer lodert (Andeutung des Scheiterhaufens?) und die beiden Schwestern die Abfahrt beobachten; rechts im Gemach stösst sich Dido dann das Schwert in den Leib; rechts aussen wird sie zum Tode erlöst durch Iris, die Regenbogengöttin, deren am Bogenende angesetzte Hand mit Didos Todesschwert die Locke abschneidet.

In einer weiteren Frontispizminiatur zum 4. Aeneisbuch einer auf das Jahr 1500 datierten Handschrift der französischen Übersetzung des Octovien de Saint-Gelais, aus der Schule von Rouen, (jetzt in Paris, Bibliothèque Nationale, ms. fr. 861, fol. 33v; Abb. 31)[28] ist der moralisierende Kommentar in die Darstellung des illustrierten Vorgangs selbst—Didos Selbstmord nach Abfahrt des Aeneas—einbezogen und als Bildallegorie visualisiert. Dido tötet sich in diesem Bild vor dem brennenden Altar des mit einer Binde vor den Augen dargestellten Liebesgottes, also des *Cupido caecus,* der die blinde Liebesleidenschaft verkörpert, als deren Opfer sie erscheinen soll.

KOSMISCHE KONZEPTION DER JENSEITSWANDERUNG

Das kosmische Verständnis der Katabasis des Aeneas ist mit Gewissheit nur im Bereich des Elysium aufweisbar. In zwei der mir bekannten Illustrationen zu *Aen.* 6 ist es sichtbar zum Ausdruck gebracht. Der Abstieg des Aeneas ist dabei in einem speziellen philosophischen Sinn interpretiert: als spiritueller Aufstieg zu Gott oder zur Weisheit. Die Maler stellen dies nicht direkt dar. Sie verfahren ebenso wie der Dichter Vergil selbst, sie beschränken sich auf Hinweise, die sie hier und dort in die Darstellung der Geschichte einstreuen, die die Bilder getreu nacherzählen.

Die wichtigste Illustration findet sich in einer Handschrift der Universitätsbibliothek in Valencia, die am Ende des 15. Jhs. in Neapel für den aragonesischen Hof, an dem die humanistischen Studien florierten, hergestellt wurde (ms. 837, früher ms. 748, fol. 161r; Abb. 32).[29] Sie gehört zu den wenigen zu Ende geführten Vergilhandschriften, die zu einzelnen Aeneisbüchern auch mehrere, in lockerer Folge in den Text eingeschaltete Illustrationen enthalten.[30] Auf die Aeneis fallen insgesamt 35 Miniaturen, davon finden sich allein 16 im 6. Buch,[31] das also ganz stark interessiert haben muss. Von diesen 16 Miniaturen illustrieren nur 3 "elysische" Szenen, 9 haben höllischen Charakter und betreffen Stationen der Unterweltswanderung der Sibylle und des Aeneas vor ihrer Ankunft in den elysischen Gefilden, in denen sich die Seligen aufhalten. Diese Ankunft an der Grenze zum Elysium ist in unserem Bild illustriert.

Im Text ist sie folgendermassen geschildert (*Aen.* 6.630-641):

> 'acceleremus' ait; 'Cyclopum educta caminis
> moenia conspicio atque aduerso fornice portas;
> haec ubi nos praecepta iubent deponere dona.'
> dixerat et pariter gressi per opaca uiarum
> corripiunt spatium medium foribusque propinquant.
> occupat Aeneas aditum corpusque recenti
> spargit aqua ramumque aduerso in limine figit.
> His demum exactis, perfecto munere diuae,
> deuenere locos laetos et amoena uirecta
> fortunatorum nemorum sedesque beatas.
> largior hic campos aether et lumine uestit
> purpureo, solemque suum, sua sidera norunt.

Die Sibylle, die ihre lange Lektion über die Strafen und Verbrechen im Tartarus beendet hat, mahnt jetzt zur Eile. In der

Ferne sichtet sie die Palastmauern des Dis mit einem gewölbten Tor. Daran soll der goldene Zweig, der als Gabe für Proserpina bestimmt ist, niedergelegt werden. Rasch nähern sie sich trotz der Dunkelheit. Aeneas geht zum Eingang, reinigt sich durch Besprengung mit fliessendem Wasser und befestigt den Zweig auf der Schwelle. Danach gelangen sie ins Elysium, eine helle und freundliche Lichtregion. Der Palast Proserpinas liegt offenbar an der Grenze zum Elysium. Hier findet die Abgabe des Zweiges statt, auf die dieser Handlungsabschnitt zuläuft. Die Göttin selbst tritt dabei nicht in Erscheinung (vgl. Abb. 35).

In dem Bild hingegen übergibt Aeneas (unten rechts neben der Sibylle) einer schönen weiblichen Gestalt, die ein langes, tiefblaues Gewand trägt und einen zarten Schleier, der halbkreisförmig um ihren Kopf steht, einen Lilienzweig. Hinter dieser Gestalt sind die ursprünglich silbernen, jetzt oxydierten Hörner einer waagerecht liegenden Mondsichel sichtbar. Die schöne Proserpina, auf deren Erscheinungsbild die Madonnenikonographie eingewirkt hat, steht also für den Mond (oder markiert den *circulus lunaris*), der als Grenze des kosmischen Hades zum Elysium hin galt. Jenseits der Grenze—sie ist durch eine Mauer bezeichnet—öffnet sich eine weite himmlische Lichtregion, und man sieht drei überirdische Gestalten in aufsteigender Anordnung (bekleidet mit einem Mantel auf nacktem Körper), die gelöst zu den Sternen hinaufblicken und mit gebärdenreichen Händen nach oben zum Himmel weisen. Wer diese drei seligen Betrachter sind, bleibt rätselhaft. Ihre Bedeutung liegt darin, dass sie das (kosmische) Elysium zum Ort der 'Himmelsschau' werden lassen und zugleich deren spirituelles Verständnis andeuten. Für den betrachtend aufsteigenden Geist beginnt hier die wie auch immer geartete *rerum diuinarum cognitio*.[32]

Der Fortsetzer des Bernardus-Kommentars bietet als Alternative zu einer ihn offenbar nicht befriedigenden rationalistischpädagogischen Aufstiegsvorstellung eine am kosmischen Aufstiegsschema orientierte Interpretation mit mystischem Einschlag an, die der in unserer Illustration zum Ausdruck gebrachten Auffassung nicht ganz fernsteht und die Verbreitung derartiger Allegoresen bezeugen kann. Er macht zu *Aen.* 6.636 den Nachtrag: *Vel aliter de ramo*[33] *dicamus ut per Proserpinam luna intelligatur subtus quam queque continentur sunt mutabilia et caduca. Ad hec percipienda vel perpetienda Eneas dum ascendisset animi consideratione, tandem ramum aureum postibus Proserpine defixit quia dum usque ad lunam hec consideratio pervenisset, vidit ibi terminari et finem habere ea de quibus homo plenus anime scire et fari posset. Illa tamen que super lunam sunt non solum hominis eloquentiam verum etiam hominis scientiam excedunt. Ibi Elisii sunt, id est campi solares et lucidi vel perpetua tranquillitas* (p. 116.17-117.2).

In der anderen hier zu erörternden Illustration (Abb. 33), einer Frontispizminiatur zu Aen. 6 aus einer von dem Paduaner Bartolomeo Sanvito im Renaissancestil kalligraphierten und wahrscheinlich auch illuminierten Handschrift, jetzt King's ms. 24 (fol. 131v) der British Library, London,[34] ist die Konzeption eines spirituellen Aufstiegs hinter einer klassizistischen[35] Fassade versteckt. In dieser Miniatur sind drei Szenen, die Aeneas und die Sibylle in drei verschiedenen Stadien der Unterweltswanderung darstellen, durch einen einheitlichen Landschaftsrahmen zu einem Bild verbunden. Dabei sind die drei Stadien so gewählt, dass sie die wichtigsten Etappen und Regionen repräsentieren und zusammen den ganzen Weg des Aeneas bis zum Ziel vorführen. Gezeigt sind:

Die Begegnung mit Charon am Flussufer. Sie bildet den Anfang der Bewegung. Rechts im Bildmittelgrund kommen Aeneas und die Sibylle zum Fluss, auf dem (in der Bildmitte) Charon auf sie zurudert; Aeneas hält ihm den goldenen Zweig entgegen.

Die Besänftigung des Cerberus, der das Tor zu dem von einer dreifachen Mauer umgebenen Hadesinneren bewacht. Auf dem Turm sitzt in Herrscherpose, ausgestattet mit Strahlenkrone und Zweizack, der Unterweltsgott Dis.[36] Diese "Höllenburg," in der die Vorstellung des Herrscherpalastes mit der der Tartarusfestung zusammengeflossen ist, steht für das gesamte Inferno der vergilischen Unterwelt.

Auf der Gegenseite, im Bildvordergrund links, abgetrennt durch eine tiefe Kluft, ist in freundlicher Landschaft die Begegnung mit Musaeus im Elysium, den die Sibylle nach dem Aufenthaltsort des Anchises gefragt hat, dargestellt. Diese elysische Szene, in der Aeneas und die Sibylle zum dritten und letzten Male im Bild gezeigt sind, verlangt unsere Aufmerksamkeit. Aeneas ist zu der würdigen Erscheinung des alten Musaeus hingewendet, der in seiner rechten Hand ein Buch, das ist ein Attribut der Gelehrsamkeit oder Weisheit, hält,[37] während er mit der linken auf die Spitze eines Hügels weist, auf dem Anchises—ἄνω σκήνων, "der in der Höhe Wohnende"—vor einer Schar lichter Seelen zu finden ist. (Dem Vergiltext zufolge [*Aen.* 6.703 mit 678] müsste sich Anchises in einem Tal aufhalten, und so ist er auch in dem alten Vergilius Vaticanus [Vat. lat. 3225], pictura 37, dargestellt: Abb. 36.) Der Maler gibt mit seinem Bildkommentar also eine behutsam andeutende Illustration des ἄνω, des Aufstiegs.

GEMINA PICTURA: CHRISTLICHER HIMMEL UND GEBET ZUM MYSTISCHEN LAMM

Fälle, in denen spezifisch pagane Vorstellungen ins Christliche übersetzt sind, finden sich in den Illustrationen zu Vergils Unterweltsbuch nicht selten, doch bleiben sie weitgehend auf den Bereich der Hölle beschränkt. Die Darstellung Didos im Höllenrachen aus dem Lyoner Manuskript ist ein bezeichnendes Beispiel (Abb. 29). Hier möchte ich jedoch nicht die Christianisierung des vergilischen Hades verfolgen.[38] Vielmehr möchte ich einen in hermeneutischer Hinsicht besonders interessanten Fall erörtern, in dem mit Hilfe doppelter Illustrierung auf zwei unterschiedlichen Bedeutungsebenen der im Text erzählte Vorgang sowohl veranschaulicht wie in einem christlichen Sinne kommentiert wird. Damit ist die Theorie der *gemina doctrina* auf die bildliche Textillustrierung appliziert und als *gemina pictura* realisiert.

Es handelt sich um eine höchst komplexe Eingangsminiatur zu *Aen.* 6 aus der schon im ersten Abschnitt unter den moralisierenden allegorischen Kommentierungen (Abb. 30) herangezogenen Handschrift der Houghton Library, Harvard University (ms. Richardson 38, fol. 174v, Abb. 34). Auch in diesem Buchfrontispiz liegt ein gemaltes argumentum vor, in dem der Inhalt des ganzen Buches zusammengefasst ist. Die Aufteilung der Bildfläche ist eine andere als beim 4. Buch. Dort ist sie gegliedert in zwei übereinander liegende, in der ungefähren Mitte durch in die Darstellung einbezogene Architekturelemente organisch unterteilte, gleich hohe Zonen, also in insgesamt vier annähernd quadratische Bildfelder—hier sind ebenfalls zwei Zonen übereinander eingerichtet, aber nur die obere ist in zwei eigens gerahmte Felder zerlegt, von denen das rechte etwas breiter ist. Die untere, fast ein Drittel höhere Zone bildet ein grosses Feld, das sich in der unteren linken Ecke öffnet zu einem vierten Feld, einem schmalen Seitenfeld, das die ganze Bildhöhe einnimmt. Die zonenübergreifende Dimension dieses Aussenfeldes ist unter den Illustrationen dieser Handschrift singulär und ganz offensichtlich von der Sache her bedingt.

Die Darstellung, die im Hintergrund des linken Teilfeldes der oberen Zone beginnt mit der Landung der Schiffe in der Bucht von Cumae am Fusse des Apollotempels und sich jeweils von links nach rechts über beide Zonen fortsetzt, springt unten rechts noch einmal zur Gegenseite über, um im linken Randfeld nach oben aufzusteigen. In diesem Randfeld drängt sich unten eine Menge nackter (oder genauer: nur mit unauffälligen kurzen Unterhosen bekleideter) Figuren, die merkwürdige Kopfbedeckungen[39] tragen, in das Portal eines hohen turmartigen Gebäudes in gotischem Stil. Im Inneren sind Treppen zu sehen, die nach oben führen und etwa in der Mitte von einem Engel kontrolliert werden. Ganz oben thront Gottvater mit Krone auf blauer Tiara(?), auf dessen linkem Knie ein Globus ruht, seine rechte Hand ist segnend erhoben. Hinter ihm stehen rote Thronengel, darunter sechsflügelige, deren unteres Flügelpaar geschlossen ist. Mit dem Portal ist augenscheinlich die Himmelspforte gemeint, die in Darstellungen des Weltgerichtes häufig an ebendieser Stelle erscheint.[40] Der Weg führt also in den theologischen Himmel der christlichen Kirche vor Gottes Thron.

Diejenigen, die dorthin gelangen, sind den im Hintergrund des unteren Feldes angedeuteten Höllenstrafen entgangen. Dieses grosse Feld enthält die Illustration der eigentlichen Unterweltswanderung des Aeneas und der Sibylle. Links oben sind sie durch die Öffnung einer Höhle in die durch einen Fluss gegliederte Landschaft eingetreten, Aeneas hält sein gezücktes Schwert hoch wie im Text, die Sibylle doziert. Zu sehen sind: zur Mitte hin vorn Charon auf dem Fluss in seinem Boot, zu dem er mit einem Seil eine am Ufer stehende Gruppe aus fünf nackten Gestalten, darunter zwei gekrönten Häuptern, zieht; sie soll offenbar übergesetzt werden. Etwas weiter hinten, etwa in der Bildmitte, steht eine schlanke weibliche Gestalt in langem dunkelbraunen Gewand und offenem blonden Haar, in dem man bei genauem Zusehen züngelnde Feuerfäden und Schlangen entdeckt; eine Furie also in auffällig freundlicher Erscheinung und eleganter Pose, gleichsam als Empfangsdame tätig, offenbar mit Wächter— und Verteilerfunktionen betraut.[41] Hinter ihr ist ein weit geöffnetes Tor, das in das Innere eines schroffen Felsmassivs führt; daraus blicken, dicht gedrängt, Verdammte mit unseligen Gebärden, in der vorderen Reihe mit hellen Körpern, weiter nach innen sind sie dunkel.[42] Zur Rechten des Tores schliessen höllische Strafstätten an: ein Feuerpfuhl, in dem Verdammte leiden, und ein zweiarmiger Galgen, an dem vier erbärmliche Gestalten hängen; zudem heller Feuerschein, Felsen, Rauch und weitere Höhlenöffnungen, aus denen Flammen schlagen. Abgebildet ist hier somit ein Inferno in der mittelalterlichen Ausprägung: als Hölle, wenn auch ohne Teufel, mit typischen Strafarten. Sie ist an die Stelle des mythologischen Tartarus gesetzt. Wie diesen lassen Aeneas und die Sibylle sie links vom Wege liegen, um zu Anchises ins Elysium zu gelangen.

Die Dreiergruppe rechts unten im Bild, die vor einem die Höllenregion abtrennenden Felsen plaziert ist, zeigt, dass die Begegnung zustande gekommen ist. Aber die Sibylle weist weiter zur Himmelspforte in der anderen Bildecke. Da soll das Ziel erblickt werden.[43]

Zu erörtern sind noch die Darstellungen in der oberen Zone, in der die Vorgänge illustriert werden, die der Vorbereitung des Abstiegs dienen. Im linken Feld sieht man zusammengedrängt: im Hintergrund drei gelandete Schiffe, links daneben Andeutungen von Tempel und Stadt; im Vordergrund tritt Aeneas bittend vor die Sibylle, die in ihrer Grotte sitzt; ganz rechts legen zwei Männer den toten Misenus nieder. Damit sind die Ereignisse von der Landung in Cumae bis zur Bestattung des Misenus vorgeführt. Die Auffindung des goldenen Zweiges mit Hilfe der himmlischen Tauben ist jedoch abgesondert und im Feld rechts daneben gezeigt.

Hier sind zwei Episoden dargestellt. Rechts stehen Aeneas und Achates vor einem Baum, in dessen Krone sich zwei weisse Tauben mit ausgebreiteten Flügeln über einem goldenen Büschel niederlassen. Achates zeigt mit ausgestrecktem Arm dahin, während Aeneas noch suchend zu Boden blickt: Diese Darstellung entspricht dem im Text erzählten Vorgang. Links daneben findet sich nun aber eine Gebetsszene, die keine wörtliche Entsprechung im Vergiltext hat. Eine (männliche?) Person in langem roten Gewand, mit kurzem blonden Haar, barhäuptig, kniet betend (mit geöffneten Händen) vor einem in einer Nische befindlichen Altar, auf dem ein weisses Lamm (mit Widderhörnern) steht. Wer diese Person ist, lässt sich nicht ermitteln. Aeneas kann es wegen der Kleidung nicht sein. Eine andere epische Figur stellt der Text nicht bereit. Pagane Götter erscheinen in unserer Handschrift nackt oder als Bronzestatue und würden auch kaum in dieser Rolle auftreten. Allenfalls wäre die göttliche Mutter des Aeneas, Venus, denkbar, von der ja die hilfreichen Tauben gesandt sind. In den Kommentaren ist sie als himmlische Liebe und kosmische Kraft ausgelegt, und in der Aeneis nimmt sie nicht nur helfende, sondern auch fürsprechende Funktionen wahr.[44] Aber die hier abgebildete Gestalt passt zu ihrem Erscheinungsbild nicht.[45] Eine fiktive Fürsprechergestalt also? Oder eine ideale Beterfigur? Man wird die Frage offenlassen müssen. Doch wirkt die ganze Szene wie die Anrufung des mystischen Lammes, das allein den Zugang zum Himmel gewähren kann.

In jedem Fall fungiert die linke Darstellung als Kommentar zu der daneben im wörtlichen Sinne illustrierten Geschichte von der Auffindung des goldenen Zweiges mit Hilfe der Tauben der Venus, einer Geschichte, die sich allein wegen ihrer mythologischen Züge als poetische Fiktion erweist, deren philosophische oder theologische Wahrheit aufgespürt werden muss. Wir haben hier also mit einer doppelten Illustration ein und desselben Vorgangs auf verschiedenen Bedeutungsebenen zu rechnen, der allegorischen und der wörtlichen—kurz: mit *gemina pictura*.

ANMERKUNGEN

1. Dazu A. Wlosok, "Gemina doctrina: On Allegorical Interpretation," *Papers of the Liverpool Latin Seminar* 5 (1985) 75-84, dort p. 75 die Belege aus Servius; besonders wichtig für unseren Zusammenhang ist Serv., *Comm. ad Aen.* 6.719 *(miscet philosophiae figmenta poetica),* zitiert unten Anm. 43. Aus späterer Zeit führe ich an: **Bernardus Silvestris**, dessen *Commentum super sex libros Eneidos Virgilii*, kritische Ed.: J.W. u. E.F. Jones (Lincoln, London, 1977) auf dieser Theorie aufbaut. Er beginnt: *Gemine doctrine observantiam perpendimus in sua Eneide Maronem habuisse, teste namque Macrobio: et veritatem philosophie docuit et ficmentum poeticum non pretermisit. Si quis ergo Eneida legere studeat, ita ut eius voluminis lex deposcit, hec in primis oportet demonstrare, unde agat et qualiter et cur, et geminam observationem in his demonstrandis non relinquere. Quoniam ergo in hoc opere et poeta et philosophus perhibetur esse Virgilius, primo poete intentionem et modum agendi et cur agat breviter dicamus* (p. 1.1-7). Zur philosophischen Intention erklärt er: *Nunc vero hec eadem circa philosophicam veritatem videamus. Scribit ergo in quantum est philosophus humane vite naturam. Modus agendi talis est: in integumento describit quid agat vel quid paciatur humanus spiritus in humano corpore temporaliter positus* (p. 3.8-11). Schliesslich folgt die Definition: *Integumentum est genus demonstrationis sub fabulosa narratione veritatis involvens intellectum, unde etiam dicitur involucrum* (p. 3.14f.). **Ioannes Saresberiensis (John of Salisbury)**, *Policraticus* 8.24, ed. C.C.J. Webb (Oxford, 1909) repr. 1965, p. 417.14-17) *Constat enim apud eos qui mentem diligentius perscrutantur auctorum Maronem geminae doctrinae uires declarasse, dum uanitate figmenti poetici philosophicae uirtutis inuoluit archana.* **Cristoforo Landino**, *Disputationes Camald-*

ulenses IV, ed. Peter Lohe (Firenze, 1980) schreibt (p. 254.32-255.8) in deutlicher Anlehnung an die oben zitierte Macrobiusstelle (*in somn. Scip.* 1.9.8): *Cum igitur . . . omnibus iam vitiis expiatum Aeneam ad earum rerum cognitionem Maro deducturus esset, quae in caelis sunt, non caelum, sed Elysios campos nominat. Miro profecto ingenio vates et qui eodem tempore et figmento suo et veritati inserviat. Nam etsi apud inferos poetarum more heroas religasset, tamen, ut haec omnia de caelo illum sentire animadvertamus, largiorem aetherem ac suum solem suaque sidera illis tribuit, ut, cum a figmento nusquam discedat, philosophiae tamen veritatem prosequatur.*

2. Vgl. dazu A. Wlosok, "Et poeticae figmentum et philosophiae veritatem. Bemerkungen zum 6. Aeneisbuch," *Listy Filologické* 106 (1983) 13-19 (wiederabgedruckt in: A. Wlosok, "Res humanae—res divinae," *Kleine Schriften*, hg. von E. Heck u. E.A. Schmidt [Heidelberg, 1990] 384-391) und, grundlegend, A. Thornton, *The Living Universe*, (Leiden, 1976) 57-69 (gewisse Vorbehalte in meiner Rezension im *Gnomon* 53 [1981] 755-758).

3. Einzelheiten bei A. Thornton a.O. 63-66 und in E. Nordens *Kommentar zu Aen. VI* (1927[3]) 23-26; vgl. A. Wlosok, *Laktanz und die philosophische Gnosis,* (Sitz.-Ber. Heidelberg, 1960) 43-47 (zum postmortalen Seelenaufstieg in pythagoreischer und platonischer Tradition). Die ausführlichsten Beschreibungen finden sich bei Plutarch, de genio Socratis, Kap. 21f. (590Aff.) und *de facie in orbe lunae*, Kap. 27-30 (942D-945D). Für den römischen Bereich wichtige Zeugnisse sind Varro, *RD* frg. 226 Cardauns, Cic., *Tusc.* 1.42f. und natürlich das *somnium Scipionis.*

4. Plutarch, *de facie* 27. 942D-F.

5. Als ein solcher Hinweis wurde immer wieder die befremdliche Angabe gegen Ende der Hadeswanderung angesehen: *sic tota passim regione uagantur / aëris in campis latis* (*Aen.* 6.886f.). Servius kommentiert die Stelle: *locutus autem est secundum eos, qui putant Elysium lunarem esse circulum.* Dieses Scholion steht in mehreren der von mir eingesehenen illuminierten Aeneishandschriften dem betreffenden Text, z.B. bei Paris, BN, ms. lat. 7939A, fol. 135v.

6. Serv., *Comm. ad Aen. 6*: *Totus quidem Vergilius scientia plenus est, in qua hic liber possidet principatum . . . et dicuntur aliqua simpliciter, multa de historia, multa per altam scientiam philosophorum, theologorum, Aegyptiorum . . .* Auch dieser Kommentar findet sich in vielen Handschriften marginal zum Anfang des 6. Buches.

7. Ich halte an dem Namen fest, obwohl die Autorschaft fraglich ist; siehe die Einleitung der Herausgeber p. ix-xi. Die zeitliche und räumliche Einordnung des Kommentars wird von der Verfasserfrage nicht wesentlich berührt.

8. *Commentum* p. 28.9-11: *quia profundius philosophicam veritatem in hoc volumine declarat Virgilius, ideo non tantum summam, verum etiam verba exponendo in eo diutius immoremur.*

9. Die Aeneis-Interpretation nimmt die Bücher 3 und 4 ein (p. 110-262). Die am fortlaufenden Text orientierte Erklärung beginnt nach allgemeinen methodischen Bemerkungen etwa bei p. 127 mit der allegorischen Deutung der Eltern des Aeneas (Venus steht als *vera Venus, quae mentem nostram ad divina erigit* p. 128.15f., für den platonischen Eros p. 125.4ff.) und dem Auszug aus Troia, bei p. 203 liegt der Übergang zum 6. Aeneisbuch, dem somit etwa 60 Seiten gelten, während *Aen.* 1-5 auf etwa 75 Seiten erörtert werden. Zur Eigenart dieses platonisierenden Kommentars, für den Vergil ein *Platonicus poeta* (p. 125.10) ist, und seinem Verhältnis zur exegetischen Tradition: C. Zintzen, Zur "Aeneis"—Interpretation des Cristoforo Landino: *Mittellat. Jahrb.* 20 (1985) 193-215. Ferner E. Müller-Bochat, *Leon Battista Alberti und die Vergil-Deutung der Disputationes Camaldulenses*: Schriften und Vorträge des Petrarca-Instituts Köln 21 (Krefeld, 1968); M. Lentzen, *Studien zur Dante-Exegese Cristoforo Landinos* (Köln, 1971) bes. Kap. IV 2; C. Kallendorf, "Cristoforo Landino's *Aeneid* and the Humanist Tradition," *Renaissance Quarterly* 36 (1983) 519-546.

10. Zu Fulgentius: G. Rauner-Hafner, "Die Vergilinterpretation des Fulgentius," *Mittellat. Jahrb.* 13 (1978) 7-49. Die seit Nordens Vermutung nicht zur Ruhe gekommene Frage, ob es einen neuplatonischen Vergilkommentar, etwa des Marius Victorinus, gegeben hat, konnte bisher nicht eindeutig beantwortet werden; vgl. J. Flamant, *Macrobe et le néo-platonisme latin*, (Leiden, 1977) 579f., 622.—Die Verbindung von Elysium—Proserpina—Mond findet sich schon in der vorneuplatonischen Homerexegese (zu *Od.* 4.563f.), auf die sich Plutarch, *de facie* 27.942D-F bezieht; später vertrat sie auch Porphyrios (bei Stob., *Ecl.* 1.14.61).

11. **Bern. Silv.**, *Comm.* p. 10.6-11: *Ubi . . . leges Venerem et Anchisem Eneam filium habere, intellige per Venerem mundanam musicam, per Eneam humanum spiritum. Dicitur autem Eneas quasi ennos demas, id est habitator corporis, ennos Grece habitator Latine. Unde Iuvenalis Neptunum Ennosigeum vocat, id est habitatorem Sygei. Demas vero, id est vinculum, corpus dicitur quia anime carcer est.* Die Herkunft der Etymologie ist unbekannt. Zur δέμας—Lehre vgl. **Macr.**, *in somn. Scip.* 1.11.3; dort 4ff. auch Ausführungen über den kosmischen "Hades."—**Ioann. Saresber.**, *Policr.* 8.24 p. 415.20-25: *Nam Eneas, qui ibi fingitur animus, sic dictus eo quod est corporis habitator; ennos enim, ut Grecis placet, habitator est, demas corpus et ab hiis componitur Eneas ut significet animam quasi carnis tugurio habitantem. Sic etiam Neptunum ennosigeum eo quod Sigeum inhabitet.*

12. **Fulgentius** erklärt *Virg. cont.* p. 98.1-3: *ramum aureum, id est doctrinam adeptus inferos ingreditur et secreta scientiae perscrutatur;* vorher gebraucht er Wendungen wie *sapientiae obscura secretaque misteria penetrare* (p. 96.2f.), *secreta sapientiae penetrare* (p. 96.5f.). Und p. 98.12-14: *discendit ad inferos atque illic et poenas malorum et bonorum retributiones et amantum considerans tristes errores oculatus inspicit testis.* Der Prozess

beginnt also mit der Einsicht in Schuld und Verfehlungen und in das Gesetz von Lohn und Strafe.

13. *Comm.* p. 30.6-9, von dem im Vergiltext gemeinten descensus: *Est autem alius (sc. descensus) virtutis qui fit dum sapiens aliquis ad mundana per considerationem descendit, non ut in eis intentionem ponat, sed ut eorum cognita fragilitate, eis abiectis, ad invisibilia penitus se convertat et per creaturarum cognitionem creatorem evidentius cognoscat.* Vgl. zu *Aen.* 6.268: **Ibant**: *Redit ad philosophicum descensum* (p. 68.21); zu 6.477: **Iter**: *contemplationem que est via a creaturis ad creatorem* (p. 97.4).

14. Der authentische Kommentar reicht in zwei Handschriften, darunter der ältesten aus dem frühen 13. Jh., nur bis zu 6.636, der Niederlegung des goldenen Zweiges an der Grenze zum Elysium. Die Fortsetzung findet sich nur in der Krakauer Handschrift, für deren Entstehung der *terminus ante* 1447 feststeht. Vgl. die Einleitung der Herausgeber p. xviif.

15. **Boccaccio**, *Genealogie deorum gentilium* 14.13 (zitiert oben S. 414). **Petrarca**, *Epist. Sen.* 4.5 (*Operum* t. II, Basiliae 1554, repr. 1965, p. 871.37): *Proinde Aeneas aduena, id est, uirtus, seu Vir fortis, carnis uictor.* Vgl. A. Wlosok, "Boccaccio über Dido - mit und ohne Aeneas," *Acta Antiqua* 30 *(Festschrift St. Borzsák),* (Budapest, 1988) 457-470. hier 468f.; J.L. de Jong, "'Sub falso tegmine vera': Dido en Aeneas in de Italiaanse kunst der Renaissance," *Hermeneus* 54 (1982) 279-288.—**Coluccio Salutati**, *De laboribus Herculis* 4.9, vol. 2, Ullman (Zürich 1951) p. 56.25: *cuncta Maronis penitissimis sunt plena misteriis;* vgl. das Kapitel *De aureo ramo,* p. 571ff.

16. Zusammenstellung illuminierter Vergil-Handschriften aus Mittelalter und Renaissance in: *Enc. Virg.* 3 (1987) 443-450 (A. Cadei); 4 (1988) 483-490 (G. Mariani Canova). Das vielversprechende Buch von P. u. J. Courcelle, *Lecteurs païens et lecteurs chrétiens de l'Énéide,* vol. 2: *Les manuscrits illustrés de l'Énéide du Xè au XVè siècle,* (Paris, 1984 [erschienen im Herbst, 1985]) ist enttäuschend und wegen der vielen Ungenauigkeiten, Fehler und mangelhaften Information nicht unbedenklich, gerade für den Nichtspezialisten, der die Angaben nicht zu überprüfen vermag. (Einzelheiten demnächst in meiner Rezension im *Jahrbuch für Antike und Christentum.*)

17. Es handelt sich um folgende Handschriften: Paris, Bibliothèque Nationale, ms. lat. 7939 A. datiert auf 1458, geschrieben in Ferrara von Leonardo Sanudo; Escorial, Bibliothek, S.II 19 und Valencia, Universitätsbibliothek, ms. 837, beide Ende des 15. Jh. zur aragonesischen Bibliothek in Neapel gehörend. [Vgl. Korrekturzusatz zu Anm. 29.]

18. Cristoforo Landino, *Disput. Camald.* p. 256.14. Ihn gilt es nachzuahmen: *Quem quidem si imitabimur, et nos corporeis pestibus liberati et nitido virtutum fonte irrigati eodem vitae genere et, dum intra haec corpora versabuntur animi nostri, gaudebimus et, cum deinde evolaverint, in nostram originem reversi aeterno aevo fruemur* (ib. 17-21).

19. Petrarca, *Epist. Sen.* 4.5, p. 871.37. Vgl. E. Müller-Bochat, "Allegorese und Allegorie. Zu Petrarcas Vergildeutung (Seniles 4.5)," in: F. Schalk (Hg.), *Petrarca 1304-1374, Beiträge zu Werk und Wirkung*, (Frankfurt a.M., 1975) 198-208.
20. Vgl. A. Wlosok, "Boccaccio über Dido—mit und ohne Aeneas" (s. oben *Anm.* 15).
21. Das Fresko des Nardo di Cione entspricht dem Plan des Inferno in der von Bartolomeo di Fruosino aus Florenz stammenden Dante-Handschrift in Paris, Bibl. Nat., ms. it. 74, fol. 1v (abgebildet bei P. Brieger/M. Meiss, *Illuminated Manuscripts of the Divine Comedy*, vol. II [Princeton, 1969] 31). Auch in vielen Einzelillustrationen zu *Inferno* 5 ist Dido namentlich oder durch charakteristische Attribute innerhalb der Gruppe der Liebessünder gekennzeichnet, z.B.: Bodleian Library, Oxford, Holkham misc. 48, fol. 8r; Mailand, Bibl. Trivulziana 1076, fol. 12v; Paris, Bibl. Nat., ms. it. 2017, fol. 63v; ferner Budapest, Univ. bibl., ms. 32 (= cod. Ital. 1), fol. 5r. (Den Hinweis auf die ersten drei Handschriften verdanke ich Marcella Roddewig/Düsseldorf.)
22. Die Handschrift wurde bereits im 14. Jh. geschrieben und dann in mehreren Etappen illustriert. Im Stil zeigt sie Berührungen mit Ateliers in Paris, Flandern und Burgund. Die Miniaturen zu *Aen.* 5-12 stammen aus der 2. Hälfte des 15. Jh. Die Qualität der Illustrationen zu Bucolica und Georgica (Anfang 15. Jh.) wird am höchsten eingeschätzt (M. Meiss, *French Painting in the Time of Jean de Berry: The Limbourgs and Their Contemporaries* [New York, 1974] 55-61. 303f. 443). Abbildungen (schwarzweiss) und Beschreibungen der Aeneisbilder bei Courcelle (s.o. Anm. 16), p. 121-127; fig. 279-290.
23. In der Eingangsminiatur zu Aen. 6 der mit dem Serviuskommentar versehenen Vergilhandschrift aus Dijon (Bibl. munic., ms. 493, fol. 123v) trägt Aeneas, der der Sibylle den goldenen Zweig präsentiert, an seiner goldenen Halskette ein Kreuz. Das ist natürlich nicht ohne Bedeutung.
24. *Eneide* 3012f. ("Er war ein Teufel, kein Mensch und hiess Charon"); Beschreibung 3049-3072. In Veldekes Vorlage, dem Roman d'Eneas (2441-2450) dagegen ist er nur "alt, hässlich und verhutzelt." Auch in der Berliner Veldeke-Handschrift des frühen 13. Jh. ist Charon nicht als Teufel abgebildet (Berlin, Staatsbibl., cod. germ. 2° 282, fol. 23r).
25. Zusammenstellung der Charon-Darstellungen aus Illustrationen zu *Inferno* 3 bei Brieger/Meiss (s. oben Anm. 21), vol. 2, 53-66; 1, 119f.; vgl. F. Vagni, "Caronte," *Enc. Dantesca* I (1970) 847-850. Aus Aeneisillustrationen sind mir Charon-Teufel bekannt in drei Manuskripten italienischer Provenienz: einer bis vor kurzem zur Collection Wellington (fol. 98r) gehörigen, inzwischen verkauften Handschrift, ms. lat. 7939 A (fol. 128r) der Bibl. Nat., Paris und ms. 185 (fol. 131r) der Bibl. Bodmeriana, Cologny-Genève. Als Teufel erscheint Charon auch in der auf das Jahr 1419 datierten Heidelberger Veldeke-Handschrift (Universitätsbibliothek, cod. Pal.

germ. 403, fol. 67r), deren Illustrator sich damit freilich an den vorgegebenen Text gehalten hat.

26. Der Höllenrachen ist in der mittelalterlichen Kunst westlicher Tradition das populärste Bild für Satan und seinen Bereich. Es war jedermann bekannt aus Darstellungen des Jüngsten Gerichtes auf Portalen und Wänden christlicher Kirchen, ganz besonders in England und Frankreich, wo er vom 12. Jh. an immer häufiger auftritt. Der Höllenrachen wurde dann auch bei der Bühnenausstattung für die Mysterienspiele verwendet, in Auferstehungsstücken etwa beim Descensus Christi. In der Buchillustration des 14. und 15. Jh. gehört er zum festen Repertoire der Illuminations-Werkstätten und wird mit Vorliebe in Stundenbüchern eingesetzt bei Darstellungen des Jüngsten Gerichtes, des Engelsturzes, der Höllenfahrt Christi, aber auch bei allen möglichen anderen Höllendarstellungen. Reiches Bildmaterial bei W.H. von der Mülbe, *Die Darstellungen des Jüngsten Gerichts an den romanischen und gotischen Kirchenportalen Frankreichs*, (Leipzig, 1911); B. Brenk, *Tradition und Neuerung in der christlichen Kunst des ersten Jahrtausends*, (Graz, Wien, Köln, 1966); R. Hughes, *Heaven and Hell in Western Art*, (London, 1968); E. Guldan, "Das Monsterportal am Palazzo Zuccari in Rom," *Zeitschrift für Kunstgeschichte* 32 (1969) 229-261; D.D.R. Owen, *The Vision of Hell*, (Edinburgh, London, 1970). Zu den einzelnen Typen s. O.A. Erich, *Die Darstellung des Teufels in der christlichen Kunst*, (Berlin, 1931) 86ff. 25ff. und die Artikel "Leviathan," "Hölle," "Höllenfahrt" im *Lexikon der christlichen Ikonographie*, vol. 2-4 (1970-1972). Auf eine mit unserer Illustration in der Figurenkonstellation vergleichbare Darstellung in den Très belles Heures de Nôtre-Dame (Brüssel, Bibl. Royale, ms. 1060, fol. 155r) weisen P. u. J. Courcelle a.O. p. 125 Anm. 9 hin. In Verbindung mit dem Descensus des Aeneas begegnet der Höllenrachen zur Bezeichnung der Unterwelt schlechthin noch in den Illustrationen der "Höllenfahrt" des Aeneas in der Heidelberger Veldeke-Handschrift aus dem Jahr 1419 (Univ. Bibl., cod. Pal. germ. 403, fol. 57r, 62r, 63v) und in den frühen Manuskripten des Ovide moralisé aus dem 14. Jh. (Rouen, Bibl. munic., ms. O. 4, fol. 355v; Paris, Arsenal 5059, fol. 199v).

27. Die 12 Aeneis-Miniaturen dieser Handschrift (ebenso das Eklogenfrontispiz—die 5 Georgica-Miniaturen sind von späterer Hand) sind von sehr hoher künstlerischer Qualität und auf Grund ihrer kompakten und in der Episodenauswahl ganz originellen Illustrationen von grosser rezeptionsgeschichtlicher Bedeutung. Verlässliche Daten zur Handschrift bei R.S. Wieck, *Late Medieval and Renaissance Illuminated Manuscripts* (1350-1525) in the Houghton Library, Cambridge, MA, 1983, p. 26f. u. 116 (mit guter Abb. von fol. 135v). Abbildungen (leider stark verkleinert und sehr dunkel) und (öfter danebengreifende) Beschreibungen der Aeneis-Miniaturen bei Courcelle p. 191-202; fig. 254-264. Nach Wieck ist das Ms. um 1465-1470 im Loiretal enstanden im Einflussbereich grosser Meister (the Coëtivy Master and the Master of Jouvenel

des Ursins) und im Auftrag eines anspruchsvollen Patrons, der freilich nicht bestimmt werden kann. P. u. J. Courcelle p. 191f. plädieren mit gewichtigen Argumenten für eine Verbindung zum Hof von Savoyen.

28. Die Übersetzung ist Ludwig XII. gewidmet. Ms. fr. 861 ist das Widmungsexemplar und enthält auf fol. 2v ein grosses Dedikationsbild. Weitere Angaben und Abbildungen aller 13 Miniaturen bei Courcelle, p. 213-218; fig. 377-388 und Th. Brückner, *Die erste französische Aeneis. Untersuchungen zu Octovien de Saint-Gelais' Übersetzung.* (Mit einer kritischen Edition des 6. Buches), (Düsseldorf, 1987) 31-33.80-93.

29. Ausführlich dazu T. De Marinis, *La Biblioteca napoletana dei re d'Aragona*, (Milano, vol. 1 [1952]); zu ms. 837 (unter der früheren Signatur: 748) vol. 2 (1947), p. 172 mit einigen Abb. in vol. 4 (1947), 255-262; Courcelle p. 219-230; fig. 389-420 (32 stark verkleinerte Abb. ohne Folio-Angaben; aus *Aen.* 6 sind 3 Miniaturen ausgelassen, darunter auch fol. 161r). [Korrekturzusatz: Vgl. jetzt die von mir eingeleitete Farbmikrofiche-Edition des Ms. 837 in der Reihe: Codices illuminati medii aevi 23, Edition H. Lengenfelder, München 1992.]

30. Bekannt sind nur noch eine etwa gleichzeitige, ebenfalls in Neapel entstandene Handschrift im Escorial, Bibl. S.II 19 und ein von dem humanistischen Schreiber Leonardo Sanudo aus Ferrara 1458 kalligraphierter Codex, jetzt Paris, Bibl. Nat., ms. lat. 7939 A. Weitere Handschriften, für die z. T. sogar auf jeder Seite eine Illustration vorgesehen war, aber nur in den ersten Büchern durchgeführt wurde, sind der in Facsimile-Edition (Florenz, 1969) vorliegende, von Apollonio di Giovanni illustrierte Riccardianus 492 in Florenz und ein Vaticanus (lat. 2761) vom Ende des 14. Jh.

31. Es sind fol.: 146r, 150v, 151r, 152r, 152v, 155r, 155v, 156r bis, 156v, 157v, 159r, 161r, 161v, 163v, 167r. In der Handschrift Escorial, Bibl. S.II 19 fallen von 64 Aeneis-Miniaturen 11 auf Buch 6, im Codex des Leonardo Sanudo (Paris, Bibl. Nat., ms. lat. 7939A) von 74 ebenfalls 11 auf Buch 6.

32. Bern. Silv., p. 114.1-9 zu 629-631: **Viam:** *contemplationem.* **Perfice**: *Quia enim agnovisti que sunt in Tartaro, restat inquirere que sint in Helisiis.* **Menia**: *Visibilibus peragratis, restat invisibilia perquirere et ideo dicit Sibilla se cernere celum, scilicet menia Ciclopum. Ciclops quasi policiculos, id est multitudo circulorum, dicitur. Per circulos enim qui fine sunt carentes et puncto indivisibili et immobili accedentes figurantur spiritus immortales et creatori indivisibili et immutabili adherentes. Ciclops ergo, id est "multitudo circulorum," est ordo spirituum; ciclopes plures spirituum multitudines. Menia ergo Ciclopum sunt celi que sunt naturales regiones spirituum.* **Conspicio**: *Patent enim intelligentie celestia;* und etwas weiter (14f.): *. . . celestia contemplatione ingredimur.*

33. Bernardus hatte ramus als integumentum für philosophia erklärt (p. 114.15, 115.4). Das genügte auch Coluccio Salutati nicht (*de*

labor. Herc. IV, p. 573.6ff.: *Allegorizator Virgilii per ramum hunc intelligit philosophiam. Ego vero. . .);* er setzt dafür sapientia ein, *que quidem est divinarum humanarumque rerum scientia, sine qua non potest esse contemplatio.*

34. Die Handschrift war das Prunkstück der Jubiläumsausstellung in der British Library vom 17.9.1982—27.2.1983 "Virgil: The 2000th Anniversary" und befindet sich jetzt unter den temporären Exponaten. Knappe instruktive Beschreibung: *Catalogue of Western Manuscripts in the Old Royal and King's Collections*, by Sir G.F. Warner und J.P. Gilson, (London, 1921) 3 p. 8. Zu den Miniaturen: F. Saxl u. H. Meier, *Verzeichnis astrologischer und mythologischer illuminierter Handschriften des lateinischen Mittelalters 3* (London, 1953) 242-244; Courcelle a.O. p. 255-261; fig. 490-501 (z.T. farbig; fol. 131v = fig. 495 ist entstellt abgebildet und an mehreren Stellen falsch erklärt). Zu Datierung und Schreiber: J.J.G. Alexander, *The Decorated Letter* (London, New York, 1978) 114; T. Kren, *Renaissance Painting in Manuscripts: Treasures from the British Library* (London, New York, 1983) 103-106; G.M. Canova, in: *Enc. Virg.* 4 (1988) p. 487f.

35. Die klassizistische Haltung äussert sich in diesem Bild u.a. in dem Verzicht auf "Verteufelung" der Unterwelt und in der würdigen Darstellung der paganen Götter. Charon z.B. ist nicht als teuflischer Dämon gestaltet (vgl. dazu o. Anm. 25), sondern als kräftiger alter Mann, wie ihn Vergil beschreibt. Auf dem Turm der "Höllenstadt" erscheinen nicht Luzifer oder höllische Furien (so bei Dante und in den Vergil-Handschriften Escorial, Bibl. S.II 19, fol. 132v und Paris, Bibl. Nat. ms. lat. 7939A, fol. 128v), sondern der klassische Herrschergott der Unterwelt Dis.

36. Das hat richtig schon Saxl (a.O. 243) gesehen: "eine Statue Plutos." Dagegen Courcelle a.O. p. 258f.: "Tisiphone en haut de sa tour," ..."dans sa main, non un fouet, mais une fourche." Diese Deutung wird allein durch die Strahlenkrone widerlegt, die freilich in fig. 495 weggeschnitten ist.

37. Vgl. schon Fulgentius, *Virg. cont.* p. 102.5f.: *Museum uidet, quasi Musarum donum, excelsiorem omnibus, qui ei etiam patrem ostendit.* Der Fortsetzer des Bern. Silv., *Comm.* p. 118.3 dagegen allegorisiert im kosmischen Sinn: *Museus dominium excelsius interpretatur, id est sol . . . MEDIUM quia ipse quasi medius inter planetas et cetera sidera . . . extat et huius ducatu Eneas patrem patrie invenit quia dum vidit omnia illuminari et calore procreari, perpendit hoc per se ita non posse fieri sed aliquo creatore ita destinari.*

38. Das soll in einer gesonderten Publikation erfolgen.

39. Eine hohe blaue oder rote Mütze in einer Krone, ähnlich, aber nicht ganz so uppig wie bei Gottvater. Diese Form kommt in der Handschrift sonst nicht vor. Sie findet sich aber z.B. in den *Très Riches Heures* des Duc de Berry (Chantilly, Musée Condé, ms. 65) in zwei Miniaturen der Brüder Limbourg, einmal bei König David (fol. 26v) und einmal für den byzantinischen Kaiser (Heraklius oder Konstantin) in der Darstellung der Kreuzerhöhung (fol. 193v).

Sollen die Figuren in unserer Miniatur als Könige und Fürsten bezeichnet werden? Oder tragen sie die "Krone des Lebens"?

40. Als Beispiele nenne ich die Gemälde von Rogier van der Weyden im Hostel-Dieu in Beaune und Hans Memling in der Marienkirche zu Danzig. Aus der Buchmalerei eine Illustration zu Ioannes Gerson, Monotessaron in ms. 17 (fol. 239v) der Univ. bibl. Gent.

41. Die Gestalt entspricht der vergilischen Tisiphone, die am Einganstor des Tartarus wacht und dem Richter Rhadamanthus zuarbeitet. Der Funktion nach vergleichbar ist eine fast gabrielhafte Wächtergestalt (ohne Flügel) mit Schwert und unauffälligem Schlangengürtel vor dem Tartaruseingang im ms. Valencia 837, fol. 159v. Auf die Placierung in der Mitte der Komposition könnte die Stellung des seelenwägenden Engels aus den Weltgerichtsdarstellungen eingewirkt haben. Die Pose der Dame begegnet in unserer Handschrift (fol. 216v) noch einmal bei der Illustration des Zeichens der Venus im 8. Buch, in der Venus als kosmische Kraft und Königin (vielleicht nach Mart. Cap. 2.181) dargestellt ist. [Vgl. den Korrekturzusatz zu Anm. 45.]

42. Die unterschiedliche Färbung könnte auch eine Zweiteilung des *Inferno* in Limbus oder Purgatorium und eigentliche Hölle als der Stätte ewiger Verdammnis signalisieren, wie sie den Vorstellungen der Zeit entspricht (vgl. z.B. fol. 113v der *Très Riches Heures* des Duc de Berry im Musée Condé, Chantilly und die Illustration zu Dante, *Inf.* 4 im gleichen Museum, ms. 597, fol. 51r = Brieger/Meiss II, 67a). Kaum dürften mit der vorderen Gruppe die vergilischen Infantes gemeint sein (so Courcelle p. 197); der Illustrator zeigt nicht einzelne Personengruppen oder Unterweltstationen des Vergiltextes (Unbestattete, Cerberus, Minos, Infantes, Selbstmörder, Liebessünder usw).

43. Der Anstoss zu dieser merkwürdigen Illustration kann von einer Passage im Vergiltext ausgegangen sein, die in den bildlichen Illustrationen sonst kaum berücksichtigt wird: der Lektion des Anchises über die Palingenesie und der damit verbundenen Musterung der vor dem "Aufstieg" stehenden künftigen Römer-Seelen im Lethetal (6.703ff.). Die Anleitung zu tieferem philosophischen Verständnis fand man bei Servius (*in Aen.* 6.719: *AD CAELVM HINC IRE PVTANDVM EST): miscet philosophiae figmenta poetica et ostendit tam quod est vulgare, quam quod continet veritas et ratio naturalis. nam secundum poetas hoc dicit: credendum est animas ab inferis reverti posse ad corpora? ut "caelum" superos intellegamus, id est nostram vitam. secundum philosophos vero hoc dicit: credendum est animas corporis contagione pollutas <u>ad caelum reverti</u>?* Für einen christlichen Leser des 15. Jh. führt der Weg in den Himmel, wie im Bilde dargestellt, in das Reich Gottes, vor Gottes Thron. Die Auszeichnung der zu Gott Aufsteigenden durch königliche Mützen könnte von der "Heldenschau" des Vergiltextes angeregt sein.

44. Zu Rolle und Bedeuntung der Venus in der Aeneis: A. Wlosok, *Die Göttin Venus in Vergils* Aeneis (Heidelberg, 1967); zu ihrer

Bedeutung bei Landino und Bern. Silv. s.o. *Anm.* 9 u. 11. Die beiden Tauben erklärt Bern. Silv. (*Comm.* p. 63.25) als *ratio* und *virtus;* dass sie vom Himmel geflogen kommen, heisse *a creatore per angelum in hominem; maternas aves* bedeute *concordes,* da die Mutter des Aeneas *concordia* sei (p. 64.3ff). Landino (*Disput. Camald.* p. 229.5ff. mit p. 220.23ff.) sieht in den *geminae columbae* die durch Hingabe an *virtus* und *religio* wiedergewonnenen Seelenflügel, die der Geist als Führer zur höchsten Erkenntnis brauche: *Illis enim ducibus ad contemplandas res tendit. Sunt autem volucres Veneris, quia oportet illas esse ab ardenti amore.* Vgl. auch Col. Salut., *labor. Herc.* p. 576.28ff.

45. Die himmlische Venus erscheint in der Frontispizminiatur des 8. Buches (fol. 216v, s.o. *Anm.* 41) zur Illustration des Himmelszeichens der Venus (*Aen.* 8.523ff.) als weibliche Gestalt in eng anliegendem roten Ober—und blauem Untergewand mit langen blonden Haaren und goldener Krone frei in grüner Landschaft; vor ihr am Boden strecken sich in den Bildvordergrund hinein zwei drachenartige Tiere, eines rötlich, das andere grünlich, beide mit aufgerichtetem Oberkörper und nach oben blickend, aber sich gegenseitig mit Waffen bekämpfend. Im Feld links daneben sieht man in kleiner Ausführung die irdische Venus, nackt, doch mit Kopfbedeckung, ihren fabulosen Gemahl Vulkan umarmen, der ebenfalls nackt dargestellt ist wie auch sonst die paganen Götter in dieser Handschrift. Das harmoniert mit der als Leseanweisung mitgeteilten Unterscheidung bei Bern. Silv., *Comm.* p. 10.4ff. (Teilzitat o. *Anm.* 11). Ein weiterer Fall von *gemina pictura?* [Korrekturzusatz: Farbabbildung und Interpretation dieser Miniatur jetzt in meinem Aufsatz: "Diva Creatrix. Das Zeichen der Venus (*Aen.* 8.523ff.) in einer Illustration des 15. Jahrhunderts (ms. Richardson 38)," in: Kotinos, Festschrift Erika Simon, (hg. H. Froning, T. Hölscher, H. Mielsch), Mainz 1992, 440-449 mit Farbtafel II und Taf. 98f.]

DISMAL DECORATIONS: DRYDEN'S MACHINES IN *AENEID* 12

W.R. Johnson
The University of Chicago

Oh, how convenient is a machine sometimes in a heroic poem!
—Dryden, 1697

The fury flapping upon the shield of Turnus is no objection to the courage of Aeneas, since (as Mr. Dryden has very well observed) it sufficiently appears from many other passages that Aeneas could well have killed Turnus without this machine, which is therefore added purely as a dismal decoration to heighten the honour and solemnity of that hero's death.[1]
—Joseph Trapp, 1731

Eccentric though Trapp's version of the Dira may now seem to us, we can see on reflection how precisely it represents the attitudes that inform various neo-classical readings of the *Aeneid* from Dryden's time down to our own. An unequivocally heroic poem, written to celebrate the glories of expanding empire, though it would accommodate ample decorations of various kinds (including the dismal), would require only the most conventional divine machinery to provide its hero with a suitably baroque triumph. In this instance, both Dryden and Trapp would perhaps have been satisfied if Venus had descended one last time, with sensational stage effects and musical accompaniment, but *briefly* and *decorously*, to furnish her more than competent offspring with just a little edge in his duel with the monstrous Turnus. But that is not the poem that Vergil wrote: Venus has to intervene twice in Book 12 before Turnus can be overcome; moreover, Juno has to change her mind (a somewhat surprising and abrupt *metanoia* given her stance and behavior throughout the preceding books), and Jupiter has to send (down from heaven!) the demonic fury to numb Turnus into stupidity, and Juturna, who is ubiquitous in Book 12, has to be forced by the fury to desert her brother before he can become the victim of Aeneas' lost temper. What we have at the close of Vergil's epic, then, is not a single, gratuitous engine of plot; what we have is a quartet of *deae ex machina* from whose discordant concord comes the bitter, dark victory that closes the poem. Each of these figures is crucial to the pattern that finally explodes the poem, but since Juturna is central to this pattern it is with her that we begin and end. Vergil doesn't always get the credit he deserves as a master of storytelling, but few narrative poets better him in the economy and elegance he shows in his treatment of Juturna.

She is summoned into the poem at 138ff. by a Juno who is clearly at the end of her tether. She has not been mentioned earlier in the poem, and no effort is made to prepare the way for her abrupt entrance with any amenities of verisimilitude. She is simply thrust onto center stage: *extemplo Turni sic est adfata sororem, diva deam*. One goddess speaking to another is a nice irony: the Queen of Heaven to an ordinary water nymph whose only distinction is to have been one of the divine king's very numerous erotic toys. In recompense for any inconvenience his pleasure might have caused her, the king of heaven had transformed the mortal girl into a minor deity, *stagnis quae fluminibus sonoris / praesidet; hunc illi rex aetheris altus honorem / Iuppiter erepta pro virginitate sacravit* (139-140). Such is the narrator's description. Juno, who is seeking a rather large favor from the nymph, is more florid than the narrator in defining her: *nympha, decus fluviorum, animo gratissima nostro* (142). Of course Juno does not ask the favor directly; she transforms it into a suggestion offered out of the kindness of her heart: since Juno can do nothing herself to save Turnus as he goes to single combat (*non possum* is deliberately vague at 151) Juturna must act quickly to rescue him from Aeneas, if this is possible. (It isn't, but Juno naturally conceals this futility with *forsan miseros meliora sequentur* [153]; her only immediate interest now is making things a little messier for as long as she can.)[2] As Juno well knows, this is a suggestion (*si quid praesentius audes, perge, decet*

[152-153]) that Juturna has no desire to refuse, and, with no answer but tears of grief, she rushes off to follow Juno's instructions: to save Turnus by inciting battle between the Latins and the Trojans, thus breaking the treaty which calls for single combat between Aeneas and her brother.

In her efforts to destroy Aeneas, Juno has forced several people to become her agents before this (Turnus was and remains one of them, Dido was one of them), but she has found none of her pawns so exquisitely fitted to her purpose as this one, and none of them offers the added thrill of vengeance that Juturna does. Juno tells the pathetic nymph that she is her own favorite among her husband's romantic victims, and she claims to have herself bestowed the nymph's immortality upon her, but of course Juno is lying: it was Jupiter who made Juturna immortal, as she will complain to him in her final tragic lament (878), and Juno is not partial to any of Jupiter's playmates (as we recall from her first speech in the poem whose image of Ganymede now enters into ring composition with that of Juturna). Juno is condemning Juturna to eternal suffering by persuading her to become part of Turnus' destruction; this will be condign punishment for the adulteress, and perhaps her suffering may cause Jupiter himself a twinge of guilt or pain.

Juno is aiming at several birds with a single stone here (Aeneas, Juturna, Jupiter), but the particular ugliness of this stratagem arises from Juno's pretense that her interview with Juturna has been motivated by compassion for Turnus' imminent doom. Her essential reason for this, her final intervention (unless it is she who wounds Aeneas, *casusne deusne* [321]), is her need to try one last time to destroy Aeneas (though she may well know that this is impossible; like a chronic gambler, she is simultaneously convinced that the next throw of the dice will be the one that counts). This obsessive need to annihilate the Trojan hero and his nation she deftly fuses with a no less unfamiliar (yet at the moment less pressing) hunger for revenge on a rival for her husband's love and perhaps on her husband.

Such are Juno's motives for pushing Juturna, a new player, into the sinister, fatal game that she has kept in motion since Aeneas left Troy (so, in this scene, *auctor ego audendi* [159]). What are Vergil's intentions (and needs) in giving Juturna so large a share in the action of Book 12 (in its plot and its denouement— say rather, its catastrophe)? His motives are varied and complex. At the most fundamental level, that of effective storytelling, he wants to tantalize us; he wants not merely to hold our attention but to increase it and sharpen it; he wants to make us need to see the death of Turnus—for even if we have no sympathy for imperial designs and may not want to see that death, it will finally be a relief to see it once the delays that Juturna effects have done their work on us. Juturna is not, therefore, mere padding; she doesn't unnecessarily protract what could have been dealt with much more briefly without her intrusion into the poem. She is the chosen instrument of the most fundamental law of storytelling, suspense.

At the same time, she performs another function, one that is hardly less crucial to Vergil's purposes. She frames for us a special perspective on the closing moments of her brother's life, that is to say, of the poem; she enacts a point of view that is constantly in evidence in Book 12 once she has entered the poem and one that comes to color, perhaps even to dominate, our own vision of what is happening at the closure of the *Aeneid*. Juno's latest and last victim, sent off on a wild goose chase to rescue her brother, trapped in a pattern of impotent attempts to snatch him from destruction, she becomes more than an object of our pity as we watch her fall: we identify with her, and her terror becomes ours.[3]

When Aeneas has recovered from his wound (420ff.) and taken the precaution of saying farewell to his son and returned to the field of battle with his Trojans, it is Juturna who knows of their coming even before Turnus and the other Latins see him: *prima ante ominis Iuturna Latinos / audit adgnovitque sonum et tremefacta refugit* (448-450). As she flees in terror, Aeneas and his companions rush forward like a storm. While his followers cut down the Latins they find in their way, Aeneas ignores the enemies he sweeps past in search for Turnus: *solum densa in caligine Turnum / vestigat lustrans, solum in certamine poscit*, 466-467. Seeing this, Juturna throws Turnus' charioteer from his chariot and assumes his form and his function, but the simile that marks this metamorphosis evokes not the look of the changed Juturna (*cuncta gerens, / vocemque et corpus et arma Metisci*, [472]), but, in a triumph of lyrical compression, in some of the most haunting verses Vergil ever achieved, the emotions that force the terrified nymph to check her flight and try to look after her brother:

> *nigra velut magnas domini cum divitis aedes*
> *pervolat et pinnis alta atria lustrat hirundo,*
> *pabula parva legens nidisque loquacibus escas,*

> *et nunc porticibus vacuis, nunc umida circum*
> *stagna sonat,*
>
> Aen. 12.473-477

The extreme hyperbaton of *nigra hirundo* (note that until we reach *alta atria* the adjective seems ominous, and it in fact remains so even after we've heard *hirundo*) designs a sense of anxiety, of something at once limitless and enclosed, of the danger of being taken, of a danger that must be faced, however, because it is dwarfed by the greater danger that the nestlings will starve without the bird's hectic, unending labors. Terrified love, the iron grip of necessity—this pain and the turbulence caught in a image of the bird's swift, fluttering movements; it is from this angle of vision that we watch Aeneas look for Turnus, that we see his anger and frustration grow as Turnus eludes him, snatched away from him again by Juturna (483ff.). And it is from the eyes of Turnus' desperate protector that we witness Aeneas capitulate utterly to the wrath he has kept getting under control, in this book and throughout the poem. When he has to stoop to miss the spear launched by Messapus and discovers that the tips of his plumes have been shorn away, the sheer triviality of the event—a brilliant touch of psychology—crystallizes all his frustration and his anger and his fruitless strivings for peace and justice:

> *tum vero adsurgunt irae, insidiisque subactus,*
> *diversos ubi sensit equos currumque referri,*
> *multa Iovem et laesi testatus foederis aras*
> *iam tandem invadit medios et Marte secundo*
> *terribilis saevam nullo discrimine caedem*
> *suscitat irarumque omnis effundit habenas,*
>
> Aen. 12.494-499

The juxtaposition of the swallow simile with this moment, the true turning point of Book 12 and its closure (and so, of the poem), increases the poignancy of the former and the ferocity of the latter. Why, since this is only a little past the mid-point of Book 12, is this the turning point? Because it is just after this image of Aeneas' uncontrollable wrath that the poet himself enters the poem with his great and by no means rhetorical question to Jupiter about why the events of his poem are taking place. That question begins with a conventional aporetic gambit (*quis deus mihi expediat?* [500-503]), but the next question, addressed to Jupiter himself, wants to know why civil wars (in a good cosmos) have to be fought, wants to know why treaties aren't kept (*aeterna gentes in pace futuras* [504]; cf. Aeneas' formulation, in his oath for the treaty with Latinus, *paribus se legibus ambae / invictae gentes aeterna in foedera mittant* [190-191]). The question is the poet's, as was the other question about the effects of anger in human history at the very opening of the poem (*tantaene animis caelestibus irae?*), but at this point in the poem, the question could almost be Aeneas' own question (or ours—or Juturna's). This destruction of *virtus* (*corruptio optimi pessima*) and the failure of theodicy that attends it are well prepared for by the picture of the good mother bird searching denatured nature to give her offspring the bare sustenance they need to survive. His eye is on the sparrow, but in a poem about world historical destiny the conflation of poignant suffering and of heroic wrath cannot do much to evoke the realities of Providence. Juturna no more needed to be in Book 12 than the swallow needed to flutter into the poem just before the wrath of Aeneas and the cry of Vergil; she is in Book 12 because, beyond her usefulness as an engine of suspense, beyond even her ability to elicit some reflected sympathy for Turnus, she creates, in conjunction with the images and themes that surround her, a powerful undersong for the last book of the poem, one that fuses with earlier similar themes and figures to countervail the poem's promise of imperial grandeur and of the theological rationalizations that nourish it.

It was, not surprisingly, Ovid who seems to have been the first to comment on the challenge Juturna makes to the imperial design of the *Aeneid*. At *Fasti* 2.583 ff., he undertakes to explain the name and nature of the goddess Muta. She had originally been a river nymph named Lara who found it difficult—so goes the universal sexist myth—to keep her mouth shut. When Jupiter enlisted the aid of Juturna's sister nymphs in her seduction, she promptly blabbed what she knew to the intended victim and even went so far as to squeal on Jupiter to his wife. Vexed, Jupiter rips out her tongue and hands her over to Mercury to escort down to hell. On the way, her guide is smitten by her and naturally rapes her, thus fathering the Lares Compitales. It is a grim story told with an outrageous lightness of touch, and its ugliness is not redeemed by the fact that in this version Juturna seems to escape (at least temporarily) from the clutches of the ruler of the cosmos. But what matters for us here is what Jupiter says to the sisters of Juturna when he talks them into giving him some help (for they all agree to grab her for him, but Lara can not help blurting out what she knows), since his words echo a crucial moment in Juturna's final speech in the *Aeneid*:

> *invidet ipsa sibi vitatque quod expedit illi*
> *vestra soror summo concubuisse deo.*
> *consulite ambobus, nam quae mea magna voluptas,*
> *utilitas vestrae magna sororis erit,*
>
> *Fasti* 2.591-594.

The *voluptas/utilitas* antithesis, emphasized by chiasmus (*magna*), brilliantly parrots and transforms the chilling recrimination Juturna makes when, recognizing the Dira and knowing who sent it, she cries out:

> *alarum verbera nosco*
> *letalemque sonum, nec fallunt iussa superba*
> *magnanimi Iovis. haec pro virginitate reponit?*
> *quo vitam dedit aeternam? cur mortis adempta est*
> *condicio?*
>
> *Aen.* 12.876-880

Juno had used the epithet *magnanimus* of her husband with bitter effect when she was insisting to Juturna that she had always been her benefactress (*scis ut te cunctis unam, quaecumque Latinae / magnanimi Iovis ingratum ascendere cubile, / praetulerim caelique libens in parte locarim* [143-145]). Whatever Juturna may have made of that peculiar claim at the time Juturna uttered it, the epithet's irony gains in power here, conjoined as it is with *superba* and *ingratum*. Ovid's Jove, sounding not a little like a traveling salesman, professes that his pleasure spells big benefits for the lucky little lady of his choice, and the crass *utilitas* precisely fixes on the immortal banality, the essential heartlessness that Juturna angrily denounces. Jupiter has let Turnus be destroyed, has in fact himself sent his destroyer, and he has let his former "mistress," whom he loved so much that he bestowed upon her eternal life, be witness to that destruction, has let be imprinted on her memory forever the sound of the coming of the monster he has sent. She does not see the evil thing beating at her brother's face and against his shield (*hanc versa in faciem Turni se pestis ob ora / fertque refertque sonans clipeumque everberat alis* [865-866]), for she is mercifully removed (*procul*) from the immediate scene, but she is in no doubt as to what she perceives means (*stridorem adgnovit et alas*) and that perception, that realization, will never be absent from her. This instant of grief and horror, which is *her* eternal return, is the immortality, the gift, the *utilitas,* that Jupiter has given her in exchange for the *voluptas* he took (Ovid leaves little doubt that it is rape that enforms the story) from her.

cur mortis adempta est condicio? It is an Ovidian question that she asks (the ways of theodicy questioned again, questioned as they were at Book 12's center, questioned here, almost at the book's and poem's end), and it is an Ovidian heroine that asks it. Aeacus at *Met.* 11.786 will bewail his lack of *copia mortis,* and not a few of the men and women, girls and boys of Ovid's poem would clearly have preferred death to divine sex and its usual aftermath: ugly transformations into unhappy existences that have no end. Juturna wants to die and cannot, but when she pulls her cloak about her and plunges into the river, it is oblivion she wants, a release from a painful tortured life, from a destiny that vicious gods have meddled with needlessly, ruthlessly, casually.

But what is this brief yet dazzling adumbration of Ovid's central intuitions doing in this poem, in this place? To observe that, especially in its final books, the poem is Alexandrian or more specifically that Vergil has feminized epic (the four *deae ex machina* in Book 12, the prevalence of Camilla in Book 11, the emphasis on Amata and Lavinia, the crucial place of Nisus and Euryalus in the poem, together with all the handsome young men that drift through these final books, much to the annoyance of Robert Graves) does not account for the prominent role Juturna plays throughout Book 12 or for the magnificent pathos that Vergil lavishes on her just when the poem is about to plunge away to its ferocious climax. Nor does narrative technique alone, Juturna's elegant resolution to problems of plot and tempo and suspense, quite explain why Vergil imagines her with such tenderness and power. Vergil could, after all, have yanked her from the poem either after she had finished putting the Latins in the mood to break the treaty (222-256) or after she had brought Turnus his sword (784-785). In Vergil's heroic model, Apollo withdraws from Hector instantly and unobtrusively once Zeus has found the balance of life and death for these two heroes (*Iliad* 22.213), so the decorums of convention give no warrant for this elaborate and tardy retreat of Juturna: even after Jupiter holds up the scales at 725ff., she intervenes, and she can't be removed from the poem until the Dira terrifies her from it. No, though she serves the closure in several ways, compressing and stylizing the narrative line beautifully, the reason for and the meaning of her final scene and its superb tirade transcend the conventions of type scene and epic narrative pattern or even the more general rules of pace and rhythm in good storytelling. Vergil's choice of her to introduce his final scene (or, to look at it in another way, his need of her for this purpose) finds no explanation in epic *langue*, in the structure of literature; Juturna is rooted in Vergil's *parole*.

This Ovidian figure, the last of Juno's pawns and Aeneas' unintended victims, indecorously summons into the poem in its closing moments an image, a memory, that had been until now studiously excluded from it. Vergil's Jupiter is a peculiar blend of the god of the philosophers and the god of history; in most of his appearances he is a clouded transparency set in front of that inscrutable, truly omnipotent Fate whose designs he executes precisely if slowly and obliquely. Almost transhuman (that is to say, not genuinely anthropomorphic) both in the perfection of his knowledge of providences and in his apparent impartialities, his devotion to justice, to the true and the good, he comes to seem to us in no need of any theodicy. This faithful minister of Fate has shed, as far as is possible (poetically, generically speaking), all the all-too-human foibles that make Homer's Zeus so paradoxical (and so attractive and so credible). But Juturna's lament, with its fierce accusation, triggers memories of the amoral yet luminous figure and of his countless infidelities, which Homer sketches and dismisses so deftly. The hidden and powerful contrast between Homer's sexy Olympian and Vergil's sour ugly recreation of him here gives this scene—or would give it, were we not in the habit of treating it as gratuitous ornament, of tiptoeing round its embarrassments—its bitter force.

But this clumsy epiphany of Zeus in the poem of Roman Jupiter and the contrast between the two it fuels radiate beyond Juturna's personal tragedy and emphasize once more the wider sufferings that litter the *Aeneid*. For if Homer's Zeus can be faulted by stern moralists for his easy sexuality, he is nevertheless mysteriously satisfying in his role of king and judge, as holder of the scales. He may wish to save Hector, but he knows, even without Athena's admonitions, that this wish is "merely personal," that he can do nothing to rescue this cherished human from his destiny. This Zeus *is* the god of all alike; as the servant of Dike, he reminds us of the spirit of balance and measure and share that we find prominently displayed at the opening of Herodotus' book when he reminds his reader that the felicity doesn't stay long in one place. Father of both Trojans and Greeks, he incarnates the rhythm of things, the Way. He can play no favorites (much as he sometimes wants to—in addition to Hector's death, he also grieves for Sarpedon's [16.433ff.]), and it is because he shapes his acts and judgments according to Dike that Thetis can accept the doom of Achilles (24.128ff.), can be reconciled to the strange blend of glory and outrage that flowers from her son's death.[4] The rightness of that death, grievous though it is to her, she must and can assent to: must because she must, can because beneath the horror of it she glimpses, mingled with the splendor of her son's death, the truth and *fairness* of it. For Juturna, the final calm of her model, isn't possible. The ugliness of Turnus' fate, fused with her own humiliation (raped, lied to, condemned to eternal misery), allows for no solace that answers that of Thetis because Jupiter isn't the god of all alike. Rather, he is the god of history, of history viewed as the accomplishment of divine plans in which what happens to people is what god wants to happen to them; in which those who win wars do so not because they are physically or intellectually or morally superior to those whom they defeat but because they are favored by heaven; in which World Historical Destiny shapes from bloodshed and plunder the best of all possible worlds, one in which Aeneas (any Aeneas) can say, *Iuppiter hac stat* (565): for God and country, God is on our side.

This god of national or world destiny is totally in his proper place in the neo-classical, baroque poem: a celebration of kingship and empire, that suits the taste of Dryden and his heirs. For such a poem (and for its readers) the 12th book of the *Aeneid* is bound to be something of an embarrassment not only in its closing verses, which must be rationalized by heaping Turnus with guilt and reducing Aeneas to a virtuous automaton, but also in its plenitude of machines, those divine females (Juno and the Dira, Venus and Juturna) who either delay the execution of Aeneas' revenge on Turnus in useless and irritating ways or who offer the regal hero assistance that he hardly needs and that distracts the reader from her growing sense of that hero's valor and from what were otherwise her now-perfected impression of the truth of the justice of his mission's divine sanction. In the sumptuously patriotic poem that Dryden, in his introduction to it, tries to coax from the poem he has translated, such delays in the poem's resolution, such constant intrusion by mechanical lady deities into this virile epic, are as bewildering as they are vexing, and they must be explained away.

The wounding of Aeneas and his mother's bringing him the magic remedy are flaws in the closing design, "difficulties," that are "not easily to be solved without confessing that Virgil had not life enough to correct his work; though he had reviewed it and found those errors which he resolved to mend, but being prevented by death and not willing to leave an imperfect work behind him, he ordained by his last testament, that his *Aeneis* should be burned."[5] *nec deus intersit, nisi dignus vindice nodus*; quoting the master, Horace, he points out that the rule that permits a mechanical god when it's absolutely necessary relates to the theatre not to epic, and he then goes on for three pages to contemplate the improprieties occasioned in the poem by the apopearance of the Dira. Dryden gives no quarter to those who argue for the Dira's entrance into the poem on the grounds that Aeneas needs help against Turnus and insists that even after Jupiter had "hung his balance and given it a jog of his hand to weigh down Turnus" he "thought convenient to give the Fates collateral security by sending a screech-owl to discourage him."[6] Nor is he impressed by those who quote Turnus' *non me tua turbida virtus / terret . . . di me terrent et Iuppiter hostis* to demonstrate that Turnus would be, without the monstrous intervention, Aeneas' match. "In answer to which I say that this machine is one of those the poet uses only for ornament and not out of necessity"; so, after a brief digression, ". . . these two machines of the balance and the Dira are only ornamental [for] . . . the success of the duel would have been the same without them."[7] In short, for Dryden, the entire narrative scheme of Book 12, with its intricate refrain of *mora/morari* (74, 553, 565, 677, 889), only gets in the way of the single genuine action left in the poem: the triumph of Aeneas. As impatient, then, with Jupiter's scales as he is with the Dira, whom he trivializes by calling her "a flying pest,"[8] what he seems to want is a burst of Tintoretto sunlight on the helmet of Aeneas (its plumes restored and massively augmented) as the hero gazes up through the swirling golden light to the heavens that will soon be his home (the corpse of Turnus, soon to be forgotten, sprawled obscurely in a dark corner of the picture). But what he gets is a closure that rivals in its desolation that of *The Trial*.

Why didn't Vergil accommodate him? Why does he station Juturna so obtrusively in that crucial, penultimate place where her accusations, where her gestures of despair, will color not only the closure but also our sense of the poem as a whole? She is, indeed, part of the stratagem, the complex engine, of delay because good storytelling requires suspense. But more important than that, Vergil doesn't want his story to end; that is to say, he doesn't want Turnus to die (as he must), not least because he isn't reconciled to the idea of his having to have Aeneas kill him.

Vergil puts considerable emphasis on the fact that Turnus and Aeneas are, essentially, evenly matched (525ff., 714ff., 788ff.; it is in the second of these passages that Jupiter's scales break a deadlock); and even after the judgment of the scales, when each hero has his proper weapon restored to him, they are once again apparently in danger of ending in a draw when Jupiter has his conversation with Juno and then unleashes the Dira against both Juturna and her brother (to warn her away from him, to put him in a daze). Dryden is, like several contemporary critics, eager to justify Aeneas' final outburst of anger by insisting that Turnus' behavior merits this anger, and this holy anger would, of course, justify the divine assistance Aeneas receives from the Dira without in any way detracting from his courage and valor in vanquishing his guilty foe: "Turnus had manifestly declined the combat and suffered his sister to convey him as far from the reach of the enemy as he could";[9] so, in the notes to his translation he remarks, "the Dira comes to denounce vengeance against him for breaking the first treaty . . . and also for violating the second treaty by declining the single combat."[10] This opinion of Turnus' cowardice and treachery is shared by Aeneas himself (*scilicet exspectem, libeat dum proelia Turno / nostra pati rursusque velit concurrere victus? / hoc caput, o cives, haec belli summa nefandi. / ferte faces propere foedusque reposcite flammis* [570ff.]), but Aeneas' ignorance is more excusable than Dryden's since he doesn't know, could not know, that Juno had engineered the breaking of the treaty (and had possibly put the finishing touches on this enterprise by wounding him herself) or that it was Juturna who had taken her brother from the battle against his will.[11] Aeneas' anger, in short, is misdirected. What he is really angry at arises from a simultaneity of multiple causes, some of them celestial in origin, some of them human; but the final triumph of the evil that unleashed them (which Juno Discordia symbolizes) comes about because, in his tragic ignorance, which he shares with Turnus, he succumbs to the very wrath he has spent much of his time in the poem attempting to subdue in others and himself.

Fate (History, the Myth of Rome) wanted Turnus dead and Aeneas victorious by that death, and some part of Vergil may have wanted that too (because he wanted peace, sometimes at any price), but another part of him wanted something else: wanted

Aeneas saved for Dike, wanted Turnus not sacrificed to Mommsen's Law,[12] wanted the truth of complex multiple causes and the truth of unintended consequences kept in mind and pondered. So he arranged for Turnus' death to be delayed by various means ("all machinery work,"[13] in Dryden's brusque phrase) until his poem could explode from the compressed force of its antinomies, its baroque shell, into glittering fragments, like Turnus' sword: *fulva resplendent fragmina haren*, (741).

For readers of the Middle Ages, even for John of Salisbury, who understood how his world and its Vergil were changing, Aeneas was a philosopher whose winning of moral wisdom, an adumbration of Christian salvation, was signalled by his plucking of the golden bough; by the Renaissance Aeneas had become the wise and virtuous prince to whom emerging nations could look when trying to find a model for their new *principes* and new *patriae*. Dryden's interpretation of the *Aeneid* shows this "modern" version of the poem (the imperial nationality as divinely ordained) in its purest state, in its gaudiest grandeur ("despotic power could not have fallen into better hands"[14] than those of Aeneas-Octavian). But it, like more recent versions of the imperial epic that it perhaps still nourishes, can only persuade us of its truth if it reduces Vergil's consummate artistry in Book 12 to a series of tawdry narrative tricks, to some regrettable errors made by a weary, distracted genius, which can only be explained away or passed over in silence. But to ignore the sorrows of Juturna or to try to justify the never-ending wrongs they symbolize is to insult Vergil's gifts and to be defrauded of the nourishment of his art.

NOTES

1. "Dedication to the *Aeneid*," *Dramatic Essays*, Everyman Library, ed. W.H. Hudson (London, 1912) 231; for Trapp, see Robin Sowerby, *Dryden's Aeneid: A Selection with Commentary* (Bristol, 1986) 247 and T.W. Harrison, "English Virgil: The *Aeneid* in the XVIII Century," *Philologica Pragensia* 10.2 (1967) 86.

2. Compare with the immediate model for her anger, Poseidon, *Odyssey* 5.290, 377-379; 13.131-133: the expanse and vehemence of his wrath is limited by the needs of the plot and the conventions of realism. Juno accepts neither these nor other constraints; see D.C. Feeney, "The Reconciliations of Juno," *CQ* 34 (1984) 183-184.

3. For the pathetic and even the tragic aspects of Juturna's narrative function, see R.D. Williams and C.J. Carter, "Critical Apprecia-

tions II: Virgil's *Aeneid* 12:843-886," *G&R* 21 (1974) 165ff.; Mario di Cesare, *The Altar and the City* (New York, 1974) 211, 218; Mihoko Suzuki, *Metamorphoses of Helen: Authority, Difference and the Epic* (Ithaca, 1989) 93-94, 148-149.

4. See also *Ody.* 24.46ff., 73ff., 91ff., where her grief is assuaged by ceremony; this solace may, intertextually speaking, cast some of its glow on her situation in the *Iliad*. See Suzuki, 142-143, for an excellent statement on the Thetis-Juturna parallel and contrast.

5. See Dryden, 247. For discerning comments on Dryden's neo-classical tamperings with his original, see W. Frost, *John Dryden: Dramatist, Satirist, Translator* (New York, 1988) 140-144. For a brilliant sketch of the royalist, imperialistic and conservative presuppositions that governed Dryden's systematic and deliberate mistranslations which were perpetrated in the interest of converting Aeneas into a "perfect prince," the fit poetical token of Charles II, see T.W. Harrison, "Dryden's *Aeneid*," *Dryden's Mind and Art*, ed. B. King (Edinburgh, 1969) 143-170; in an earlier, two-part essay (*op. cit.* [n. 1 above] 10.1, 1-10 and 10.2, 80-91) he traces the rejection of the Dryden version (and of Augustus and Vergil along him) by Whigs in the early eighteenth century, then Vergil's partial comeback, in preparation for the nineteenth century, as a virtuoso of the sublime and pathetic. By Victoria's reign, both the Imperial and the Pathetic Aeneas will be available, alone or wonderfully fused, in commentaries for the sixth form. This droll hybrid still saunters among us. Contrast Michael West's interesting remarks on Dryden's "sentimental hero," "Dryden's Ambivalence as a Translator of Heroic Themes," *Huntington Library Quarterly* 36 (1973) 351.

6. Hudson, *op. cit.* 247-248.

7. *Ibid.* 248.

8. *Ibid.* 247.

9. *Ibid.* 249.

10. *Dryden's Works*, ed. W. Frost, v. 6 (Berkeley, Los Angeles, 1987) 836.

11. F. Cairns repeats these old accusations in his *Virgil's Augustan Epic* (Cambridge, England, 1989): "Turnus immediately restarts the battle" after Aeneas is wounded "by a cowardly arrow" (75) whose bowman interests Cairns as little as does the fact that Turnus is as ignorant of what Juno and Juturna are up to as Aeneas himself. This oversight, combined with a total lack of interest in Juturna and the Dira, allows Cairns to transmute Turnus into a collage of the evil suitors whom Odysseus legally slaughters (324ff.). For Cairns, who is even less tolerant of the conventions of divine machinery than Dryden, Juno and Allecto are rather cumbersome gimmicks for representing human psychological drives (see 69, n. 26). One wonders what psychological drive Cairns imagines that

Athena represents in her question to Zeus at the close of the *Odyssey* (24.472ff.) just before, with her father's permission, she plunges back into the poem to give it its abrupt, inadequate, ramshackle closure (it is interesting to recall that the words of this question find some echo in Vergil's question to Jupiter in *Aen.* 12.500ff.). A not dissimilar disregard of the machines of Book 12 leads P. Hardie to not dissimilar conclusions in his *Vergil's* Aeneid: *Cosmos and Imperium* (Oxford, 1986); he too pays no attention whatever to Juturna and the Dira, and he rarely notices Juno for anything that does not relate to her meteorological significances (93, 104, 332); Allecto (253) is somehow a token of unbridled growth and expansion.

12. "A nation which has constituted itself a state will absorb those neighbors who are not of an age politically; a civilized nation will absorb neighbors who are not spiritually of age." See J. Linderski, "Si Vis Pacem, Para Bellum: Concepts of Defensive Imperialism," *Papers and Monographs of the American Academy in Rome* 29 (1984) 138. His essay examines this influential delusion with wit and enviable delicacy.
13. *Ibid.* 232.
14. *Ibid.* 218.

RECEPTION OF GIBBON'S *DECLINE AND FALL* IN AMERICA IN THE EARLY NATIONAL PERIOD

Meyer Reinhold
Boston University

In Europe Edward Gibbon's *magnum opus, History of the Decline and Fall of the Roman Empire*, was accorded instant acclaim—and vituperation.[1] On this side of the Atlantic, however, reaction was slow in coming, partly because his history made its appearance in the turbulent years from 1776 to 1788, from the beginning of the independence movement to the promulgation of and debates over the Constitution, and also, at a time when passions ran high, because of Gibbon's Toryism and his support of the crown against the American colonies.[2] Moreover, the first and second editions of the first volume were sold out quickly in England and did not reach the American market. In addition, while history, especially ancient history, was of intense interest to the Founding Fathers as a major source of "useful knowledge," they studied intensively the decline and fall of ancient republics but had little interest in the annals of the autocratic Roman Empire.[3] Still, as early as 1778, John Adams had some knowledge of Gibbon's work, for on his voyage to France in March of that year, during a severe storm at sea he wrote: "Neither Milton in Verse, nor Gibbon in prose could have given any adequate Idea of it...." And Washington in his small library had a copy of some of the volumes (edition of 1783).[4]

A few Americans who were abroad during those years soon became aware of Gibbon's acclaim and notoriety. Henry Laurens, distinguished South Carolinian, who had been a prisoner of war (in the Tower of London) in the early 1780s, not only read *Decline and Fall* but afterward actually met and talked with Gibbon.⁵ Jefferson, in France as American envoy, quickly sensed the importance of the work, and recommended Gibbon as a bridge between ancient and modern history (from Augustus through the Roman Empire, to the Middle Ages and the Byzantine period). From Paris, in 1786, he wrote his young relative Thomas Mann Randolph, Jr., to read the ancient historians in the original and not in translations—and to read Gibbon, adding that "the transition from Ancient to modern history will be best effected by reading Gibbons [sic!]." And in 1787, he ordered from Paris the volume of *Decline and Fall* containing Gibbon's treatment of the Emperor Julian. Like many readers of the time—and ever since— Jefferson spotted an error in Gibbon.⁶ An oddity is the favorable reaction to Gibbon by Francis Kinloch, eccentric scion of a wealthy South Carolina family, who in London in 1777, warmed to Gibbon's critique of Christianity, and compared him to Tacitus, Horace, Juvenal and Hume.⁷ James Madison was quick to sense the importance of Gibbon's history. Early in 1783 among the books he ordered for Congress' library, he included the first three volumes of *Decline and Fall*, the only parts thus far published, together with 15 other titles of works on classical authors and on ancient history.⁸

The first hostile judgment on Gibbon in America came from Benjamin Rush, friend of John Adams and Thomas Jefferson, and first Surgeon General of the United States. In 1789, in his thoughts on the proposal to establish a federal university, he singled out Gibbon for criticism. It was not Gibbon's methods and views as historian that were repugnant to Rush, but his literary style. In rejecting British authors in general as models of style for the United States, which to Rush was still in "the age of simplicity," he criticized as unnatural "the purple glare of Gibbon."⁹ Rush's brief comment on Gibbon was soon elaborated by Noah Webster, who added to strictures on the "false taste of the English" in literary style, major faults of Gibbon as historian. Webster rejected "the promiscuous encomiums . . . bestowed on Gibbon," concluding that, except for some excellent chapters on the history of the Roman Empire, "His work is not properly a '*History*' of the Decline and Fall of the Roman Empire,' but a 'Poetico-Historical Description of Certain Persons and Events.'" Gibbon's history, Webster averred, should be entitled "A Display of Words." For Gibbon was more concerned with displaying his talent as writer than to collect, marshal and elucidate the facts accurately. Indeed, Gibbon's aim was not to instruct but to please the ear with ornament. "Let a man read his volumes with the most elaborate attention, and he will find at the close that he can give very little account of the 'Roman Empire'; but he will remember perfectly that Gibbon is a most elegant writer." Yet on stylistic grounds Gibbon is at fault in his affected use of allusive terms, in his "figurative poetical manner," and his addiction to terseness. Most of those who read Gibbon admire and praise his style, but few understand the historical matter. Still, in the end Webster lauded Gibbon's scope, erudition and industry, recognizing that people turned to his work because there was no other English work that bridged ancient and modern times. It was, in sum, Gibbon's literary style that Webster deemed reprehensible as being unsuitable for Americans.[10]

Despite the growing accessibility of Gibbon to Americans, it is noteworthy that his history was not used by John Adams in his massive *Defence of the Constitutions of Government of the United States of America* (1787- 1788) nor in the debates at the Constitutional Convention in the summer of 1787, nor in the *Federalist* papers, nor in the various state ratifying conventions.

With the constitutional debates behind them and the national life formally launched, Gibbon's popularity among Americans soared markedly in the 1790s.[11] In Philadelphia, New York, Boston and elsewhere, the *Decline and Fall* was steadily imported and advertised by many bookdealers,[12] both in full sets and in abridged form. The work now also appears in lending libraries and in college and private collections.[13] Jefferson's great second library, later sold to Congress, contained a Gibbon, and in 1790 he promised his daughter Mary (then about twelve years of age) a copy of Gibbon.[14] Aaron Burr, too, considered Gibbon essential reading for his brilliant daughter, Theodosia, whom he had educated in the traditional classical curriculum, the so-called "masculine education."[15] In 1795, the Rev. John Clarke, giving advice to a student at Harvard College, recommended standard works for the study of history, but demurred about Gibbon's *Decline and Fall*, criticizing his style and prejudices. "If we admit the rules prescribed by Cicero for this species of composition," he wrote, "Gibbon must appear to a great disadvantage, both as writer and as a man."[16]

For many Americans, as well as for Europeans, Gibbon's Chapter 44, on the history of Roman law, was the most brilliant and enduring. In 1794, James Kent, Professor of Law at Columbia University and Chief Justice of the State of New York, who had a profound influence on American jurisprudence, paid tribute to Gibbon as "eminent Author" on legal studies.[17] Two decades later, David Hoffman, Professor of Law at the University of Maryland, while criticizing Gibbon for "meddling with theological polemics," commended him for decrying "pedants" and "useless erudition" on the part of those whom Gibbon would have called the *erudites* and *philosophes* of Europe, for they lacked systematic methodology and a transcending purpose in their work. In the field of law Hoffman recommends Gibbon's Chapter 44 as "having high merit," as a "concise but elegant and learned exposition of Roman jurisprudence," and a "masterly view of Roman law," "unrivalled" as a summary, "luminous, learned, succinct, and satisfactory."[18]

At the end of the century, William Vans Murray, brilliant young Marylander and legal scholar, shared with John Quincy Adams an interest in some passages of Gibbon, and an anonymous American noted that Gibbon came to regret his Chapters 15 and 16 (on Christianity as cause of the decline of the Roman Empire) because many Englishmen, attached to what he called "the shadows of Christianity," raised objections.[19] In 1794, William Cobbett, a conservative Englishman who had emigrated to the United States, in attacking Joseph Priestley in the context of American revulsion toward the French Revolution, denounced also "the infidel philosophy of Voltaire, Gibbon, . . . and the rest of that enlightened tribe."[20]

In 1799, in an extended comparison of Hume, Robertson and Gibbon as historians published by "O" (perhaps Charles Brockden Browne), Gibbon was rated last. Conceded are Gibbon's literary charm, the importance of his theme, and his great learning. But these merits are put in the shade by hostility to Christianity, in which "He excelled all former and contemporary writers." In this he was guilty of "hypocrisy and malice," "misrepresentation, as well as sophistry," suppressing or disguising evidence favorable to Christianity. The author also faulted Gibbon for his pervasive indecencies, his "lascivious allusions," which stemmed from a "polluted and debauched imagination." Moreover, Gibbon's literary style was rejected as tiresome, often obscure, unrelieved in its pomposity, artificiality and affectation, as well as his addiction to trite figures and epigrammatic brevity.[21] Similarly, Samuel Miller, in his comprehensive summary of the achievements of the eighteenth century, rated Hume and Robertson among the great modern historians; but as for Gibbon Miller faulted him for deviations from the truth and "shameful obscenity," "insidious and malignant zeal to discredit religion," and "circuitous obscurity and the meretricious ornament of the style." On the whole, Miller concluded that despite the fame of Gibbon's celebrated work and despite his great learning, "he is far from having furnished a model that can be safely imitated, or conferred any real improvement on this department of English literature. Nor is his work less hostile to all the interests of decorum and virtue than to the best rules of taste and criticism."[22]

Nevertheless, the popularity of Gibbon remained high in America. Between 1804 and 1826 (the fiftieth anniversary of the first volume), four American editions of *Decline and Fall* were published in Philadelphia and New York.[23] Even the acerb Fisher Ames read and admired Gibbon's work, reminding Americans of the early nineteenth century that "we have produced nothing in history."[24] John Adams classed Gibbon with Robertson and Hume, and *Decline and Fall* was on the youthful reading list of Ralph Waldo Emerson.[25]

Gibbon was in the libraries of the Adams family. John Quincy Adams, in January of 1830, recorded in his diary: "I can never read this author without indignation. Yet his irony, his bitter indifference, and his art of insinuation may be studied to advantage. His heaviest sarcasms upon Christianity and the Bible are in distant allusions. His philosophy is shallow, and always infected with anti-religious acrimony."[26] His son Charles Francis Adams, both as student at Harvard in 1824 and as omnivorous reader in the 1830s was ambivalent about Gibbon, whom he read through methodically. He could admire his "research learning," and his "skillful manner of attack," but deplored his style as "difficult to read," cumbersome, tiresome, monotonous. His chapters on Christianity and Julian are worth studying even if perversions of history. The chapters on Christianity, he wrote more than once, "excite in me nothing but disgust." Still, he was at times intrigued by Gibbon's style and his mastery and deploying of the material, even if used for a bad cause. "His chapters upon the Christian religion are worth studying not so much for the matters as the skilful manner of attack." He is "masterly," "in most respects unique"; Gibbon, he concluded was an "amazing master of his weapons but used in a bad cause."[27]

As modern critical methods began in the second quarter of the nineteenth century, and as Greek and Roman history were being transformed by principles and strategies that replaced the traditional Humanist and Enlightenment uses (and abuses) of history, one might have expected that in America attention would be paid to the faults of Gibbon as chronicler of historical events.

But, in general, the same criticisms of Gibbon prevailed as in the past. When the fourth American edition appeared, Caleb Cushing again called attention to Gibbon's hostility to Christianity and "gross indelicacy," though he acknowledged his erudition, understanding and untiring industry. Impurity and irreligion aside, wrote Cushing, his work merits "a high station among the great classics of our language," "unsurpassed and perhaps unrivalled by any historical work of ancient or modern times," a work, which, despite defects of style, shines with "teeming greatness of thought."[28] Similarly, William H. Prescott praised Gibbon for his great learning, vast range of subject, and "liberal and elegant scholarship." But to Prescott, one of America's great historians, Gibbon's faults were conspicuous: perversion of learning to accord with his preconceived prejudices, hostility to Christianity, indecencies ("with Iago-like duplicity"), scepticism, absence of moral sentiment, egotism, pomposity and "bloated dignity of expression," stylized rhetoric, which, despite an "exhilarating glow" of "literary enthusiasm," repels because of a "succession of strained, convulsive efforts."[29]

In 1835, the distinguished Edward Everett, who had been the first Eliot Professor of Greek Literature at Harvard and was then a member of the United States House of Representatives, admired Gibbon's undertaking of a grand theme, "with a giant's strength." But his work is "cold and cheerless. You pace through the resounding halls, sad and unsatisfied with their splendors. You are fatigued with the soulless beauty of this history; exhausted with its dreary learning; and rise from the perusal of the twelve admirable volumes, without having experienced one thrill of virtuous excitement."[30] The same year, Thomas H. Shreve wrote an extended favorable appreciation of Gibbon, regretting that one of the great writers of the eighteenth century, one of "the master spirits of the earth," was so little known in the United States. His subject was of no great interest, he noted, to Americans.[31] But Shreve urged Americans to study him and "learn to admire" his "distinguished intellectual greatness." To this end Shreve even attempts to mitigate Gibbon's antipathy to Christianity and to elevate him to a place among the six greatest historians of all time, placing him beside Herodotus, Thucydides, and Tacitus. Gibbon's style is "suited to the majesty of the subject." In sum, "There is in no language a work which will more amply repay the intimacy of the student or which contains a richer and more varied resource of imperishable treasure than the *History of the Decline and Fall of the Roman Empire.*"[32]

That same year the negative assessment of Gibbon reappeared in an attack by Leonard Withington, who deprecated "Gibbon's infidelity." Though he found him superior to Hume in diligence of research, Gibbon's sceptical dogmatism, his hostility to religion, and his "genteel sneer" were reprehensible. Though he is diligent in documenting the narrative, his unrelieved uniform style and methods fail to give signals to the reader of "the very different gradations in which the events stand in point of probability." "No writer ever blended facts and opinions with such fatal skill." Especially reprehensible are his chapters on Christianity, which did great harm in inculcating infidelity. "However, his day is over; all the harm he can do is probably done."[33] In the late 1830s Andrews Norton again criticized Gibbon's style as monotonous and pompous, and his addiction to apothegms that are "trivialities disguised by ... formal style." These faults are, however, overshadowed by his numerous errors, hostility to Christianity, lack of moral sensitivity and indecencies. He is neither a sound historian, nor a philosopher, Norton wrote. "His work is a *misrepresentation* throughout. Everything is modernized and discolored. . . . His work is like an exhibition on an ancient stage."[34]

"Mistakes in Gibbon" used to be a favorite sport. But despite the enormous advances in the last century in our knowledge of the Roman Empire and its successor powers in Europe and the Near East, Gibbon's work is still read as a classic, for the grandeur of its conception, learning, elegance and wit. J.B. Bury in his masterful edition of *Decline and Fall*, at the end of the nineteenth century, singlehandedly provided a corrective commentary, brief and random. A new comprehensive commentary in the light of the new learning we now possess together with a variorum edition of *Decline and Fall* is a desideratum. It will require today a large team of specialists to update what Gibbon, two centuries ago, achieved singlehandedly.

NOTES

1. On the reception of Gibbon in his own time and the subsequent two hundred years see P.B. Craddock, *Edward Gibbon: A Reference Guide* (Boston, 1987) xiii-xlv; and *Edward Gibbon, Luminous Historian, 1772-1794* (Baltimore, 1989) *passim*.
2. Yet Gibbon was not just a passive backbencher supporting the government's policies on the American colonies, as many Americans thought. From 1774-1779 he tried to hear both sides of the Ameri-

can problem and his appraisal of the American cause was tempered. See *The Letters of Edward Gibbon*, ed. J.E. Norton (London, 1956) 2.45-51; "Gibbon's Correspondence," *Philadelphia Reporter and National Recorder* 1 (April 24, 1819) 295-296.
3. See M. Reinhold, *Classica Americana: The Greek and Roman Heritage in the United States* (Detroit, 1984) 38-39, 48.
4. *Diary and Autobiography of John Adams*, ed. L.H. Butterfield (Cambridge, MA, 1962) 4.24; E.E. Prussing, *The Estate of George Washington, Deceased* (Boston, 1927) 418-433.
5. D.D. Wallace, *The Life of Henry Laurens* (New York, 1915) 381.
6. *Papers of Thomas Jefferson* (Princeton, 1950) 10.307; 11.523; 13.460. In 1793, he recommended Gibbon for study by John Garland Jefferson (*Writings of Thomas Jefferson*, Memorial Edition [Washington, D.C., 1903], 19.104) though he added, "As I do not suppose you can get a copy of Gibbon you may leave him for the next winter when I shall have mine in Virginia." Cf. H.T. Colbourn, "Thomas Jefferson's Use of the Past," *William & Mary Quarterly*, 3d Ser., 15 (1958) 56-70.
7. On Kinloch, see H.F. May, *The Enlightenment in America* (New York, 1976) 145-147, 376.
8. *Papers of James Madison*, ed. W.T. Hutchinson and W.M.E. Rachal (Chicago, 1969) 6.77.
9. *Letters of Benjamin Rush*, ed. L.H. Butterfield (Princeton, 1951) 1.492-493.
10. Noah Webster, *Dissertations on the English Language* (Boston, 1789) 367ff. *The Massachusetts Magazine* 1 (July 1789) 441-443, 475-476, reprinted "Webster's Criticism upon Gibbon's History," at the request of Z.M., who commended Webster's "superior abilities, wise discernment, and correct taste."
11. May, *op. cit.* 118-119, 340.
12. E.g., *Catalogue of Books, Stationery, Cutlery, Ec., for Sale at Cary, Stewart & Co.'s Store* (Philadelphia, 1791); *Hugh Gaines's Catalogue of Books Lately Imported from England* (New York, 1792); *Thomas and Andrew's Catalogue of Books* (Boston, 1793); *Catalogue of Books, Ec. Now Selling at Ross & Douglas, Booksellers and Stationers* (Petersburgh, VA, 1800). Cf. W. Reitzel, "The Purchasing of English Books in Philadelphia, 1790-1800," *Modern Philology* 35 (1937-1938) 163.
13. E.g., *Catalogue of Books for Sale or Circulation by John Dabney at his Bookstore and Circulating Library in Salem* (Salem, 1790); *Catalogue of Books Belonging to the Library of Rhode-Island* [later Brown University] (Providence, 1793); *Catalogue of Books in the Boston Library* (Boston, 1795); Thaddeus Mason Harris (Librarian of Harvard College), *A Selected Catalogue of Some of the Most Esteemed Publications in the English Language Proper to Form a*

Social Library (Boston, 1793); *Catalogue of Books in the Library of Hon. Robert A. Livingston of Clermont* (Poughkeepsie, 1800). See also L.H. Harris, "A Virginian Moves to Kentucky, 1793," *William & Mary Quarterly*, 3d Ser., 15 (1958) 208-209 (this small library contained a copy of Gibbon).

14. *Catalogue of Library of Thomas Jefferson*, ed. E.M. Sowerby (Washington, D.C., 1952-1959) 1.47-48; *Papers of Thomas Jefferson*, 17.239. As late as 1825 Thomas Jefferson continued to recommend the study of ancient history in the original authors or in translation: "For its continuation and the final destruction of the empire we must then be contented with Gibbon, a compiler." See *Writings of Thomas Jefferson* (see n. 6, above) 16.125.

15. *Correspondence of Aaron Burr and his Daughter Theodosia*, ed. M. Van Doren (New York, 1929) 8 (letter of Dec. 18, 1793).

16. John Clarke, *Letters to a Student in the University at Cambridge, Massachusetts* (Boston, 1795) 64-65.

17. James Kent, "An Introductory Lecture to a Course of Law Lectures" (New York, 1794) in *American Political Writing During the Founding Era (1760-1805)*, ed. C.S. Hyneman and D.S. Lutz (Indianapolis, 1983) 2.945.

18. David Hoffman, *A Course of Legal Study* (New York, 1836^2; repr. New York, 1974) 42-43, 479, 521-523. The first edition, 1817, did not differ in its comments on Gibbon.

19. *Letters of William Vans Murray to John Quincy Adams, 1797-1803* (Annual Report of the American Historical Association for the year 1912), ed. W.C. Ford (Washington, D.C., 1914) 407 (letter of Dec. 14, 1798).

20. Cited by May, *op. cit.* 222.

21. "Parallel between Hume, Robertson and Gibbon," *Monthly Magazine and American Review* 1 (April 1798) 90-94. *The New England Quarterly Magazine* 1 (July-September 1802) 264, rated Gibbon's first volume the most polished, the second and third inferior. Charles Brockden Browne, "On the Style of Sir. T. Browne, Dr. Johnson and Mr. Gibbon," *The Literary Magazine and American Register* 4 (1805) 58-60, wrote a negative evaluation of Gibbon. He regretted Gibbon's popularity among young readers, commenting that his literary charm conceals his infidelity, that his unrelieved style pattern was tiresome, and that his affectation tended to obscurity. "He has confounded the diction of a *poet* with that of a *historian*."

22. Samuel Miller, *A Brief Retrospect of the Eighteenth Century* (New York, 1802) 2.13, 135-136, 155.

23. On early American editions of Gibbon's *Decline and Fall*, see J.E. Norton, *A Bibliography of the Works of Edward Gibbon* (Oxford, 1944) 102, 112-114.

24. From his essay "American Literature," in *Works of Fisher Ames*, ed. W.B. Allen (Indianapolis, 1983) 1.35, 507.
25. *The Spur of Fame: Dialogues of John Adams and Benjamin Rush, 1805-1813*, ed. J.A. Schutz and D. Adair (San Marino, 1966) 152; K.W. Cameron, *Emerson's Early Reading List, 1819-1824* (New York, 1951).
26. *Memoirs of John Quincy Adams*, ed. C.F. Adams (Philadelphia, 1876) 7.163.
27. *Diary of Charles Francis Adams*, vol. 1, ed. A. Di Pace Donald and D. Donald (Cambridge, MA, 1964) 276; vol. 4, ed. M. Friedlaender and L.H. Butterfield (Cambridge, MA, 1968) 193, 197, 213, 223-224, 247; vol. 8, ed. M. Friedlaender *et al.* (Cambridge, MA, 1986) 173, 199, 205-206.
28. *North American Review* 28 (1829) 312-313.
29. *North American Review* 29 (1829) 302-304.
30. *North American Review* 40 (1835) 115.
31. This view was expressed by Alexis de Tocqueville in the 1840s in *American Democracy*. He wrote: "Democratic communities ... care but little for what occurred at Rome and Athens." An anonymous American wrote in 1835: "There is not a country on earth, where there is less reverence for antiquity than in the United States." See Reinhold, *op. cit.* 195, 203.
32. *Cincinnati Mirror and Western Gazette* 4 (Feb. 14, 1835) 129ff.
33. *Literary and Theological Review* 3 (1835) 38-57.
34. *North American Review* 45 (1837) 403-404. Similar observations on the "glaring faults" of Gibbon were made by F. Bowen, *North American Review* 56 (1843) 367. For some aspects of the reception of Gibbon in the United States see Craddock, *Edward Gibbon: Luminous Historian (op. cit.)* 356-357.

TRADIZIONE E ORIGINALITÀ NEGLI STUDI CANADESI SU VIRGILIO

❦

Mario Geymonat
Università di Venezia

A livello internazionale—e non solo in Canada o in Italia—assistiamo oggi ad una diffusa rivitalizzazione degli studi classici, sia in ambito accademico sia nel mondo editoriale. Il merito di questo rinnovato interesse per la cultura greca e latina va attribuito anche, io credo, al progresso degli studi sulla tradizione classica, che fino alla seconda guerra mondiale erano coltivati solo assai saltuariamente (ma con lodevolissime eccezioni, come il *Virgilio nel Medioevo* pubblicato in Italia da Domenico Comparetti già nel 1872, oltre un secolo fa).

In questi ultimi anni la storia della tradizione classica ha favorito in effetti il moltiplicarsi dei rapporti fra classicisti e studiosi di discipline anche molto lontane, discipline però che in vari periodi e in paesi diversi hanno subito una influenza profonda, nel metodo e nel contenuto, da parte della filologia e della critica del mondo antico.

Senza questo nuovo fiorire di studi e di interessi non sarebbe stata possibile in Italia, ad esempio, la realizzazione della *Enciclopedia Virgiliana*, in cinque volumi (1984-1991), alla quale hanno collaborato non solo filologi classici, archeologi e storici antichi di livello internazionale (e fra essi numerosi importanti studiosi d'oltre oceano), ma anche ricercatori delle letterature medievali e moderne, linguisti, musicologi e storici dell'arte.

Testo riveduto della relazione letta il 13 dicembre 1988 al convegno "Italy-Canada-Research," organizzato dal Centro Accademico Canadese in Italia presso il Consiglio Nazionale delle Ricerche a Roma.

Negli ultimi anni hanno preso il via pure altre ambiziose iniziative, e fra queste ricordo almeno quella di pubblicare nel 1992, in occasione del cinquecentesimo anniversario della "scoperta dell'America," ben sei volumi della grandiosa collezione tedesca *Aufstieg und Niedergang der Römischen Welt* dedicati a *The Classical Tradition and the Americas*. Il progetto ha ottenuto il convinto sostegno soprattutto degli Stati Uniti e della Germania ed è stato affidato a una stretta collaborazione fra le università di Tübingen e di Boston: a Tübingen insegna Wolfgang Haase, condirettore dell'intera collana di De Gruyter, mentre Boston è stata scelta perché fu la prima città del Nord America a dare impulso agli studi classici e all'insegnamento del greco e del latino (già all'inizio del secolo XVII) e perché è sede oggi del prestigioso "Institute for the Classical Tradition," fondato nel 1983 ma già provvisto di una cospicua biblioteca in materia.

Nella *Preliminary List* distribuita ai collaboratori si leggono i titoli di circa 200 contributi affidati a studiosi di vari paesi. Obiettivo delle ricerche sembra essere la mediazione che la cultura rinascimentale europea ha saputo svolgere fra "memoria classica" e "nuovo mondo" americano. Saranno toccati argomenti specifici come *On the History of the Idea of "Bellum iustum" Up to and Including the Spanish Discussion on Treatment of the Indians* (W. Nippel, Bielefeld), come l'epica in lingua latina sulla scoperta dell'America (a partire da *Lorenzo Gambara's 'De navigatione Christophori Columbi'*: G. Demerson, Clermont-Ferrand), come *The Myth of the American Amazons in the Renaissance Period* (F. Lestringant, Mulhouse), come *On the Transfer of Classical Grammatical Categories to American Indian Languages* (E. Weisshar, Tübingen) o ancora come *The Americanization of German Scholarship in Nineteenth-Century America* (W.W. Briggs, Jr.; Columbia, SC). Fra i contributi significativi per l'argomento di cui mi occupo segnalo qui almeno *Recent Trends in Anglo-American Scholarship on Vergil (1950-1990)* (R. Glei, Bochum) e l'intero quinto volume, tutto dedicato a *The Classical Tradition in Canada* (esso conterrà fra l'altro ben due articoli di A.G. McKay· *Classical Elements in the Novels of Hugh MacLennan* e *Classical Education in English Canada*).

Nei prossimi anni la bibliografia sugli studi classici in Canada sarà dunque abbastanza ampia. Ora tuttavia mi sono dovuto accontentare di due soli articioli specifici (*Latin Studies in Canada*, di A.G. McKay, nella rivista brasiliana *Romanitas* del 1962,[1] e *The Classics in Canada: Recent Developments*, di A. Barrett, nel periodico statunitense *The Classical Outlook* del

1972²) e della relazione sul Canada presentata al congresso internazionale di Roma "La filologia greca e latina nel secolo XX" del 1984 (i cui "Atti" a stampa sono disponibili però solo dal 1989).

Dovuta a Douglas E. Gerber, il pindarista della University of Western Ontario, la relazione *Canada: Greek and Latin Philology*³ non contiene alcun riferimento esplicito agli articoli sopracitati di A.G. McKay e di A. Barrett: fornisce peraltro le date di nascita delle più importanti riviste canadesi di filologia classica (*Phoenix*, 1946; *Classical News and Views/Echos du monde classique*, 1957) ed offre un apprezzabile resoconto degli studi di letteratura greca in Canada fra il 1950 e il 1980. Troppo rapida appare invece la trattazione degli studi di latino, mentre addirittura sorprendente mi sembra l'affermazione d'apertura che gli studi classici in Canada avrebbero avuto inizio solo dopo la seconda guerra mondiale: "The vast majority of my references pertain to material published during the past thirty years or so. This is not because such works have appeared in the period with which I personally am most familiar, but because it is only since the end of the Second World War that much publishing has been done by Canadian Classical scholars" (p. 797).

Al contrario un recente articolo di A.G. McKay,⁴ che si muove in un ambito storico molto più vasto, mi convince che i più importanti autori antichi furono letti nel collegio gesuitico del Quebec fin dalla metà del secolo XVII, e che in particolare il VII e l'VIII libro dell'*Eneide* rappresentarono uno stimolo anche per le prime esplorazioni del Canada settentrionale. Del resto i testi greci e latini ebbero una cospicua influenza sulla sorgente letteratura canadese già nei secoli scorsi, e non si deve dimenticare che: "For many years the classics have enjoyed a favored position in Canadian education. During the nineteenth and early twentieth centuries English Canada shared the British notion of the importance of the classics in a liberal education and of the rigorous training in grammar and syntax for the formation of character. In French Canada the strong influence of the Roman Catholic church has sustained interest in the classical languages, especially Latin" (A. Barrett, p. 37).

Anche in Canada d'altra parte gli studi classici hanno subito negli ultimi decenni le critiche e gli attacchi di chi vorrebbe che l'educazione fosse tutta rivolta al presente e non tiene conto che, dimenticando il passato, si corre il rischio di perdere il senso del valore da dare allo stesso futuro dell'umanità. Per fortuna anche in Canada si è saputo reagire a queste rischiose posizioni estreme;

come afferma lo stesso McKay (nell'articolo citato su *Romanitas*, p. 324): "The challenge to recovery was met with determination and resource by militant, dedicated Latinists who sought to improve, even erase, the threadbare content and drab appearance of High School texts; the curriculum was revitalized, and new paedagogic approaches were adopted. Grammars and texts were judiciously revised or scrapped entirely and replaced with new versions. Lively emphasis was laid on aspects of Roman life, biography, and archaeology. New teaching devices were brought to bear on the situation: colored slides, photographs, maps, models, numismatic and epigraphical materials, archaeological artifacts and, above all, personal reports and observations by teachers who had visited or even fought within the classical countries" (nella seconda guerra mondiale, naturalmente!).

Della relazione di D.E. Gerber non mi sento di condividere un punto in particolare, là dove egli afferma: "In contrast to the strong interest shown in Catullus and Horace, relatively little has been written by Canadians on Vergil" (p. 806). Al contrario mi sembra doveroso notare infatti che il Canada è stato sede per anni della redazione di *Vergilius*, la prestigiosa rivista della Vergilian Society of America, e che in quasi tutti i Departments of Classics delle università canadesi operano in questi anni studiosi seriamente interessati a Virgillo, e a volte si tratta di filologi e critici di riconosciuto livello internazionale.

Di alcuni mi limiterò qui a fare solamente il nome, rinviando per una disamina più approfondita del loro contributo scientifico all'articolo promesso da Reinhold Glei per *Aufstieg und Niedergang*. Ricordo dunque il già nominato Anthony Barrett, della University of British Columbia a Vancouver, di cui di recente ho letto l'articolo *Pessimismo* nel IV volume dell'italiana *Enciclopedia Virgiliana*, ma anche Charles E. Fantazzi della University of Windsor, che già nel 1966 pubblicò su *American Journal of Philology* un buon contributo sulle *Bucoliche* in relazione alla poesia neoterica ed elegiaca romana, e ancora Hermann Lloyd Tracy, a cui si devono articoli sull'*Eneide* in *Phoenix*, *Greece & Rome* e *Vergilius*. Ma penso anche agli studiosi canadesi che hanno pubblicato le loro opere più importanti all'estero, o che sono addirittura andati ad insegnare materie classiche in altri paesi: è il caso ad esempio di Raymond Clark, di origine britannica ma ora canadese, che insegna alla University of Newfoundland e che ha stampato ad Amsterdam nel 1979 un interessante volume *Catabasis: Vergil and the Wisdom-Tradition*, o di Robert John Getty, autore di articoli virgiliani su *Phoenix*, su

Classical Philology e su *Transactions and Proceedings of the American Philological Association*, che è emigrato negli Stati Uniti per insegnare alla University of North Carolina.

Per evidenziare il buon livello degli studi canadesi su Virgilio è utile in primo luogo ricordare la presenza e l'attività in università di quel paese di studiosi stranieri di grande prestigio (finora però nessun classicista italiano!). Il più noto è forse George Goold, un inglese ora professore a Yale ma che negli anni Cinquanta e Sessanta è stato attivo nelle università canadesi di Manitoba e di Toronto. G. Goold è negli Stati Uniti in questi anni uno dei responsabili del troppo lento progetto harvardiano per una nuova edizione di Servio (in particolare per il commento alle *Bucoliche* e alle *Georgiche*), ma già in Canada egli si era fatto promotore di studi importanti in questo campo, guidando fra l'altro l'eccellente dissertazione di Paul Ch. Burns (ora alla University of British Columbia a Vancouver) *The Vatican Scholia on Virgil's* Georgica*: Text and Analysis*, un lavoro di cui non può fare a meno chiunque si occupi seriamente dei complessi problemi della scoliografia tardo-antica al poeta.

Cospicui meriti nella crescita degli studi canadesi su Virgilio ha avuto anche un altro studioso europeo, Herbert Huxley. Nato nel 1916 da una famiglia inglese molto modesta ma allievo di St. John's Cambridge, Huxley ha insegnato successivamente a Leeds, Manchester, Dublino (Trinity), Rhode Island (Brown) per trasferisi infine come professore di materie classiche alla University di Victoria. Autore di una significativa edizione commentata al I e al IV libro delle *Georgiche* (Londra, 1963) e di una serie di articoli di argomento virgiliano su riviste inglesi ed americane, Huxley, diventato cittadino canadese di pieno diritto, è tornato negli ultimi anni a Cambridge e qui ha svolto egregiamente l'incarico di curare il XIX numero dei *Proceedings of the Vergil Society* (1988).

Nella serie dei maggiori studiosi di Virgilio approdati da altri continenti in Canada non si può infine dimenticare Kenneth Fleming Quinn. Di nascita neozelandese, dopo aver diretto fin quasi a cinquant'anni di età il Department of Classics della University of Otago (Dunedin) negli antipodi, venne nominato nel 1969 professore di latino a Toronto, e qui "as a literary critic... has made a considerable impact on [the Canadian] understanding of Latin literature" (Gerber, p. 805). Quando giunse in Canada, Quinn aveva già dato alle stampe il suo più importante contributo virgiliano (*Virgil's* Aeneid: *A Critical Description* [Ann Arbor, 1968]), ma a Toronto egli ha prodotto ancora una serie di articoli su vari problemi di letteratura latina, ed ha rappresentato molto degnamente il Canada al Convegno mondiale scientifico di studi su Virgilio del settembre 1981 (quando anche io ebbi l'occasione a Mantova di conoscerlo personalmente).

Ho lasciato volutamente per ultimi i due studiosi che in questo secolo hanno contribuito con maggiore originalità, a mio giudizio, agli studi e alla passione canadese per il grande poeta latino: Norman Wentworth DeWitt e Alexander Gordon McKay. Il fervore della loro attività di insegnanti e di studiosi e la serietà dei loro contributi scientifici danno buone speranze per il proseguimento degli studi virgiliani in Nord America anche fra le generazioni future.

Fu proprio con una attenta lettura dei primi libri dell'*Eneide*, condotta alla luce di Apollonio Rodio e dei tragici greci, che N.W. DeWitt esordì e si affermò nei primi anni del secolo come uno dei classicisti più intelligenti e preparati che fossero usciti dalle università del nuovo mondo. Nato nel 1876 sulla riva canadese del lago Ontario, De Witt iniziò gli studi a Toronto, nel proprio paese, per concluderli poi a Chicago, negli Stati Uniti. La sua tesi, *The Dido Episode in the* Aeneid *of Virgil*, un centinaio di pagine di grande intensità e dottrina, venne stampata in volume da Briggs a Toronto nel lontano 1907, e può considerarsi il primo volume canadese di filologia classica effettivamente noto a livello internazionale: fra i suoi recensori già nel 1908 ricordo Henry R. Fairclough, uno dei maggiori studiosi dell'*Eneide* negli Stati Uniti della prima metà del secolo (su *Classical Philology* 3, pp. 221-222), e l'italiano Vincenzo Ussani (sul *Bollettino di filologia classica* 14, pp. 61-62). Come ha rilevato Francis Cairns nella breve voce dedicata allo studioso canadese nel II volume della *Enciclopedia Virgiliana*,[5] "la dissertazione su Didone assegnò a De Witt un posto onorevole nella storia degli sudi virgiliani," e infatti "la sua trattazione, nuova e provocatoria, mette in rilievo questioni che non avrebbero dovuto essere trascurate dalla critica." Certo ancora a metà degli anni Trenta il breve volume di De Witt ha avuto una indubbia influenza sulla monumentale edizione del IV libro dell'*Eneide* di A.S. Pease.

In seguito N.W. De Witt continuò a stimolare una attenta lettura di Virgilio nei circoli colti e nelle maggiori università del nuovo mondo e a pubblicare articoli specifici su importanti riviste come *Classical Journal, Classical Philology, Classical World, American Journal of Philology, Transactions and Proceedings of the American Philological Association, Vergilius* (non esistevano in quegli anni riviste di filologia classica specificamente canadesi!).

Ma bisogna pure dire che alcuni contributi di De Witt appaiono oggi culturalmente invecchiati e scientificamente improponibili, come ad esempio la breve nota *Virgil's Copyright* pubblicata su *Classical Philology* del 1921, una difesa commossa ma troppo ingenua del cosiddetto pre-proemio dell'*Eneide*.

Non fu un caso dunque la presa di distanza della critica europea dal secondo volume virgiliano di De Witt, *Virgil's Biographia Litteraria*, stampato a New York-Toronto nel 1923 dalla American Branch della Oxford University Press, una ricostruzione appassionata ma troppo immaginosa della vita del poeta, basata su notizie accolte in modo acritico soprattutto dall'*Appendix* (erano anni però in cui anche uno studioso italiano celebre come Augusto Rostagni la riteneva sostanzialmente autentica!). Recensito con qualche riserva ma con parole lusinghiere dal caposcuola dei virgilianisti harvardiani E.K. Rand ("A Romantic Biography of Virgil," in *Classical Philology* 18 [1923] 303-309), che definiva l'opera "another stimulating book on Virgil," "the work of a lover of Virgil" che "will be read by all true idolators of Virgil with gratitude and delight," il volume dello studioso canadese fu invece duramente stroncato dal francese H. Goelzer, uno dei più avveduti filologi e conoscitori di Virgilio di quegli anni ("Virgile et ses oeuvres de jeunesse," nel *Bulletin Budè* dell'ottobre 1923, pp. 27-44), ed il suo giudizio è ancor sostanzialmente condiviso dalla critica moderna.

Il parziale insuccesso del suo secondo volume su Virgilio indusse De Witt a dedicarsi ad altri grandi autori classici: Demostene e soprattutto Epicuro. In collaborazione con il figlio Norman Johnston lo studioso canadese curò per la Loeb nel 1949 il VII volume delle orazioni di Demostene, mentre per quanto riguarda Epicuro è da ricordare soprattutto il suo ultimo libro, il più fortunato e famoso, *Epicurus and His Philosophy*, pubblicato a Minneapolis nel 1954, quattro anni prima della sua morte. Ma va certo ricordato in questa sede che l'interesse di De Witt per la filosofia epicurea prese spunto proprio da una lettura acuta e originale delle *Bucoliche*, e lo si può ben vedere rileggendo oggi il breve e intenso articolo "Vergil and Epicureanism," pubblicato da De Witt in *Classical World* del 1932.

Assai diverso e tutto in crescita è stato l'itinerario culturale di Alexander Gordon McKay, il maggiore dei virgilianisti canadesi della seconda metà del nostro secolo.

Laureatosi nel 1950 a Princeton con una tesi sulle relazioni fra Atene e la Macedonia nel VI e nella prima metà del V secolo a.C., McKay si è occupato di tragedia greca (di Eschilo in particolare) ed è stato editore (con D.M. Shepherd) di due fortunati volumi di poesia latina: *Roman Lyric Poetry: Catullus and Horace* (Londra, 1969) e *Roman Satire: Horace, Juvenal, Persius, Petronius and Seneca* (New York, 1976).

Ma con il passare degli anni, passando dalla Grecia a Roma e come attratto ineluttabilmente dalla forza superiore del Fato, A.G. McKay si è andato appassionando sempre più soprattutto a Virgilio, con la produzione di un'ampia serie di contributi di interesse generale e particolare e con indagini originali nel campo della topografia antica e della bibliografia. Il primo articolo virgiliano di McKay, "The Greeks and Cumae," è stato pubblicato ormai più di trent'anni fa,[6] mentre ha quasi vent'anni il suo volume più apprezzato, *Vergil's Italy*,[7] e recentissime sono le sue voci sull'*Enciclopedia Virgiliana*, come *Canada* e *Repertori Bibliografici*. In particolare scrivendo di "repertori bibliografici" McKay non poteva tacere di se stesso, delle bibliografie critiche su Virgilio da lui pubblicate prima su *Classical World* (1964-1973) e poi annualmente su *Vergilius*, esemplari per chiarezza, leggibilità e facilità di consultazione, strumento indispensabile di consultazione per chiunque in questi ultimi vent'anni abbia lavorato scientificamente sul poeta.

Accennando al progetto dell'editore De Gruyter di dedicare alcuni volumi a *The Classical Tradition and the Americas*, all'inizio di queste pagine, ho sottolineato l'importanza della mediazione rinascimentale europea fra memoria classica e mondo americano. Nel caso di McKay assistiamo curiosamente ad un itinerario inverso: è proprio l'interesse culturale profondo per l'antico che ha spinto lo studioso d'oltre oceano verso l'Europa, sulle rive del Mediterraneo, nel *locus amoenus* dove gli affascinanti miti classici furono cantati dai grandi poeti greci e latini. Sensibile alla complessa organizzazione dei contatti internazionali fra studiosi, A.G. McKay ha condotto in Italia generazioni di canadesi e statunitensi lettori di Virgilio o appassionati di archeologia, e a loro ha dedicato la sua ultima fatica, *Roma Antiqua: Latium and Etruria, a Source Book of Classical Texts* (Washington, 1986): un libro molto bello, dove rovine e paesaggi non sono tanto memorie da guardarsi con occhio romantico e decadente, ma nodi indissolubili per collegare strettamente le nuove generazioni con il mondo antico.

NOTES

1. *An.* IV, 5.323-331.
2. *Ibid.* vol. L, 4.37-38.
3. *La filologia greca e latina nel secolo* XX (Atti del Congresso Internazionale 17-21.IX.1984), 2 (Pisa, Giardini, 1989) 797-808.
4. "The Northern Passage to Hesperia: Vergil and Quebec," *The Augustan Age, Occasional Papers* 1 (1987) 19-30.
5. (Roma, 1985) 38.
6. *The Vergilian Digest/Vergilius* 3 (1957) 5-11.
7. Edito nel 1970, due anni prima del parallelo libro dell'italiano Francesco della Corte, *La mappa dell'Eneide*.

A LATE TWENTIETH-CENTURY READING OF VERGIL'S *ECLOGUES:* THE SHEPHERD AS ARTIST

Harry C. Rutledge
University of Tennessee

Vergil's concern in the *Aeneid* for the plastic arts, the artist, and artisans is well known. Famous examples are the great mural of the Trojan War on the Juno temple in Dido's Carthage (1.456-493), Daedalus's depiction of Minoan Crete on the doors of the Apollo temple at Cumae (6.20-33), and the shield of Aeneas with its detailed scenes from the history of Rome (8.626-728). When in Book 1 Aeneas is made visible to Dido, the beauty of his appearance is likened to a carving in ivory, or to silver or marble which have been embellished with gold (1.592-593). Especially arresting is the description of the blushing Lavinia as Amata and Turnus discuss her future—her blush as crimson as the red dye painted by an artist on a piece of Indian ivory (12.67-69).

The whole of the *Georgics* on a primary level is concerned with the art of husbandry. The shepherd-farmer as an artist is brilliantly celebrated at the end of the poem in the famous Aristaeus epyllion, with its inset of the story of Orpheus and Eurydice (4.315-558). The thrilling power of Orpheus, the archmusician's song, is so great that Hell with all of its ghastly works comes to a standstill (4.481-484). Orpheus the musician is a complement to Aristaeus the shepherd of the bees. In the juxtaposition of Orpheus and Aristaeus, Aristaeus becomes enobled. The shepherd-farmer, exemplified by Aristaeus, is an artist equal to Orpheus.

What of Vergil's *Eclogue Book?*[1] As I make the presentation which follows, I want it to be clear that I see the unity of the ten poems in the *Eclogue Book* as described by John Van Sickle in his book, *The Design of Virgil's* Bucolics (1978). Moreover, as I survey the works of Vergil, I can only agree with the general opinion that the *Eclogue Book* and the *Georgics* are stepping stones to the *Aeneid*. I believe, however, that the two earlier works have their own independent strength and brilliance. With regard to the *Eclogue Book* in particular, I think it can be seen to speak to the reader today, even if the reader is not familiar with Vergil's Rome or the poetry of Theocritus. Furthermore, my appreciation of the *Eclogue Book* has been enhanced by Eleanor Winsor Leach's book, *Vergil's* Eclogues: *Landscapes of Experience* (1974), and the impressive connection it makes between Vergil's poems and contemporary landscape painting. (I think that all of the Augustan poets could only have been alert to the great Augustan building program and what could only have been the powerful presence in Rome of scores of artists over a number of years.)

More pointedly, I would make the suggestion that since the characters in the poems of the *Eclogue Book* are so continually concerned with song and singing, the atmosphere in which they speak and sing suffused with "the sound of music," might we not consider what the work as a whole seems to say about the life of the artist? There has been and is great interest in art and the artist in this century. The throngs who attended the Picasso Retrospective at the Museum of Modern Art in New York in 1980 were astonishing. Similar crowds were in Montréal in 1985 to see the huge exhibition of Jacqueline Picasso's Picassos. Fanfare attended the later opening in Paris of the Picasso Museum. Since its premiere in 1896 there has been no more popular opera in the repertory than Puccini's *La Bohéme*, a depiction of the life of artists. Thomas Mann took up several times the position in modern life of the artist, as in *Tonio Kröger* (1903), *Death in Venice* (1912), and *Doctor Faustus* (1947). Picasso himself exalted the artist in his suite of etchings, *The Sculptor's Studio* (1933-1934). Surely the most intense fascination with art and the artist is to be found in the series of photographs made of the painter Jackson Pollock at work in the 1940s and 1950s. The restoration of Claude Monet's water-garden at Giverny, opened to the public in April 1980, is one of the most devoted acts of homage to an artist since the heyday of Ptolemaic Alexandria.

The *Eclogue Book* opens to the sound of music. The musical shepherd is Tityrus, playing on a reed pipe, *sub tegmine fagi* (1.1) Tityrus is at ease beneath the shade of a beech tree—*lentus in umbra* (1.4). The shadow of the tree is a protected spot, a haven.

To the passing Meliboeus, Tityrus freely confesses that he owes his bliss to a veritable god in Rome. A special beneficence has provided him with the freedom and the pleasure to make his music. In sharp contrast, Meliboeus has been denied such bliss. He can only envy Tityrus the *frigus . . . opacum* (1.52), the cool shade. For him there is no more singing (1.77), no more life in the *viridi . . . antro* (1.75), the green cave. Although Tityrus invites Meliboeus to spend the night, the conclusion of the poem intimates that Meliboeus pushes on, into the night.

In the second *Eclogue*, the shepherd Corydon is utterly alone. He longs for the companionship of Alexis. In his soliloquy he remarks on his gifts both as a skillful shepherd with a thousand lambs (2.21) and as a singer the equal of Amphion (2.24). Corydon goes on to remark that if Alexis were with him, a major occupation for them would be the making of music (2.31). Corydon has a marvelous pipe which Damoetas gave him long ago (2.36-37).

As Corydon dreams of such happiness, he then appeals to Alexis, describing the superb bouquet of lilies, irises, poppies, and narcissi which he will create for him (2.45-50)—a veritable work of art suggesting the great swags of fruits and flowers carved on the inner shell of the Ara Pacis, or a Baroque or Impressionist flower painting. At the height of his fantasy, however, Corydon realizes that such bliss is not to be his. He should tend to his flower beds (2.58-59), prune his vines (2.70), and occupy himself with the making of a basket (2.71-72).

It is in the third *Eclogue* that the shepherd takes on a clear definition as artist. Damoetas has beaten Damon in a contest of piping and singing (3.21-22). Menalcas is incredulous (3.25-27). Damoetas boldly challenges Menalcas to a match, with Palaemon as the judge (3.50).

Damoetas puts up as his wager a heifer. Menalcas, however, stakes a pair of beechwood cups, both adorned with clusters of grapes, the vine and trailing ivy (3.38-39), one of which depicts in relief Conon, the third-century astronomer, paired with a nameless astronomer who is, in Robert Coleman's view (in his college text, 1977) probably Eudoxus, because Menalcas says that the second astronomer was famous for his agricultural advice. The cups of Menalcas embody Dionysian inspiration as well as the great poet-scientists of the Hellenistic era. Our two shepherd-poets are humorous reflections of the carved figures.

The third *Eclogue* proceeds as an amoboeic duet which is virtually a catalog of musical subjects, including: Jupiter (3.60-61), Phoebus (3.62-63), Galatea (3.64-65), Phyllis (3.76-79), the wolf and the rain (3.80-81), the poet, Pollio (3.88-89), the lurking snake (3.93), the treacherous stream (3.96), and subtle riddles (3.104-107). The themes are so rich and ingenious that Palaemon declares the match a draw (3.108-109).

We begin to see the world of the shepherd-artist. Singing, the playing of the pipe, music, are ubiquitous. The stage is the *antrum*, whether the cave made by the shade of the spreading beech or a natural cave or a place which has the feeling of a *reducta vallis* (as in Horace, *Odes* 1.17). In these three poems which open the *Eclogue Book* we move from the passive shepherd-artist, Tityrus, to the isolated but vigorously imaginative Corydon, to a display of poetic subjects.

It is in *Eclogue* 5 that a closer focus is made upon art and its significance. Mopsus and Menalcas are ready to compete in singing. Mopsus wants an *antrum* to be the stage (5.6-7). It is an *antrum* made especially private by a spreading vine over its entrance (5.6-7). We are in a private studio, the private world which is so characteristic of Hellenistic art.

Mopsus goes first, singing of the death of Daphnis. Daphnis was the arch-shepherd, the tamer of nature (5.29-30). He was a second Dionysus as he led revellers on the festal day of Bacchus (5.30-31). In his power, he graced all nature. He was the *decus omne* (5.34). His death made a desert. Daphnis has the exuberant invention of such artists as Claude Monet and Tennessee Williams. Daphnis as shepherd was *formosi pecoris custos* (5.44), the keeper of a beautiful flock; but he transcends his subjects, he is *formosior* (5.44). Daphnis, even in death, is the artist transcendent.

Menalcas, hardly to be outdone by Mopsus, sings of the destiny of Daphnis, his apotheosis. The shepherd-artist becomes sublime, a god to be worshipped. We are reminded of the early death of Dylan Thomas, and the great admiration his work continues to enjoy. For an ancient comparison, there is the same admiration for Art and the Artist in the famous relief in the British Museum, the *Apotheosis of Homer*, by Archelaus of Priene. Menalcas and Mopsus can only reward each other for their wonderful arias. Menalcas gives Mopsus a fine reed pipe (5.85). Mopsus gives Menalcas a bronze-studded crook (5.88-90), the perfect gift for the artist-shepherd who rules his world.

And so to the magical sixth *Eclogue*. Whereas Daphnis in *Eclogue* 5 is the Platonic Idea of the Artist, with the attributes of the Life-God, Dionysus, in *Eclogue* 6 we have the practicing artist, Silenus, the old retainer of Dionysus. Silenus, the woodland artist, is persuaded to perform. Neither Apollo nor Orpheus could give so much joy (6.29-30).

The song of Silenus has been much discussed. The 11 subjects of the song, which I take to be a paean to life, celebrate the primeval world beginning with creation, coming down to early Athens. (The range of the Song makes it a miniature of Ovid's *Metamorphoses.*) We hear of Pyrrha, Saturn, and Prometheus (6.41-42); the expedition of the Argonauts (6.43-44); much of Cretan Pasiphaë and her love gone wrong (6.45-60); Atalanta and Phaethon (6.61-63); Scylla, the enemy of Ulysses (6.74-77, and thus we come to the Trojan War); finally of Tereus and Philomela (6.78-81, Philomela, a princess of early Athens). The song is a hymn of creation, history, and love, especially love's trials. Into the midst of it strolls Vergil's contemporary, Gallus, in the Aonion hills (6.64-65). Nothing in the song of Silenus is strange to the arch-poet. The world of creation, imagination and love is the very world of the arch-poet. Gallus and Silenus are one. Together they are Art and Artist; Gallus and Silenus both exist on a plane where Art and the Artist are one.

It is *Eclogue* 8 which provides the full demonstration of *ars poetica* in what I will now freely regard as Vergil's presentation of the shepherd as artist. If we ask the question, what is art?, the perfect reply comes in the songs of Damon and Alphesiboeus in the eighth *Eclogue*. The opening lines make clear that this poem is a celebration of song (8.1-5):

> *Pastorum Musam Damonis et Alphesiboei,*
> *immemor herbarum quos est mirata iuvenca*
> *certantis, quorum stupefactae carmine lynces,*
> *et mutata suos requierunt flumina cursus,*
> *Damonis Musam dicemus et Alphesiboei.*

> The Muse of the shepherds, Damon and Alphesiboeus!
> —the heifer marveling at their recital was
> oblivious to the grass; lynxes were spellbound
> by their song; rivers diverted sought their courses
> —let us hymn the Muse of Damon and Alphesiboeus.

The song of each shepherd is a pastoral love song. I take them as exemplary pastoral love songs, the culmination of the genre from Theocritus to Vergil. Damon sings with deep poignancy of his unrequited love for Nysa. He has loved her since he was twelve years old (8.39). Love is a hard god, however; Nysa will have nothing to do with Damon. Proof of Love's harshness is found in the tale of the mother-murderess, Medea (8.48-49). Damon could die (8.58-60).

In contrast, the song of Alphesiboeus is a pulsating incantation designed to bring the beloved Daphnis back to the lover. The song spells out the stages of the magic rite which will charm Daphnis into returning. The fire goes ablaze as Daphnis draws nigh.

The singing of Damon and Alphesiboeus is not a contest, it is a recital—two superb art-songs by two masters of the form. Each artist is so fine that there is no rivalry.

Yet the world of art does know rivalry. There are third prizes and honorable mentions. First prize is for the best of the best. The seventh *Eclogue* illustrates the world of keen competition. The contest in *Eclogue* 7, as witnessed and reported by Meliboeus, is between Corydon and Thyrsis. The spirit of the encounter is truly, "Anything you can do, I can do better."

Corydon opens the match by invoking the example of Codrus (7.21-22). Thyrsis boasts of his own superiority (7.25-28). Corydon vows a marble statue to Diana if he wins (7.31-32); Thyrsis promises a golden statue to Priapus (7.35-36). And so it goes. Corydon praises the summmer (7.45-48), Thrysis the winter (7.49-52). Corydon sings of Alexis (7.55-56), Thyrsis extolls Phyllis (7.59-60). Meliboeus concludes his description of the contest with the report that Thrysis lost and Corydon was pronounced superior (7.69-70). Thus, the world of art is not isolated creativity. It is also an intensely personal world of rivalry, competition, and selection. In the seventh *Eclogue* Vergil brings to pastoral life the spirit of the panhellenic games. The contest between the shepherd-artists is a bucolic miniature of the Pythian Games. It is fun, like the games of *Aeneid* 5, but it is not silly. Vergil is not ready for the *Aeneid*, but the *Eclogue Book* is certainly couched in terms of Vergil's later exposition of the Greco-Roman world.

The ninth *Eclogue* gives us the fragility of art, the strangely transitory nature of both life and art. The bravura songs of the eighth *Eclogue* are framed by the seventh *Eclogue* with its ambience of fierce competition and the ninth *Eclogue* with its elegiac commentary on the relation of art to life when there is no place for art. The tenor of *Eclogue* 9 is that of *Eclogue* 1—the harsh world of soldiery and deprivation surrounds the two shepherd artists, Moeris and Menalcas. Moeris tells their mutual friend, Lycidas, of the sorry turn of events. Lycidas has heard that Menalcas has been allowed to keep his hillside because of his poetry (9.7-10). Moeris sadly contradicts Lycidas, observing bitterly (9.11-13):

> *sed carmina tantum*
> *nostra valent, Lycida, tela inter Martia quantum*
> *Chaonias dicunt aquila veniente columbas.*

But our poetry, Lycidas, is no more effective
against the arms of War than they say the doves
of Dodona are when an eagle swoops among them.

Lycidas is horrified, but is thankful that Menalcas at least is alive, and praises him by quoting from one Menalcas's poems (9.23-25). Moeris, for a moment distracted from his misery, also salutes their poet-friend by quoting three lines from a poem on Varus by Menalcus (9.27-29).

Caught up in the delight of poetry, Lycidas and Moeris continue their musing, with Lycidas asking Moeris for some verses of his own. Moeris sings from a Galatea-poem (9.38-43), lines which invoke an enchanted world of pure springtime. Lycidas compliments Moeris by quoting verses from one of Moeris's poems on Daphnis and Caesar (9.46-50). There can be no joy for Moeris, however, even in his art. Reality is too pressing. He says, with deepest rue (9.51):

> *Omnia fert aetas, animum quoque ...*

> Time takes away everything, even the spirit ...

The happy singing of his boyhood is lost forever (9.51-52).

All this while the two friends have been walking along the road. They come to the tomb of Bianor. Lycidas proposes that they pause there for more singing, but Moeris wants only to push on. The tomb is only too suggestive of Moeris's plight. Our Moeris knows full well the condition of life summed up in the celebrated epitaph, *Et in Arcadia ego.*

The ninth *Eclogue* has two concluding lines. As Moeris walks away from the tomb, he has the feeling that life must go on (9.66):

> ... *quod nunc instat agamus—*

> We must see now to what is pressing ...

Menalcas is bound to return. Then will be the time for singing (9.67). The artist and art will not be defeated.

I have saved for last the most famous of the *Eclogues*: 4 and 10. Attention has been lavished for centuries on the meaning of the fourth *Eclogue*. In Ward W. Briggs' *Eclogue Book* bibliography for the years 1927-1977, the citations for the fourth *Eclogue* occupy 14 closely printed pages.

In the context of the present reading, the fourth *Eclogue* is a "portrait of the artist as a young man." If the subject of the poem is seen as the emerging, developing artist, then the poem offers a glorification of the artist perfectly attuned to the depiction of the artist in Picasso's suite of etchings, "The Sculptor's Studio." Vergil's exalted language in the poem is right for such an intention.

The child is to be born, destined to mingle with the gods and the heroes (4.15-16). Because of this destiny, his childhood is a state of bliss. The countryside blooms; cattle have no fear of wild beasts (4.18-22).

The child enters early manhood. The world is still a paradise, but he, the young apprentice, is not omniscient; he must study and practice. There are many arts to learn in shipbuilding and sailing (4.32), building walls (4.32-33), managing the soil (4.33), venturing forth into unknown realms as though he were an Argonaut (4.34-35); in his dealings with men he must have the bravery and courage of a veritable Achilles (4.35-36). Vergil's metaphor on growing up fits many walks of life—the great and lasting beauty of the fourth *Eclogue* is in its generality—but especially that of the artist in his early development. The histories of Michelangelo, Rembrandt, Van Gogh, Henry James, Flaubert and Tennessee Williams easily come to mind.

The child becomes a man in his full powers. Art flows from his hands. No challenge is too great. Like Thomas Mann's brilliant writer in *Death in Venice*, Gustav von Aschenbach, everything he touches has a marvelous result. Like a magician the artist can render pasturing rams in every color (4.42-45). No matter the instrument or medium, the artist can create anything he sets his mind to. This is, of course, a supremely gifted and stunning versatile artist, a Victor Hugo or Pablo Picasso.

And the world pays homage (4.48-52):

> *adgredere o magnos (aderit iam tempus) honores,*
> *cara deum suboles, magnum Iovis incrementum!*
> *aspice convexo nutantem pondere mundum,*
> *terrasque tractusque maris caelum profundum;*
> *aspice, venturo laetentur ut omnia saeclo!*

> O come, great honors (now is the time),
> precious child of the gods, great offspring
> of Jove! Behold the universe nods with its
> burgeoning weight, as well as the earth, the
> vastness of the seas, and the deep sky.
> Behold, as all things rejoice in the age to come.

The narrator of the fourth *Eclogue* then movingly declares that if he can tell the story of this life to come, he will equal, if not surpass, Orpheus, Linus, Calliope, Apollo and Pan himself (4.55-59). The narrator will have such power because his subject, the brilliant, surpassing artist, is more than equal to the great artists of myth and poetry. In the meanwhile, our genius is yet to be born. As a newborn babe he must smile at his mother, if he is later to have the life of a god (4.62-63).

The tenth *Eclogue* gives us the full-grown man, the archpoet, Gallus. As a poem encapsulating the Artist's Life, it embraces such subjects as the loneliness of the artist, imagination and inspiration, the relative madness which often seems to mark the great artist.

Again and again in the history of art we find the artist leading the life of the outsider. In his giftedness, he is separate. The great treatment of this condition is in Thomas Mann's novel, *Doctor Faustus*, the story of the composer, Adrian Leverkühn. Gallus longs for the departed Lycoris. Lycoris represents life abroad, beyond the confinement of the study or studio. Gallus lies beneath a lonely rock (10.14) as though he were in an *antrum*. Apollo, Silvanus, Pan come to him—these the gods of both inspiration and productivity (10.21-30). It is Apollo who asks Gallus why he is mad, there being little hope for the return of Lycoris (10.22-23).

Gallus will not be comforted. He sees himself dead, his death honored by the Arcadian musicians gathered around him (10.31-34). Then Gallus wishes he were an ordinary shepherd (10.35-40). But, alas, he is required to be a soldier. Here we have a complex frustration. Gallus would have love, he would have the life of a shepherd-artist, but there are other demands upon him. In the broadest context, can we not see Vergil's Gallus as the young T.S. Eliot? Eliot experienced such conflicts and frustrations in his unfortunate first marriage, his life in the bank and his simultaneous life as a poet. We can see Gallus as the prototype of other artists of our time. Picasso stayed behind in Paris during

World War II. He was both Gallus and Tityrus. On the other hand, Thomas Mann was forced to flee Hitler's Germany; he was a Meliboeus. Gallus wants to be everything to everyone—artist, soldier, lover—he is Mann's Adrian. Gallus must reconcile these frustrations and ambivalent attitudes. We have seen in the *Eclogue Book* that to be an artist is total commitment.

Gallus' mind wanders as he contemplated a life without Lycoris (10.50-68). He believes that he can never write poetry again (10.62-63). He is the subject of Amor (10.64). But is he? Is not the famous concluding line of Gallus's soliloquy (10.69) the most ambiguous verse in all of Vergil's poetry?

omnia vincit Amor: et nos cedamus Amori.

Cannot Love and Art be one and the same?

In the following two lines our narrator leaves Gallus, concentrating on the weaving of a basket. He wants the basket to be acceptable to Gallus. Is not Gallus likely to return to art? Is not love of art, whether as artist or admirer of art, one of the supreme human passions? Do we not study art because, first of all, we love it?

On this gripping, thrilling, ambiguous note, Vergil ends the *Eclogue Book*. The arch-poet, Gallus, in Vergil's rendering, is as many-faceted as a Cubist portrait by Picasso. What is the life of art? What is the artist's life? Vergil, in the *Eclogue Book*, offers a description of art and the artist which is in perfect accord with our complex appreciation today of the making of art and the significance of the life of the artist.

NOTES

1. This tribute to that deep student of Rome and the ancient culture of the Bay of Naples, Alexander G. McKay, began as a banquet address before the Ohio Classical Conference, October 1985. With considerable abbreviation, but with fresh adjustments, the paper was presented before the Southern Section of the Classical Association of the Middle West and South in November 1988. The work of R.D. Williams and E.W. Leach on Vergil and art are well known. My study is more specifically concerned with Vergil in the *Eclogues*, and the Artist. My own concern with the Artist in the world is similar to that of Thomas Mann who gives us the supreme artist, crippled and transcendent, in his character of Adrian Leverkühn, *Doctor Faustus* (see my essay, "Classical Latin Poetry: An Art for

Our Time" in *The Endless Fountain*, ed. M. Morford, 1972). Meanwhile we watch the career of the greatly appreciated poet, Richard Wilbur, and the intensely examined careers of Tennessee Williams and Andy Warhol. Vergil's life was that of these twentieth-century figures. This paper profited from the reading by Professor Ward W. Briggs, Jr., bibliographer of the *Eclogues*, 1927-1977 (*ANRW* II.31.1, 1981), in the summer of 1985. The Latin text is that of R.A.B. Mynors (Oxford, 1969); the English translations my own.

FALLGRUBEN FÜR DEN KLASSISCHEN PHILOLOGEN

Viktor Pöschl
Universität Heidelberg

Fallgruben? Ach, deren gibt es so viele, dass es unmöglich ist, sie in grösserem Umfang auch nur andeutungsweise ausfindig zu machen. Einfach ist die Wahrheit, vielfach der Irrtum, und wir alle fallen ihm zum Opfer. Dabei spielen wissenschaftliche Moden, denen man kaum ausweichen kann, eine verhängnisvolle Rolle. Die Anziehungskraft gewisser Arten von Erklärungen ist nun einmal ganz überwältigend, wie Wittgenstein meinte. Ich kann mich nur auf einige wenige Beispiele beschränken und muss mich mit Stichworten begnügen, die ich willkürlich auswähle. Es wäre nicht schwer, ein ganzes Buch darüber zu schreiben. Ein jeder wird imstande sein, zahllose Beispiele zu jedem Stichwort hinzuzufügen, und ebenso leicht wird er die Stichworte selbst vermehren können. Mir kommt es nur darauf an, einige Fehlerquellen namhaft zu machen, die wir allzuleicht vergessen.

DIE TYRANNEI DER METHODE

Die Hauptaufgabe der klassischen Philologie war lange Zeit die Herstellung zuverlässiger Texte, die Methode war die Textkritik, wie sie namentlich Lachmann entwickelte (vgl. S. Timpanaro, *Lachmanns Textkritik*). Das Seltsame und Verhängnisvolle war, dass die textkritische Methode auf die Literaturkritik übertragen wurde. Ein Beispiel hierfür bietet Leos Rekonstruktion der verlorenen hellenistischen Elegie (vgl.

Verf. *Heidelberger Jahrb.* 3 [1959] 95ff.). Leo kam es darauf an, die griechischen Vorgänger der römischen Elegie zu ermitteln, die für ihn unter der Annahme des Gattungszwanges, den er als verbindlich ansah, nur griechische Elegiker sein konnten. Er ging dabei von Übereinstimmungen zwischen Plautus und der römischen Elegie aus. Plautus war Nachahmer und weitgehend Übersetzer von Stücken der Nea. Von diesen übernahmen, wie Leo glaubte, hellenistische Elegiker bestimmte Motive—hier war der Gattungszwang merkwürdigerweise ausser Kraft gesetzt— und ihnen folgten wieder die römischen Elegiker. Aus diesen Übereinstimmungen wurden also Motive der verlorenen hellenistischen Elegie rekonstruiert. Dass hier die Textkritik das Muster war, ist evident: von dem 'Original' der griechischen Komödie wurden zwei Zweige abgeleitet: auf der einen Seite die römische Komödie, auf der anderen Seite die hellenistische Elegie, von der wiederum die römische Elegie abhängig war.

Zur Textkritik gehörte es, Interpolationen aus dem ursprünglichen Text zu eliminieren. Dies war das Leitprinzip für Eduard Fraenkels Bestreben, *Plautinisches in Plautus* (1922) ausfindig zu machen. So schied er witzige Partien als plautinische Zusätze aus, indem er glaubhaft machte, dass der Text nach Ausscheidung des Zusatzes ohne weiteres dort anknüpfte, wo der Einschub einsetzte, die witzige Partie also eine plautinische Interpolation war. Ich habe keinen Zweifel, dass diese Methode zu einem beträchtlichen Teil zu richtigen Ergebnissen führte. Dass sie durch Funde von Originaltexten der griechischen Komödie widerlegt werden könnte, ist trotzdem nicht auszuschliessen. Im übrigen ist die in den ausgefahrenen Spuren der Textphilologie sich bewegende Plautus-Forschung vielen Fehldeutungen erlegen, weil man Plautus nur als Text und nicht als Theater begriff.

Die Methode, die nach dem Prinzip arbeitete "Schneide heraus was du herausschneiden kannst," hat in der Textherstellung des Iuvenal (z.B. bei Ulrich Knoche) oder in Jachmanns Arbeit über die Binneninterpolation bei Euripides zu merkwürdigen Auswüchsen geführt. Der gleiche Jachmann, im übrigen ein hervorragender Gelehrter, hat aus der Properz-Elegie 2.15 die Verse 23-28 als Interpolation eliminiert, weil dort Properz den Wunsch äusserte, seine Geliebte möge mit einer Kette an ihn gefesselt sein, die nie gelöst würde (*Rheinisches Museum* 34 [1935]). Man könne doch nicht, sagte Jachmann, eine Kette ins Bett mitnehmen. Dass die Kette metaphorisch gemeint war, scheint ihm nicht in den Sinn gekommen zu sein.

Eine noch viel verhängnisvollere und weitreichendere Folge der Übertragung der Textkritik auf die literarische Kritik war, dass man die lateinische Literatur als Ganzes als einen mehr oder weniger minderwertigen Abklatsch der griechischen betrachtete, wobei der geringere Wert der abgeschriebenen Handschrift gegenüber dem Archetypus das prägende Paradigma war. Die lateinischen Autoren waren nur wichtig, insofern man glaubte, aus ihnen verlorene griechische Autoren rekonstruieren zu können. Leo war nicht eigentlich an Plautus interessiert, sondern an den verlorenen griechischen Vorbildern; Pasquali suchte in seinem *Orazio lirico* (1920) vor allem hellenistische Lyrik zurückzugewinnen, was er später selbst, wie er einmal zu mir sagte, für einen Irrtum hielt. An einer Geringschätzung des Römertums war vor allem in deutschen Kulturbereich freilich nicht nur das Prägemuster der Textkritik schuld, sondern die Griechenreligion der Goethezeit (Walther Rehm, *Griechentum und Goethezeit, Geschichte eines Glaubens* [1936]) und der antirömische Komplex (W. Rüegg, *Cicero und der Humanismus*, [1946]). Eine Rolle spielten aber auch Äusserungen der Römer selbst, und damit kommen wir zu einer weiteren Fallgrube: *Die verfehlte Berufung auf einseitig ausgewertete Belege.*

Hier haben die berühmten Verse des Virgil *excudent alii* (Aen. 6. 847) viel Unheil angerichtet. Was Virgil hier vor allem sagen will, ist doch, dass die Römer in der Kunst, Völker zu führen, Zivilisation zu verbreiten *(paci imponere morem)* und bei kriegerischen Unternehmungen Härte und Milde richtig einzusetzen, andere Völker übertreffen werden. Darauf liegt jedenfalls der Hauptakzent. Die gängige Auslegung geht aber in andere Richtung. Sie legt den Ton auf die Unterlegenheit der Römer in der bildenden Kunst und der Redekunst. Ob darin eine Unfreundlichkeit gegen Cicero zu vermuten ist, wage ich nicht zu beurteilen. Dabei ist Virgil diskret genug, die Poesie nicht zu erwähnen. Die einseitige Auslegung der Virgilstelle, auf die man sich berufen zu können glaubte, ist mit daran schuld, dass man die Qualität, die Substanz, das humane Potential der römischen Literatur solange verkannte, dass z.B. Teuffel seine römischen Literaturgeschichte mit dem Worten beginnen konnte: "Den Römern fehlt . . . "

Einen anderen überbewerteten Beleg bildete Ciceros Satz *nemo fere saltat sobrius nisi forte insanit* (*Murena* 13). Da geht es dem Redner darum, den Vorwurf Catos zu entkräften, der Murena einen saltator genannt hatte. Dieser Beschimpfung, die dem übertreibenden Stil der kämpferischen Publizistik in Rom entspricht, stellte Cicero eine Behauptung entgegen, die ihrerseits übertrieben war. Daraus aber hat man gefolgert, dass die Römer überhaupt nicht hätten tanzen dürfen, und dies veranlasste Pasquali dazu, die Aufforderung zum Tanz am Beginn der Kleopatra-Ode (c. 1.37) nicht ganz allgemein zu verstehen, wie jeder unbefangene Leser sie verstehen muss, sondern ausschliesslich auf den rituellen Tanz der Salier zu beziehen. Hierin manifestiert sich *der Hang, wirkliche oder vermeintliche Widersprüche zu beseitigen.*

Dies ist verhängnisvoll, weil das Leben und jeder Mensch voller Widersprüche ist. Einem rationalistischen Interpreten fällt es offenbar schwer, Widersprüche zu ertragen. Er ist von einem Bestreben geleitet, die Dinge zu vereinheitlichen. Manche Deutungen des Horaz können dies bezeugen. Z.B. werden die hochtönenden Huldigungen des Horaz an Maecenas in der ersten Ode und in der Vorschlussode 3.29 von Eduard Fraenkel ironisch aufgefasst, während doch in einer Gesellschaft, wo Ahnenstolz eine grosse Rolle spielte, ein Mann, der der römischen Nobilität nicht angehörte, diesen Mangel auf andere Weise auszugleichen suchte, und dies müssen wir für Maecenas annehmen, dem der Hinweis auf etruskische Könige, von denen er angeblich abstammte, genehm sein musste. Auch die Gewalt der Liebesleidenschaft, die so deutlich aus vielen Horazoden spricht, suchte man ironisch zu verstehen oder als Auswirkung des Gattungszwanges. Wenn Horaz Leidenschaft äussert, folgt er—so schien man zu glauben—den grossen griechischen Lyrikern. Während die Leidenschaft dort noch echt war, soll sie es bei Horaz nicht mehr sein. Dass man echte Empfindungen in überkommenen Formen ausdrücken kann, wollte man nicht wahrhaben.

VERFÄLSCHUNG DURCH REZEPTION

Auch dies ist ein immenses Kapitel, für das ich nur ein bezeichnendes Beispiel bringen möchte. Es ist auch heute noch allgemein üblich die Bukolik Virgils unter dem Begriff "Arkadien" zusammenzufassen, wie ihn beispielsweise Bruno Snell darlegte ("Arkadien, Die Entdeckung einer geistigen Landschaft" in: *Die Entdeckung des Geistes*, [Hamburg 1955³] 371-400). Hier wird das Goldene Zeitalter, das Elegische und die Konzeption der sentimentalischen Dichtung, wie sie Schiller charakterisierte, in die Deutung der virgilischen Bukolik hineingetragen. Dies aber ist wie E.A. Schmidt überzeugend nachwies (*Antike und Abend-*

land 21 [1975]) eine Nachwirkung der Arkadienvorstellung, wie sie Sannazaro in seiner "Arcadia" entwickelte. Sannazaros Arkadien ist als Symbol der Renaissancesehnsucht nach der Antike zu begreifen. Diese neuzeitliche Arcadienvorstellung ist fälschlich auf Virgils Bukolik übertragen worden, die in erster Linie als "Dichtung über Dichtung" zu verstehen ist.

IDEALISIERUNG UND VERDRÄNGUNG DES BEFREMDLICHEN.

Die Deutungen der Worte '*urgentibus imperii fatis*' in einem berühmten Satz des Tacitus (*Germania* 33) veranschaulichen die Gefahr der Verdrängung des Unerfreulichen. Der Satz lautet: *urgentibus (iam) imperii fatis nihil (iam) praestare fortuna maius potest quam hostium discordiam.* "Da das Verhängnis des Reiches schon drohend andringt, kann uns Fortuna nichts Besseres geben als die Zwietracht unserer Feinde." R. Reitzenstein (*Göttinger Gelehrte Nachrichten* [1914]) hat das ganz anders übersetzt: "Jetzt, wo das Fatum der Römer zur Erringung der Weltherrschaft vorwärtstreibt, ist die Zwietracht der Germanen besonders wertvoll." Das schrieb Reitzenstein im Jahre des Ausbruchs des Weltkrieges. Hier spürt man den Zeitgeist des kaiserlichen Deutschlands. Heinze lehnte zwar diese Deutung ab, aber auch er wagte nicht, den klaren Sinn der Worte wiederzugeben, indem er vorschlug, "Das Reich ist durch Schicksalsfügung in schwerer Bedrängnis." Auch er blieb also auf halbem Wege stehen. Den Pessimismus des Tacitus wollte er nicht in seiner ganzen Schwere wahrhaben.

Auch sonst blieb er der Achtung vor königlicher Macht offenbar allzusehr verpflichtet, so, wenn er im Horazkommentar zum Schlussgedicht des dritten Odenbuches die Worte (*monumentum*) *regalique situ pyramidum altius* mit 'höher als das das Königsgrab der Pyramiden' wiedergab, während *situs* hier wie immer in ähnlichem Zusammenhang etwas ganz anderes, nämlich Moder, Verwitterung bedeutet. (Zur Begründung im einzelnen vgl. Verf., *Horazische Lyrik* [1970] 250ff.) Das seltsame ist, dass Heinzes Kommentar zu epi. 2,118 (*vocabula rerum*) *quae situs informis premit et deserta vetustas* mit den Worten kommentiert: "*situs* wie *od.* 3.30.2 vom Schimmel und Moder des Alters." Hier ist offenbar ein Ausgleich zwischen der älteren und richtigen Deutung der Ode *Exegi monumentum* nicht hergestellt und die neuere falsche Deutung glücklicherweise *nicht* berücksichtigt worden. Ein anderes Beispiel für das Bemühen,

Befremdendes zu beseitigen und mit dem Zeitgeist in Einklang zu bringen möchte ich nur kurz erwähnen, es sind die Bemühungen, die Verherrlichung kriegerischer Grosstaten, zu denen auch militärische Härte und Brutalität gehört, wie sie in der Aeneis einen für uns so beklagenswerten breiten Raum einnehmen, umzudeuten. Hier versuchte z.B. Kenneth Quinn in einem Vortrag, den er bei der 2000-Jahrfeier in Rom hielt, Virgil von unserem Standpunkt aus zu exkulpieren, indem er die betreffenden Schilderungen als ironisch zu erklären und dem römischen Dichter die gleiche Kritik zu unterschieben suchte, die wir hier zu üben geneigt sind.

Ein weiteres eindrucksvolles Beispiel liefert Mommsen, der die römische Kapitalstrafe nicht als Todesstrafe deutete um die römische Praxis zu entlasten. Da musste erst E. Levy kommen, um das zurechtzuweisen (Levy, *Die römische Kapitalstrafe,* Sitzungsber. der Heidelberger Akademie [1931]).

Auch die Deutung der Necessitas-Strophe der Fortuna-Ode des Horaz c. 1.35 gehört hierher, wo man die grauenhaften Attribute, mit denen die Necessitas daherkommt, in harmlosere umdeutet, und zwar nachweislich schon seit dem 18. Jahrh., vielleicht noch früher. Was führt sie mit? Balkennägel, Keile, den strengen Haken und das flüssige Blei. Das sind, wie jeder Unbefangene zunächst annehmen wird, Folter und Hinrichtungsutensilien (vgl. meine Ausführungen *Horazische Lyrik* [1970] 27ff.). Wohl können sie, wenn auch sehr gezwungen, auch als Werkzeuge des Bauhandwerks gedeutet werden, aber die Epitheta *saeva* der Necessitas und Epitheton *severus* des *uncus* sprechen entschieden gegen diese Deutung, die trotzdem von allen neueren Interpreten akzeptiert wird. Der Grund ist natürlich die Scheu, die necessitas mit so grausamen Werkzeug auszustatten, wie es der von Lessing zitierte Sanadon andeutete: "Je ne peux pas souffrir cet attirail patibulaire." Die hier praktizierte Verdrängung des Grauenvollen, das leider auch zum Leben gehört, hat übrigens einen gefährlichen Aspekt. Wie kann man Wirklichkeit bewältigen, wenn man die schwarze Seite nicht sieht? Bei der Missdeutung der Attribute der Necessitas kommt noch etwas anderes hinzu, worauf ich in meiner früheren Behandlung nicht hinwies, nämlich *die suggestive Macht von Parallelstellen*.

Bei Horaz c. 3.24.5ff. steht der Satz: *si figit adamantinos summis verticibus dira Necessitas.* Es scheint nicht ganz klar, wo die Necessitas die Nägel einschlägt (so die Interpreten). Ich fürchte, es ist ganz wörtlich zu nehmen. Auf jeden Fall handelt es sich um eine grauenvolle Umschreibung des Todesverhängnisses. Weniger grausam sind mehrfach bezeugte sprichwörtliche Wendungen, so Cicero, Verr. 5.33: *ut hoc beneficium quemadmodum dicitur clavo trabali figeret*, und Petron 57.7: *quod semel dessinavi, clavo trabali fixunst*, wozu Nisbet-Hubbard peremptorisch bemerken: *These passages are sufficient to refute the old notion* (1.35.18). Aber abgesehen davon, dass auch diese Stellen nicht völlig eindeutig sind, kann man nicht übersehen, dass Balkennägel sowohl in der Baukunst wie bei der Kreuzigung verwendet werden können. Es kommt auf den Zusammenhang an.

Mit der Gefahr der idealisierenden Tendenz hängt auch zusammen, was man unter den Stichworten *Prüderie und Lebensfremdheit* subsummieren könnte. Die Deutungsgeschichte einer Horazstelle ist da höchst aufschlussriech (*Epi.* 1.19.28):

temperat Archilochi Musam pede mascula Sappho.

Eine vollständige Doxographie der vielgeplagten Stelle kann ich selbstverständlich hier nicht vorlegen. Ein paar Belege müssen genügen. Britannicus (Kommentar zu Juvenal 2.47, Ausgabe des Juvenal 1480) moralisiert: *tale monstrum libidinis dicitur Sappho excogitasse, unde mascula est appellata.* Turnebus (1512-1557), Joseph Scaliger (1540-1609) und Pierre Bayle, *Dictionnaire Historique et critique*, 1695-1697, deutsch von Gottsched 1741-1744, verbinden fälschlich *pede* mit *mascula* und beziehen es auf den Sprung vom Leukadischen Felsen. Immerhin bemerkt Bayle zum Sappho-Gedicht φαίνεταί μοι κῆνος "Die Ode ist nicht in der Schreibart einer Freundin, welche an die Freundin schreibt; alles schmeckt nach der Liebe der Fleischeslust" (in Gottscheds Übersetzung 4. Teil S.147). Völlig zutreffend bemerkt P. Buttmann (*Das Geschichtliche und die Anspielungen des Horaz*, Abhdlg. Berl. Akad. d. Wiss. [1815]): "Das Beiwort *mascula* konnte nicht so gefasst werden, ohne einen Nebengedanken zu erwecken." Ganz anderer Meinung war F.G. Welcker (1784-1868). 1816 veröffentlichte er einen höchst lebendigen und unterhaltsamen Aufsatz "Sappho von einem herrschenden Vorurteil befreit," der eine grosse und verhängnisvolle Wirkung hatte. Durch diese Schrift wurde das Urteil über Sappho bis auf den heutigen Tag in eine falsche Richtung gelenkt. Welcker nämlich bezeugte sein "Erstaunen über die unsägliche Gemeinheit, welche sich oft, vordem und neuerlich, über die Sappho ausgesprochen hat." Er bestreitet aufs heftigste, dass Sapphos Liebe zu ihren Freundinnen "anstössig und gar gemein, sinnlich und strafbar gewesen sei." Hier kann man nur eine seiner Formulierungen auf ihn selbst anwenden: "Verschiedene Zeitalter haben oft in abweichenden Urteilen ihren eigenen Geschmack ausgedrückt" (*Kl. Schriften* II [1845] S.80). Dabei wollen wir nicht vergessen, dass der Satz auch auf uns anwendbar ist.

Es war nur konsequent, dass Welcker die naheliegende Deutung, dass in der *mascula Sappho* des Horaz eine homoerotische Anspielung liegen könnte, ablehnt. Sie bezeichnete vielmehr "die männlich freie Sprache in ihren Liebesliedern." Ganz ähnlich meinte Th. Kock (*Alcaeus und Sappho*, Berlin [1862] 27), mit *mascula Sappho* sei "die ungewöhnte Stärke ihren Gefühls" ausgedrückt: "Dies allein meint Horaz."

Welckers Urteil über Sappho hat dann Wilamowitz übernommen und verstärkt (vgl. W.M. Calder III, F.G. Welcker "Sappho-Bild and its reception in Wilamowitz," in: W.M. Calder III u.f. (Hrsg.), F.G. Welcker, *Werk und Wirkung Hermes Einzelschriften* Heft 49, (1986) 131-156. In einer Besprechung von Pierre Louys, 'Les chansons de Bilitis' schriebt er (*Göttinger Gelehrte Anzeigen* 1896): "Dieser Liebe (der Sappho) irgendetwas grob Sinnliches zuzuschreiben ist nicht nur sündhaft, sondern zeugt von einer groben Unfähigkeit, Texte zu verstehen." Kiessling-Heinze und Eduard Fraenkel stehen ganz unter der Wirkung des gleichen Vorurteils. Kiessling-Heinze: "(Sappho) ist in ihrem Kunstverstand eher einem Mann vergleichbar als einem schwachen Weibe, darum '*mascula*.'" Eduard Fraenkel, *Horace* 346: "It is, Horace suggests, extraordinary for a woman to walk in the footsteps of that most virile poet Archilochos, but Sappho, θαυμαστόν τι χρῆμα, could do so, for the power of her poetry was as great as any man's." Er fügt dem eine aufschlussreiche Anmerkung bei: "When Philipp Buttmann knew that he was soon to die, he felt it heavy on his conscience that he had done a grave injustice both to Sappho and to Horace by reading, with many others, the vulgar slander into *mascula*. He therefore prefixed to the second volume of his *Mythologus* a special note, at the end of which he says 'meine wirkliche Schuld gegen beide / *Sappho and Horace* / gut zu machen, halte ich für eine meiner heiligsten Pflichten, ehe ich aus diesem Kreise der redenden Menschengeschlechter scheide; welche ich hiermit erfülle'. The note is dated 'February 1829.' He died four months later."

Trotz dieser Bemühungen ist die homoerotische Anspielung aus der Horazstelle ebensowenig wegzubringen wie das homoerotische Element aus den Gedichten der Sappho selbst. Ich glaube, dass Ovid die leidenschaftliche Liebe der Sappho zu ihren Gefährtinnen so verstanden hat und so verstehen durfte:

Heroides 15: *quas non sine crimine amavi* (von Welcker und anderen durch die Konjektur *quas hic sine crimine amavi* beseitigt). *Ars amandi* 3.321: *nota sit et Sappho, quid enim lascivior illa? Tristien* 2.365: *Lesbia quid docuit Sappho nisi amare puellas?* Diese Bemerkungen des Ovid sind keineswegs nur, was man natürlich wollte, der Libertinage seines Wesens zuzuschreiben, sondern fanden eine Stütze in den Gedichten der Sappho selbst, in denen, die wir kennen, und sicherlich auch denen, die uns verloren sind.

Es ist unvorstellbar, dass man bei Horazens *mascula Sappho* an solche Zusammenhänge nicht gedacht hätte. Ganz falsch wäre es jedoch, wollte man daraus eine moralische Verurteilung herauslesen. Es ist bei Horaz vielmehr eine liebenswürdige Anspielung, mit schalkhaftem Augenzwinkern gesagt, wie es dem heiteren Konversationston einer urbanen Gesellschaft entspricht. Dass damit ein wenig Medisance verknüpft ist, versteht sich von selbst. In dem Missverständnis freilich, dass ein so zähes Leben hat, manifestiert sich die Kluft zwischen weltmännischer Freiheit und moralischer Enge und gelehrter Lebensfremdheit, und deshalb bin ich auf diesen Fall etwas ausführlicher eingegangen. Bewunderung von Schönheit lässt sich von erotischen Gefühlen nun einmal nicht völlig trennen.

Was aber das Phänomen Sappho betrifft, darf ich auf eine Deutung hinweisen, die Wolfgang Rösler in einem noch ungedruckten Vortrag "*Homoerotik und Initiation: Über Sappho*" (innerhalb eines Vortragszyklus *Homoerotische Lyrik,* den der Anglist Stemmler veröffentlichen wird) einleuchtend begründet hat. Im Kreis der Sappho wurden junge Mädchen in fundamentale Verhaltensweisen eingeführt, die sie im späteren Leben benötigten: körperliche Kultur, musische Ausbildung, religiöse Erziehung, sexuelle Unterweisung gehörten dazu. Dies aber lässt sich dem Kulturphänomen der Initiation zuordnen, wie es Mircea Eliade (*Das Mysterium der Wiedergeburt,* Zürich-Stuttgart [1961]) dargestellt hat.

Ich möchte noch auf zwei weitere Horazstellen hinweisen, die aus der gleichen Ursache wie die *mascula Sappho* falsch verstanden wurden. In der Horazode 3.20.7f.

> *grande certamen, tibi praeda cedat*
> *maior an illi*

ist *illi* einhellig überliefert. Gleichwohl wird die Konjektur *illa* von P. Hofmann Peerlkamp (1862) fast überall beifällig aufgenommen, so in den Ausgaben bzw. Kommentaren von Kiessling (1884), den späteren Auflagen von Kiessling-Heinze, H. Schütz (1889), Klingner (zuerst 1939 und in den späteren Auflagen), P. Maas (*Studi Italiani di Filologia Classica* 1956 = Kl. Schriften, München 1973, 227f.) G. Williams (1969), D.R. Shackleton-Bailey (1985). Nur Nauck (6. Aufl. 1868), Wickham (1901ff.) und Borszák (1984) halten die Überlieferung. Erfolgreich verteidigt wird sie von Kraggerud (*Symbolae Osloenses* 57, [1982] 101-108). Das Hauptproblem liegt in der Deutung von *praeda maior*. Was damit gemeint ist, geht aus dem Zusammenhang klar hervor. In dem Gedicht ist von einem Kampf die Rede, der zwischen zwei Rivalen ausgetragen wird, dem Pyrrhus und der 'Löwin,' einem Mädchen, deren Name nicht genannt wird. Der Umkämpfte ist der schöne Nearch. Der Kampf geht aber nicht darum, wem von beiden Nearch gehören soll, sondern wem die *maior praeda* gehören wird, was jeder unbefangene Leser als die grössere Beute verstehen wird, d.h. beide Rivalen werden etwas von Nearch bekommen, aber mehr das Mädchen. Merkwürdigerweise weichen sämtliche Interpreten diesem Sinn aus, selbst Kraggerud. Er denkt an eine "Rivalität auf dem offenen Liebesmarkt." "Wir brauchen unter solchen Umständen nicht zu glauben, dass der Verlierer Pyrrhus überhaupt nichts gewinnen werde, wenn er auch der erstrebenswertesten Prämie verlustig geht." Die *grösste und beste Beute*, so übersetzt er, wird die Nebenbuhlerin davontragen. d.h. er eskamotiert den Komparativ *maior*. Weshalb alle Interpreten dies tun ist leicht einzusehen. Kiessling-Heinze sprechen es aus, man könne doch dem Horaz nicht die Kopflosigkeit zutrauen, dass er hier an eine Teilung der Beute gedacht hätte, ebenso Syndikus: "Sie kämpfen ja nicht darum, wem das grössere Stück von der Beute gehört." Eben dies aber tun sie, und, eben dagegen sträuben sich die Interpreten, weil sie sich nicht vorstellen können, dass zwei sich in einen Partner teilen können. Sie sind ein Opfer ihrer Lebensfremdheit, ihres Mangels an Welterfahrung geworden. Pirandello hätte keine Schwierigkeit gehabt, das zu verstehen, der in der Komödie '*O di uno o di nessuno*' von zwei Studenten erzählt, die zu arm waren, um sich zwei Geliebte zu halten und sich deshalb in eine teilten.

Anhangsweise möchte ich noch zwei andere Beispiele nennen, wo die gleiche Person von zweien geliebt wird. Weil man das intolerabel fand, hat man das Anstössige einmal durch eine Konjektur, das andere Mal durch Umdeutung der geliebten Person beseitigt.

In der Allius-Elegie des Catull lesen wir (68.67ff.)

*isque domum nobis isque dedit dominam
ad quam communes exerceremus amores.*

Dass Catull und sein Freund Allius *communes amores* betrieben, beseitigte man durch die auch stilistisch abscheuliche Konjektur *dominae*, die wiederum von den meisten Editoren akzeptiert wird. *Communes amores* bezeichnet dann nur die Liaison zwischen Catull und Lesbia, wobei freilich die Beziehung von *ad quam* auf *domum* eine weitere stilistische Monstruosität darstellt.

In der Horazode 2.12 identifizierte man Licymnia, der sowohl Horaz wie seinen Freund Maecenas huldigen, unter Berufung auf Pseudo-Acro mit Terentia, der Gattin des Maecenas, wozu Syndikus bemerkt: "Die antike Gleichsetzung mit Terentia ist heute allgemein anerkannt." Abgelehnt wurde sie jedoch von B.R. Morris and R.D. Williams, (*Philological Quarterly* 42 [1963] 145-150) und ausführlich von G. Davis (*Philologus* 119 [1975] 70-83). Davis will freilich nur die Liebschaft des Horaz zu Licymnia anerkennen. Die klare Aussage der beiden Schlussstrophen, die den Höhepunkt des Gedichtes bilden und ganz eindeutig von der Liebesleidenschaft des Maecenas sprechen, verfälscht er, indem er abschwächend paraphrasiert (a.O. s.76: Would you (i.e., *if you were in my position*) exchange such a girl as I have described for excessive riches?" Er tut dies aus dem gleichen Bedenken, dem der unbekannte Gewährsmann des Pseudo-Acro erlag und das H. Schütz formulierte: Wollte man Licymnia für eine Geliebte halten, "müsste man unsinnigerweise annehmen, dass Horaz und Maecenas eine gemeinsame Geliebte gehabt hätten." Dass jedoch beide von dem Liebreiz der Licymnia fasziniert sind und Maecenas ihr Haar nicht gegen die Schätze des Achaemenes und Phrygiens vertauschen möchte, wird deutlich genug gesagt. Ist es so schwer, das, was da steht, unbefangen zu verstehen?

FOUR "NEOCLASSICAL" POEMS

George Thaniel
1938-1991

For Alexander G. McKay, on His 65th Year

At Hadrian's Villa (Tivoli)

Hadrian
emperor on a grand scale
was aware of how the cosmos
moves from macro- to micro-
and vice versa
and often talked
to his *animula*.

And I, standing now
at the Great Hall of Philosophers
am caught by the struggling plant
in the ceiling
and the ghost-like fish
in the greenish waters
of the *Teatro Marittimo*
small fish
custodians of absence.

Note: Two of the four poems are associated, somehow, with Dr. A.G. McKay. The idea for "At Hadrian's Villa (Tivoli)" was given to me initially in the summer of 1968 during a tour of antiquities in Campania and Latium by the Vergilian Society of America. The reference to Lucilius in "New Year's Eve at Times Square" derives from some notes I took on Roman satire after leafing through A.G. McKay and D.M. Shepherd, *Roman Satire* (St. Martin's Press, 1976).

New Year's Eve at Times Square

Just after midnight
broken glass and empty cans
litter the ground
while the mounted police
rushes the crowd
made wild by the anticipation
of a new year.

Tonight is festival
which you couldn't plainly describe
in hexameters.*

*After Lucilius: *Servorum est festus dies hic, quem plane hexametro versu non dicere possis.*

Bath (England)

Somebody mentioned
that a nondescript Venus
was once unearthed in these quarters.
We found no Venus
but a Minerva Sul
in her protective cube of glass.

No need of priestesses of love
great need of spiritual nurses.
That might be the message
of the "Jesus Saves" team
by the entrance to the baths—
inspired young man
drawing symbols of salvation
on a board
wrapping them in words of faith,
another catching up with us
mere photographers of reality
to ensure that the seed of logos
had hit some nest inside.

Bath is a beautiful city
could have adorned the shield of Achilles
or better that of Aeneas
since Vulcan rather than Hephaestus
held sway here once
and may still lurk
behind the steaming waters
that rush lasciviously
out of the earth's womb.

Sic Itur Ad Astra

Nec tellus nostrae, nec patet unda fugae
Restat iter caeli: caelo temptabimus ire.
                                            Ovid, *Ars Amatoria* 2.36-37

The Voyager II has just skirted Neptune
Daedalus is still at his game
man wants a way out
of his Trojan land
of his Aeschylean sea,
even the silver-fingered moone
the virgin of the forest
has been demythologized,
even the sun, the great sun
is trapped into green houses
where he grows revengeful.

Yet, there is no way back
since Adam bit at that apple
since Prometheus stole that fire.
Man is destined to forge ahead
Icarus will again tempt the air
the sun may again have his way.

Another cycle and another *saeculum*
another trick of unpredictable time
which stands by the humble cyclamen
but also makes Hiroshimas possible—
Cronos swallowing his own children
one always escapes.

LIST OF ILLUSTRATIONS

Illustrations found within text:
Alexander Gordon McKay 13
Vergil Mosaic, Bardo National Museum, Tunis 37
The Villa Vergiliana, Cumae, Italy 255

Illustrations found within Plate section:
1. *Orestes and Pylades: detail of copy of the Timomachus painting (see Plate 5) from Casa del Citarista, Pompeii.*
2. *Iphigenia before the Temple of Artemis; detail from copy of the Timomachus painting, Casa del Citarista, Pompeii.*
3. *Orestes and Pylades before Iphegenia; pinax from House of Vettii, Pompeii.*
4. *Orestes and Pylades are led before Iphigenia; sarcophagus (307 A.D.) from Glyptotek, Munich.*
5. *Orestes and Pylades before Iphigenia: copy of the Timomachus painting from Casa del Citarista, Pompeii.*
6. *"Vendita di amorini" (from Stabiae), Museo Nazionale, Naples: Inv. No. 9180; Andreae, Kat. Nr. 267, pp. 192, 217.*
7. *"Erotenverkauf" (copy by Tischbein), Dusseldorf: Andreae, p. 223; Trevelyan, pp. 45, 125.*
8. *"La Marchande d'Amours" (by Vien, 1763), Fontainbleau: Trevelyan, p. 62.*
9. *Abbildungslegende: Mailand, Soprintendenza Archeologica della Lombardia Inv. ST. 5986. Patera von Parabiago. Hirmer Fotoarchiv Nr. 562.3110.*
10. *Artist's rendering of a silver plate from Spain showing various ways in which a spring served the community.*
11. *Map of the known spas of Roman Campania.*
12. *Restored terra-cotta pot with four holes found in garden in House of the Ship Europa, Pompeii. (Photo: Stanley Jashemski.)*
13. *Restored pots from Garden of Hercules, Pompeii. (Photo: S. Jashemski.)*
14. *Cast of tree root in pot in Garden of Hercules. (Photo: S. Jashemski.)*

15. *"Sombrero" formations in garden in House of Polybius, Pompeii. (Photo: S. Jashemski.)*
16. *West part of peristyle garden in House of Polybius. (Photo: S. Jashemski.)*
17. *Plan of peristyle garden in House of Polybius; roots are indicated in black, stakes by circles. (Plan courtesy Soprintendenza alle antichità della Campania-Napoli; garden details by S. Jashemski.)*
18. *Southeast portico garden in villa at Oplontis. (Photo: S. Jashemski.)*
19. *Plan of villa at Oplontis. (Plan courtesy Soprintendenza alle antichità della Campania-Napoli; garden details by S. Jashemski.)*
20. *Pots each with two small stake cavities, found in garden of villa at Oplontis. (Photo: S. Jashemski.)*
21. *Pots found in planter-pool garden in villa at Oplontis. (Photo: S. Jashemski.)*
22. *Ornamental pots in Casa dei Cervi, Herculaneum. (Photo: S. Jashemski.)*
23. *Pots found in garden in winter palace of Herod at Jericho. (Photo: courtesy E. Netzer.)*
24. *Pot found in garden in Hadrian's villa. (Photo: F. Luciolli.)*
25. *Cast of tree root in half amphora, in sculpture garden in villa at Oplontis. (Photo: F. Hueber.)*
26. *The Canopus in Hadrian's villa. (Photo: F. Luciolli.)*
27. *Discarded amphoras, cut in two, and used as planting pots in Canopus garden. (Photo: F. Luciolli.)*
28. *Adonis gardens. (Furtwängler-Reichhold, Griechische Vasenmaleri, pl. 78.1.)*
29. *Bibliothèque municipale de Lyon. ms. Palais des Arts 27. Virgile. L'Enèide. Fol. 137r°. Descente aux Enfers et reconcontre d'Enée et de Didon.*
30. *Cambridge, MA, Houghton Library, Harvard University, ms. Richardson 38, fol. 135v (8.4 x 9.5 cm.). By permision of the Houghton Library, Harvard University.*
31. *Paris, Bibliothèque Nationale, ms. fr. 861, fol. 33v (14 x 19 cm.).*
32. *Valencia, Biblioteca de la Universitat de València, ms. 837, fol. 161r (13.1 x 13.9 resp. 17.4 cm.).*
33. *London, British Library, King's ms. 24, fol. 131v.*
34. *Cambridge, MA, Houghton Library, Harvard University, ms. Richardson 38, fol. 174v (9.7 x 9.5 cm.). By permision of the Houghton Library, Harvard University*
35 and 36. *Biblioteca Apostolica Vaticana, Vat. lat. 3225, pict. 36 u. 37 in den Stichen von Carolo Ruspi (19. Jh), aus: T.B. Stevenson, Miniature Decoration in the Vatican Virgil (Tübingen, 1983) 72f. (verkleinert im Verhältnis 4.5).*

INDEX KEYED TO LINE NUMBERS

Note: Italic page numbers refer to line references made in footnotes.

Aeschylus
Agamemnon:
866-868 287
Supplices:
223f. *166*

Aesop
62 213
83 214
84 214
344 214

Ammianus Marcellinus
17.13.32 211
25.4.15 211

Anthologia Palatina:
16.128 .... *279*
16.151 65

Apollodorus, *Bibliotheca:*
3.15.7 .... *91*
3.15.8 .... *91*

Apollonius, *Argonautica:*
2.1266f. *177*
2.404f. *177*
2.933-935 .... *165*
4.14f. *177*
4.1541-1546 .... *165*
4.162 .... *177*
4.1682-1688 .... *165*
4.933-936 .... *165*

Appian, *Mithridates:*
115 225

Apuleius
Apologia:
55f. 350
de deo Socratico:
(*passim*) 63
Metamorphoses:
3.29 351
11.3-6 350

Aristides (Aelius Aristides)
Orationes:
32 (Keil) 349

Aristophanes, *Nubes:*
762 299

Aristotle, *Poetica:*
3.2 312
11 (1452b 6-8) *278*
14 (1454a 7) *278*
16 (1454b 30-35) *278*
16 (1455a 6-8) *278*
17 (1455a 18) *278*
17 (1455b 10-12) *278*

Athenaeus
6.253D-F *354*
318D 351

495

Augustus, *res gestae:*
- 3 241
- 4.7 .... *144*
- 13 .... *333*
- 30.1 .... *333*
- 32.3 .... *333*
- 34.1 .... *333*

Aurelianus (Caelius Aurelianus) *Chron. Dis.:*
- 2.48 .... 357, 360
- 5.126 .... 359, 363
- 5.77 .... 357, 359

Ausonius
Epigrammata de diuersis rebus:
- 14 214
- 118 65

Mosella:
- 1-22 403
- 11-22 403
- 23 403
- 152-160 401
- 163-169 402
- 178 402
- 320-329 402
- 435 .... *407*

Bernardus Silvestris
Commentum super sex libros Eneidos Virgilii:
- p. 1.1-7 .... *423*
- p. 3.8-11 .... *423*
- p. 3.14f. *323*
- p. 9.8f. 411
- p. 10.4ff. *432*
- p. 10.6-11 .... *425*
- p. 24.7-10 413
- p. 25.1.18-20 413
- p. 28.9-11 .... *424*
- p. 30.6-9 .... *426*
- p. 30.20f. 410
- p. 63.25 .... *432*
- p. 64.3ff. *432*
- p. 68.21 .... *426*
- p. 93.22 413
- p. 94.12ff. 413
- p. 95.12ff. 413
- p. 95.16 415
- p. 97.4 .... *426*
- p. 114.4-9 .... *429*
- p. 114.15 .... *429*
- p. 115.4 .... *429*
- p. 116.17-117.2 419
- p. 116.23-117.1f. 411
- p. 118.3 .... *430*
- p. 118.11f. 411

Boccaccio, *Genealogie deorum gentilium:*
- 14.13 .... *426*
- 14.13 p. 722.27-723.12 414

Brittain, V.
Testament of Youth: 197

Cato
de Agricultura:
- 43 380
- 51 374
- 52 374
- 133 374
- 143 (134) *353*
- 148 (139) *353*
- 150 (141) *353*

frag.:
- 36 219

Catullus
- 35.3-6 298
- 35.11-18 298
- 55.1 300
- 55.18-22 300
- 62.57 .... *301*
- 64 .... *62*
- 64.78 .... *91*
- 66.39 69
- 67.1-2 297
- 67.12 .... *301*
- 67.15-16 297
- 67.19 .... *301*
- 67.2 297
- 67.31-34 297

67.45-48	296
67.6	297, *301*
67.6-10	297
67.9	296
68.67ff.	488

Celsus, *de Medicina*:
2.17.1	357

Cicero
de Amicitia:
24	273

Brutus:
60	209
81	209

C.M. (de Senectute):
21	213

de Diuinatione:
1.40 (87)	209
2.7.18	222
2.14.33	222

Epistulae ad Atticum:
14.12.2	357
15.27	210

Epistulae ad Familiares:
16.24.2	357

de Finibus:
2.67	210
2.79	*279*
4.10	210
5.63	*279*

pro Murena:
13	480

Orationes Philippicae:
3.32	*63*
18 (5) 12	220

de Oratore:
1.18.1	210

Partitiones Oratoriae:
109.5	210

pro Plancio:
65	357

ad Quirites (Post Reditum ad Populum):
18	*63*

de Republica:
1.25	407
1.29	407
2.29.51	*155*
2.30.52	*156*

Rhetorica ad Herennium:
3.28.1	210

pro Sulla:
62	298
62-66	*301*

Tusculanae Disputationes:
1.42f.	*424*
4.6-7	190

in Verrem:
5.33	484

CIL:
1.2.76 (= ILS 880)	*301*
4.5285	345
10.1163-1164	*370*
10.1177-1180	*370*
10.1707	362, *370*
10.3714	*370*
10.3811	361
10.4559	*370*
10.4718	*370*
10.4734	362
10.4792	*370*
10.4865	364, *370*
10.4884	364, *370*
10.6786	359
10.6786-6799	359
10.6787	359
10.6790	359
10.6793	359
10.6795	359
10.6796	359
10.6797	359
10.6798	359
10.797	102
10.8348	101

Columella, *de re rustica*:
3.21.11	*390*
5.10.6	*375*
10.133	*363*

Dante, *Inferno:*
  3.82-177 415
  5.60 414
  5.61 413

Degrassi, *ILLRP:*
  10-12 .... *107*
  1271 .... *107*

Dio Cassius
  48.52 386
  51.15.5 .... *355*
  51.19.7 344
  54.29.3 .... *405*
  63.29 386

Diodorus Siculus
  1.4 209
  1.46-49 212
  1.52 212
  1.63 212
  1.64 212
  1.66 212
  2.1 219
  2.46 209
  4.61.3 .... *91*
  11.62 212
  14.113 219
  19.87 212

Dionysius of Halicarnassus
Antiquitates Romanae:
  1.4.2 95
  1.25 .... 215, 221
  1.61-62 .... *143*
  1.64.5 .... 101, 240, *242*, 277
  1.72.2 93
  1.73.3 .... *106*
  2.58 221
  4.62 210
  5.2.2 216
  6.69 78
  9.2.5 216
  9.3.8 216
  10.2.17 216
  13.1.30 216
  15.3.7 216
  16.18 216
  17.1.B 216

de Compositione Verborum:
  1.1 312
  1.1-9 311
  1.10-20 312
  1.13 312
  1.20 312
  1.21-24 312
  1.25-26 312
  7-15 315
  11.13 315
  26.1-5 315
  26.11-12 315
  26.13 315
  26.14-16 315
  26.6-10 315

de Demosthene:
  1.2 318

Donatus, *ad Vergil, Aen.:*
  12.945 239

Elegiae in Maecenatem:
  123 .... *63*
  134 .... *63*

Euripides
Andromache:
  1140f. *166*
Hecuba:
  547-552 272
  563-565 272
Hercules Furens:
  1326 .... *91*
Hippolytus:
  1253f. *294*
Iphigenia Taurica:
  38-39 .... *278*
  72-73 272
  455-457 272
  508-509 277
  510-569 .... *277*
  584 271
  584-847 .... *280*
  621-622 .... *278*
  622 272

624 272
636 271
674-686 272
725 272
760-787 .... *280*
769 272
774-775 272
1444-1445 272
1477-1478 271
1487 272

Festus
  178L 221

FGH:
  4.F84 93
  240.F29 .... *107*
  560.F4 .... *106*
  564.F5 = 840.F14 103
  566.F59 99
  819.F1 .... *107*

Fulgentius
*Expositio Virgilianae
continentiae secundum
philosophos moralis:*
  p. 94.17ff. 412
  p. 96.2f. *425*
  p. 96.5f. *425*
  p. 98.1-3 .... *425*
  p. 98.12-14 .... *425*
  p. 99.18ff. 413
  p. 102.5f. *430*
  p. 120.12 411

Galen
  10.363-366K 363
  11.392K 357
  20.50-54K *370*
  20.343-46K *370*

Gellius (Aulus Gellius), *Noctes
Atticae:*
  1.1.9 210
  2.10 215

Herodotus, *The Persian Wars:*
  1.50 211
  1.66-68 212
  2.44 212
  2.106 212
  2.121 212
  2.129-130 212
  2.135 212
  2.189 212

Hesiod, *Theogony:*
  1011-1016 .... *107*

Historiae Augustae
Marcus Antoninus:
  3.5 348
Marcus Aurelius:
  18.5f. 348
Septimius Severus:
  21.8 211
Severus Alexander:
  29.2 348
  31.5 348

Homer
Iliad:
  1.22-23 321
  1.118-119 321
  1.169-171 .... *326*
  1.231 .... *326*
  1.231-232 .... *326*
  1.232 .... *322*
  1.278-281 321
  1.287-289 321
  1.292 .... *326*
  1.293 .... *326*
  1.293-294 320
  1.295-296 321
  2.478 .... *165*
  3.338 .... *326*
  4.75-77 158
  4.275 .... *165*
  5.242ff. *126*
  5.438ff. *165*
  5.529 .... *326*
  5.574 .... *327*
  6.437 .... *326*

6.98f.	*127*	16.482-484	*165*
7.208	*165*	16.616	*326*
9.387	322, *327*	16.665	*326*
9.647	322	16.827	*326*
9.647-648	322	16.837	324
10.110	*326*	17.38	323
10.135	*326*	17.65	*165*
11.292	*165*	17.111	*326*
11.295	*165*	17.201	324
11.390	*326*	17.282	*165*
11.414	*165*	17.443-447	324, 325
11.441	323, 324	17.670	*327*
11.452	323	18.12	*326*
11.549	*165*	18.54	323
11.604	*326*	18.86-87	158
11.813	*326*	18.162	*165*
11.816-818	324	18.180	*327*
11.836	*326*	18.455	*326*
12.1	*326*	18.590-606	158
12.147	*165*	19.24	*326*
12.22ff.	*126*	19.208	*327*
12.41	*165*	19.287	323
12.295	*165*	20.169	*326*
12.298	*165*	20.208ff	129
12.349	*326*	20.215-240	*407*
12.362	*326*	20.297ff.	*128*
12.451	*165*	20.307ff.	*407*
12.802	*165*	20.398-400	196
13.177-181	158	20.416-418	196
13.178-180	*165*	20.493	*165*
13.278	321, *326*	21.27ff.	*204*
13.389-391	158, *165*	21.218ff.	*126*
13.492	*165*	21.270-273	112
14.12	*326*	21.272	112
14.414-417	*165*	21.279	112
15.482	*326*	21.463-466	323
15.581	*165*	21.465-466	325
15.605	*165*	21.493f.	*166*
16.59	322	21.493-495	158
16.209	*326*	22.25-32	*155*
16.264	*326*	22.26-31	323
16.278	*326*	22.76	323, 325
16.307	*326*	22.169-170	324
16.345-350	196	22.213	440
16.433ff	442	22.337ff.	*126*
16.477ff.	*126*	22.431	323
16.482-484	158	23.65	*327*

Index Keyed to Line Numbers

23.105 .... *327*
23.175ff. *204*
23.221 .... *327*
23.222 .... *165*
23.223 .... *323*
23.262-897 158
23.358-538 158
23.431-432 .... *165*
23.455-456 .... *165*
23.598-599 .... *165*
23.692-693 .... *165*
23.712-713 .... *165*
23.760-762 .... *165*
23.783-784 .... *165*
23.845-846 .... *165*
24.128ff. 442
24.508 324
24.516 324
24.518 320
24.525 320
24.525-526 .... 323, *327*
24.531-533 .... *327*
24.767 322

Odyssey:
2.5 .... *165*
4.563f *425*
5.12 .... *165*
5.290 .... *445*
5.295-314 110
5.296 111
5.297 111
5.298 112
5.299 111
5.305 111
5.312 111
5.313f. 111
5.377-379 .... *445*
5.394 .... *165*
6.151 .... *128*
9.19f. 121
9.480ff. *127*
9.537ff. *127*
10.133ff. 115
10.158-175 .... *156*
10.174ff. *127*
10.189ff. *127*
10.287 175

10.304 .... *178*
11.157-159 168
11.321 .... *91*
12.73ff. 116
12.208-217 117
12.298ff. *127*
13.131-133 .... *445*
16.1ff. *407*
16.17 .... *165*
16.183ff. *128*
16.210ff. *407*
17.111 .... *165*
17.397 .... *165*
24.46ff. *446*
24.73ff. *446*
24.91ff. *446*
24.472ff. *447*

Homeric Hymn to Demeter:
371ff. *341*

Horace
Ars Poetica:
60 63
Epistulae:
1.15.8 357
1.16 264
1.19.28 484
2.118 482
Odes:
1.1.1 .... *405*
1.7.30 119
1.7.30-32 119
1.17 470
1.35 483
1.35.18 484
1.37 481
2.1.4 259
2.1.7 262
2.1.16 266
2.1.25 260
2.1.25-26 266
2.1.31 266
2.1.37-38 262
2.1.39-40 262
2.10.1 263
2.10.5 263

2.10.5-6	264
2.10.13-15	264
2.11.1	266
2.11.17	260
2.12	488
2.12.1-2	266
2.12.9-10	266
2.12.9-16	260
2.12.21-22	266
2.12.24	266
2.13.2-4	265
2.14.6	260
2.14.6	264
2.14.9-12	264
2.14.13	264
2.14.15-16	264
2.14.17-18	265
2.14.21-22	265
2.16.1-2	266
2.16.5	266
2.16.6	266
2.16.17	265
2.16.19	265
2.16.29-30	265
2.16.31	265
2.16.32	265
2.16.34-35	265
2.17.2	260
2.17.3-4	260
2.18.5	266
2.18.9-11	264
2.18.32-34	264
2.18.38-39	264
2.2.3-4	262
2.2.6	262
2.2.9	262
2.2.10-11	266
2.2.17	266
2.2.22-23	262
2.2.23	262
2.2.39	262
2.3.1	263
2.3.4	263
2.3.25	263
2.6.1	266
2.6.1-4	259
2.6.2	266
2.6.3	266
2.6.18	260
2.6.21-24	259
2.7.1-2	260
2.7.5-6	260
2.7.9-10	260
2.7.13-15	260
2.7.27-28	260
2.8.13-14	265
2.9.2	266
2.9.4	266
2.9.5	260
2.9.10	263
2.9.19-20	263, 266
2.9.20	266
2.9.21	266
2.9.23	266
2.20.6-7	260
2.20.13-20	267
3.207f.	486
3.23.3f.	*353*
3.24.5ff.	483
3.29	481
3.30.2	482
4.5.31-36	344

Sermones:
1.10.81	263
2.3.164f.	*353*
2.5.12f.	*353*
2.6.2	213

Hyginus
Fabulae:
41	*91*

Poetica Astronomica:
2.5	*91*

ILS:
63	101
5004	102

Ioannes Saresberienis
Policratus:
2.15 p. 90, 22f. Webb	410
8.6 p. 261.13f. Webb	413
8.24 p. 415.20-25 Webb	*425*
8.24 p. 416.16-19	413

Index Keyed to Line Numbers

8.24 p. 416.27-29 413
8.24 p. 417.14-17 .... *423*

Ion, *Phaedra:*
265ff. (Nauck) 316

Josephus, *Antiquitates Judaicae:*
3.245 376
13.372 376

Justin
18.6.1-8 65

Juvenal, *Saturae:*
2.47 484
4.451 209
9.137f. *353*
12.89f. *353*

Kipling, R.
The Last Ode . . .: 187, *188*

Lactantius, *Divinae Institutiones:*
1.22 221

Landino (Cristoforo Landino)
Disputationes Camaldulenses IV:
p. 183f. (Lohe) 414
p. 120.12 (Lohe) 411
p. 190.9f. (Lohe) 411
p. 220.23ff. (Lohe) *432*
p. 229.5ff. (Lohe) *432*
p. 253.12 (Lohe) 410
p. 254.1f. (Lohe) 411
p. 254.32-255.8 (Lohe) *424*
p. 255.1f. (Lohe) 411
p. 255.3f. (Lohe) 411
p. 255.7f. (Lohe) 411
p. 256.14 (Lohe) *426*
p. 256.17-21 (Lohe) *426*

Livius Andronicus
frag. 16: (Morel) *126*

Livy, *ab urbe condita:*
1.2 101
1.2 220

1.13 220
1.25 219
1.55 .... 215, 221
5.33.3 219
5.40 215
7.15 .... *227*
8.11.15 101
10.2.4 223
24.21.9 223
25.40 .... 224, 226
29.8 216
29.18 216
29.19 216
31.12.1 216
31.13.1 216
40.29 221
40.219 215

Lucan, *Pharsalus:*
9.15 226
9.961 225

Lucilius
598 (Warmington) *278*

Lucretius, *de rerum natura:*
6.273 .... *177*
6.745-748 .... *177*

Lycrophron, *Alexandra:*
1261-1262 .... *81*

Macrobius
Commentarii in Somnium Scipionis:
1.9.8 .... 408, *424*
1.11.3 .... *425*
Saturnalia:
1.21.7ff. 338
1.22.4 338
2.4.18 .... *155*
3.11 .... *252*
5.175 73

Martial, *Epigrammata:*
9.93 .... *352*

Naevius, *Bellum Punicum frag.*:
- 7M 100
- 8M 100
- 10M 100
- 17-21 66
- 24 ..... *62*

Nepos (Cornelius Nepos)
- 18.1 209

Orphic Hymn:
- 294.53 (Abel) *176*

Ovid
Amores:
- 2.6.15-16 270

Ars Amatoria:
- 1.16 299
- 2.20-98 299
- 2.36-37 491
- 3.321 486

Epistulae ex Ponto:
- 1.2.77-78 271
- 2.8.1-4 347
- 2.8.2 347
- 2.8.5-9 347
- 2.8.9f. 347
- 2.8.10 347
- 2.8.25-36 347
- 2.8.28 347
- 2.8.38 ..... 347, *353*
- 2.8.43ff. 347
- 2.8.44 ..... *353*
- 2.8.45-50 348
- 2.8.51 ..... 347, *353*
- 2.8.52 347
- 2.8.58 347
- 2.8.60 347
- 2.8.64 347
- 2.8.67 347
- 2.8.70 347
- 3.1.159-164 ..... *353*
- 3.1.162-164 ..... *353*
- 3.1.163-166 ..... *353*
- 3.2.33-34 276
- 3.2.43 277
- 3.2.43-96 268
- 3.2.45 277
- 3.2.45-60 276
- 3.2.45-93 ..... 271, 277
- 3.2.53-54 ..... 276, 277
- 3.2.55-56 277
- 3.2.59 277
- 3.2.62 276
- 3.2.67-70 277
- 3.2.71-72 ..... 277, 278
- 3.2.75 ..... *278*
- 3.2.77 278
- 3.2.77-79 277
- 3.2.77-84 277
- 3.2.81-82 277
- 3.2.83-90 277
- 3.2.85-86 277
- 3.2.85-90 277
- 3.2.89 277
- 3.2.90 277
- 3.2.91 277
- 3.2.92 ..... 277, 278
- 3.2.93-94 277
- 3.2.94-95 278
- 3.2.95 277
- 3.11.17f. *353*
- 4.4.63-82 277
- 4.8.21 ..... *353*
- 4.9.105-110 347
- 4.9.108 347
- 4.9.111-112 347
- 4.9.113-116 348
- 4.9.127 349
- 4.9.129-134 349

Fasti:
- 2.143 ..... *301*
- 2.583ff. 438
- 2.591-594 439
- 2.633f. *353*
- 2.637f. 244
- 5.145f. 345

Heroides:
- 2.41 ..... *301*
- 11.101 ..... *301*
- 15 486

Metamorphoses:
- 1.492-495 ..... *294*
- 4.715 299

Index Keyed to Line Numbers

6.218ff. 281	6.511-520 286
6.385ff. 281	6.513 289
6.388f. 287	6.513-515 285
6.390-395 287	6.514 .... 284, 286, 289, *294*
6.394f. 287	6.515 .... 285, *293*
6.407ff. 282	6.516-518 .... 285, 289
6.412-423 285	6.516f. 285, 287
6.422 286	6.519-521 .... *293*
6.423f 285	6.520f. 287
6.424 285	6.521 288
6.425 .... 285, 289	6.523 .... *294*
6.426-428 290	6.525 289
6.428ff. 288	6.527-529 285
6.429ff. *294*	6.533 285
6.430 289	6.535 .... *293*, *294*
6.430f. 289	6.537f. 284
6.430-434 289	6.539 .... *293*
6.438-440 286	6.544-547 288
6.440 .... 287, 288, 289, *295*	6.545 284
6.443f. 291	6.546f. 288
6.444-446 286	6.549 287
6.451-454 287	6.551f. 289
6.455-457 .... *294*	6.555f. 284
6.455ff. *294*	6.557 287
6.460 .... *294*	6.559 285
6.460-466 284	6.561 282
6.461-466 290	6.562 283
6.464 287	6.565-567 282
6.466 .... *294*	6.566 .... 282, *293*, *294*
6.469 284	6.566f. 289
6.470-474 284	6.571-572 286
6.471f. *294*	6.572f. 288
6.472-473 286	6.574 .... 282, 288, *294*
6.472f. 288, *294*	6.575f. 288
6.474 .... 285, *293*	6.576ff. 289
6.482 .... 285, *293*	6.577-578 282
6.483 289	6.581 .... 287, 291
6.486-487 286	6.581f. 282
6.486ff. 288, *294*	6.582 282
6.487-494 286	6.582-586 288
6.488f. *293*, *294*	6.583 .... 282, 284
6.491 284	6.583-585 .... *294*
6.492 .... *294*	6.583-586 282
6.496 .... *293*	6.585 .... *294*
6.498 .... *293*	6.587 .... 288, *295*
6.503 .... *293*	6.587-588 286
6.504 .... *294*	6.588-590 .... 286, *294*

6.590	288
6.591-595	289
6.594	288
6.594f.	288
6.595	287
6.596	286, 288
6.597	288
6.598	*293*
6.598f.	288
6.600	288
6.601	291
6.604	289
6.605f.	284
6.609	*294*
6.609f.	*294*
6.610f.	*294*
6.611f.	289
6.612	289
6.614	289
6.614f.	*294*
6.617	289
6.617f.	287
6.621f.	291
6.622f.	*294*
6.623	284
6.624-635	290
6.626	289, *295*
6.628	*294*
6.629	*293*
6.632	289, *294*, *295*
6.635	*293*
6.636f.	285
6.639-642	290
6.640-642	284
6.643	289
6.645	289
6.645f.	*294*
6.652	286, *294*
6.653	284, 286, *294*
6.653-655	284
6.657	289
6.659f.	284
6.660	284, *294*
6.662	289
6.663f.	288
6.665	*294*
6.666	289
6.666-674	285, 289, 291
6.669-670	283
6.669f.	283
6.673f.	285, 287
6.677f.	290
6.682ff.	290
6.685	*295*
6.687ff.	290
6.707ff.	291
6.708	291
6.711	291
6.712f.	291
6.714-718	291
6.717-718	*295*
6.720f.	291
7.297ff.	282
7.340-342	*295*
7.394ff.	282
7.739f.	*294*
9.640ff.	*293*
10.3-8	*294*
10.62	*293, 294*
10.104f.	*341*
10.134	*293*
10.476ff.	*293*
10.706	299
11.786	440
12.526	*293*
13.457-472	272

Remedia Amoris:
589	270

Tristia:
1.7.27-28	271
1.7.29-34	271
2.365	486
3.2.39-42	*280*
3.2.55-56	*280*
3.2.57	*280*
3.2.59-60	*280*
3.8.13f.	345
3.8.14	346
3.8.15	346
4.4.5	269
4.4.63	277
4.4.63-64	270, 272, 277, *278*
4.4.63-82	268
4.4.65-66	269

Index Keyed to Line Numbers

4.4.65-82	273
4.4.66	277
4.4.67-68	277
4.4.68	270
4.4.69	269
4.4.69-72	277
4.4.72	273
4.4.73	269, 277
4.4.73-78	269
4.4.74	270
4.4.75-76	270, 273, 277
4.4.79	277
4.4.79-82	270
4.4.80-81	272
4.4.81	270
4.4.81-82	277
4.4.82	270
4.4.87	272
4.4.87-88	270
5.2.45-46	346
5.2.45-78	346
5.2.51f.	346
5.4.25	271

Owen, W.
Fragment: Cramped in That Funnelled Hole: 199
Strange Meeting: 202

P.G.M.:
4.2719 .... *176*
4.2751 .... *176*

Paneg. Lat.:
12.6.4 349

Pausanias, *Periegeta:*
1.27.10 .... *91*
4.35.12 362
8.7.3 362

Persius, *Saturae:*
2.28 299

Petrarca
Epist. Sen.:
4.5 .... *426, 427*

Petronius, *Satyricon:*
38 222
46 210
47 210
50.1 .... *352*
57.7 484
60.7 .... 344, *352*
60.8 344
88 222
128 222

Phaedrus, *Fabulae:*
28 214

Philo, *Leg. ad Gai:*
22.151 351

Philostratus, *Vita Apollonii:*
8.5,152 (299 Kayer) *355*
8.7,157 (310 Kayer) *355*

Pindar, *frag.:*
95.96 .... *341*

Plato, *Hippias Minor:*
285d 209

Plautus
Asinaria:
277 213
655 213
Aulularia:
(argument) 213
7 213
12 213
26 213
240 213
266 213
354ff. *252*
575 .... *252*
Bacchides:
10 .... *252*
953ff. 247
Captivi:
123 .... *252*
Curculio:
676 213

Epidicus:
  177 .... *252*
frag.:
  172 (Lindsay) 246
Mercator:
  82 250
  163 213
  641 213
Miles Gloriosus:
  1064 213
  1285 250
Mostellaria:
  144 250
  865 213
  979 250
Poenulus:
  625 213
Pseudolus:
  84 213
  628 213
Rudens:
  1206ff. *353*
Trinummus:
  (argument) 213
  149 213
  642 250
  783 213

Pliny the Elder
Naturalis Historia:
  2.93 .... *155*
  5.14 (13) 220
  7.20 223
  12.14-16 375
  12.15 376
  12.16 375
  12.83 210
  13.27.84-87 221
  13.84 215
  15.2 220
  15.136-137 386
  17.64 .... 374, 376
  17.80 380
  17.97 375
  17.98 375
  23.105 375
  25.26 .... *178*

  31.6-8 360
  31.8 .... 357, 362
  31.9 .... 357, 359, 363
  31.10 357
  31.11 357
  31.12 361
  31.59 357
  34.26 103
  34.84 225
  34.105 220
  34.137 222
  35.136 .... 274, 279
  36.12 227
  36.99 220

Pliny the Younger
Epistulae:
  4.4 350
  5.1 350
Panegyricus:
  10 (2) 2.5 .... *354*
  30.5 350
  44 331
  44.2 .... *334*
  45 331
  45.3 .... *334*
  45.6 .... *334*

Plutarch
Aemilius Paulus:
  32.5 225
  33.4 225
Camillus:
  20 215
  22.3 103
de facie in orbe lunae:
  27.30 (942D-945D) *424*
  27.942D-F *424, 425*
de genio Socratis:
  21f. (590Aff.) *424*
Flamininus:
  1.1 225
Numa:
  22 221
  22.2 215
Pompeius:
  2.4-5 216

Publicola:
19.8 219
Quaestiones Romanae:
2 .... *301*
Romulus:
14.3-5 220
Sulla:
12.9 216
Theseus:
15 .... *91*

Polybius
3.22.1-3 .... *107*

Priscian, *Panegyricus:*
185f. 73

Probus, *Vita Verg.:*
73, BR.10 .... *204*

Proclus, *Hymn:*
6.2.14 .... *176*

Propertius
1.15.31 62
1.16.15-16 306
1.16.17-44 305
1.16.45 307
1.16.45-46 306
1.9.23 299
1.9.23-24 298
1.9.24 299
1.9.26 299
1.9.33-34 300
2.1.37-38 270
2.1.38 .... *278*
2.20.1 .... *302*
2.25.23-28 479
3.10.28 299
3.12 264
4.11.33 .... *301*

Ptolemy
3.1.68 364

Quintilian, *Institutio Oratoria:*
2.7.4 211
10.1.2 211
11.2.1 211

Sallust, *Catilina:*
6.1 93

Salutati (Coluccio Salutati), *de Laboribus Herculis:*
4.9 p. 52.25 .... *426*
p. 571ff. *426*
p. 573.6ff. *430*
p. 576.28ff. *432*

Sassoon, S.
Suicide in the Trenches: 198
A Soldier's Declaration: 198

Seneca
BNF (de beneficiis):
1.15.6.8 210
6.43.3.33 211
de Ira:
3.33.4 211
Epistulae:
51.6 357
56.1-2 366
78.5 .... *369*
86.8-11 362
115.5 211
V.B. (de vita beata):
24.2.22 210

Servius *auctus*
ad Vergil, Aen.:
1.3 (= fr. 1P) *108*
1.92 .... *126, 128*
1.92ff. *128*
2.152ff. *128*
2.687ff. *128*
2.801 .... *127*
3.167 .... *143*
3.176ff. *128*
3.263ff. *128*
4.203ff. *128*
5.232ff. *128*

5.685ff. *128*
9.16ff. *128*
10.667ff. *128*
10.844ff. *128*

Servius
ad Vergil, Aen.:
1.6 .... *252*
1.8 .... *252*
1.16 .... *251*
1.58 .... *252*
1.135 .... *248*
1.181 .... *248*
1.191 .... *251*
1.208 .... *248*
1.233 .... *251, 252*
1.273 100
1.340 .... *92*
1.378 .... *251*
1.399 .... *248*
1.435 .... *251*
1.460 .... *245, 252*
1.543 .... *251*
1.573 .... *252*
1.601 .... *252*
1.636 .... *251*
1.647 .... *252*
1.657 .... *252*
1.686 .... *252*
1.703 .... *245*
1.724 .... *251*
1.730 344
1.738 .... *251*
2.3 .... *252*
2.12 .... *252*
2.51 .... *245, 251*
2.60 .... *252*
2.93 .... *126*
2.155 .... *248*
2.206 .... *251*
2.324 .... *252*
2.424 .... *252*
2.463 .... *252*
2.531 .... *252*
2.610 .... *252*
3.15 .... *143*
3.42 .... *251*
3.46 .... *251*
3.108 .... *142*
3.121 132
3.140 .... *252*
3.167 .... *143*
3.217 .... *248*
3.278 .... *252*
3.477 .... *252*
3.686 .... *251*
4.1 .... *62, 244*
4.31 .... *252*
4.83 .... *248*
4.133 .... *249*
4.166 .... *253*
4.194 .... *251*
4.229 .... *245*
4.267 .... *251*
4.301 .... *251*
4.318 .... *253*
4.373 .... *245*
4.424 .... *251*
4.435 .... *252*
4.534 .... *252*
4.608 .... *251*
5.80 .... *252*
5.122 .... *252*
6.90 .... *251*
6.229 .... *251*
6.383 .... *245*
6.544 .... *252*
6.719 .... *423, 431*
6.890 .... *248*
7.49 .... *252*
7.268 .... *252*
7.427 .... *252*
7.715 .... *251*
8.84 .... *248*
8.127 .... *245, 252*
8.310 .... *246*
8.577 .... *253*
8.632 .... *251*
9.44 .... *252*
9.327 .... *251*
9.399 .... *245*
9.482 .... *253*
9.641 .... *251*
9.645 .... *251*

Index Keyed to Line Numbers

9.693 .... *251, 252*
9.778 248
10.529 .... *252*
10.532 245
10.532 .... *251*
10.559 .... *252*
10.727 .... *251*
10.848 248
11.160 .... *252*
11.343 245
11.361 .... *251, 252*
11.373 .... *252*
11.537 .... *253*
12.296 .... *252*
12.342 .... *252*
12.519 245
12.538 .... *253*
12.547 245
12.694 .... *252*
12.940 .... *239*

ad Vergil, *Ecl.*:
1.58 245
3.1 .... *252*
3.16 .... *251*
3.106 248
5.58 .... *251*
6.50 .... *252*
6.58 248
7.3.1 .... *252*
8.71 .... *251*

ad Vergil, *Geo.*:
1.74 .... *251*
1.94 .... *252*
1.125 .... *252*
1.189 .... *251*
1.248 .... *252*
1.266 .... *251*
1.344 .... *252*
2.288 245
3.305 .... *252*
4.170 .... 245, *251*
4.171 .... *252*
4.296 245
4.459 .... *252*
4.561 .... *251, 252*

Shakespeare
Henry V:
4.1 200
Romeo and Juliet:
2.1.220-225 299
Sonnet 130: 304

Silius Italicus, *Punica:*
1.273 220
12.13f. 226
14.529 299

Sophocles, *Ajax:*
550ff. 241
562 241

Statius, *Silvae:*
2.2.18-19 363

Stobaeus, *Ecloguae:*
1.14.61 .... *425*

Strabo, *Geographica:*
1.4.5 224
5.2.3 216
5.2.8 216
5.2.60 219
5.3.1 357
5.3.6 362
5.4.3 364
5.4.4 219
5.4.6 .... 219, 362
5.4.7 .... 219, 361
5.4.9 .... 219, 359
6.1.14 .... *81*
6.3.1 224
6.3.5 219
6.3.9 219
6.281 77
7.6.1 224
8.7.23 217
8.8.23 224
9.2.25 227
9.3.8 212
10.2.9 (452) 209
12.5.3 224
13.1.19 224

13.1.26-27 227
13.1.30 .... 224, 238
13.1.53 .... *107*
13.3.2 224
13.3.31 224
14.2.48 209
14.11.19 224
15.3.7 225
17.1.27 225
17.1.43 225

Suetonius
Caesar:
81 .... 215, 221
Caligula:
52 225
Divus Augustus:
7.1 348
15 195
17 .... *355*
72.6 219
86 210
98.2 351
Galba:
1 386
8 221
9 221
10 221
Vespanian:
7 222
8 223
12 .... *227*
Vitellius:
2.5 347

Symmachus, *Epistulae:*
6.17 363

Tacitus
Agricola:
2.3 .... *333*
3.1 .... *333*
44.5 .... *333*
Annales:
1.11.2f. *404*
2.53 226
2.59 226

2.61 226
4.32.6 .... *334*
12.66 362
16.1 217
16.1-3 217
Dialogus de Oratoribus:
21.4 210
37.2 210
42 210
Germania:
3.3 .... 220, 482
Historiae:
1.1 328
1.1.4 .... 331, *333*
1.15-16 330
1.15.1 .... *333*
1.16.1 .... *334*
1.56.3 331
1.72 362
4.42.6 .... *334*
4.53 .... *227*

Terence
Adelphoe:
93 249
134 249
195 249
196 248
197 .... *253*
311 249
329 248
330 249
373 249
376 .... *253*
381 249
415 249
498 .... *252*
537 .... *252*
665 .... 248, *253*
668 248
679 249
966 248
985 248
Andria:
55 248
74ff. 248
83 248

Index Keyed to Line Numbers

99	250
164	248
218	250
282	248
294	*253*
538	*253*
849	*252*
868	248
933	247
980	248

Eunuchus:

12	213
46	248, 249
48	248
67	248
236ff.	248
445	247
604	*253*
1053	247

Heautontimorumenos:

239-240	249
301	*252*
374	249
465	250
476	248
481	250

Phormio:

5	245
74	*253*
248	248
549	*253*
575	*253*

Tertullian, *de Testimonio Animae:*
33.9 .... *73*

Theocritus, *Idylls:*
2.12f. *176*

Thucydides, *The Peloponnesian War:*
1 209

Tibullus, *Elegies:*
1.1.21f.	*353*
1.3.34	*353*

1.10.15ff.	*353*
1.10.26	*353*

de uiris:
3.2 221

Valerius Maximus:
1.1.11	221
8.15.7	*352*

Varro
Ap. Aug. Civ. Dei:
7.34 221
de Lingua Latina:
5.144 102
de re rustica:
frag. 226 .... *424*

Veldekes (Heinrich von Veldekes), *Eneide:*
3012f. *427*

Velleius Paterculus
2.25.4 361

Vergil
Aeneid (1):
1.2	233
1.8-11	*63*, 120
1.13	233
1.23	111
1.33	135
1.38	131, 233
1.39	75
1.41	76
1.68	233
1.84-86	109
1.92	111
1.93	112, 123
1.94	120
1.96f.	112
1.102	111
1.103	111
1.113-119	43
1.123	*63*
1.142-156	*165*
1.152	247

1.161-163 .... *156*	1.450ff. *128*
1.170 82	1.453ff. 123
1.180ff. 111	1.456-493 467
1.184-194 .... *156*	1.462 .... *188*
1.184ff. 115	1.463 .... *128*
1.190ff. 116	1.468 .... *91*
1.192 82	1.469-473 .... *91*
1.192ff. 119	1.470 .... *128*
1.192ff. *128*	1.474-478 .... *91*
1.194 116	1.479 75
1.195-206 116	1.479-482 .... 75, *91*
1.198ff. 115, *127*	1.482 .... 75, 76
1.199 119	1.483-487 .... *91*
1.200 117	1.488-493 .... *91*
1.201 117	1.490 69
1.202f. 119	1.490-504 .... *165*
1.203 93	1.506 .... *92*
1.205f. 120	1.511-514 158
1.207 120	1.544-545 152
1.208-209 119	1.553 .... 230, 235
1.220 118	1.553-554 .... 229, 230, 231
1.242-249 .... *50*	1.554 .... 230, 235
1.250-253 121	1.555 131
1.259-260 240	1.583 .... *128*
1.261 247	1.592-593 467
1.263 193	1.603-605 123
1.263ff. 121	1.609f. 122
1.279 .... *62*	1.617-618 138
1.283-285 104	1.632 .... *62*
1.295f. 121	1.647 .... *62*
1.305 118	1.647-652 .... *156*
1.309 119	1.657ff. *128*
1.314-320 .... *165*	1.667 .... *62*
1.317 69	1.673-674 .... *62*
1.326ff. *128*	1.685f. *294*
1.338ff. *128*	1.730ff. 123
1.358-359 206	1.755 82
1.364 .... *92*	*Aeneid (2):*
1.375-376 .... *62*	2.13 246
1.378-379 135	2.15 75
1.378-380 133	2.16 75
1.378-385 121	2.31 75
1.382 121	2.112 75
1.383 82	2.163 76
1.385ff. 248	2.170 76
1.387f. *62*, 122	2.171-175 76
1.437 125	2.186 75

Index Keyed to Line Numbers 515

2.196 248
2.199-227 .... *80*
2.213-217 .... *92*
2.225-227 76
2.226 76
2.238 172
2.298-308 159
2.347-360 159
2.355 .... *243*
2.370-385 .... *165*
2.404-405 76
2.413-419 159
2.425 76
2.431ff. *126*
2.457 44
2.469-475 159
2.486-490 44
2.491-505 159
2.515-517 .... 158, 162
2.615-616 76
2.616 .... 75, 76
2.624-631 .... *165*
2.624-633 159
2.693f. 163
2.693-694 158
2.717 135
2.763ff. 67
2.766-767 44
2.772 67
2.780-784 139
2.781 .... *142*
2.796-798 .... *50*
2.932-935 162

Aeneid (3):
3.12 135
3.84 123
3.94-99 130
3.95 137
3.96 138
3.101 138
3.103-112 162
3.105 130
3.106-110 237
3.107 130
3.111 130
3.111-115 131
3.121-123 132

3.140 43
3.148-168 135
3.148ff. 136
3.161-171 131
3.167 133
3.168 135
3.179-188 132
3.180 132
3.190 .... 39, 43
3.253 231
3.253-254 .... 230, 231
3.254 235
3.384-469 161
3.432 .... *127*
3.433 123
3.435ff. *127*
3.486 77
3.488 77
3.489 44
3.500-501 139
3.503 135
3.521-524 229
3.523 .. 229, 230, 231, 233, 234
3.523-534 231
3.524 .... 230, 231, 234, 235
3.530-540 .... *80*
3.530-545 77
3.554ff. 117
3.555 .... *127*
3.569ff. 117
3.594ff. 248
3.715 .... 114, *127*

Aeneid (4):
4.15ff. 71
4.24ff. 125
4.55 125
4.68-74 132
4.69 250
4.73 77
4.78 250
4.91 250
4.95 .... *63*
4.144-146 132
4.165 .... *92*
4.170 71
4.172 71
4.173-188 416

4.215	*156*
4.221	250
4.259ff.	125
4.260f.	*62*
4.264	77
4.265-275	*63*
4.266	77
4.267	250
4.271	250
4.279-280	232
4.302	*295*
4.332	*62*
4.339	71
4.345	232
4.345-346	231, 234
4.345-350	*156*
4.346	231, 232
4.347	71
4.350	232
4.351-353	*63*
4.365	135
4.381	232, 234, 235
4.393-396	184
4.408	248, *253*
4.435	232
4.534	249
4.550	*63*
4.563	*62*
4.576-579	123
4.590	248
4.596	*63*
4.606	249
4.625-626	138
4.626	138
4.638-640	138
4.646-647	138
4.657-658	138
4.661-662	138

Aeneid (5):

5.1-34	*164*
5.5	159
5.6	159
5.17-18	234
5.35-83	*164*
5.73	44
5.84-93	158, 160
5.84-595	*164*
5.85	82
5.137-150	158, 160
5.145-147	162
5.160	*145*
5.210-219	158, 160
5.242-243	*164*
5.268-281	158, 160
5.278-279	162
5.284	78
5.301	44
5.311ff.	114
5.317	*164*
5.319	*164*
5.387	44
5.404-405	*90*
5.437-442	160, *165*
5.439-442	158
5.443-452	158, 160
5.453-460	158, 160, 163
5.519-532	158, 160
5.573	44
5.580-595	158, 160
5.588-593	132
5.594-595	158, 160
5.604-778	41, *164*
5.604-871	158
5.609	157, 161
5.615ff.	70
5.621	43
5.624-625	43
5.626	82
5.645-652	237
5.704-707	78
5.709-718	41
5.715	39, 40
5.724-739	41
5.729-730	42
5.730	43
5.730-731	42
5.737	43
5.744	135
5.750	40
5.750-754	42
5.750ff.	70
5.754	44
5.755-761	42
5.762	43

Index Keyed to Line Numbers 517

5.762-771 43	6.202 .... 171, 173, *177*
5.762-778 42	6.205-207 168
5.779-871 .... *164*	6.209 .... *177, 236*
5.785 43	6.211 174
5.801 43	6.212 170
5.833 .... *145*	6.232 87
5.854f. 88	6.234f. 171
5.867 87	6.237 174
Aeneid (6):	6.237-238 172
6.1-263 180	6.237-242 173
6.9-11 .... *177*	6.237ff. *177*
6.13 169	6.238 172
6.14-33 132	6.240f. 174
6.20 83	6.241 173
6.20-22 .... 83, 88	6.242 173
6.20-33 467	6.243ff. *176*
6.23-30 84	6.247 168
6.27 84	6.257f. 167
6.28 .... *91*	6.260 176
6.30-33 90	6.264-294 180
6.38 87	6.268 .... *426*
6.38-39 85	6.290-294 176
6.42ff. *177*	6.294-332 180
6.61 234	6.333-383 180
6.100-102 .... *178*	6.357 233
6.106 174	6.384-385 180
6.106-109 168	6.413 .... *156*
6.109 168	6.426-439 180
6.126 .... *176*	6.426f. *188*
6.131 .... *176, 177, 236*	6.430 .... *188*
6.131-132 169	6.431 .... *188*
6.131ff. *177*	6.440-547 181
6.136-137 171	6.442-449 85
6.136ff. 168	6.444 170
6.138 171	6.448-449 86
6.138-139 171	6.450 .... 183, 413
6.138f. 172	6.456 68
6.142 174	6.467-468 184
6.156-235 171	6.475-476 183
6.176 87	6.477 .... *426*
6.185-211 170	6.477-478 181
6.186 171	6.505 238
6.186ff. 171	6.544 248
6.187-189 88	6.546 233
6.188 172	6.548-627 181
6.195f. 172	6.562 131
6.201 .. 171, 172, 173, 174, *177*	6.576 174

6.625	138
6.628-678	181
6.630-641	417
6.636	418, *426*
6.636-650	400
6.638	170
6.640	*407*
6.646	*90*
6.648	131
6.650	135
6.658	170
6.678	419
6.679-892	182
6.701	161
6.703	419
6.730-743	182
6.756	135
6.764	67
6.783	82
6.784f.	*339*
6.791-807	*165*
6.792-793	*135*
6.800	*90*
6.840	76
6.847	480
6.851-853	401
6.852	141, 189
6.853	241
6.882	88
6.883	182
6.883-884	88
6.886f.	*424*
6.893-901	182
6.893f.	185, *188*
6.900	40

Aeneid (7):

7.2	40
7.10-14	78
7.15-20	78
7.21-24	79
7.25-36	*108*, 139
7.120-123	140
7.121-122	136
7.154	75
7.205-211	133
7.206	133
7.209	133

7.239-244	137
7.241	137
7.242	139
7.300-303	291
7.367-370	*144*
7.385-405	291
7.401	*236*
7.563ff.	*177*
7.570	*177*
7.648	*128*
7.805	79
7.805-806	79
7.805ff.	69

Aeneid (8):

8.7	*128*
8.37	138
8.184-305	148
8.278f.	123
8.336	135
8.367	*156*
8.407-415	74, *165*
8.409-410	79
8.412	79
8.412ff.	248
8.413	80
8.435-438	75
8.448	82
8.470	131
8.513	131
8.523ff.	*432*
8.602	*236*
8.626-728	467
8.671-674	157
8.678-684	136
8.684-686	141
8.685	68
8.688	68
8.695-713	68
8.699	75, 77

Aeneid (9):

9.30	*90*
9.153-155	47
9.172	87
9.180	87
9.201	39
9.216-218	39
9.217	40

Index Keyed to Line Numbers

9.217-218	46
9.259	135
9.329-801	*165*
9.391-393	87
9.435	88
9.436-437	88
9.449	87
9.473-475	*50*
9.476	78
9.477-485	*80*
9.489	78
9.499	78
9.503-504	78
9.535	*145*
9.669	*165*
9.672f	*92*

Aeneid (10):

10.8	193
10.106	193
10.108	193
10.113	193
10.124	44
10.130	*236*
10.153-160	141
10.163-214	140
10.166	141
10.166-169	140
10.167	140
10.168	140
10.170-174	140
10.172	140
10.173	140
10.175	141
10.175-180	140
10.179	140
10.180-184	140
10.183	140
10.184	140
10.185-186	140
10.186-187	140
10.198-206	140
10.200	140
10.201	140
10.207-212	140
10.254	*145*
10.270-278	*165*
10.284	248
10.302-306	175
10.314	191
10.323	191
10.325	89
10.326-327	89
10.327	89
10.329-330	89
10.337	191
10.341	191
10.348-349	191
10.349	191
10.352-610	*165*
10.390-396	*92*
10.394	191
10.396	191
10.397-411	*165*
10.403-404	191
10.414-415	191
10.415-416	191
10.486	191
10.489	191
10.513	191
10.519	192
10.519-520	*204*
10.536	192
10.540-541	192
10.545-546	192
10.557-560	192
10.576-601	*92*
10.589	192
10.601	192
10.636-644	*165*
10.698-699	192
10.699-700	192
10.730-731	192
10.734-735	194
10.736	193
10.778	193
10.812	87
10.815-816	193
10.821-822	88
10.822	87
10.825	88
10.826	87
10.844ff.	*128*
10.861ff.	248
10.880	124

10.890-891	193
10.901	195
10.907-908	193

Aeneid (11):

11.24-28	48
11.34-35	40, 48
11.35	40
11.42	88
11.54	*236*
11.57-58	49
11.57f.	241
11.65-70	88
11.72-75	151
11.72-77	77
11.92-93	49
11.139-141	*50*
11.165-166	47
11.477-485	79
11.480	68, 71
11.484	79
11.532ff.	89
11.535	69
11.593	89
11.620	141, *145*
11.648-663	*165*
11.661	69
11.663	89, *90*
11.715-724	158, 162
11.819	89
11.829-830	89
11.835f.	*63*
11.891-895	45
11.904	89

Aeneid (12):

12.1-480	*165*
12.41	233
12.57-58	47
12.67-69	467
12.74	443
12.75	*156*
12.99-100	*156*
12.138ff.	72, 434
12.139-140	434
12.142	434
12.143-145	439
12.151	434
12.152-153	435
12.153	434
12.159	435
12.190-191	438
12.194	67
12.216-221	*156*
12.222-256	440
12.289	141
12.296	248
12.321	435
12.324-340	*165*
12.420	44
12.420ff.	436
12.436f.	241
12.441-442	*156*
12.441-926	*165*
12.448-450	436
12.456	237
12.466-467	436
12.469ff.	72
12.472	436
12.473-477	437
12.483ff.	437
12.493ff.	70
12.494-499	437
12.499ff.	70
12.500-503	437
12.500f.	*447*
12.504	438
12.525ff.	444
12.553	443
12.565	442
12.565	443
12.570ff.	444
12.600	71
12.618	247
12.676ff.	72
12.677	443
12.697	241
12.703	241
12.714ff	444
12.725ff.	440
12.741	445
12.784-785	440
12.785	72
12.788f.	444
12.794	*243*
12.794-795	240

Index Keyed to Line Numbers

12.821	45
12.827	45
12.833	*156*
12.843	*236*
12.865-866	439
12.872	72
12.876-880	439
12.878	435
12.889	443
12.892	*236*
12.925	82
12.934	47

Culex:

210-231	397
413-414	397

Eclogues:

1.1	468
1.4	468
1.19-25	395
1.27ff.	*406*
1.35	*406*
1.38f.	*406*
1.40	*406*
1.52	469
1.75	469
1.77	469
2.21	469
2.24	469
2.25-27	469
2.31	469
2.36	*90*
2.36-37	469
2.45-50	469
2.58-59	469
2.70	469
2.71-72	469
3.21-22	469
3.38-39	469
3.50	469
3.60-61	469
3.62-63	469
3.64-65	469
3.76-79	469
3.80-81	470
3.88-89	470
3.93	470
3.96	470
3.104-107	470
3.108-109	470
4.1	402
4.2	398
4.3	398
4.5	398
4.6-17	*407*
4.10	398
4.15-16	474
4.18	398
4.26	396
4.32	474
4.32-33	474
4.33	474
4.34-35	474
4.35-36	474
4.42-45	474
4.48-52	474
4.55-59	475
4.60	396
4.62-63	475
4.89	396
4.183	396
4.208	396
4.212	399
5.6-7	470
5.29-30	470
5.30-31	470
5.34	470
5.44	470
5.85	470
5.88-90	470
6.29-30	471
6.41-42	471
6.43-44	471
6.45-60	471
6.61-63	471
6.64-65	471
6.74-77	471
6.78-81	471
7.21-22	472
7.25-28	472
7.31-32	472
7.35-36	472
7.45-48	472
7.49-52	472
7.55-56	472

7.69-70	472
8.1-5	471
8.39	472
8.41-43	247
8.48-49	472
8.58-60	472
9.7-10	473
9.11-13	473
9.23-25	473
9.27-29	473
9.38-43	473
9.46-50	473
9.51	473
9.51-52	473
9.66	473
9.67	473
10.6	64
10.14	475
10.21-30	475
10.22-23	475
10.22f.	*62*
10.31-34	475
10.35-40	475
10.50-68	476
10.62-63	476
10.64	476
10.69	64, 246, 476
10.72	64

Georgics:

1.18-19	*80*
1.29-31	*355*
1.146	*407*
1.365-366	158
1.365f.	162
1.373-429	158, 163
1.493-497	206
1.511-514	162
2.3	*80*
2.179	*80*
2.420-425	*80*
2.490	*204*
2.535	82
3.105-107	162
3.105f.	158
3.355	*91*
3.381	*91*
3.414-439	*165*
3.416-424	158, 161
3.422-424	161
4.78-81	158, 163
4.207	*91*
4.210	399
4.210-218	399
4.213-314	399
4.215	400
4.228-229	206
4.292	*90*
4.315-558	467
4.467	*177*
4.481-484	467
4.507	*91*

Robert McKay Wilhelm is a professor of Classics at Miami University in Oxford, Ohio. His specialties include Latin literature, Vergilian studies, classical mythology, and Greek and Roman art and archaeology. He earned his Ph.D. from The Ohio State University.

A professor of Classics at McMaster University, Howard Jones is the author of several books including *Pierre Gassendi: An Intellectual Biography* and *The Epicurean Tradition*. He received his Ph.D. from Indiana University.

Anne Bell, of Oxford, Ohio, provided invaluable editing and proofreading assistance in addition to doing the typesetting and mechanicals for this book.